NETWORK ARCHITECTURE AND
DEVELOPMENT SERIES

Network Performance Baselining

Daniel Nassar

MACMILLAN
TECHNICAL
PUBLISHING
U·S·A

Network Performance Baselining

By Daniel Nassar

Published By:
MTP
201 West 103rd Street
Indianapolis, IN 46290 USA

International Standard Book Number: 1-57870-240-2

Library of Congress Catalog Card Number: 00-100403

04 03 02 01 00 7 6 5 4 3 2 1

Interpretation of the printing code: The rightmost double-digit number is the year of the book's printing; the rightmost single-digit number is the number of the book's printing. For example, the printing code 00-1 shows that the first printing of the book occurred in 2000.

Composed in Palatino and MCPdigital by MTP

Printed in the United States of America

Trademarks

Warning and Disclaimer

Publisher
David Dwyer

Associate Publisher
Brad Koch

Executive Editor
Al Valvano

Managing Editor
Gina Brown

Product Marketing Manager
Stephanie Layton

Acquisitions Editor
Theresa Gheen

Development Editors
Katherine Pendergast
Lisa M. Thibault

Senior Editor
Kristy Knoop

Copy Editor
Keith Cline

Indexer
Christine Karpeles

Manufacturing
Jim Conway
Chris Moos

Book Designer
Louisa Klucznik

Cover Designer
Aren Howell

Proofreader
Debbie Williams

Composition
Amy Parker

Contents

About the Author

Daniel J. Nassar is president of LAN Scope Incorporated, a Havertown, Pennsylvania-area based international Network Baseline Consulting and Training firm. The firm specializes in emergency network troubleshooting, network baseline studies, application characterization and remote protocol analysis. Dan is personally active in the firm's training division, where he teaches courses on network baselining subjects.

As president of Eagle Eye Analysis Incorporated, another Pennsylvania-based network consulting firm, Dan evaluates industry products such as network analyzers or new networking devices such as switches and routers. Dan provides remote evaluation and writing services direct to industry manufacturers that includes documentation design for industry white paper reviews, training manual design, and overall product assessment.

Skilled in an extensive range of networking disciplines including network design, network implementation, troubleshooting, and network management, Dan is highly regarded throughout the industry as the global markets chief scientist in the area of network baseline evaluation and reporting.

Dan can be reached at (610) 446-3831 or (610) 359-3573, or on the Internet at nassard@lanscope.com or nassard@eagleanalysis.com.

About the Technical Reviewers

These reviewers contributed their considerable hands-on expertise to the entire development process for *Network Performance Baselining*. As the book was being written, these dedicated professionals reviewed all the material for technical content, organization, and flow. Their feedback was critical to ensuring that *Network Performance Baselining* fits our readers' need for the highest quality technical information.

Brian Honan is a Senior IT Consultant and head of COMIT Technical Services, which is part of The COMIT Gruppe based in Dublin, Ireland. Brian advises clients of The COMIT Gruppe on technical infrastructure issues, strategic planning of local and wide area networks, and on designing and implementing core network services.

Marc Charney has 12 years of experience in the computer industry. After receiving his degree from the University of California, Berkeley in 1987, Marc worked for the Federal Reserve Bank of San Francisco, where he helped design computer models of the United States economy. Marc then moved on to Sybase, where he helped develop its sales-office integration, automation, and networking strategy. In his next position at Delta Life & Annuity, Marc managed a complete overhaul of its network and systems infrastructure. Currently, Marc is an Internet Security and Intranet Development Manager at First Tennessee Bank where his efforts are focussed on Web integration of current bank systems.

William McLuskie is a Senior Consulting Partner with Acentron Technologies, Inc. (http://www.acentron.com). He specializes in the development of n-tiered, web-based applications for national and international clients. Most of his development work is done on the Microsoft Windows platforms using IIS, MTS, ASP and Visual Studio. Additionally, he has taught object-oriented design, component development and various programming languages at several universities, as well as in the corporate sector. He holds a B.Sc. in Computer Science and a M.Sc. in Computer Information Systems. William lives in Charlotte, NC with his wife Brenda and daughter Caitlyn. When he is not coding, he is an avid student of Japanese martial arts and the Chief Instructor at Aikido of Charlotte. He can be contacted at william@mcluskie.com or through http://www.mcluskie.com/william/.

Paul Hinsburg MBA, MCSE is the owner and operator or CRSD Inc., a computer consulting company in the Silicon Valley region. Paul also serves as a Senior Consultant with CRSD and has 14 years of experience with PC networking and enterprise systems, including Windows NT and Microsoft's BackOffice suite of products. Working as a software developer, Paul designs tools and utilities to augment his network consulting efforts. Some of the tools are included in commercial products. In addition to consulting, Paul has developed technical training courseware and has served as the author/co-author of such books as *Windows NT Performance: Monitoring, Benchmarking and Tuning*, New Riders, 1998 (ISBN:1-56205-942-4) and *Windows NT Applications: Measuring and Optimizing Performance*, MTP (ISBN: 1-57870-176-7). He also works as an instructor for Learning Tree International. An enthusiastic sports participant, Paul can be found playing roller hockey or coaching one of his four kinds in his free time. Paul can be contacted at `paulhins@home.com`.

Dedication

To my beloved true friend and partner in life, my wife Kathleen. You have always shone upon me the moral character and compassion that I lack. You have been my mentor and my guide in life. Thank you for showing me what the heart is all about. I may have not always followed the right path, but without you, I would not be on any road. You are the reason I endure.

Acknowledgments

First, I would like to thank the personnel at MTP. The team has been amazingly patient with me for the long period in which I have been working on this manuscript. To Mr. David Dwyer and Mr. Al Valvano, thank you for giving me the opportunity to bring this work to the networking marketplace. To Ms. Theresa Gheen, thank you for guidance during the writing and production phases. To the Developement Editors, Ms. Katie Pendergast and Ms. Lisa Thibault, thank you so much for reading this complete manuscript and at the same time maintaining the concentration to deal with my redundant writing style. I would also like to thank all the technical editors, especially Brian and Mark for their technical guidance through the writing of this technically abstract book. Final thanks are also due to the complete staff at MTP in the copy editing and layout departments.

I would like to thank my colleagues, Ms. Janice Pellegrini and Mr. Marco Fiore for their support. Specifically, my friend, Janice, was instrumental in helping me develop this book through providing me with the required transcribing services needed to transfer the technical material in this manuscript from my mind to paper. While I was busy writing this book, my new friend, Marco, assisted me, with some of the day-to-day technical duties that we engage in at LAN Scope.

I cannot forget to thank my friend, Mr. Tim Barnard. Tim engineered all of the graphics in this book. With my technical, hand-scratched concepts, Tim was able to create the required art to relay the technical material in this book in a true graphical manner.

There are also individuals in this industry with whom I have interacted over the past 25 years, and to whom I must partially dedicate this book. These are the individuals whom I must label as the non-believers. This book finally culminates all of my consulting and writing work at LAN Scope over the past 11 years. From the heart, I developed the concept of network baselining to ensure the networks in this world run in a stable and reliable fashion performing at the highest level. It has also been my personal mission to ensure the industry networking personnel in the marketplace, who work in the trenches day-to-day supporting networks under corporate rule, the opportunity to receive the knowledge transfer that they require to perform their jobs. To the non-believers, I hope you all can finally see that network baselining was my vision and mission, and there is not a dark wall in this world that can block the shining light that network baselining can spread upon today's networks.

This book would not have been at all possible without the love that I received from my family. To my mother Jean, thank you for being there when I really needed you. To my brother David, I am proud of you, and thank you for your support. To my children, Danny, Mikey, and Joey, without you guys there would have not been a driving force to allow me to create this work. You boys are the world to me.

Tell Us What You Think

As the reader of this book, you are the most important critic and commentator. We value your opinion and want to know what we're doing right, what we could do better, what areas you'd like to see us publish in, and any other words of wisdom you're willing to pass our way.

As the Executive Editor for the Networking team at MTP, I welcome your comments. You can fax, email, or write me directly to let me know what you did or didn't like about this book—as well as what we can do to make our books stronger.

Please note that I cannot help you with technical problems related to the topic of this book, and that due to the high volume of mail I receive, I might not be able to reply to every message.

When you write, please be sure to include this book's title and author as well as your name and phone or fax number. I will carefully review your comments and share them with the author and editors who worked on the book.

Fax: 317-581-4663

Email: nrfeedback@newriders.com

Mail: Al Valvano
           Executive Editor
           New Riders Publishing
           201 West 103rd Street
           Indianapolis, IN 46290 USA

CHAPTER 1

What Is Baselining

With the onset of the new millennium, networking has entered a new era. Network stability, reliability, and performance is a must. It is our mission. We, as network analysts, have a clear charter. We must use our inherent and finely developed skills of abstract-geared network astronomy to systematically view network point-to-point dataflow and then to analyze complex network communication sequencing. In this process, we must extract accurate metrics to surgically expose "real-world" issues that affect our network's operation and performance. We must then closely review the extracted issues to develop a concise technical synopsis supported by a clear-cut recommendation.

We then face the task of inserting the results in a final report that accurately displays a network baseline study. The final network baseline study report must accurately reflect a network's current state of operation. Therefore, we must ensure that statistical measurements which characterize the data workload applied to our network infrastructure, reflect our findings and recommendations. This methodology, which enables us to utilize metric reflection to extract relevant issues, is critical for the process of building a true proactive and reactive view of the network design integrity, network operational health, and final end-node–to–end-node performance. Figure 1.1 represents a high-level concept of network baselining.

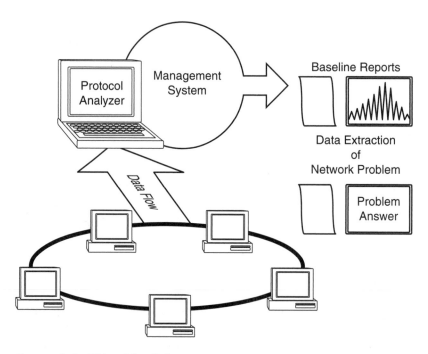

FIGURE 1.1 *Network baselining.*

The galaxy of network infrastructure that we have created is now multi-symmetrical. The endpoints, which communicate throughout the galaxy, are not always visible to the average eye. Our networks have evolved to internetworks. Many complex topologies and protocols now interconnect for the express purpose of transmitting data from one point to another and gaining access to remote resources on different end systems. In a perfect world, our goal is to transmit the most data in the fastest amount of time with absolute fluency. This concept can be thought of as *flawless network communications*.

We must use a specific methodology to plan our vector for a focused network baselining workflow process. This methodology must include a structured data-acquisition plan via protocol analysis. After the data-acquisition plan is in place, we must then use a structured workflow-analysis, data-gathering engine to ensure that we gather all essential information. At that same time, we must be dynamic enough to cross-examine all the required metrics that dictate changes in our data-gathering process. We can obtain the metrics that we use from a view via a network management system or a network protocol analyzer. As we capture the metrics, we must review the data closely through exact protocol analysis specifically to extract problematic and exception-based dataflow to identify issues. To develop a defined technical synopsis, we may then adjust our final data-acquisition process to actually verify issues. This process may require us to closely adjust our focused viewpoint of the network galaxy dataflow with our protocol analysis scope and tools via measurement processes, such as filtering and triggering. After we have truly isolated a network-affected issue and the applied cause, only then can we start to draw possible conclusions or to offer recommendations.

We must always keep in mind that the goal of network baselining is to use quantitative statistical measurements to expressly identify key network issues relevant to our mission.

Now that we have defined network baselining, let's move forward with the dynamics of data capturing and obtaining a true network baseline. Network baselining has always been my goal, and has now become a reality as well as a requirement in our global networking industry.

1.1 Understanding When to Perform a Network Optimization Project

Every day on an internetwork, many scenarios that require on-the-fly decisions by a network analyst surface. When faced with a network problem, the analyst's immediate impulse is to react. Even in the quiet moments and days, when standard technical tasks are planned and the network is stable, an analyst ponders ways to enhance the network's overall performance and operational features. This is the time when the analyst considers adding new products or features to a network to make it more effective.

Network optimization refers to using the art of network baselining to obtain network metrics to enhance the network's capability to reach a higher altitude of *dataflow energy (DFE)*. *Maximum dataflow energy* (MDFE) is defined as sending the maximum amount of data in the fastest amount of time with optimal fluent protocol cycles (see Figure 1.2). A plateau of MDFE can be defined as "perfect network communications."

Many reasons compel us to optimize a network through the art of network baselining. One main reason is reactive problem analysis. Many of us face day-to-day troubleshooting issues that require an immediate response. Throughout this book, the discussion identifies specific ways to use protocol analysis and network monitoring tools to resolve critical network problems and to attack this monkey on our back that we constantly encounter.

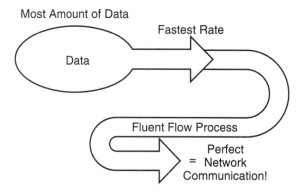

Most Amount of Data

Fastest Rate

Data

Fluent Flow Process

Perfect
= Network
Communication!

FIGURE 1.2 *Maximum dataflow energy.*

Network baselining, for example, enables us to isolate certain low-level topology and medium-based errors that may be causing intermittent problems that affect our network's stability. By using protocol analysis to locate the devices that cause these errors when the error generation cycle is dormant, we can partially optimize our network.

Another reason to perform proactive network analysis is to ensure that our network is always operating in a stable and reliable fashion. Considering the number of reactive network problems that we must face on a daily basis, this may seem an impossible task. The path to achieving the goal of using consistent proactive network sampling in our daily schedule is always impeded by the time and resource restraints that result from constantly handling daily network problems. We can actually use network baselining and optimization techniques to reduce the occurrence of reactive problem situations and move into a proactive stance.

By using daily trend analysis of certain metric statistics, for example, we might locate network workstation logon-sequence inefficiencies. By using specific techniques, such as filtering of a user via protocol analysis, we may be able to extract data that shows clients redundantly generating protocol calls on certain server-based files while accessing servers. If we capture this event, we may also find that the protocol-redundant events actually increase the user's startup time (that is, the time it takes the user to log on to the network). Next, by cross-threading our analysis process and checking other key measurements, such as peak utilization, we may also find that this event negatively affects endpoint connection integrity by increasing the use of a complete network area and causes further problems in other application access modes in a certain network user domain.

Another reason to use baselining techniques for optimization is to monitor network modifications and new product implementations. As network analysts in today's networking world, we must rapidly implement many changes on our networks. Some of these changes or implementations are planned cyclical migrations, while other changes are required on a dynamic and immediate basis to accommodate unpredicted network operational cycles or business application changes.

Later in this book, you learn actual techniques that enable you to wrap a working methodology based on protocol analysis around a network modification and implementation cycle process to ensure that network configuration changes and product deployment occur in a smooth and solid process.

During the course of network migration planning and implementation, it is important to recognize the benefits of network baselining—specifically, that network baselining enables us to predict how a new migration process being implemented may impact a network. It is also critical that we verify whether the change to configuration or product implementation is properly deployed against our network infrastructure. We must use protocol analysis in a pre- and post- mode to ensure that we actually realize the predicted effect or benefit of the change or product implementation cycle. Again, it is vital that other operational areas of our network environment not be negatively impacted when the change or product implementation is activated in our network.

Network baselining enables us to use key analysis methods in a network migration cycle to optimize a network.

By properly using protocol analysis to focus on endpoint-to-endpoint dataflow and to monitor reactive, proactive, and network change implementation cycles, we can ensure network stability and reliability. After we have become consistent and technically competent in the required protocol analysis techniques, the overall network that we support will benefit from our own internal technical skills. By studying the technical measurement and data-decoding techniques presented in this book, you will significantly enhance your network support skills. As analysts, it is imperative that we develop a real network baselining methodology that inherently focuses on constantly optimizing our complete internetwork.

Finally, one of the most important goals of network baselining is to predict the effects of application deployment on an internetwork. Today, application deployment is the key activity that drives the network design, implementation, and support cycles of the MIS community. Network analysts know with certainty that the complete internetwork infrastructure exists primarily to employ critical business applications. Applications are the entities that drive the need for a strong foundation within *local* and *wide area network* (LAN and WAN) infrastructures. It is crucial to understand the importance of the application entity to the business and to ensure that steps be taken to accurately measure the impact of applications on a network infrastructure.

It is critical to ensure that the network infrastructure can accommodate the required applications of our business. Again, we must never forget that the entire reason for network infrastructure is to support business applications.

Network baselining involves a set of complex analytical steps that comprise part of a complete methodology.

As noted, this methodology requires that we understand how to plan for data acquisition, perform actual data acquisition via protocol analysis, and report on our complete data-acquisition cycle. After we have completed this process, it all comes down to ensuring that we can support the flow of critical business applications. Having said that, we can now discuss network baselining goals. (You will learn how to achieve these goals later in this book.)

Foremost, the network must be stable, reliable, and must perform. We must ensure that business applications perform in a positive manner. We must also predict and gauge the impact of applications on the network to ensure that the internetwork can support the application component. We must maximize all our network technologies, and we must ensure that our network communication channels are available and can handle the capacity required for the business dataflow. All network devices and endpoints throughout the galaxy of our network infrastructure must be interoperable.

To gain the full return on our investment, networking technology must operate at peak performance. After all, networks comprise the critical infrastructure that makes global networking possible.

With these facts clearly in mind, the discussion now turns to the technical knowledge required to obtain and effectively use network metrics. To determine a network baseline, we must develop a skill set in key analytical measurement areas, such as protocol analysis dissection and decoding, as well as a process methodology.

1.2 New Network Implementation and Modification Analysis

It is a new day. We have many new network implementations planned. We have a schedule. Let's keep it. No, let's not. Why don't we take a quick break? Let's review the implementation plan. How many of the projects scheduled are really required? Do we need to perform all the steps we have outlined? Did we verify whether the actual products offered by our vendors are real requirements? Did our vendors and integrators draft the vector for our next implementation cycle or did we pave our own network migration path.

Many new implementations are painstakingly thought out, but many are not. That's okay, it's reality. But we have to take a break. Let's grab the wheel. Let's take the opportunity to own our network implementation cycle. It's where we live. Is the network so complex that we can't take a minute, a day, or a week to actually review the required implementation? It would be helpful to our mission. To truly manage new network implementation, we should use the art of network baselining. By using network baselining, we can review our implementation cycles. We can verify network implementations by using pre- and post-protocol analysis sessions. A definite component of network baselining is using protocol analysis and certain network metrics as gauges to properly plan and evaluate the success of network implementations.

These network implementations include such things as new products that we might introduce into our internetworks on daily cycles. We might also deploy new products, such as workstations, servers, new routers, and so on. We might also make changes to such things as the workstation software image, network interface card (NIC) drivers, and switch firmware. Network baselining enables us to verify these types of implementations. Many new products have specifications and benefits designed to be brought forward through actual implementation.

Did we realize the expected benefit? That is the question. Protocol analysis enables us to measure an area of our network as it relates to new product implementation. Measurements can be taken prior to deploying the product on the network in a pre-protocol analysis mode, and a comparative measurement can be taken after the implementation in a post-protocol analysis mode.

If we schedule a new server to replace a current server, for example, we must qualify the actual benefit of implementing the new server. Let's say, for this example, that the new server is required to generate higher effective throughput and faster response time than the current server (as related to housing and serving a critical business application). In this case, it would be beneficial if prior to deployment we were to engage a protocol analyzer in a pre-measurement mode to examine the current server's interpacket response time in handling inbound and outbound file Read and Reply sequencing. We would also benefit from checking the server's *effective file throughput* (EFT) and channel performance when multiple end nodes actually access the business application. For the purposes of this discussion, these are key measurements that enable us to view end-to-end data transfer performance criteria. (You learn how to measure delta response time (DRT) and EFT later in this book.)

After the new server is implemented, it would then be beneficial from a post-protocol analysis standpoint if we were to closely monitor the new server for the same measurements. It may be very clear that the new server does in fact generate a higher effective throughput and a faster DRT when our user base accesses the critical business application. We can only see this, however, through the process of pre- and post-protocol analysis. Figure 1.3 shows the use of pre- and post-protocol analysis to thoroughly review the impact of a new implementation or change on a network.

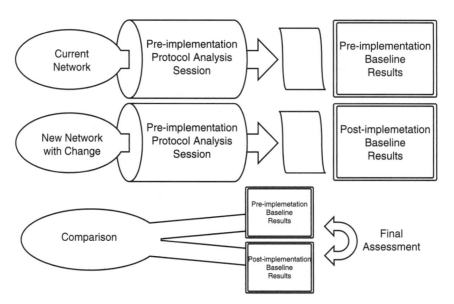

Figure 1.3 *Network modification analysis.*

These performance components, although inherent through many network management systems and high-end application monitoring systems, are only truly seen in an intricate and exact way through accurate pre- and post-protocol analysis. This book presents the actual methodologies and specific critical statistical measurement steps required to view this particular area of network implementation so vital to our network infrastructure and performance.

Circumstances may arise, for example, when we face a technical task that calls for a configuration change to accommodate our network operation, or for the implementation of a new product. Because of the real-world rapid work cycles in MIS, we may not always have time to conduct a preplanned protocol analysis session for statistical measurement prior to a change. It should always be possible, however, to use protocol analysis after a change in configuration to benchmark the effect of the change on the network environment. The important point here is that protocol analysis, when engaged properly against our network, enables us to view the product implementation and configuration change in a focused process mode. (Otherwise, we would make a limited rudimentary benchmark assessment of the network environment by just logging daily operations or by monitoring the end user's perception, perhaps by reviewing a daily help desk log.)

Keep in mind that network protocol analysis via structured techniques enables us to use statistical quantitative measurements to view our network implementations on a proactive and reactive basis. Many devices, products, and applications, along with software modules related to operating systems, are implemented on our network on a daily, weekly, or monthly basis. Many of these implementations are scheduled. From my many years of field experience, it is clear to me that many of these implementations and changes are not monitored closely throughout their implementation cycle. Is this because we do not have the time? Or is this because we do not have the necessary structured processes within our technical workflow model? Or perhaps we have not focused on the value of protocol analysis as an overall enhanced insurance related to our overall network operation and stability. The final message is simple: It is critical that we use protocol analysis and statistical measurements through structured network baselining processes when implementing a new network product or when changing a network configuration.

We must remember this important fact in our future project management!

1.3 Reactive Problem Analysis and Extraction

"Hey, I got a call from the help desk to troubleshoot a performance issue. I have a busy day implementing a new router. I'll hand the ticket to the Level 1 user support team; they will close out the issue. It will be a non-factor tomorrow. Fewer problems, fewer headaches, right?"

"Well, let's see, what if the same problem comes back tomorrow. That will not be viewed positively. We can mask the occurrence in this week's support meetings; and if it comes back next week, then we'll call in the top guns."

As an industry consultant who specializes in network baselining, these situations mean more business. We're going to get another call for emergency protocol analysis.

In today's network environment, in the fast climate of MIS support and operations, however, it is critical that networks be supported in a reactive and rapid fashion. To do this, we must take responsibility for a network reactive situation and must establish an understanding of the term *mean time to repair* (MTTR). MTTR refers to the time required to resolve or repair a network problem. The term MTTR is used consistently in the glass-house support world of mainframe computers as a measure of uptime factors in computing.

We must minimize the amount of time required to resolve critical network issues in LAN and WAN environments. Just as this was part of the mainframe environment and also related to mini-network support, it is also a real factor in today's network environment (as related to internetwork support for critical business applications).

Consider, for example, the CIO who puts his business reputation on the line, guaranteeing that the internetwork will support a new critical business application. Well, we (as network analysts) have to watch his back. It's our job. Better yet, it's our mission, because it's real life and because we care. So what's the deal?

We can use network protocol analysis to react to problems and also for extraction analysis. This statement is a clear fact. By using protocol analysis and properly deploying network analysis tools, we can analyze and troubleshoot most critical network issues and then find and propose specific recommendations at a rapid pace.

To accomplish this, we must use an exact methodology. The methodology must implement rapid network baselining to move quickly through statistical measurement processes. After we have moved through the statistical measurement processes and have developed a benchmark, we can then move forward with exact problem extraction using protocol analysis techniques. You can read about these techniques throughout this book. The key element to understand, however, is this: Workload characterization statistical measurement via network baselining is the front-end process to actual problem extraction!

Too often, we turn to conventional methods of problem determination to troubleshoot a network problem (because those methods seem familiar and easy). We must learn to rapidly measure our network infrastructure through baselining techniques, however, to extract data that clearly points to an exact cause of a network problem. This is the only way we can truly step to the plate when attempting to hit a home run on reactive problem and extraction analysis. Figure 1.4 represents the high-level concept of using protocol analyzers and associated management systems to rapidly troubleshoot network problems.

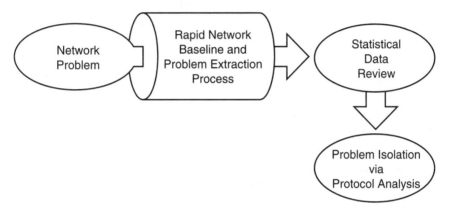

FIGURE 1.4 *Reactive problem analysis.*

Throughout this book, you learn how to use a protocol analyzer to resolve critical network problems. Simply put, however, you must follow a sequenced process in which you use workload characterization measurements to review key statistics, such as utilization, protocol percentages, error rates per topology, and so on, before actually reviewing the analyzer trace data to extract the problem. After you have extracted the problem, many other techniques enable you to analyze the data to determine the exact cause of the problem. These techniques also entail a structured and regimented methodology; however, they also demand a free-form dynamic mental process whereby you actually thread data to the network problem to prove the exact cause. This book presents other processes that are required to document the data items extracted via protocol analysis. To ensure that the final baseline report correctly represents how certain statistics and actual data points to the cause of a network problem, it is important that you use these documentation processes. More technical material appears later in this book (on both network documentation and key items to document in a network baseline report).

It is critical to use network baselining to review and document certain statistics on an ongoing basis (even when faced with emergency problems on a network). When troubleshooting, network baselining enables you to determine the exact problem. By using the network baselining methodology, you can develop an "on-target" technical synopsis of a problem's actual cause and can then make clear-cut recommendations to solve that problem!

1.4 Proactive Internetwork Analysis

In the network support world, rarely do we have time to think proactively. When we do find an opening in our schedule, sometimes it's nice just to focus on reading the current issue of a network magazine. As important as keeping current with the literature is, perhaps (if we can push ourselves) it may be better to take any extra time to think about what proactive internetwork analysis can do to ensure our network stability, reliability, and to enhance performance.

Is it possible to actually use our internetwork analysis tools in a proactive way for our network operation? Are the network analysis tools properly deployed? Let's take a look and see. Have we set up the network analysis and monitoring tools and adjusted them in such a way that the configurations and thresholds meet our unique network dataflow? Are they set on default? Or are they set in such a way that enables us to determine whether issues that affect our network stability occur on a daily basis?

Is it time to determine whether some of the network tools that we have implemented are properly integrated? Are they interoperable? Have we created a network management and analysis tool umbrella that truly cross-links and extracts the critical statistical metrics and data from certain tools that are valuable for our viewing capability? Have we tied our tools together in a proper manner and allowed them to intersect at a common area so that we can actually see the required statistics and data from a centralized viewpoint? Are the tools configured so that we can extract the required data for final baseline reporting?

Do we understand that the tools we have deployed are extremely powerful? Do we thoroughly understand these tools and use them to their maximum? We face these questions and challenges on a day-to-day basis.

A good time to become proactive is when all network operations are stable. By focusing on centralized internetwork analysis in a proactive stance, we may have a unique opportunity to get a strong handle on our network's current operation. By doing so, we can help to ensure the network's future stability, reliability, and performance. Remember that time may not be available in the future for this important process.

To move forward into a proactive stance, we must first review our network analysis tools. We must understand how they operate, and how they are configured, both internally as individual tools and tied together and applied against our unique network design. When we understand these facts, we then have the option of moving forward, using the tools in their default operation or possibly using a modified or adjusted setup of the tools that may provide for a better fit with our network. In other words, if we are at a point where we understand how the tools are configured and adjusted, it is then key that we move forward with any final adjustments required to enhance their effectiveness for our internetwork and our dataflow operation.

Most network monitoring and protocol analysis tools have a standard (or socalled default) configuration. In the default configuration, the tools may only be set up to gather and display certain types of statistics and data. Each network has a different design. An analyst can adjust certain parameters on most tools and thereby gather additional information and possibly display the results in a unique way. We must configure and adjust any tool we use for our internetwork operation in such a way that the tool relates specifically to our actual dataflow.

In summary, it may be necessary to modify the tools to form-fit our environment. This may require us to actually review the tool's configuration design, review the tool's thresholds that set alarms or display data, and adjust the tools to ensure that they can properly measure the actual dataflow within our unique network infrastructure.

After we have optimally implemented all the different monitoring and analysis tools, we must consider whether any overlap in features or operation exists among the tools. Some of the tools may include network management systems, application modeling tools, protocol analyzers, and predictive analysis tools.

The discussion here focuses mainly on the operational cross-threading of different tools. This relates importantly to proactive monitoring and data-analysis extraction. When we understand whether any overlap in features exists, in which the different tools represent common data types or statistics, we can then identify the overlap metrics that are more powerful in certain tools and less useful in other tools. Next, we can eliminate any non-required output from certain tools. By so doing, we can focus in a more proactive fashion and use the tools to their maximum potential, not becoming overloaded with redundant similar statistics and data from many different tool sources. Figure 1.5 shows the process of using protocol analyzers and high-level network management systems to produce structured baseline reports that include statistical measurements and data related to the network baseline process.

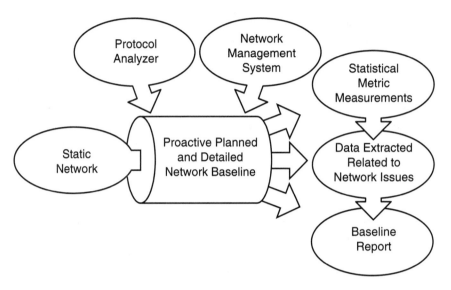

FIGURE 1.5 *Proactive network analysis.*

The final area to focus on in proactive analysis is network baseline reporting. We can have all the data and statistics in the world, but if we cannot accurately pull the required data from the tools and use the information to create a simple focused report on real network issues, the tools are useless. We have to learn how to drill down through all the statistics and data and find the relevant information. Next, we must extract the required proof to support our findings. Then we have to apply the information to a simple and focused documentation process to create a network baseline report.

Throughout this book, you learn key requirements of network baselining. We discuss in detail the monitoring and analysis tools most effective in today's networks. You learn how to use these tools to measure the network, using specific techniques that involve a real, working methodology. The art of data extraction will become your most valuable skill. Finally, you learn how to apply the gathered data to a real reporting process to create a network baseline.

At this point, you should understand the need to use proactive internetwork analysis. Proactive internetwork analysis is the most positive step you can take to ensure that your reactive problem cycle is minimal and that the application environment impacts on your network infrastructure in a positive manner. As discussed earlier, you should be prepared to use proactive internetwork analysis for new pre- and post-analysis implementation cycles.

We must never forget a critical thread throughout proactive internetwork analysis: Quantitative and statistical measurements are only *real* if an analyst can surgically remove the required data to present important issues to the appropriate technical and management personnel!

We must also never forget that our internetwork dataflow is the core of our business infrastructure. As we move forward, we must keep in mind that key parties must be able to view this data and make critical business decisions. Although some of these parties may be technical personnel, some may not be. Either way, we must create both critical exception reports and complete network baseline reports. Some of these reports may be reactive, but many may be proactive. Overall, by correctly using proactive internetwork analysis techniques, we can create a vanguard of energetic information to help us to ensure that reactive issues do not come to the surface.

Our job is to use the art of proactive internetwork analysis to extract the important information required to ensure that the network is both reliable and can support the business.

1.5 Application Impact Analysis

As mentioned earlier, application deployment is now one of the more critical technical cycles related to network infrastructure that we must face on a day-to-day basis (in terms of network design, implementation, and support). After all, application deployment across the infrastructure is the primary reason for a network's being. Early in networking, it was common for network users to launch a business application from one central file server. As networking moved forward during the late 1980s and throughout the 1990s, many network applications were structured with a centralized server design but were deployed in abstract fashion across internetwork architectures. This became more of a factor in client/server-based network deployment architectures. This natural evolution of application deployment has made network support that much more complex.

When applications are deployed in a centralized server process, it is much easier to track application usage through server and network operating system management processes. When the deployment of server applications became more abstract, it was due to the cross-pollination of application modules throughout internetwork infrastructures. As application component modules were spread across multiple points, such as client workstations and multiple servers, the support issues became even more complex.

Specifically, to actually troubleshoot or analyze networking issues related to application performance or application usage in a decentralized network design, we must deploy and use a troubleshooting process across many different areas of our internetwork infrastructure.

Because many applications require custom protocol flow sequencing through more than one server in today's networking architectures, we must deploy application modules across many different endpoints of our internetwork galaxy.

In many instances, application usage requires a launch from a specific client endpoint, and then an initial connection to a specific server. After the initial connection has been established, the dataflow may sequence and chain and process associated dataflow threads through multiple servers within an internetwork infrastructure. As this occurs, it is quite a complex task to actually track this type of dataflow. The only way to do so from an accurate technical standpoint is by using strategic protocol analysis techniques. This specifically means using protocol analysis dataflow capture techniques at multiple network area intersection points. This requires a skill set that includes an in-depth understanding of the methodology of network protocol analysis positioning for the express purpose of application characterization.

Throughout specific sections of this book, such as in the chapters on network baselining and the subchapters on application characterization and modeling, we identify the technical steps required to truly study today's application environment.

You learn how to use network analysis data-acquisition planning, network analyzer positioning, and application decoding and modeling techniques required to accurately characterize the applications deployed across today's internetworking environment. Figure 1.6 shows the use of protocol analysis and application monitoring tools to determine how an application will impact our internetwork infrastructure.

Techniques discussed include how to capture an application and review the events that occur within an application's process. Among these events may be sequences, such as a user connection, logon, application file access, application printing or scanning, and other specifics related to a certain application. You learn how to track the application's process through a technique called frame marking. The frame-marking techniques presented in this book teach you how to capture application data in such a way that you can go back into the traces at a later time and extract specific symptomatic problems and statistics related to the application (and relevant for certain analysis exercises).

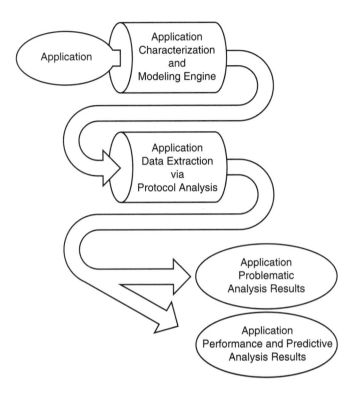

FIGURE 1.6 *Application characterization.*

One of the specific focus areas is measuring how applications impact the specific network area on which they are deployed. This requires using such analysis techniques as marking time sequences and data-transfer blocks for cumulative data. After reviewing these techniques, the discussion turns to how to investigate the dataflow for the specific chain and threading sequences through multiple devices and servers. The only way you can accomplish this is by applying the precise art of application characterization analysis.

Determining how applications impact the network is one of the most critical reasons in today's internetwork infrastructures to engage the art of protocol analysis and to present network baselining as a high-level umbrella process. It is essential to ensure that we are properly designing, implementing, and supporting today's business applications on our networks!

Chapter 2, "Baselining Goals," presents specifics on some of the key goals of network baselining.

CHAPTER 2

Baselining Goals

An analyst must keep certain goals that are important in networking in mind when performing a network baseline study. All networks must be stable and reliable. All network components must perform at the maximum specification for design. It is also critical that network devices work together to produce true interoperability.

2.1 Ensuring Network Stability

In any large internetwork, it is important to ensure that the physical foundation for protocol communications is 100% stable. User workstations requiring access to servers must be able to locate and connect to those servers. Today's large internetworks house many servers and other devices that must be accessed to facilitate final end-to-end communications. Locating these devices requires a stable physical network and a structured device-addressing scheme.

Complete internetwork communications can be easily obstructed if a network device, such as a server on a single segment in a *local area network* (LAN) cannot be located. The same is true if a server on the other side of a router within a LAN environment or even in a *wide area network* (WAN) remote resource area cannot be located. Such events can negatively impact the foundation of basic internetwork communications.

Many different scenarios can cause problems in a large internetwork. Certain problems may affect the capability of one device in a specific network area to locate and connect to another device or even possibly prevent initial communications from commencing.

An example is a physical network medium with excessive errors that may be impeding upper-layer dataflow fluency because the basic physical frame communications are not operating properly. The foundational basic frame processes can be impacted in a Token Ring network with an excessively high number of ring purges or in an Ethernet network with an extremely high collision rate. By engaging a proper network baseline process, an analyst can verify the physical foundation of a LAN topology (see Figure 2.1).

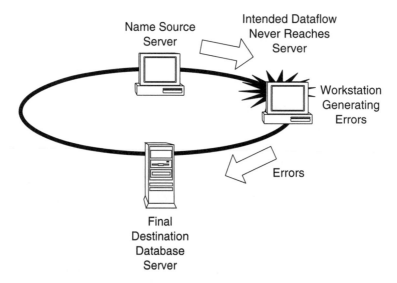

FIGURE 2.1 *Network medium with errors impacting application dataflow.*

Evaluation of a physical area of a LAN or WAN requires examining the particular medium. Large internetwork composite designs may require thorough investigation of certain physical media along the path route from one device.

An *end-to-end channel* can be defined as the complete network channel, which can be composed of multiple network areas and devices that connect two specific endpoints.

An example of an end-to-end channel is a workstation connecting to a server across a set of five individual Ethernet segments connected together by local switches and routers (see Figure 2.2).

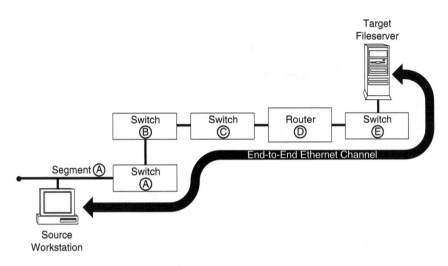

FIGURE 2.2 *End-to-end network channel.*

Note that all five Ethernet segments must be separately analyzed. The switch and the routers in the complete channel should also be examined for configuration and operation. To examine all five segments, you need a proper network baselining plan to use for network analyzer positioning. Chapter 13, "Network Baseline Planning Data Acquisition, and Final Reporting," discusses project planning in more detail. The goal is to ensure that the complete communication end-to-end channel from the workstation to the final server is physically sound. It is extremely important that the physical network provide a strong foundation so that devices can communicate between specified points in the overall design of the end-to-end channel.

It is important to evaluate whether all network devices can intercommunicate. For communication to commence, all main network devices must initially locate other devices.

An example of a network intercommunication problem is when one device is trying to find a physical address or the network layer *Internet Protocol* (IP) address of another device (see Figure 2.3).

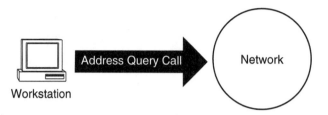

Workstation

FIGURE 2.3 *Device address query.*

Locating an address sometimes requires using certain upper-layer protocol sequencing, such as *Address Resolution Protocol* (ARP). As noted in Chapter 7, "LAN and WAN Protocols," a workstation can use an ARP sequence to generate an outbound broadcast to LAN network routers or hosts which can provide the required address information back to the workstation attempting to locate another device.

Each protocol environment uses addressing algorithms specific to that protocol suite or *network operating system* (NOS) interaction. This commonly requires the use of a central address table, such as a routing table, a bridge information table, or an associated host-addressing depository.

To start a communication session, an endpoint workstation usually attempts to communicate to a local host or a router that actually holds a specific addressing table or routing table. The workstation queries information from the device, which may contain the information of other key devices within the internetwork (see Figure 2.4).

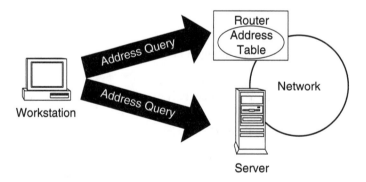

FIGURE 2.4 *Specific device location query process.*

Sometimes a workstation must call on a server to locate another server or servers. This may require the server holding most of the large internetwork information to maintain a consistent and accurate addressing table that references the location of other servers that can be located on the complete internetwork (see Figure 2.5).

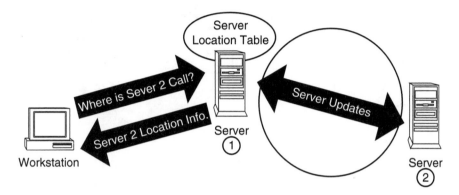

FIGURE 2.5 *Workstation-to-server query.*

When devices communicate across a large internetwork infrastructure, specific network communication sequences may occur.

Assume, for example, that we have multiple file servers in a large infrastructure NOS environment, such as Novell NetWare. The different file servers must provide each other with information related to their location and the service that they provide on the Novell internetwork. This can be referred to as *server synchronization*. Based on the NetWare release of the NOS loaded on the file servers and workstation, along with the type of the internetwork design, the server synchronization may be performed in different ways.

In the Novell environment, mainly used in older server designs, the NOS releases use the *Service Advertising Protocol* (SAP). Chapter 7 analyzes Novell in greater detail. The Novell SAP sequencing uses a process in which internetwork-based NetWare file servers cross-generate periodic, but frequent, SAP updates to other file servers. The updates include information detailing server locations and intervening network count and a service provided by all NetWare-based servers. In today's large Novell internetworks, *Network Directory Services* (NDS) provides a less-intensive protocol communication between the servers. The Novell NDS process is used so that when a user logs in to one Novell file server, they actually log in to the complete internetwork database of file servers. Both SAP and NDS processes engage server synchronization. The important fact for this discussion is that server synchronization is critical for workstation devices to locate certain servers and services (see Figure 2.6).

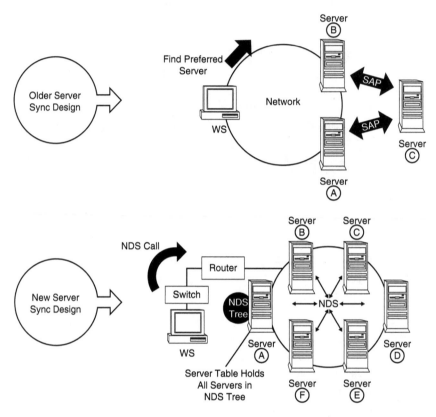

FIGURE 2.6 *Server synchronization.*

To ensure that the information is correct, specific protocol communication sequences must occur on a consistent basis between the servers. If the protocol sequences fail—if the update of an addressing profile is incorrect or corrupted, for example—the stability of the complete internetwork can be affected. The *Open System Interconnection* (OSI) protocol model directs how NOS and application vendors can help to ensure this process. (See Chapter 7 of this book for a further description of the OSI protocol model operations.)

If an end user using a workstation is logging on to a server on a local segment but cannot locate a remote server on another segment, for example, a non-stable situation results (see Figure 2.7).

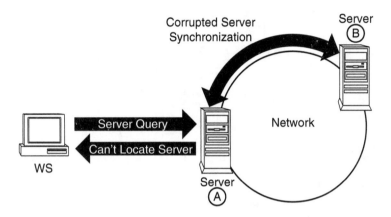

FIGURE 2.7 *Server location failure occurrence.*

Another condition that could result in a network stability problem is when a workstation requires access to a remote device, but the workstation knows only the assigned IP address. The station attempts to call out the IP address to a localized router that should answer with a physical address route.

An example of this is ARP. Chapter 4, "Quantitative Measurements in Network Baselining," discusses the Address Resolution Protocol in more detail. In this type of circumstance, if the router holding the address table related to ARP cache (address holding area) does not have an accurate routing table, or if there are problems on the network surrounding the router, it is very possible that the routing table will not contain correct or consistent information.

Many situations can cause problems related to server synchronization or to the update of certain router tables within a large internetwork. Some anomalies are timing latency, low throughput conditions, or problems in a configuration of a certain device, or even possibly a non-stable physical network.

The key message here is that network stability is a major issue.

True network stability requires a solid and fluent operation of all physical network mechanisms, such as the Token Ring *Media Access Control* (MAC) operation or a WAN circuit operation. It is also important to maintain address integrity on routing tables across routers and associated critical servers and hosts within the infrastructure (see Figure 2.8).

Through the process of protocol analysis with the proper techniques applied, you can thoroughly investigate these areas and verify overall network stability.

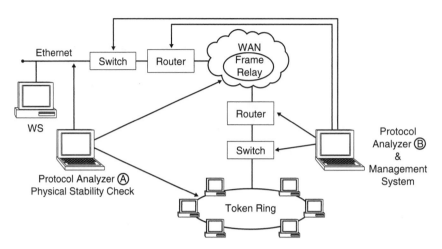

FIGURE 2.8 *Network stability check.*

You can use protocol analyzers to review a physical medium on an Ethernet, Token Ring, or WAN Frame Relay network. Investigating the physical stability of each LAN or WAN network topology requires a specific protocol analysis approach and methodology. If the network is not stable, the upper-layer protocols will not have a foundation to flow on and application data performance can be negatively affected. The overall addressing schemes must be reliable. By using protocol analysis, you can investigate server synchronization sequences, routing update sequences, and other key communication sequences on the internetwork, any of which may affect overall network stability of routing tables and server host tables.

One of the key goals of network baselining is to ensure network stability by examining physical integrity on all network medium areas and reviewing address schemes for accuracy.

2.2 Ensuring Network Reliability

The next main investigation area that must be established as a goal when performing a network baseline is the reliability of the network. Many of the upper-layer applications present in today's enterprise networks require connection-based processing during communications from one device to another. Connection-based processes of network protocol communications are discussed in Chapter 4 "Quantitative Measurements in Network Baselining," Chapter 5 "Network Analysis and Optimization Techniques," and Chapter 6 "Documenting the Network for Baselining"; this chapter does, however, touch on the subject.

When critical communications take place between network devices, such as a workstation and a server, it is important to maintain a consistent connection. A database application requires a stable protocol communication channel to be established between a workstation and a server before and after a file transfer occurs, for example. This is particularly true if the application design is intended to transfer multiple files in the overall application event operation. In this particular case, the NOS and the application developers may utilize a connection-based protocol to provide the required mechanism.

For an application design, an efficient connection protocol to use is *Transmission Control Protocol* (TCP). The TCP protocol is an extremely strong transport layer protocol. Chapter 7 discusses TCP in more detail.

For this discussion, the following notes apply:

- TCP is one protocol type that provides for enhanced transfer of data in a stream process.

- A constant connection can be maintained between two specific devices on the network.

This connection is possible through the process of opening a data port on each endpoint so that the ports can communicate with each other. Even when data does not flow back and forth, TCP provides updates to maintain the connection between the two devices by sending sequence and acknowledgment packets to the ports. This is referred to as a *poll* or a *network connection maintenance sequence*. In this situation, it is extremely important that the port connection between the two devices remain open and maintained, even when data is not flowing between the two ports. If the connection ever breaks abruptly, the upper-layer application level communications will not be able to commence when required (see Figure 2.9).

This can cause a network reliability problem across the infrastructure of a large internetwork!

In most large internetworks, specific devices are positioned to be critical to endpoint communications. Connection handling or maintenance between specific endpoints is usually a must. Most internetworks also use redundant channel design between critical device points, such as routers and switches. Specifically, you can design an internetwork infrastructure that allows for redundant channels to be accessed in the case that a critical device outage occurs. The key is that reliability is critical.

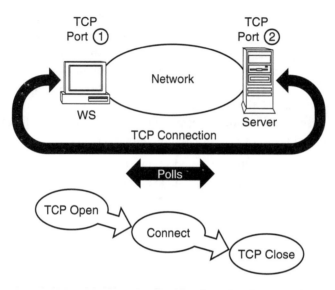

FIGURE 2.9 *Connection reliability factors.*

Reliability relates somewhat to stability because if the physical network operations are stable, there next must be an area of network protocol communications responsible for maintaining consistent dataflow operations. This specific area is mainly engaged at the transport layer within protocol communications. Through protocol analysis, it is possible to use a focused approach to examine network reliability. This process involves deploying a protocol analyzer and filtering in specific areas of the network on specific devices. The required filtering mechanism and applied techniques is discussed in Chapter 4, as well as throughout the rest of this book. For the purpose of this discussion, *filtering* refers to a technique used in protocol analysis that allows for focusing on a specific set of data. The key point here is that by using filtering when using a protocol analyzer, an analyst can effect an exact focus technique. By using an exact methodology, a network analyst can examine the reliability of a network communication session.

When using a protocol analyzer to focus on communication sequences for the purpose of ensuring network reliability, you should closely examine the transport protocol layer packet communication from a data-review standpoint.

The connection layer protocols that process communication across network endpoints hold key information. By using protocol analysis, you can examine this information (which is valuable to an analyst). You can review specific information, such as the connection state, stability level, and the response time between two specific devices (see Figure 2.10).

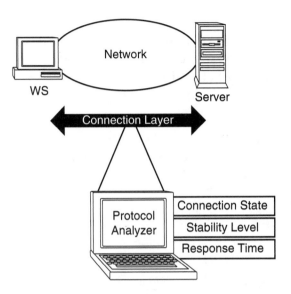

FIGURE 2.10 *Connection layer review.*

You can consistently monitor two endpoints communicating or maintaining a connection across a large internetwork infrastructure. If you closely monitor the endpoints, you can review specific statistics or metrics with the proper protocol analysis platform. An important area to review is how often a connection is maintained or updated when data communication is not occurring. This can relate to the occurrence of polling events and the timing pattern in which a polling event occurs.

The actual polling intervals can be reviewed for consistency, and you can determine the capability of each endpoint to communicate back with data size transmissions and the availability for handling data. These items are specific to each protocol type and topology environment. If two endpoints can maintain a connection and there is no interruption to the connection process, basic reliability is in place. Note also that servers and the workstations that communicate to each other across a large internetwork require a clear data path and a consistent capability to communicate in a reliable fashion. As noted earlier, it is important that all internetwork critical devices, such as routers and other devices that provide end-to-end passthrough routes for communication work in a 100% stable operation.

Simply put, it is important to investigate network communication connection sessions to ensure the final connection state of operations. It is also important to investigate the final passthrough route for true reliable communications so that when the application layer generates a data transfer, the transfer occurs in a 100% positive fluent basis (see Figure 2.11).

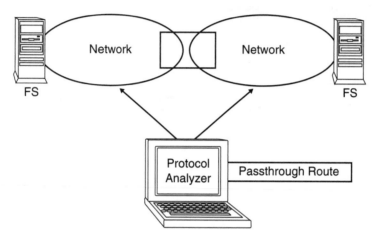

FIGURE 2.11 *Passthrough route analysis.*

The main message is that examining network reliability via protocol analysis is an important goal when baselining a network!

2.3 Achieving Maximum Performance

After you have thoroughly investigated network stability and reliability via protocol analysis, the next network area to review is internetwork performance. This can be as simple as monitoring two devices communicating or examining the complete internetwork performance. When examining the complete enterprise internetwork, the protocol analyst must use a large pallet of statistical measurements that would most likely include using management systems and protocol analysis in a combined fashion. When monitoring just two devices for performance, the analyst must focus on examining how much data is transferred within a certain amount of time related to a specific communication event, such as file transfer. The analyst can monitor the file transfer for *effective file throughput* (EFT). Chapter 5, "Network Analysis and Optimization Techniques," discusses the measurement techniques required for performance analysis (see Figure 2.12).

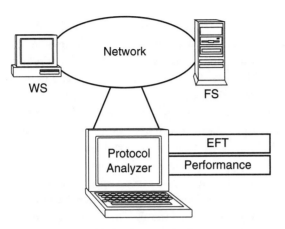

FIGURE 2.12 *Performance analysis.*

The performance level of network communications is also measured by users and our operations staff (in terms of how the network response time is rated). This is actually just a perceived response time. A major end user complaint is that the network is slow or that it is not performing well. When a user issues complaints, we must closely examine the problem. To do so may require interviewing the user before using any troubleshooting processes. When interviewing the user, it is important to determine whether any portion of the application delays the user is experiencing is related to the application, workstation, or the network. Many times a user just does not properly use an application or execute a workstation. When this is the case, the delays can be labeled "Business Transaction Delays." This type of delay is not the same as an actual application or network delay, because the delay is affected by the business user (see Figure 2.13).

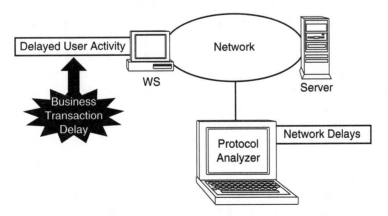

FIGURE 2.13 *Business transaction delays versus network delays.*

Large internetworks include complex designs built on a foundation that implements multiple servers throughout the infrastructure. Some designs include devices, such as routers, communication servers, and firewalls, that require access to multiple resource endpoints. This type of design can lead to many complex issues. When workstations are communicating to servers, it is important to determine whether the maximum performance level is being attained. When dealing with different topologies and different protocols, the final performance achieved as related to specifications may vary based on the network technologies involved. There are performance specifications as to how much data can be transferred on a LAN medium, and certain specifications relate to a WAN medium. When performing a network baseline study, you can use various measurements to verify these items. Chapter 6, "Documenting the Network for Baselining," and Chapter 7 cover baselining LAN and WAN networks. Another area that can affect final performance is the NOS and the protocols deployed (which affect final end-to-end communication). The overall application design or the application traffic profile applied against the specific internetwork design can also affect performance.

A protocol analyzer enables an analyst to use a technique to examine how a workstation and a server are communicating across an internetwork. Through a close review of the communication sequence, the analyst can benchmark the actual performance level. After the analyst obtains the end-to-end performance benchmark, he can extract certain details from the session—for example, a workstation communicating to a remote server at a data rate of 200 kilobytes per second (Kbps).

Next, it is important to investigate whether this is an optimal level as related to the physical topologies involved, the associated NOS, and the combined application transfer requirements. If end users are complaining about the speed of an application or the network in general, it is important to use protocol analysis techniques to surgically investigate the location of delays. Through analysis, you can pinpoint the delays to a network area or a device that may be negatively impacting the end-to-end channel and lowering the related internetwork throughput. This may require reviewing the EFT on a specific user segment, then investigating the throughput across a specific router, and then finally investigating the throughput on the target network. It may even be necessary to investigate the actual server handling or inter-throughput time on a specific device. Through the measurements applied, you may be able to determine how much of the end-to-end 200Kbps throughput rate is applied in the local workstation, LAN, WAN, remote server, or the actual application and any delay noted. The process of examining and pinpointing network latency may become involved. The actual techniques used, as well as the configuration and deployment of protocol analyzers, and the final analysis positions chosen to review achieved performance are extremely critical (see Figure 2.14).

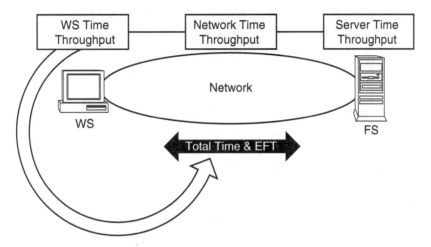

FIGURE 2.14   *Time and throughput tracking analysis.*

The most outstanding concept from this particular area of the book is that maximum performance is an important goal in network baselining and must be reviewed via protocol analysis.

2.4 Ensuring Application Efficiency

When establishing a set of goals for a network baseline, the next main area that an analyst must investigate after reviewing stability, reliability, and performance is application protocol sequencing. We can review an application in many different ways through many different custom management and analysis tool platforms.

The main objective of reviewing an application is to determine whether the application is efficient and is performing at the maximum level in terms of the application design and intended operation. Each application must be investigated thoroughly through an exact process, using a technique known as *application characterization*. Application characterization is the process of profiling an application via analysis tools by capturing dataflow related to events that occur when individual steps of an application are engaged. We can use protocol analysis tools to filter specific application transfers between workstations and servers. By observing how the application is operating within specific events, we can determine whether the application is efficient as related to the original design. Chapter 4 discusses specific details on application characterization along with the methods for using an application study.

Many times when applications are deployed on large internetworks or rolled out in a migration cycle, they are not deployed in the most efficient manner. When an application is originally designed, it usually has a certain efficiency rating or performance level that should be attained within a network configuration. When the application is deployed "live" on a large internetwork, network issues in various areas may impact the application or cause problems related to the final efficiency. You can deploy an application against a network topology design in many ways. Using application characterization techniques makes it possible to monitor each event of an application, such as a logon, file access, or printing, and to examine how rapidly data is processed and how much data is processed within an individual event sequence. You can also examine use effects on a particular network area and examine the units of data actually sent from one endpoint to another. This process is extremely involved, but is also very critical to the final review of internetwork communications.

It is a fact that networks exist for the express purpose of providing application access or remote access to key critical resources. Due to this fact, application characterization is a critical step in our network analysis baselining goals (see Figure 2.15). It is also important to reinforce the fact that a network must be stable, reliable, and with optimal performance to provide a foundation for true application efficiency. As noted, application characterization is discussed in much more detail in Chapter 4.

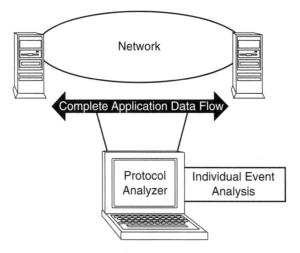

FIGURE 2.15 *Basics of application characterization.*

2.5 Maximizing Technologies

In today's large internetworks, we face many different network technologies from a design, layout, implementation, and support standpoint. There are hardware technologies, operating system technologies, and application technologies. Within the physical hardware technologies, there are many different server platforms, many different router platforms, and many different workstation or unique peripheral platforms. Some of these devices are intended for a specific technical purpose as related to LAN or WAN topology and internetwork architecture design. At times, network devices and software are designed for a specific purpose and operation, but may have different specifications as to performance, data-rate handling, response-time capability, or other possibly unique configurations. It is important that we understand that these technologies must be maximized to allow for application efficiency and maximum performance to occur across an internetwork. Hardware platforms or NOS configurations are usually deployed on an internetwork with initial default configuration settings. These default configurations may not always be optimal for final internetwork communication operation. It is extremely important to determine whether servers are responding at the highest specification level possible, or whether routers can provide the highest throughput possible, or whether applied NOS configurations are causing problems where the technology is not maximized. Protocol analysis enables us to examine whether a technology is being deployed and maximized against the top-level operating specifications.

Consider, for example, that an Ethernet *network interface card* (NIC) is deployed in a server that can use a *maximum transmission unit* (MTU) of 1518 bytes at the physical Ethernet frame level. A frame MTU can be described as the specified maximum size for a physical frame as related to a certain LAN or WAN topology. Specifically, the NIC can generate a packet up to a maximum of approximately 1500 bytes. If a server is deployed and properly configured against the internal NOS and can also transmit packets that allow end-user workstations to negotiate packet sizes with the server up to 1500 bytes, this would be a maximum applied configuration of the NOS to the physical Ethernet NIC MTU operation. If the application deployed against the workstation and server limits the packet size through initial TCP communication sequencing and reduces the *maximum segment size* (MSS) to approximately 500 bytes, this would be a negative configuration. This would cause packets to be negotiated down to the 500-byte level instead of utilizing the 1500-byte MTU within the Ethernet physical NIC and the NOS configuration. This is just one example of a specific area of a possible misconfiguration, where technologies are not being maximized and the cause in this area would be the application. Throughout this book, various case studies and discussions address the critical process of reviewing our technologies to ensure that they are maximized in terms of their original configuration (see Figure 2.16).

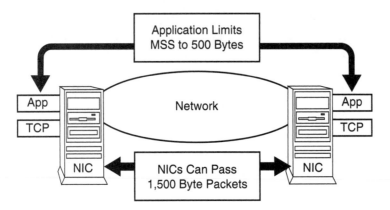

FIGURE 2.16 *Transfer without maximized design.*

Reviewing hardware and software technology operation via protocol analysis is a key goal in network baselining because it enables an analyst to view network traffic to verify network configurations.

In summary, by using protocol analysis in a focused manner, we can examine whether the technologies across our internetworks are being maximized.

2.6 Sizing a Network Communication Channel

LAN and WAN designs have specifications in terms of the maximum data capacity that can be handled. Routers and certain other data-passthrough devices, such as switches, also have specifications as related to throughput or maximum dataset handling capability. It is important to understand that when a workstation talks to a remote file server, many different network areas and devices might provide passthrough routes for dataflow. Many different devices and network segment areas may be utilized for final end-to-end communications. The workstation is one endpoint and the server is another. If they are on the same LAN segment, the network communication channel is simple to review. It is important when performing an internetwork baseline to examine each individual network area and device for capacity and data-rate handling.

For example if you have a workstation that is communicating to a server across a local Ethernet segment, you would need to apply a process to ensure that the communication channel is properly sized. You can use a protocol analyzer to review the workstation communication capability to access the Ethernet and the Ethernet medium's handling capability to transfer the data. The next area that you could study is how the server responds back to workstation requests and the server capability to use the Ethernet channel. Note also that you can use certain measurements, such as utilization, effective throughput, and others to verify this area. This is an example based on just one specific Ethernet end-to-end channel.

Another example would be if the same server is placed on a remote LAN four networks away (or four hops away) and two additional LAN segments and a WAN network must be traversed for the workstation to reach the remote server. In this case, the overall network end-to-end channel becomes much more complex. There could even be multiple topologies deployed (considering that the WAN channel is involved). In this particular case, different capacity levels and applied data-rate handling are involved, and these affect the final EFT and overall performance of the complete end-to-end channel. Depending on the topology, a device configuration from the workstation all the way through the four-network segment area to the actual server a final capacity will be required. The overall end-to-end network communication channel should be designed to effect an equal level in terms of load distribution and capacity handling. In this example, the final message is that when multiple network areas and devices are involved in the complete channel, the protocol analysis techniques become more involved. In other chapters of this book, you learn exactly how to analyze communication channel capacity and to effect a design that allows for maximizing the internetwork end-to-end channel performance (see Figure 2.17).

Some of the potential network communication channel sizing issues are resolved in the design, but sometimes design issues are not calculated properly. It is also a fact that when network migration cycles are implemented, such as in large rollouts, certain network communication channels are not maximized. In these situations, you should use protocol analysis to review the sizing of a network communication channel. You can review the basic design specifications and examine the general performance end-to-end matching configurations. It is important that the overall end-to-end network communication channel be properly sized, however. Each topology has a specific tolerance as related to maximum capacity that can be achieved for a certain time period. Certain topologies tolerate the maximum capacity being exceeded or the capacity close to being exceeded better than others do. For example, the Ethernet CSMA/CD access method engages a contention-based process that creates a more sensitive environment on the physical medium as related to high-burst utilization of available bandwidth. This is the opposite as compared to deterministic access-based topologies, such as Token Ring, which can sustain high levels of utilization and still provide each node equal access per node. The key factor here is that through the use of protocol analysis, we can investigate the end-to-end communication channel between two devices.

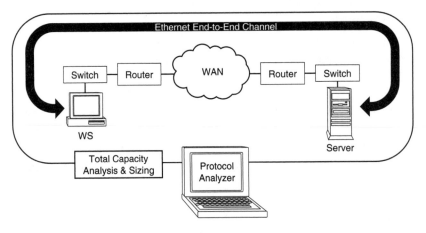

FIGURE 2.17 *End-to-end channel capacity analysis and sizing.*

In today's internetworks, because many multiple topologies and applications are deployed in a fashion that they must work together, it is important to review how the communication channel is sized against the overall performance match. Protocol analysis, enables us to review critical statistics with a dynamic and structured process. Throughout this book, you learn about capacity measurements, throughput measurements, and response-time analysis techniques that enable an analyst to properly size a network communication channel.

Remember that it is important that the largest amount of data can be sent across the complete network channel in the least amount of time. To do so, it is important to understand that network topologies must be configured to allow for a certain portion of the communication channel to be available on a consistent basis. It is not always correct to apply maximum use against an available capacity channel. It is always a good maneuver to leave a certain portion of the capacity available (for upper-layer communication sequencing or other events considered external to general application dataflow). What is important to remember is that the critical application dataflow must be able to access the communication channel at any given time in the most rapid fashion.

Protocol analysis techniques enable us to investigate a complete network communication channel. It is important to determine whether the required internetwork design has been applied to allow for a properly sized configuration. The complete channel must adequately handle the end-to-end application and session dataflow at a maximum level.

2.7 Network Interoperability

Many different devices are deployed across today's large internetworks. With all the different hardware platforms, software platforms, and different applications deployed, it is important that all devices work together in concert in a positive fashion. This concept can be defined as *network interoperability*.

In the early days of networking, it was simple to design a network that would provide for interoperability. After all, only a limited pallet of physical network topology devices, and basic workstations, and server platforms were available. Also, there were only basic router and bridge platforms available. In today's large internetworks, a multitude of devices have to work together to provide for true end-to-end interoperability.

Routers, for example, have to be thoroughly investigated for their overall configuration and interaction with other routers on the internetwork. New switches should be reviewed for parameters to define whether they are properly configured for a certain network area. NOSs also have to be deployed carefully to ensure that they are properly configured for frame sizes, which are interoperable with certain topologies. It is also important that the actual physical frame communication configuration be properly implemented. After the NOS has been deployed, other parameters may affect applications in terms of interoperability. You can adjust certain timing parameters on workstation clients and servers to allow for operating systems to maintain connections. Also, at times, configuration parameters are applied that are not 100% effective when considering the final application handling and performance requirements. If network devices are not properly designed for true interoperability, the overall stability, reliability, and performance levels of the complete internetwork can be affected in an extremely negative fashion (see Figure 2.18).

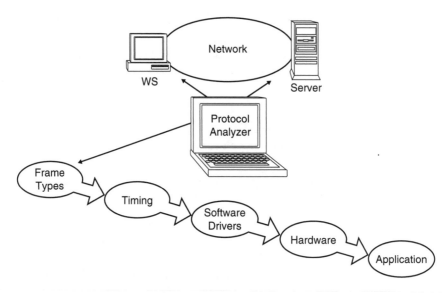

FIGURE 2.18 *Network interoperability factors.*

It is important to review all devices on an internetwork related to hardware platforms, software platforms, and final application designs to ensure that they are interoperable. Protocol analysis enables us to examine how network devices, NOSs, and applications communicate with each other on an internetwork. When using protocol analysis, we can examine actual dataflow for communication sequences, which will unveil whether the device, NOS, or application is configured in an interoperable fashion for the specific implementation. There are specific protocol error sequences that may be clearly evident when using a protocol analysis tool but that would not be evident through a configuration review process. Protocol analysis is the only way to truly examine network interoperability.

Another example is that if a router is deployed on a network it must be investigated for how often it updates another router. If all the other routers already deployed on the internetwork have a certain synchronization sequence, it is very possible the new router will have to be investigated for how often it provides an update. Using protocol analysis, we can view this update (see Figure 2.19).

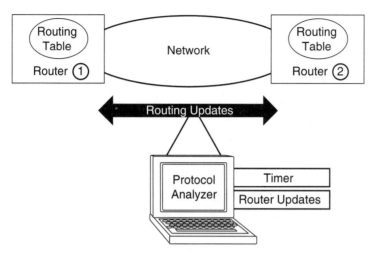

FIGURE 2.19   *Router synchronization analysis.*

One more example is that if new servers are deployed across a network and are preconfigured for certain Ethernet frame types, it is important to examine their frame type configuration as related to cross-ring interoperability. The server frame types must be verified to ensure that they are configured for the required frame types to communicate with all local and remote workstations that may require access to the servers. If the frame type is not properly configured on the servers, they may not communicate with the workstation devices deployed on the network.

In certain cases, you may have to reconfigure and adjust new servers for the proper Ethernet frame type. Protocol analysis enables an analyst to review all network devices for the type of Ethernet frame being used for active transmission. Any issues with regard to non-compatible Ethernet frame types can be quickly identified via network analysis. This type of analysis is further described later in this book.

The overall message here is that protocol analysis is the only way to truly examine network interoperability when performing a network baseline!

The next chapter discusses in detail industry-recognized protocol analyzers, network management tools, and unique application characterization programs. It is important for an analyst to understand the tools required for a network baselining study.

This book then moves into the deep world of network baselining using the art of protocol analysis!

CHAPTER **3**

Network Baselining Tools

This chapter presents some of the key network protocol analyzers along with other tools used to capture and evaluate the relevant data and statistics required when performing a network baseline study. Various tools can be combined with some of the tools mentioned in this chapter that are custom to certain networking infrastructure environments. Some of these tools include network management systems for internetwork hubs, switches, and routers. This particular chapter is dedicated to a review of specific tools in the category of network-based protocol analyzers, which can capture data and enable an analyst to view that data from a LAN and WAN analysis viewpoint.

Specifically, this chapter covers some of the most popular and technically competent protocol analyzers used to analyze LAN and WAN network topologies, and associated higher-layer protocol suites that travel across LAN and WAN mediums. Some of the tools are considered industry-standard products for network analysis, whereas other tools are somewhat unique and apply to a particular analysis or monitoring requirement.

3.1 Network Baselining Tool Usage Methodology

To perform a network baseline efficiently, an analyst must use a protocol analyzer with proficiency. This section presents a general description of protocol analysis and performance tuning. From a methodology standpoint, protocol analysis can be considered the process of using a protocol analyzer to capture data from a network, to display the data, and then to next review the data and analyze how certain protocols are operating within a particular network architecture.

Also from a methodology standpoint, *performance tuning* is the process of using workload characterization measurements gathered from a protocol analyzer and using the statistics for the purpose of tuning a specific component of a LAN/WAN environment. It is always the goal when performing a network baseline study to ensure stability, reliability, and enhanced performance within a particular internetwork architecture.

Before an analyst can tune a specific network topology, such as a Fast Ethernet or ATM network topology, the analyst must understand the particular topology specifics. Chapter 7, "LAN and WAN Protocols," covers the exact protocol analysis methodology that should be applied to a specific LAN/WAN topology or protocol environment when performing a network baseline study. The reader should refer to these chapters to truly understand the required methodology for analysis within a specific topology or protocol environment.

When performing a LAN/WAN baseline study, it is also important for an analyst to have the required skills to interpret the upper-layer protocols while performing a protocol analysis decoding exercise.

If an analyst is using a protocol analyzer on an Ethernet network that utilizes Novell servers, for example, the analyst should have experience in decoding Ethernet packets and Ethernet protocol layers within the Novell protocol suite, such as IPX, SPX, and NCP. This is just one example of the exercises an analyst may be required to perform. If an analyst were studying a 16Mbps Token Ring internetwork architecture with Windows NT Servers, the analyst might need to closely review the Token Ring packet for the general physical and header information as related to the Token Ring physical layer. The analyst would also need to understand the NT protocol suite within the packets captured in the applied baseline session. This would include protocols such as IP, TCP, NetBIOS, and *Server Message Block* (SMB). Chapter 7 discusses, among other things, how an analyst should review certain protocol environments such as the Novell NetWare protocol suite and the Windows NT protocol suite.

In summary, it is important for an analyst to understand that both the topology and the network protocol suite components combine to create a network architecture that should be reviewed in a network baseline study.

With that said, it is also important for the protocol analysis tool being used for the baseline study to be able to decipher the physical topology header information and display the information within a clear protocol analysis view. The protocol analyzer must also have the capability to provide an expanded, detailed decode of the particular protocol suite being analyzed.

In reality, protocol analysis is an art that must be used by an analyst when performing a network baseline study. To perform a network baseline study, an analyst must develop the required technical skill set to competently perform protocol analysis. After an analyst has developed a solid technical understanding of the LAN and WAN topologies and protocol suites that must be analyzed, it is next important that the analyst become inherently familiar with the process of troubleshooting and performing a network baseline study.

It is a given that developing the skill set and technical underpinnings required to engage protocol analysis and performance tuning requires time, and a methodical learning approach is needed to truly understand network baselining.

Before performing any type of network baseline study, an analyst needs to understand a specific protocol analyzer's use and operation. This chapter presents some of the general features available among the popular protocol analyzers. The analyzers have similar features. They enable an analyst to capture the data, display the data in different views, and also perform an analysis process (reviews) on the data in many different ways (based on the tool). Some protocol analyzers are more advanced than others; some even have artificial intelligence–based Expert systems that enable an analyst to immediately capture certain statistical data and to review result measurements on the data prior to even stopping the analyzer tool capture mode and decoding the information gathered.

Note also that some tools are rather rudimentary and only enable the analyst to capture the data and view it in basic form.

The discussion now turns to a brief description of a high-level methodology for protocol analysis and performance tuning, and then moves into an overview of some of the key industry tools. Chapter 4, "Quantitative Measurements in Network Baselining," and Chapter 5, "Network Analysis and Optimization Techniques," provide more detailed methodology and a description of the required steps for engaging protocol analysis and performance tuning.

3.1.1 Data Protocol Analysis Methodology

A protocol analysis session requires specific steps considered basic to the function of capturing and decoding data packets during a LAN/WAN baseline session. These steps include the following:

1. Preparing the analyzer for data capture

2. Capturing the required data

3. Setting up the analyzer for proper display views

4. Decoding the data in the display view and reviewing data from a general analysis standpoint

5. Examining the data for key statistics

6. Checking the data for physical errors

7. Reviewing the data captured for general performance for end-to-end communications

8. Focusing on problems in the data through further automated display feature views, such as filtering, triggering, time-structured mark setting, and setting other display features to isolate the scope of vision on the problem to a detailed level

The key to a highly effective protocol analysis is to get as much network data as possible to analyze. The analyst can do this by using a wide-spectrum horizontal approach as to a scope of vision. For the analyzer to capture relevant information, the analyst must apply certain filters and triggers (discussed later in this chapter). After the data has been captured and saved, the analyst must then concern himself with setting up the analyzer for a proper display view. The analyst must then, when a "good" view is attained, analyze the data and extract any key statistics, such as utilization, along with other metrics, such as physical problems or errors in the data. Overall, it is important that the performance of the baseline session be measured for general benchmarks (discussed in more detail in Chapters 4 and 5)(see Figure 3.1).

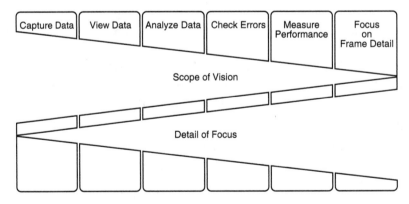

FIGURE 3.1 *Data protocol analysis methodology.*

The last focal point of any network analysis session is to refine the protocol analysis session review process by closely examining any detailed information that may relate to the baseline study session or to the problem being analyzed. The key here is that at the end of the protocol analysis process, the analyst should be able to accurately focus on specific statistics, data, and any problematic issues.

3.1.2 Performance Tuning Methodology

During a performance tuning session, an analyst will most likely be reviewing a new device in the network, or a recent implementation or change. As discussed earlier, there is a strong emphasis when performing a network baseline to ensure that any new devices or products added to an internetwork are implemented properly in terms of configuration, design, and operation. This applies to hardware, software, and application components, and even to network operating system changes.

If a new router is implemented between two key locations, for example, a pre- and post-analysis method should be used. If the older router is reviewed with a pre-protocol analysis approach, the analyst can benchmark statistics such as frame-per-second forwarding rates, effective throughput forwarding rates, and various information related to how the preceding router provided connectivity and performance between two specific LAN sites. This "pre-baseline analysis session" should be saved. If the router is changed and a new router is implemented with a higher-performance criteria, the analyst can use performance tuning methodology to ensure that the router implementation is effected positively.

Several steps are considered basic to the methodology of implementing changes to a network and performing a tuning exercise with a protocol analysis tool. Some of the key steps include the following:

1. Perform a pre-analysis session on the network area prior to the change.

2. Perform a post-analysis session and review any details regarding statistical change that may be required.

3. Pinpoint any differences noted in statistics or trends in the data analysis session that may enable you to further identify issues in the trace and to fine-tune the configuration.

4. Identify any errors or problems that point to a required tuning step to improve performance.

5. Define and document the changes necessary to fine-tune the network analysis session.

6. Perform a configuration change by implementing new hardware or software or reconfiguring, as required, to implement the final change operation.

7. Perform an additional post-protocol analysis session to see whether the implemented changes are valid and effective.

8. Document, in detail, the findings from the pre- and post-analysis session.

In summary, if a new device such as a router is implemented within a network, an analyst can use protocol analysis to evaluate the new router and thereby fine-tune the network's performance. If the results from the first post-protocol analysis session show that the router is not forwarding the correct size frame, for example, the analyst can analyze the data, review any problems, and pinpoint an exact cause. The analyst can then reconfigure one of the router's parameters (if that is the cause of the problem). When doing so, the analyst might identify parameter changes that could enhance network performance in other areas (the data-forwarding rate, for example). He can document potentially favorable changes, implement them, and then review the data after the change(s). The final step is to document the final fine-tuning process (see Figure 3.2).

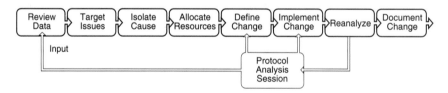

FIGURE 3.2 *Performance tuning methods.*

3.1.3 Protocol Analyzer Operational Methods

As noted earlier, an analyst needs a thorough understanding of the network topologies and protocols involved when performing a network analysis session. To be extremely effective in a complex internetwork environment, an analyst must have a full understanding of the following:

• **The LAN/WAN architecture involved.** This includes understanding the topologies and the associated protocol suites within the dataflow of the internetwork.

- **The correct approach for a network baseline session.** This includes protocol analysis methodology and performance tuning methodology. Chapters 4 and 5 detail the specific methods that an analyst should follow when conducting a network baseline session. However, a thread of information about network analysis methodology runs throughout this book. An analyst must keep in mind that a network baseline session requires a structured approach for each specific occurrence.

- **The protocol analysis and network baselining tools being used.** This includes an understanding of the basic function and operational modes of those tools.

The first two items are extremely important, because it is vital for an analyst to understand the LAN and WAN architecture of an internetwork, as well as to understand the steps required for a successful network baseline session. The easiest portion of the process is understanding the operation of a particular protocol analyzer.

Most protocol analyzers provide strong documentation online when using the analyzer, as well as a reference manual to assist with the tool's operation. An analyst should try to receive some training on the specific tool's operation. If an analyst knows how to use the analyzer, but does not understand the LAN architecture, topology, or protocol suite operations, or does not have a handle on the correct methodology, the analyst will most likely not be effective when using the protocol analyzer in a network baseline session. Again, understanding the specific tool operation is the easiest portion of the network baseline process. Such an understanding requires knowledge of how a protocol analyzer is configured.

The following is brief description of the basic components of a protocol analyzer.

Most protocol analyzers and network baseline tools are both hardware and software device platforms that enable an analyst to view data on a LAN/WAN. The protocol analyzer usually has a *network interface card* (NIC) that can physically connect to the LAN/WAN and create interconnection capability. In intrusive connections, such as WAN connections, the analyzer may have special cables, pods, or NICs that allow for a unique connection. The protocol analyzer usually has a special built-in NIC that interfaces with a specific suite of protocol layer decodes, which make it possible for the analyzer to interpret packets captured from the network. The protocol analyzer connects to the LAN or WAN topology point and functions as a separate node on the LAN or WAN area. When the protocol analyzer is activated for capture, it can capture all packets on the internetwork channel to which it is connected (versus just packets identified for a specific node). In other words, the device can operate in "promiscuous" mode and can captures all packets traveling across the LAN or WAN topology point where the analyzer is connected.

The NIC captures the packets and then passes data into an internal protocol-processing engine, which enables the analyst to quickly execute the "review decode" function and to display and review the captured data. Network analysis software models tend to be based on specific layer model designs. Most protocol analyzers include a base operating code along with a specific code for decoding certain data captured for specific topology and protocols. Most protocol analyzers, based on their design, vary as to their type of base operating code for the use of the analyzer—that is, the specific code that allows the analyzer tool to function.

The next important feature of a protocol analyzer to consider is its capability to look at a specific topology. Most protocol analyzers have a built-in NIC that allows connectivity to a LAN or WAN topology. One protocol analyzer might be configured with an Ethernet interface card or Token Ring interface card, for example, whereas another analyzer might be configured for WAN topologies. It is important to understand that the protocol analyzer, depending on its NIC configuration, will also have an associated code on the hard disk that allows for the topology packets to be interpreted.

Another area of importance in the network analysis software model for a protocol analyzer is the protocol suite decodes. These are the software module decodes that allow a protocol analyzer to properly interpret any of the decodes for protocol suite layers that can be displayed in the analyzer, such as IPX, SPX, or NCP in the NetWare suite, or IP or TCP in the TCP/IP suite.

The analyzer software modules work together to form the network analysis software model that works with the protocol analyzer hardware components, such as the NIC or the pod, that connect to the network. Again, the key network analysis software model protocol layers include the operating code, the topology code, and the protocol suite code (see Figure 3.3).

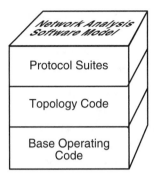

FIGURE 3.3   *The analyzer software layer model.*

3.1.4 Main Functional Modes of a Standard Protocol Analyzer

The main functions of most protocol analyzers used in a network baseline session are as follows:

- Preconfigured capture setups

- Active capture operation

- Display setup and processing configurations

- Detailed display features for focusing on data issues that involve complex schemes such as filtering or triggering

All protocol analyzers feature basic capture setup, active capture, display, viewing and decoding of a packet captured. Certain protocol analyzers are more advanced than others and have more features built in for general operation. Some of the more advanced analyzers even have Expert systems that provide automated review of statistics and data captured. Other protocol analyzers are rudimentary and just provide the actual data displayed onscreen.

Other more-advanced protocol analyzers display symptomatic statistics that enable an analyst to immediately identify a problem as data is being actively captured on the network. This is an enhanced view of protocol analysis and is built in to the more high-end analyzer tools, such as the Network Associates Sniffer, Shomiti analyzers, and the Wavetech Wandell Goltermann Domino line.

Most of the mid-range to more-advanced protocol analyzers provide detailed review and display features. Some of the main display and detail features include triggering and filtering.

Triggering is a technique that allows a protocol analyzer to start capturing upon the triggering of a specific event, such as when a specific workstation or server attaches to the LAN or WAN. In this case, the analyzer triggers upon this connection event and starts capturing data upon transmission from that device.

Filtering techniques are also available from the advanced protocol analyzers. *Filtering* enables an analyst to set up the analyzer in a precapture mode to filter out data types such as one particular protocol suite. Certain analyzers can also filter a specific protocol suite after the data has been captured, if properly set up prior to analysis. An analyst could, for example, set up a protocol analyzer to filter just on *NetWare Core Protocol* (NCP). In such a case, the analyzer would capture and save data for display related to the NCP suite only. No other data would be present in the final trace, if so set in a precapture mode for NCP. If the analyzer is set in a nonactive precapture mode, the tool could capture all the data, which could then be saved to disk. In this case, a post-capture display filter could provide for review of the NCP, and removal of the filter would enable an analyst to review all the other data in the captured trace.

When performing a network baseline exercise, triggering and filtering can be excellent aids. These steps are interlinked and described in detail in Chapters 4 and 5 (see Figure 3.4).

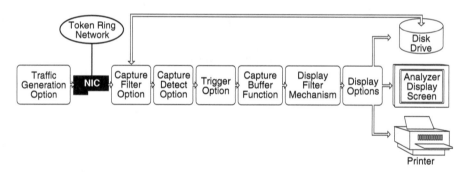

FIGURE 3.4 *The internals of a protocol analyzer.*

Note that cabling problems cause a high percentage of network problem symptoms. In the past, troubleshooting of a possible bad cable required many medium-testing techniques. Today most protocol analyzers provide internal testing features that engage a *Time Domain Reflectometer* (TDR) for testing the physical medium of the network area medium being studied. A TDR testing feature is a device mode operation within a protocol that can generate a specific signal on a LAN or WAN medium and then monitor the cabling medium for certain physical characteristics.

TDR testing modes are helpful for cause isolation when engaging a network baseline study related to physical problems that may be present on LAN and WAN media. Some TDR tools are separate, handheld devices; others are built in to a protocol analyzer.

3.2 Network Protocol Analyzer and Monitoring Tool Reviews

This section describes some of the most prominent network protocol analyzers and network management tools relevant to a network baseline study.

Keep in mind that other tools are also available within most of the large internetworking environments and that an analyst can use these other tools in direct conjunction with a portable protocol analyzer. Because of the limited scope of this chapter, only a brief review of the key protocol analyzers is given. Note that some of the key network management systems for internetwork hub, switch, and router infrastructure also have built-in features that provide automatic baseline processes. Included among these management systems are tools such as HP OpenView, which can provide device status and discovery capabilities for topology review along with many other statistical metrics. Also available are internetwork hub management systems such as CiscoWorks, Cabletron Spectrum, and Bay Optivity. All these management systems have the built-in capability to provide assisted baseline statistic metric gathering and also may assist in the baseline study process.

3.2.1 Network Associates Sniffer Analyzers

In the late 1990s, the Network Associates corporation acquired Network General, a company that developed and produced the original Sniffer analyzer (well-known to the protocol analysis market). Network Associates has developed and released a series of technology enhancements related to operational features of the original Network General Sniffer product line.

The new Network Associates Sniffer Pro is an extremely powerful analyzer that provides for a cross-internetwork visibility of many issues that may affect a network topology and protocol infrastructure. The Sniffer Pro offers an intuitive capability to monitor data traffic on a network area as related to dataflow activity on a real-time basis (see Figure 3.5).

FIGURE 3.5 *The Network Associates product family.*

Many different statistics and metrics can be gathered in a detailed view, such as utilization, error statistics, individual node-by-node station statistics, and error rates. Historical monitoring is available for statistical metric views of utilization, protocol percentages, error rates, and other key statistics over a selected time period. Intuitive alarms are built in to the Sniffer Pro system. An analyst can set these for immediate identification and associated isolation of issues.

The Sniffer Pro analyzer can monitor a network and can also generate traffic on a real-time basis. With this tool, an analyst can evaluate response times and associated latency on the internetwork. The Sniffer Pro is built to operate on and take full advantage of the multibit-level Windows operating system features. The Sniffer Pro product has been fine-tuned so that it can be colocated and can coexist in core residency with other applications without any major issues occurring (as related to the capture capability of the tool or its operational performance). The Sniffer Pro is an extremely high-performance system that supports most main topologies, including Ethernet, Fast Ethernet, and Gigabit Ethernet, along with Token Ring engaging 4Mbps and 16Mbps data rates, *Asynchronous Transfer Mode* (ATM), and key WAN network analysis modes such as T1, Fractional T1, *High-Speed Serial Interface* (HSSI), and basic and primary ISDN networks.

In the near future, Network Associates will introduce Sniffer Pro connectivity for higher-speed broadband technologies such as SONET, and other key high-capacity and high-speed network product lines.

The Sniffer Pro platform offers two major features from a network capture standpoint: analysis and monitoring. These features are comparable to the original Network General Sniffer in that they offer monitoring and capturing capability.

In the monitoring mode, the Sniffer Pro has various screens that can be viewed quickly to gain an assessment of the internetwork traffic statistics and dataflow metrics.

The Sniffer Pro Monitoring view offers the following:

- Dashboard view

- Matrix view

- Host table view

- Protocol distribution view

- History view

- Global statistical view

- Smart Expert screen

- Physical layer statistics

- Switching statistics

In a capture mode related to the Analysis view, the Sniffer Pro offers the following:

- Real-time analysis for statistics produced by an expert artificial intelligence engine for true cause-and-effect isolation

- Display features for reviewing data at a decode level for Summary, Detail, and Hex views

- Host Table view

- Protocol Distribution view

- Matrix view

- Statistical view

One of the key features of the Network Associates Sniffer Pro product line is that the tool provides simultaneous statistical monitoring from a full-spectrum viewpoint and, in direct correlation, the capability to immediately view the trace data captured that is producing the statistics in the monitor mode. This differs from the original Network General Sniffer product line, which separated the two products (such as Ethernet Monitor and Ethernet Analyzer). In today's Sniffer Pro product line, these processes coexist and can be operated in parallel, so an analyst can quickly transition between statistical views and data trace analysis views.

If an analyst requires Expert system capability assistance, the Sniffer Expert system decoding engine can be launched immediately to help isolate cause-and-effect issues.

The monitoring feature in Sniffer Pro enables an analyst to immediately review network load statistics, including a review of a percentage of utilization as related to general utilization, along with broadcast and associated frame and byte counts. Error statistics are available for most major topologies. When monitoring Ethernet, for example, the Sniffer Pro enables the analyst to quickly review CRC errors, long and short packets, fragments, jabber conditions, bit-alignment errors, and collision counts. For Gigabit Ethernet and Fast Ethernet conditions, CRC errors, code violation errors, jabbers, and runts can be quickly reviewed.

In a Token Ring environment, standard soft errors and hard errors can be monitored (such as a beaconing). The analyzer also enables an analyst to monitor ring purge counts and ring change events at the physical Token Ring MAC layer.

Protocol statistics are available for all major protocol suites. Individual stations can be monitored in a node-by-node mode, and packet-size distribution counts can be quickly monitored. All these features are integrated through a toolbar based on a Windows *graphical user interface* (GUI) in a monitor application window.

The Sniffer Pro dashboard feature is unique: It provides a real-time view of the internetwork traffic flow in a quick graphic display mode that shows packet-per-second count, errors per second, and utilization percentages. The gauge counters move quickly to show the actual changes as related to real-time traffic.

One of the key features in the monitoring process is the Host Table feature. The Host Table view offers an instant view of the LAN adapter statistics and metrics for each LAN network device active on the network. Physical addresses, network layer addresses, and application layer addresses can be quickly viewed. For high-speed platforms such as ATM, the host table shows a speedy view of the *permanent virtual circuit* (PVC) and *switched virtual circuit* (SVC) for ATM UNI and NNI connections. At the WAN level, virtual circuits can be viewed for Frame Relay, HDLC, and T1 connections (required for analysis review). The complete view is again integrated through a GUI.

One of the real benefits of the Sniffer Pro monitoring features is the matrix screen. The Matrix view shows real-time communications traffic flow from node to node across the monitored internetwork. An analyst can quickly view the matrix and associate the traffic map with actual real-time traffic occurrences back and forth across the internetwork. This view works for both LAN and WAN monitoring.

The Historical Sampling view available in the monitoring mode provides a rapid review of key samples, such as packet-per-second error rates, utilization, packet counts, broadcast levels, and physical error rates, along with packet-size indications from a historical standpoint.

The Protocol Distribution view is extremely powerful because it covers such a wide range of protocols. Some of the key protocols supported are IPX, SPX, NCP, NCP Burst, IP, TCP, NetBIOS, AppleTalk, and DECnet. Sniffer Pro can decode the IBM SNA, NetBIOS, OS/2, IBMNM, SMB, Novell 2x, 3x, 4x, 5x, and 4x plus NDS decodes, XNS: MSNET, Banyan VINES, XNS, SUN:NFS, ISO, PPP, SNMP v.1 and 2, LAPD, Frame Relay, FDDI and FDDI SMT, DLSw, X Window, X.25, SDLC, and HDLC. Also supported are many of the process application layer protocols for the TCP/IP model such as FTP, TFTP, NFS, Telnet, SMTP, POP2, POP3, HTTP, NTP, SNMP, Gopher, X Window, and many other key protocol suites (see Figure 3.6). The key factor is that the protocol screen is extremely dynamic for viewing protocol percentages on an internetwork.

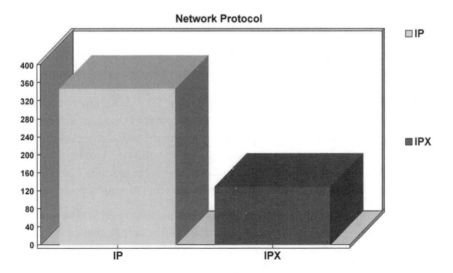

FIGURE 3.6 *Protocol distribution view comparing IP and IPX.*

The Global Statistics screen offers a quick view of the statistics required for an analyst to understand some of the key general workload utilization measurements.

Some statistical display views called smart screens are also available for some of the high-speed broadband technologies such as ATM. With the ATM adapter interface, an analyst can quickly review cell traffic as related to cell type, cell frame counts, OAM cell types, and LMI cell types. This is an extremely dynamic process.

Physical layer statistics can be viewed on an ATM network for each device operating in a PVC- or SVC-established connection, along with error rates. You can also view the exact cell traffic–to–error counts as related to ATM physical medium.

During a WAN network physical layer statistic review, an analyst can review traffic from a DTE-to-DCE perspective, quickly and in a clear graphical table.

The Switched Statistic screen is one of the new features and is extremely useful when monitoring *virtual LAN* (VLAN) configurations and switching statistics in a high-speed channel Ethernet environment. Each switched module connected and configured by Sniffer Pro for review can be quickly monitored. The switch module status, the port status, the VLAN assignment, and the traffic rates in and out of each port assigned from the switch can be quickly monitored. Error statistics can also be quickly viewed.

The Sniffer analyzer also offers a set of complex alarm features that are extremely dynamic and assist in managing the overall alarms that are preset by the analyst prior to starting the baseline analysis review.

The Sniffer Analyzer enables an analyst to filter on network data when capturing and displaying by protocol via data pattern matching and addresses filtering. The Sniffer Pro offers excellent time-relationship data views that an analyst can trigger when capturing and displaying by external and internal pattern matching. The display features enable the analyst to view in both numeric and graphic formats. An analyst can configure multiple view windows to view the summary of packets, packet detail, and hex representation on the same screen.

The Network Associates Sniffer Pro is an extremely powerful platform that offers an automatic fault isolation and true-performance enhanced management for small to large internetworks. The Sniffer Pro high-speed analyzer can quickly enable an analyst to isolate issues and identify problems and make recommendations. It enables true visibility across multiple internetwork topologies and protocol environments.

Network Associates also offers a software-only analyzer called *Sniffer Basic*. The Sniffer Basic tool offers the main statistical screens and some basic decoding engines for certain protocols. It does not offer any real Expert analysis and does not enable an analyst to use certain high-end filtering processes for cause isolation and analysis featured in the Sniffer Pro tool.

The Sniffer Pro tool evolved from the original Network General Sniffer. Network Associates will be adding many features to Sniffer Pro on an ongoing basis, and will offer enhanced support for all product lines. The original Network General Sniffer is still used by many analysts. Because of this, the following brief presentation of some of the features in the original Network General Sniffer is offered.

The original Sniffer analyzer product family offered many different configurations, including portable analyzers and complex distributed Sniffer configurations. The portable analyzer was offered in three versions:

- A preconfigured PC analyzer packaged in either a Compaq or Toshiba portable
- A PCMCIA version for most compatible laptops
- A NIC/software package for configuring the Sniffer Analyzer in a PC

The *Distributed Sniffer System* (DSS) supports the same analysis functions as the portable analyzer, but its main operation is to monitor an internetwork of distributed analyzers from a central-point console that inter-communicates with analyzers dispersed across multiple LANs. The DSS product line has three main components: SniffMaster Consoles, Sniffer Servers, and DSS application software.

The DSS Sniffer Servers are placed on different network segments as slave devices and continuously monitor the data and statistics for these segments. The DSS slave units communicate inband across subnetwork areas to the SniffMaster Console. The SniffMaster Console acts as a central client for main DSS server operations and gathers the dataflow and statistics from the Sniffer Servers.

The DSS hardware and software provide all the main Sniffer functions, but from a distributed view against multiple network areas. The Sniffer DSS data can be imported into a Sniffer and RMON combination, which allows for cross-platform views with SNMP management systems such as HP OpenView.

The original Sniffer supported most major protocol suites. The original Sniffer main menu option included a traffic-generation feature and a cable tester. The traffic-generation feature enabled an analyst to load a network with traffic. The cable tester operates as a TDR.

The original Sniffer offered a software module separate from the main Sniffer protocol analyzer software known as the Sniffer Monitor. The module's main purpose was to monitor and display vital Token Ring or Ethernet network statistics. Displays were available for Station Statistics, Transmit Timing, Error Statistics (including CRC, collisions, and TR hard and soft errors), Protocol Statistics, Packet-Size Statistics, Traffic History, Routing Information, Reporting Writer Tool, and Alarms Indicator. The Routing Path was a unique feature that could show the location and percentage of packets routed through a multiple Token Ring environment, in relation to each ring (see Figure 3.7).

```
Frame Status Source Address  Dest. Address      Size Rel. Time     Delta Time Summary
   1 M        NETWARE-XT      1111.FFFFFFFFFFFF  113 0:00:00.000    0.000.000  NSAP: R NETWARE-XT
   2          1111.IBM002FEB  NETWARE-XT          67 0:00:00.000    0.000.057  NCP: C F=0000 AC08 0200 Read 4 at 166
   3          NETWARE-XT      1111.IBM002FEB      61 0:00:08.244    8.244.112  NCP: R OK, 4 bytes read
   4          1111.IBM002FEB  NETWARE-XT          67 0:00:08.254    0.009.995  NCP: C F=0000 AC08 0200 Read 256 at 1604
   5          NETWARE-XT      1111.IBM002FEB     313 0:00:08.274    0.020.025  NCP: R OK, 256 bytes read
   6          1111.IBM002FEB  NETWARE-XT          65 0:00:08.284    0.010.015  NCP: C Scan bindery for *
   7          NETWARE-XT      1111.IBM002FEB     112 0:00:08.424    0.140.224  NCP: R OK, Found SUPERVISOR
   8          1111.IBM002FEB  NETWARE-XT          65 0:00:08.434    0.009.994  NCP: C Scan bindery for *
   9          NETWARE-XT      1111.IBM002FEB     112 0:00:08.454    0.020.035  NCP: R OK, Found GUEST
  10          1111.IBM002FEB  NETWARE-XT          65 0:00:08.464    0.010.033  NCP: C Scan bindery for *
  11          NETWARE-XT      1111.IBM002FEB     112 0:00:08.484    0.020.007  NCP: R OK, Found HARRY
  12          1111.IBM002FEB  NETWARE-XT          65 0:00:08.494    0.010.010  NCP: C Scan bindery for *
  13          NETWARE-XT      1111.IBM002FEB     112 0:00:08.514    0.020.032  NCP: R No such object
  14          1111.IBM002FEB  NETWARE-XT          65 0:00:08.524    0.010.012  NCP: C Create Bindery Object JIM
  15          NETWARE-XT      1111.IBM002FEB      55 0:00:19.109   10.585.227  NCP: R OK
  16          1111.IBM002FEB  NETWARE-XT          74 0:00:19.129    0.020.026  NCP: C Create property for JIM
  17          NETWARE-XT      1111.IBM002FEB      55 0:00:19.149    0.020.021  NCP: R OK
  18          1111.IBM002FEB  NETWARE-XT          81 0:00:19.159    0.010.016  NCP: C Create property for JIM
  19          NETWARE-XT      1111.IBM002FEB      55 0:00:19.179    0.020.050  NCP: R OK
  20          1111.IBM002FEB  NETWARE-XT          79 0:00:19.189    0.009.994  NCP: C Create property for JIM
  21          NETWARE-XT      1111.IBM002FEB      55 0:00:19.209    0.020.025  NCP: R OK
  22          1111.IBM002FEB  NETWARE-XT          90 0:00:19.229    0.020.031  NCP: C Add JIM to set
  23          NETWARE-XT      1111.IBM002FEB      55 0:00:19.249    0.020.033  NCP: R OK
  24          1111.IBM002FEB  NETWARE-XT          88 0:00:19.430    0.180.257  NCP: C Add JIM to set
  25          NETWARE-XT      1111.IBM002FEB      55 0:00:19.450    0.020.027  NCP: R OK
  26          1111.IBM002FEB  NETWARE-XT          88 0:00:19.490    0.040.061  NCP: C Add EVERYONE to set
  27          NETWARE-XT      1111.IBM002FEB      55 0:00:19.510    0.020.027  NCP: R OK
  28          1111.IBM002FEB  NETWARE-XT          63 0:00:19.540    0.030.044  NCP: C Get bindery object ID for JIM
  29          NETWARE-XT      1111.IBM002FEB     109 0:00:19.560    0.020.025  NCP: R OK, Received JIM
  30          1111.IBM002FEB  NETWARE-XT          68 0:00:19.570    0.010.021  NCP: C Create handle for SYS:MAIL
```

FIGURE 3.7 *Sniffer Pro protocol decode summary screen.*

The original Sniffer then allowed analysts to quickly launch a separate program known as the *Sniffer Analyzer*. The original Sniffer Analyzer offered most of the capture, decode, and analysis display views as the new Sniffer Pro, but was mainly based on a DOS engine. The original Sniffer Expert system assisted an analyst with automatically locating problems on a network and offered advice on resolving particular network issues or problems. This system has been significantly enhanced in the new Sniffer Pro product line to offer an integrated data view of real-time statistical issues, along with direct hotkey mapping of error occurrences to real data (see Figure 3.8).

```
- - - - - - - - - - - - - - - - - Frame 1 - - - - - - - - - - - - - - - - - -
 Frame Status Source Address   Dest. Address     Size Rel. Time    Delta Time  Summary
     1 M       NETWARE-XT      1111.FFFFFFFFFFFF   113 0:00:00.000   0.000.000  NSAP: R NETWARE-XT
DLC:  ----- DLC Header -----
DLC:
DLC:  Frame 1 arrived at  06:41:47.725; frame size is 113 (0071 hex) bytes.
DLC:  FS: Addr recognized indicators: 00, Frame copied indicators: 00
DLC:  AC: Frame priority 0,  Reservation priority 0,  Monitor count 0
DLC:  FC: LLC frame,  PCF attention code: None
DLC:  Destination = Functional address C00000800000, NetWare_Stns
DLC:  Source      = Station IBM2  0033BF
DLC:
LLC:  ----- LLC Header -----
LLC:
LLC:  DSAP Address = E0, DSAP IG Bit = 00 (Individual Address)
LLC:  SSAP Address = E0, SSAP CR Bit = 00 (Command)
LLC:  Unnumbered frame: UI
LLC:
IPX:  ----- IPX Header -----
IPX:
IPX:  Checksum = 0xFFFF
IPX:  Length = 96
IPX:  Transport control = 00
IPX:        0000 .... = Reserved
IPX:        .... 0000 = Hop count
IPX:  Packet type = 4 (IPX)
IPX:
IPX:  Dest    network.node = 1111.FFFFFFFFFFFF, socket = 452 (NetWare Service Advertising)
IPX:  Source network.node = 1111.IBM0033BF (NETWARE-XT), socket = 452 (NetWare Service Advertising)
IPX:
NSAP: ----- NetWare General Service Response -----
NSAP:
NSAP:  Service type = 0004 (File server)
NSAP:  Server name = "NETWARE-XT"
NSAP:  Network = 00001111, Node = 10005A0033BF, Socket = 0451
NSAP:  Intermediate networks = 1
NSAP:
```

F I G U R E **3.8** *Sniffer Pro protocol detail summary screen.*

The Sniffer Analyzer's strengths are clearly the expanded range of support for all major network topologies and protocol suites.

The built-in Expert system capability to isolate issues on-the-fly and help an analyst identify the cause of network problems is a significant plus because of the accuracy, along with the online Expert help system that is available to an analyst. The Sniffer Pro report-generating features are excellent for creating network baseline data reports. Almost all the network statistics gathered with Sniffer Pro can be quickly viewed in multiple windows and then fed directly to the reporting engine and also can be printed in various standard formats and fed into most major PC third-party applications for management reporting (see Figure 3.9).

```
Network Associates Expert Object Report
Connection : TCP Connection: Port 4704-23
```

Protocol	Telnet	
Station Function	Workstation	Workstation
Network Name	[36.53.0.195]	[36.56.0.208]
Network Address	[36.53.0.195]	[36.56.0.208]
DLC Name	3Com2 115176	3Com2 063841
DLC Address	02608C115176	02608C063841
Subnet	[36.53.0.0]	[36.56.0.0]
Port	4704	23
Frames transmitted	28	15
Data bytes transmitted	574	314
Zero windows	0	0
Average Ack Time	41ms	270ms
Window Size Range	512	4096
Keep Alives	0	0
Retransmissions	0	0

	Response Times
Requests	14
Total Response Time	3s 827ms
Maximum Response Time	1s 172ms
Minimum Response Time	40ms
Average Response Time	273ms

Applications
Telnet Application

Alarms:

Ack Too Long (1172ms)	TCP Connection: Port 4704-23
Ack Delta Time	1s 172ms
Maximum Ack Time	826ms

FIGURE 3.9 *Sniffer Pro expert screen.*

3.2.2 Shomiti Systems Inc. Analysis Tools

The Shomiti Systems Inc. network analysis tool company offers an excellent palette of network analyzers and monitoring tools for small, medium, and large internetworks.

One of the key tools that Shomiti has introduced is a Windows platform analyzer called *Surveyor*. Surveyor offers the capability to monitor an internetwork quickly through the Windows platform. Real-time analysis display views are available for multiple topologies. Surveyor can sample and enable an analyst to review network physical layers. The tool also provides decoding capabilities for a multiprotocol layer model, including all seven layers for many major protocols. There is also an artificial intelligence analysis engine Expert module built in to the system, called the *Expert module for Surveyor*. This system offers automatic problem detection capability for network issues. The Expert module enables a network analyst to be quickly notified of any issues that may require further decoding and corrective actions via cause analysis. The Expert system works dynamically with the main Surveyor analyzer engine and enables an analyst to quickly associate problems and issues to actual data trace internals captured with the Surveyor tool. The symptoms can be reviewed on standard LANs and on VLAN systems (see Figure 3.10).

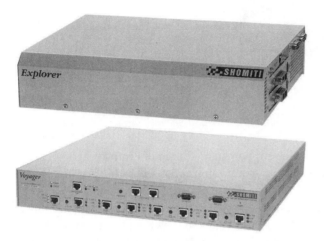

FIGURE 3.10   *A product family shot of the Shomiti tools.*

Many unique symptoms can occur on a network. Because of this, the Surveyor Expert system enables an analyst to isolate physical issues and transport retransmission issues as well as application layer communication problem-based issues. These are just some of the symptoms that can be quickly identified with the Shomiti Surveyor analyzer. The analyst can then engage a filter to quickly move to the trace analysis data area where the problem may be present.

The main Surveyor analyzer engine supports most of the main physical LAN topologies, such as 10Mbps and 100Mbps Ethernet, and 4Mbps and 16Mbps Token Ring. A real-time monitoring capability enables an analyst to gain statistical views of utilization, frame-per-second rate counts, protocol percentages, and error-rate statistics for all the key topologies. The main Surveyor analyzer platform has many display views in the statistical mode comparable to other tools. The Surveyor offers Protocol Distribution views, and Host Table views are available for node-by-node associated statistics, along with multiple upper-layer decoding capability for key statistics. In summary, the Shomiti Surveyor statistical mode enables an analyst to quickly view statistics such as utilization and frame-size distribution, protocol distribution, physical MAC layer statistics, network layer statistics, and application layer statistics, along with the top transmitters and receivers at the physical, network, and application layers (see Figure 3.11).

FIGURE 3.11 *Screen display from a statistical Shomiti Surveyor Analyzer.*

The Surveyor product line supports a full range of protocols. For a list of these protocols and further manufacturer information, refer to Appendix B, "Reference Material." For the purpose of general discussion, the Surveyor tool supports full MAC layer data investigation for all major Ethernet frame types, Token Ring frames, and other key suites such as the PPP suite and the Cisco suite. At the network layer and transport layer, the IP layer is supported, along with the TCP layer. The analyzer engine also supports the IPX, SPX, and NCP protocols and all other protocols in the Novell suite.

The Microsoft Windows NT layer can be monitored for SMB Plus, SMB, and CIFS, along with MMPI. All process application layer protocols are available for decoding and viewing, including the TCP/IP DOD model for TCP/IP, such as SNMP, TCP, Telnet, TFTP, UDP, UNIX, Web, NFS, XDR, XDM, MCP, X Window, and UNIX Remote Services. The Surveyor application database processes can be reviewed for the Oracle suite, such as TNS and Sybase. Other key protocol suite decoding is supported, such as AppleTalk, DECnet Phase IV, the IBM protocol suite including SNA, NetBIOS, and NetBEUI, along with the Banyan VINES suite. The Surveyor analyzer supports decoding for application suites including cc:Mail and Lotus Notes. All these decodes are available for display view via network analysis within the seven-layer model.

The Surveyor tool also offers an automatic traffic-generation capability that is used as a module, called the *Packet Blaster Engine*. The Blaster Engine offers advanced traffic-generation capabilities that allow for an immediate traffic stream to be generated from the NIC in the Surveyor analyzer. Data traffic patterns can be created in a unique and custom format by an analyst and then sent outbound for generation onto the network. This feature should be used only when proper planning as to analysis and traffic-generation exercises are engaged in predeployment testing and in the process of troubleshooting (but always in a careful manner). The Packet Blaster is inherently designed to enable an analyst to capture a file off the network and can replay the precaptured traffic file back in simulated real-time fashion against the network. This enables a user to create certain test scenarios for application testing and characterization that can also be used for predictive modeling in an application environment. Certain network physical issues can also be isolated through generating traffic and reviewing any effects on certain network devices via the Surveyor monitoring analysis engine.

The Shomiti company also offers extremely high-speed platforms that make it possible to capture data at high data rates through certain additional hardware-partner tools, such as the Shomiti Explorer. The Explorer is a hardware platform system that interconnects to the main analysis engine.

The Explorer system is a hardware platform that can be deployed throughout the internetwork in various areas or can be mounted in a main computer room rack. The Explorer system has a form factor approximately the size of a standard rack-mounted platform. The system can connect to a 10Mbps, 100Mbps, or Gigabit Ethernet medium and allows for automatic sensing and detection of data rates. This tool enables an analyst to rapidly deploy the Explorer in any specific area of an Ethernet internetwork, and then to remotely review data and statistics that the Explorer captures. The Explorer can connect to multiport and single-mode fiber connections and offers full- and half-duplex interconnection schemes. A network analyst can quickly use the Explorer for a real-time view of high-speed broadband transfer on Gigabit Ethernet channels. As noted, the Explorer can be deployed across the internetwork at certain points and then the Explorer can be activated to connect to the medium. When connected to the medium, data and statistics are transmitted through the Shomiti Surveyor engine for analysis and monitoring.

Another key tool offered by Shomiti is the Voyager platform. The Voyager platform is a separate hardware and software platform tool that allows for RMON1- and RMON2-compliant monitoring capability for both full- and half-duplex 10- and 100Mbps Ethernet LANs. This tool is a separate device with a form factor that again can be mounted in a standard rack or physically placed throughout an internetwork configuration. It offers an immediate synchronized view of half- and full-duplex Ethernet channels and can also monitor Fast Ethernet channel environments such as in the Cisco platform. It can automatically configure host tables and has multiport-capturing capability. The Shomiti Voyager platform is based on a silicone-accelerated multiport RMON2 engine and is extremely capable of keeping up with the high-speed data rates on the internetwork. It is built on *application-specific integrated circuit* (ASIC) technology and can filter the real-time line rate. Monitoring ports are available on the main platform for 10/100Mbps Ethernet, along with external taps that can be utilized as required.

The Shomiti product line also offers a seamless product purchase capability to acquire Shomiti Century taps, which have been available for quite some time. These taps allow for interlink taps of uplinks and key channels in networks for 10BASE-T Ethernet, 100BASE-TX Ethernet, and Gigabit Ethernet. The taps enable seamless interruption of traffic flow, so an analyst can monitor key network traffic channels such as *intermediate distribution facilities* (IDF) or user closet areas to *main distribution facilities* (MDF) or main computer rooms uplinks that cannot normally be interrupted for analysis.

3.2.3 Wavetek Wandel and Goltermann's Domino Analyzers

Wavetek Wandel and Goltermann (W&G) has been a long-time leader in the protocol analysis tool marketplace. W&G is well known for its robust protocol analysis engine tools such as the DA30 protocol analyzer. The DA30 tool has been used heavily for several decades by network product manufacturers for protocol analysis along with end-market enterprise protocol analysis.

In the 1990s, W&G also developed a product line for protocol analysis that was more geared toward the corporate enterprise in terms of network support: the WAVETECH *Wandel and Goltermann Domino*. W&G has enhanced the Domino product line with many intelligent features for the end user, such as the Domino Wizard, which creates automated reporting capabilities for network baseline purposes.

W&G has introduced the WAVETECH *Wandel and Goltermann Mentor*, which is an artificial intelligence Expert-based system designed to guide a network analyst through protocol analysis exercises. W&G also offers lower-end analysis tools to clients who may not have a requirement for high-end platforms. This product line includes the *W&G LinkView Pro analyzer*.

The following is a brief description of some of the products that Wandel and Goltermann offers to the networking industry (see Figure 3.12).

FIGURE 3.12   *The W&G domino family product.*

It should be mentioned that Wandel and Goltermann recently merged with Wavetek, and the new company is now known as Wavetek Wandel Goltermann. The company is headquartered in the United States out of Research Triangle Park, North Carolina and also has international primary offices in Germany.

The Wandel and Goltermann Domino DA30 product line is not heavily discussed in this chapter, because it is mainly geared toward the higher-end market—that is, the manufacturer product line for analyzing networking devices such as routers, switches, and other key devices. Specifically, product manufacturers use the DA30 tool because of its high-end capability to test products before release.

The Domino analyzer product is a small, portable device that really fits the end-user market in the enterprise internetwork support area. The tool form fits a normal laptop size and can just fit underneath the laptop. The Domino analyzer can interface directly with a personal computer at the parallel port on a specialized cable. Specific software is loaded from the Domino interface analyzer software family that allows applications to run and Domino to display key statistics along with network traffic decodes. The Domino is the actual protocol analyzer and links to the network interface, such as a Token Ring network and Ethernet 10/100 or Gigabit Ethernet LAN. The Domino analyzer is a pod unit, which then interfaces with a PC laptop and directly links through a parallel port to the PC's Windows interface. Within the Windows interface, an analyst can view captured data and monitor traffic statistics, examine decodes, and also transmit network traffic.

The Domino analyzer platform enables an analyst to view key statistics such as utilization, protocol percentages, error rates, and other key station-by-station statistics relative to traffic flow in the internetwork. The W&G Domino interface, as it relates to the GUI operations of Windows, enables the user to quickly move through the Domino analyzer functions.

The base Domino software offers the following key modes of operation:

- Monitor

- Capture

- Examine

- Transmit

The analyzer monitor screen allows for a comprehensive review of all key statistics, such as the Domino analyzer main status as to its operation, along with network statistics for utilization, frame count, and other key workload statistics. The protocol distribution pie chart gives the analyst a quick view of protocol percentages. There is also a frame-size area graph that illustrates frame-size distribution. In Monitor mode, internetwork traffic flow can be reviewed for all key workload characterization measurements. In the Domino Capture mode, an analyst can configure and start the Domino for active capture of data live from the network or from a precaptured file. The Examine mode enables an analyst to view a summary breakout of packets along with Detailed and Hex view. The Examine view provides many different display views of patterns of particular data and protocols.

In the Examine mode, an analyst can quickly stop the Monitor mode and go directly into a trace review of all frames that were captured. All the main protocol layers can be reviewed, from the physical layer through the application layer model. Hotkey filtering systems are available along with strong filtering systems that allow for extraction or internal inclusion of frame types or specific field data types. In addition, automated applications can be run on network analyzers via a toolbox bar from which specialized W&G tests can be engaged on a live network. The Domino offers a result data trace to be captured and imported into a *common separated value* (CSV) file format, and then data can also be imported into spreadsheet charting programs such as Excel and Lotus. The tool also has built-in reporting macros that can be engaged for unique baseline and statistical charting.

The Domino supports Standard, Fast, and Gigabit Ethernet. Different Domino pods can be purchased, depending on the end-user requirements. If all standard Ethernet types are required, one specific pod can cover the complete interconnection scheme. The Domino product line also supports analyzer pods for Token Ring, 4/16Mbps, FDDI, most major WAN network types, and other major network interfaces. There is also a Domino product platform for ATM interconnection analysis.

A notable factor is that the Domino platform is portable so that the actual Dominos can link together and then link into the PC. This enables multiple Domino sessions to be run simultaneously and viewed in one PC through the Windows interface, such as Ethernet and ATM (thus, the name Domino). There are restraints, however, related to the PC configuration and how it should be built to handle multiple Dominos running simultaneously. Most of the processing is actually done in the Domino physical engine, but, for the record, the actual PC platform is also critical as related to memory and processor speed to allow multiple sessions to run simultaneously.

As mentioned earlier, the Domino product line introduced the Domino Wizard in the 1990s. This particular tool is excellent for monitoring an internetwork from a baseline perspective. Automatic baseline statistical view capabilities can be stored in a database and then saved to different formats, such as a CSV file. Automatic reporting features are also built in to the tool; an analyst can use these tools to automatically chart generation for historical baseline requirements. An analyst's efficiency increases by monitoring and baselining a network with just one tool. An analyst can actually decode and baseline a network at the same time!

An analyst may also decide to use another tool on the same segment to complement the baseline study, such as the Domino Wizard. The wizard can be used for charting the network from a historical standpoint. Key workload characterization measurements can be charted, such as utilization, frame rate, broadcast rate, multicast rate, and physical error rate. The analyst can then decode the traffic using another analyzer in a correlating fashion. It is possible to use the Domino Wizard in direct correlation with the standard Domino Examine software and simultaneously perform active decoding of data while charting a network with the wizard product. One concern is that at times, this type of process may cause a gap in the overall charting method, depending on how configurations are applied in the PC running the Domino Wizard and Examine software. If everything is fine-tuned in the PC configuration, it is possible to use the tools at the same time and perform one baseline with the tool in a seamless fashion.

The Examine software engine in the Domino allows for performing LAN traffic analysis against the decodes for all the main protocol layers. The Examine decode engine offers an internal decode quick-filtering capability for more than 225 protocols based on the W&G examine engine. Quick filters are available for protocols, patterns, and station addresses, and protocols can be reviewed from multiple topology types. The protocol suite support is widespread; the following protocols are some of the key types included: 802.3 MAC, 802.5 MAC, LLC, LLC2, TCP/IP, UDP, OSPF, TFTP, SMTP, SNMP, Telnet, FTP, PPP, ARP, IPX, SPX, NCP, ISO, HDLC, SDLC, SMB, SNA, QLL, NetBIOS, Sun, DECnet Complete, X.25, Frame Relay, S.75, LAPB, LAPD, Cisco, AppleTalk Complete Suite, VINES, XNS, and SMDS.

Wandel and Goltermann offers other tools that allow for statistical analysis review, such as LinkView Pro. LinkView Pro provides an automated capability to examine traffic with the combined W&G examine engine, but also enables an analyst to gather immediate statistics through key tools such as discovery topology map features. The LinkView product allows the topology map to be discovered quickly and for statistics to be built for metrics on the network being analyzed. The result is a network analyzer platform that allows for statistical measurements at the same time that a network analysis is being performed. Traffic analysis statistics are available via station audit discovery and protocol distribution, top traffic generators and receivers, along with historical long-term statistics for all key protocol layers including the TCP/IP protocol layers (see Figure 3.13).

The W&G Mentor product is an interactive Expert analysis system that allows for automatic artificial intelligence review and detailed analysis of data in an immediate drop-down mode. The W&G Examine decode engine can be reviewed at any time when running Mentor. The key factor is that when symptoms occur on the network, the interactive W&G Mentor can pose a question to an analyst, such as whether the network is operating properly or whether there is a performance problem. Depending on the answer provided by the analyst, the W&G Mentor, which runs under a Windows GUI, can in most cases offer an immediate recommendation related to traffic analysis indications based on the live capture in conjunction with the analyst's answers to the automated questions that were posed (see Figure 3.14).

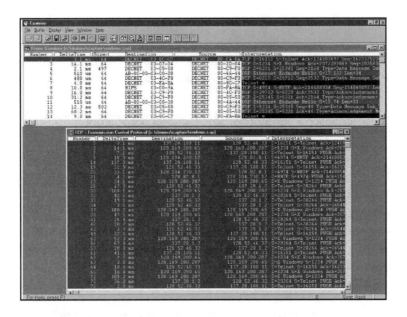

FIGURE 3.13 *Examine decode mode.*

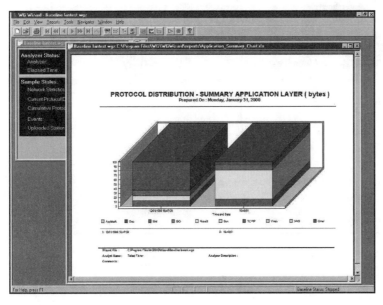

FIGURE 3.14 *W&G Wizard baseline application mode.*

The W&G Mentor offers immediate diagnostic capabilities that enable an analyst to find a specific area that may need to be worked on further through a detailed analysis. From a quick analysis standpoint, an analyst can engage W&G Mentor and quickly answer a series of questions, start a statistical analysis session, and forward through a major and minor symptom map to a specific area that may be causing a problem. The W&G Mentor helps an analyst to quickly focus on the issues at hand within the network traffic analysis session.

One of Domino's key positive points is the separate processing engine designed into the separate hardware unit.

Today, many manufacturers are moving away from hardware. W&G appears dedicated to supporting a separate hardware platform for the capture and analysis of data, which allows for processing data on high-speed network topology links without loss of any packet during traffic analysis. The product line also offers a very user-friendly interface with true multitasking network baseline monitoring features and real-time data analysis (see Figure 3.15).

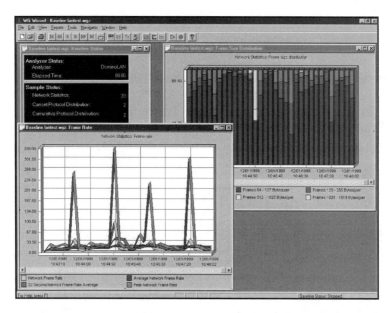

FIGURE 3.15   *W&G Wizard historical frame rate analysis mode.*

3.2.4 Novell LANalyzer for Windows

The Novell software LANalyzer product is a software analyzer that can analyze Ethernet and Token Ring LANs. The LANalyzer runs under Windows. The tool allows for monitoring and analyzing data traveling on an Ethernet and Token Ring LAN. Traffic can be analyzed for troubleshooting and for network baselining reasons.

The LANalyzer offers strong monitoring features for statistical metric views. The LANalyzer has a screen that presents a graphical view of frame-per-second rate, utilization, and errors. The screen is called the *Dashboard*. It runs in a gauge-type format and provides an analyst with a rapid view of key network statistics. This feature enables an analyst to see problems when they start to occur. The Dashboard is excellent for gaining an initial view of the main workload characteristics. Further review can be performed against specific stations by querying stations for statistics as related to individual data flow on a node-by-node basis. Metrics can be obtained and displayed as views of network traffic, such as packets per second, broadcast rates per second, and multicast rates.

The LANalyzer also provides a Display mode screen that presents individual station statistics: the *Station Monitor*. An analyst can capture data and stop the analyzer to review the internal trace data. The decode screens are fairly simple to engage. The data captured can be viewed in a Summary mode, Decode mode, or full Hexadecimal View mode. The LANalyzer software requires a robust platform. It is recommended to use a high-end PC with a high-level memory configuration. Only certain types of NICs are compatible with the software.

The LANalyzer for Windows versions include a full decode palette for all major protocol suites, but is biased toward the Novell NetWare suite. Support is available for other suites, such as the TCP/IP protocol suite, AppleTalk, and others. Certain third-party manufacturers offer sets of extra decode software modules that can be added to the core engine and can be used for protocol suites that Novell is not currently offering.

The LANalyzer software also offers a scaled-down reporting engine. Statistics can be viewed in the detailed packet window, and historical legends can be configured for utilization over a specific time period. This information can be imported into third-party spreadsheet charting applications. Most data files that are captured can also be saved into a CSV file format. One of LANalyzer's strengths is its built-in capability to perform rapid physical layer analysis in both the Ethernet and Token Ring LAN environments. The tool's internal capability to filter on individual stations makes it somewhat comparable to certain hardware analyzers. The LANalyzer is an analyzer that offers a cost-efficient way to quickly view data and statistics on a network that usually can only be viewed through more sophisticated protocol analyzers.

3.2.5 Hewlett-Packard Network Advisor

Hewlett-Packard has released many different analysis tools, along with other test equipment. The HP *Network Advisor* is a standalone platform unit based on RISC architecture and is still used for protocol analysis in many networking environments. The HP Network Advisor is a high-performance tool that engages RISC-based hardware architecture, enabling an analyst to capture data quickly on high-speed media and review the data in a technical format that is intuitive as to problem resolution.

The Network Advisor product supports most major LAN and WAN topologies. Most major protocol suites are supported, including IBM SNA, NetBIOS, Novell, TCP/IP, Novell, Windows NT, DECnet, 3Com, and XNS.

The Advisor main menu presents subdisplay menus for access to the Advisor Control, Config, and Display Setup. The Network Advisor presents key workload characteristic statistics in unique gauge-type displays that change based on real-time dynamic traffic cycles.

The Network Advisor engages a unique feature for artificial intelligence systems called the *Finder Expert System*. This feature dynamically analyzes captured data from an analysis session and then presents an analyst with recommendations to resolve issues based on cause analysis. This system enables an analyst to focus on the symptoms that are occurring while still allowing the data analysis capture to continue. This process enables an analyst to rapidly locate the cause of network problems more efficiently.

3.2.6 Optimal Software Application Expert and Application Preview

The Optimal Software company has introduced one of the more revolutionary analysis and network management products available today. With the amount of application deployment now affecting the internetwork community, it is important that applications be critically monitored.

Because applications are being deployed at such a rapid pace and are deeply impacting networks, it is important to understand how applications are deployed from a predeployment standpoint, and it is critical to ensure that they are properly planned for deployment. Such an understanding enables an analyst to determine whether the network is available to support the application and whether network adjustments are required.

We can also quickly evaluate whether the application needs to be fine-tuned to apply for a proper performance level on the internetwork from a planning standpoint. Even in situations where the application has been deployed, and we are in a post-review phase related to reactive analysis, problematic issues require rapid cause analysis.

Optimal Software has introduced a tool that allows for immediate isolation of critical issues (see Figure 3.16).

FIGURE 3.16   *The Optimal Software tools.*

The discussion now focuses on a general review of one of the main Optimal products: the Application Expert.

Application Expert is a unique tool because it allows for a rapid capture and data review of application traffic models across key internetwork points. The Optimal Application Expert system can monitor network application performance and application events at a rapid but concise and technically competent level. The platform is built on a multiple data-analysis engine system that includes multiple views of application traffic flow in very unique ways. Some of the key views involve very innovative screens that enable an analyst to isolate issues rapidly.

One of the key views is called an *Application Thread*. This particular view enables an analyst to capture an application trace via another network analysis platform, such as the Network Associate Sniffer, or directly from the Optimal Application Expert tool. The Optimal Expert system platform NIC can be configured to capture the traffic directly off the network. The Optimal Expert Threading System view feeds the trace analysis results from a packet trace and processes the binary data into an application thread. The thread can be defined as a sequence of application events that occur on the network.

If a packet trace is captured via the network analysis platform or Optimal Application Expert, for example, there may be 50,000 frames or 100,000 frames. One of the key features is that the Optimal Application Expert can actually interpret all the frames and display the simple events that occur as related to application dataflow. For example, 100,000 frames may break down to only 10 or 20 main application events. This is a very unique view and makes it possible to determine how application data movement is affecting the internetwork.

One of the key features is that when the actual thread is identified (such as a read file call from a workstation to a server for an Oracle database), the application threading tool shows the device addresses at the physical or network layer, along with the number of data in bytes and packets that are moved in transmission, along with the amount of time and latency for a server turn time and workstation turn time, and network transmission time. These are just some of the views that can be quickly displayed via the Thread Analysis screen display and report.

The thread analysis report integrates with a Bounce Diagram view in the Application Expert tool. The *Bounce Diagram view* enables an analyst to make an immediate assessment of the timing measurements and the gaps involved in traffic bursts. If a client sends a specific packet across the internetwork, for example, the time that it took to send that packet can be quickly viewed, and the behavior of the overall event as related to the application thread can be cross-correlated. The Bounce Diagram view is integrated with the actual

Application Threading screen. The bounce diagram also offers an immediate view of traffic efficiency, and any inefficiency is identified in certain colors. Actual traffic types and direction of traffic can be quickly viewed in timing modes.

Another important feature is the *conversation map*. The conversation map is a unique view of how dataflow occurs from an application standpoint from one node to another across an internetwork. During an application analysis, analysts may have a general understanding of the application dataflow from one device to another. When a data trace is actually fed into the Optimal Application Expert or captured from the Expert tool, however, the analyst may be surprised to find that the conversation map is showing another view as to exactly how data is flowing.

On communication from a client to a server, for example, an analyst may also discover many other servers are quickly contacted and briefly reviewed. It is also possible when running data-trace analysis results into the Optimal application conversation map that an analyst can quickly see the servers that are being contacted at other sites that he was not aware of prior to viewing the conversation map.

This allows for an immediate understanding of how data flows through an internetwork from point to point. This is an extremely useful tool from a general network analysis review standpoint and from a reporting perspective.

Note that if excessive traffic is captured with the Optimal Application Expert, the conversation map can be edited so that only those devices relevant to the analysis process can be viewed.

The tool offers other key features, such as a direct view of a packet trace. At the present time, the packet trace works up through the network layer area only, but it will most likely be enhanced in the future to include multiple layers and offer true trace analysis capabilities. At this time, it is quite easy to use another network analyzer such as the Network Associates Sniffer, take a data capture, and then feed the data trace into the Optimal Application Expert. It is also possible to directly capture a packet trace from the Expert system. The key factor is that an analyst, by using the Optimal Application Expert, can quickly review a trace analysis screen for packet trace data and then quickly cross-view the actual application threads that occur. The analyst can then quickly transition to the conversation map and view the dataflow that actually occurred with the application events as packets traveled through the internetwork when the application was captured.

Other features of the Optimal Application Expert include the following:

- The payload versus overhead screen
- The response-time analysis screen
- The time plot screen

In the *payload versus overhead screen*, an analyst can quickly separate data frame overhead and protocol overhead from actual data payloads. This is a very useful screen from a graphical and reporting viewpoint. The Expert tool can also offer *response time analysis*, where the response time can be monitored right down to the timing metrics of an actual application event. *Time plots* can also be produced on a historical basis. The key is that the response-time analysis graph allows for rapid review of application traffic on a node-by-node basis, and then the client-to-server network time can be quickly cross-correlated.

All these features work together to produce an awesome capability to visualize network traffic from an application standpoint, and to visualize how the application threads are actually occurring on the network. The threads are the events that actually take place related to the main application data transfer on the internetwork. Network analysis is also a unique way to look at data-trace applications through the processes noted in this book as *application characterization* (see Chapter 4). Note, however, that the Optimal Application Expert enables an analyst to quickly identify application threads and event cycles that take place on a dynamic basis. By quickly reviewing the thread process, sometimes a more simplistic determination can be made of what is actually occurring with the application data movement.

The Optimal Application Expert correlates and works with another tool called the *Application Preview*. The Application Preview product allows for a streamlined view of predictive modeling related to application deployment.

An analyst can use Application Preview to design a topology for an area where an application will be deployed. The analyst would use certain features of the Application Preview to perform this task. The first task for the analyst would be to build the topology map. This would include using automated icons from Preview, such as network segment, router, or switched devices. After the topology has been built, an analyst then would build a user profile. The user profile would allow an analyst to decide how many types of users would be deployed and where they would be deployed against the topology that was built. The user profile building process enables an analyst to decide what types of user profiles will be using a certain application data file and what types of tasks will be performed. By using the automated feature, the profile can then be built. The analyst can then take Preview and deploy the users across the internetwork. To do so, the defined user profile step along with the deployed user step requires an import of the trace data that is going to be deployed. This is where Application Preview interfaces with Application Expert. The trace is taken from Application Expert or a Sniffer file, and then is cross-threaded into Application Preview. The steps in "deploy user profile" create an automatic step to perform this exercise. In the deploy user phase, the analyst actually deploys the users against the topology that is performance, once the user profile is established. At this point, the traffic analysis results from the application capture via Application Expert are being applied against the topology that was built and the user profiles that were designed.

The final step is to perform a reporting process and set load levels on the internetwork being used for predictive modeling. To do so, the analyst must determine capacity load levels on specific segments of the topology that was built for the Application Preview process. After the load levels have been set, the analyst can then run reports related to capacity and timing latency that are required in the preview process.

The reports that are run allow for WAN recommendation views of the target load levels, the current bandwidth, the recommended bandwidth, and the background load. Capacity reports also allow for determining a resulting load level, a target load level, and the current bandwidth assessment. This enables an analyst to build a topology, identify a user group, characterize traffic and import traffic, and deploy traffic against the topology model. This process enables the analyst to then produce a predictive assessment of what the traffic loads and the resulting latency issues may be for deployment (see Figure 3.17).

An analyst can cross-thread final result information from Preview back into Application Expert to produce an application assessment and predict user response times. The analyst would normally take the capture from the Application Expert system and thread Application Expert results into the Application Optimal Preview. After the topology map and user profiles have been built, the analyst can then identify the application usage and apply it against the topology and user groups created. The user groups then can be assigned against the geographical or logical areas of the topology. Then the analyst can specify final load values. In a final view, the bandwidth recommendation and capacity reports can be run and then cross-threaded back into the Optimal Application Expert to understand final latency and response time effects on the internetwork (see Figure 3.18).

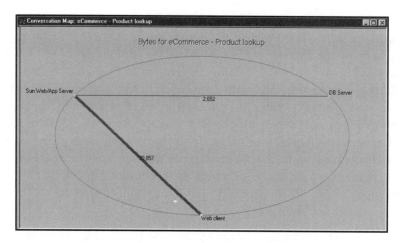

FIGURE 3.17 *Optimal Software conversion map screen shot.*

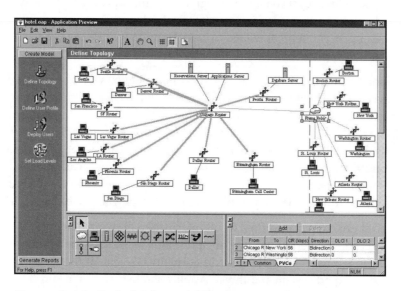

FIGURE 3.18 *Optimal Software Application preview displaying topology map.*

In summary, this tool is extremely powerful for high-performance application deployment predictive modeling and application assessment, in both reactive and proactive network baseline exercises (see Figure 3.19).

Link Name	From	To	Resulting Load Level (%)	Target Load Level (%)	Number Of Users	Current Bandwidth	Background Load (%)	Recommended Bandwidth
Phoenix Link	Phoenix Router	Chicago Router	26	60	6	1544	25	666
Phoenix Link	Chicago Router	Phoenix Router	27	60	6	1544	25	685
Denver Link	Denver Router	Chicago Router	23	60	6	56	0	22
Denver Link	Chicago Router	Denver Router	43	60	6	56	0	41
Seattle Lirk	Chicago Router	Seattle Router	66	60	9	56	0	61
Seattle Lirk	Seattle Router	Chicago Router	35	60	9	56	0	33
Dallas Link	Dallas Router	Chicago Router	35	60	9	56	0	33
Dallas Link	Chicago Router	Dallas Router	65	60	9	56	0	61
San Diego Link	San Diego Router	Chicago Router	39	60	10	56	0	37
San Diego Link	Chicago Router	San Diego Router	72	60	10	56	0	68
SF Link	Chicago Router	SF Router	86	60	12	56	0	81
SF Link	SF Router	Chicago Router	47	60	12	56	0	44
Las Vegas Link	Chicago Router	Las Vegas Router	92	60	13	56	0	86
Las Vegas Link	Las Vegas Router	Chicago Router	51	60	13	56	0	48
LA Link	LA Router	Chicago Router	54	60	14	56	0	51
LA Link	Chicago Router	LA Router	101	60	14	56	0	94
Peoria Link	Peoria Router	Chicago Router	52	60	27	512	40	446
Peoria Link	Chicago Router	Peoria Router	50	60	27	512	40	425
Birmingham Link	Chicago Router	Birmingham Router	53	60	89	1544	30	1374
Birmingham Link	Birmingham Router	Chicago Router	42	60	89	1544	30	1094

WAN Report for Reservations System Deployment, Phase II

FIGURE 3.19 *Optimal Software WAN capacity report.*

3.2.7 Compuware's EcoSCOPE

Compuware Software has introduced the EcoSCOPE product line. The EcoSCOPE product line is an extremely intuitive platform that enables an application analysis engine to work in a master monitoring mode via a high-speed probe that can be placed in the internetwork. The product line offers a probe based on a physical PC platform device that usually utilizes a high-speed platform such as a Compaq server. The high-speed computer platform is engaged with a specialized internetwork interface card to act as probes. The probes can be placed on the inbound or outbound uplinks or channels of major local and wide area network points within a complete internetwork infrastructure.

The EcoSCOPE platform is based on a Super Monitor operational feature tool that works with Windows NT–based software operating systems. The EcoSCOPE product allows for immediate analysis of data traffic and discovery of devices, protocols, and application traffic statistics. The Super Monitor can monitor all key statistics that are required for workload characterization measurements, such as utilization, protocol percentages, and other key error statistics. The highlight of this tool is that it offers integrated application review traffic capability for application response times, transaction times, and throughput between different key areas of the internetwork.

The Super Monitor can be configured remotely or internally on both exterior and interior edges of an internetwork for monitoring multiple probes. In other words, the probes can be placed in LAN-based uplink channels or at WAN network points, and the EcoSCOPE Super Monitor can view the devices remotely.

From a single view, the topology map can be quickly built and reviewed, and point-to-point traffic ratios can be monitored as to how protocols are flowing from one point to another.

The EcoSCOPE monitoring feature offers an immediate view where the topology will be displayed onscreen in a logical format and can be discovered on an ongoing basis. The tool offers techniques that can highlight actual application traffic flowing from one point to another. That traffic will continue to show updates, and graphic, colored views are available to see the traffic patterns from one point of a local or wide area network to another. This enables an analyst to quickly identify, for instance, where a TCP is flowing across an internetwork, or even where a certain application such as Lotus Notes is flowing across an internetwork. By clicking on the automated application monitoring screen within EcoSCOPE, an analyst can collect data from the network, review the reports quickly, and zoom in on a certain traffic application dataflow sequence. This is possible because the EcoSCOPE line intuitively picks up the application data movement by watching actual well-known application calls.

After the application call has been identified, an analyst can click on the call sequence and actually see the real-time data movement across the network topology, and can associate the actual response time of the application between two specific points. The application response time can be monitored to see how servers and workstations are responding, and what kind of internetwork latency may be present. The transaction time for the application can also be monitored, so an analyst can quickly use EcoSCOPE to monitor transaction response times for specific applications and even database movement such as Oracle, Sybase, and Microsoft SQL.

This is a very popular analysis tool because of the need to truly understand application behavior upon networks and how application deployment affects the internetwork from an impact standpoint, capacity analysis, and performance optimization standpoint.

EcoSCOPE can monitor all major protocol platforms and suites, including Windows NT, 3Com, AppleTalk, Banyan VINES, DECnet, ISO, NetBIOS, Novell NetWare, SNA, XNS, TCP/IP, and many other traffic types (see Figure 3.21).

3.2.8 Ganymede Software's Chariot and Pegasus Monitoring Tools

Ganymede Software Inc. has introduced a unique product called *Chariot*. This tool is designed for immediate performance analysis measurements across network end-to-end points in distributive networking environments. Specifically, the Chariot software offers a component called the *Chariot Console*. The Console software component would load on one particular device within a networking environment, and Chariot End Point could then be loaded on another device within the same networking environment.

The Chariot Console could be loaded in Segment 1, for example, and the Chariot End Point could be loaded on Segment 2. If Segment 1 and Segment 2 are connected by a switch or a router, the Chariot Console could communicate with the Chariot End Point across the Ethernet Segment 1, over the router, and then communicate on Segment 2 to the actual endpoint. The devices communicate with each other on an end-to-end conversation mode for certain traffic analysis output requirements.

The Console is the main program interface to the overall Chariot system. It is where the actual tests are created and the monitoring software resides to start the test operation and to provide the traffic analysis. The endpoint is the actual point that communicates back to the Chariot console. Note that there can be multiple endpoints, as discussed later.

A quick test can be designed where a certain type of traffic pattern can be generated from the Console directly to the endpoint. The endpoint would then respond with communication via the traffic generation test. Specifically, the test mode would normally be described in the product line as a test script. The *test script* is a small traffic pattern similar to normal application traffic in the market.

One specific traffic pattern could be a platform such as Lotus Notes, for example. The general Lotus Notes operation has specifically been built into a defined test script mode. It can then be executed from the Console to the remote endpoint. The endpoint would then provide communications back and forth based on the script. The Console would collect statistics that would be valid for the purposes of the output of the use of the product. The main output modes include response time, transaction time, and throughput time for the Lotus Notes script. These variables are excellent from an overall performance testing standpoint.

The main reason the Chariot platform is so powerful is that it allows for an immediate view of response time, throughput, and transaction time related to the type of test script that is generated.

There are many open possibilities for using the Chariot tool during a network baseline study. An analyst could place different endpoints throughout the network infrastructure and place the Console in one key point (for instance, the main computer room) during the network baseline study. By running the scripts simultaneously or consecutively, an analyst could determine the throughput, response time, and transaction time output across each point of testing. This could enable the analyst to understand latency and overall performance between different IDF closets within a network enterprise infrastructure.

There is also the capability to load multiple endpoints within one specific area. In this case, an analyst could test multiple stations against other key stations within one specific IDF domain.

For example, this would allow for testing of older stations as compared to newer workstations that just received a memory upgrade. The response time, throughput, and transaction times should be higher on the newer workstation platform. Ganymede Software offers the Chariot product line multiple node count packages that include 10 to 500 nodes and higher in custom packages. This tool can obviously be used in a major simulation for application predeployment rollout as related to network topology design.

The program is fairly quick. It also allows for multiple test scripts to be run; these are already preconfigured by Ganymede. Over 500 tests of predetermined common scripts, such as Lotus Notes, Novell, and NT-based scripts, are already available to run. The tool can also capture a trace analysis session related to a specific application and, through a certain binary conversion process, create a test script that is actually similar to the application that is going to run. This makes immediate predictive modeling analysis possible and enables the analyst to use the tool in the application characterization mode.

The Chariot tool allows for a quick operation where the Console program is started. A specific IP address is configured into the Console. One or more endpoints are configured with IP addresses at different points within the internetwork. Either a script is launched from the predetermined scripts loaded in the program, or an analyst may modify certain variables in the scripts as required. The analyst starts the test, and the script activates whether the console will communicate to each one of the endpoints across the internetwork channels. After the tests have been completed, the analyst can view the results and the summaries, such as the throughput, transaction, and overall response time screens. The data can be saved in different modes, enabling viewing of the data in HTML format or in other spreadsheet programs such as Excel or 1-2-3 (see Figure 3.20).

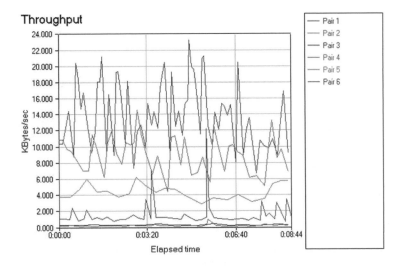

FIGURE 3.20   *Chariot throughput graph.*

The output test screens are excellent. They allow for an immediate view of transaction, throughput, and response time testing modes. In relation to the actual throughput testing mode, an analyst can look at throughput on an average between the Console and endpoint pairs, along with a minimum throughput and a maximum throughput. A confidence interval is applied by Ganymede Software up to a 95% level, along with a relative precision and final measured time. The transaction rate can also be monitored for average, minimum, and maximum, along with confidence interval, measure time, and relative precision. The response-time measurement also offers an average, minimum, maximum, and a confidence interval and relative precision measurement (see Figure 3.21).

The key factor is that all these output screens can actually be viewed in graphical format for multiple traffic portions of the overall script. This enables an analyst to quickly view the output from a visual standpoint.

Note also that these are excellent attachments for a network baseline study. By reviewing response time and throughput alone, an analyst can cross-map these output metrics to the procedures discussed in Chapter 4 under workload characterization measurements (see Figure 3.22).

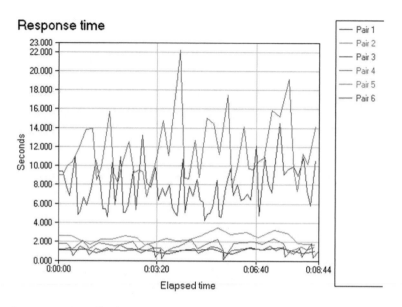

FIGURE 3.21 *Chariot response time graph.*

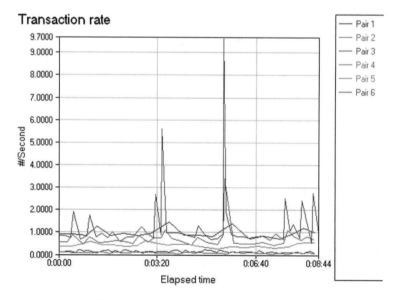

FIGURE 3.22 *Chariot transaction rate graph.*

Note that Ganymede Software also offers a remote monitoring tool that works with the Chariot Console and End Point software, called *Pegasus*. Pegasus is more of a remote monitoring network analysis center monitoring tool, which would be used by a remote control center monitoring multiple Chariot operations being tested throughout several enterprise sites.

For more information on the Chariot product line, refer to Appendix B, "Reference Material."

3.2.9 Antara Testing Products

The Antara company recently introduced a product line that offers the capability for testing Fast and high-speed Ethernet products and associated traffic links in both the manufacturing and corporate environment. The Antara product line was originally designed for the network testing process and large networking product manufacturer environments. The product suite was developed by the original founder of Kalpana, which was acquired by Cisco Systems in 1994.

The Antara product line is a strong testing tool for today's high-speed medium topologies and includes a major platform called the *Port Authority GT*. This tool is a device and simulation test tool used quite frequently in the manufacturing test environment. The tool can also be used in the corporate enterprise environment. The tool is an enhanced product line switching matrix tool that allows for automatic traffic generation and data capture from high-speed Fast Ethernet channel and Gigabit Ethernet channel links. The tool can be used for burn-in and traffic generation of switches, and hubs with internal capabilities that operate via its automated monitoring software to burn in network product platforms prior to release to the network industry. This would include network Ethernet switches and other key Ethernet high-speed interconnection channel hub devices. The product can also be used in the corporate environment by network implementation teams to test switches prior to rollout.

The Port Authority GT utilizes a five-slot chassis with an integrated Pentium server. Users can plug in a keyboard, mouse, and monitor to directly control the GT. The GT supports a port capacity of up to 32 10/100 Ethernet ports that can be either UTP or fiber. User security is optional. The GT provides many internal test features to enable an analyst to configure traffic patterns. The engineering engines that engage the traffic generation mode are based on powerful ASIC technologies. Each port can capture and generate traffic at wire-speed. By engaging custom onboard processors, the Antara products enable an analyst to create, generate, and capture results based on policies for specific traffic types.

Although the Antara Port Authority GT product line is designed specifically for product manufacturing environments, it also allows for quality assurance in the corporate enterprise environment (see Figure 3.23).

Figure 3.23 *The Antara product line.*

Antara also offers a *Port Authority IT* product line, which is more of a growth-geared testing solution that can be used for online response-time analysis and traffic analysis straight from the Ethernet link. It is now quite common to see the Port Authority IT product and the GT product used in the corporate enterprise environment as staged within an Ethernet uplink. In this particular case, the tool can be used to test Ethernet uplink network channel links from a traffic monitoring and traffic generation standpoint using gigabyte Ethernet tools (see Figures 3.24 through 3.26).

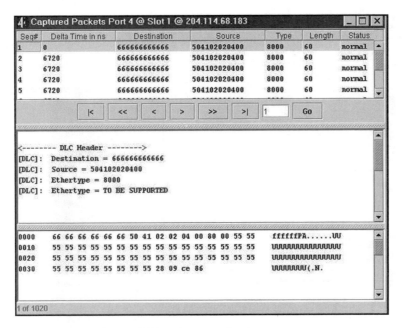

FIGURE 3.24   *Antara GTDecode screen shot.*

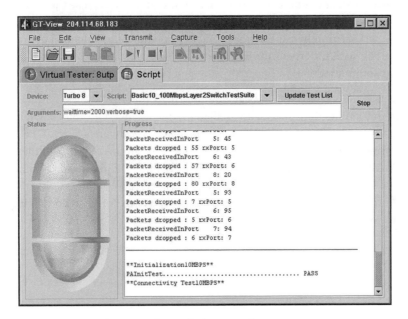

FIGURE 3.25   *Antara packet analysis screen shot.*

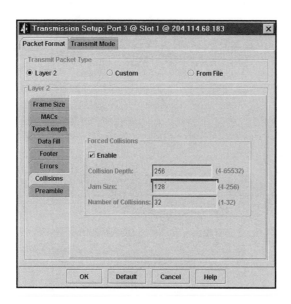

FIGURE 3.26 *Antara collision review screen shot.*

The tool can be used to test Ethernet uplinks between IDF and MDF areas, along with testing the products that provide the uplinks, such as the main Ethernet switches within the platform. Overall, the product line offers a way to rapidly and accurately test Ethernet switches on end-to-end channel operations, along with Ethernet uplinks for true integrity within the data transmission capability mode.

The Antara tools also offer a passive monitoring capability via the passive-fiber monitoring points that enables an analyst to quickly insert a protocol analyzer such as a NAI Sniffer or other key tools such as Compuware's EcoSCOPE monitoring tool. This allows for passive monitoring in the case of an Ethernet uplink within a corporate environment. The GT and IT Tap Module minimizes a loss of signal by regenerating the signal into mirrored operations. Even if the Port Authority product were to lose power, the passive board could continue monitoring, enabling an analyst to continue completing a baseline mode.

The Antara product line is an excellent platform to assist in staging an actual network baseline study. Its accuracy and technical test features provide a nonintrusive way to sample high-speed networking channels and also concurrently test main site networking product platforms such as Fast and Gigabit Ethernet switches that interconnect main network areas.

3.2.10 Fluke LANMeter

This network monitoring tool product line is considered a partial protocol analyzer and a TDR. Fluke Corporation offers a handheld meter that can function as a Layer-1 physical testing tool and a Layer-2 and -3 analysis tool. The instrument is based on a platform that enables an analyst to gather and view network statistics for a LAN, including such things as errors, network utilization, broadcast levels, node-by-node utilization factors, and protocol percentages. Naming features are supported for address-to-name mapping. This feature is useful when troubleshooting is required when analyzing multiple network segments.

The Fluke meters are full-blown TDRs that also enable an analyst to gain a comprehensive view of the cabling infrastructure while still monitoring certain valuable statistics from Layers 2 and 3 of the protocol model. This portable tool is helpful for network implementation projects and rapid reactive network baselining, and is also excellent for field troubleshooting of network issues.

3.3 Closing Statement on Network Analysis Tools

The two previous chapters defined network baselining and the required goals to engage a proper study. This chapter has presented how a network protocol analyzer is composed, along with descriptions of some of the key platforms used for analysis when performing a network baseline study.

Remember that many of the tools can be used individually or together, depending on the required output of the baseline study. The next chapter presents the methodology and steps required for an analyst to understand how to effectively use the tools presented to perform a network baseline study.

CHAPTER 4

Quantitative Measurements in Network Baselining

When conducting a protocol analysis for the purpose of proactive review of a network's operation, many different metric and statistical measurements prove valuable for each session. This is also true when performing a reactive network emergency troubleshooting analysis.

Certain statistical metric measurements are considered standard and are required to effectively perform a network baseline session. The required measurements can be gathered from a protocol analyzer and specific management systems. Figure 4.1 shows the main network baseline statistical measurements.

The main network baseline measurements include the following statistical metrics:

- Utilization
- Utilization for station traffic statistics and associated node by node
- Protocol percentages and level statistics
- Error statistics' types in association with various network topologies and devices
- Physical frame statistics related to certain topology mechanism operations

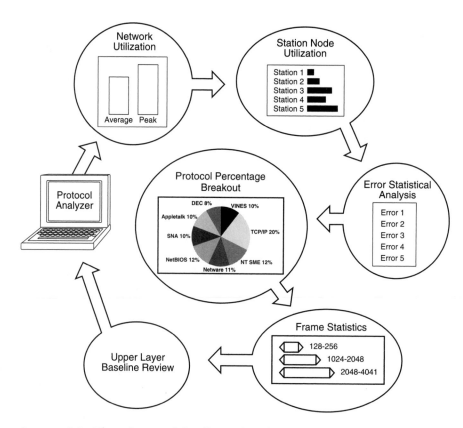

FIGURE 4.1 *The main network baseline statistical measurements.*

4.1 Utilization Analysis

The measurement for network utilization as related to capacity is a foundational component of a network baseline analysis session. Utilization is critical because only a certain amount of available capacity on any network medium can be used for data communication.

Available capacity refers to the allocated portion of bandwidth available for the transfer of data upon a particular topology medium. Each network topology and associated medium has a standard assigned capacity. The assigned capacity is based on the design, configuration, and final implementation of the topology within a network.

Utilization is defined as the amount of available capacity absorbed by a specific network device or set of devices as combined with data communication that is also associated with network process operation. Figure 4.2 clearly shows how utilization is engaged against available capacity.

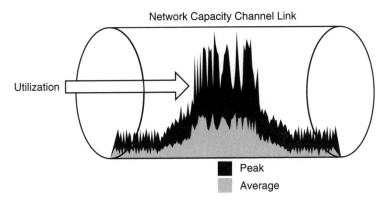

FIGURE 4.2   *Utilization engaged against available capacity.*

Consider, for example, the original standard 10 *megabits per second* (Mbps) capacity available in the early Ethernet topology environment. On a 10Mbps Ethernet network, 10 million bits of data could be transferred on the wire within an assigned time interval of one second. This interpretation relates to the fact that the original Ethernet network design was based on a baseband transmission process. Chapter 8, "Ethernet," discusses the Ethernet topology and architecture in greater detail.

When moving to a Fast Ethernet design, such as 100Mbps, the available capacity increases to allow for up to 100 million bits of data to be transmitted across the Ethernet medium within one second.

When the Ethernet network is used for data communications, such as logging on to the network or for application file transfer, a specific portion of the available capacity is utilized. Depending on the type of Ethernet configuration involved, such as shared Ethernet or switched Ethernet, the available capacity level varies according to the configuration of the complete internetwork. In a switched configuration, for example, only one user may be utilizing a specific Ethernet port and the capacity assigned may be 10Mbps or 100Mbps. If other particular ports in the switched Ethernet configuration are also receiving a high number of inbound broadcasts from other devices across the enterprise internetwork, it is very possible that some of the available capacity on the designated switched Ethernet port may be utilized by dataflow not associated with the connected device to the switched port.

Another example is a shared media Ethernet environment based on approximately 30 users. If the user count increases by 100% to 60 users, it does not necessarily mean that the shared Ethernet media's available capacity will be split across twice the number of users based on the original configuration. In other words, the utilization effect change may not be an exact duplicate, based on the user count. Specifically, if the user count increases from 30 to 60 workstation nodes, this does not necessarily cause a 100% increase in utilization. It is a fact that the final utilization reached will also be affected by the type of traffic profiles that each user is adding to the Ethernet medium. The point here is that a certain amount of available capacity is present on an internetwork, and that the utilization component is based on the type of traffic combined with the type of user connection applied to the specific topology medium.

Measuring utilization achieved versus capacity available is an ongoing challenge in network analysis that must be identified throughout a network baselining session. To do so, the use of a protocol analyzer tool proves extremely valuable. Protocol analyzers allow for monitoring of utilization in many different profile categories.

There are three main profile categories for reviewing the utilization statistic for close analysis review during a network baseline session. Figure 4.3 shows the main components of network utilization that can be measured in a network baseline study.

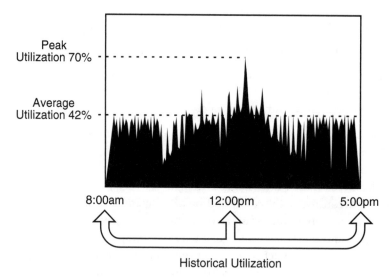

FIGURE 4.3 *The main components of network utilization.*

These three main statistical measurement categories for utilization are as follows:

- Average utilization

- Peak utilization

- Historical utilization

4.1.1 Average Utilization

Average utilization is the amount of network capacity achieved on a specific network medium from the available capacity within a specified time interval. The time interval required to gain an accurate view of average utilization on any Ethernet medium area or on a switched Ethernet port is contingent on the requirements of the network baseline study.

As discussed earlier in this book, network baselining is essentially the process of utilizing management systems and protocol analysis tools for the purpose of profiling a network's state of operation over a specified period of time. With this process description in mind, the use of the average utilization measurement would apply to the length of the baseline study. Average utilization should be closely monitored using a protocol analysis tool or a network management system over the period of the network baseline session.

If the baseline session is staged for an eight-hour cycle based on the business operation profile, the average utilization component should be monitored from a statistical standpoint over the eight-hour period. Determining the time period required for a network baseline session to be engaged against sample points as related to a complete network baseline study requires an extremely in-depth and technical planning process. Chapter 13, "Network Baseline Planning, Data Acquisition, and Final Reporting," presents a detailed process related to network baseline data-acquisition planning. For the purposes of this discussion, it is important to understand that a network baseline should be performed for a period of time that compares to or mirrors the business operation on the network. If a branch office network for a bank is going to be baselined, the logical time period to study the network for a complete session view is an eight-hour period from 9 a.m. to 5 p.m.

The baseline analyst determines the network areas that the network management platform or the protocol analyzer are deployed against. Again, this book presents detailed data-acquisition methodology related to positioning points later in this book.

It is important to state here that the average utilization component should always be gathered against selected monitoring points for the duration of the entire network baseline session.

A protocol analyzer or network management tool just counts the utilization at a certain sampling interval over the time period that the tool is deployed against the network area for sampling. If a protocol analyzer is used and deployed against the Ethernet segment, for example, it monitors utilization every second within a one-minute period. The one-second period is then accumulated on one-minute intervals and time stamped against an historical chart. The message here is that average utilization can change every second. A one-second interval in an Ethernet medium may show 2% utilization in the first second, and then may change in the next second to 4%. In the third second, the utilization may move to 6%, and then quickly move up to 9% on the fourth second point. In the fifth measurement second, the average utilization may drop to 1%.

The protocol analyzer keeps track of the utilization changes on one-second intervals and averages out the utilization over the time period being tracked against the overall network baseline. Most analyzers offer this feature. This measurement becomes cumulative and adds up over a period of time. This is considered the average utilization component. Figure 4.4 shows the concept of measuring average network utilization.

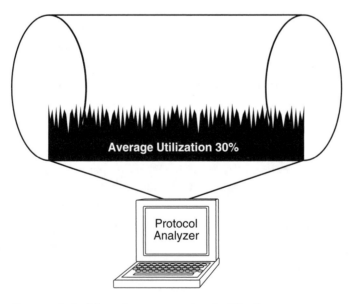

FIGURE 4.4 *Measuring average network utilization.*

The average utilization component is extremely useful to determine the kind of network utilization sustained against the available capacity on a shared network medium, a switched port, a *wide area network* (WAN) port, or any area where a network baselining session is being performed over a specified period of time. Average utilization can relate to a trend of data traffic on a network medium.

This is a critical measurement and can be used in troubleshooting sessions. As a note to the next section, if the available capacity is 100% and the average utilization exceeds 50%, the peak transition utilization will most probably be much higher.

Average utilization should be closely monitored and marked throughout a network baseline session.

4.1.2 Peak Utilization

The peak utilization measurement is one of the more critical statistical measurements in a network baseline study. Peak utilization occurrences must be measured and individually monitored over the complete time period of a network baseline session. Specifically, peak utilization transitions can occur instantaneously, but should be tracked over a period of time.

Peak utilization is a spike transitional utilization event that occurs in direct parallel with standard average utilization. Peak transition or spike utilization events can be directly caused by applications invoked on the internetwork or by other network operational sequences such as device failure.

Peak utilization events can be captured with a protocol analyzer and on certain network management systems. Peak transitional events occur very rapidly, in microsecond, millisecond, or in multiple-second intervals. Peak utilization can relate to specific events. A long peak transition utilization occurrence, combined with a high level of utilization, can very easily negatively impact a network medium, or an application and user environment across the enterprise internetwork. The two key points of consideration are the time period and the level of the utilization peak occurrence. Figure 4.5 shows how peak utilization can be measured via protocol analysis.

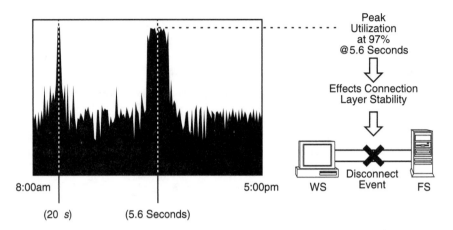

FIGURE 4.5 *Measuring peak utilization via protocol analysis.*

Consider, for example, a Fast Ethernet environment with a switched port configuration that can handle a 100Mbps maximum capacity per port. In this case, the peak utilization capacity level is 100Mbps per port. A brief utilization spike that could be considered a nonimpact event would be a peak transition utilization spike that is marked at 98% by a protocol analyzer for a timing duration of 200 *microseconds* (µs). Such a spike may not necessarily cause an outage on the switched port link. This is because the capacity level is not sustained for longer than 200µs. However, another example would be a condition when a similar spike event reaches the 98% utilization peak transition level, but occurs for a 5.6-second time period. This timing duration may be long enough to interrupt active upper-layer protocol sequences, such as *network operating system* (NOS) or application traffic that engaged. This level of peak utilization occurring for 5.6 seconds could interrupt data application ports that are active and open for communication between a server and a workstation. This could present a problem if a server/host is actively handling Transmission Control Protocol (TCP) communications or other upper-layer application traffic with a set of user workstations that requires port maintenance to occur under the 5.6 interval. The connection TCP port maintenance processes such as polling events may not be able to maintain sequencing through the channel due to peak saturation occurrence. It is quite possible that dropped connections would result for one or more of the workstations maintaining a connection with a server/host. Note also that the cause of the peak transition could be completely unrelated to the workstation connected to a specific port and could be the result of an inbound broadcast storm, a physical failure of the Ethernet switch, or even an application process that would be considered abnormal or combined in correlation with colocation of multiple applications between the server and workstation.

The key point is that the peak transition utilization measurement area of network baselining is critical.

Most network management systems for switch, hub, and router do not allow for measuring peak transition on a consistent basis at extremely rapid time intervals. It is important to view peak utilization for the actual level and exact time period of occurrence when involved in emergency troubleshooting cause analysis or problem extraction. The focus of measuring peak utilization becomes an ongoing task that can be extremely tedious.

Normally this measurement is used when performing a network baseline on a specific segment, switched port, or network area such as a WAN link, during the initial portions of the actual baseline study.

It is important throughout a network baseline session to closely measure peak transitions by monitoring the appropriate screens on the protocol analyzers or network management systems. If utilization peaks occur frequently, it may be necessary to set up specific filtering or triggering mechanisms on the analysis tools utilized, which will allow for capturing the peak transition metric and then will also allow for mapping the event to a specific protocol or to application sequence events. This is possible only by first carefully measuring peak transitions.

Most protocol analyzers enable an analyst to quickly view a peak utilization transition and then to stop the analyzer and turn on certain display features when reviewing data, such as an internal network utilization view in the data trace. The marked network utilization peak levels that are marked can then be located by decoding the trace and matched to protocol and application data events with a protocol analyzer. The timing duration can also be marked by using certain techniques such as relative time marking. The process of identifying peak utilization overload occurrences is discussed later in this chapter in the section titled "Network Response Time Analysis" and throughout other key sections of this book.

The final message here is that the peak utilization transitional spike measurement process is important to profile specific areas of an internetwork for peak utilization occurrences and then to map the occurrences to a protocol or application event. By performing this process, an analyst can perform associated troubleshooting and cause analysis of high utilization occurrences while baselining a network in active dynamic process.

4.1.3 Historical Utilization

Historical utilization is an extremely important measurement that requires the review of utilization over a given time period. If a network baseline session is configured and set up to monitor a network area such as an Ethernet shared medium at 10Mbps for an eight-hour time frame, it would be beneficial to have an historically based utilization chart in printed form that shows average utilization and peak transitions combined at certain sampling points over the same eight-hour period. Because sampling points can occur every second, or even in subsecond intervals on certain management systems and protocol analyzers, the actual sampling point used to build a historical chart must be chosen carefully.

A five-minute sampling interval for average and peak point transition marking is standard, and certain tools enable an analyst to do this. Various protocol analyzers are extremely accurate in quantitative historical measurement charting. Certain network management systems can be also utilized.

The key point is to mark and chart utilization for the average and the peak transitional points on an historical basis over a time period that profiles against the network baseline sampling time period. If a baseline is performed for an eight-hour period against a 10Mbps Ethernet, for example, the utilization should be marked and charted for the average and peak utilization over the eight-hour time period. Through this process, you might note that at approximately 9:50 a.m., and then also from 1:30 p.m. to 2:30 p.m., peak transitions are high and network saturation above the 80% level of utilized available capacity occurs for 1 to 1.5 seconds. You might also see that the average utilization stabilizes over the eight-hour sample at 42%. This process enables you to clearly view the business-day network utilization occurrences map the utilization chart against business application traffic modeling and the engagement of business processes across the enterprise internetwork composite. Historical process review and charting provides an extremely useful view for network baselining. Figure 4.6 shows how historical utilization measurements can present unique data events.

This method can also be applied when charting a historical utilization model during a baseline that was performed a month earlier in the calendar year, and then engaging a comparative network baseline to view the historical differences when a similar study is performed several months later. This method allows for comparative reviews of the network when different application profiles are deployed, and when changes to the network are made on an ongoing basis. This can also provide a reference to many historical measurements. This measurement is used extensively in proactive network baselining.

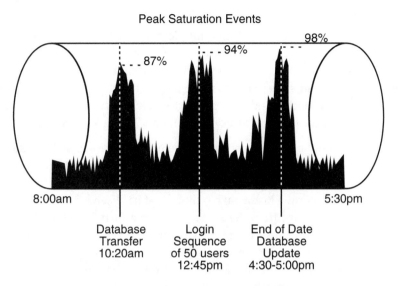

FIGURE 4.6 *How historical utilization measurements can present unique data events.*

In closing the utilization measurement discussion, average utilization should always be applied as a statistical measurement metric when performing network baselining on a proactive basis. Peak transitional utilization measurements are used extensively during both proactive network baseline studies and reactive troubleshooting or in emergency cause analysis. The historical method view is intended for proactive network baselining and is not recommened for engagement as often in emergency network troubleshooting or cause analysis because of the time required to gather the historical chart.

4.1.4 Station Statistical Review and Node-by-Node Analysis

This measurement is the second main category of statistical review metrics gathered for use in a standard network baseline study. After having reviewed average utilization and identified and cross-mapped any peak transitions to protocol or network level application and operational occurrences and after having established an historical view, an analyst should begin a network station statistical review of node-by-node utilization and traffic profiling.

Next, it is important to determine which portions of the overall bandwidth in a network area are utilized against each of the stations accessing the medium. In a network baseline that involves a shared medium architecture, which would apply to shared Ethernet or Token Ring architecture or *Fiber Data Distributed Interface* (FDDI), a station-by-station analysis is extremely relevant. This is because multiple devices share a restricted medium. This process is also relevant on a WAN connection, in which multiple devices are sharing a dedicated leased line or a Frame Relay circuit. After gaining an overall understanding of average, peak, and historical utilization, it is important to compare the actual individual component's use to the absolute overall utilization on a per-device relative basis. This concept and process is extremely important to shared architecture analysis in the *local area network* (LAN) and WAN environments.

Consider, for example, an Ethernet environment with approximately 45 devices on a 10Mbps shared Ethernet hub. A sample baseline session may show an average utilization of 30% and the highest peak transition at 92% for a three-second duration. After the historical baseline chart has been established, the next focus is to determine from the 45 stations on the shared medium, which devices are utilizing and absorbing relative utilization components as related to the absolute utilization against the entire shared area. The absolute utilization factors would be noted as the 30% average and the peak transition of 92%. The relative utilization components would be broken out by utilizing the station statistical analysis and node-by-node utilization review. Figure 4.7 shows how relative utilization compares to absolute utilization.

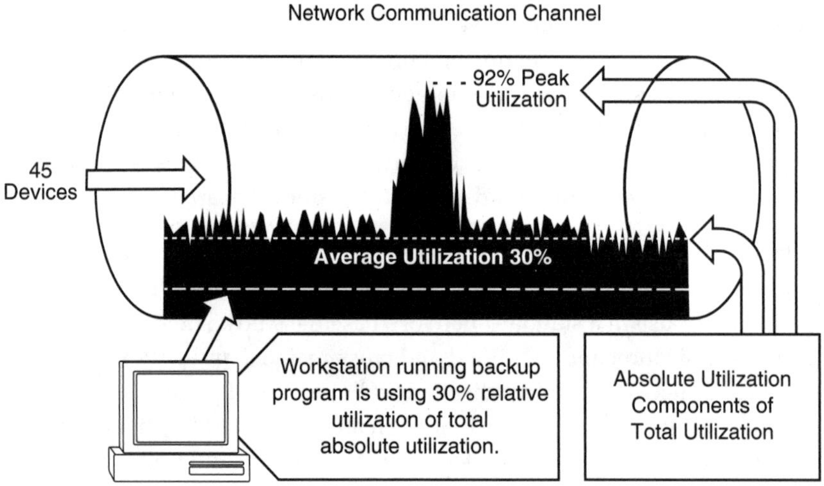

FIGURE 4.7 *How relative utilization compares to absolute utilization.*

With some protocol analyzers, you can conduct a station-by-station review. The protocol analyzer station review screens usually list each device address on the shared medium, showing the associated relative utilization component as related to the complete average and complete transition. This review process yields a picture of how each station is affecting the shared medium's utilization of the available capacity.

Percentage measurements can be broken down on a per-physical-device address basis. This process enables discrete cause analysis for any possible problems. This is extremely relevant if a specific device is absorbing more than a relative 30% of the overall absolute utilization. The 30% level creates an uneven distribution as to other devices sharing the medium. This is both a proactive and reactive measurement that should be taken during a network baseline study.

Consider another example. If a specific device shows an average utilization of approximately 51% of the overall absorbed average utilization, this indicates that one device is responsible for 51% of all the utilization on the shared medium. If out of 45 devices, one device is found to have this percentage assigned, this could be cause for concern. If the device is investigated and found to be a localized server for logon and print share services, you probably don't have a major problem. If, on the other hand, the device is located and found to be assigned as a workstation that should not be absorbing the achieved bandwidth, you might have a problem. Further investigation of the device reveals that the device is running an application related to backup across the LAN during the business time frame, which was not intended. This process is then found to account for the relative utilization being so high (51% of the overall absolute usage). This situation warrants immediate cause analysis and troubleshooting of the backup process, and possible removal of the application event from the workstation on the Ethernet medium during the business day. In this example, the positive factor is that the station statistical review and node-by-node analysis (via a protocol analyzer) enables an analyst to isolate the component causing the problem and therefore to troubleshoot the issue to cause.

Switched Ethernet presents situations in which certain monitoring points represent only one device on the particular network link or channel. This could mean that the average and peak utilization could all be attributed to the one station, and that the station-by-station statistical analysis may not necessarily apply. In such a situation, by reviewing the station's average and peak utilization on the port (applying the first category of basic utilization measurements, and then applying a station statistical analysis review), an analyst might find that many devices are communicating to the device from other segments, even though the device is placed on the unique individual switched port. Based on the inbound and outbound traffic levels, such as frames sent to the port and received from the port to other multiple devices, it may be possible to decide whether a full internetworkwide station review should be performed. The decision could be made based on conditions such as a high number of other device addresses communicating with the single station. In certain cases, there may be inbound traffic not related to communicating with the device on the switched port, but rather internetworkwide broadcast packets impacting the switched port. This technique facilitates an understanding of the traffic array that is inbound and outbound from other network devices communicating with the device on the individual switched port.

Other statistical measurements help an analyst to monitor a device to determine how a station's bandwidth component is relative to a utilization component. Each station may have statistics for average and peak utilization achieved, along with specific other metrics such as average frame size and frame-per-second rate. These statistical components are discussed later in this chapter.

It is important to note in this section that some analyzer and management program features enable an analyst to conduct a discrete station statistical analysis related to endpoint analysis. These display features enable an analyst to see how a station contributes to absolute bandwidth capacity utilization levels in a shared or switched architecture. New programs (now available), such as Vital Signs, enable an analyst to quickly review statistics critical to an endpoint's allocation on a specific design. Other statistical programs are available from vendors such as Cisco (CiscoWorks) and INS (Enterprise Pro); with these, an analyst can monitor statistics on a per-port basis.

The key point here is that an analyst can engage various protocol analysis processes along with management processes to review station statistics associated with node-by-node utilization.

4.1.5 Protocol Level and Type Analysis

When performing protocol analysis, one of the simplistic measurements, often ignored or not considered an important metric measurement, is a basic protocol percentage-breakdown measurement. This is an extremely vital measurement and should never be viewed as not important. Many MIS analysts view this measurement as a basic profile that matches the deployed operating system environment. The fact is that this measurement can point to many variances of normal network operations.

Most protocol analyzers and key network management systems offer a discrete review of the amount of traffic associated with each protocol. The review is usually based on all the packets captured within the protocol analysis or management capture session.

Each internetworking environment in today's enterprise usually has multiple protocols deployed. The protocols are invoked by the various network operating systems and applications working with the specific internetwork architecture.

Consider a Novell environment, for example. It may employ several protocols such as *NetWare Core Protocol* (NCP), *Internetwork Packet Exchange* (IPX), *Sequence Packet Exchange* (SPX), and *NetWare Core Protocol Burst* (NCPB). In the Windows NT environment, it is common to see *Server Message Block* (SMB), NetBIOS, TCP/IP, and the IP protocols. Figure 4.8 shows how protocol percentages can be measured in a network baseline study.

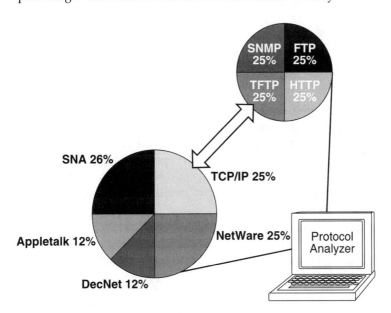

FIGURE 4.8 *Measuring protocol percentages.*

When starting a protocol analysis session from a network baseline perspective, it is important from an analyst's standpoint to keep a wide-open view of which protocols are present on the network. By understanding the protocol percentages within a certain user area or server area, or switched link, the analyst may be able to determine the type of application dataflow present in the specific network area during the baseline exercise.

As discussed later in this book, many data-acquisition points may be chosen during a complete network baseline study. By closely monitoring protocol statistics throughout every session in a sitewide network baseline study, it is possible to locate issues where applications are being deployed. Sometimes applications are found operating in network areas where they are not intended. Sometimes this measurement offers a brief statistical review of the protocol percentages applied to a certain network area, where every statistic appears to be in alignment with the applications deployed. In this particular case, the measurement is considered informative and benign as to problems and a positive statistical logged result for the network baseline study.

An example of a reactive problem would be a network area with approximately 30 Token Ring networks in a central city location. From the main city location, there is also a remote site that has only six nodes deployed on a small Token Ring network. The small Token Ring deployed in the remote location is based on a protocol sequencing across the wide area, mainly utilizing the IPX protocol (a network layer protocol in the Novell protocol suite). The users in the remote area servers are complaining about performance and are having outages when communicating to the main headquarters location over a 128K dedicated link. By deploying a protocol analyzer at the remote location and performing an initial basic set of baseline measurements such as average, peak, and historical utilization, and station-by-station node analysis, it is revealed that the utilization on the remote 16Mbps Token Ring is excessive, showing a 92% peak utilization level (compared to a previous month's network baseline session that showed a 15% peak utilization). Further discrete network baseline measurements show that the station-by-station node utilization reveals that the WAN link router has a relative utilization of 80% of the overall utilization on the local medium at the remote site. By next running a protocol percentage measurement on the remote ring, an 85% NetBIOS protocol percentage is determined. The NetBIOS protocols are found to be present on the remote Token Ring. It was noted that the previous month's baseline sample showed that NetBIOS was not present on the Token Ring at the remote site. Through further decoding processes that included drop-down drill analysis against the frames, it was found that there were inbound NetBIOS storms from the headquarters location. The storms were all NetBIOS packets at over 800 frames per second and found to have saturated the WAN link to the remote site. The NetBIOS storms were not present at the remote site in previous network baselining sessions. This clearly shows that using a basic statistical metric process early in the cause analysis troubleshooting session helped to pinpoint the problem at the site quickly. This proved to be an extremely beneficial measurement in this case.

Consider now the example of a high deployment of NetWare and TCP/IP protocol suites across a large internetwork. This particular site did not show any exception problem issues during an internetwork baseline session in the spring of a certain year; in the summer (second quarter) of the same year, however, another baseline session revealed a high number of DECnet protocols on the internetwork. Even without problems on the internetwork, the DECnet protocol should have been investigated for application profiles to determine why the protocols were present on the network. If problems had been present, they might have been caused by a new application deployment adding high traffic levels by engaging communication via DECnet protocols.

These examples are intended to point out that protocol percentages are extremely important to the network baseline process. Protocol percentage measurements can be gained from a network analysis platform using a protocol analyzer or through utilizing a network management system that may be proprietary or applied to intelligent architecture at the site.

4.1.6 Statistical Error Review

Before investigating any upper-layer protocols during a network baseline session, it is important to closely review any physical errors on any topology medium being sampled. This is true for Ethernet environments, Token Ring environments, and any other main topology environments, even WAN media. Physical medium error analysis is a critical step in the network baselining process. This is because it is essential to ensure that the physical medium carrying the network layer, transport layer, or application layer protocol traffic is 100% foundational and working in a positive manner.

Consider this example of a problematic circumstance: Suppose a Token Ring network experiences a high number of physical errors that eventually cause the active monitor device to move into a high ring purge occurrence state. Upon this occurrence, the Token Ring *network interface card* (NIC) across the specific Token Ring will all have to be physically reset at the NIC physical level for a brief time period. This may cause the requeuing of certain upper-layer protocol transmissions from certain stations on the ring. This can cause an extremely high ring purge level, and the physical Token Ring medium can continue to escalate in medium recovery and eventually the errors from even just one station may cause problems on the complete ring. If the process continues, next it is possible that upper-layer protocol transmissions will be interrupted. This type of event can have a negative impact on a completed internetwork. The upper-layer protocols in certain workstations and servers could eventually attempt to reestablish communications by retransmitting at the network or application protocol layer.

Continuous retransmissions at a high level could then cause a disconnect from the connection-based layer protocol, or all the way up through the application layer event. The same type of problem could occur on a physical Ethernet medium, such as in a shared design when the *carrier sense multiple access collision detection* (CSMA/CD) mechanism, which could start Ethernet medium errors to escalate above the 2% to 3% level. The key factor here is that the physical error rate on the physical Ethernet medium will disrupt the capability for Ethernet end-node devices to share the available medium for normal upper-layer application traffic flow communication. The problem could even be translated to a WAN medium using a Frame Relay design. The Frame Relay physical architecture allows for a physical error-generation process to be exhibited through the forward congestion and backward congestion bits, FECN and BECN, which indicate congestion on data transmission in the Frame Relay header. Depending on the level of congestion in a Frame Relay circuit from one point to another between two LAN locations communicating across a WAN, it is very possible that the upper-layer protocol and application traffic transmissions intended for the WAN link could be disrupted by the congestion levels.

To closely examine the physical health of a medium being sampled during a network baseline analysis, it is essential to engage tools associated with the network baselining process that can capture physical errors on that medium. When using a network management system, you may need to adjust parameters to apply physical error analysis techniques When using a protocol analyzer tool, simple threshold settings and standard default settings usually enable the protocol analyzer to just display the errors present on that particular topology medium. The analyst performing the baseline analysis study must closely examine the physical medium during the network baseline study before moving into an upper-layer protocol analysis process. Figure 4.9 displays how error analysis can be performed via protocol analysis.

This is a very important portion of the methodology path of statistical metric measurements when starting a workload characterization event cycle in an overall network baseline. It is important to always thoroughly investigate the physical medium on any area of the internetwork infrastructure. When performing a large baseline study across an enterprise internetwork where many physical medium areas are involved, an analyst must be selective as to which physical media are checked via physical network protocol analysis. This will vary on a case-by-case basis depending on the data-acquisition plan that is chosen.

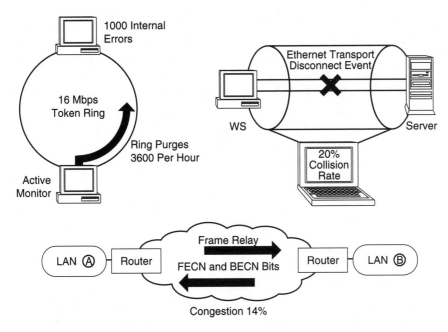

FIGURE 4.9 *Performing error analysis via protocol analysis.*

4.1.7 Physical Frame Layer Process and Statistical Review

When performing a network baseline exercise, the physical frame health of a network architecture must be checked carefully. Whereas some physical mediums may require examination of physical frame communications, other physical mediums may not. In the Ethernet environment, for example, none of the physical frames that are communicated and processed across the medium actually holds information about the physical medium operation. This is not the case in a Token Ring environment, because there are 25 main *Medium Access Control* (MAC) frames that may be encountered, and which may contain valuable information about the physical medium health.

On a Token Ring environment, certain frame types or sequencing at the physical layer may indicate problems, including the Ring Purge MAC frame, Report Soft Error MAC frame, and token-claiming events. All these types of MAC frames include information related to the physical medium's state of operation, general physical health, and possible error state. It is important to understand that certain physical architectures process frames at the physical level.

Another topology that uses physical frame generation is the *Fiber Data Distributed Interface* (FDDI) physical topology. The FDDI physical topology utilizes a MAC layer that can generate events such as a MAC beacon trace, which can indicate problems. The FDDI physical architecture also allows for generation at the physical level of *station management layer*–based frames. These frames can report occurrences such as resource support concerns or the status of certain management states of the physical FDDI medium NIC at the physical medium level. It is important to understand that critical frames such as the FDDI SMT-based *Status Reporting frames* may report on other specific errors that may be encountered at the physical FDDI level and that must be investigated. Figure 4.10 shows physical frame analysis being performed in a network baseline study.

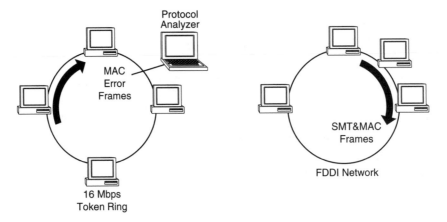

FIGURE 4.10 *Performing physical frame analysis.*

4.1.8 Summary

Overall, it is important to keep in mind when performing network baselining exercises, that certain physical topologies may have to be examined for frames generated at the physical level which may contain important error-based information. However, not all topologies perform this type of process. Therefore, when performing a network baseline, before data-acquisition planning is engaged, it is important to closely examine the network architecture to identify any physical topologies that may require physical frame analysis. Based on the review, it may be necessary to deploy physical frame analysis techniques for the specific topology concern. Later chapters of this book, such as the chapters that discuss analyzing Token Ring and analyzing FDDI, contain detailed information on how to examine the physical frame processes of these unique topologies. The final point here is that when performing a network baseline, the physical frame analysis step should be considered a key workload characterization measurement process.

Let's now move forward into the deep unique world of analyzing upper-layer protocols.

4.2 ULP Data Unit Measurements

After the required steps for standard characterization statistical measurements review are performed in a network baseline, it is next important to very carefully investigate the *upper-layer protocols* (ULPs), such as NCP or TCP protocols, that may be present within the traces taken.

When performing a network baseline across an internetwork with many subnetwork areas and multiple possible sampling points, a set of specific data-acquisition points needs to be chosen. Later in this book, a presentation details methods for choosing data-acquisition sampling points. After the sampling points have been chosen and all the required network baselining workload characterization measurement statistics have been obtained, the next step is to closely examine the ULPs. Doing so requires an analyst to have a developed skill set and to follow exact methodology.

The discussion now focuses on the methodology that should be followed when examining the ULPs from an initial standpoint. Investigating ULPs involves an in-depth understanding of networking technology, including the applied network topology and how the protocols are composed. There are also areas of data analysis that must be understood related to investigating packet formation and compiling techniques. It will also be a helpful skill set if an analyst also understands design techniques that are used on medium-to-large internetworks.

The initial steps discussed examine block and packet-size formation, network transfer fluency and integrity, and finally network packet compatibility.

4.2.1 Block and Packet-Size Examination

When investigating ULPs during a network baseline study, it is important to ensure that a protocol analyzer is placed on the network area that was most recently sampled through baseline characterization measurements. This provides for a comparative analysis. Specifically, wherever the workload characterization baseline measurements were taken is the exact area that should next be sampled for ULP analysis review.

After the protocol analyzer has been positioned within the area of the network, an analysis capture should be configured and then started. The protocol analyzer sampling point could be a specific port on an intelligent hub connecting a shared Ethernet collision domain or a port on a hub in a Token Ring network, or a *Frame Relay Assembler/Dissembler* (FRAD) link to a WAN link.

After a data capture that fills an initial buffer of data in the protocol analyzer has been completed, the analyzer should then be stopped. Some analyzers include artificial intelligence or Expert systems that allow for intuitive investigation of data based on programmed rules-based intelligence review of data gathered in the protocol analyzer. If this type of analyzer is being used, it may be beneficial to analyze the Expert system data prior to stopping the initial capture. Either way, the main point here is that to begin a session of reviewing ULPs, one full buffer of upper-layer data should be captured.

The next step taken should be a close investigation of any Expert system data in artificial intelligent–based systems of the protocol analyzer or management tool. Some Expert systems may include information related to the physical medium being tested and other information related to the upper-layer protocols being examined. Some artificial intelligence–based systems are extremely advanced, such as the *Network Associate Incorporated* (NAI) Sniffer. The NAI Sniffer enables a dynamic detailed review of certain protocol layer communications. The Expert system in the Network Associate Sniffer facilitates review of the physical layer, the network layer, the connection-based layer processes, and the application layer dataflow. Certain symptoms are logged and then applied diagnoses related to the artificial intelligent system may be presented. Review of these statistics when using this type of tool will yield a roadmap of the types of problems that may be present in the ULP data section of the trace data captured. This will allow for a more defined identification of network issues that may require further investigation or cause analysis by the analyst. Figure 4.11 displays how upper-layer protocols can be viewed in a network baseline study.

Notes should be taken from the Expert systems that are applied via the protocol analysis or management tool used. Also, certain statistics can be saved or printed out to certain management systems or file formats, such as a *Common Separated Value* (CSV) file format platform. The CSV file format can be imported into most commercial spreadsheet and reporting systems, from where these statistics can then be reviewed for network baselining exercises.

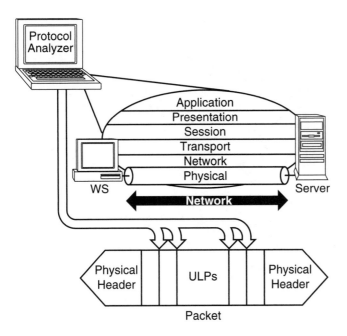

FIGURE 4.11 *Viewing upper-layer protocols.*

That said, the main process that must be emphasized is the overall investigation of the upper-layer protocols by examining specific areas. This is the discrete review of areas in the different protocols within the analyzer data-trace capture that is completed. All protocols must be examined for specific criteria. Chapter 7, "LAN and WAN Protocols," discusses this in more detail. One of the key areas that must be investigated is the protocol-layering technique used on the particular network. Certain protocol-layering processes can be captured with a protocol analyzer. The type of protocol layering captured is affected by the topologies, network operating systems, and applications deployed. Figure 4.12 shows how protocol layering can be analyzed in a network baseline study.

An example is a Novell NetWare operating system deployed against a certain physical topology. In the case of analysis review of data captured , it will be common to see the IPX layer, the SPX protocol layer, and the Network Core Protocol layer present in dataflow when network devices are communicating across the LAN or WAN.

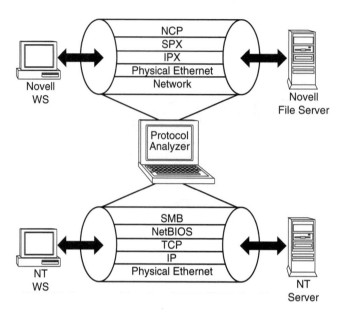

FIGURE 4.12 *Analyzing protocol layering.*

If the Windows NT protocol suite is deployed, it is common to see the *Internet Protocol* (IP) layer processed for network layer communications, the *Transmission Control Protocol* (TCP) layer processed for connection-based protocols, and NetBIOS engaged for session layer data transfer. It is also common to see the SMB protocol layer present for calls on the NT Server from the NT Workstation environment.

These are just some of the examples of protocol-layering investigation processes that an analyst might encounter. Note that when upper-layer data, such as application data, is sent across a LAN or a WAN, the data may have to be encapsulated in a specific format.

Encapsulation refers to the internal packaging of data within certain protocols, which is then packaged with other protocols, and eventually within a topology-based frame.

A packet is actually formed through encapsulation techniques based on the topology of a certain LAN architecture, the NOS deployed, and the application environment across an internetwork.

Another term for encapsulation is enveloping or multiprotocol layering, which are both common terms. The concept is that a packet is formed by certain factors. To be more specific, the packets are formed by the physical frame of the topology and are also affected by the NOS deployed, which engages certain protocols such as IP at the network layer or TCP at the transport layer. The final data is then encapsulated, possibly within the TCP layer. The final packet protocol forming factor is the application.

Note that the term *packet* is normally associated with a topology frame that includes or encapsulates protocols and data. The term *frame* is associated with a topology frame that is empty as to holding any ULPs or data (therefore, just a frame). Both terms are interchangeable in general discussion across vendors and industry personnel when discussing protocol analysis. Figure 4.13 illustrates the packet versus frame concept.

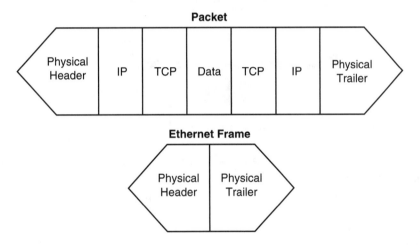

FIGURE 4.13   *Packet versus frame.*

In summary, the actual packet size is determined by the following three simple factors:

- Frame type or physical maximum transmission unit

- Network operating system and applied protocols

- Applications deployed and data unit packaging techniques

These three factors form the final packet and affect the type of protocols engaged in the packet layer encapsulation scheme. Figure 4.14 presents the main packet-forming factors.

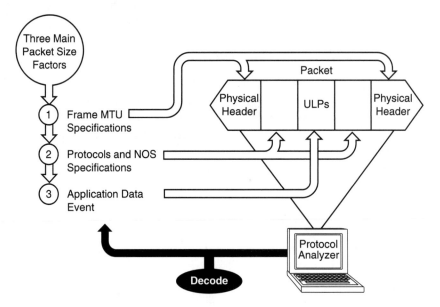

FIGURE 4.14 *Main packet-forming factors.*

Note that the actual packet size is also determined by these forming factors. If an Ethernet topology is used, for example, the maximum size of the packet is always in the 1514 byte range. The actual type of protocols deployed within the Ethernet packet, if utilizing a Windows NT environment, include IP and TCP. The final data may be deployed inside the actual TCP layer and this will be determined by the application invoked.

Inefficiencies in packet size formation can negatively affect performance. Some of these circumstances can be located through protocol analysis of ULPs.

An example could be a case where the full Ethernet *maximum transmission unit* (MTU) is not utilized. In this case, an application utilizes TCP and limits the *maximum segment size* (MSS)
to approximately 500 bytes. In this case, the application may only include approximately 400 bytes of data. The 400 bytes of data are called the application *protocol data unit* (PDU). The PDU would then be encapsulated inside the

TCP header, which would be encapsulated inside the IP header, which then would be encapsulated inside the actual Ethernet physical frame. The final packet size might only be somewhere between 500 to 550 bytes in final size when captured with a protocol analyzer. The limiting factor is the TCP MSS invoked by the application operation as related to the TCP layer process.

The investigative process of using protocol analysis against the initial captured trace is for the express purpose of understanding the type of protocol-layering techniques used and the type of packet sizes formed. As mentioned earlier in this book, it is clear that *maximum dataflow energy* (MDFE) is based on the maximum amount of data transmitted in the most amount of time with the highest amount of efficiency. As noted, the size of final data packets are formed by three main factors: the physical network, the NOS, and the application. With this said, if high efficiency is not being seen and the network or an application is not performing during an application characterization session, it is possible that the investigation of the ULP layers may identify certain areas that may be able to be fine tuned to improve performance. The areas requiring tuning could include the application or the type of NOS utilized, or the type of physical topology engaged. The key is to increase the maximum the size of data to increase efficiency.

It is now clear that this is a critical step in a network baselining exercise. From a methodology perspective, it is important to remember that when completing the network workload characterization metric phase of a baseline study, it is important to next engage a review process against the upper-layer protocols. The technique is to engage a wide-open capture and closely review the trace by moving through the data in a frame-by-frame process. It is critical to examine the layering sequences and the size of packets engaged in the particular network baseline session against the area being sampled. Later in this book, further techniques are presented on how to examine data internally within a protocol analysis trace through a process called *paging through the trace*.

4.2.2 Network Transfer Fluency Review

After completing a review of the ULPs, as related to the packet-size formation and layering applied, the next area to review is the data network transfer fluency process. The network transfer process can be thought of as the end-to-end communication sequencing between specific devices in the network baseline session. It is important to review the fluency of a network transfer session when performing a network baseline by engaging protocol analysis.

When examining a shared LAN area such as Ethernet or Token Ring, many devices in an initial upper-layer protocol layer capture will be encountered as communicating back and forth to each other throughout the data session. A protocol analysis trace can include thousands of frames, up to 100,000 packets or more. Many of the various packets involved relate to different end-node conversations and may interleave because there are different time slots in one second where different devices share the medium. When this occurs, it is important to apply protocol analysis techniques such as filtering to examine discrete conversations between selected servers and workstations in the network baseline session. The key is to examine these sessions at a network transfer level.

This process can actually be started by first taking a wide-open capture of upper-layer protocol data in the network sampling area during the network baselining process. When completing the upper-layer capture, the analyst should save the data capture and then display the data to closely examine all the key workstations and servers that are communicating by using UPLs. The next step is to extract the top traffic generators from an outbound traffic talking standpoint and from an inbound receiving standpoint. This process is sometimes called examining the network transfer sessions for the top traffic generators and top traffic receivers. After identifying the top traffic sessions, each one of the identified top generating and receiving sessions should be closely examined. This usually involves a process of filtering on certain workstations communicating with certain servers. Specific transfer processes have to be closely examined. As noted later in this book under a section that discusses analysis techniques, many different negative traffic flow events can be captured and identified with a protocol analyzer. The key factor here is that the overall session end-to-end capability between two devices should be examined for network transfer integrity. After workstations and servers have been filtered during in a network baseline session, the capture should be closely examined for fluency.

An example of a consistent fluent transfer operation is when a workstation calls on a server for a particular remote file to be read. If the file is transferred in a consecutive mode to the workstation and eventually the file is closed without any errors, the session can be thought of as fluent.

Another example is that when performing a network baseline and moving directly into this process, the analyst sees that a particular set of stations are not generating in a fluent manner. If abnormal errors are occurring—such as high levels of file retransmissions, transport retransmissions, long response times, or errors are being encountered in the network analysis based on an

Expert system and they appear to be consecutive in an ongoing basis—it is very possible that a nonfluent transfer has been encountered. Later in this book, further details on techniques used to examine end-to-end transfer are presented.

A nonfluent transfer, when considering the example of a file transfer that is interrupted by a high retransmission rate, can start to become more predominant as a network problem and be considered a more critical issue when occurring on a consistent or ongoing basis.

The key factor again, moving back to the discussion of MDFE or perfect communications, is that it is important to transmit the most amount of data in the most rapid amount of time, with the truest integrity.

Another example is that if a file transfer is occurring on a network and the file transfer usually requires only 2,000 packets to transfer approximately 20000 bytes of actual data, but an additional 5,000 packets are engaged, this approximates to a 25% retransmission rate. This would be an extremely nonfluent situation because a high amount of redundancy is in place, specifically file retransmissions, to allow the data transfer to finally take effect. In this particular case, this would be considered a nonfluent condition and would affect the final efficiency of the performance of the overall end-to-end network transfer condition. Figure 4.15 displays the concept of measuring network data-transfer fluency via protocol analysis.

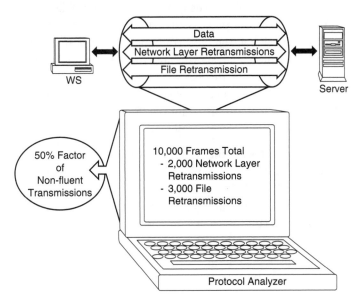

FIGURE 4.15 *Measuring network data-transfer fluency via protocol analysis.*

For the purposes of this section of the book, it is important to remember that when performing a network baselining session, the next step in upper-layer protocol investigation after examining packet-size formation techniques is to examine the fluency of the overall network communication sessions. There may be many sessions in place in a wide-open capture and it is important to be selective. You should choose the top traffic generators and the top traffic receivers in any network communication session when this process is followed.

4.2.3 Network Packet Compatibility

When investigating upper-layer protocols, the next area of network baselining is to review packet compatibility. When multiple devices communicate across a network, the packet types engaged must be compatible at the physical frame and ULP layers. Specifically, packet compatibility can be a factor at the physical level and also at the upper-layer protocol level. Certain types of physical frame technologies require packet compatibility. One example of this is the Ethernet architecture. The Ethernet architecture allows for multiple possible frame types, such as Ethernet II, 802.3 Raw, 802.3 IEEE Accepted, and 802.3 SNAP.

An example of incompatibility is when the Ethernet frame types used for application transfer on a large network are not similar in configuration between a workstation and a server on a particular end-to-end Ethernet channel link. In this case, there is a very strong possibility that Ethernet communications will never commence or complete.

Another type of packet compatibility issue concerns the network layer (specific-version technologies, for example). Assume, for instance, that an internetwork at one site uses IP version 4 (the most common version of Internet Protocol), but when performing analysis you note that certain devices using IP version 6. You then find that the devices with IP version 6 applied to the workstation IP protocol configuration are not connecting to certain servers. The lesson you learn is this: It is important for the IP versions to be compatible across a particular IP-based network implementation for true transfer fluency.

A Novell environment provides another example. Assume, for instance, that two different versions of SPX are deployed. The site workstations are configured for SPXI and SPXII. Although the two versions can coexist in certain configurations, for true fluency and high transfer rates to occur without occurrence of any abnormal conditions, it is important to implement a common version of SPX. It is important for the SPX versions to compatible across the Novell-based network implementation.

Packet compatibility can be examined with a protocol analyzer when examining a capture of an upper-layer protocol trace in a network baseline session. Figure 4.16 presents the concept of packet compatibility analysis.

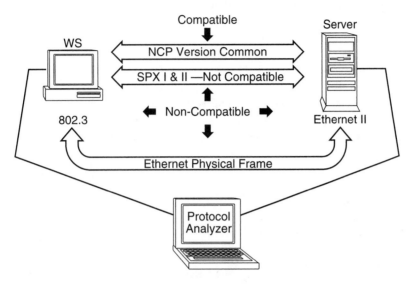

FIGURE 4.16 *Concept of packet compatibility analysis.*

It is a critical step to ensure that the physical networks are compatible by reviewing topology frame-type headers. It is also important that all network, transport, session, presentation, and application layer protocols communicated across a LAN or WAN be compatible. It is important to examine this area of network communication as to frame types and protocol versions for compatibility for all endpoints involved.

4.2.4 Summary

After investigating the upper-layer protocols by examining how packets are formed from a protocol-layering and packet-size formation standpoint, it is then important to examine the overall fluency of general communications and to closely examine packet compatibility at the physical and multiprotocol level.

The discussion now turns to other critical measurement techniques in network baselining, such as network timing and throughput analysis.

4.3 Network Performance Reviews

The next step in network baselining is to examine performance. Performance is probably the most closely monitored operational feature by the users in the network environment. It is critical that applications perform; after all, they are supporting the business.

To achieve performance, certain features must be available and operational in the design of the network. Performance must also be considered when configuring and implementing the network. It is possible to use protocol analysis tools very effectively to examine network performance. Two important components of network performance lend themselves to statistical measurement review via protocol analysis and network management systems.

The following two main components must be closely monitored to review performance:

- Network response time

- Network throughput and transaction analysis

The following is a description of these critical measurement metrics and how important they are to the analysis of a session gathered during a network baselining process.

4.3.1 Network Response Time Analysis

Network response time analysis can be defined as the process of using a protocol analyzer or a network management–based platform to examine the response time on a network. This measurement is usually applied between specific endpoints. There are many different reasons to examine response time. Response-time measurements can be used in both reactive and proactive analysis. Response-time analysis should be used in a careful and planned manner when performing network baselining. The measurement techniques can also be used in a very rapid and exact manner when performing network troubleshooting or cause analysis. The main types of metric timing measurements used in a network baseline session, in both proactive and reactive modes, are as follows:

- Absolute time measurements

- Delta time measurements

- Relative time measurements

Timing measurement techniques are considered universal. Many different protocol analyzers allow for these metrics to be closely examined. Many different management systems also allow for these statistics to be reviewed.

It is important to start with a general review of each measurement process, and then to apply it to a network analysis session or baselining process.

Absolute time refers to the time that a packet is captured via a network protocol analysis tool. There are different times when packets are generated onto the network; these are the absolute generation time. If the network analyzer or management system is positioned on a network three hops away from the source device that generated the packet, however, the actual capture time of the packet at the three-hop position is identified as the absolute time within the upper-layer protocol analysis trace of the analyzer. For certain processes, the identification of this time proves very valuable.

If a help desk is encountering problems at 10:20 a.m. every day and a protocol analyzer is deployed properly, for example, it may be possible to isolate this event to cause very quickly. With most protocol analyzers, an analyst can pre-configure a certain time metric to capture of a particular event. If the analyzer is set to capture on a specific area at 10:00 a.m., and the problem does occur at 10:20 a.m., it may next be possible to capture the event and then review the data by turning on the absolute time feature of the analyzer. This enables the analyst to review the trace analysis data results at 10:20 a.m. for a possible protocol analysis event that caused the problem. This is an extremely useful tool process for network baselining, and the process could be cross-threaded for multiple network baselining stages.

One example of absolute time usage in network baselining is mapping protocol or application events against the absolute time of the data-trace process captures.

The delta time measurement is also extremely critical. *Delta time* refers to the amount of time between two consecutive packets captured in a trace analysis session. Depending on how the protocol analyzer is configured, the delta time may be more relevant to locating the exact specific cause of a problem or specific identification of a certain issue. When using the delta time measurement, it is extremely effective to use a protocol analyzer and filter on specific station communications such as a workstation and server communicating to each other. With the proper filter, it is very easy to review requests or response sequences from a workstation to a server and back to the workstation. This facilitates the examination of request and reply information in forward and reverse sequences via delta time. If the packets are consecutive, it is very simple to look between the packets with the delta time measurement activated.

This enables the analyst to view the amount of time that it takes for the workstation and the server to respond.

Another factor to consider here is whether the workstation and server are placed on the same physical network. If they are, the actual response time from the server and the workstation could be considered accurate by viewing the delta time between server and workstation packets. If the devices are different networks, the network transmission time must be taken into account for calculation. Specifically, the delta time would show the amount of time that it takes for the workstation to request information and how long it takes for the server to actually respond. Next, the delta time metric can be cross-mapped and identified as the interprocessing time of the particular device. When dealing with multiple architectures in a large, multi-tier internetwork, the timing metrics become more complex.

Consider, for example, a situation in which two hops separate a workstation and a server when communicating across a router-based network. If one protocol analyzer is positioned on the source segment where the workstation is located, and another analyzer is placed on the destination segment where the server is located, and a data transfer is generated, certain measurement criteria can be obtained. The source-segment analyzer shows the workstation generation time and also shows the destination server response time as well as the network time traversed for the packet to be received back on the source segment. The server-segment analyzer shows the server generation or interprocessing time and the workstation response time, but as combined with the network time involved in the response back from the workstation to the server segment. In this case, it may be beneficial to use both protocol analyzers to perform a comparative analysis and extract the difference between the workstation interprocessing time and the server interprocessing time related to two different traces in a comparative mode. This enables an analyst to extract the network transaction transfer time between the networks across the two-router hop. This is just one example of how network timing can be so useful in the network baselining session.

The next measurement that is important is relative time. Relative time can be an extremely useful measurement for the purpose of examining the exact metrics related to certain protocol sequencing events. *Relative time* refers to the amount of time between two specific packets marked in a protocol analysis session. Most protocol analyzers allow for the relative-time metric to be turned on as active. If two devices such as a server and workstation are communicating on a network and the data-transfer session is captured with an analyzer in a filtered session, and a file open protocol call occurs at packet 1, it is then possible to mark packet 1 with a 0-marked base through the relative-time measurement. If packet 54 shows the close completion on the file transfer, the time between packet 0 and packet 54 is considered the time for the file transfer to occur. The key point is that the file transfer time can be measured by using the relative time metric. By zeroing at packet 1 and then examining packet 54, the relative time measurement would accumulate or build in the relative-time column in the protocol analysis tool. This is an extremely useful measurement technique, because it enables an analyst to measure the difference in time between a file open and the file close, which could be considered the time for the file transfer. This time measurement can be used for other key purposes such as measuring the time between polling events of other network event operations.

Other examples of using relative time include measuring other protocol analysis sequencing events—such as the amount of time between two broadcasts from a router; this would enable an analyst to understand the frequency of *Routing Information Protocol* (RIP) updates—or the amount of time between two polls from a specific printer to a print server. This technique proves extremely powerful in a network baselining session.

Network timing measurements are extremely important in terms of performance review via network baselining. It is important to understand that these measurements may need to be engaged in a troubleshooting occurrence or a reactive situation in a more rapid manner. Network timing measurements can be used quickly to determine why a delay is occurring across an internetwork. Figure 4.17 displays the three main timing measurements.

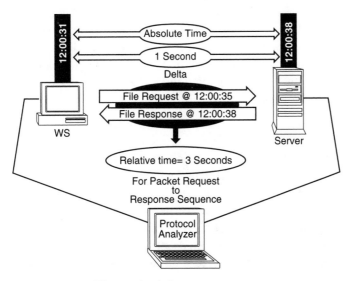

FIGURE 4.17   *Three main timing measurements.*

In a proactive network baselining session, it is important to examine the first several upper-layer protocol traces to examine key workstations and servers to see how they are responding from a general response-time basis; this examination enables an analyst to understand how performance is being achieved during the network baseline study.

The proactive use of this measurement is extremely important. If the right devices are selected, certain criteria can be benchmarked in the network baseline study, such as the average delta time or average relative time for certain file transfers. The network timing measurement process is a powerful tool when performing a network baselining exercise.

4.3.2 Throughput and Transaction Measurements

The next important measurement in network baselining is throughput and transaction measurement analysis. *Effective file throughput* (EFT) is defined as the amount of time that it takes to transfer a specific number of cumulative bytes related to a certain measurement of time.

It is important to understand that throughput, which can be considered the movement of data against time, can be measured by analyzing many different network protocol sequencing events. Network throughput is normally measured in *kilobits per second* (Kbps) during network baselining or troubleshooting-based cause analysis sessions. With that said, it is not considered beneficial to investigate throughput for network protocol sequencing that is not consecutive, such as network logons, broadcast events, or events considered business transactions and which are not consecutive. The only way to truly measure throughput, as to the movement of data, is to closely examine file transfer. File transfer when taking throughput measurements into account, can be examined by filtering on a workstation and a server. The next step is to closely examine the workstation and server data communications by observing actual file transfer events by examining effective file throughput. To do so, an analyst must use EFT-based measurements during protocol analysis.

Most protocol analyzers, including the Network Associate Sniffer, Wandell & Goltermann Domino, and other industry management tools, such as the Ganymede Chariot product, allow for immediate effective throughput measurements to be obtained based on certain file transfer events. When using a protocol analyzer or management system, it may be necessary to set up specific filters on a workstation or server to extract true EFT transfer. It may also be necessary to engage a file transfer process by using an actual file transfer event (requesting a user to do so in the network area being sampled). There are also predetermined data scripts that generate application traffic models that can be played through certain network management systems, such as the Ganymede Chariot system. The Chariot system is extremely valuable when investigating throughput or data-transaction processing, because it allows for data scripts to be played across two specific endpoints of an internetwork channel. The endpoints are defined by the Chariot application module software and the two endpoints actually communicate with each other by predefined data scripts. The scripts are then played from endpoint to endpoint and are considered non-intrusive against the network channel. The Chariot software then just charts the throughput achieved.

This is an extremely useful process, and there are many different products that allow for this type of EFT channel analysis. The Optimal Software Application Expert system allows for throughput measurements to be determined in a system review of application operation thread analysis and other features within the Optimal platform. With this in mind, when using a protocol analyzer an analyst should use the EFT measurement process as his base measurement process.

To begin this process, an analyst should deploy a protocol against the network baseline sampling area. Key workstations and servers should be defined as top traffic generators and receivers. After specific devices have been designated as primary devices engaging a file transfer, other devices need to be extracted from the display view so that the devices chosen for the network EFT measurement process can be reviewed in a focused mode. Certain applications may need to be invoked to enable file transfer to occur. The protocol analyzer needs to be set up in a filtered and a focused mode to examine data-transfer processing.

One key step is to start the protocol analyzer and have it set up to filter on the workstation physical MAC address at a certain user area. When the file transfer is engaged, the protocol analyzer captures the file open and closed statements, which will allow for the file transfer to be examined. After the upper-layer protocol data-trace capture has been completed and saved, the trace can then be opened for review. Certain measurement metrics may need to be activated, such as relative time and cumulative bytes. With these two metrics active within the data-trace review, it is possible to zero out the relative-time based on the start of the file transfer by finding the file open request. When the file open request is found and the zero-base mark is applied, the cumulative byte column will also be set to a zero mark.

Next, the analyst should identify the file transfer close process. If the file close process is found to be 200 frames later and marked, it is now possible to examine the time from the start of the file transfer to determine the relative time of the complete transfer, and the amount of data moved in the file transfer can also be examined for data movement or total cumulative bytes transferred in the file exchange process. This will allow for the EFT measurement to be closely marked or identified. Multiple file transfer events should be examined for a true benchmark or comparative analysis of this critical measurement. Figure 4.18 displays the concept of measuring EFT.

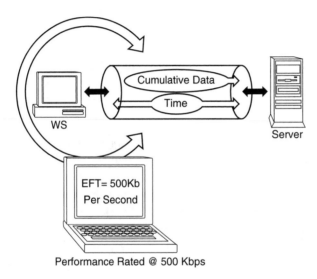

FIGURE 4.18 *Measuring effective file throughput.*

In overview, EFT measurements and transaction analysis can be applied to a network baselining session. This process can be used for emergency network troubleshooting to examine slow file performance events and to perform cause analysis on performance problems. It can also be deployed when performing large network baseline studies related to examining effective file transfer on a per-segment area as related to a large internetwork baseline study. When baselining a network, EFT measurements should be closely examined in the user areas and also in the main computer room area. This allows for an understanding of how effective file transfer is across different areas of the internetwork. There are times when bridges, routers, or switched channels in an internetwork design will increase the latency and decrease the EFT finally being achieved. This is a critical benchmark of overall internetwork performance.

4.3.3 Summary

Network timing measurements in direct association with the EFT measurements enable an analyst to understanding the complete performance model of a particular user session. This can be true when measuring how a user is communicating with a specific server or when evaluating the performance of a complete network baseline study (perhaps when performing a large internetwork study). Timing and EFT measurements are critical when performing a large internetwork baseline study. Note that when performing a large internetwork enterprise audit, many different analyzer positioning points must be chosen and many different captures as related to timing and EFT measurements apply to the overall network baseline process.

4.4 Analyzing an Internetwork for Reliability

When moving directly into the mid-portion phases of a network baseline study, the next focus is to closely examine the reliability of dataflow communications. This is a necessary review stage whether the purpose of the study is for a rapid reactive determination of cause or for the purpose of performing a proactive network baseline on a specific segment area within a small or large infrastructure.

To examine internetwork reliability a protocol analyzer can be effectively used for the purpose of studying certain phases of network communication. With network operational communication dataflow, certain processes must take place to allow for final file transfer to commence. As noted earlier in this book, the reason that a network exists is for the express purpose of accessing remote resources or accessing remote data from another device. Keeping this in mind, it is important to understand that for basic file access and transfer to occur, many other different phases of network communication must also take place.

For a workstation to transfer a file to server, for instance, it first must connect to a server. Next, the workstation user must log on or authenticate to the server. After a connection has been established and authentication has been resolved in terms of the logon process, the next step involved is for the user to invoke one or more applications from the server. This is a standard networking process.

During many unique events, the user workstation cycles through an application launch sequence and the application is engaged. Either way, whether the application is launched immediately or the process is determined by how quickly the user decides to access the application, in certain circumstances the user workstation must maintain a connection with the server. This type of connection maintenance is referred to as a *polling event* or a *keepalive sequence*. The method of using a poll operation is usually determined by the application and the NOS operational modes. Depending on implementation requirements, polling may or may not be engaged, because it is an optional dataflow operation. After the polling event is active, the application event cycle is then engaged. Sometimes the process is unique as related to the type of NOS deployed or the type of application being utilized.

Next, to start an application operation, specific files must be obtained from a file server or remote host. To access these files, a workstation may send a protocol call sequence for the file or search for the file. This file search process can be involved, sometimes requiring normal or excessive data transfers to locate the file. At times, anomalies can occur during this key phase in network communication. After the connection has been established, the logon authentication approved, the keepalive or polling event process engaged, and a file search sequence launched, a file access event or transfer occurs to remotely access the application. Figure 4.19 shows how protocol analysis should be used for measuring internetwork reliability.

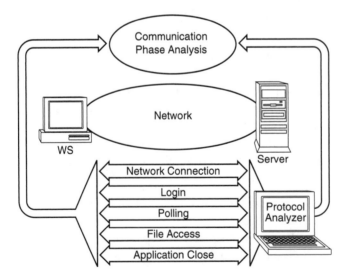

FIGURE 4.19 *How protocol analysis should be used.*

File transfer analysis is extremely involved, but is a very critical portion of network baselining related to analyzing phases of network communication.

Other types of communication can also take place in an internetwork, such as internetwork addressing, routing protocol updates, and packet identification. If a specific device needs to be located across the internetwork, internetworking addressing sequence algorithms are engaged.

If specific routers have to synchronize with each other and establish routing tables, routing protocol update sequencing is engaged.

Some unique phases of network communication involve broadcast sequences or updating sequences between key servers, which can be classified under unique packet identification concerns.

To ensure that an internetwork is reliable when performing a network baseline, the following phases of network communication should be examined:

- Network connections
- Logon sequences
- Network keepalive connection transmissions
- File search sequencing
- File access and transfer
- Internetworking addressing
- Routing protocol update sequencing
- Packet identification analysis

The following sections discuss each one of these unique areas of network analysis. Figure 4.20 displays the main phases of network communication.

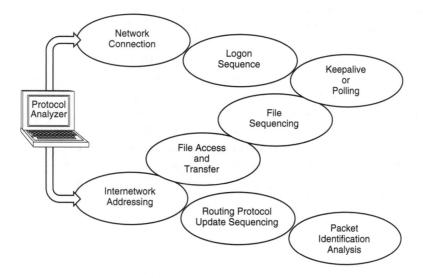

FIGURE 4.20 *Main phases of network communication.*

4.4.1 Network Connection Analysis

When starting a network communication session, a network device establishes a connection with another device to commence the communication. Network communication connection processes vary based on the type of NOS and the applications deployed on the internetwork.

An example of a simple network connection process is when a workstation is attached to a Token Ring or Ethernet network in a Novell environment. After a workstation has connected to the physical medium, it usually next attempts to connect to the main Novell file server within the facility. This process can be configured to be automatic or invoked by the user. Depending on the Novell operating system release, the workstation calls out a request to find the Novell file server that is desired for connection. After the file server has been located, it responds back and establishes a connection with a server. A protocol analyzer is useful here to examine the network connection process.

In older Novell release operations, the workstation can attempt to locate a server first by performing a protocol sequence utilizing NCP to find the nearest file server. NCP is discussed in detail later in this book. After the NCP "find nearest server" command has been received by the closest server, that server then responds to the workstation with a connection established. Then the workstation establishes a connection with the server and obtains information on properties of the server most desired. After these properties have been received, the workstation then destroys the connection with the initial server and attempts to locate the main server for file access through a directed command obtained from information on the first property's call command on the server-connection process. This is an involved connection process, but it can be examined with a protocol analyzer. With some of the newer releases of Novell network operating systems, it is common to encounter *NetWare Directory Services* (NDS). NDS enables a user workstation to log in to the complete internetwork. In this case, the workstation protocol call sequences will differ. The differences will clearly be seen with a protocol analysis tool. The key message is that it is common for an analyst to capture on a workstation engaging NetWare connection processes and examine the overall connection sequencing and event cycle. Figure 4.21 presents the concept of analyzing network connection and login sequences.

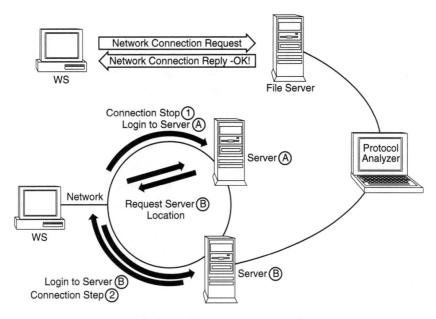

FIGURE 4.21 *Analyzing network connection and logon sequences.*

Connection processes for establishing workstation-to-server connections in different NOS environments such as Novell or Windows NT environments all vary based on different factors such as the requirement of a connection cycle, the location of the workstation, and the server devices. The important point to understand is that a protocol analyzer can be used to closely examine this process.

The protocol analyzer needs to be set up and situated to filter on the workstation, and a connection process has to be invoked by the analyst or the user to examine the connection sequence. After the connection sequence has been captured, the analyst should closely reviewed it. It is possible to use this process in a proactive network baseline stage or in a reactive stage for certain analysis requirements.

4.4.2 Logon Sequence Analysis

When determining reliability, the next important network baselining step is to ensure that network-based workstations are establishing a consecutive logon sequence with servers. The logon process should be consistent, fluent, and rapid, but without excessive redundant communication.

By filtering on a workstation with a protocol analyzer, the logon sequence can be investigated. During a logon sequence, a workstation may search for server-based files to engage the logon process or to develop an authentication process for the workstation user to enter the username and password. For an actual logon to be considered approved by the server, many steps occur including file search, file open/file close operations, and username and password sequencing. After a logon has been approved by the server, the workstation user is then considered connected and "logged on" to the server's NOS.

A protocol analyzer can be used to monitor this event. A logon sequence can consume 100 frames or thousands of frames. It is possible to use tuning processes via analysis to locate issues in a workstation image file, such as the logon script. This enables an analyst to tune network configuration for network access sequencing used by site workstations and servers so as to limit the logon sequencing by modifying the search path or the location of certain logon files. If a username or a password is incorrect, authentication failures show up during network protocol analysis.

Examining the logon sequence is a very valuable step during network baselining for both reactive and proactive analysis concerns.

4.4.3 Network Keepalive Connection Analysis

All protocol environments, whether they be Novell, Windows NT, or *Systems Networking Architecture* (SNA), have internal processes that can engage polling events or keepalive transmissions. Certain application designs do not require the constant maintenance of a poll or keepalive connection between a workstation and a server. Specific applications allow for a connection to be reestablished and an application dataflow process to commence. Other applications require constant maintenance between the device and the server, such as print servers and critical database connections. In these instances, a protocol analyzer can be used to examine network keepalive connection transmissions or polling events.

When the connection is initially established with a workstation and a logon sequence is invoked and authenticated, the next event that usually occurs in upper-layer data communications (if an application is not being launched) is a keepalive or a poll event. A protocol analyzer or management system can be used to closely monitor a workstation or a server for polling event cycles if they are occurring. When observing upper-layer protocol events during a network baselining session, an analyst should closely examine polling events and keepalive connections. This will allow for discrete analysis in this critical area and close examination of the overall network communication session.

Polling events can be clearly seen as outbound requests and replies that do not include high amounts of data internally within the upper-layer protocol packaging area. Usually certain fields are active in the transport layer of a packet, indicating acknowledgment and sequence number polling event cycles as concurrent with consistent polling processes. A protocol analyzer can examine polling event cycles in many different environments. Figure 4.22 presents the concept of analyzing network polling events.

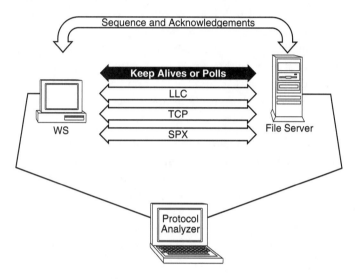

FIGURE 4.22 *Analyzing network polling events.*

In a Windows NT environment, for example, TCP sequence and acknowledgment numbers can be examined. In an SNA environment, *logical link control* (LLC) polls can be examined. In a Novell environment, SPX layer sequence and acknowledgment numbers can be reviewed.

This is an extremely important part of network baselining methodology. Polling events and keepalive connection transmissions should be examined in all multiprotocol environments.

4.4.4 File Search and File Access Sequencing and Analysis

After a device has established a connection to a host and a logon authentication process has been approved, and the polling event has been found to be either active or inactive, the next sequence that should be examined is the file searching or file access process.

It must be mentioned again that the main reason for internetwork architecture to be present in our enterprise environment is for access to remote resources or files from different hosts and locations. File search and file access activity is a critical area of network protocol analysis. By closely examining file search and file access processes, the overall efficiency of internetwork transfers can be examined, and it is possible to examine application sequences at a very discrete level.

During logon sequences and application launching processes, various files are searched by different stations throughout the internetwork. When starting a network baseline, it is important to plan to closely examine from each data-acquisition point how file search activity is being performed from specific workstations and user stations within a particular network area. This determines how efficient the user workstation file location process is for distributed or centralized access of different applications and critical files in the internetwork architecture.

An MIS team may place files on workstations and servers that are considered normal under the initial design and implementation process of that particular internetwork. When multiple applications are deployed across a large architecture, however, it is very common to find files that are misplaced or that could be more efficiently placed on the local workstation drive or a centralized server. Depending on the situation, protocol analysis can be used to review what files are searched and the type of file access occurring. This is a critical process for examining reliability in a large internetwork.

Note that file search activity should be kept to a minimum. File sequencing analysis can be examined with a protocol analyzer. If a workstation is filtered on and a file search appears to be redundant and the file is not found on the server for 1,000 or 2,000 frames, this is excessive or abnormal redundant communication that could possibly be minimized by implementing a hard search path or putting the file locally in the workstation.

An example of file access is the actual opening of a file. This is one of the more critical steps in upper-layer protocol analysis. It is always important to examine the upper-layer application protocols via network baselining to review file open and close packet sequences and thereby determine how files are accessed. The file open command contains critical metric settings that the protocol analysis tool will unveil to the analyst. Some of these settings show items such as file search attributes for open, close, security access, and other key information related to the file.

The file open response from a server may show the file size and location, and certain search attributes such as read, write, and update capability. The file close statement clearly shows that the file is closed and has been received by the station.

By examining the file search and file access process packets, an analyst can determine how efficient the overall internetwork is in terms of serving the user environment for the main purpose of file access on a remote device. Figure 4.23 presents the concept of analyzing network data file transfers.

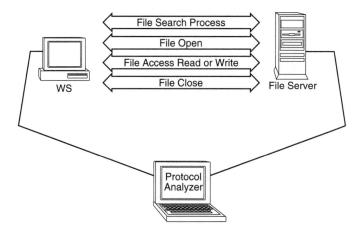

FIGURE 4.23 *Analyzing network data file transfers.*

This is a critical part of network baselining and should be used for all internetwork baseline studies and engagements. This measurement process should be used during both reactive and proactive analysis.

4.4.5 Internetwork Addressing Analysis

In every network, small and large alike, there is always the need for one device to locate another device or devices per a communication requirement. Sometimes the addresses are available and a source device knows the address of the destination device with which it must communicate. For example, this can be established by setting a default gateway for a workstation that needs to locate a router or server in a particular network location on a user station. Another area where concerns may arise is the set up of unique addressing schemes that allow for address resolution, such as *Domain Name Services* (DNS).

Many different address-resolution schemes allow a device to locate another device.

One example is *Address Resolution Protocol* (ARP), which is used in the TCP/IP environment. If a workstation knows the IP address of the device that it wants to communicate to, but it has no understanding of what the physical network address is for the device, it performs an ARP call packet sequence with a target IP address to locate a target hardware address. A local router can be designed, or a local device can be set up with an addressing system that intercepts the ARP request and maps the IP address to a physical address. This establishes and engages a packet response to the workstation sending the ARP as to how the physical address can be attached to in order to obtain the final communication sequence.

It is important that internetworking addressing always be operative, because it is a key factor in internetwork stability and reliability. If internetworking addressing problems exist, a protocol analyzer will reveal an address-resolution failure occurrence to an analyst. An analyst can use a protocol analyzer effectively and examine internetworking addressing schemes. Figure 4.24 shows how internetwork addressing can be examined via protocol analysis.

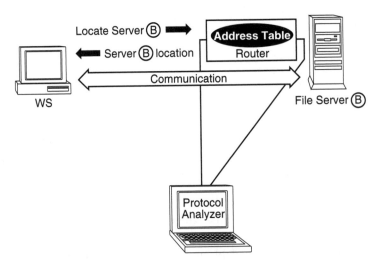

FIGURE 4.24 *Examining internetwork addressing.*

By closely examining internetwork addressing during upper-layer protocol analysis, an analyst can understand the reliability factors involved. All network layer addressing schemes should be investigated for proper addressing assignment. This would be extremely relevant in the IP addressing process, because network and subnet schemes need to be closely examined. In a Novell environment, even the network layer scheme for IPX should be examined for integrity, such as the network node.socket process.

There are many different networking addressing levels. A typical packet contains a physical network address, and depending on the protocol environment, may also contain a network and a transport layer address.

A TCP/IP packet, for example, contains a physical address, an IP layer address, and a TCP port address relevant to internetwork address review.

It is important to engage protocol analysis to examine internetwork addressing call sequences to ensure that resolution is occurring for devices attempting to locate other devices. It is also important to investigate the internetwork addresses assigned to different protocol layers when examining an upper-layer protocol trace in the first several capture sessions of a network baseline process.

This measurement technique can be used to examine an internetwork for reliability in a proactive or reactive network baseline study.

4.4.6 Routing Protocol Updates

Routing protocol update sequences are another important area in internetwork architecture. The purpose of routing protocols in a large internetwork is to ensure that the routers are updating each other upon locating the various devices for which they are maintaining routing tables. Various routing protocols are available, such as distance vector protocols or link-state-based routing protocols. Chapter 7 discusses these protocols in more detail.

An example of a distance vector protocol is the standard RIP. An example of a link-state-based routing protocol is *Open Shortest Path First* (OSPF). As explained later in this book, routing protocols are extremely important, and their analysis is also important.

Note that an analyst can use a protocol analyzer to examine routing protocol update sequencing. It is possible to filter on a specific router in an internetwork and examine how often protocol update requests and sequence updates are sent to other routers. It is also possible to identify abnormal events where routing protocols are not occurring. The time between routing protocol events can be determined by engaging the relative-time process measurement, as noted earlier in this chapter. The point here is to examine the routing protocol update sequencing closely when performing a network baseline study. Figure 4.25 shows how routing updates can be examined via protocol analysis.

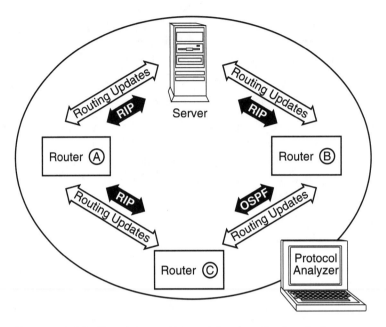

FIGURE 4.25 *Examining routing updates via protocol analysis.*

This is important for both proactive and even reactive analysis in the event that routing update problems or routing table integrity issues are present.

4.4.7 Unique Packet Identification Problem Analysis

When performing upper-layer protocol analysis for reliability, the final area to be examined is packet identification analysis. Many different types of packets in an upper-layer protocol data-trace session can exhibit problems.

Examples of these unique packets are broadcast sequences or specific error packets that relate to different network, transport, or application layer protocols. Some packets are not even defined in the key phases of network communication mentioned earlier such as network connections, logon sequencing, or polling events. These unique packets may require immediate identification, and the only way to identify these types of packets is to page through the data trace, which is the method of carefully moving through the data captured carefully to examine the trace for any abnormal packet sequences that do not appear to fit the form of the trace analysis session.

Examples of this type of occurrence include an SMB incorrect version packet transmission, or an NCP unique read error. These are upper-layer protocol application-specific packets, but they also fall into the category of packets that should be identified for problems via network analysis. Figure 4.26 shows how unique packets in network traffic can be examined via protocol analysis.

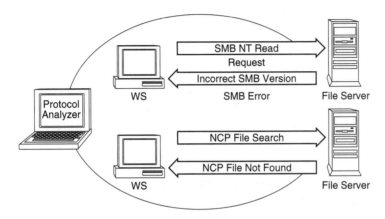

FIGURE 4.26 *Examining unique packets in network traffic via protocol analysis.*

The key factor here is that the analyst should always keep an eye out for abnormal packets within a trace by paging through the trace and noting the results. It is recommended to page through the trace carefully on all upper-layer protocol traces before completing a network baseline session when examining upper-layer protocols.

4.4.8 Summary

When examining an internetwork for reliability, remember to use a protocol analyzer to examine a network connection and ensure that the user logged on properly and efficiently. Examine any polling events for timing intervals and requirements. Closely monitor the file search and sequencing and file access process for a smooth file open and close. Examine internetwork addressing sequences for quick address resolution and proper address assignment. Examine routing protocol update sequencing for normal operations and routing protocol fluency. Closely review the trace for any unique packet identification problems that may be relevant to the baseline study. Take careful notes on the findings and establish a "running issue list" for any issues found and store the information in either a database or written notes to facilitate an understanding of the information when examining the final baseline results.

Remember that this may only be the initial baseline sample of many different sampling points or ports in a large internetwork study, and it is important that these areas be closely noted for future reference.

At this point, all main baseline steps should have been followed. The analyst should have moved through the network baselining process by examining network metric measurements, upper-layer protocol block and packet size, transfer fluency, and packet compatibility. Network performance reviews should have been executed and the network should have been examined for reliability by closely monitoring the phases of communication.

The next main and final step of quantitative baseline measurement is to examine the applications deployed across the internetwork. This is achieved through application characterization tuning and modeling analysis. This is an extremely important process in network baseline analysis, and is considered the pinnacle process in baseline analysis review.

The following section describes application characterization tuning and modeling analysis.

4.5 Application Characterization Tuning and Modeling

One of the important areas of performing a network baseline study is to determine the baseline of how applications are performing on a network. Whether the network baseline is performed on a simple network or on a large internetwork, the applications must be closely monitored. One of the terms used when monitoring an application is *application characterization*, which refers to the process of using protocol analysis and application review management systems to closely study how an application impacts a network, and how the network supports the application.

Various application event cycles can be monitored with a protocol analysis tool. Some of the basic event cycles in any application that can be characterized or monitored are event cycles such as application launch, application authentication process, application module access, and other application event processes such as database access, printing, scanning, and so forth. The key here is that a protocol analysis approach allows for the examination of an application by capturing the actual application dataflow on the network.

Through the process of application characterization, it is sometimes possible to identify the presence of abnormal occurrences in the application's operation on the network. It is also possible to identify how well a network supports the application's deployment. Based on some of the facts found through protocol analysis and application characterization modeling with management tools, it is sometimes possible to tune the application design, or adjust the network configuration or design, to allow for better performance of the application. After all, distributed application usage is one of the main reasons for the existence of the network.

It is also possible to examine how applications should be deployed on multiple user-count sequences. Doing so requires a process known as *application modeling*. Application modeling can be extremely involved and may require extensive skill sets. The following sections discuss some of the key processes followed in application characterization, tuning, and modeling. Figure 4.27 presents the main concepts of application characterization, tuning, and modeling.

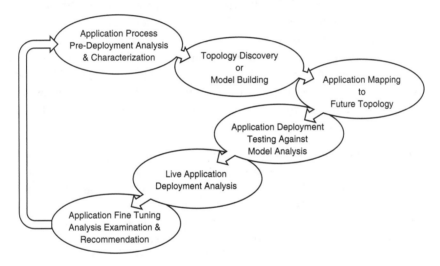

FIGURE 4.27 *Application characterization, tuning, and modeling.*

4.5.1 Application Deployment Analysis Considerations

In today's large internetworking environment, it is clear that the nature of a particular business dictates the day-to-day event cycle of the MIS community. After all, business requirements are the primary reason for the existence of an internetwork. For a business to be supported properly by an internetwork, it is important for all applications to be closely studied.

It is important that the internetwork provide access to rapid applications that serve the business. Some of these applications include email or e-commerce, Internet access, and database access for critical data storage.

Many large companies are experiencing a tremendous growth of users on the internetwork for the express purpose of application access. Even with today's basic business applications, it is important that high performance and reliability be in place to support the application access process. If these attributes are not in place, the business cost model and the business bottom line can be negatively affected. It is important that all MIS communities motivate network analysts to engage protocol analysis and management tools to properly characterize, tune, and support applications, and properly plan for application deployment through modeling exercises.

When considering application deployment, one of the key factors to consider is the time element involved in properly deploying an application. Quite often an analyst or MIS team will find themselves in the position of reacting to an application problem after it has already been deployed or is in a post-deployment analysis process. This is not a positive situation, but one that can be tackled with a proper application characterization approach or application modeling exercise. It is important to understand that organizations such as MIS teams will have limited talent in this area, and due to the increasing complexity of interaction among different applications, it is important to keep in mind that the deployment process must be closely examined.

Different tools enable an analyst to examine certain factors, such as the application's initial operation or its specific event cycle. Engaging these tools allows for true assessment of the application. After the application has been assessed, it is possible that the application assessment model may need to be examined in modeling tools or deployment profiling tools. These types of tools enable an analyst to understand how the application assessment on a one-user or multiple design would apply to higher counts in a multiuser deployment and against different topologies and architectures within an internetwork composite. Specific measurements must be examined, such as how the application operates in terms of response time, performance level, and behavior. Vital statistics must be closely examined to understand how the application traffic is operating and how efficient the application is from a transfer standpoint.

One of the basic consequences of an application's operation that must be examined is how the application affects the utilization of the available capacity or bandwidth on a network. It is also important to understand how quickly the application operates in term of response time for critical events such as launch, database access, and scanning operations. It is possible to examine the internetwork latency, which may be an added factor related to the application's deployment.

Prior to deploying an application or when troubleshooting an application, it is important to know the latency involved in any internetwork channel or the current load related to utilization in any channel. With these two factors as main points of concern, note that it is possible to determine the effect of the application's deployment on the specific network area.

Consider, for example, an Ethernet segment with a 50% load and a 2ms latency from device to device within one Ethernet collision domain. These metric statistics would be considered the load and latency factors. Now suppose another Ethernet segment is going to be connected to this segment through a router and a workstation and server placed on each side of the Ethernet end-to-end two-LAN channel. Specifically, a workstation will be placed on the old Ethernet segment along with a main file server and 10 new Ethernet users are placed on the new Ethernet segment. In this example, it may be possible to determine what kind of additional load and additional latency would be introduced across the router and two LANs when adding the application. Another key factor that could be determined is how the original source network is affected by the additional traffic load of the new 10 workstations accessing the server from the new segment. To do this, the application would have to be captured for an initial characterization or event review as to how it operates and how certain application steps are performed. This is sometimes referred to as *event threading* or *event chaining* of specific application cycles. The key is that the application needs to be closely captured via application characterization. Figure 4.28 presents the concept of using protocol analysis for application deployment.

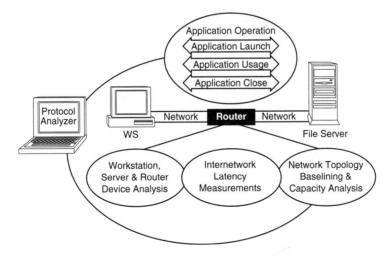

FIGURE 4.28 *Using protocol analysis for application deployment.*

The point here is that after the application has been captured and characterized, the load of the application (the new 10-user model in this example) is determined. The determined load can be added to the current load and the new latency level can then be determined.

It is most likely that the latency in certain areas of the end-to-end channel will increase slightly because of a higher deployment of load. These are just some of the areas that need to be considered upon application deployment.

The key is that it is necessary to identify what applications need to be characterized within an internetwork infrastructure. This type of information should be gathered and determined in the early stages of baseline planning.

After the applications have been identified, they should be closely examined against user profiles. There are certain user profiles, such as users who access one application or two applications in a combined fashion. Each user profile may differ slightly. One user may access word processing and a computer-aided design application, whereas another user may access word processing and a database application. There may be different user profiles and different application loads that may be applied to different areas of the internetwork. When these factors are understood as to how the applications are deployed on the network and the user profile is determined, an application audit process can be developed into the data-acquisition plan of a network baseline study. The process can detail a plan on how to profile the applications in terms of characterizing the application, troubleshooting the application, tuning its performance, or the network support of the application, and possibly modeling the application for increased deployment. These are critical steps to be considered when performing a network baseline study.

4.5.2 Blueprinting or Characterizing an Application Sequence Model

When studying or characterizing an application, a key term used by high-level analysts is *blueprinting the application*, which refers to capturing the application from an initial standpoint.

A protocol analyzer should be used to filter on a specific workstation within the network segment area being sampled for the network baseline study. When the workstation is filtered on, this is the initial capture setup for the protocol analyzer. Prior to this step, an analyst should outline the event sequences of an application.

An example of an event sequence outline could be the access to a database such as Lotus Notes. Event sequence 1 is the user accessing the network by connecting. Event sequence 2 is the logon or authentication process to the server environment to allow for access to launch the Notes application. Event sequence 3 is the launch of the Notes application by clicking on the Notes application icon. After the database has been accessed, other event sequences can be noted such as updating the database, modifying the database, saving the database, and printing a database file. The final application sequence is closing the Notes application and logging off the network.

These event sequences can then be developed and documented in an application table that lists the application event cycle algorithm. That process enables the analyst to note the events as a chain or a thread.

It is then possible to filter on the workstation with a protocol analyzer and start the application sequencing. The application sequencing should be closely monitored for each event. The protocol analyzer can be used to mark the frames or packets transferred in each event, and certain metrics can also be measured in accordance with this process. The metrics can include utilization, bytes transferred, relative time, and average frame size, or protocol sequencing such as polling or unique events per application event. This is an extremely focused view of characterizing or blueprinting an application. Figure 4.29 presents the concept of blueprinting an application.

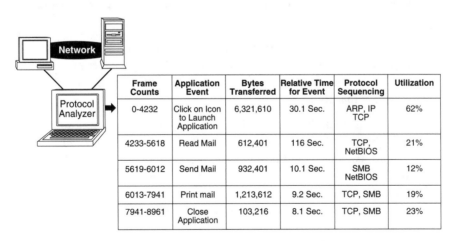

Frame Counts	Application Event	Bytes Transferred	Relative Time for Event	Protocol Sequencing	Utilization
0-4232	Click on Icon to Launch Application	6,321,610	30.1 Sec.	ARP, IP TCP	62%
4233-5618	Read Mail	612,401	116 Sec.	TCP, NetBIOS	21%
5619-6012	Send Mail	932,401	10.1 Sec.	SMB NetBIOS	12%
6013-7941	Print mail	1,213,612	9.2 Sec.	TCP, SMB	19%
7941-8961	Close Application	103,216	8.1 Sec.	TCP, SMB	23%

FIGURE 4.29 *Blueprinting an application.*

After an application has been truly characterized, the data should be stored in a tabular format within a spreadsheet or database. This will yield a blueprint to determine how the application operates on the network.

It is important to study an application on a single-user model, and then consider deploying multiple tests at different points to get comparative reviews.

An application could be characterized and tested across multiple network areas, such as a one-user area and then another user area, and then in the computer room. This enables the analyst to establish three separate points that show how it responds and reacts to different points-of-location access within a large internetwork. It is extremely critical to understand interpacket latency across all key internetwork channels and how the application is affected by the complete network.

After application characterization steps have been taken, and the application has been captured at multiple points, the trace analysis results should be closely examined for conditions (as noted earlier in the upper-layer baseline review process).

Examining the internetwork reliability sequencing—such as network connection, logon, polling, file search and access—is critical. Using this method of discreet review against the blueprint is an extremely intuitive way of characterizing or blueprinting the application. This is an extremely valuable step in network baselining, and is considered a pinnacle measurement sequence in the network characterization process.

It is also important to note that after the application has been characterized and blueprinted, it is next possible, by examining the upper-layer protocols via the reliability analysis sequence discussed earlier, to investigate those areas of the application that could be fined-tuned.

An example would be if an application code operation is engaging an extremely small PDU size input such as 36 bytes inside a maximum Ethernet MTU of 1500. This would be an inefficient use of the Ethernet MTU channel and possibly the TCP maximum segment size. One possible remedy would be for the application development team to increase the PDU size to 1400 bytes maximum to boost the efficiency of the application. This could lead to the application utilizing an Ethernet MTU to have an increased packet size to a maximum level within the Ethernet end-to-end channel. This is just one example of application tuning.

Also, by examining the reliability chain of network communication after blue-printing, it may be possible to identify problems in site routers, switches, and network infrastructure devices that negatively impact the application's performance.

If the application is putting a maximum data unit in the topology MTU and a maximum Ethernet packet is being formed upon output generation of a packet from a server to a workstation, this is positive. A negative occurrence is if the packet traverses a switch or router that then limits the maximum MTU to a smaller packet size, such as 500 bytes. This effect would impact the data transfer across the complete network in such a way as to hinder the capability of properly supporting the application to true efficiency. A possibility may be to modify the router for a larger MTU setting to allow the Ethernet end-to-end channel to be maximized, thus enabling the application to reach its true efficiency.

Another example is a circumstance when too many users are deployed in a network area, such as in a highly dense Ethernet collision domain. This could be determined through network baselining measurement analysis, which would clearly determine whether an Ethernet area is over-saturated and user density is high. However, an application blueprint process may reveal, for example, that the application is attempting to generate burst transfers from the server that effect a 60% or 80% utilization factor at brief peak transitions of 800ms. However, these types of transitions could not coexist positively in the highly dense or extremely high level of collision domain with excessive saturation. In this case, the Ethernet partitioning design may need to be revisited to accommodate a new application being deployed.

These are some examples of how important it is to truly blueprint and characterize an application before deployment.

Characterizing an application is critical to the network baselining process!

4.5.3 Reviewing an Application Against the LAN and WAN

Many factors are involved when deploying an application against a large LAN or WAN design. The network must be baselined and examined for peak utilization levels, such as average and peak transition and historical views. It is very important to identify busy traffic periods and how they may affect the application deployment. Certain user groups have to be identified and user profiles have to be established. It is important to understand when an application is going to be engaged and how the different transactions affect different periods of the business day. It is important to know what types of clients are deployed and how dense the clients are in certain user or server areas, and how this will affect the deployment of the application.

Placement of file servers is also critical. It is important that file servers be reviewed for proper placement (either a remote decentralized design or a centralized architecture). It is important that all the clients that access servers have a low-latency channel and balanced channel to allow the application to operate smoothly.

In certain cases, it is positive for an application server to be placed in a centralized location so that all clients in a localized LAN can access the server without failure.

If the server is remote and an application blueprint model reveals that high latency is present even though no symptoms are exhibited, however, this serves as a warning flag not to place more clients across the WAN circuit; doing so would just introduce additional latency.

These are examples of the circumstances that should be taken into consideration when deploying an application. As can be seen from these examples, it is important when initially deploying an application to consider what its rollout effects will be on multiple users against this application profile.

An MIS department should prepare for application rollouts by predetermining what the rollout level counts will be and where users will have to be placed. It is critical to understand how users should be placed against the internetwork infrastructure to access the application. Based on this determination, it may be necessary to place several servers on the internetwork to synchronize or transfer information to prevent stations from traveling long routes to access key file server centralized database or server resources. In the case of flat internetwork architecture or large Ethernet LANs, this may not be a factor.

When introducing WAN architectures against the scheme, however, many considerations must be taken into account.

If multiple users are going to be placed across the other side of a WAN and they require access to a centralized server environment that already has a high level of LAN access from its local user-node standpoint, it may be necessary to place a remote server at the remote LAN site that will hold the key information for the application at the remote site. It may also be possible to design and provide database synchronization so that all information is updated on a consistent basis from the remote site to the headquarters site for all the key server central architectures related to the application flow. Figure 4.30 shows how to analyze an application in a LAN and WAN layout.

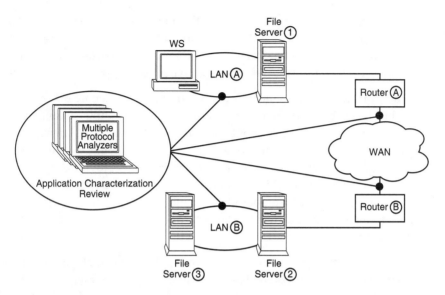

Figure 4.30 *Analyzing an application in a LAN or WAN layout.*

These are just some of the elements that should be considered upon deployment of an application across a large internetwork. Another factor to consider is how the links are utilized on large internetworks or LAN links. It is important to determine the overall load and latency factors on certain areas of the internetwork prior to application deployment. This prevents problematic circumstances from occurring after deployment.

If troubleshooting processes are engaged after an application is deployed, this is considered a post-deployment situation. Under this condition, some of the application remote access models may have to be deactivated to understand the base load and the latency of the internetwork.

4.5.4 Final Application Impact Analysis and Modeling

Many unique tools enable an analyst to assess the impact of an application on an internetwork. It is optimal to utilize some of the techniques discussed in this section, such as characterizing or blueprinting the application before its deployment. It is always beneficial to characterize or capture an application from a lab environment before it is deployed on a live internetwork. In a lab environment, the application can operate in a very native environment that is considered benign and not problematic.

Another factor to be taken into account is the number of users across the inter-network who will be accessing the application, as well as where the users will be placed. Based on these components, it is next important to determine how the network is running from a baseline perspective prior to application deployment.

The network baselining techniques discussed in this chapter are extremely valuable. Load should be determined (utilization, for example). Standard response time measurements should be employed to determine latency and delay on a specific network area or across a network channel, switch, or router channel that is going to be affected by the application deployment. All file servers and key hosts should be examined for performance. It is important to understand how they are responding at an interpacket delta level within the main computer room to determine how the device platforms will support additional application load.

Any users' segments where the application is going to be deployed should be closely examined using general baseline characterization techniques. This is extremely important in shared architectures and even switched architectures, for proper planning.

The workstation hardware and software configuration profile designs must be examined for hardware and software build design to accommodate the application's coexistence with other applications. Often, MIS departments fail to properly plan the workstation profile design to accommodate additional application uses when other applications are already resident.

After these steps have been taken via a thorough baseline study that engages quantitative baseline measurements, upper-layer protocol analysis review, performance review, and internetwork reliability assessment, the next step is to properly blueprint or characterize the application. After the blueprint or characterization of the application has been performed, the investigation of the application fluency should be examined by closely observing the model of the application dataflow against the phases of network communication that have been discussed.

After these factors have been determined and all assessments have been performed by the analyst, it is important to next document all the findings. A true application characterization should include a blueprint or a characterization table of the application, along with an application assessment write-up of any issues or problems located. The topology and architecture should be discussed (regarding where the application is going to be deployed). Any assessment concerns related to network topology or problematic concerns that may impact the application's fluency should be documented and addressed (as related to network design and implementation).

After these elements have been taken into account, it will then be possible to take the application characterization data trace from the blueprint model and feed it into modeling programs that will allow for a daisy-chaining or threading model to be built on how the application threads protocol-sequencing events. It is then possible to multiply the number of users from the application characterization blueprint data trace to a multiuser account that correlates with the rollout objectives. Figure 4.31 shows how to thread and analyze an application.

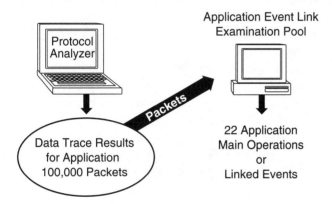

FIGURE 4.31   *Threading and analyzing an application.*

If one user model has been captured and 20 users are going to be deployed, for example, it is possible to multiply this load in the application characterization modeling tool.

The next step is to actually deploy the application against the new topology requirements. In this case, the topology can be physically designed into modeling programs or possibly discovered, depending on the application modeling program.

The network analyst has many unique tools from which to choose, such as the Optimal application platform tools that employ Optimal Application Expert and Optimal Preview. These tools work together to allow the application to be closely threaded and deployed against a large internetwork. It is possible to carefully capture the application and perform a blueprint with a protocol analyzer. It is then possible to use the trace taken from a protocol analyzer, such as the Network Associate Sniffer, and feed the data into an Application Expert program from Optimal. The application can then be assessed and the information can be pulled into the Optimal Application Preview program, which is a modeling program. The application model would then be deployed against the topology built by the analyst using the Optimal Preview program. After the initial traffic blueprint is applied against the topology model, certain reports unload and additional latency changes can be assessed and fed back into the Optimal Application Expert program for cross-review, response time prediction, and possible impact on the overall network model.

It's important to remember that without even using a modeling program and using the protocol analysis skills, it is possible to capture the application, characterize the application, assess the internetwork through a baseline study, examine the characterization steps, the performance model, and the reliability, and then properly lay out a topology in a modeling program. The topology layout model should then be directly affected by an applied traffic model consistent with the rollout objectives. This process helps to determine how the deployment of 20 new users on a physical topology may affect a live internetwork. This is considered a network modeling exercise and is an extremely intuitive way of understanding the impact of applications on a network and how the applications support the application deployments across a network.

4.5.5 Summary

This is obviously the pinnacle measurement area of network baselining. This is an extremely important factor in network baselining exercises. Never underestimate the importance of application characterization. Application characterization techniques (as discussed under the blueprint process and characterization technique) can be used for reactive troubleshooting when applications are not performing well. Also, this technique can be used on an ongoing basis for proactive baselining and the proper deployment and careful assessment of how applications are implemented across enterprise internetworks.

This is a very important process and should be followed closely throughout an analyst's network baselining career.

Case Study 1: Utilization and Capacity Analysis

There is a finite level of capacity available on any local or wide area network medium that is tested during a network baseline study. Specifically, the available capacity is the maximum level of area of bandwidth that can be utilized across a specific local or wide area network medium. This case study describes a troubleshooting process that was performed using protocol analysis via network baseline methodology. The troubleshooting scenario at this particular site could have been avoided if a proper capacity-planning exercise had been engaged prior to a recent network operating system upgrade to the internetwork involved in this case study.

The internetwork facility in question was based on a 10BASE-T architecture with approximately 200 nodes. The site was moving forward with a series of migrations planned over a six-month time frame. The migration cycles included replacement of workstations throughout the facility to a more robust and higher-speed processing platform, along with a stronger hardware platform in the file server infrastructure. Also included in the migration plans was an eventual upgrade to the Ethernet channel capacity from 10Mbps to 100Mbps switched architecture. Another planned migration step was to upgrade the network operating systems of the site servers in the Novell NetWare environment from a 3.x to a 4.x release.

The migration-planning process originally had called for the workstation and server upgrades to be implemented as Phase 1, and the Ethernet channel capacity upgrade to be implemented as Phase 2. The network operating system upgrade along with other minor application-balancing exercises were planned as a Phase-3 step during the six-month time frame. Because of the unavailability of new Ethernet switching hubs and the required implementation teams needed for the Ethernet channel upgrade, the Phase-2 step was moved to the end of the migration cycle; Phase 3 and the network operating system upgrade were moved up to the middle of the cycle, Phase 2.

The site six-month migration implementation started with the workstation and the server platform upgrades throughout the facility. The facility removed all prior workstation platforms that were using older processors with 486 workstations and any using a processor under a Pentium build, because there were a large number of older Ethernet workstations based on 386, 486, and Pentium I platforms. The new Pentium II and higher platforms with a minimum of 128MB of memory were implemented at workstation platforms throughout the user community. The file server environment was upgraded significantly to a new manufacturer platform that involved over 1GB of memory and added an extensive disk raid architecture and interserver clustering design.

All the migration steps in Phase 1 appeared to be positive, and there were no complaints about performance. In fact, immediate higher performance was evidenced in the form of a lower ratio of problematic calls into the site MIS help desk. The user community was extremely pleased with their new workstations and the higher performance level being achieved on the network.

In the middle of the migration cycle, Phase 2, the server team next implemented the Novel 4.x release. Upon this implementation, intermittent performance problems were noted throughout different portions of the user community. This implementation coincided with different applications that were installed that were also part of the Phase-2 step. Several applications were moved from one server to another server and so forth throughout the facility. Some of the architecture steps were carefully planned from a project-planning standpoint, but certain issues came to the surface that would not have been caught without a proper network baselining exercise in a test lab, or without an extensive understanding of network dataflow.

During the Phase-2 migration cycle, various symptomatic problems were being reported to the help desk; these included slow performance with various applications and intermittent disconnects from the server environment.

The LAN Scope analysis team was contacted to analyze the internetwork environment. Because the environment was still based on a 10BASE-T Ethernet architecture in a shared Ethernet collision domain design, the general baselining exercises were fairly straightforward. The Ethernet segment was based on a three-segment design.

The LAN Scope analysis team deployed a network analyzer in each of the three 10BASE-T hub shared media areas. We started general baseline exercises and measured general utilization across all three shared areas. We noticed that the shared areas showed an average utilization of 50%, with peaks transitioning between 85% to 100% in all three areas. This was a major concern, because all the servers were still placed on segment two, which was extremely saturated with an average utilization of 75%, flushing a 100% peak utilization for five seconds and above frequently throughout the business day.

With these kinds of peak transitions in utilization being seen, we noted that the protocol percentages all appeared to be in check, with the exception of the Ethernet physical medium frame percentage, which showed an 802.3 percentage level of 6% to 8%. This rate directly correlated to an extremely high collision level that was being induced by the high impact of utilization on the shared medium area.

The physical medium on Ethernet, when based on a *carrier sense multiple access collision detection* (CSMA/CD) design, has an inherent design where collision levels will increase upon extremely high utilization of the medium. This is an intrinsic design that the Ethernet NICs connected to the medium will engage to listen for network availability and then transmit and receive for the data communications process and to continue. Ethernet shared media is based on a contention-based architecture and collisions are part of the Ethernet access method. When utilization on shared Ethernet exceeds the approximate 30% level, however, low throughput problems can occur. As throughput starts to decrease and utilization reaches the 60% to 80% level of overall usage, collisions can become highly excessive at more than 5% and can escalate to cause further problems, such as network layer retransmissions and application layer file retransmissions. Eventually, communication can be broken down to create a negative situation that breaks down connectivity at the transport level. This can eventually disrupt complete communications on an Ethernet shared medium when utilization levels are extremely high.

Based on the high utilization levels and the corresponding high physical-error levels, the LAN Scope analysis team next focused on the upper-layer protocol decoding process.

Upon investigating the upper-layer protocols, it was noted that packet sizes of 1500-byte MTUs were being utilized on cross- workstation–to–server communication quite frequently throughout the medium. It appeared as though maximum packet sizes were engaged at very low delta time processing intervals. It was clear that the low latency and extremely rapid rate of transmission from workstations to servers resulted from certain factors from the Phase-1 migration step, including the new robust workstation and server platforms, along with the new NIC implementation that was introduced through the inherent motherboard design on the workstations throughout the facility. All workstations were performing rapid *frame-per-second* (FPS) rate-generation capability transmissions on the network, along with extremely rapid server response times. Transmissions from site Ethernet nodes were clearly seen to be in the millisecond and even microsecond range upon inbound and outbound frame transmission.

It was also noted that when upper-layer protocol packets were composed in a normal and healthy manner, the packet sizes were again well above 1500 bytes. We found frequent collision and CRC errors throughout the upper-layer protocol analysis, frame-trace analysis results. These errors appeared to be present every 10 to 20 frames throughout the data-decoding analysis sessions. These errors were present even in data traces that had 80,000 to 100,000 frames. The frame collision rate along with the CRC rate exceeded 18% upon final analysis in all three areas, and was considered a major concern.

The LAN Scope analysis team held a meeting with the MIS support team at the site to investigate why the packet data size was so large. Upon investigation of the data, we could clearly see by examining the internal detail of the Ethernet frame that the maximum Ethernet MTU was engaged upon general data transmission (see Figure CS1.1).

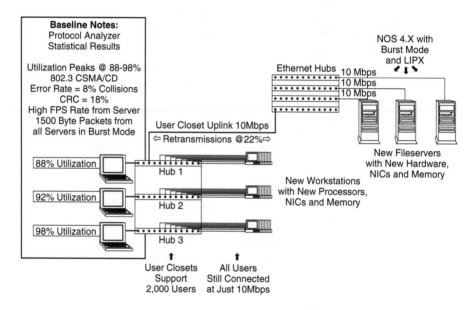

FIGURE CS1.1 *Utilization and Capacity Analysis*

The protocol layering scheme was based on Ethernet 802.3 Raw with LIPX, SPX II, and *NetWare Core Protocol Burst* (NCPB). We identified the highest protocol-layering scheme of using NCPB as a possible concern, because of its inherent capability to transmit larger packets sizes at faster rates.

We also noted that the application data appeared to be utilizing the maximum area of data size within the Ethernet frame. Our concern initially was whether the application movement had increased or whether the NOS application data movement had increased.

We performed a characterization exercise to examine one user accessing the network. When the user launched the PC upon the network and logged on to the network for certain drive mapping exercises to access applications, we noted that upon connecting to the Novell server, a packet size was negotiated with a Get Max Packet Size call from the user workstation and a Packet Size Okay reply was sent by the server and received to utilize a maximum Ethernet MTU of approximately 1500 bytes. This appeared to be standard to our technical team members for normal network communications in the NetWare 4.x environment. It also appeared as though the application environment was normal.

We briefly requested to review the traces that were taken at the facility on a previous network analysis session performed by a member of the MIS team at the facility. Upon reviewing these traces, it was clear that the Novell 3.x release was utilizing standard IPX through the 3.x release. A Novell 3.x server without an LIPX, which engages a larger internetwork packet exchange patch applied, will negotiate packet sizes down to below a 576-byte level, if one hop count is seen exceeded by a server in the Transport Control field upon packet-size negotiation. It was clear that upon the recent Novell NOS release upgrade in the server environment, along with the workstation shell and image release upgrade, that a larger packet size was now being engaged upon the site internetwork.

Upon the final review of our findings, we developed a technical synopsis that the NOS release did in fact allow for the larger packet sizes to be engaged, which the application took advantage of and utilized a maximum PDU insertion of the Ethernet MTU. This was found to be a normal occurrence and was noted as a clear finding.

Our next finding was that the Ethernet contention-based shared media architecture based on 10Mbps—or 10 million bits on the wire in one second, versus 100Mbps being available for capacity—was an issue. The designed current capacity channels on the Ethernet internetwork at this particular client site were not ready to handle Novell 4.x, which engaged the large Internetwork packet exchange Ethernet transmission capability. It was also clear that the application data movement utilizing larger packets would also increase all general packet sizes throughout the facility.

We noted in the previous traces that the average frame size was well under 200 bytes and the packet sizes throughout the traces did not appear to exceed 250 to 300 bytes.

It was clear that the site should have stayed on the original migration track of implementing Phase 3 on schedule.

Specifically, the Ethernet capacity upgrade to 100Mbps was clearly needed prior to the upgrade to a Novell 4.x release, which will engage and utilize and engage a full Ethernet MTU.

The findings clearly pointed to the fact that too much data was implemented against the Ethernet channel capacity present on this particular enterprise internetwork architecture design. When the larger packet sizes were engaged, the available capacity was utilized to the maximum level, which impacted the physical layer and created a "bounce" effect on the physical level. The bounce effect was clear due to the fact that the utilization levels impacted the physical layer, which then caused problems at the network layer, the transport, and eventually at the application layer.

Therefore, the client actually "bounced a ball" of high-level utilization on the physical medium, which then increased problems and caused the ball to bounce back up to affect the upper layers.

This network baselining exercise and troubleshooting process was extremely useful in resolving the client's issue. The client backed off the new NetWare 4.x parameters in such a way that a smaller packet size was utilized for negotiation. This involved extensive work on the server environment and a reload of the client PC imaging software.

The Phase-3 100Mbps upgrade was affected within one month of our analysis. The 100Mbps upgrade involved a switched architecture, in which each user had a switch port operating at 100Mbps half duplex. All the servers were then placed on separate switched ports at 100Mbps full duplex.

Upon this implementation, the LAN Scope analysis team remeasured the general performance at the facility through post-protocol analysis network baselining techniques and found that the packet sizes were maximized and that the interpacket delta times were even more rapid—that is, packets in and out of the workstations upon delta time were all seen within the microsecond level. There were no complaints about performance and the facility was operating in a stable and reliable fashion. Performance was also noted at a high level and the user complaints regarding any of the application access points were nominal.

This was a completely successful exercise and clearly represents how network baselining can be an advantage in terms of measuring utilization for various capacity-based issues.

Case Study 2: Throughput Analysis Issue

Recently, one of LAN Scope's clients contacted us with a request to analyze a poor performance concern at their location. As can be seen from some of the previous case studies, the most common complaints are in the areas of slow performance, poor connectivity, or general slow response time.

In this particular case study, the issues surrounded a Token Ring architecture that involved a Token Ring internetwork based on approximately 30 rings at a large location. The Token Ring architecture was rated at 16Mbps, which had been in place for approximately 10 years. Previous to that, the architecture was based on 4Mbps (see Figure CS2.1).

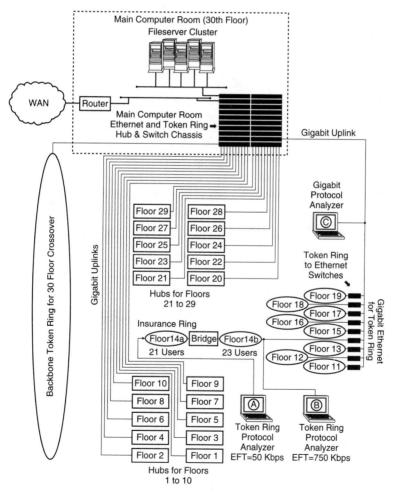

FIGURE CS2.1 *Poor performance issue involving a Token Ring*

The site also was starting to implement Ethernet user areas and Ethernet high-speed servers on Ethernet-switched ports at certain points of the enterprise architecture. An eventual migration cycle was planned over a two-year time-frame to move to a shared environment, and eventually to a pure Ethernet environment.

In the short term, the concern was that most of the users throughout the facility had been experiencing major performance problems over the past six months. The LAN Scope analysis team sat down with the MIS team at the site and conducted an extensive entrance briefing. We were briefed that the site user Token Rings appeared to show low average and peak utilization based on the management systems at the facility. We were told that the site MIS team took extensive efforts to segment the rings to low user-node counts, because a large application deployment was ongoing at the facility during the current year. As more application data was being moved across the internetwork based on user rings at a data rate of 16Mbps, there was sensitivity definitely in place to ensure that the nodes counts were partitioned down to smaller rings so as not to exceed capacity. Despite the segmentation applied, however, the users still complained about poor performance upon each new application being added to the environment.

We noted that the file server environment which had been added within the past six months and the applications that were added in direct correlation with new servers were all installed on high-speed full-duplex Ethernet-switched channel ports, which had a direct internal backplane link via an Ethernet–to–Token Ring switching blade via a high-speed chassis switch-based router at the facility. This particular channel device had a 10-gigabit backplane with an interpacket latency level that was extremely low according to general specifications. Based on a review of this configuration along with the fact that the Token Ring networks had no more than 20 users per ring, it appeared from an entrance briefing standpoint that utilization should be in check and would be low in levels.

The LAN Scope analysis team asked a series of questions relating to physical network architecture, symptomatic problem history, and the migration cycle that had occurred and was ongoing throughout the upcoming year. We also focused on the application deployment based on our review of certain user profiles that were applied to workstations throughout the facility. With all this information in hand, we developed a project plan for the location.

The project plan enabled us to vector our process to immediately troubleshoot one of the user rings that was experiencing slow performance. A ring on the 14th floor, noted as the Insurance Ring, had an extremely high number of complaints related to poor performance. We positioned a network analyzer on this ring.

Over a four-hour period, the network analyzer showed an average utilization of 12% with a peak of no more than 38% on the 16Mbps Token Ring. The Token Ring protocol percentages appeared to be normal, with the percentage splits expected at the site for Novell- and Windows NT–based protocols, TCP/IP, and SNA-based protocols for workstation emulation to the mainframe host environment.

The physical error rate for Token Ring appeared to be nominal, with minor line and burst errors upon ring insertion. The Token Ring frame communication was normal with a stable neighbor notification rate of an even seven seconds. Everything appeared to be in check up to the upper-layer investigation area.

The LAN Scope analysis team started to perform effective throughput measurements on the ring. We noted upon outbound communication to file servers at the facility that general EFT was low, approximately 50 to 70Kbps. This was a major concern because a Token Ring operating at such low utilization levels using maximum packet sizes of 4K should achieve a much higher EFT.

We followed the network design layout path routes and noted that the users on this particular floor Token Ring (14A) were also sharing a crossover bridge with another Token Ring (14B) on the same floor, which then connected to a switch passthrough connection to cross-floor gigabit Ethernet channel backbone that connected all site user area networks to the main Token Ring server backbone and to the new Ethernet-switched server backbone that traversed a multiport configuration. Specifically, between each floor network areas was a Token Ring–to–Ethernet switch that provided a connection to an Ethernet gigabit link between each one of the main floors.

The main concern was that for communication from users on the Token Ring 14A on this floor to site servers to take place, it was necessary for all packets to pass through a Token Ring bridge that was rated at 16Mbps that was connected to Token Ring 14B. The bridge was placed between rings 14A and 14B and was wide open as to filtering configuration and did not apply for any protocol filtering because filtering was provided within the network Layer 3 circuitry of the Token Ring–to–Ethernet switch on each floor edge switch. The LAN Scope analysis team took this into account and noted it in our network analysis results.

We moved to Token Ring 14B on the same floor and performed the same type of analysis exercises. We found that Token Ring 14B showed an average utilization of 6% and a peak of 18%. There were 23 users on Token Ring 14B, whereas Token Ring 14A had only 21 users. Comparable node counts were seen from average node-by-node utilization comparison. The protocol percentages also appeared similar. The physical error rate was stable and the Token Ring frame communications were normal.

Our next step was to investigate effective throughput measurements by measuring cumulative bytes against relative time for certain file transfer sequences. We just continued to mark file open sequences against file close sequences from users from the 14B ring when sending outbound requests to the file server and performing consecutive file reads against certain file servers. The effective throughput on Token Ring 14B ranged between 300 and 400Kbps, and periodically reached as high as 750Kbps. The Token Ring 14B levels were excellent as to EFT levels achieved.

Some concerns were definitely noted regarding Token Ring–to–Ethernet translation delays or possible latency that could be induced in this area. The main concern was that the effective throughput on Token Ring 14B showed an extremely higher ratio than on Token Ring 14A.

Clearly there was a problem between Token Ring 14A and Token Ring 14B related to transmission across the bridging circuitry. We reviewed the architecture and operation of the vendor bridge and noted that the specifications called for a throughput capability of at least 1000Kbps. The only concern was that when investigating the actual configuration, certain issues were taken account such as the actual build of the bridge and the architecture platform.

The bridge was based on a two–Token Ring NIC design, based on the software and hardware platform specified by the manufacturer. Specifically, the implementer of the bridge has the capability to use different PC platforms when designing the bridge architecture. We noted that the platform chosen was based on an old CPU processor architecture using a 386 processor that was not compliant with the high-speed NIC channel architecture for the particular ring passthrough operation.

Based on this concern, we reviewed this issue with the MIS team at the facility. The MIS team addressed our concern and immediately provided us with a high-speed Pentium platform PC along with a more robust internal CPU bus channel and higher memory levels. We implemented this new hardware platform and installed two newer and even more robust Token Ring 16Mbps card with high receive buffer capability at the physical level.

Upon doing so, we reanalyzed the Token Ring 14A area for achieved EFT. We noted immediately that the effective throughput levels increased to 200 to 300Kbps. Some minor latency was still present and lower throughput was still present because another bridge had to be traversed prior to moving into the Token Ring–to–Ethernet switching channel high-speed backplane translation.

The lesson learned here is that the older bridging architecture between the rings definitely was affecting the overall throughput for users who had to pass through the ring, and eventually pass through another ring-shared medium area based on Token Ring deterministic architecture and then travel through a Token Ring–to–Ethernet switch to move through the Gigabit Ethernet channels to access the high-speed Ethernet servers.

Effective throughput measurements are extremely important in network baselining. It is important to understand the throughput received upon network connection, and to understand that network logon always differs from the final EFT received through eventual application file access. This is because throughput directly relates to a user's performance and eventual perceived performance of a complete internetwork architecture.

Case Study 3: Response Time Baseline Analysis

One of LAN Scope's major clients recently contacted us to analyze a "perceived response-time issue" with a set of applications that surrounded a file server (X1) at their main facility. The MIS team help desk personnel had been fielding an excessive number of complaints regarding general application access through-out the facility; however, most of the problems also appeared to be based on one specific application (Microsoft Exchange, which resided on server X1).

The MIS team that supported the enterprise environment was broken into two groups:

- **The network support team.** The network highway group that supported the general network architecture, internetwork hub architecture, and topology build areas

- **The application and server support team.** The team that supported the application balancing, NOS, and workstation shell compliancy overlay as related to the enterprise design

Based on the perception issues related to slow performance and general slow response time with the application and the main file server, X1, it was evident that both support teams thought that the problem resided across the line in the other group's support area. This posture is quite common in a large MIS environment. Both teams displayed a team approach and were willing to take responsibility for any issues that resided in their area. But it is quite often a political situation in which one team attempts to support their technical design specification and their implementation processes, until another group can prove otherwise.

Based on this situation, the director of the information group for this client requested that the LAN Scope analysis team review this issue. We began our review with a standard entrance briefing during which we reviewed the file server configuration at the site along with the most recent implementation of Microsoft Exchange. We noted that the file server environment was based on a high-speed performance platform design on a very robust channel architecture. We were told that the NIC topology connection for the server was based on a high-speed, full-duplex Ethernet connection. We also noted that the file server also was used as a backup domain controller for the NT environment.

One of the immediate configuration issues that we noticed was that there were two NICs in the file server. The first NIC was connected to the main internet-work switching architecture in the main computer room for the complete environment. This NIC channel was for all intended site user traffic, so the backup domain controller could be accessed as required, along with any other applications on the server, such as Microsoft Exchange. The application team noted that only approximately 20 users were using the Exchange application at the time, which should not have caused a major impact.

We were also briefed that the second NIC was connected to an Ethernet segment based on Internet access. Duplicate NIC channels in a server can cause latency in a server's capability to respond and perform (see Figure CS3.1).

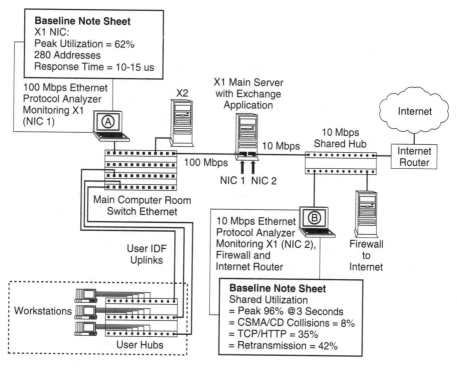

FIGURE CS3.1   *Response Time Baseline Analysis*

After obtaining all the necessary information during the entrance briefing, we understood all the issues at hand and immediately developed our initial project plan. Our first project plan was to examine the server's response time in its closest environment, which is a process we typically engage in network baselining. We placed a protocol analyzer in the main computer room on a switched port, only three ports away from the server port handling the backup domain controller X1 server's connections for both NICs.

We engaged a port-mirroring exercise on the switch and started examining traffic on each one of the server's NIC channels separately. We noted that the server had IP forwarding turned on as a mechanism in utilizing two NICs. The client told us that the IP forwarding configuration was for the express purpose of accessing the Internet via an Internet segment where a firewall was placed. We also noted in the entrance briefing that only approximately 50 users in the facility were accessing the Internet.

We began our standard baseline analysis exercise by starting with general utilization measurements against each one of the X1 server's channels. On the main network channel NIC 1, the X1 server showed an average utilization of 35% with a peak of 62%. These utilization levels did not appear abnormal. We closely examined the utilization level for the number of connections accessing the server, and identified that more than 280 network layer addresses were accessing the channel. It appeared as though the physical layer was stable and general Ethernet frame communications were operating in a normal fashion. There were no CRC errors, short or long frame errors, or abnormal frame communication at the physical Ethernet switch channel level.

We started with a general comparison related to the X1 server's NIC 2 channel that connected to the firewall Internet segment. This segment was connected to a firewall channel that had a 100Mbps NIC connected to the other port on the same switching module for the same switch the server X1 NIC 1 was connected to. We noted immediately upon reviewing the firewall that the other side of the firewall channel was based on a 10Mbps shared medium NIC connection to a shared 10Mbps hub that also connected to a T1 router for the firewall. This particular shared medium area hub was found through our audit of the computer room, and was not noted in the entrance briefing.

We immediately brought an additional protocol analyzer into the site to analyze the shared Internet segment and started baseline measurements in this area. The Internet segment, which was based on a 10Mbps shared media Ethernet design, showed saturation with utilization levels averaging 45% and peaking at 96% for durations of 3.5 seconds and higher. The protocol percentage appeared to be mainly based on TCP/IP, utilizing HTTP for application to the Internet at a very high level. Collision levels were noted between 7% and 8%, and appeared extremely high.

We then focused back on the channel NIC 2 card for the X1 server and noticed that there was an extremely high number of retransmissions, of more than 35%, related to network layer communications in and out of the segment on communications to the firewall subchannel for that area of the computer room. Retransmission levels combined at the network and transport level for TCP/IP were noted between 36% and 42%.

Based on this extremely high level of nonfluent retransmissions along with the findings on the Ethernet shared area on connection to the Internet firewall router, it was clear that there appeared to be a large amount of access to general HTTP-based Internet access channel communications.

We moved directly back to our analyzer positioning point one on the NIC channel 1 for the server link for X1. We next focused on application layer analysis in our statistical screen, along with upper-layer protocol decoding. We found that a high number of the protocols based on TCP/IP, which were more than 70% of the protocols in the general percentage base for breakout, were based on HTTP. In other words, the absolute TCP/IP-based usage was 80%, as compared to a 20% NetWare-based utilization on the Internet for the users at the main LAN facility. The amount of process application protocols for TCP/IP relative to the total TCP/IP usage of 70% based on HTTP to the Internet were noted at well over 50% of all site data communications.

This finding specifically focused our efforts on the fact that the Internet usage was much higher than actually perceived by the MIS team, as noted in the entrance briefing.

We brought this to the attention of the MIS team at the facility, and they immediately agreed with us, based on our findings, that many users throughout the facility were starting to access the Internet and they really were not monitoring the actual increase in this usage.

Based on this concern, we immediately identified that the IP forwarding channel in the NT-based backup domain controller was possibly being overloaded and causing response-time concerns for the server's internal I/O processing at the facility.

It should be noted that in our X1 server analysis session, we found that many of the users at the facility were receiving interpacket delta response time from the domain controller upon high utilization levels of 10 to 15ms when monitoring from the computer room area. This was extremely high. The levels should have been at 1 to 3ms, maximum.

Such an extremely high analyzed delta time would explain why performance would be slow upon extremely high access and applied utilization levels on the server. There are obviously times when access levels are high on a main server that is taking on the role of a backup domain controller, as well as serving new important applications such as Exchange and also handling internal routing for IP forwarding to the Internet channel, such as designed at this particular facility.

Based on this concern, we noted the interpacket delta time as extremely high and brought all the issues to the MIS team member board for general review. Upon review of our findings, they thought that instead of continuing with further testing in the user area, it would be beneficial to have the IP forwarding disabled in the X1 server and to then break out the TCP/IP usage for the Internet firewall into a specific separate switch port on the main switch within the computer room. In other words, because the Internet access levels were found to be so high, they thought that separation of the Internet access through the server would be beneficial and would obviously be a positive architecture direction for general application and topology layout concerns.

The MIS team made an immediate change control decision, and on the next business event disabled the IP forwarding on server X1 and brought a direct link from the Internet firewall into a main switch in the computer room. They also upgraded the 10Mbps link between the firewall to the router to 100Mbps, which was a simple modification parameter on the switch, to allow for the change to 100Mbps through the firewall channel. This allowed for a higher-speed access for site users accessing the Internet directly through a switch to the Internet firewall and then through the router for the final Internet access.

The next business day, the LAN Scope analysis team sampled the server interpacket delta time in the main computer room on the X1 NIC 1 channel, which was now the only active NIC for the server. We noted that the interpacket delta time appeared to drop and was now rated between 300 microseconds and 1 millisecond maximum.

The issues identified were clearly the factors causing the perceived response-time problems throughout the facility that were being blamed on the new implementation of Microsoft Exchange.

Based on our findings, the Exchange application rollout migration went forward in a positive manner. The server was performing at a higher level and more than 90 users were added in the following three weeks without any outage to the facility as related to access to the main server X1.

In this particular baselining exercise, the network protocol analysis methodology used was extremely crucial to the overall isolation of the cause of this problem.

Case Study 4: Packet Size Analysis

A garment manufacturer in New York City contacted LAN Scope to analyze an accounting based application problem that they were experiencing. Their issue was that one of the applications at the facility which they had been using for accounting for quite some time, had been re-engineered and re-developed to be placed on a larger internetwork platform that they recently implemented within their headquarters facility.

Most of the processing for this site application had been performed in a mini computer environment through the mid 1990s. They only moved forward into local area networking heavily within the past several years.

As the company moved forward into local area networking, many of the different applications that they were using were basic office applications for word processing or general spreadsheet usage. At that time, many of their core business database applications were still placed on the host environment and accessed through a front end processor.

The main concern was that the application which was used in a small defined area by only 10-15 users, was now required for application access as related to accounting reviews for a much larger volume of business that was beginning to develop within their infrastructure. The company was starting to develop channels to their distributors, which increased their sales by almost four times in the past year. Based on this increase in business flow, the accounting application was starting to be accessed by many subsidiary managers that were responsible for profit and loss, as well as other accounting personnel throughout the facility. Application usage was up by almost five times and had grown to approximately 50-60 users (see Figure CS4.1).

The application performance issues were present on a new infrastructure based on High-speed Ethernet and a server environment that was extremely robust. Also, their general Ethernet channel utilization levels, according to their hub monitoring systems and even their own network analysis platforms were showing below 20% peak utilization.

The LAN Scope analysis team began the study with our normal entrance briefing process and reviewed the network configuration. We found that the site was using Ethernet architecture rated at 100Mbps half and full-duplex, based on both shared and switched architecture. The architecture was designed in such a way that high-speed channel architecture was not a concern from our technical standpoint. We also felt positive about the initial review of the brand new internetwork hub deployment switched architecture along with new robust workstation and server platforms. Our concern was that there may be an issue with the main file server or possibly the application.

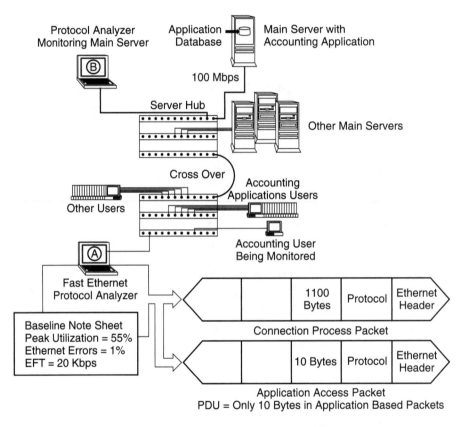

FIGURE CS4.1 *A garment manufacturer in New York City with an accounting based application problem.*

We reviewed the symptomatic history with the problems as related to application access, as well as the growth as related to the application's deployment. We designed a project plan that involved sampling the application closely while still performing network baseline exercises. Our primary focus was to examine how the application performed for one specific user from an initial standpoint.

We moved to the main Ethernet switch in the main computer room and set up a port mirrored process on a user who accessed the application quite frequently. This particular user launched the application against the general file server on a consistent basis.

We started with a general port baseline sample review, or what we term a rapid baseline, against the user's port. The user's port access showed an average utilization on a 100Mbps half-duplex port of approximately 30%, and a peak of 55% utilization for no more than 500 microseconds. Protocol percentages showed an even split of TCP/IP and NetWare throughout the channel, which was expected. The Ethernet error rate was nonexistent with a flat CRC rate at well under 1%. The overall health of the link and general operation appeared to be normal. The user was on a half-duplex link and collisions were present, but again fell well under the 1% level.

The server environment was based on both NT and Novell in the main computer room.

We noted that the broadcast filtering was applied to the Network Layer (3) switch environment within the computer room, and the broadcast levels were also well under 5%. Any broadcast levels being seen were required for the particular user port access.

The network layer symptomatic levels were extremely low and general symptoms across the statistical screen of the analyzer appeared to show no problems in the physical, network, transport or application layer. The only concern that we did note was that the application layer was showing an effective throughput of under 20Kbps upon application access. This immediately indicated that there was some sort of performance problem within the facility server environment, application, switch or possibly related to the specific user.

We then performed a more controlled exercise and had the user access the application upon a clean reboot. Our main focus in this particular exercise was to examine the application through characterization processes which we would perform, if required. We started upper layer protocol analysis trace decoding upon the initial launch and access of the application, and then stopped our analyzer to just review the general application data before we would perform a controlled application characterization exercise. In this event analysis, we started to examine the internal frame area of the application's access.

Upon connection to the network, we noted early in the trace that the user's packet size appeared to float between 300 and 1500 bytes in size upon access of connecting to the server and logging onto the server from a clean reboot. As soon as the application was launched, accessed, and certain executable files were accessed, the average packet size inside the main level of data trace review of the analysis session showed the application's packet size at approximately 150 bytes maximum. Most of the packet sizes ranged from 120 and 130 bytes upon read/write access of the application transfer between the user and the server for the accounting-based application.

We opened up various packets and found that these were clear packet file access calls utilizing the Ethernet frame 802.3 IEEE accepted encapsulation mode which engaged an Ethernet frame with an LLC encapsulation header. The IPX header was then encapsulating NCP, which encapsulated the application Protocol Data Unit (PDU). We then investigated the size of data in each read and write transfer from the server back to the workstation. Upon reads, we noted that exactly 10 bytes of data appeared to be consistently sent from the server to the workstation in each particular packet. We investigated this consistently through the trace analysis session, and found this to be common throughout every event accessed on a read of the application for accounting queries from the workstation user operation. This was an immediate concern, based on the fact that we felt that the protocol data unit size was extremely small.

To cross-verify this issue, we then picked another user from a completely different area and performed the same set of exercises with our network baseline analyzer. We had to set up an additional port mirroring session on another port to do so. When we finished our exercises, we came up with the same findings and then developed our technical synopsis.

The synopsis included the facts that the maximum Ethernet frame size was negotiated upon occurrence of connection to the server. In other words, when the workstation user would connect to the server and logon and move through the authentication process, a normal 1500 byte Ethernet *Maximum Transmission Unit* (MTU) packet size was negotiated. In this case, the topology was providing the maximum MTU for Ethernet and the network operating system was providing maximum access to the actual Ethernet MTU processing capability. This proved that the network operating system along with the workstation image shell were correctly configured.

It was clear from this analysis that the application itself was designed for a small amount of data to be placed in the application for transfer. We immediately identified these concerns and relayed them to the site manager. The site manager could clearly see that the packet sizes were the factor in question. With the packet sizes being so small upon general application access, the application could be considered chatty. The packet sizes were small, and the small data unit was not due to the network topology or the network operating system configuration in the file server or the workstations, but rather due to the application design process.

This finding was beyond the control of the MIS environment within the facility and they immediately contacted the application developer.

The developer agreed that this was a possible concern and brought forward the issues to the development engineers within the company. They made modifications to the application and produced a new application patch which allowed for a larger packet size to be negotiated upon read calls for the properties of the file upon access of an open and close process. After the modification patch was applied, the LAN Scope analysis team was asked to re-analyze the issue.

We returned to the facility with the focus of examining the original user. It was immediately seen that the user was now utilizing maximum application based PDUs of approximately 1000 bytes within each packet. The users throughout the facility also saw an immediate performance increase upon the patch being applied throughout a widespread configuration at the facility.

This is another clear example of how network baselining and protocol analysis decoding methodology allowed our analysis team to zero in on a specific problem. Without the specific baseline tests performed against utilization, protocol percentages and error rates, that we perform in workload characterization network baselining exercises, the application manufacturer may have challenged the MIS team and not have followed through on the patch.

Based on the fact that our technical synopsis information was backed up by clear technical data and proof, they immediately responded to their client by providing a patch and concurred that the problem was definitely due to their own development cycle as related to the application's design.

In this particular case, the company worked with the application vendor and continued to improve relations. The application vendor was also able to apply this patch to other key clients throughout the industry.

In this type of situation, everybody wins, due to the fact that we all worked as a team, but we utilized the process of network baselining and protocol analysis to identify our concern.

Case Study 5: Application Characterization and Modeling Analysis

One of LAN Scope's clients, a large medical provider, recently contacted us to perform an application characterization and modeling exercise on a critical medical-based application. The client internetwork was based on several large hospital locations, medical-care facilities, and administrative offices. The application that we were to analyze involved a medical record program used to compile medical records on a patient for eventual submission for approval of payment to major insurance companies. The program was called a medical-record accumulator program.

The analysis exercise requested was for our team to review how the application was performing in a small implementation phase of approximately 10 users. We were told that the application would eventually be rolled out to approximately 100 users within the next six months. We were also advised that three separate locations would require access to the application. There were concerns as to whether distributed servers would be required or whether remote access from the three locations could be achieved over the WAN with application performance being retained. Performance problems had already been noted by the users on the rollout of approximately 10 stations when accessing the application (see Figure CS5.1).

During LAN Scope's entrance briefing meeting, we reviewed the network topology and architecture layout. We also reviewed the application event process along with any symptomatic occurrences that had taken place. We also reviewed the past and future migration phases of the application as related to the rollout cycle.

The application event cycle included a process in which a medical clerk would launch the application. After the application had been launched, the clerk would then enter a new patient record. The new patient record name would be entered into the database as a registered patient. The next phase included entering testing results from the various clinical or medical facilities as related to the patient's history. Various information for different test procedures or general healthcare would be entered in detail. Some of the information involved scanning documents at the medical clerk's station. The medical clerk's workstation area was designated as the "accumulator area." This included a workstation with a scanner and a printer. Overall, the medical accumulator workstation was the central point of entering all the data and scanning any medical records, as required.

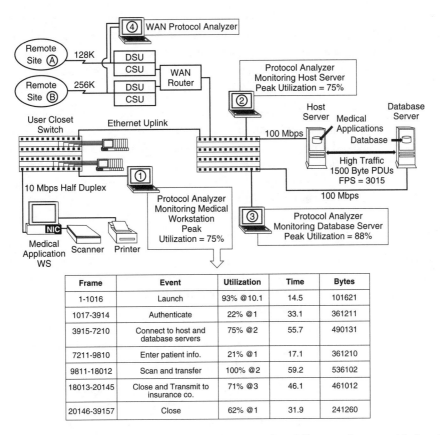

FIGURE CS5.1   *An application characterization and modeling exercise on a critical medical-based application.*

The information would then be transferred during different processing phases to a main host server in the main computer room at the facility. The host server would interactively communicate with a database server that would update all the key information. Upon accumulation of all the data related to the medical record of the patient, the information would then automatically be submitted as a final record to the insurance company via transmission over a wide area link. The record would then be considered a recorded database record on the patient.

Different medical facility areas of the overall health care vendor could then add to the database submission with regard to the client history. The final goal was to create, maintain, and submit a patient medical record for billing to major insurance companies.

Based on this event cycle, the main concern was whether the workstation design in the accumulator area was properly designed to handle the transmission for true stability, reliability, and performance in this area. It was also a concern as to whether the database servers or host servers could be distributed to different WAN sites to increase performance.

Based on the review we received in the entrance briefing, LAN Scope began our application characterization process. We decided to start our testing at the medical record accumulator station. The testing would include a close review of the application by filtering on the medical clerk's launch of the application and access of different phases of the application. It would also include reviewing certain processes such as scanning and final database record transmission. We also had intentions to study the main server room environment, where the host and database server were placed.

As we began our application characterization of the user station, we focused closely on general baseline statistics as an immediate way to understand how the station operated without the application launch. We asked the user to launch all other applications that would normally be co-resident in the workstation memory such as word processing, mail, and other programs that would be used at any given time. Our focus was to baseline the user node without the new medical application applied.

The user was configured against at 10Mbps switched port configured for half duplex. We closely monitored the user via a port-mirroring process to examine the general transmission for the key statistical metrics. One of the metrics we closely monitored was utilization, which was noted at an average of 30% and peaked at 52%. We also monitored general protocol percentages, which showed a high percentage of TCP/IP at 80%, with smaller percentages of NetBIOS, AppleTalk, and DECnet. These protocols were noted as external to the port area and inbound as related to broadcast levels. These percentages were mainly due to the fact that the switch the user was connected to for access did not have network Layer 3 broadcast filtering applied, and the user was seeing inbound broadcasts from the complete medical internetwork environment domain.

With this noted, we closely focused on the physical error rate. Collision levels were noted at 1% to 2% and appeared to be benign in terms of causing any problems. Based on the statistics noted, we then requested that the user launch the new application. This was initially noted as Test 1. During this test, we had only one analyzer positioned on the medical clerk's accumulator station. Watching the station, we asked the user to start different phases of the application. In each event of the application, we just marked the amount of inbound and outbound frame counts on the analyzer so that when we completed the analysis, we could determine where the information for each event would reside in the data trace. This exercise is called frame marking.

We frame marked each event of the application, which included the following:

Step 1. Launch the application.

Step 2. Log on and authenticate the application.

Step 3. Connect to the host. (Note that this step involved connecting and logging on to the host server in the main computer room.)

Step 4. The user would then open a new data record, which would then involve communication where the host server would connect to the database server in the computer room to open a new record.

Step 5. The medical clerk would then enter information on the patient. Different subevents would then launch, such as enter history information (address and other information related to the patient, for example). Other information could then be added such as patient history in different areas of the hospital for various procedures, surgery, prescriptions, and other medical information.

Step 6. Certain information records would have to be supported by scanning in information from the local accumulator station.

Step 7. After the patient record was built, the record was closed and selected for transmission to the insurance company that supported the medical patient billing situation.

Step 8. Then the application would be closed.

These events were closely monitored. We noted that upon launch of the application and also in certain events such as scanning, between 95% to 100% utilization was reached on the user-port connection channel frequently for peak utilization. The average utilization on the 10MB half-duplex ranged between 60% and 75%. The peak transition levels were extremely high, and lasted for more than 10.5 seconds, with the highest time duration noted at 16.3 seconds.

These saturation levels completely absorbed all the available capacity for the medical clerk accumulator workstation port on the switch. Based on this observation, we immediately had an issue related to Ethernet channel capacity as well as concerns regarding the general workstation handling capability.

By viewing certain statistics on our network analyzer during multiple sessions, we noted that the workstation performance appeared to be affected by certain operations such as scanning and transmission of records.

We also noted in particular that the protocol analyzer showed a large amount of connectivity potential drops with TCP window size exceeded along with long acknowledgment times. We stopped the first application characterization trace and saved the trace. We filled out an application and closely measured each event for cumulative bytes transferred, relative time for event, and a peak utilization on the port affected for each event.

All our statistics were carefully noted along with symptomatic problems per event incurred on the analyzer statistical screen. Our initial technical synopsis from the information brought forward was that we thought that the port access was designed on an extremely low capacity for the application movement that would be applied on the port. We thought that the workstation configuration for a medical accumulator station would require some hardware platform upgrades to handle the application transfer when co-resident with other critical applications such as general mail, scheduling, or any other applications that the medical clerk would utilize.

We then moved the next phase of the application characterization study to the computer room. In the computer room, we placed a network analyzer in a port-mirrored situation on the host server and a third network analyzer in a port-mirrored situation on the database server. At the same time, we kept a network analyzer placed on the medical clerk area on the accumulator station. We staged a one-step, three-position analyzer-synchronized process in which the medical clerk would launch the application. We placed one analyst in the computer room and one analyst in the medical clerk area. The analyst in the computer room was monitoring both analyzer two and three, which were positioned on the host server and database server. The analyzer in the medical accumulator station area was analyzer one.

Our approach here was to examine what kind of interaction occurred on the servers in terms of bandwidth and overall interaction as related to the application that would not been seen from the accumulator station point of view via analysis. This was important to determine whether the MIS department could distribute the application through database servers or host servers to other sites, based on the amount of traffic flow and how distributing servers could impact the WAN in terms of performance with regard to the planned migration.

The analysis results in the medical clerk accumulator area were similar to those from our preceding session. In the computer room, what we immediately saw by monitoring each one of the servers, which were both on 100Mbps full-duplex ports, was an extremely large amount of traffic for an Ethernet channel capacity in Fast Ethernet from server to server. Average utilization for the host server was noted at 42%, peaking at 75%. The database server showed an average utilization of 53% with a peak of 88%. This was extremely high, and was noted as verified via our full-duplex Ethernet analyzers.

Based on this utilization level alone for multiple event cycles of the application, we had a concern regarding capacity levels from the onset of our analysis. We also noted that during scanning transmission and select final data transmission to insurance vendor, that the number of frames that transmitted between the host server and database server counted for more than 80% of all the frame transmissions involved in these event cycles. These were inner–computer room file transfers across one particular backplane of one switch. Our concern here again was the amount of traffic that would be applied to any WAN channels if these servers were to be separated for any reason. Based on this immediate vector, even in the statistical screens, we thought that this area needed further investigation.

We stopped all the traces and saved the data. In both the accumulator area and the computer room, we built three application tables. One table was designed for the medical accumulator station, the second for the host server, and the third application or blueprint table was applied against the database server.

In the computer room, we spent most of our time investigating the internal trace data and the size of frames as related to average frame size and throughput of cumulative data between the servers. Because the host and database servers were placed in the computer room, the actual channel access provided for high throughput and data transfer. This was beneficial because the maximum packet size was engaged for most of the time at more than 1500 bytes on the MTU. Full PDUs were being inserted by the application vendor into the maximum Ethernet packet size. Transfer rates for EFT between the two servers were noted; these ranged between 1000Kbps and 1200Kbps. This clearly showed on our final analysis that this application would require the host and database server to coexist in a common area throughout the infrastructure of the medical enterprise internetwork.

We saved all our information and developed a blueprint understanding of how the application operated against the topology within the enterprise internetwork in this particular configuration. We contacted the MIS team and received further information on the rollout specifications. They told us that approximately 50 users would be added within this facility and another 40 to 50 users would be rolled out as medical clerk accumulator stations in various hospital locations. We then requested information on the WAN topology and noted that the current WAN topology was based on fractional T1 circuitry, with some of the circuit channels only allowing for either 128K or 256K fractional T1 links.

Based on this concern, we thought that it would be beneficial to the application modeling exercise to properly deploy a rapid baseline procedure against two of the key remote locations where the rollout would occur. We implemented a WAN analysis approach to do so on a key WAN circuit rated at 128K. We found out that the 128K circuit location was running at approximately 50% average and 80% peak bandwidth. This is extremely high for a fractional WAN T1 link. This was without the new application deployed across the link, and for just general office mail and word processing application transfer to the hospital headquarters. We also monitored a 256K link and noticed that the 256K links at certain sites, based on node concentration level being doubled at these sites, showed similar high utilization.

Based on our findings in these areas, we developed the following technical synopsis from the application characterization phase. We took the position that the user station in the medical clerk area and at the headquarter location will require a minimum memory upgrade of approximately 128MB and a processor upgrade to a Pentium II level. (Older workstation platforms were currently being used; they were based on 486 and Pentium I, along with 32MB of memory.) We determined that the NIC design should be based on a more robust platform of 100Mbps minimum half-duplex design, based on a higher and faster bus channel in the PC platform in the workstation area.

We presented this information to the MIS team, and a new workstation platform design was immediately noted as an excellent recommendation to be considered for rollout. With that out of the way, we then stated that within the computer room the database server and host server would have to coexist in any key location. The client examined the budget and rollout capabilities and agreed that to implement multiple server environments in multiple locations would create a significant dollar outlay and would also impact MIS security for centralized processing policy, which was preferred at the time.

With this being noted, they reviewed their WAN topology. It was decided that the best way to proceed was to consider restructuring of the WAN architecture to Frame Relay with higher bandwidth levels at the sites that would utilize this application. The Frame Relay architecture from a WAN standpoint would also allow for burst transfer over the a predetermined *committed information rate* (CIR), which would allow for a more open channel burst handling of data on the WAN.

The client requested that we perform a brief modeling exercise with 10 users across one of the 256K links. To do so, we implemented an application modeling process. This process included taking the traces that were captured in the application characterization phase and feeding the network protocol analyzer data traces from the application characterization phase into an application modeling program. The program requested us to input a characterization in a specific data screen as to the amount of previous bandwidth applied to the WAN links. Based on our WAN characterization, we filled out the average and peak bandwidth along with the latency that we had previously seen on the channels. It also required that we perform a topology building exercise to show the LAN and WAN topologies as connected. We built this topology map and applied the utilization and latency levels against the current model to develop a basic understanding of how the current WAN topology was operating with the protocols that were applied at the time. The application modeling program then just requested us to apply the data traces taken at the headquarters location against the remote locations. Each station that was added was considered one medical accumulator station. We just applied the data traces taken and multiplied them by 10 stations. The application modeling program immediately produced an output that characterized and simulated what the effective utilization increase would be at each site. Obviously, based on the characterization levels that we provided and input levels of the circuitry already showing an 80% peak on the 128K and 256K remote channels, the application modeling program noted that the bandwidth was exceeded.

Using the modeling program, we were able to increase the bandwidth channels in a cumulative manner until we eventually saw a drop in utilization against available capacity. When we moved the channels to 768K with applied burst rates up to a full T1 for Frame Relay, we noted that the average utilization, even with the 10 accumulator stations at a remote site, would still allow for an average utilization bandwidth of no more than 30% and a peak of approximately 52%. This was considered an achieved level that was successful, because the Frame Relay circuits could be upgraded further in the future.

Based on this information, we produced a model of what the wide area requirements would be for the client. The client MIS team then developed a relationship with a new router and WAN vendor and implemented a new Frame Relay internetwork based on our recommendations.

The MIS team then requested a formal application characterization and modeling report on the complete exercise. We put together a report that reflected our technical findings on the application characterization phase, and referenced all our application characterization tables, technical synopses, and applied recommendations.

The application characterization report included recommendations on upgrading the workstation platform along with the port channel speed link. It also verified that the two main servers should be combined in any main computer room, based on the heavy interaction in data movement. We also recommended the WAN for any remote site with 10 users be upgraded and verified to a higher level for capacity channel rates at a minimum of 768 CIR with a burst up to a T1 level.

After these recommendations were formally presented, the client implemented several migration steps that included upgrading any workstations that would be utilized as medical record accumulator workstations for this particular application. These medical clerk stations received a new PC platform based on a 100Mbps full-duplex switched link, which was then connected via a switch through an Ethernet gigabit link to the main computer room, thus providing for a high-speed channel. Any remote-user locations were limited to a maximum of 10 to 12 stations, and were upgraded to a new Frame Relay separate FRAD channel as required, via a WAN Frame Relay link to the main medical facility computer room where the servers resided. This baseline analysis and application characterization process served to reduce the impact to other users at the remote site and prevented absorption and over-utilization of the available capacity on a WAN link that could not handle the traffic. This created a nonimpact situation upon final rollout of the application.

Within four months, the medical site was able to roll out approximately 120 users without incident, and the application is operating in a positive fashion. This is a very robust application and will require continued protocol analysis upon rollout, because the application has the capability to move excessive levels of data based on some of the event cycles in the application process.

In this case, the application characterization and modeling exercise was extremely positive. The methodology allowed for a baseline analysis approach that was extremely thorough. It also allowed for an application characterization approach for mapping out the events of the application and the impacts on the network. Identification of issues related to network configuration, topology, and application operation were blueprinted in this characterization phase. The rollout phase of the application was properly targeted, by carefully monitoring the LAN via baselining, characterizing the application, and then thoroughly examining the wide area impacts of the application. By utilizing the modeling program, we were able to properly predict what the WAN channel design should look like on a future upgrade or migration cycle to accommodate the application's impact.

This is the proper way to perform network baselining and application characterization as a combined process. This method allows an analyst to ensure how applications will impact internetworks and to determine how internetworks are built to support the rollout of applications.

CHAPTER 5

Network Analysis and Optimization Techniques

When performing a network baseline study, specific techniques enable an analyst to troubleshoot network issues. Some of these techniques involve processes discussed earlier in this book, such as utilization and quantitative measurement analysis. Unique methods exist to isolate specific traffic flow events, which can be very helpful during isolation and statistical baselining.

First, an analyst must engage the standard methodology as presented in the preceding chapter. Next, the analyst should apply techniques that provide a more focused review of dataflow from each specific baseline session. Some of these techniques can be applied to cause isolation; others can be used to optimize a network's performance (see Figure 5.1).

Among the techniques involved are the following:

- Physical health analysis

- Broadcast storm analysis

- Network capacity overload analysis

- Network throughput analysis

- Network end-to-end interpacket timing analysis

- Transport and file retransmission analysis

- Packet route and path cost analysis

- End-to-end file transfer analysis

- Drill-down data-decoding steps and specific techniques

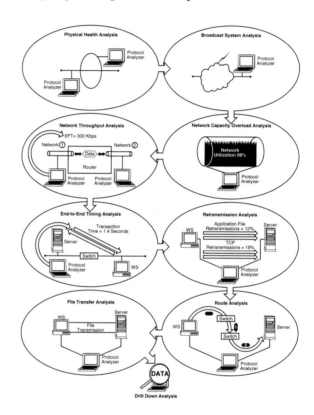

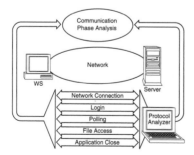

FIGURE 5.1 *The main network optimization techniques.*

The techniques listed above will yield a palette of data information that will be extremely valuable in problematic and network baseline data profiling situations.

When reviewing a data trace during a network baseline session, an analyzer's Expert system output information, or the internal indications in the data trace, may immediately point to a specific type of problem, such as excessive physical errors. Rather than quickly taking the information from the Expert system and immediately attempting to troubleshoot the specific area of the network flagged as troublesome, the analyst should also further examine the internal data-trace results. It is highly likely that the data-trace internal view holds additional information that should also be reviewed and cross-mapped to a higher-level report information-extraction engine or Expert system screen results. Further examination of the data trace will most probably result in a more exact cause analysis mapping of the problem, yielding a more exact technical synopsis and applied recommendation.

This chapter describes each analysis technique. These techniques should be applied when performing a network baseline study. This is important so that you can isolate issues to their exact cause and profile data for optimization reasons.

5.1 Physical Health Analysis

Taking into account the many physical topologies in the *local area network* (LAN) and *wide area network* (WAN) environments, it is natural to assume that many different physical error types may be encountered. When performing physical health analysis in a network baseline session, it is important to quickly note all information gathered in an Expert system or management system platform. Information related to error type, time of the error event, the associated addresses or network segment involved with the area in question, and protocol event sequence involved with the error must be clearly documented. The internal data-trace analysis results should then be cross-mapped to the output report of the error.

Many different host systems and internetwork device platforms (such as routers and switches) have their own internal method of reporting errors through various management platforms. Many different protocol analysis and management tools report error-count levels and time-of-occurrence conditions. All these systems yield valuable Error log or error-report information, which is a primary focus area when reviewing data. The Error log information must always be carefully gathered and documented.

For the purposes of illustrating error-report gathering, the following discussion describes how to apply this approach using a protocol analyzer tool.

5.1.1 Using a Protocol Analyzer for Error-Report Gathering

A protocol analyzer used during a network baseline session enables an analyst to quickly assess the types of errors encountered, the error count, and the time of occurrence. This relevant information proves extremely valuable because it assists in identifying the error event and the possible impact of the error on a network. In a reactive analysis session, this information is crucial and relevant to a rapid troubleshooting process. In a proactive network baselining session, this information is also important; however, the information can be quickly noted and documented for later review through the baseline process. This is especially important during a large internetwork study involving many different network areas, because certain physical errors may repeat and show a pattern of events that might be related to a center networking device, such as a main computer room hub, switch, or router. Within the protocol analysis capture, the error event is contained within a frame or a packet sequence, depending on the LAN or WAN topology.

It is important to cross-map the statistical Error log or output report from a specific management system (if one is present). It is important to map the Expert results with the internals of the protocol analysis dataflow events. The protocol analyzer error-reporting screens should be carefully examined for the key error event. After the error event information has been noted, the protocol analyzer should be paused or stopped. The capture should then be immediately saved to disk to ensure that the error frame or error frame occurrence is stored properly within the protocol analyzer platform. The data trace should then be opened and reviewed carefully, following a "page through the trace" process. The process of paging through the trace just involves slowly moving through the internal data gathered by the protocol analyzer to locate any unique anomalies. Some protocol analyzer Expert-based systems have a hotkey filtering system to quickly filter to the error event inside the data-trace results.

A protocol analysis trace taken during a network baseline session, may contain a large number of packets and frames. Some data traces could contain 50,000 or 100,000 frames or even more within one single capture. It can be quite cumbersome to page through the complete data trace after the trace has been opened for review. An Expert system feature provides a hotkey filtering system can facilitate an immediate extraction filter based on the error occurrence in the particular analyzer Expert system screen. The approach in this case is to highlight the error on the analyzer Expert system or statistical monitoring screen. After the error has been highlighted, an analyst can use this feature to quickly filter to the area within the set of packets within the overall data trace to the exact area of the error occurrence. After the error event has been found, other relevant information in packets surrounding the error occurrence frame may also be identified; these may point to the actual cause of the error.

An inexperienced analyst may too quickly map the cause of a problem to an Expert system error-output report or a management system Error log. By using the actual data-trace error event and packet-sequence review process to access packet data around the error, it is possible to be more defined and accurate as to the cause analysis. In summary, a thorough review of the error frames within the trace may uncover packets or frames surrounding the error occurrence that may pinpoint the cause of a problem.

Consider, for example, 16Mbps Token Ring network that is operating abnormally from an upper-layer application standpoint. Users are complaining significantly about performance. In this case, the analyst should immediately deploy a protocol analyzer, because this is a rapid baseline situation (or a reactive analysis event).

As stated earlier, certain quantitative baseline measurements must be taken prior to topology error analysis, such as utilization, protocol percentages, and other statistical measurements. If the analyst moves through the initial steps in the quantitative baseline measurement process and notices a high number of error reports from the protocol analyzer indicating a high ring purge error *Media Access Control* (MAC) occurrence, this is a relevant event.

Assume, for example, that through an analysis session a high number of ring purge MAC frames are found within a Token Ring environment. The protocol analyzer could then just stop the capture, save the information, and filter on the ring purge events via a hotkey filtering system. The analyst could identify the ring purge MAC frames within the Token Ring trace analysis session. If, prior to the ring purge MAC frames, it is noted that excessive ring insertion failures are associated with a specific device, or excessive Soft Error Report MAC frames, this might indicate the cause of the ring purge error noted in the Expert system or Error log. Chapter 9, "Token Ring and Switched Environments," discusses Token Ring issues in more detail. This is just one example of how internal data-trace analysis, as associated with Expert system mapping, facilitates a cross-review process that yields a more accurate analysis.

Another illustration is an Ethernet internetwork that is showing a high number of corrupted CRC frames within the analyzer Expert system analysis screen. If the protocol analyzer filters on the artificial intelligent Expert screen displaying the CRC corrupt Ethernet errors, the analyst should then move directly to the internal area of the trace that shows the CRC-corrupted error frames involved. By doing so, the analyst can determine that prior to the CRC frames, and possibly after the frames, certain frames indicate a high number of communication events on the Ethernet medium. Because the Ethernet medium engages a *carrier sense multiple access collision detection* (CSMA/CD) sequence that is an ongoing process and is part of the Ethernet architecture, the cause analysis can be somewhat complex. Certain Ethernet frames, when including errors such as a CRC type, may be shorter than normal and may have physical addresses that cannot be interpreted. Because of this, sometimes the source and destination addresses may not be able to be read related to the CRC error cause. If prior to the CRC error frames, the trace shows that a certain set of devices are communicating, it is quite possible (based on the operation of CSMA/CD within Ethernet) that these devices are involved in conversations when a high number of CRC errors are occurring.

If retransmissions of frames at the Ethernet level are occurring, it is very possible that the CRC errors that are not readable are related to the frames that communicated most recently prior to the CRC error. This is another example of how a cross-mapping of the internal data-trace results as related to the analyzer Expert system are invaluable to protocol analysis and network baselining.

Later in this book, specific topology techniques such as analysis of Token Ring errors, Ethernet errors, and WAN errors is discussed in detail. In the context of this discussion, however, the point is that more is involved in isolating errors via network baselining other than just a simple review of protocol analyzer Expert screens or management system Error logs. All error reports encountered in these types of systems should be backed up by a close review of the internal data-trace results. The information should be cross-mapped between the management or Error log systems and the internal data-trace results. This method allows for a more accurate physical health analysis technique (see Figure 5.2).

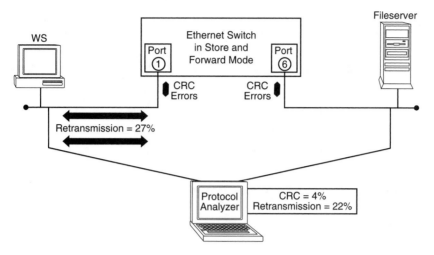

FIGURE 5.2 *Approach of physical health analysis.*

5.2 Broadcast Storm Analysis

When encountering a broadcast storm in a network baseline session, an analyst can apply a specific technique to isolate the cause of the storm and the possible effect of the broadcast event on the internetwork.

A *broadcast storm* is a sequence of broadcast operations from a specific device or group of devices that occurs at a rapid frame-per-second rate that could cause network problems.

Network architecture, topology design, and layout configurations determine the network's tolerance level as it relates to frame-per-second broadcasts.

Consider, for example, a frame-per-second rate related to a broadcast storm generation of a specific protocol (*Address Resolution Protocol* [ARP], for example). Such generation, at more than 500 frames per second and on a continuing basis, is considered an abnormal protocol-sequencing event and can be extremely problematic.

The key here is to understand the difference between a normal broadcast event and an actual broadcast storm. When a normal broadcast event occurs, the broadcast is engaged from a specific physical device on a network for the express purpose of achieving a network communication cycle. There are conditions when a device, such as a router, broadcasts information to update other routers on the network to ensure that routing tables are maintained as consecutive and consistent related to internal route table information. Another standard broadcast event is when a device attempts to locate another device and requires the physical address or *Internet Protocol* (IP) address of another device.

When a specific workstation device has a default gateway assigned, a "normal" broadcast event can occur. The device knows, for example, the target IP address of a device on the internetwork. It is common for this device to broadcast an ARP sequence to attempt to locate the target hardware address. ARP broadcasting is discussed in detail later in this book.

A workstation that broadcasts an ARP sequence to locate a target server but doesn't establish a broadcast resolve and doesn't receive a target hardware address for the server provides an example of an "abnormal" broadcast event. If the target device fails or the source broadcast operation mechanism or protocol-sequencing mechanism of the device fails, the source workstation device could start performing a loop ARP sequence that could be interpreted as a broadcast storm. Such an event in itself could cause a broadcast storm.

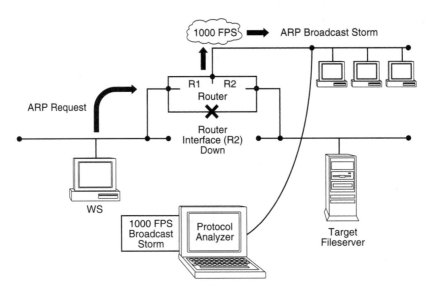

FIGURE 5.3 *Broadcast storm analysis.*

The point to be made here is that the frame-per-second rate of the broadcast sequence and the frequency of the broadcast sequence event occurrence can constitute an abnormal event.

Another example can be found in a Novell environment, when the *Service Advertising Protocol* (SAP) sequencing is engaged by specific servers. If the servers are broadcasting an SAP on standard NetWare sequence timing, the occurrence may take place on 60-second intervals. If there are hundreds or thousands of servers, the SAP sequence packets generated may become highly cumulative and affect areas of the enterprise internetwork that are not utilizing Novell processes.

In large internetworks, many of these concerns are addressed through protocol filtering within routers and switches in the network Layer 3 routing design. When a problem does occur because of an anomaly or possible misconfiguration of an internetwork, it is important to capture the information upon occurrence.

By applying an exact technique with a protocol analyzer, an analyst can very quickly capture a broadcast storm and identify the cause of the broadcast storm and develop a method to resolve the storm. Many different tools enable an analyst to achieve this. Almost all management systems for internetwork hubs, routers, and switches facilitate broadcast storm identification. The threshold that determines what is an actual broadcast occurrence versus an actual broadcast storm is usually set by the network manager or the configuring analyst of the network management platform.

The following discussion details the use of a protocol analyzer for broadcast storm analysis. When performing a data-analysis capture, a protocol analyzer is a useful tool for capturing a broadcast storm. Many protocol analyzers have thresholds that allow for an artificial intelligent–based Expert system to identify a broadcast storm. A storm can be identified by preconfiguring and studying a trigger or threshold for determining what would constitute a storm occurrence. When performing a network baseline, an analyst should always engage the threshold setting on the protocol analyzer prior to a baseline session.

5.2.1 Using a Protocol Analyzer for a Broadcast Storm

Based on the network architecture, the protocols, and the node count on a site being studied, an analyst must determine what constitutes a broadcast storm. This requires the analyst to be quite familiar with the topology and types of protocols and applications being deployed. A general benchmark is that a broadcast sequence occurring from a single device or a group of devices, either rapidly or on an intermittent cycle at more than 500 frames-per-second, is a storm event. At the very least, the sequence should be investigated if it is occurring at 500 frames-per-second (relative to just a few devices and a specific protocol operation).

After the threshold has been set on the protocol analyzer, a data-trace capture should be started. After the capture has been invoked, and a broadcast storm event has occurred in the Expert system with notification or in the statistics screen, the time of the storm and the devices related to the storm should be carefully noted. The addresses should be noted in a log along with the time of the storm and the frame-per-second count. Most protocol analyzers provide this information before the capture is even stopped. As soon as the broadcast storm occurrence takes place, the analyzer should be immediately stopped to ensure that the internal data-trace information is still within the memory buffer of the protocol analyzer. The data trace should then be saved to a disk drive or printed to a file to ensure that the information can be reviewed. The data-trace capture should then be opened and the actual absolute storm time noted from the Expert system or the statistical screen. Based on the absolute time, it may be possible on the protocol analyzer to turn on an absolute time feature. When turned on in the data trace, the absolute time feature enables an analyst to search on the actual storm for the absolute time event. This may immediately isolate and identify the cause of the broadcast storm.

Certain protocol analyzers offer hotkey filtering to move directly within the data-trace analysis results of the storm event. Either way, by using absolute time or hotkey filtering, the broadcast storm should be located within the data-trace capture.

Other metrics can be turned on in a protocol analysis display view when examining a broadcast storm, such as relative time and packet size. After the start of the storm has been located, the key devices starting and invoking the storm should be logged. Sometimes only one or two devices cause a cyclical broadcast storm occurrence throughout an internetwork, resulting in a broadcast storm event across many different network areas. The devices communicating at the time closest to the start of the storm inside the data-trace analysis results may be the devices causing the event.

After the storm has been located, the Relative Time field should be zeroed out and the storm should be closely reviewed by examining all packets or frames involved in the storm. If 500 or 1,000 frames are involved, all frames should be closely examined by paging through the trace. After the end of the storm has been located, the time between the start of the storm and the end of the storm should be measured by using a relative time process. This is achieved by just zeroing out the relative time at the beginning of the storm occurrence and examining the cumulative relative time at the end of the sequence. This provides a clear picture of the storm device participation and processes, the packet-size generation during the storm, and the source of the storm location.

The initial several packets located for the broadcast storm should be investigated for the physical, network, and transport layer addressing schemes that may relate to the storm occurrence. This helps an analyst to understand the sequence of the storm event.

This is an extremely important process in network baselining and should be engaged in proactive and reactive analysis. In proactive baselining, an analyst must configure the proper broadcast storm thresholds on the protocol analyzer. This way, the storm events will show during the network baseline session. In a troubleshooting (reactive) event, it is important to know whether certain failure occurrences or site network failures are also being reported by the users; these may relate to the time of the storm occurrence. If this is the case, just isolating and identifying the broadcast storm may make it possible to isolate the devices causing the storm or the protocol operations involved. It may then be possible to stop the storm occurrence. This will increase performance levels and optimize the network.

5.3 Network Capacity Overload Analysis

When examining utilization, it is important to understand both the available capacity on any network medium and actual achieved utilization levels from an average, peak, and historical perspective. Every network LAN or WAN topology has an available capacity. Determining the utilization levels of a topology is important, but equally important is identifying any problematic utilization levels or saturation utilization levels. As discussed earlier, saturation of any main network medium can cause outages on a network related to an end-to-end session. Peak utilization and time measurement methods must be used to identify any outages.

Other conditions exist when the capacity, even if available, may be in an overload condition in certain topologies.

Consider, for example, a 10Mbps shared media Ethernet topology operating at 60+% utilization levels. The Ethernet topology in a shared configuration normally allows for a specific maximum capacity of 10Mbps or 100Mbps. Can the shared Ethernet medium sustain the applied utilization levels and continue to operate in a positive manner? Although capacity levels may only be operating at a peak transition of 60% or 70%, and approximately 30% to 40% of medium may appear available, the CSMA/CD mechanism of shared Ethernet could trigger an excessive collision problem at this level. As noted later in this book, in shared Ethernet media the collision-detection mechanism can increase to a level that causes problematic events at the physical level when utilization exceeds 30% of available capacity. In this example, a level as high as 60% of the available capacity can constitute a network overload condition.

With most network analyzers and management systems, an analyst can set a threshold that will immediately identify whether a specific LAN or WAN is in overload. The thresholds of certain internetwork management systems are specific to switches, hubs, and routers, and usually facilitate this process.

For the purposes of this discussion, a protocol analysis approach is followed. When performing a network baseline, the protocol analyzer should be preset for a network overload threshold setting (if an available option). This feature is usually found in an artificial intelligent Expert system threshold setting mode. An analyst should determine whether a network overload threshold setup feature is available prior to a baseline session. The next focus is the exact type of topology and protocol sequencing being examined. A 16Mbps Token Ring network requires a different overload threshold setting than a 10Mbps Ethernet environment requires.

Another consideration factor is the type of application traffic and NOS environments that are deploying various protocols across the architecture. The combined topologies and protocols create a specific architecture that must be considered when assessing an overload condition during the network baseline process. In a network continually sustaining a 50% utilization level, for example, setting an alarm below this level will trigger abnormal error occurrences or will cause already well-known information to be continuously logged. Presetting the threshold setting is somewhat of an intuitive process on the part of the analyst. The message here is that the analyst must understand the type of topology and protocol environment deployed and determine what type of a condition will cause a utilization overload of the available capacity. Figure 5.4 illustrates the concept of analyzing a network overload event.

A dedicated-circuit WAN with a fractional T1 link engaging a 256K circuit provides another example. You should not continue to run data across the circuit at 80% to 90% capacity. This type of level could cause excessive retransmissions and overflow of some of the buffers in the end-to-end router platforms between two specific wide area sites. If more than 80% to 90% utilization is being achieved, even though there is still 10% available capacity, it would be better to upgrade the circuit to increase performance levels. The other factors involved in making this decision would be the type of router technology, the type of protocols, and the consistency of this traffic level. There are many factors related to this occurrence.

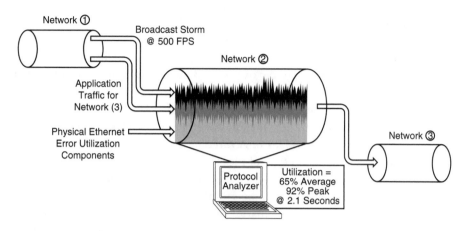

FIGURE 5.4 *Analyzing a network overload event.*

A protocol analyzer example illustrates this technique. A protocol analyzer can be deployed across a certain network topology. When the network baseline session is initially configured, a threshold can be set for the proper overload condition. This is the alarm that occurs when the overload event happens. If the network baseline process is active, and the analyst encounters a network overload alarm, the protocol analyzer should then be stopped and the capture should be saved. The analyst should note the network overload event as to the time of occurrence and the type of devices involved. The data-trace capture should then be reviewed by isolating high-utilization occurrences within the trace. Some, but not all, network analyzers enable an analyst to turn on network utilization as a metric within the data-trace view results. The key is to properly mark the absolute time of the occurrence from the analyzer Expert system or the management system. The Absolute Time field should be turned on within the data-trace capture results.

Whether the network overload is located through a hotkey filtering system or absolute time, the overload occurrence should be closely examined. Most likely, a set of devices is involved in communication when the network overload occurrence takes place.

The network utilization column in the data trace should be examined and noted. The internal trace results should also be closely examined for the type of packet size used during the data movement when the utilization overload condition occurred. As noted earlier, utilization is a component of data size and rate of data movement. If an overload condition of 90% occurs when packet sizes are increased above 2K from an area of 100 bytes, this clearly indicates that larger blocks of data are present at a consistent data rate (increasing utilization on the medium). The actual protocol event sequences can then be examined for the cause of the overload. Based on the start time of the overload occurrence identified within the data trace, it may be possible to note the data-trace events in the first several packets identified at the time of the occurrence. Several features can be activated in the protocol analysis detail review to examine information such as Hex or ASCII data view of packet internals to identify the opening of a certain type of file. The application layer protocol could also be examined for a specific file sequence that has been opened. By identifying the types of files opened and the protocol events occurring at the time of the network start sequence, an analyst can relate the utilization overload to a specific application operation or occurrence on the network—a server synchronization event, a unique application launch, or a communication cycle such as database transfer, for example.

Figure 5.5 shows how changing the size of data movement affects network utilization.

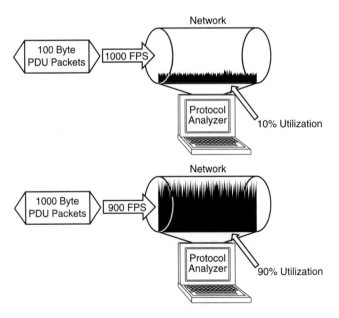

FIGURE 5.5 *Changing the size of data movement.*

It is critical to perform network capacity overload analysis during network baselining. An analyst can use this technique in both a reactive analysis for emergency troubleshooting, as well as in a proactive way to examine capacity overloads.

5.5 Network Throughput Analysis

When performing a network baseline, effective throughput should always be considered a standard measurement. The most accurate way to perform *effective file throughput* (EFT) analysis is to measure EFT against exact file transfer. General throughput measurements can also be taken against a specific network LAN or WAN area.

A specific technique applies to performing throughput analysis consistent with protocol analysis methodology in a network baselining session. This technique involves cross-mapping throughput measurements obtained from a protocol analyzer statistical or Expert screen with the throughput within the actual data-trace results.

When performing throughput analysis, it is very important to mark the beginning of a file open and a file close sequence. This is because after a file transfer begins, the transfer of data units in packets between two specific devices is usually a consecutive process and data movement can be consecutive and rapid.

Marking the file open and close sequences helps the analyst to determine the throughput across the internetwork channel in a LAN or WAN area. The following discussion focuses on measuring EFT with a protocol analyzer.

Prior to the study, the protocol analyzer deployed on the network should be set up for a network baseline study, and any Expert system threshold in an artificial intelligence–based protocol analysis or statistical screen threshold should be set. Several effective throughput levels are standard. During the network baseline study, the analyst should be familiar with the internetwork architecture and aware of the throughput typically achieved in the particular internetwork architecture. After the standard throughput levels for the specific network have been determined, they should be entered into the Expert system.

If the required achieved level of effective throughput for a network baseline study is 500Kbps, for example, this threshold level should be set in the protocol analyzer prior to a capture session. After the 500Kbps threshold has been set, the protocol analyzer alarm triggers or a statistical screen is identified while a capture is active when a file transfer drops below the 500Kbps mark. The analyst should mark the time of the effective throughput drop and note any devices involved in transfer during the low effective throughput drop. It is next important to identify the timing event of the actual low effective throughput alarm occurrence. Most analyzers include an absolute time mark in the statistical output screen or the Expert analysis screen. With these items being noted, a low EFT event could then be cross-mapped to the internal area of the trace by using the effective throughput measurements discussed earlier in this book.

After the trace analysis data has been saved and the detail trace opened, it is then possible to view the data and locate the low EFT occurrence within the data by cross-mapping the statistical absolute time or hotkey filtering to a low effective throughput event.

When a low effective throughput occurrence is found within the trace, it should be verified by setting relative and cumulative bytes and adding the relative-time metric against data movement that is cumulative to determine the effective throughput achieved for the dataflow operation.

Figure 5.6 displays the technique of measuring EFT.

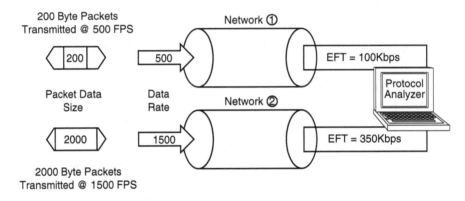

FIGURE 5.6 *Measuring EFT.*

It is also possible to trace throughput on a consistent basis by setting several protocol analyzers or management systems at specific threshold levels. This is another unique technique, because it enables the analyst to consistently capture the throughput levels of various devices communicating across an internetwork. Most protocol analyzers can develop multiple sets of views against certain devices communicating with application- or connection-based protocols within a LAN or WAN topology. When specific devices are being tracked in a statistical or Expert screen of a network analyzer, it is possible to monitor the ongoing effective throughput by examining statistical screens.

Measuring effective throughput is not only valuable for low effective throughput occurrences, but also for ongoing tracking of file transfers. The technique for this process is to set up the thresholds correctly and to consistently view the specific devices being reviewed for throughput during the baseline.

An example is to monitor the client stations related to the most critical servers at the site. Specific applications could be launched and the throughput could be compared for different applications. This enables an analyst to determine the data movement and the data-rate for standard throughput; it also enables an analyst to compare application *protocol data unit* (PDU) inputs within different application profiles. This identifies throughput differences in certain areas of the internetwork and also the throughput differences related to certain application sequencing.

This is a critical technique that should be followed in proactive baseline studies. This process can also be used in reactive analysis for low throughput or performance problems.

5.5 Network End-to End Interpacket Timing Analysis

Network communication involves at least two devices communicating with each other: a workstation and a server; or a server communicating with another server (at a minimum).

Specifically, any two devices communicating across an internetwork identifies an end-to-end communication channel. A data communication sequence occurs across a network channel and data is processed and a data transfer is achieved.

It is possible to use protocol analyzers and network management systems to examine the network end-to-end timing between two specific devices. As discussed under the timing section in the last chapter of this book, several different timing metrics or statistics can be activated in a protocol analyzer when measuring this process. Some of these metrics or statistics include absolute, delta, and relative time.

A specific technique applies, however, when examining how workstations and servers are communicating as to timing in a network baseline session. This is accomplished by determining the time difference between Request and Response sequences.

A workstation and server across any topology usually invoke a specific protocol sequence to transfer information, and may engage another protocol sequence to call on a specific server file and so forth. Later in this book, there are extensive discussions on specific protocol sequencing methods for different protocol types and suites such as Novell and *Transmission Control*

Protocol/Internet Protocol (TCP/IP). For the purposes of this discussion, it is important to understand that there is an exact technique for measuring end-to-end interpacket timing that enables an analyst to quickly determine how various workstations and servers are responding to each other in terms of performance across the internetwork. The process of using a protocol analyzer is used for illustration.

When using a protocol analyzer for end-to-end interpacket timing analysis, it is first important to set the proper thresholds that will trigger alarms when an excessive response time occurs between a workstation and server. Many network analyzers and management systems have threshold settings that set off an alarm when a server or workstation responds over a certain time period. Normal internetwork end-to-end channel communications on a LAN with multiple segments should take no more than 10 to 15 *milliseconds* (ms), and in fact it is common to see response time well under 5ms on most internetwork infrastructures. Across WAN infrastructures, interpacket latency for end-to-end sessions can be as high as 50ms. A response time of less than 20ms is more typical, however. Some WAN designs are based on different deployment design criteria, such as whether servers are centralized or decentralized across an infrastructure. The server positioning design must be considered when deploying several protocol analyzers against the end-to-end channel.

An example of this process includes a multiple protocol analyzer data-capturing session against an Ethernet end-to-end channel that involves three segments including a WAN. For example, a multiple analyzer positioning "map" relative to the complete internetwork layout can be drawn up. Segment 1, for example, involves a shared Ethernet segment, which connects to a router and then connects to a WAN Frame Relay circuit. That circuit interconnects another WAN site noted as the remote location with an additional router, which is connected to another shared Ethernet segment, Segment 2. This mapping involves the following three specific network areas that must be traversed:

- Segment 1

- The WAN Frame Relay cloud, and

- Segment 2

With this example in mind, at least four protocol analyzers are required to examine an end-to-end channel communication session. One protocol analyzer could be placed on the Segment 1 location in the shared Ethernet area. An second protocol analyzer could be positioned at the exterior side of the WAN router connected to Segment 1 and connected to the Frame Relay cloud or the

Frame Relay Assembler Dissembler (FRAD) link. A third protocol analyzer could be positioned at the remote site on the exterior side of the WAN analyzer connected to the FRAD link at the Segment 2 site, and a fourth protocol analyzer could be connected to the remote Ethernet shared Segment 2. This setup places four network protocol analyzers in a parallel mode for synchronized analysis.

Figure 5.7 shows how end-to-end channel analysis can be used in a network baseline study.

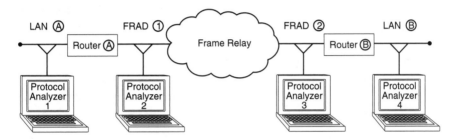

FIGURE 5.7 *Engaging in end-to-end analysis.*

The next step is to synchronize all the protocol analyzers in terms of date and time to ensure that all the relative base measurements for time in each analyzer platform are as close as possible. Some network protocol analyzers offer synchronization of time through GMT synchronization, depending on the manufacturer. Other inband and outbound triggering mechanisms in different analysis tools also enable an analyst to configure synchronization.

After the analyzers have been engaged, application characterization techniques can then be deployed against a network end-to-end channel being timed. An application can be launched from a local workstation at one segment to access a server at a remote site. This would be valid if a distributed server is placed at the remote site. The application, when launched, can be monitored by all four protocol analyzers. With absolute time set as active, it is possible to trace a specific packet, such as a TCP or a Novell SPX packet, by monitoring the sequence number as it travels from the source workstation to the remote server.

It is also possible to track the TCP or *Sequence Package Exchange* (SPX) response by examining the sequence and acknowledgment number as well as the identification fields of the networks traversed in the network and transport layer protocols of each packet.

By tracking the packets sent and received, the end-to-end network channel interpacket timing measurements can be determined. An analyst can make delta time active on the Section 1 analyzer to examine the request outbound process from the original workstation and to examine the inbound server response. Even by just using the first analyzer, however, the actual time spent across Section 1, across the WAN Frame Relay cloud, across Section 2, and across the remote segment is all compiled into the remote response. By using several analyzers, an analyst can determine how much time is spent on Segment 1, how much is related to the internal turn time of the workstation or delta time on Segment 1, how much time is spent across router one at the local station, how much time is spent traversing the Frame Relay cloud, how much time is spent traversing remote router two at the remote site, and how much time is spent accessing the server on the remote Ethernet segment at the remote site. An analyst can actually determine the amount of time spent in the server, the server turn time, as well as the server delta time at the remote site.

Timing analysis is an extremely valuable technique, but it must be very carefully configured and engaged. By applying this technique, an analyst can examine the appropriate analyzer screens and cross-map high response time or long acknowledgment time errors, as well as other conditions such as slow responding servers. The analyst can check these occurrences against actual timing events in the internal data-trace analysis results. This technique enables the analyst to accurately isolate the cause and results in extremely on-target information.

This process can be coupled with multiple application-characterization techniques, such as launching certain events. It is then possible to determine delays that may be related to the application processing or delay event sequences that take place when packets are traversing routers or switches on large internetworks.

Various tools enable an analyst to process data scripts across an internetwork based on this sequence.

Some of the most valuable tools available for this type of process include the Chariot platform offered by Ganymede Software and Optimal Software's Application Expert. The Chariot tool allows for immediate generation of data scripts across the internetwork; this will quickly show defined data movement, and allows for viewing transaction time, throughput, and response time operation. Chariot tools can be placed at multiple network points.

Network analyzers can also be placed at the same points to extract data. Optimal's Application Expert provides response-time prediction and data analysis in a multipositioning process, but adds a feature to examine an application's thread across an internetwork.

Many different management systems offer unique platforms and features that can engage tests similar to Ganymede's Chariot and Optimal's Application Expert.

The key factor to remember is that timing measurement is a valid process and should be configured and performed very carefully. By so doing, an analyst can isolate delays and perform specific optimization tuning against internetwork transfer.

This is a valid technique and should be used consistently by an analyst in both proactive and reactive analysis situations.

5.6 Transport and File Retransmission Analysis

When conducting either a proactive or reactive network baseline study, it is important to monitor the transport layer and application layer for retransmission events. A retransmission occurrence can cause an inefficient situation in terms of final data communication. A retransmission is a redundant dataflow event that adds to the amount of cumulative bytes transferred on a network to effect a final transmission of an intended application process or *network operating system* (NOS) data.

The specific purpose of the transport layer mechanism operation is to ensure connection. Most transport layer protocols engage a connection process that invokes a sequence-and-acknowledgment cycle between two specific end nodes. This sequence-and-acknowledgment maintenance cycle causes, in certain cases, a higher transmission of redundant data. This is common if there are delays or other abnormal occurrences in the communication channel between two end devices. Later in this book, an extensive discussion is presented on various types of transport layer protocol operations and processes.

For the purposes of this discussion, the main function of the transport layer in network communication protocol sequencing is to ensure that there is a transport mechanism in place for transferring data from specific protocol port areas within certain workstations and hosts across an internetwork. In certain cases, the transport layer also generates packet traffic that allows the transport channel created to be maintained for connection.

Protocol analysis enables an analyst to monitor the transport channel that has been established between a workstation and a file server for general operation and transfer of data across the channel. The analyst can also monitor the transport layer for recurrences of transmission of data considered redundant. In this case, the focus would be monitoring transport layer retransmissions.

Because the transport layer is essentially in place to establish a network channel for data port communication and, at times, to maintain the communication channel in a consistent and reliable state, it is critical to monitor this area through a network baseline process to ensure connectivity.

If a transport layer connection is established with TCP, two specific ports for TCP may be opened on a respective end-to-end channel on an internetwork. The endpoints could be a workstation and a file server, each of which would have a TCP port open. The transport layer protocol TCP would maintain the connection. Polling events between the two protocol ports in the two devices would take place that would allow for maintaining the TCP port transport layer channel that is open related to the port transmission activity.

With the aid of a protocol analyzer, an analyst can monitor this channel. If a delay is present in the internetwork, or if one of the two devices encounters a problem, the end-to-end communication may be negatively affected. Again, this might result from internetwork delays or because one of the devices has an internal issue related to resource handling or processing of data. When this occurs in the TCP environment, the transport layer may show extensive retransmissions of data because it is attempting to ensure that the data required for achievement of an application process is sent on a continuous basis. When retransmissions occur, redundant data is sent. One of the endpoints—for example, the workstation—could encounter a situation in which it is not receiving required data responses from the server because of delays. As this occurs, it is likely that the workstation will re-request the data on a continual basis. Under certain conditions, the host may retransmit the data for integrity purposes, based on the inherent operation of the transport layer protocol TCP.

Figure 5.8 shows retransmission analysis being engaged.

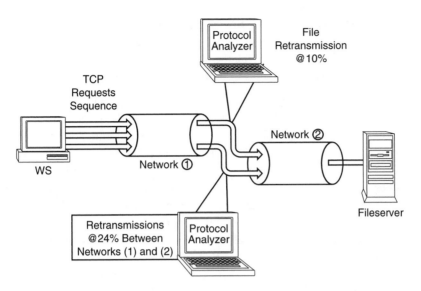

FIGURE 5.8 *Engaging in retransmission analysis.*

After a protocol analyzer has captured the retransmissions, an analyst can mark the percentage of data related to retransmissions as related to standard data process transmissions to understand the retransmission level. An extremely high retransmission level, such as 20% or 30% of all frames transmitted, shows an excessive level of redundant communication.

This example clearly shows how transport layer transmissions can become an issue. The simplest way to monitor transport layer retransmissions is to use a protocol analyzer.

5.6.1 Application-Based File Retransmission

Application-based file retransmission is another type of retransmission event that can take place in application operations when communication occurs between workstations and servers. In most cases, a complete file retransmission is usually invoked by application operational sequencing, or developers may intentionally code it into the application process for redundant cycles to enable integrity checks in the application transfer.

When a file is sent across a network, a file open and a file close sequence is usually invoked. A protocol analyzer enables an analyst to monitor how often files are opened and closed. If some files are opened and closed on a consistent basis in consecutive order, the application code or the application process may very well be invoking the file retransmissions. When this type of situation occurs, it is critical to monitor the event with a protocol analyzer. Doing so enables the analyst to identify the inefficiently designed applications causing redundant excessive communication on a network.

To monitor transport retransmissions, the network protocol analyzer should first be set for the appropriate thresholds to capture this error. Some network protocol analyzers enable the analyst to set up a predetermined threshold or filter for this type of event. After the network baseline session has been started, if any of the transport layer retransmissions alarms are triggered, the error occurrence and time can then be documented. A hotkey filtering system can then be invoked after the file has been captured and saved. The hotkey filtering system can be engaged or the time of the transport layer retransmission can be marked from the appropriate analyzer screen. After the time event of the retransmission event has been identified and noted, the internal areas of the data capture can then be examined for the actual retransmission event.

In some cases, it is possible to mark the transport layer sequence and acknowledgment fields for the retransmission event. Some protocol analyzers highlight this alarm; with others, only a detailed analysis can identify this concern. The technique involved is to cross-map any statistical alarms on the analyzer from an Expert or statistical screen against the retransmission event inside the data trace.

After the retransmissions have been found, they should be correlated to any file open and close sequence prior to the retransmission. This process enables the analyst to identify the file being transferred and to possibly identify the application being involved. If the retransmissions are excessive, the amount of retransmissions in terms of the data transfer frame count for normal retransmitted frames should be compared and documented. A percentage of retransmissions should be calculated against overall standard data transmission events. If retransmissions exceed 10% of overall traffic, this is a problematic level that could cause redundant communication and additional utilization on the medium. Retransmission levels as high as 20% and 30% could cause application integrity issues and/or application failures. The level of retransmissions should be carefully noted.

Figure 5.9 presents the concept of file fluency analysis.

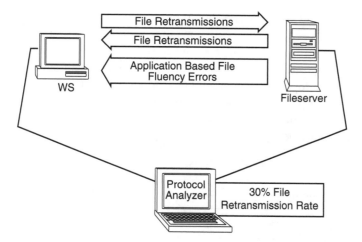

FIGURE 5.9 *File fluency analysis.*

When monitoring application-based file retransmissions, it is also important to set up a protocol analyzer prior to starting a network baseline to capture any concerns related to this type of event. Some protocol analyzers enable an analyst to set up a filter or an Expert system threshold to trigger an alarm. When performing a network baseline session, if a file retransmission alarm is triggered, or if a statistic is reported on a screen for an event, the analyzer can then be stopped and the data. should be saved for review.

The event occurrence from the statistical or Expert screen should also be noted for the absolute time of occurrence and the devices involved in the file retransmission. It may also be possible in some circumstances to mark the protocol type or application invoked. Usually this is just noted as the protocol layer engaged and not the application type.

After the capture has been saved, the data trace should then be opened and the event should be located by hotkey filtering or matching of the absolute time of occurrence. After the file retransmissions have been located, the type of files being opened should be examined and, if possible, cross-mapped to an application engaged at the site. It is sometimes possible to turn on Hex or ASCII data display views with an analyzer to examine the internals of the file open statement (if the application layer does not report the file type, for instance). This enables an analyst to identify the application access that is occurring.

Next, the file open and close process should be monitored for how often the file is opened and closed in a consecutive manner. A file opened and closed once is a normal event. If a file is opened and closed 25 consecutive times with the same data being transferred, this is an excessive file retransmission event. The application development team should be contacted to investigate whether this is an intended application event or whether this is an abnormal event. In most cases, this issue can be resolved by working in tandem with the application development and NOS server support teams.

Figure 5.10 shows file access-error analysis.

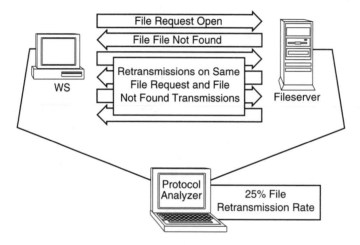

FIGURE 5.10 *File access-error analysis.*

Both steps of examining transport and file retransmissions via network baselining are extremely important. These techniques assist in identifying redundant communication that can be eliminated from a communication session. These steps also assist in identifying network-based foundational or application process issues.

5.7 Path and Route Analysis

During a network baseline, it is important to always investigate the route of packet transfer across a network or internetwork channel. It is also important to determine the number of hops or paths taken across internetwork interval points when transferring information.

The use of protocol analysis in this area is an extremely valuable process. Path route and path count analysis can be used in proactive and reactive network baselining sessions. To examine path route concerns, it is important to understand that within network layer protocols, and also internal to some of the data involved above the physical layer inside a packet, there is information that may identify the route that a packet has taken through an internetwork.

When examining a simple Token Ring frame, for example, it is very common to examine a Routing Information field. The Routing Information field includes specific information as to the bridge, router, or switch that been traversed, and how many hops have been taken related to the Token Ring packet. An analyst can use a protocol analyzer to capture this information.

Figure 5.11 illustrates route and path analysis in a Token Ring network.

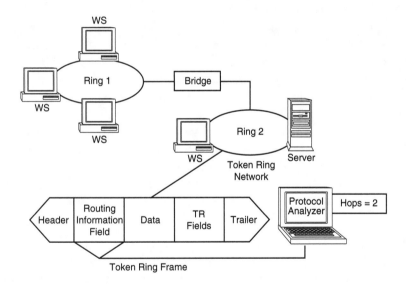

FIGURE 5.11 *Route and path analysis.*

Several network layer protocols can also be examined—such as IP, IPX, and even *Datagram Delivery Protocol* (DDP) in the AppleTalk environment—for a Hop Count field. A Hop Count field can be examined and reviewed for a quick view of how many routes have been traversed. It is important to associate the hop count with the point of capture and where the packet is traveling through the internetwork.

Certain network layer protocols, such as IP, provide even more information. The IP protocol provides a Hop Count and combined Time in Transit field, associating how long a packet has spent on a network in the term of actual seconds or time metrics. This a combined field and shows *time-to-live* (TTL). This field is discussed in detail later in Chapter 7, "LAN and WAN Protocols."

The technique of examining packet, route, packet count, and path count is extremely important and can become intuitive for analyst.

Most protocol analyzers enable an analyst to immediately examine the internals of a packet or frame in a detailed manner. Some protocol analyzers have alarms settings for excessive hop counts or path routes traversed. The protocol analyzer should be set up for any alarms or thresholds required.

After the capture has occurred, if any events take place in a network baseline session, the information related to a path count exceeded or a hop count exceeded field should be noted. The absolute time, the occurrence of the event, and the devices involved should also be noted. The capture should then be stopped and saved. When the data trace is opened, the event should be located through absolute time cross-mapping or hotkey filtering. When the frames showing the event are located, the frames should be opened in a detailed mode. The information related to path route or hop count should be examined. In most cases, this examination focuses on the network protocol involved. Most network layer protocols usually just display the source network, source node, and sometimes the socket or protocol port being communicated to across the internetwork. By examining the source network relative to the destination network, the hop count can be determined for the data communicated across a set of routes.

In a flat internetwork, such as a switched Ethernet environment, a hop count marking in a Hop Count field within a network layer protocol may not be valid or exist. By examining the source and destination network, however, an analyst can determine whether a device is located across an Ethernet end-to-end channel that involves two, three, or four switches. Again, it is extremely important to understand that, in most instances, the network layer protocol holds this information.

Figure 5.12 illustrates route analysis of an Ethernet network.

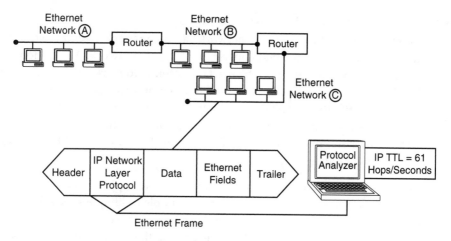

FIGURE 5.12 *Route analysis of an Ethernet network.*

The source and destination networks involved should then be marked, and then the devices should be mapped against the physical topology of the network. By just locating the source and destination network, the devices can be reviewed against a physical architecture or topology map. By locating where the devices are positioned on the network and associating this with the route taken, it is sometimes possible to identify inefficient design or incorrect implementation of servers and workstations across an internetwork. Remedies can then be taken, such as relocating a server or reconfiguring switches or routers in such a way that fewer routes are traversed.

At times, excessive multiple-route occurrences can be identified. In some cases, routing loops or delays can be identified in this sequence. Sometimes a passthrough route through a server that provides for IP forwarding or has multiple NICs can be located through this technique.

This is extremely important and allows for route protocol analysis to be used to examine the route that a packet actually takes and the number of hops that the packet encounters when traversing the internetwork from the source to the destination.

The ability to map this to an actual sequence flow or roadmap taken through the internetwork is an invaluable process to a network baseline study, in both a proactive and reactive mode.

5.8 End-to-End File Transfer Analysis

Another important technique in network baselining is end-to-end file transfer analysis. File access is the main operation of an internetwork. As mentioned earlier, a protocol analyzer can be used consistently to mark a file open and a file close sequence. An analyst can review when files are opened and closed, and can identify the source and destination devices related to the transfer. As discussed earlier, the analyst can examine the internal time sequences between a file transfer and mark the timing related to the file transfer event as well as the amount of data moved.

Taking into account the techniques presented in the application discussion of this book, it is next important to note that a simple technique should be followed during every network baseline study to examine end-to-end file transfer. When performing a network baseline, even with the absence of errors, it is important to constantly monitor file transfer events when examining the internal levels of protocol analysis–based traces captured during a session.

A simple way to do this is to ensure that any protocol analyzer or network management tool used is set up for the appropriate thresholds that will enable identification of any abnormal occurrences of this type. Some protocol analyzers enable an analyst to set up a threshold that will alarm when a certain file is opened and not closed in a relative amount of time.

Figure 5.13 illustrates a file transfer delay event being analyzed.

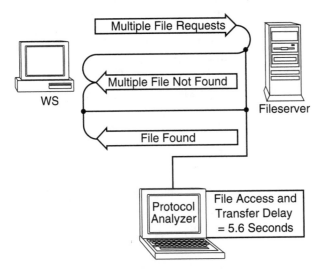

FIGURE 5.13 *Analysis of a file transfer delay.*

An analyst can also identify this process by setting specific alarms, such as alarms to a nonresponsive host environment or a slow responding server. In certain conditions, this may enable the analyst to immediately identify any abnormal end-to-end file transfers within a data capture.

A normal process is for a file to be opened, accessed, and closed. In some cases, a file is opened, accessed, and then abruptly stopped. Sometimes the event can be caused by delays on the network or failure of the NOS or failure of the application itself.

Often a device failure in the workstation or file server causes this event. It is important to examine this event on a consistent basis as a thread throughout many network baselining sessions in an enterprise internetwork study.

A protocol analyzer can set up in a predetermined configuration prior to a network baseline session to allow for a threshold alarm to activate upon incorrect file closures or any nonresponsive conditions on workstations and servers.

After the protocol analysis network baselining session has been started, it is then possible to identify any alarms that may be triggered. If any alarms occur related to file transfer sequencing, the devices involved and the absolute time of the occurrence should be noted. After the capture has occurred, the data trace should be saved. The data captured should be opened and the abnormal file transfer located through a hotkey or absolute time cross-mapping sequence.

In the event that alarms are not triggered, a page through the trace exercise enables the analyst to examine file open and close sequencing. If the error is located, the file open and close process can be examined. Once marked, the open and close process should be considered the start and stop point for a file transfer. The packets should next be examined from the open state to the close state for redundancy or abnormal retransmission events. In some instances, the trace data will show an abnormal stop and file close as even be present in the trace.

The key factor here is that normal consecutive file open and close sequencing is essential to a positive network communication process. It is also the main reason that we have file open occurrence, an access event such as a data transfer, and a file close. Most of the time, the application layer protocol is monitored for this type of cycle. Application layer protocols include such types as NCP and Windows NT's SMB. Further information on application layer protocols appears later in this book.

In closing, it is important to examine end-to-end file transfer in every network baseline study session.

5.9 Trace Decoding Techniques

When performing a network baseline, the final technique is the actual method used by the analyst to identify specific events and perform trace decoding. Earlier in this book, a brief discussion was presented on a process termed "paging through the trace."

When moving through a data capture, the data must be examined on a consecutive basis and reviewed closely by carefully moving through the trace information. Large data captures can include multiple frame sequences that can involve thousands of frames. Some network baseline capture sessions involve anywhere from 30,000 up to 100,000 or more frames. Because of this, it is important to have a technique that allows for quick examination of the frame sequencing. One technique is to use an Expert or statistical screen for cross-mapping event errors and quick hotkey filtering to the area in the trace that shows the problem. At times, an Expert or statistical screen may actually show the frame number prior to stopping the capture when an error event occurs.

When performing a network baseline, careful notes should be taken from the Expert system or the statistical screen prior to stopping the capture. If critical information is noted, such as absolute time of occurrence, devices involved, or frame numbers related to error occurrence, an analyst can move through the trace more quickly after the capture has been saved for review. Even if an Expert system is not available, there are ways to page through the trace to obtain important information that is essential for a network baseline session. This is an extremely valuable step in network baselining.

Figure 5.14 illustrates the concept of trace note taking during a network baseline study.

The following is an example of using a protocol analyzer to page through the trace. First, the analyzer must be preconfigured for the proper metric thresholds to ensure that event alarms will trigger and show absolute time and areas of occurrence for frame category marking prior to the error event. Watching the protocol analyzer closely while the capture is occurring will also allow for marking this type of event.

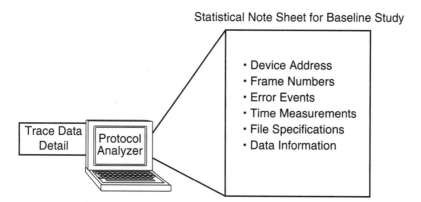

FIGURE 5.14 *Trace note.*

After the capture has been started, the analyst should closely monitor the protocol analyzer. This is extremely important when performing reactive troubleshooting analysis for rapid cause isolation. If an error alarm for a retransmission is triggered on the analyzer statistical screen when frames are being received into the analyzer NIC and the analyzer is showing an inbound frame count of 5,325 frames captured, the frame number 5,325 can be quickly noted as a possible frame area in the data trace as associated with the retransmission error.

The error and the devices involved with the error should be recorded on a statistical notebook, along with the frame area within the trace that is inbound. Thus, when the data capture is saved and the event examined, the analyst can swiftly move to frame 5,325 for cause isolation.

Figure 5.15 illustrates the concept of frame marking during a protocol analysis session.

This is just one example of this type of cross-mapping of an ongoing rapid dynamic process throughout a network baseline session. Again, the analyst must be extremely involved with the protocol analyzer while the capture is occurring for this technique to be helpful.

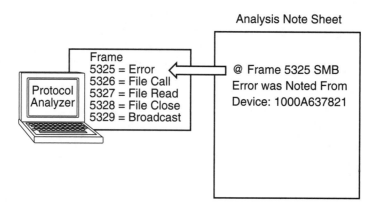

FIGURE **5.15** *Frame marking.*

After the protocol analyzer has been stopped, whether an Expert is active or inactive, the analyst can move through the data in a page through the trace process to investigate certain data. If any events are located during the live capture dynamic session, the cross-mapped technique of reviewing the data associated with certain frame numbers or with absolute time occurrence should be followed. Hotkey filtering should also be used, when possible. This will allow for quick use of an Expert system or an artificial intelligence statistical screen to quickly key to the type of error within the data capture.

After a problematic frame or packet has been found, certain types of information should be clearly recorded in a statistical mode by the consultant or analyst performing the network baseline.

An analyst should note information related to the following:

- Address(es)

- File access and name(s)

- Time frame(s)

- Frame structures for field length

- Routing information

- Specific protocol(s)

5.9.1 Address Marking

When examining a trace, it is first important to note the various levels of addressing. The physical address should be noted inside any packet that has an error. The network layer address should also be noted, along with any transport layer ports that are opened. This will assist in identifying any events related to an error frame that could be associated with certain devices or specific network applications.

An analyst might, at times, capture the trace information and identify a specific area of the trace that shows the problem. Depending on the analyst's experience and understanding of the internetwork, however, the analyst may or may not be able to identify the device or application associated with an error. By properly marking the information in a log and forwarding it on to an appropriate MIS person, it is quite possible that specific servers or applications can be pinpointed as the cause of the problem.

5.9.2 File Access and Name Marking

It is also important that the analyst note any file open and close sequences associated with error occurrence. After the file open and close sequences have been marked, the file being called on in the application layer protocol, the Hex code, or ASCII code that shows the file being opened should be noted. This information can then be forwarded to the appropriate MIS personnel who may be able to identify the application associated with the error. Again, the analyst may not always understand which devices or applications are involved. By clearly noting the file sequencing or the file that is opened and closed in an analysis log from a protocol analysis standpoint, however, other MIS team members may be able to identify the application or area of the internetwork related to file server location causing the problem.

5.9.3 Time Frame Marking

As discussed throughout this chapter, it is important to record the time frame of an error event. The absolute time frame of a packet is usually marked within the upper-layer physical header inside the detail level of a packet area. It is also possible to turn on the absolute time within the data-trace summary screen to review the absolute time of any error frame occurrence. Each time an error is noted in a baseline session, the network analyst should always record the time frame occurrence in a statistical analysis log.

5.9.4 Frame Structures for Field Length Marking

Occasionally, a network baseline analyst will encounter a frame structure error. Frame structures are usually designed for a specifically defined operation. For example, a typical Ethernet frame is based on a frame size ranging from 64 bytes to 1518 bytes. A 4Mbps Token Ring frame is limited to 4096 bytes. An analyst should always mark the frame size associated with any error frame occurrence captured.

Specifically, if an error frame is detected when examining a data trace, the frame size and protocol layer sizes should be noted, as well as the data payload. Each packet will always have a certain *maximum transmission unit* (MTU) size and specific amounts of data will be associated with the protocol layers. It is important to mark the payload of data transferred in any frames where errors occur. This information should be recorded in the analyst's statistical log.

5.9.4 Routing Information Marking

Another key area to monitor is the Routing Information field. As discussed earlier in this chapter, frames contain specific information that indicates to an analyst the route taken or the path hop count achieved. When performing a data-trace analysis session that involves cause analysis or standard network baselining for error mapping, the analyst should clearly mark any critical routing information, such as the route or path taken. If routing update sequences are captured between routers or switches, or other key devices on the network such as servers or hosts, the analyst should also record any routing update sequences when performing error-mapping analysis.

5.9.4 Specific Protocol Marking

Specific protocol marking is also important. This book does not discuss certain event occurrences. These are abnormal occurrences that do not fit any specific profiles, such as an abnormal error from a certain application, or an abnormal type of protocol event that has not been seen before in a network baseline session. If any abnormal event occurs, the analyst should document as much information as possible about the event. This would include the absolute time of occurrence, the devices involved, and any protocol sequencing taken.

When performing a network baseline session, it is extremely important to be in a constant review mode, which involves statistical documentation of the occurrences. Statistical documentation involves recording and documenting information prior to stopping the data capture. It is also vital that information be saved to a trace file save mode or a *Common Separate Value* (CSV) file format when possible so that the information can be reviewed later in the network baseline process.

Some of this information will be extremely critical to the final data-acquisition decoding and final reporting process of the network baseline study.

It should never be assumed that information is not required or is unimportant. All information should be documented in a concise and detailed basis. When performing a large internetwork baseline involving several baseline areas, such as a 10 to 15 segments in an Ethernet environment, for example, some of the information found in Baseline Session 1 may be relevant in Baseline Session 7. It is important that every network baseline session be consistently documented through statistical save modes for trace file captures, along with general note-taking and statistical marking during a trace analysis session.

5.10 Conclusion

It is extremely important that all the techniques discussed throughout this chapter be followed during a network baseline session. These techniques are extremely valuable when roving from session to session across large internet-work baseline studies. They are also valuable when performing a simple network baseline study. These techniques apply in both proactive and reactive analysis sessions.

When performing a network baseline, it is vital that a clear documented file on the network be available for reviewing topology maps, address assignments, and other key configuration information. The following chapter discusses the importance of network documentation during a baseline session and of cross-mapping the documentation to the results found in a trace analysis session.

CHAPTER 6

Documenting the Network for Baselining

When performing a network baseline, an analyst should have a complete set of network documentation. Certain documents, such as a network topology drawing, prove extremely valuable to the network baselining or data-acquisition planning process. Documentation that specifies server configurations, router and switch configurations, operating system profiles, and protocol configuration details are also very valuable during the network baseline planning cycle.

An analyst must sometimes perform a network baseline session on a network that has not been documented properly. In this case, it is more difficult to plan the network baseline process because certain parameters—such as where to position network protocol analyzers or management systems for the network evaluation cycle—may not be clear.

More information regarding the data-acquisition planning process for developing a network baseline program appears later in this book. This chapter discusses the importance of network documentation as it relates to the process and program of network baselining.

A clear and accurate set of network documentation assists the analyst with the network baseline planning cycle, enabling the analyst to produce a more accurate network baseline final report. Note also that a properly performed network baseline study yields additional information upon completion that further augments or creates a more in-depth set of network documentation. In other words, by actually performing a network baseline study, you can extract additional information that enables you to update the network documentation for a particular internetwork.

The discussion now turns to some of the important facts related to network documentation when performing a network baseline study.

6.1 Using the Network Baseline Results to Document the Network

During a network baseline study, it is very common to encounter a physical *network interface card* (NIC) address or network layer address (such as an *Internet Protocol* [IP] address) that is not identified or noted within the network documentation. Quite often major network devices, such as switches or routers, are located in data-trace results. These devices might have been omitted from previous network topology diagrams or network layout documents.

It is important to always note these types of items during the network baseline process to ensure that you can refer to them at the end of the study to investigate problems and also to ensure that you can update the site network documentation after the final baseline process output.

When examining a specific enterprise internetwork with a large infrastructure, this is an important phase of the overall analytical procedure.

When examining protocol analyzer trace files, you might identify certain NIC or network layer addresses that do not directly correlate with the network documentation available prior to the network baseline study. If you follow the proper note-taking procedures (such as those discussed in the past several chapters) when paging through a data trace or a set of protocol analysis session results, you can most probably identify any key conflicts. In other words, you must log any addresses and server names not documented in the initial network documentation that you referenced prior to the study. You should log this information when performing the analytical procedures of reviewing or paging through the data trace.

Quite often after a large-site baseline study has been completed, several baseline sessions are cross-referenced from one large baseline study to identify a common thread such as a device or several devices that do not appear on the network diagram or in the documentation. Usually when this occurs, an analyst can contact the appropriate personnel within the network support division and attempt to identify the physical or network layer addresses identified in the trace analysis session as "not active on the network." Very possibly, the network support team won't be aware of the device addresses in question. You can further investigate the addresses by reviewing previous network documentation and then reviewing the data traces in more detail to identify the physical location of the devices within the internetwork. The analyst and the support personnel can work together as a team to identify these locations. This method often helps to locate devices that were missed during the compilation of the previous network documentation.

Under certain conditions, an undocumented address may also correspond to a network problem or event, such as a routing loop or a misconfigured server or switch on the infrastructure design. When this type of event occurs, it can be extremely beneficial to immediately update the network documentation. In certain cases, you may also need to reconfigure the network when events such as these take place.

Documenting the network is an important part of the network baseline cycle. Network documentation is vital to the network baseline process and, as noted, the process itself often yields information that you can use to update the final network drawings to make them more accurate and on-target and therefore more useful during future troubleshooting processes.

Poor network documentation can negatively affect an analyst's ability to rapidly troubleshoot a critical network problem.

If a physical router is placed on an internetwork in a direct parallel line with another physical router, for example, problems can occur. Assume, for example, that two routers are placed as exterior routers from a *local area network* (LAN) to a *wide area network* (WAN) location. The LAN is configured as an Ethernet LAN with approximately 10 segments in one main location. The original network documentation shows only one main physical router (Router A), which provides an exterior router separation between the interior LAN and the WAN for the rest of the corporation at this particular location. Upon trace analysis of the LAN, another router is identified (Router B) and its address noted. Router B does not appear in the current network documentation and support personnel don't know whether it's actually connected or active on the network. Further review of the trace analysis files shows two routers using different routing protocols and causing the routing tables to refresh more frequently than normal in each of the main routers.

If certain workstation devices throughout the internetwork with the multiple Ethernet segments on the local LAN are set up to use one router (Router A) as a default gateway to the WAN, problems can occur if the router tables refresh too frequently. This may cause a situation in which addresses cannot be located (a non-reliable network, as discussed earlier in this book). In this type of situation, an analyst could identify the address of the other router (Router B) that does not appear to match the network documentation received prior to the study. The analyst could contact the appropriate support personnel or router team, and work hand-in-hand with them to identify the newly located router. If the new router is found and placed directly in line with Router A, which was considered the main exterior router, it may be possible to reconfigure the new router (Router B) that was not previously documented or in place on the configuration (see Figure 6.1).

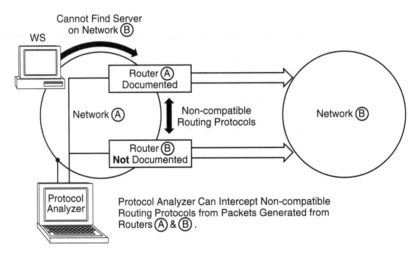

FIGURE 6.1 *How non-documented routers can affect a network's operation.*

This may sound like an unusual problem—unlikely if a network design team is extremely thorough. In large internetwork infrastructures, however, it is quite common to encounter such situations. In this particular instance, immediate action could possibly be taken to remove the new router located through protocol analysis from the current configuration and place it in a different location within the LAN. After all, the router may be in place for a reason—such as a WAN link that is not part of the main WAN, but which may be a link to another company or a specific Internet link.

In this example, the newly identified router may have been purposely configured without a direct line to the main computer room, possibly to come off
another Ethernet segment for some other reason. It may be possible to reposi-
tion the new router within the site design.

It is very possible that the second router could have two interfaces and one of
the interfaces could be connected in line with the main exterior router, as noted.
In this case, it is possible that even a condition such as a routing loop could take
place. (Chapter 7, "LAN and WAN Protocols," discusses routing protocols and
methods.) In this type of condition, packets could flow in and out of the LAN
from the WAN and possibly take multiple routes to the LAN segments through
the two parallel routers. This setup could prove extremely problematic and
cause extensive delays. The trace protocol analysis results of the baseline sessions may show high multiple router symptom errors along with route validity
changes and route cycle changes as related to the router configurations. This
could show that the two router tables are being refreshed too frequently and
would also possibly correspond to other protocol analyzer symptoms such as
long response time for workstations communicating over the WAN, along with
timeouts and non-responsive conditions for upper-layer communications. This
is considered an important identification item in a protocol analysis session.

This particular example shows how critical it is to use a network analysis session to identify any anomalies related to network documentation and how
important it is to immediately identify an unknown device and redesign a
configuration that could be causing problems on the network.

In summary, it is important to always have the most current set of network
documentation prior to beginning a network baseline study. Such documentation includes information such as the network layout configuration, network
blueprints, file server and workstation documentation, any LAN and WAN site
maintenance and service logs, and any topology-specific documentation such
as LAN and WAN configurations or drawings, along with network protocol
configurations and router/switch diagrams and configurations.

The discussion now turns to network documentation as it relates to the
network baseline process.

6.1.1 Understanding Network Layout Documents

Various types of network documentation can assist an analyst when performing a network baseline session. Some network layout documents relate directly
to the topology or the configuration of a specific area of the network. Other
relevant network layout documents include network blueprints or documents
that contain information related to file server and workstation configuration.
LAN and WAN service logs may also prove useful (see Figure 6.2).

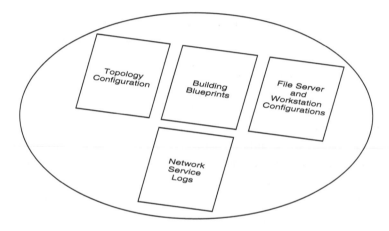

FIGURE 6.2 *The main types of network documentation required for a network baseline
study.*

Thorough network documentation is very important to the network baseline
process. Quite often when performing a network baseline or when making an
emergency protocol analysis, an analyst must immediately locate a certain
device within a large enterprise internetwork.

Sometimes a protocol analysis trace from a network baseline study shows that a
device is generating physical errors on certain topologies. A network baseline
study might also show that a device is generating network or upper-layer communication errors that also cause performance problems evident in the baseline
data-trace flow. These problems may relate to symptomatic occurrences affecting
the user base at the site.

By following the proper methodology for network baselining as discussed
earlier in this book—such as performing utilization measurements, reviewing
protocol percentages, and reviewing certain statistical metric measurements
such as error statistics—an analyst can most likely immediately identify the
address of the device causing site problems. The analyst can then contact

the relevant network support personnel to locate the device based on the type of error (physical, network, or application). If the network support group can find the device, both the analyst and the network support team can then quickly review the device's operation. They can also assess the impact of the network error on users' day-to-day operations, including application performance within a particular network area. Without current or accurate network documentation, however, finding the specific device can take a much longer time. Even after the device has been located, its impact on the LAN may take longer to understand if certain configuration information is not available. Obviously, network documentation can be extremely important to quick problem identification and problem resolution.

6.1.2 Building Blueprint Documentation

When performing a large network baseline, an analyst faces a slower process if he cannot locate problem devices (identified during data-trace analysis sessions). The process is also slowed if the analyst doesn't have the relevant configuration information (hardware and software builds, for example). Such missing information may impede the analyst's ability to immediately identify technical issues, and may therefore thwart the network baseline progression. The analyst might become bogged down in the data-acquisition process and not be able to move rapidly through the full network baseline cycle.

Among key documentation important to a successful network baseline is a building blueprint that includes an overleaf diagram of the network's cabling. The blueprint must show the building's physical layout as well as the network cabling point-to-point configuration. Each cable run should be labeled on all ends to match the blueprint and the cabling diagram. All patch panels should have affixed labels that show cable-to-cable linking.

A mere network topology diagram may not give an analyst all the necessary information. Even though a network topology diagram may point out LAN segments, WAN location points, and router/server configurations, it may not show exactly where these devices are located within a building.

The building blueprint, very importantly, should document the correlation between the network configuration diagrams and the location of devices within a building. When designing, configuring, and implementing any type of network, it is important to always update a building blueprint with the location of key devices in the network (such as internetwork hubs or switches that provide connections to the user area). Important information also includes main computer room file server locations and key router and switch platform placement within a particular network infrastructure.

A building blueprint should serve as a main reference document during the network design and implementation process. All network devices implemented on a network—such as hubs, switches, routers, and servers, and even possibly key workstations and printers—should be documented on the building blueprint.

Network support personnel should have a duplicate of the main building blueprint so that they can document any network changes. All network design and implementation personnel should try to ensure that the placement of any key network devices and cabling runs is properly marked on the blueprints (see Figure 6.3). This documentation is vital to a network baseline analyst and to any troubleshooting personnel.

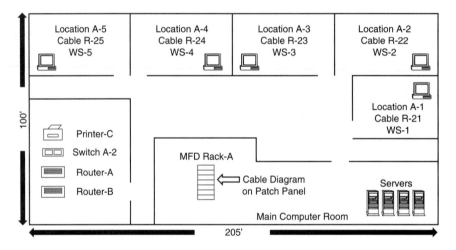

FIGURE 6.3 *A building blueprint.*

This documentation will be vital to a network baseline analyst or any troubleshooting personnel in the future when troubleshooting ongoing network problems within an enterprise infrastructure.

Often during a protocol analysis session, an analyst can locate a physical or network layer address that identifies a problem device. Even if the analyst identifies the device via the network baseline session, the network support personnel must be able to locate the actual device within the facility.

Even if the address appears to be active on the main file server within a location and the device is active on the network, it can sometimes be a challenge to locate the actual internetwork hub where the device is connected. And even if the network blueprint references the specific location of the internetwork hub, it may be necessary to follow a specific cable run throughout the facility to find the device (in a particular office or cubicle, for example).

In this particular case, an analyst with a detailed building blueprint can refer to the blueprint and determine the location of the address or device in question more rapidly. The analyst may then be able to quickly find the device and review its configuration (to hopefully determine why errors captured via the network baseline session generated). The detailed blueprint enables the analyst to isolate a network problem more rapidly.

Configuration documentation of servers or station devices within a facility is also vital to network troubleshooting and network baselining. Critical internal documentation includes hardware and software builds of a network file server or a main workstation in a facility.

The discussion now focuses on the important LAN file server or workstation configuration information as it relates to a network baseline study.

6.2 Network File Server and Station Documentation

When performing a network baseline session, it is important to review the configuration of any and all problem devices (identified as such during trace analysis). When reviewing a file server or a workstation, certain information is critical.

When performing a protocol analysis session, if a server is found to show an extremely slow response time, an analyst should immediately review the server's configuration. Certain server configuration information is critical (for example, the type of NIC as well as the card's software driver). The analyst should identify the physical network address of the server along with any network layer address information, such as an IP address. Certain hardware configuration information is also relevant, such as the memory allocation of the server (from an original hardware design standpoint). The analyst should review the server operating system parameters and active monitoring screens for the memory used throughout an operational cycle. By doing so, an analyst might find a memory-related problem (such as maximum use) in a server. Such a memory problem might be causing an excessive utilization of the server process modes and eventually causing slow response times (for attached users attempting to access the server). The analyst must also review other memory parameters, such as blocks of memory in use and blocks of memory free. It is also important to monitor processor utilization; the design or the hardware build of the server (such as the type of bus design) can affect processor utilization.

The analyst should monitor all utilization metrics for average and peak transitions of server usage. To do so, the analyst can closely monitor the configuration hardware build of the server and then monitor server statistical screens (perhaps by using a network operating system monitoring program). In a Novell server environment, the analyst can use a Novell monitoring program; in a Windows NT environment, the analyst can use a Performance Monitor program.

Other critical statistics for file servers include original cache buffers and total cache buffers utilized. Some server environments, such as Novell, have unique statistics that must be monitored, such as packet received buffers. Minimum and maximum server configuration settings can sometimes be adjusted; doing so enables you to fine-tune a server so that it performs more rapidly. A server usually has a minimum and maximum number of assigned connections as well. An analyst must review these configurations as well.

An area of importance in the server configuration is the amount of disk drive allocation available for maximum use and the amount of disk drive actually used (see Figure 6.4).

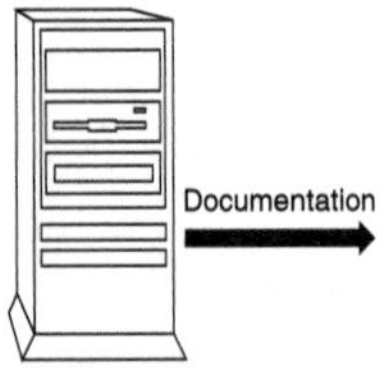

Customer: XYZ Corp.		Date: 10/10/99	
Server Name	XYZ_1		
NIC Driver and Card	Driver Version 3.02 3COM NIC		**Utilization**
MAC Address	3COMFB2104		
Server Version	NT 4.0		62%
Build Number	6125.6		
Service Pack Level	4		
Total Memory	512MB		21%
Memory in Use	385MB		
Virtual Memory Total	400MB		12%
Virtual Memory in Use	22%		
Virtual Memory Peak in Use	80%		19%
Processor Utilizatrion Average	13%		23%
Processor Utilization Peak	92%		

Documentation → Server XYZ_1

FIGURE 6.4 *A simple way to document a server configuration for access during a network baseline study.*

When reviewing a server environment, it is also important to consider the types and number of applications balanced or configured against a server. Quite often, after a network has been designed and implemented and a server layout configuration has been planned, new application deployment causes the applied user-connected configuration to increase rapidly.

In light of this, it is important for an analyst to understand that, from a baseline perspective, specific data may show that a network server is operating in a slow or over-maximized condition. In such a circumstance, the server may start to show slow response time or slow interpacket delta response time or general long acknowledgment time when responding to workstations attempting to access the server. When this type of error occurs, the analyst may be able to quickly work with the network support team to review the server's configuration, to identify suspect areas of the configuration, and to adjust certain settings to improve performance. In certain cases, it may be possible to immediately reconfigure the server; in other cases, it may be necessary to add hardware components to the server along with software updates to improve the server's performance.

Assume, for example, a server configured for basic word processing– or spreadsheet-type programs. For the first several months of the initial implementation, the server appears to operate quite well. Three to four months into the server's rollout cycle, the server starts to show slow performance when users access the server. The problem appears to be site wide and many users complain about performance issues. A baseline analyst can deploy a network analyzer in the main computer room and closely monitor the server. After setting a filter on the server, the baseline analyst can then monitor the server's response or delta time and the overall *effective file throughput* (EFT) as well as the general operation. If the server appears to show slow response time and extremely low EFT, the analyst can review the server's configuration. If the analyst determines that the server is highly utilized related to memory and utilization parameters, the analyst can search for a hardware configuration issue. If the number of actual user connections appears to have increased (relative to the assigned users), this may indicate that the problem partially relates to an under-balanced server (relative to the number of user connections applied).

Another error condition might result after new applications are deployed on the server (a new *Transmission Control Protocol* (TCP) application, for example). The server's original design might not have anticipated a new application's operational effect on the server's own operation. Assume, for example, that the analyst determines that the server is operating at 50% capacity with regard to the new TCP application. The baseline analyst may then be able to more closely identify the problem. When performing a protocol analysis session, the analyst might find TCP window errors (size exceeded, size frozen parameters, and TCP window not updating, for example). This could indicate that the server's TCP window (discussed later in this book) is not configured appropriately to deal with the actual application usage demanded by the user community.

Although a server may have adequate hardware resources (memory, disk space, and processor configurations, for example) to handle a new application, certain configurations may need to be changed to accommodate new demand. (For example, simple TCP configurations such as window size may have to be increased, for instance from 16KB to 32KB, to facilitate a more fluent TCP stream for all the new users accessing the new application.) The previous examples show just a few possible misconfigurations and the importance of network documentation to a network baseline exercise.

Site workstations throughout a facility have similar types of parameters that call for review. Such workstation parameters include memory, hardware configuration build, processor type, NIC configuration and driver type, as well as other parameters such as the *Network Operating System* (NOS) operating shell and certain drivers that enable users to access specific server environments (for example, Novell and Windows NT).

The important thing to note here is that a baseline analyst must always remember to immediately document any protocol analysis results that show anomalies and then forward them for baseline analysis review. If an analyst determines that a particular device needs configuration review (during the baseline analysis process or during the final reporting process), the analyst must contact the network support personnel who support that particular device. The analyst must also immediately check the network documentation for items such as a file server or a workstation. Properly documented information enables the analyst to more rapidly identify a reconfiguration or an adjustment parameter or possibly an additional design implementation required to resolve network issues. This is a key tie-in between network analysis and network documentation, which must be clearly noted.

The discussion now turns to the importance of documenting any adjustments to a network configuration (through network maintenance or service, for example).

6.3 Network Maintenance and Service Logs

During the mid-1960s and through the 1970s, it was always important to document all maintenance and service to mainframes and mini-hosts. A network service or consultative technician usually documented any maintenance to the main host. Just as in those early days of computing, we should still clearly note all service in a maintenance or service log. Relevant information must include service problems and their solutions. This information must be updated for a new configuration or a new application. As LANs and WANs became more widely implemented during the 1980s and 1990s, minor network service calls or adjustments to certain areas were often not recorded (because of the rapid deployment cycle of LANs and WANs to support enterprise applications).

It was not a major factor due to the amount of notes deployed or the importance of the main applications that were configured against the LAN or WAN. LANs and WANs now comprise the core infrastructure of many business operations. Because of this, it is vital to document all network maintenance as well as device upgrades (especially any that involve hardware or software configuration for operating systems as well as even application deployment modules) after each implementation. This documentation should enable analysts to relate any abnormal events to recent changes or modifications to the LAN or WAN.

When an analyst performs a network baseline session, the analyst will more than likely identify errors or anomalies in the trace analysis results that relate to the initial network documentation received prior to the baseline study. The analyst should immediately note the error and contact the network support personnel. Documentation showing recent changes to network devices (a new firmware implementation on a router module, a recent change to a type of switch made during a service call for a software upgrade, or even a new application deployment within a particular area, for example) may enable network support personnel to isolate the cause(s), troubleshoot, and resolve the problem more rapidly.

Network service personnel dealing with LAN and WAN infrastructure issues need ready access to all relevant information (including all "change" information). All such documentation should be kept on a database of some type within the network support area. Many large enterprise internetwork support teams do document all relevant information and make such readily available to service personnel. As the number of nodes being serviced in LAN and WAN environments increases, it is common for the documentation process to be skipped after a final problem resolution. This lack of documentation results because network support personnel are in a reactive mode and have to resolve issues quickly. Because of time constraints or other pressures, quite often the documentation of the network change or the network reconfiguration is not completed (see Figure 6.5).

Date	Device	Location	Service Note	Tech Name
10/1/99	Router 22-CR13	BLD 6 Location A-16	Placed Module-2 Refreshed ARP Cache Cold Boot Retested O.K.	D.N..
10/19/99	Server X22	BLD 1 Location MFD	Upgraded Memory from 128MB to .5 GIG Retested O.K.	D.N.

FIGURE 6.5 *A simple way to document LAN and WAN service records in a log.*

No matter what the situation, this step should not be skipped, and all changes and implementation or software upgrades in any LAN or WAN area should be clearly documented.

A simple approach that can be implemented within an enterprise internetwork support team is called "change control." The change control process involves submitting a planned request for a network modification or previous emergency change already applied to a board of individuals who monitor, approve, and document changes. Many large companies have implemented this approach, but many times a gap exists between the time when the change is made and when it is actually documented. When performing a network baseline session, an analyst should always keep an eye out for this type of occurrence.

An analyst should always keep in mind that when protocol trace analysis results show certain physical, network layer, or application events that do not appear to be normal, it may be possible that recent changes on the network have not yet been documented. A baseline analyst should focus on properly taking notes while paging through the trace and performing the processes discussed earlier in this book. The analyst should then take the documentation immediately to the network support team to review the occurrence. If the analyst thinks that the protocol analysis results from a network baseline study show a change related to a particular process evident in the network traffic flow, this event should then be communicated to the network support team. The network support team may be able to identify a recent change in the service log and relay to the analyst that the change is verified and that the event is normal.

Assume, for example, that a protocol analyst runs an analyzer in a main computer room and filters on a certain router. If the router appears to show a routing protocol update utilizing a routing protocol such as *Open Shortest Path First* (OSPF) and the analyst is not familiar with the protocol being configured (as noted in the original network documentation), this would be a notation that the analyst would quickly make. The notation could be as simple as this: Router 22A is generating OSPF updates on a certain frequency. During a follow-up session with the network support team, the analyst could quickly note that a router was recorded as generating OSPF and that the other routers throughout the facility are using *Routing Information Protocol* (RIP) on standard 30-second intervals. Because RIP updates are based on a distance vector routing protocol type (as discussed later in this book) and OSPF is a link state–based routing protocol (also discussed later in this book), the two routing protocol types would be identified as possibly incompatible but may not be configured for a fine-tuned routing update cycle. The network support team could review the routers and then relay to the analyst that they are aware of a recent server log entry for the OSPF modification and that the site team will be updating other routers in the facility to OSPF (see Figure 6.6).

This process enables the baseline analyst to modify how the network baseline sampling session related to this event will be reviewed. This event could then be logged as an anomalous event that is not of major concern, and the baseline analyst could then move on to further network analysis focus items more critical and relevant to the session. This is just one example of the type of event where the network service or maintenance logs or change control logs could prove extremely helpful.

Issue	Router 22-A Incoming route change every 30 seconds. Router required a 3.2 patch for OSPF. Router was running RIP V.2.0
Action	Performed upgrade & rebooted network. Route 22 changes non-existent.
	D.N. 10/31/99

FIGURE 6.6 *How detailed information related to a network modification can be entered into a service log.*

All network service implementations and network changes should be fully documented in a logbook or database within the facility. On large internetwork infrastructures, the database or custom program approach works best for the documentation review. Within certain NOS environments, such as Novell and Windows NT, various third-party applications are available for this process.

The key point is that change and modification information must be documented. In the computer room of critical servers, hosts, and other devices such as routers and switches, it may even be advantageous to include a logbook close to the device in the computer room so that it can be referenced out upon the change. The logbook could serve as the physical entry point and could be reviewed on a weekly basis and updated in a change control program and automated database.

The following section discusses the key topology documentation vital to a network baseline session.

6.4 Examining Topology-Specific Documentation

When performing a network baseline session, it is always beneficial to have network diagrams or topology information available prior to the session. This information enables an analyst to quickly decide how the network baseline plan for deploying a network analyzer should be built. Later in this book, you learn some of the key data-acquisition planning processes required for a full network baseline study. For the purposes of this discussion, it is important to emphasize that topology documentation is critical to planning a baseline process.

When planning a baseline study, a key item to consider is the position of analyzers for a network baseline session. Such consideration and determination requires an understanding of the network topology.

Prior to a network baseline study, an analyst should always attempt to gather any network documentation that shows the topology diagram of the LAN and WAN areas of the network. Other important information includes the network protocols and operating system documentation, along with router and switch configurations within a facility. This section discusses these key items.

When performing a network baseline, the LAN layout must be documented. On a LAN diagram, it is important to note items such as the number of nodes configured and how they interconnect to a specific area within each site. With regard to the user area, it is important to understand that in each user area of the LAN a specific number of users may connect to a hub, switch, or router within a main closet that is closest to the user community accessing the network. On certain technical layout documents, this may be identified as a user closet or an *Intermediate Distribution Facility* (IDF). The user closet or IDF area may have a device such as a switch or hub that connects all the users through a cabling scheme to that closet. It is vital to document and update the number of users connected to that device, and then to specify the type of device in the configuration that connects the user community in that area. This particular IDF point will most likely have a cabling path that links to a main computer room or other areas of the internetwork, such as a WAN location router. The key is that the link from the main user IDF link up to the main computer room or a *Main Distribution Facility* (MDF) should be clearly, yet simply shown on the diagram as an uplink or cabling channel to the main computer room or MDF.

The main computer room or MDF may have a set of main hubs, switches, or routers that serve as central devices connecting all the user closets throughout a large enterprise infrastructure; these devices must be documented. The MDF devices may interconnect to a critical WAN router that connects to several other LAN locations (such as 10–20 LAN locations linked through a WAN).

On the highest level diagram of a global network, the main computer room or MDF router used for WAN connections should show a channel link, such as a Frame Relay, or a dedicated WAN link to other LAN locations. A flat layout diagram can show the links to the WAN sites. The WAN site can be clearly, yet simply identified on the diagram and the type of router or switch that connects to the WAN can also be shown. With this type information in hand, the analyst can review a one-page document that diagrams the global enterprise internetwork.

Consider, for example, a main computer that connects three user-area IDF closets. The main high-level diagram would most likely show an MDF room with a
centralized router/switch linking down to the multiple IDF closet areas. The
link down to each closet area would be clearly diagrammed and the IDF closet
areas would show a switch, router, or hub that services the particular user area.
The number of users in each IDF could be noted as IDF downlink runs (showing 24 or 48 users connected to an IDF closet area, for example). This information follows across the one-page diagram and shows all three user areas as
within the one LAN site. If the centralized MDF computer room also houses
main servers, these could also be placed on the high-level diagram. The main
computer room could show the interconnection to the 10 WAN network sites by
showing the type of WAN link symbol and the type of WAN router or switch at
the remote sites. The remote site could be named on the high-level diagram.
Such a high-level global diagram can show a company's local area internetwork
(see Figure 6.7).

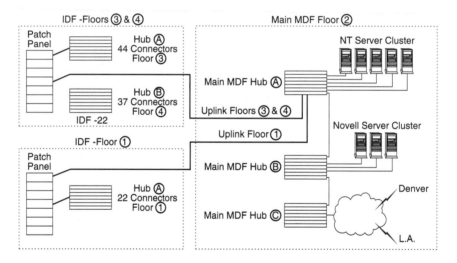

FIGURE 6.7 *A diagram of a one-city location internetwork can be documented for
reference during a network baseline study.*

A further breakdown of each area of the network into separate subdiagrams
could prove beneficial. If one user IDF area (User Area 1) uses a hub within the
computer room that is based on a switched platform, the main diagram header
would be "User Area 1." The diagram would show the user hub area (1) and
the links down to the 24 or 48 users within the user area. The user connections
could be clearly shown on the diagram. This type of diagram could then be
duplicated for all three IDF layouts.

A MDF subdiagram could further document the main computer room. A detailed diagram could show the main computer room or MDF housing the servers and also show the main internal router switch within the computer room that links to the three user areas along with the link to the WAN router within the main MDF area. Any critical file servers located within the facility could also be indicated on a main computer room or MDF subdiagram (see Figure 6.8).

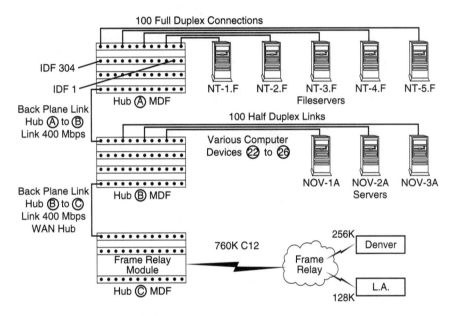

FIGURE 6.8 *Documenting an internal one-site LAN MDF room.*

A WAN network diagram could also prove beneficial to an analyst dealing with a large infrastructure. A WAN topology diagram (for a Frame Relay network, for example) could show extensive detail of a Frame Relay internetwork. All the sites could be illustrated on a one-page diagram. Each WAN site could show the type of router in a simple picture format along with the assignment of addressing formats, such as the IP address and the location of the device in the WAN. The type of Frame Relay link could then be identified and the inter-switching system cloud of the Frame Relay link related to the Frame Relay cloud could be shown on a one-page diagram. All the WAN network sites could be tied together in a logical layout. The allocation of the assignment for the Frame Relay link could also be identified, such as the *data-link control identi-fier* (DLCI). Each site could also have a standard bandwidth allocation as well as a committed and burst allocation for Frame Relay. The bandwidth allocation on the Frame Relay channels could also be identified on a one-page diagram (see Figure 6.9).

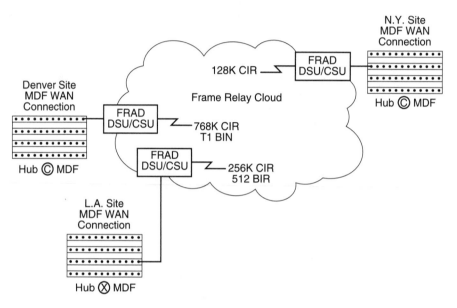

FIGURE 6.9 *Documentation of a global cross-city location can be documented for review during a network baseline study.*

When reviewing other topology information, it is important to keep in mind that device operating systems may be relevant or active on the routers or switches and that these may affect operation and performance. Some servers may be running various protocol stacks while other servers are running com-patible or different protocol stacks that relate to the computing channels or application profiles. Descriptive protocol notes should always accompany any devices placed on a diagram.

A server noted as Server 1, for example, could have the application profile noted (Lotus Notes, Word, or any other type of active application, for example). The active protocols on the NICs could also be diagramed (for instance, TCP active on NIC 1 *or* Novell protocols active, such as IPX and SPX, on NIC 2).

At times, certain channels of the network, such as WANs and LANs, may be used for certain protocol dataflow. In such cases, the network channels could be diagrammed on the network and could show the protocol types intended and defined to the network channel.

In WAN designs, it is common to separate certain protocol types, especially in large computing enterprise internetworks such as TCP/IP and Novell. In some cases, it may be necessary to have separate *Frame Relay Assembler Dissembler* (FRAD) channels for protocol or application separation. In this type of situation, the WAN diagram should reference the protocol communication across the channel. These few examples illustrate the importance of documenting network protocols with a network diagram.

When considering critical network passthrough devices, such as switches or routers, it is important to accurately document the configuration of a bridge, switch, or router.

Multiple interface cards within a switch or router may connect to different segments in the LAN or WAN infrastructure. Each segment connected to routers and switches should be identified by the physical and any network layer address assigned, such as an IP address.

Other parameters may also be important, such as cut-through or store-and-forward switching in the switching environment.

In the router environment, other parameters are important such as routing protocol update frequency, keep alive timing, buffer size, maximum transmission unit size, encapsulation type, queuing strategy, interface statistics such as input and output rate, as well as packet conditions that relate to physical conditions such as resets, collisions, and general queuing operations.

Proper documentation of switching, routing, and internetwork hub devices facilitates rapid cause isolation and troubleshooting when performing a network baseline session (see Figure 6.10).

Often you will detect delays when analyzing and filtering on the switches and routers in the computer room during a network analysis session. Clear router or switch configuration information assists in determining whether the particular device has a parameter that may be limiting the *maximum transmission unit* (MTU) type or the maximum frame size forwarded, or it may show a parameter problem related to packet loss or packet drop.

Device Name	MTU Size	Keep Alive	Queuing	Routing Protocol
Router Ⓐ Interface ②	1500	60 Sec.	FIFO	RIP V2
Router Ⓑ Interface ③	4500	60 Sec.	FIFO	RIP V2
Router Ⓒ Interface WAN	1500	60 Sec. & Link State	FIFO	RIP V2 or OSPF

FIGURE 6.10   *How router and switch parameters can be documented.*

During a protocol analysis session, for example, an analyst may encounter excessive broadcast traffic levels in a certain user area. If the broadcast traffic level is centered on Novell and AppleTalk and appears to show inbound broadcast traffic from an exterior WAN location that has packet traffic flowing inbound to the specific area being monitored but has no correlation for devices or servers used in this area, an abnormal condition may be indicated. If the frame-per-second rate of the broadcast is in the storm category area, the switch or hub in the main IDF user closet in question may not be configured to filter out the protocol traffic from the other sites.

In this case, the configuration may not prevent the IDF users from experiencing unneeded inbound broadcast packet storms from exterior protocols. By performing the proper protocol analysis session, identifying the issue, and then contacting the network support team, you may be able to reference the documentation related to the switch in the IDF closet. If the switch is found to have a backdated version of software that is not compliant with broadcast filtering or Network Layer 3 routing, it would be wise to consider this switch for a Network Layer 3 routing or broadcast domain control implementation via virtual LAN configuration.

The important thing to note here is that through network baselining you can identify issues and take notes that you can present to the network support team for their reference. Upon referencing the documentation, it may be immediately clear that the version of a switch or a particular router configuration does not allow for network layer 3 filtering, and this may be the heart of the problem. Obviously, if everything is clearly documented in the switch and router area, you can more rapidly isolate the concern.

6.5 Closing Statement on Network Documentation

This chapter has discussed the importance of network documentation as it relates to network baselining and network troubleshooting. Many programs enable database logging of key physical network addresses and network location information for devices and operational configuration. Other programs enable you to create extremely useful visual documents (such as diagrams). VISIO is one such extremely robust program that relates to network topology and LAN and WAN documentation. Many large enterprise internetworks throughout the global networking environment use this program. The VISIO program is easy to configure and use and extremely important for network documentation. The program enables you to implement most of the key network LAN and WAN channel links currently used in topology and protocol environments of large infrastructure enterprises. The program enables you to configure the different types of switches, bridges, and routers used throughout the infrastructure. Other programs on the market also enable you to create this type of documentation.

It is important for an analyst to know that *prior* to a network baseline study, network documentation will be valuable. If no network documentation is available (such as from a LAN or WAN topology program), the analyst may feel less inclined to properly plan a network baseline session. At the very least, prior to a baseline session the analyst should walk through a facility and review the placement of devices and determine how the placement relates to the available network documentation. Even such a limited scenario assists the analyst in planning a proper baseline study from a data-acquisition positioning standpoint. Data acquisition planning procedures are discussed in more detail later in this book.

For the record, certain documentation related to the placement of devices within a facility is critical. Accurate building blueprints are definitely required for critical network troubleshooting processes.

Information related to server, workstation, switch, router, and hub internal configurations is extremely valuable to the network baselining and troubleshooting process. During the network baseline process, an analyst may encounter many conditions where the protocol analysis results identify slow performance or anomalies in traffic flow. It is very important that the documentation for file servers, critical workstations, printers, hubs, switches, and routers be available for review after isolation of problems during a protocol analysis session.

In closing, the LAN and WAN diagrams are among the highest level and most important type of diagrams required for network baselining. When reviewing the discussions on network topologies and protocols presented later in this book, keep in mind that network documentation plays an important part when performing an accurate network baseline session in a rapid manner and when isolating problems through cause analysis and when troubleshooting with a protocol analyzer.

6.6 Moving Forward

Throughout this book, and specifically in chapter 7, you will explore some of the unique case studies that have been encountered throughout my consulting career in the industry as a lead baseline analysis in the LAN Scope analysis team. The LAN Scope analysis team has studied more than 8500 networks in 11 years. The case studies presented are relevant to many network topology and protocol configurations. It is likely that you will find at least one or two of these case studies relevant to your networking environment.

These case studies present some of the benefits and "real world" experiences that were encountered through network baselining and protocol analysis by my work with the LAN Scope analysis team.

Detailed methods in reviewing protocol types such as Windows NT, Novell, TCP/IP, and other main protocols are presented in this material. A detailed discussion on network topology specific analysis techniques for various topologies such as Ethernet, Token Ring, FDDI, ATM, and WAN infrastructures proceeds.

Real world network baselining processes such as data acquisition planning, data acquisition, and final network baseline report development discussions help to wrap up the book.

CHAPTER **7**

LAN and WAN Protocols

This chapter discusses the major protocols that can be captured, decoded, and reviewed using protocol analysis during a network baselining exercise. The protocol types chosen for review in this chapter include most of the major protocols encompassed within the *local area network* (LAN) and *wide area network* (WAN) environment in today's enterprise internetwork infrastructure.

When performing a network baseline project, it is necessary to completely investigate and decode the packets received during a protocol analysis session. Each captured packet contains a specific set of protocol layers encapsulated inside the physical frame header.

For instance, an Ethernet frame could contain the *Internet Protocol* (IP) or *Internetwork Packet Exchange* (IPX) protocol at the network layer within a particular packet. Other protocol layers could also be used such as the transport layer, which could include the encapsulation of protocols such as *Transmission Control Protocol* (TCP) or *Sequence Packet Exchange* (SPX). The protocol-layering systems usually change depending on the *network operating system* (NOS) and the applied protocol suite.

Another example is that in a Windows NT transmission it is common to capture packets that use a physical frame header, which would then encapsulate the IP protocol at the network layer, the TCP protocol at the transport layer, along with the NetBIOS protocol at the session layer, and *Server Message Block* (SMB) at the application layer. This is just one example of a particular protocol-layering sequence.

Protocol information for individual packets can be clearly displayed within the layers of each packet by viewing a protocol analyzer summary and detail display window. The display of the protocols depends on the type of network analyzer being used during the session. An analyst must be able to monitor the internals of a packet to understand the type of protocol layering involved, and how the protocol layering relates to the interaction of the network communication session being investigated.

Every protocol suite involved in a network transmission is affected by the NOS design, which is invoked by the vendor providing the workstation-to-server communication scheme for the particular LAN or WAN environment. For instance, the Novell protocol suite differs from the Windows NT protocol suite.

It is also important to understand that each protocol suite has specific layers that are used for certain processes. Each specific layer within a protocol suite is mentioned as a separate protocol within its own right. Each individual protocol has field categories specific to the protocol type.

During a baseline analysis session, an analyst must keep a technical notebook to carefully reference any key information identified in the baseline session. This process does take time, but proves extremely valuable to the development of an analyst's required technical skill set.

The following sections of this chapter present the key protocol-layering mechanisms used for each protocol, along with techniques for analyzing the protocol suite. This chapter covers most of the major protocols within the internetwork environment.

Some of the protocols presented may have varying fields related to internal operations, which may change depending on update releases of the NOS or variations of software patches provided by vendors. The material presented in this chapter is based on the base specifications for each one of the protocol types as engaged by a particular protocol suite.

Some general analysis techniques should be noted before moving forward with this chapter. When investigating a packet within a protocol analysis session, it is important to understand the particular protocol-layering mechanism. After a data trace capture has been completed and saved, the analyst must display the internal data in both a summary and detailed screen view. Next the analyst can invoke the "paging through the trace" process, as mentioned earlier in this book, and just take notes on the type of physical header used and any other types of protocols used for encapsulation. The analyst should carefully note the network layer protocol, along with the type of transport protocol, if engaged, and whether connections are being maintained. Next, note the type of application protocol involved.

An analyst must understand the type of protocol-layering schemes working between workstations and file servers. It will be helpful to carefully analyze individual packets to truly understand the application process flow and the internetwork operations involved in such.

Some NOS and software application development engineering teams choose to use certain NOSs expressly to engage the protocol layers inherent in the operating system's design.

As noted earlier, with the Windows NT protocol suite, the NOS inherently uses IP at the network layer and TCP at the transport layer. Because of this alone, many application developers have chosen the Windows NT operating system as a protocol suite because it is compliant and form-fits their particular application dataflow requirements. In certain cases, the application developers may also invoke different fields within protocol layer operations that will cause the application layer, transport layer, or other layers of the protocol suite to produce various custom operations for an application.

The only way to understand this process is to fully analyze the protocol-layering scheme at the start of an upper-layer review analysis session.

As noted earlier in this book, it is important to take detailed notes on the protocol-layering scheme. Most protocol analyzers used for network baselining can usually display the protocol-layering schemes in the summary level and show all active layers. If the protocol analyzer being used does not have this feature, the individual packets may have to be decoded at a detailed level, and the actual internals of the packets investigated.

This chapter now focuses on each one of the major protocol suites, along with a review of the key layers of the protocol suites and associated technical fields. Certain specialized techniques relate to specific protocol suites.

7.1 Analysis of the Novell Protocol Suite

The Novell protocol suite is well known throughout the global networking industry. The Novell protocol suite was introduced in the mid-1980s when the original Novell NetWare NOS was unleashed. The Novell NetWare operating system achieved immediate success. The NetWare NOS was designed specifically to fit small-to-medium internetworks from an original design standpoint. The popularity of Novell NetWare NOS grew, because it adequately supported general node-to-node communications for local area networking processes. It also was very user friendly in terms of access for general application deployment throughout the internetworking environment. Companies of all sizes found the Novell NOS to form-fit their requirements for distributed communications between PCs in both the LAN and WAN infrastructures.

The Novell protocol suite was originally designed and based on the implementation of an application layer protocol called *NetWare Core Protocol* (NCP). This protocol was designed to operate inherently between a workstation and a server for access. The NCP was also designed to work internally with a network layer protocol process that engaged a protocol called *Internetwork Packet Exchange* (IPX). The transport layer protocol that was engaged for connection-based processes was called *Sequence Packet Exchange* (SPX). Certain components of the Novell protocol suite were somewhat similar in design to layers of the Xerox protocols. The Novell NetWare protocol IPX is comparable to the *Xerox Networking Systems* (XNS) protocol for network layer operations, for example. The Novell SPX protocol is similar to Xerox's *Sequence Packet Protocol* (SPP) for the transport layer protocol design.

When the Novell NetWare operating system was originally unleashed, the applied protocol suite included five main protocols for general communication. The IPX protocol was intended for general network layer communications, the SPX protocol was intended for general transport layer communications, and NCP was intended for access and update for workstation to file server communication calls. Novell also implemented a routing protocol-layering system. Novell *Routing Information Protocol* (RIP) is a Novell version of the *Transmission Control Protocol/Internet Protocol* (TCP/IP) RIP version, but Novell RIP is based on a 60-second update. Novell NetWare was also designed with a protocol to advertise the services of NetWare servers for updates every 60 seconds through a protocol called *Service Advertising Protocol* (SAP). The Novell SAP updates allow different Novell servers to maintain a database of all available Novell services. The NetWare protocol suite was enhanced after the original release to allow for a more robust application layer protocol process through a derivative of NCP called *NetWare Core Protocol Burst* (NCPB) (see Figure 7.1).

The following sections detail some of the main protocol-layering schemes used in the Novell protocol suite.

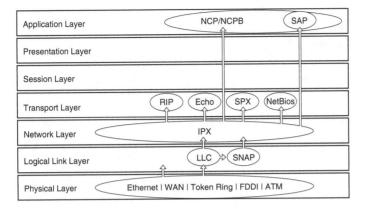

FIGURE 7.1 *The Novell protocol suite model.*

7.1.1 IPX

IPX was designed to allow for network layer communications to occur. There is no connection actually maintained within the IPX protocol. It does not actually guarantee a final delivery of any data across an internetwork channel. However, it does allow for two nodes to initiate communication and for communication to commence. It does not maintain a connection for the actual protocol sequencing.

The IPX protocol does allow for setting up of the communication channel between two NetWare nodes and the transfer of data in relation to a unit of measure. The IPX protocol is not normally used for extensive broadcasting, but there is currently a derivative of standard IPX called IPX WAN broadcast processes, which does allow for a higher broadcast sequencing cycle (see Figure 7.2).

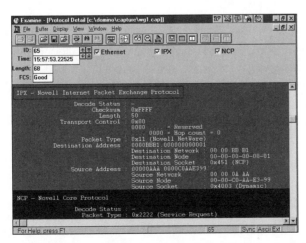

FIGURE 7.2 *A IPX packet from an internal view as layered with NCP.*

The IPX packet has the following specific field configurations:

- **Checksum field.** This field is normally used for an algorithm check to occur in communications of two nodes using an IPX transmission. The field is based on an algorithm check that engages a *cyclical redundancy check* (CRC). The field is 2 bytes long.

- **Length field.** This field represents the length of the IPX protocol layer, plus any other protocol layers encapsulated within IPX, along with any data within the IPX encapsulation cycle. This field is 2 bytes long and again identifies the total length of the IPX header, plus other protocols and data involved.

- **Transport Control field.** This field is used by the IPX header to identify how many hops or IPX-based networks have been traversed across a network-generated transmission cycle. This is also called the Novell hop-count field. The Transport Control field is based on a 1-byte length configuration.

- **Packet Type field.** This 1-byte field identifies the next upper-layer protocol that will be encapsulated inside the IPX packet.

- **Source and Destination Network fields.** These fields are normally 4 bytes long and indicate the source or destination Novell network number assigned for the IPX transmission.

- **Source and Destination node.** These fields indicate the Novell device communicating, such as a workstation or a server. This field normally includes a physical address such as a *Media Access Control* (MAC) address used for higher-layer identification. This is a 6-byte field.

- **Source or Destination socket.** The source or destination socket within the IPX header indicates the actual type of upper-layer protocol process within the Novell protocol stream being communicated to for operation. In this type of call, there can be an identification, such as a NetWare server or an actual NetWare application process, or types of custom socket as designed by an application developer. This field is a 2-byte field that allows for an identification of a protocol communication area and is somewhat similar to a port in the TCP nomenclature (see Figure 7.3).

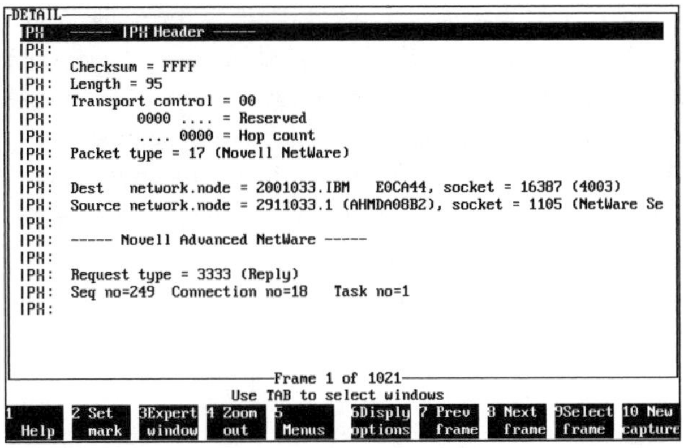

```
┌DETAIL─────────────────────────────────────────────────────────┐
│ IPH     ───── IPH Header ─────                                 │
│ IPH:                                                           │
│ IPH:  Checksum = FFFF                                          │
│ IPH:  Length = 95                                              │
│ IPH:  Transport control = 00                                   │
│ IPH:       0000 .... = Reserved                                │
│ IPH:       .... 0000 = Hop count                               │
│ IPH:  Packet type = 17 (Novell NetWare)                        │
│ IPH:                                                           │
│ IPH:  Dest   network.node = 2001033.IBM   E0CA44, socket = 16387 (4003)│
│ IPH:  Source network.node = 2911033.1 (AHMDA08B2), socket = 1105 (NetWare Se│
│ IPH:                                                           │
│ IPH:  ───── Novell Advanced NetWare ─────                      │
│ IPH:                                                           │
│ IPH:  Request type = 3333 (Reply)                              │
│ IPH:  Seq no=249  Connection no=18    Task no=1                │
│ IPH:                                                           │
│                    ┌Frame 1 of 1021┐                           │
│                    Use TAB to select windows                   │
│ 1    2 Set 3Expert 4 Zoom 5      6Display 7 Prev 8 Next 9Select 10 New│
│ Help   mark window out   Menus  options  frame  frame  frame capture│
└────────────────────────────────────────────────────────────────┘
```

FIGURE 7.3 *Another view of an IPX header with all main fields active.*

7.1.2 SPX

The SPX protocol is normally used in a Novell transmission environment that requires maintenance of a connection. The SPX protocol is engaged by the Novell NOS or an application developer for the express purpose of maintaining a connection in a Novell internetworking environment. SPX is a transport layer protocol.

The connection is maintained by engaging certain fields such as the Connection Control field, the Sequencing and Acknowledgment Number fields, and the Allocation field. Two devices within the Novell internetworking environment, considered network nodes, can communicate back and forth using the SPX protocol layer to encapsulate data for transmission while also maintaining a connection sequence process.

The actual connection sequence can be continuous with data flowing on an ongoing basis, or the SPX layer can be used just for a polling and acknowledgment cycle (to maintain a connection, for example).

The NetWare protocol suite has two versions of active SPX: SPXI and SPXII. The SPXII version protocol allows for a packet larger than 576 bytes to be used for a *Protocol Data Unit* (PDU) inside the SPX header and also allows for variances in operation as related to the allocation and windowing design within the SPX protocol header.

The SPX protocol is specialized, because some fields allow for polling on event cycles, as required. An internal end-to-end acknowledgment and sequence process can be maintained through endpoint monitoring. The SPX process engages an examination between two NetWare nodes of the sequence acknowledgment and allocation-based fields. The following fields are considered active as SPX configuration fields and are important for analysis (see Figure 7.4).

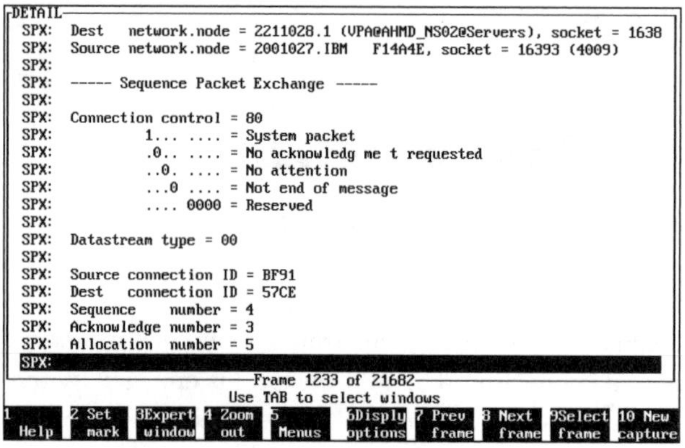

```
┌DETAIL──────────────────────────────────────────────────────────────────────┐
│ SPX:  Dest    network.node = 2211028.1 (VPA@AHMD_NSO2@Servers), socket = 1638│
│ SPX:  Source network.node = 2001027.IBM   F14A4E, socket = 16393 (4009)      │
│ SPX:                                                                         │
│ SPX:  ----- Sequence Packet Exchange -----                                   │
│ SPX:                                                                         │
│ SPX:  Connection control = 80                                                │
│ SPX:               1... .... = System packet                                 │
│ SPX:               .0.. .... = No acknowledg me t requested                  │
│ SPX:               ..0. .... = No attention                                  │
│ SPX:               ...0 .... = Not end of message                            │
│ SPX:               .... 0000 = Reserved                                      │
│ SPX:                                                                         │
│ SPX:  Datastream type = 00                                                   │
│ SPX:                                                                         │
│ SPX:  Source connection ID = BF91                                            │
│ SPX:  Dest    connection ID = 57CE                                           │
│ SPX:  Sequence    number = 4                                                 │
│ SPX:  Acknowledge number = 3                                                 │
│ SPX:  Allocation  number = 5                                                 │
│ SPX:                                                                         │
└──────────────────────────Frame 1233 of 21682───────────────────────────────┘
                           Use TAB to select windows
┌──┬─────┬───────┬──────┬─────┬─────────┬───────┬───────┬───────┬────────┐
│1 │2 Set│3Expert│4 Zoom│5    │6Display │7 Prev │8 Next │9Select│10 New  │
│Help│ mark│ window│ out  │Menus│ options │ frame │ frame │ frame │capture │
└──┴─────┴───────┴──────┴─────┴─────────┴───────┴───────┴───────┴────────┘
```

FIGURE 7.4   *An internal view of an SPX protocol header.*

- **Connection Control field.** This field is used to identify the type of connection active between two specific NetWare nodes. Certain active connection processes can be identified, such as system, acknowledgment process active, connection active, attention active, and process inactive or process ending. This is a 1-byte field.

- **Data Stream Type field.** This field is identified in an SPX header, and is intended to internally flag to the upper-layer application sequence the type of data encapsulated within the SPX header. If there is an end-of-the-message cycle, this field configuration is also active. This field is 1 byte long.

- **Source and Destination ID field.** This particular field identifies the main virtual assignment from the NetWare NOS of the SPX virtual assignment for the transport connection process. This is somewhat similar to a TCP port assignment. The source and destination ID is a virtual assignment applied upon connection when using the SPX protocol for transport between two NetWare nodes. A virtual source and destination ID is assigned to each Novell node endpoint (relevant to the internal process using SPX for a connection-based cycle). This field is 2 bytes long.

- **Sequence Number field.** This field indicates the sequence of the SPX transmission between two NetWare nodes. The sequence number alternates upon transmission between two nodes on an ongoing basis. The sequence number increases depending on the sequence of data being transmitted in relation to the connection being maintained. This field is 2 bytes long.

- **Acknowledgment Number field.** This field is engaged in direct correlation with the Sequence Number field, but in converse correlation of the sequence number used between two NetWare nodes utilizing SPX for communication. The Acknowledgment Number field updates upon dynamic assignment in reverse order with the Sequence Number field between two nodes communicating with the SPX-based connection. Note that the bidirectional dataflow between the two devices is consistently updated within the acknowledgment number sequence on an ongoing basis. The acknowledgment number and the sequence number work together to maintain the connection sequencing between the two NetWare nodes communicating via SPX.

- **Allocation Number field.** This field indicates the number of Novell receive buffers available for transmit and receive as to available count between the source and destination virtual SPX ID assignments. This is somewhat similar to a TCP windowing scheme for inside the TCP operation for available window size. The Allocation Number field operates somewhat differently in the Novell environment, and is based on the allocation as related to receive buffers between the two NetWare endpoints communicating with SPX for connection.

- **Data field.** This optional field includes the PDU, and if active is variable in length. If the field is not active, the SPX protocol usually includes application layer protocols as encapsulated inside the SPX header. An SPX packet can carry pure data, and data can be encapsulated; the size of this field varies in length depending on the data size or requirements in this particular field (see Figure 7.5).

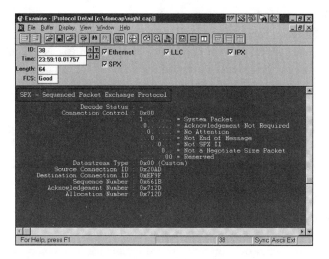

FIGURE 7.5 *Another view of a SPX header with all fields active.*

7.1.3 Network Core Protocol

The Network Core Protocol was the first application layer protocol that was developed and used by the Novell operating system development team. The protocol was key to the success of Novell NetWare, because its main purpose was to allow a workstation to call on a server for a particular type of access (such as a connection, login, or file access). The server uses the same protocol to respond to the respective requesting Novell NetWare workstation node.

This particular protocol is very clear and easy to investigate via protocol analysis. Tips on analyzing NCP are offered later in this chapter.

The following is a description of the key internal field configurations for NCP. Note that the NCP is based on a request-and-reply sequence for standard NCP. The NCPB protocol uses a different type of request-and-reply mechanism.

The focus now turns to the standard NCP basic mechanism operation. The communication mechanism used is a standard Request sequence, in which a workstation performs an NCP Request and a NetWare server then provides an NCP Reply on a per-packet basis.

The following list identifies the NCP Request sequence configuration fields, along with the NCP Reply sequence configuration fields (see Figure 7.6).

FIGURE 7.6 *An NCP request header.*

- **Request Type.** This field is normally used by NCP clients, such as a workstation, to request information from a Novell server. This field is normally noted as a Code 2222 for standard NCP request operations (a file access or file read sequence call to a server, for example).

  This field can also be active for other key request types such as a Code 1111, which requests NCP to create a service connection. Code 5555 requests a connection breakdown. If burst mode is active, which would only be active and used in NCPB, Code 7777 applies. This is a 2-byte field that indicates the request type.

- **Sequence Number.** This field allows for the sequencing of a transfer related to NCP to be referenced on a cyclical basis between a workstation and a server. The sequence number updates upon each transmission. Each outbound request from a workstation that is replied to is eventually followed by another sequence number that normally increments by one. This may vary depending on the type of transmission involved in the overall data cycle. Normally, the sequence number is tracked and is incremental depending on the number of requests from a workstation. This is a 1-byte field.

- **Connection Number Low.** This field is used to identify the type of connection number assigned to the NetWare node as compared with the NetWare NOS task-tracking connections. This can be cross-reviewed in the Novell monitoring screens. The key is that the connection number will be assigned to low if the NOS is configured for connections under a certain node count level. This is a 1-byte field.

- **Connection Number High.** This field identifies the type of connection if the node count is exceeded based on a NOS-specific identification separation level. Certain operating systems in the NetWare environment allow for a higher number of connections, depending on the high count of connection. The Connection High field is used to identify the connection number, which is also going to be similar to the connection number low assigned by the NOS for the Novell workstation node. This is a 1-byte field.

- **Task Number.** This particular field identifies the actual I/O cycle task assigned by the Novell NetWare operating system to the particular workstation node. Note that the task number will change, depending on the requirement of the operating system (which assigns different tasks on an ongoing dynamic cycle). This is a dynamic field and is not consistently tracked in network analysis because it changes so rapidly, depending on the I/O cycle of the server. This is a 1-byte field.

- **Function.** This field is extremely important to network analysis and includes the actual function of the NCP request sequence. Note that the Function field changes based on the request type chosen, such as open a file, close a file, or create a connection. The NCP function is the actual NCP vector for the type of workstation NCP request being performed on the server. The field indicates the request type identification. The function identifies the actual action being requested by the workstation node. This is a 1-byte field and directly affects the following two fields: Subfunction and Subfunction Structure Length.

  - **Subfunction.** This field acts as a subvector off the main Function field and identifies a subfunction such as "read all files with a modify flag active." In other words, this is a subfunction of the main function called on by the NetWare workstation node. This is a 1-byte field.

- **Subfunction Structure Length.** This field further identifies any more specific operations related to the main function or subfunction that are required by the workstation endpoint communicating with the NetWare server. This is a 2-byte field and allows for varied communication as related to custom structuring for the function request.

- **Data (variable).** This field is a variable-length field and may include actual data if encapsulating data is active in the NCP reply process. This is usually not active on a request cycle and is normally only active on a Reply sequence. This is a valid field format, however, for the NCP request header (see Figure 7.7).

FIGURE 7.7 *An NCP reply header.*

- **NetWare Core Protocol Reply.** This field indicates the type of reply from the NetWare server and response provided back to the NetWare workstation node. The server normally replies with a Code 3333 if all functions are active and the NCP reply is responding to a direct correlated NCP request Code 2222. If the NCPB mode is active a Code 7777 is used, which would not directly correlate to standard NCP. If a particular server operation cannot respond to a NetWare inbound request Code 2222 and the server is busy related to task I/O or other server functions discussed later in this chapter, an NCP reply Code 9999 may be provided. This indicates that the request is being processed and the server may be busy. If all active communications are normal, this field is normally decoded as a standard Code 3333 mode reply. This is a 2-byte field.

- **Sequence Number.** This field indicates the server-based sequence NCP reply to an inbound NCP request from a workstation. If a workstation NCP Request sequence number is noted as 128, an NCP reply with sequence 128 should also be provided for the Request sequence number 128. On the next inbound request of 129 from a workstation, the server should reply to active sequence number 129 and so forth. This will directly correlate to inbound requests from certain workstations, based on the actual task assigned for the server I/O cycle. This is a 1-byte field.

- **Connection Number Low.** This field is used to maintain the connection-sequencing operation upon reverse dataflow between a workstation and a server. The actual connection number is assigned based on the assignment level within the NOS. This will also directly correlate to the main operating system function. This is normally a 1-byte field.

- **Connection Number High.** This field is active if the connection between the workstation and the server is being maintained is above a certain operating system level based on a certain deployment for license at the account. This is normally a higher number than, for instance, 285 on active communications. This is a 1-byte field.

- **Task Number.** This field identifies the dynamic I/O cycle task assigned between the workstation and the server for communication on a Reply sequence mode. This is a 1-byte field.

- **Completion Code.** This is an extremely important field for analysis. This field indicates how a server is responding related to an exact function response to the main function request from a workstation. If a workstation requests information on a basic 2222 request, with a function read, and the server NCP reply completion code is responded with a "file not found," this completion code is considered an FF or a "failure to find" the file. If the file is found, the completion code would be normal and this field would be considered actively noted as OK in the code response. This field can be monitored, and it is designed on a 1-byte field and directly correlates to the workstation NCP request inbound and is considered the actual server NCP reply to the function request from the inbound workstation.

- **Connection Status.** This field normally indicates the response from the NetWare server as to the connection and whether the communication cycle between the workstation and the server is considered active within the operating system connection mode. This field is a 1-byte field.

- **Data.** This field is extremely important to upper-layer protocol analysis. By using a protocol analyzer properly in a network baseline session and turning on the hexadecimal and ASCII displays, it is possible to investigate this field from the NCP header to examine the exact type of data encapsulated in NCP. Data can be sent back and forth upon transmissions, depending on application design, and the NCP reply carries the data. This field indicates the size of the data and is variable size (see Figure 7.8).

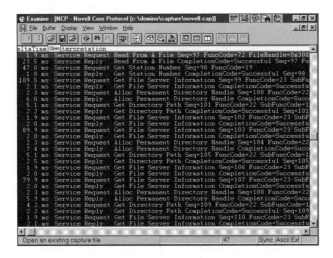

FIGURE 7.8 *An NCP conversation from a summary view via protocol analysis.*

7.1.4 Other Key Layers in the Novell Protocol Suite

The following protocol descriptions are summary reviews of other protocols used in the NetWare protocol suite enterprise processing environment. The following descriptions do not include actual field breakouts because of the extensive nature of the particular protocol type. Appendix B, "Reference Material, lists other manuscripts that detail the actual fields related to the following protocol types. If an analyst requires more information on a NetWare decode, the vendor should be contacted for any public documents available for review. It is always recommended that a protocol analyst have the most common public documents related to reference or white paper information on a protocol type. Protocol type fields can change, based on NOS release functions that are also modified on different versions of operating systems. Protocol operations can also vary when patches are provided for an operating system and the protocol suites used within the operating system type.

7.1.4.1 NetWare Core Protocol Packet Burst Mode

The standard NCP layer was basically designed for a small-to-medium-sized internetwork operation. In a standard NCP operation, a workstation may request a file open and a file read, and upon a file transfer from the server to the workstation would reply with one packet. For each other portion of the file required, the workstation would have to provide a request and another reply would then be provided by the server. This would be an ongoing reverse cycle that is considered somewhat chatty for large internetwork structures.

Because of this, and the increasing count of network nodes throughout many global network environments, the Novell NetWare development team provided a modification to NetWare Core Protocol: the *NetWare Core Protocol Burst* (NCPB).

The NCPB mode sequence allows a workstation to provide a request for a sequence of the data required, and the server to reply with multiple replies in a particular sequence.

This allows for a complete stream of communication to be sent back and forth in multiple sequences in a less-chatty operation, in which there is a constant request for every reply required from a server.

Basically, the complete stream transmission for NCP operations is provided with multiple sequences that includes multiple cycles of replies from the server that match a single request from a workstation.

Specifically, NCPB allows a workstation to request certain information from a file server, and the server can then reply with multiple replies for the single request. The workstation then requests any additional information related to the sequence, and the server continues to provide multiple packets for reply. An analyst can decode NCPB by just reviewing the server request type and the server reply type, which will always be active as a Code 7777. Also incorporated into the NCP operating system burst mode operation is the capability for the IPX packet to be engaged with a *Large Internetwork Packet Exchange* (LIPX) header that increases the standard IPX header length by more than 576 bytes. This allows for a larger PDU to be used in certain topology environments that allow for larger packet sizes, such as Token Ring and FDDI. In most cases when NCPB and LIPX are engaged, packet sizes can be engaged up to the maximum transmission unit of the applied topology.

The burst mode configuration field format allows for an extensive field breakout that includes a Request and Reply sequence, tracking of sequencing acknowledgment numbers, actual the actual transmission of sequence numbers, burst length, and burst offset fields. For large PDU transmission requirements, fragmentation fields allow for length offset and breakouts as related to fragmentation transmission. After the file has been opened and requested, different timing parameters can even be tracked, on a consecutive basis, such as delay times, sequence numbers, and acknowledgment numbers.

7.1.4.2 Novell Routing Information Protocol

The Novell protocol suite was originally configured to allow for a routing information protocol to be used for each Novell router, or any servers acting as routers, to update on a consistent basis. Any key information could be updated as to server location, device location, and the amount of time or length to actually reach that location. The Novell RIP is a distance vector routing protocol that is somewhat similar to standard Internet Protocol–based RIP. The main difference in Novell RIP is that the RIP updates are provided on a 60-second cycle rather than the 30-second update used in the IP environment. The RIP protocol operation can be activated on the NetWare server and NetWare-specific routers, such as multiprotocol routers.

The fields within the NetWare RIP that are important to decode and analyze are specific information fields that identify the location of the device within the Novell internetwork and the actual length of time to reach that device as related to a specific metric.

The Novell RIP packet configuration format includes a network address for devices running RIP. A Novell device running RIP can broadcast a RIP sequence that identifies the routing table within the particular device. In this case, each available Novell server and router can usually be identified within the Novell RIP update. The RIP update table is presented in the RIP packets transmitted from the Novell device generating a RIP broadcast. Novell RIP updates include the Novell router location and ID. Also included is the time away as related to delay to reach the router in a metric called TICK, set for 1/18 of a second in timing for each TICK. An analyst can closely examine Novell RIP sequences, which should occur on 60-second updates on an ongoing basis between key servers and routers (see Figure 7.9).

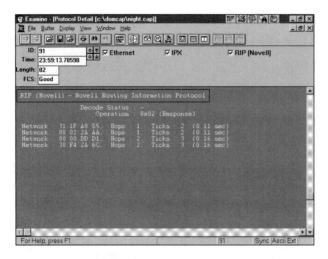

FIGURE 7.9 *A Novell RIP header.*

7.1.4.3 Novell Service Advertising Protocol

The Novell SAP has been around since early versions of the NetWare operating system. It allows a server to advertise its available services to other key Novell servers, routers, and other devices throughout a Novell internetwork. The normal update sequence occurs on a 60-second interval. The Novell server advertises its current Novell services to other internal Novell servers of which it is aware. That awareness is based on the current SAP table, which is consistently maintained.

An outbound Service Advertising Update includes the Novell servers available, along with detailed information about the server type, server location, and the server process location as related to transmission.

The Novell SAP packet header relies on an IPX encapsulation technique to be transmitted across Novell bridges and routers throughout an infrastructure involving Novell devices. The SAP packets normally include a request and reply format. This is because, at times, a server must locate another server. Therefore, a Novell SAP request can be generated by a server, and then another Novell server can reply directly with a Novell Service Advertising reply from the device attempting to be located in the Novell internetwork. In this case, a server may request information on another server, and then other servers within the Novell internetwork can reply (see Figure 7.10).

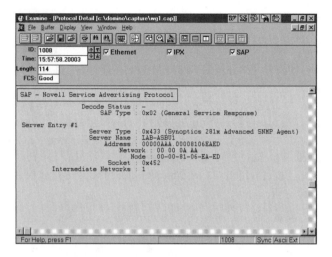

FIGURE 7.10 *A Novell SAP header.*

This is considered a very chatty protocol on large Novell internetworks, which have server node counts of 50 and more. In smaller Novell internetworks this is a very useful protocol because it allows the Novell server environment to maintain a hooked operation in which each server is available and also aware of the location of other servers throughout the Novell internetwork.

In large Novell internetworks with multiple Novell servers, the server location and mapping scheme usually involves an implementation of *NetWare Directory Services* (NDS). NDS allows a NetWare workstation or other NetWare nodes to log in to a complete Novell internetwork and essentially eliminates the consistent requirement for Novell SAP processes. Also, the implementation of *NetWare Link State Protocol* (NLSP) has allowed for a more consecutive and nonintrusive process with less-frequent updates (see Figure 7.11).

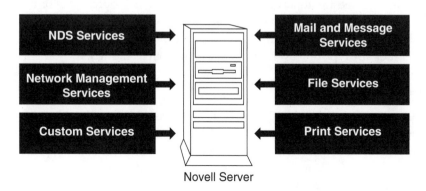

FIGURE 7.11 *The Novell NDS operational concept.*

7.1.4.4 NetWare Link State Protocol

In the 1990s, Novell introduced a protocol that could update standard NetWare servers and routers as to the state of a particular device, its service offered, and the location within the Novell internetwork. NLSP is based on a link-state routing update operation rather than a distance vector approach (which is normally used in the Novell SAP or RIP cycles). The NLSP is much less intensive to the overall network operation traffic cycle with regard to constant transmission. The only updates provided to a router or server running NLSP in the Novell environment are based on a changed-state occurrence or on timing intervals based on an hourly sequence, which is less intensive than the standard Novell RIP and SAP 60-second sequence.

The NLSP also addresses larger internetworks by providing longer routing address fields, allowing for more than 127 Novell networks. The NLSP uses more than 128 network hop counts rather than the standard Novell RIP limitation of 16 network hops.

7.1.5 Tips on Analyzing the Novell Protocol Suite

The following are analysis techniques that can be used to examining certain Novell protocol suite layers encountered during a network analysis session. As previously noted, the overall fields have been presented as to their configuration and operation. The following are notes on actual analysis techniques for the protocol layer type.

7.1.5.1 IPX Analysis Techniques

The IPX protocol is extremely valuable for analysis because it includes the Novell nomenclature for the internetworking addressing schemes on the packet being investigated. When using a protocol analyzer and investigating a Novell NetWare IPX layer within a packet, the Novell source and destination network number are clearly noted, along with the Novell network node. These two fields alone are important to identifying the actual source node or device transmitting a packet within the Novell internetwork. A protocol analyst should always closely monitor these fields when investigating a Novell error packet or any type of Novell communication, such as file access. These fields identify the source network and node, along with the final destination network and node.

Also contained within the IPX header is the Transport Control field, or Hop Count field. By closely analyzing this field with a protocol analyzer, an analyst can identify how many hops the packet has traveled before it was captured. By analyzing this field, an analyst may be able to identify any routing loops or improper routes that may be present.

The Addressing and Hop Count fields enable an analyst to identify vector address situations, along with path routes taken in a network analysis session.

The Protocol Type field shows the next protocol layer up in the packet sequence, which can also be analyzed by moving through the packet detail process.

7.1.5.2 SPX Analysis Techniques

When analyzing the Sequence Packet Protocol in a Novell connection sequence, an analyst can closely examine a Novell source and destination virtual ID when the two nodes are maintaining a connection. By monitoring the connection-based sequence, an analyst can determine whether the NetWare connection is maintained on a consistent basis. If the connection is broken, the SPX header of the field shows this.

The other key factor is that if the communication is consistent and ongoing, and a connection is maintained in a normal way, the SPX field shows this as well.

If several devices on a Novell internetwork have problems and a user complains about connection drops, an analyst can just filter on the SPX communication for the user's ID if it is found that SPX is used for connection maintenance. By consistently filtering on the SPX communication and monitoring the summary view of the SPX communication between the two source and destination IDs, it may be possible to follow the connection Sequencing Acknowledgment and Allocation fields in the SPX header to identify a connection break. It may then be possible to vector into the connection break sequence and investigate any ASCII or hex data that was active or any other upper-layer protocol in process when a connection break occurred. This may also enable an analyst to identify high timing in interpacket delta time differences in between the sequences where the SPX connection breaks. An analyst may also be able to identify timing delays on the internetwork. Either way, by closely monitoring the SPX fields and monitoring the Sequence Acknowledgment and Allocation field between two NetWare nodes, an analyst can use the summary screen to follow the NetWare connection sequence.

By following the connection communication cycle, an analyst can determine whether the connection process is operating normally.

7.1.6 NCP Analysis Techniques

When examining NCP, an analyst should closely focus on the outbound requests from a workstation and the subsequent reply from the server. In most cases, the NCP indicates what the workstation is requesting and how the server replies in relation to the function request. The upper-layer protocol communication fields of the NCP are usually clearly displayed in most protocol analyzers. At times, if there is a problem with a server responding to a request, the NCP reply indicates the type of failure (a file not found, a bindery error, a server operating system error, for example).

Analysis of the NCP layer is extremely important for investigation of how workstations are requesting information from servers and how servers are replying.

The key to analyzing NCP in most cases is to use a summary view in a network protocol analyzer. Just focus on the NCP requests from certain devices to the server and how the server responds.

In problem situations that identify a specific device on the network having a problem, an analyst should filter on the device by using a physical or network layer Novell IPX layer filter to watch the two devices communicate.

NCP is active, depending on the encapsulation and operation of the IPX header. By monitoring the NCP communication inbound and outbound sequences from the server as related to a specific station, an analyst can follow the NCP communication sequence between the Novell workstation and server.

For example, a workstation may attempt to connect to a server, and the server provides the connection. The workstation may then attempt to log in to the server, and the server provides the login function. The workstation then may request authentication, and the server may reply with "authentication failed" because of an improper password. By examining NCP, an analyst can actually see this failure code come back from the server in the NCP reply in the authentication sequence request-reply operation. The process of protocol analysis is key in investigating and locating this type of problem. In this particular case, the problem could be as simple as an incorrect password. The main lesson here is that by examining NCP in a focused analysis and by using proper filtering schemes, actual NCP problems can be identified (workstation connection problems, login problems, file access problems, for example).

When examining any session via network baseline process, it is important to keep a close eye on NCP frame communication between workstations and NetWare servers by examining NCP at the summary and detail level with a protocol analyzer.

7.1.7 SAP Analysis Techniques

SAP is a simple protocol used by Novell servers to periodically update services available related to Novell resource service types. It is important to filter on Novell SAP sequences and monitor the services available from servers. By decoding SAP transmissions, an analyst can locate servers, identify server functions, and the delay of the server as related to its position within the internetwork. It is also important to watch the frequency of Novell SAPs to investigate whether too many NetWare servers are being broadcast as available in a NetWare area that does not require access to the servers. In large Novell internetworks, SAP updates can cause high traffic levels. In such a case, it may be necessary to put filters on a router or a switch via a network Layer 3 filtering within certain internetwork environments.

7.1.8 Novell RIP and NLSP Analysis Techniques

RIP analysis process is focused on the area of analyzing standard 60-second Novell RIP updates along with any outbound RIP requests from a router trying to locate another router within a Novell internetwork. When analyzing the packets, it is important to examine the address of certain routers, the number of hops away for the router, and the amount of time away related to the TICK field for the 1/18-of-a-second process.

A protocol analyzer can be positioned on a Novell internetwork to capture RIP updates by setting a protocol display filter wide-open trace, or presetting a pattern match filter with certain protocol analyzers just to investigate Novell RIP sequence timing and Novell internal RIP sequence information data.

As noted, Novell recently identified the requirement to reduce the amount of broadcast traffic associated with standard SAP and RIP operations. The standard RIP updates are keyed on 60-second standard intervals. This is because of standard distance vector implementation of Novell's version of RIP. The new NLSP allows for a link-state routing protocol implementation.

NLSP produces less network overhead traffic and timing by reducing the overall routing update frequency. This in turn reduces the overall amount of processing required for NetWare-based servers related to routing operations. The updates are sent in hourly intervals and only during router and server operational changes. The NLSP protocol also addresses internetwork size concerns by allowing routing between 127 hop counts rather than the standard RIP limitation of 16 network hop counts. The NLSP processes can also be more easily managed by host management platforms.

NLSP updates should be closely monitored with an analyzer. The key is to monitor the standard NLSP updates of the linked routers and to watch for out-of-normal time sequencing.

7.1.9 Novell Communication Process Analysis Techniques

Many Novell communication processes require exact analysis techniques and a specific analysis view from a baseline perspective. The following sections describe these unique processes.

7.1.9.1 Novell Delay Packet or Busy Packet Communication

When file servers in a Novell environment are operating at a high inbound I/O task level or are incorrectly designed with regard to hardware/software configuration, or if too many users are applied for connection or too high of an application balance is applied to the server, a server may operate in a busy mode. The NetWare operating system has an inherent technique for a server to provide an outbound communication packet in responses to NetWare work-station requests with this type of occurrence. In standard NCP, a reply of a Code 9999 in the NCP reply packet indicates a NetWare busy operation. In a situation where the NCPB mode is active, a NetWare busy flag can be flagged in the field header of the format of an NCP flag format for the NCPB operation.

In this type of circumstance, an analyst can just review certain upper-layer pro-tocol traces in the NetWare baseline session to find this type of situation, or in certain cases an analysis can preset filters to determine whether servers are busy in the NetWare environment.

When performing a large baseline study in a situation in which there are critical NetWare file servers, it is sometimes beneficial to filter on the NetWare servers through physical MAC addresses or network layer IPX addresses.

In doing so, after the address filter has been applied, another pattern-match data filter can be applied against the NCP reply field indicating whether a server is busy. In an NCP environment, an extra pattern match would be required matching the pattern of Code 9999 being engaged in the reply on an outbound server transmission for the hex offset of an NCP reply sequence. Upon capturing any packets matching the pattern, these sequences would be identified as busy packets by just reviewing a summary level of the screen. If NCPB mode is active, server busy conditions can be identified by closely exam-ining the NCPB flag fields as related to the busy flag hex offset in the pattern of data. With NCPB busy flags, a capture and display protocol analyzer filter can also be set to examine the same occurrence (see Figure 7.12).

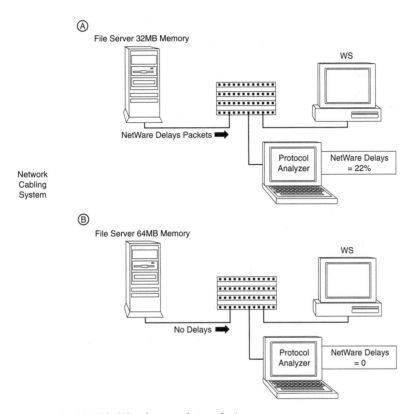

FIGURE 7.12 *NetWare busy packet analysis.*

The key factor here is that by closely examining NetWare servers for NetWare busy packets, it may be possible to identify NetWare servers that have inadequate resources as related to memory, hardware, or other possible software configuration issues. When a server is busy, it is usually because the server has software or hardware configuration issues. The application layer may be overbalanced, and there may be too high of an application load or too high of a user count assigned to the server. In this case the server can be investigated based on the analysis results.

NCP or NCPB mode busy indications from a server that exceed 200 to 300 per hour indicate a server inundated with requests which cannot be replied to by the NOS I/O task handler. This again can be because of internal problems within the server or an overbalance of user connections or applications.

7.1.9.2 NetWare File Access Failure Packet Analysis

A network analysis session sometimes indicates file access errors. The normal process is this: A file is requested by using a search command. After the file has been located, it is either opened for the either writing or reading. The file is eventually closed.

In certain circumstances in NCP or NCPB, a workstation attempts to locate a file on a server but fails.

This can be because of file misplacement or misconfiguration of Novell mapping in the Novell workstation and server infrastructure. Problems also arise when workstation path statements are incorrect as related to Novell server drive mapping configurations for the workstation image. For either condition, the key factor is that by properly using a network protocol analyzer and analyzing NCP or NCPB, file access errors can be captured.

Some of the key access errors clearly seen are identified in the NCP Reply sequences in standard NCP or in standard NCP burst replies from the server. The area to closely examine is the Function field for the NetWare request, along with the NCP reply from the server. If replies are found showing that files are not found or file access fails, subfunctions of the NCP request and reply fields should be investigated for data relating to the cause (see Figure 7.13).

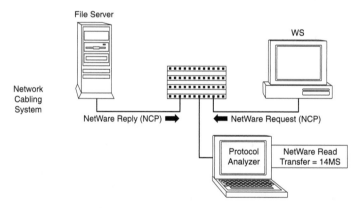

FIGURE 7.13 *NetWare file fluency analysis.*

In certain circumstances, the reply command may indicate whether the file could not be accessed because of improper attributes based on a search attribute request or file access parameters in the request that are not valid. In some cases, a file may not even be located on the server being searched. In any

case, it is important to always examine NetWare file access communication by
closing studying the inbound workstation NCP request and then closely examining the outbound server NCP reply. The detail area of the NCP or NCPB
header is where the information is indicated upon reply from the server. This
type of information should be carefully noted in a technical analysis log when
encountered by an analyst.

7.1.10 NetWare Bindery Error Analysis

Prior to the release of the newer NetWare 4.x and 5.x operating systems, some
of the older Novell operating systems contained a bindery configuration. The
NetWare bindery allows for the general linking of the database of resources
important to the NetWare operating system—that is, for linked files for which
the server provides resources to the user community. If a bindery is corrupt, an
NCP reply is provided on the network packet transmission with a completion
code indicating a bindery error.

This is just encapsulated in the NCP as an NCP reply with bindery error. A network analyst can use a protocol analyzer to capture NetWare bindery errors by
just applying a pattern match for the bindery error after capture during the initial session.

After the initial session has been captured, the hex offset along with the
Bindery Error Type field should be identified and a pattern match can be set up
for a precapture filter to further investigate the frequency of occurrence.

If bindery errors occur at a rate of more than 1% of all absolute traffic, there is a
critical problem in the NetWare bindery. In this case, the bindery may have to be
repaired or the NOS may need to be reloaded. In a Novell NDS environment,
this is not an issue because of the infrastructure change of the overall design of
an NDS container and the general operation without an active bindery.

7.1.11 Novell NetWare Login and Authentication Analysis

A Novell internetwork may have many different login request processes. In a
standard NCP operation, a workstation just logs in to one server may request
information from one server about another server via a specific NCP call, and
eventually links to other servers throughout the internetwork. In a NetWare
NDS design, a workstation logs in to the complete internetwork of servers.

The following login process occurs in a standard NetWare core protocol
environment.

7.1.11.1 Standard NCP Login Process Analysis

The workstation attempts to locate the nearest server on the internetwork and attempts an initial connection. The workstation negotiates a packet size and buffer size with the server and establishes initial connection. The workstation may destroy connection from the primary initial server, which was found from the "get nearest server" command, and then connect to the preferred server for login processes to access certain information on the client/server cycle. Next, a workstation usually attempts to locate and download the LOGIN.EXE file from a primary server and establish user privileges associated with the file.

A protocol analysis approach can be used to examine a Novell login process. In some circumstances, based on certain login shells or certain menuing systems used, the NetWare access login cycle can be examined in detail. By creating a connection with a server, negotiating file server information, along with buffer size, packet size, and the actual connection to the initial server, it is possible to actually watch a NetWare workstation establish the initial connection. It is easy for the analyst to also examine the summary login mode. An analyst can determine how a workstation establishes a login process through authentication of the login key and eventual password process to negotiate access to the server. The analyst can monitor a workstation connecting to the main system drive in the NetWare server for connection and eventual connection to other applications.

During examination of the login process, an analyst might identify abnormal occurrences. Login sequences should be fluent. If there are excessive instances of "files not found" or "login files cannot be located" errors, or other information related in NCP shows connection or login sequence as not fluent, it is possible to identify the cause. In certain cases, the cause can be menuing systems or mapping of the workstation. In other cases, the server may be improperly configured.

NetWare login analysis is critical. Many users complain of delays when they log in to the internetwork. One of the key rules of a NetWare analysis is to limit NetWare login sequences to a minimal level (to the most minimal level for I/O). By using protocol analysis and network baselining, it is possible to investigate how long a NetWare login sequence takes. A normal sequence contains less than 1,000 frames. If 3,000 or more frames are identified, it is possible anomalies exist in the NetWare login sequence.

In certain situations, the server may indicate specific conditions such as "access to server denied" or an error message generated from the ATTACH.EXE process. Other circumstances also indicate errors (a workstation attempting to log in to a server, the server responding with "unauthorized workstation," for example). Other common errors include "cannot route to a key file server" and "bad local network address." These are just samples of errors that might be encountered in a protocol analysis session when investigating NetWare login sequencing.

Investigation of a NetWare login sequence requires an understanding of the standard authentication and analysis processes. The NetWare login cycle includes a process in which the workstation invokes an encrypted private key unique to the user and should be valid to the specific user. There is also the RSA public key (the Rivest Shamir and Adleman process) that it used for the authentication services to validate user information. This key is part of the normal requester in the RSA process.

The authenticator is a special credential operation created and engaged by a client, including a specific session information that is utilizing a user's complete name, workstation address, or validity period. A signature is considered a background authentication credential, which is engaged within the combination of multiple packets such as the authenticator and encrypted private key.

The final proof is the encryption technique used in a LAN or WAN in a Novell environment, which is constructed by using the message, signature, and user's private key in a random number generator to ensure that each message is unique. When conducting a network analysis session, different levels of security must be considered.

A client requests authentication by invoking the DOS requester from the client endpoint. The operating system then returns an encrypted key. The server key can only be decrypted with the proper password. The user then provides a valid password to decrypt the key. The client receives an encryption link called a signature, using the authenticator and the private key, and the key is then removed from memory. The signature is used as a background authentication review, and the client then requests access using a proof. The proof is then sent across the network to prevent it from being captured. Every proof from a workstation has a different proof because of the random number generation process. The user in then authenticated. After the proof has been received and validated by the server, the access to the Novell server is pending the completion of the second layer of authentication, which is considered the final detailed level, if required. The second level is not always used, depending on the level of security assigned.

7.1.11.2 NetWare Directory Service Analysis

The NetWare Directory Service is inherent to NetWare 4.x and 5.x releases, and allows a workstation to log in to a complete Novell internetwork of servers. It is based on an object-oriented database and allows for NetWare resources to be designed into an hierarchical tree.

The NDS tree is distributed throughout the complete enterprise server internetwork from one centralized approach. This differs completely from the bindery system that preceded the NDS operation. In an NDS operation, the user logs in to the complete internetwork and all the servers within the Novell enterprise environment. This login capability allows for an enhanced security process for the login cycle. In NDS, a full computing environment can be accessed by one user from one single point within the internetwork.

Some synchronization concerns apply in large NDS trees because all servers must be constantly aware of each other in terms of NetWare server location, function, and access points to allow for the NDS tree to be designed.

The NDS tree structure is comprised of a main container and subordinate leaf objects. The top level of the tree container is called the root. From that point, there is an *organization* (O), a *country* (C) and an *organizational unit* (OU). The tree is designed on a partitioned segmentation strategy.

The NDS tree can be split into many different segments, and databases can be distributed and replicated throughout the Novell server environment. By distributing the segments and the databases throughout the NDS tree, it is possible to have a more fault-tolerant and smoother internetwork design.

Partitioning allows an administrator to take pieces of the NDS tree and distribute them to various servers. Note that the main root is considered the key portion of the tree. The backup copies of the NDS tree off the main root can be considered replicas and can be transmitted across multiple trees and customized by the NetWare administrator.

There are four types of NDS replicas. A read/write copy of the original partition is considered the master. A read/write copy that is a copy of the partition. A partition may have multiple read/write copies. If changes are made to one of the replicas, these changes must be communicated to all servers that have a copy of this replica. A read-only is one that can be viewed but cannot be modified, and a subordinate reference is a replica that is created by the NDS and is sent to other portions of the tree for just pure fault redundancy. The parent replica does not reside in this reference and this is considered a subordinate reference for redundancy only.

The replication strategy in an NDS server-to-server environment is extensive. The process allows a main server with a master replica to go down the list of the NetWare environment and produce replicas by copying the affected partitions. The replication traffic can actually be viewed through functional programs in the NetWare environment, such as DS Trace.

The key is that by also using a network analysis tool, such as a protocol analyzer during a network baseline session, the NDS tree updates can be examined. This can be achieved by examining NDS updates, such as location pointers to where the updates are traveling.

In large internetworks, too many replicas designed against the master replica may cause excessive traffic as well as excessive updates of objects between the NDS tree. This could also put a severe load on the network.

NetWare administrators must always be concerned as to whether they are creating the proper number of replicas and what the effect is on the overall internetwork.

When performing network analysis, it is important to review the NDS tree operation via protocol analysis. One of the key areas to be examined is NDS replica distribution. When the subordinate references are created in their pyramid design and transmitted throughout the internetwork, a network analyzer can be used to examine the frequency and the traffic impact of the sync procedures in relation to the replicas on the internetwork traffic level. As more NetWare servers become involved and the NetWare NDS tree becomes more complex, larger NDS synchronization patterns will be clearly present in Network analysis sessions. The use of a protocol analyzer is extremely valuable in these cases. The sync procedure should be closely analyzed to ensure that the NDS tree is properly configured and the replicas are being properly distributed in an efficient manner without extensive traffic load.

Also, the standard NCP traffic alarm log with interactive NDS traffic can show an analyst how often a synchronization occurs.

For further information on NDS operation, see Appendix B.

7.1.12 Closing Statement on NetWare Analysis

When analyzing the NetWare environment, it is important to keep in mind that the protocol analyzer platforms available facilitate a clear view of NCP, and in most sequences, NCPB. Investigation of the network and transport layer protocols such as IPX, SPXI and SPXII, are also simple from a standard analysis standpoint.

The key factor in analysis is to monitor workstations communicating to servers. It is important to be able to determine whether the connection, login, and file access processes are fluent. Another important factor is whether file access on an ongoing basis is consistent and shows fluent communication. The main point here is that NetWare workstations should be able to connect to servers, log in to servers, and access files on a consistent basis.

NDS traffic should be minimal and should allow for smooth login processes. Any problems seen in the NetWare environment will most likely be identified through a close analysis of the NCP upper-layer protocol layers on request and reply analysis, along with NCPB Request and Reply sequence analysis.

7.2 TCP/IP Analysis

TCP/IP is a architecture that was designed for the large enterprise internetwork. The TCP/IP suite was originally designed in the early 1970s as a protocol that would allow for broad communication across diverse computing environments, such as mini-computers and LAN operating system file servers. The protocol was primarily designed to enhance interaction of communication between application and resource data node points spread across a large global enterprise infrastructure. TCP/IP directly relates to the discussion of the key network layer protocol, *Internet Protocol* (IP), and the transport-based connection protocol, *Transmission Control Protocol* (TCP).

Quite often, the entire group of protocols that rely on TCP and IP, which involves many protocols, is referred to as the TCP/IP suite. This is because all the key process application protocols, which include protocols such as *File Transfer Protocol* (FTP) and Telnet, rely on the IP and TCP layer for a network communication to be developed for a transfer of data and for a connection process to be maintained. Most of the process application protocols, which are discussed briefly in this chapter, rely on and preside on the TCP/IP.

Note also that TCP/IP was developed and engineered to accommodate the original development of the Internet. The Internet is a medium spread across the worldwide global infrastructure that interconnects many computing environments, including government and corporations.

The TCP/IP suite was developed in late 1969 and was directed by the U.S. Defense Department through an agency called the *Defense Advanced Research Project Agency* (DARPA). DARPA developed the TCP/IP protocol through an initial network called the *Advanced Research Project Agency Network* (ARPANET). The original direction of the ARPANET internetwork was to develop a large interconnection based on packet-switching technology. ARPANET was tested for initial evaluation in four key locations: the University of Utah, the University of California at Santa Barbara, Stanford Research Institute, and the University of California at Los Angeles. The original configuration was based on a design for the IP host configuration in the testing of TCP/IP, which was based on a Honeywell platform. In the late 1970s, the *National Science Foundation* (NSF) decided to augment the development effort and named a production system the *Computer Science Network* (CSNET).

As things progressed, eventually DARPA decided there should be a clear division of the two organizations to divide the ARPANET into *MILitary NETwork* (MILNET) for military traffic and the ARPANET for nonmilitary traffic.

Eventually the ARPANET network was redefined into a network called National Science Foundation NETwork (NSFNET), which was maintained by the *Office of Advanced Science and Computing* (OASC). This was done to allow for further development of the TCP/IP protocol.

The TCP/IP protocol was actually defined for standards in 1973 by the RFC standards. The model was defined under the *Department of Defense* (DOD) model.

The DOD model compares to the *Open System Interconnection* (OSI) model in the following way. There are four specific DOD layers rather than seven OSI layers. The DOD model includes the network interface layer, the Internet layer, the host-to-host layer, and the application processing layer.

The network layer involves the physical data link processes of key devices that communicate throughout the physical infrastructure, such as the physical layer, the NIC area, and other physical entities such as connectors, firmware, and hardware.

The Internet layer directly relates to the IP protocol itself and is involved with the movement of a unit of data in the encapsulation data of other upper-layer protocols. The IP layer allows for the identification of addressing schemes for internetwork routing and for the transfer of units of data between two IP nodes.

The host-to-host layer is involved with the final delivery of data between two specific devices that are considered IP nodes. The point of connection between the two devices is a port. Two protocols are used at the host-to-host layer: TCP or the *User Datagram Protocol* (UDP). The TCP protocol uses a connection-based process and is much more reliable and stable. The TCP layer involves a high amount of end-to-end node packet interaction that is separate from data transmission (to maintain true connectivity and stability). The UDP protocol involves less overhead and only communicates between the endpoints via UDP ports when data is being sent and does not maintain a connection.

The highest layer in the TCP/IP protocol model is the application layer. This layer involves several protocols such as FTP, Telnet, *Simple Mail Transfer Protocol* (SMTP), *Trivial File Transfer Protocol* (TFTP), SMNP, and other key protocols (see Figure 7.14).

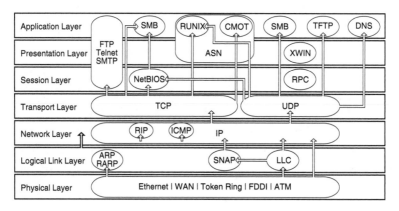

FIGURE 7.14 *The TCP/IP suite model.*

This discussion focuses on the IP, TCP, and UDP layers, as well as other surrounding protocols required for analysis, such as ARP and *Internet Control Message Protocol* (ICMP), which is an error-based reporting protocol in the IP node environment. The following section considers the TCP protocol layers.

7.2.1 TCP/IP Layer Configuration Fields

Prior to presenting an in-depth discussion of the IP, TCP, and UDP, this section first discusses some additional protocols considered important for general analysis when a solid physical DOD model is required underneath the process application protocol layer.

Note that any application that uses a process application protocol in the TCP/IP environment requires a solid transfer of data across all IP-based gateways and reliable port transfer of data at the transport level. Specifically, the IP layer must be stable and the transport layer must be also reliable at the TCP and UDP levels, regardless of whether a connection is being maintained. The endpoint host port access must be available via TCP and UDP. The IP and TCP layers require the physical layer to be solid.

With that said, other protocols below the process application layer are also involved in the TCP/IP protocol suite; the following sections discuss these.

7.2.1.1 ARP

This protocol is used when a TCP node requires access to a physical address of a device that will be used for general access to resources, routing, or switching communication transfer across the internetwork. It is also sometimes necessary to locate a specific physical device on the network, such as a server, which is required for communication. In this particular case, a device in an IP network can be configured with a known IP address but without knowledge to the physical location or physical device address to locate the device. In some cases, the sought device may be on the other side of a router or a switch. ARP has been developed to allow for this type of situation.

A TCP/IP host node can transmit a packet to another host node with an identification of the IP address that it is trying to locate. The target hardware address field will be empty. Upon transmission, the device transmits its source IP address and its source hardware address, along with its target IP address and a target hardware address as unknown (see Figure 7.15).

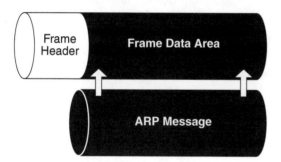

FIGURE 7.15 *ARP encapsulation.*

Any device that intercepts the ARP, such as a router, a switch, or a server directly correlated to the target IP address, can respond with the IP address so the source device can transmit to the physical address for physical layer communications to commence (see Figure 7.16).

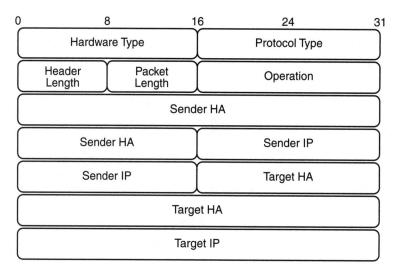

0	8	16	24	31

Hardware Type / Protocol Type

Header Length / Packet Length / Operation

Sender HA

Sender HA / Sender IP

Sender IP / Target HA

Target HA

Target IP

FIGURE 7.16 *ARP layer concepts.*

In the case of a router, a router intercepts an ARP and establishes an investigation process in which the router operation process reviews the ARP cache table within the router to cross-map and return the target hardware address to the source IP device for communications. This type of reply, when received by the original device, allows the original device to continue communication.

There is also a process called *Reverse Address Resolution Protocol* (RARP). This same process can be used in a reverse cycle. The source node typically knows its own IP address and may know certain physical addresses of other hosts. However, it may not have the required target IP address. In this situation, an RARP can be used to obtain a remote IP address.

Proxy ARP is another protocol that can be used in the address mapping process. Gateways and routers in an IP environment use proxy ARP. Proxy ARP allows routers and switches to provide the actual hardware address or destination nodes of devices on another side of a router to a source node performing an ARP request with an IP address that is not on the same logical network. Basically, the router or the switch assumes a proxy mask mode of the actual target device.

7.2.1.2 Internet Addressing
The Internet addressing scheme is extremely involved and is detailed in many different texts, some of which are mentioned in Appendix B. Many different IP addressing schemes can be used and there are many different ways to assign

IP addresses. Various devices can engage technologies, such as *Dynamic Host Control Protocol* (DHCP) and *Boot Protocol* (BOOTP), for device IP address assignment; any DHCP or BOOTP packet transmissions should be referenced for exact protocol analysis investigation with a protocol analyzer during a network baseline session.

For the purposes of this discussion, the current IP addressing schemes are based on either IP version 4 or IP version 6. The overall concept of an IP addressing scheme is based on a logical 32-bit address assigned to an IP physical node within the network. The Internet address is required for the IP datagram to be used for communication from one IP host to another IP host. Different classes of IP addresses are available: Class A, Class B, Class C, Class D, and Class E. The IP version 4 addressing scheme is briefly discussed in the following subsections (see Figure 7.17).

7.2.1.2.1 Class A IP Network Address

Class A is the highest area in the IP addressing design. There are 128 class A network addresses. Each of the 128 networks can address up to approximately 16 million hosts. In a Class A network, the first byte is the network address, and the last three bytes are the host address. The first bit must be set to zero, making the first byte in the range of 0 to 127. As displayed earlier, 73.34.103.4 is a Class A address.

Class A addresses are designed for very large networks. They are identified through the first 8 bits: 0 through 7. This area identifies the network. Again, the first byte 0 is reserved. Bits 1 to 7 actually identify the network. The remaining 24 bits identify the host. There are only 128 Class A network addresses available; 0 and 127 are reserved.

7.2.1.2.2 Class B IP Network Address

Class B is in the second highest area in the IP addressing design. The first byte must be in range of the 128 to 191 area. The first two bytes are used for the network area assignment, and the last two bytes are for the host. An example of a Class B address is 134.64.23.5.

Class B addresses are more common. The first two bits have a binary value of 10, which is standard. The next 14 bits identify the network. The next remaining 16 bits in the total 32-bit address configuration identify the host. A total of 16,384 Class B addresses are possible, but the addresses for 0 and 16,383 are reserved.

7.2.1.2.3 Class C Network Address

Class C addresses are the bottom area in the IP address design. The first byte is always in the 192 to 223 area. The network is assigned in the first three bytes, and the host is assigned by the last byte. An example of a Class C address is 209.43.12.4.

Class C addresses are generally used for smaller networks. The first byte begins with a binary 110. The next 21 bits identify the network address, and the remaining 8 bits identify the host. A total of 2,097,152 Class C addresses are possible.

7.2.1.2.4 Class D Network Address

Class D addresses begin with a binary 1110 and are intended for multicasing.

7.2.1.2.5 Class E Network Address

Class E addresses begin with a binary 1111 and are reserved for future use.

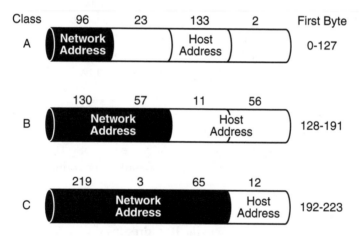

FIGURE 7.17 *The IP version 4 addressing model.*

The scope of this book does not include subnet discussions or version 6 IP addressing. (For more information on IP addressing, refer to Appendix B.)

7.2.2 IP

The IP is an extremely robust protocol that allows two devices to communicate across an internetwork. It is based on the design of one device that communicates with the IP to another device that communicates with the IP. These two devices are IP nodes or hosts. The IP nodes transfer data in a packet called a *datagram*. This datagram an IP message unit for a unit of measure transfer of data. The IP datagram provides for a unit of measure of up to 65K in size. This is an extremely large unit of measure for a transfer of data. Because of this fact, IP allows for inherent fragmentation within the overall configuration fields assigned to the general communication process.

Although guidelines apply to the transfer of data, they are not 100% reliable because there is no connection maintained. The overall tiered service allows for a data transfer process to occur. The transfer of data is effected between two IP nodes through an initial connection between the two nodes, which is established but not maintained. This is considered a connectionless protocol and provides only for a unit of data transfer. Guidelines within the IP fields apply, and these allow for the transfer of data to occur between nodes in an organized way. Fields are used for specialized processing, such as a Service Type field. In a Service Type field, type of service routing can be engaged for high-performance routing in certain routing algorithms, such as *Open Shortest Path First* (OSPF), that work with *Type of Service* (TOS) routing. Fragmentation is also possible for large datagram transfers of up to 65K; these can be broken up into multiple packets and tracked on transfer from node to node. Again, there is no reliable connection mechanism, but the fragmentation can be tracked through the identification flag and certain flag fields. An IP packet can also avoid excessive routing through an internetwork because of the *Time-To-Live* (TTL) field, which assigns a TTL interval or hop count to the field process. This is also an inherent design within the IP system (see Figure 7.18).

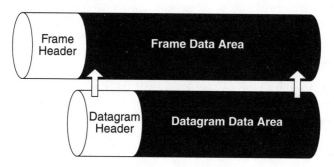

FIGURE 7.18 *The IP datagram encapsulation concept.*

- **IP Version, 4 bits.** This field identifies the current version of IP used. IP software modules check this field to ensure version.

- **IP Header Length, 4 bits.** This field identifies the length of the IP header. This field is measured in 2-bit words.

- **IP Service Type, 8 bits.** This field identifies how the IP packet can be processed by a destination host. The Service Type field is divided into five internal fields:

  - 3 bits, Priority Area (0 normal, to 7 critical).

  - 1 bit, Requests Low Delay Processing.

  - 1 bit, Requests High Throughput Processing.

  - 1 bit, Requests High Reliability Processing.

  - Bits 6 and 7 are not used.

- **IP Total Length, 16 bits.** This field identifies the total length of the current IP packet. The length includes the IP header and Data field. The largest size of an IP datagram is approximately 65535 bytes.

- **IP Identification, 16 bits.** This field is engaged for fragmentation control. Each network topology may limit the size of a *maximum transmission unit* (MTU). The IP software will then have to fragment packets. When fragmentation occurs, packets must be divided and reassembled when transmitted. It is considered standard for IP routers to handle packets of at least 576 bytes. This field identifies the unique datagram when fragmentation process is active.

- **IP Flags, 34 bits.** This field assists with controlling the fragmentation process. The first bit is a "do not fragment" identifier. If active, this bit indicates that the IP datagram should not be fragmented. The second bit is a "more fragments" identifier field. When nonactive, this indicates that the IP packet holds the last fragment of a IP transmission.

- **IP Fragment Offset, 13 bits.** This field is used when fragmentation occurs. The destination node requires this field for reassembly because packets may not flow in order. This field identifies the current offset area for data that is internal in the packet as related to the total datagram. The value is set from zero to the highest offset.

- **IP TTL, 8 bits.** This field is important for protocol analysis and it identifies how long in actual time an IP packet can flow on a network. Time is measured in seconds. The IP software puts an internal starting value in this field. Any IP-based host or router that processes an IP packet on an internetwork transfer must decrease the TTL value by at least one second. All IP hosts and routers must also decrease the TTL of the IP packet by the actual time in a second count for internal processing time when routing across the channel. If the IP field is ever found to drop to zero in value by an IP router or host, the IP device discards the IP packet. This prevents an IP packet from traveling in network loops (see Figure 7.19).

```
IP: -IP Header-
IP:
IP:  Version = 4, header length = 20 bytes
IP:  Type of service = 00
IP:  000.  . = routine
IP:   0  . = normal delay
IP:   . 0  = normal throughput
IP:   . .0.. = normal reliability
IP:  Total length = 51 bytes
IP:  Identification = 7052
IP:  Flags = 0X
IP:  .0.. . = may fragment
IP:  ..0. . = last fragment
IP:  Fragment offset = 0 bytes
IP:  Time to live = 64 seconds/hops
IP:  Protocol = 6 (TCP)
IP:  Header checksum = C87C (correct)
IP:  Source address = [132.163.200.15]
IP:  Destination address = [129.6.16.4]
IP:  No options
```

FIGURE 7.19 *An IP trace decode.*

- **IP Protocol, 8 bits.** This field indicates the next upper- or higher-layer protocol, which is further encapsulated after the IP Data field.

- **IP Header Checksum, 16 bits.** This field uses a basic algorithm to perform a verification on the IP header but not on the IP Data field.

- **IP Source and Destination IP Address, 32 bits each.** This field includes the IP address of the endpoint host in an IP packet.

- **IP Options, variable length.** This field is not required and considered optimal. The field can be used for testing. The options field contain an IP code, IP option class, and IP option number. This field can be used for special operations. Examples include routing and time-stamp adjustments.

- **IP Data, variable length.** This field carries actual data. The padding of zero bits may be used to ensure that the final size of the IP datagram reaches at least a 32-bit word (see Figure 7.20).

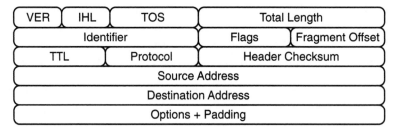

VER	IHL	TOS	Total Length	
Identifier			Flags	Fragment Offset
TTL		Protocol	Header Checksum	
Source Address				
Destination Address				
Options + Padding				

FIGURE 7.20 *The IP header breakout for the IP trace decode shown in Figure 7.19.*

7.2.3 UDP

The UDP is a transport layer protocol and is the simplest version of a transport mechanism that allows for an open port communication between two IP host nodes. The basic design is two devices in an IP network are considered hosts and communicate to each other across the IP network. Each host is assigned an IP address and communicates through the IP datagram services. The IP datagram encapsulates a transport-based protocol that assigns a port communication area to each endpoint. Each endpoint will have a port area assigned for communications. These ports are assigned through either UDP or TCP at the transport layer.

In the case of UDP, the ports are just assigned and based on the application port access at the process application layer. UDP does allow for integrity checks on the Data field if the checksum is valid. UDP is not a connection-based protocol and has no inherent connection-based process (see Figure 7.21).

UDP Source of Port	UDP Destination Port
UDP Message Length	UDP Checksum
Data	

FIGURE 7.21 *The UDP internal fields.*

The following is a description of the UDP field configurations:

- **UDP Source Port, 16 bits.** This field contains the UDP-assigned source port identifier in a host.

- **UDP Designation Port, 16 bits.** This field contains the UDP-assigned destination port identifier in a host.

- **UDP Message Length, 16 bits.** This field contains the length of the UDP header plus and any assigned upper-layer protocols and the Data field length.

- **UDP Checksum, 16 bits.** This field provides a checksum verification process for UDP header and any attached data. This field is considered as optional because of overhead processing concerns. At times it is invoked for integrity checks to occur on the data, because the IP datagram does not check data.

- **UDP Data, variable.** This field contains any data encapsulated in the UDP headers.

7.2.4 TCP

TCP is a protocol used for operation at the transport layer. As its name implies, the protocol operates at the transport layer and allows for extensive control over communications. Two ports are assigned to each endpoint IP host through an involved synchronized process, in which the port is opened for communication. The TCP process and internal mechanism operation allows for a TCP port to be assigned and a connection to then be maintained. This process relies on the IP datagram to provide an overall unit of measure and transfer across the internetwork as related to IP addressing schemes. The TCP mechanism, just as UDP, assigns a port. But the port, once assigned, is maintained through a consecutive connection process, which engages sequence and acknowledgment numbers on consecutive communication (see Figure 7.22).

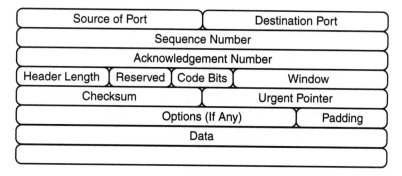

FIGURE 7.22 *The TCP layer model.*

The TCP also has an inherent capability for a window size to be advertised. The TCP window size is advertised in bytes and allocates the amount of data available at the endpoint of each TCP/IP node connection within the host data area for the TCP port allocation assignment as related to TCP stream transfer.

TCP is based on a stream transfer process. The stream transfer allows for a stream of data to be transferred in segments across the IP datagram transfer channel. The segments sent in a TCP stream rely on each one of the IP datagrams or packets within the IP datagram process for transfer. The TCP connection is actually maintained through the acknowledgment and sequence number ports. The availability of TCP ports on each end are advertised through the TCP window mechanism.

A source TCP host node starts a TCP connection by communicating with another TCP destination host node by sending a TCP packet with an initial sequence number. This TCP packet identifies the start of communication and the start of a three-way handshake. On the other endpoint of the TCP communication process, the TCP destination host node responds by providing an immediate response to the initial sequence number by providing a TCP packet transmission an acknowledgment, and also assigns its own initial sequence number for the bidirectional transfer of data. When the TCP source node receives this packet, it then understands that the TCP destination node communicates on an active session in a bidirectional TCP open state and sends a TCP packet with an acknowledgment to the initial sequence number from the destination node. This is considered the third packet of transmission or third IP datagram with the internal TCP three-way handshake active.

On the fourth packet transmission, the original node that started the TCP transmission begins to send regular sequence numbers rather than initial sequence numbers. These sequence numbers are consistently updated when transfer of data or data length is actually sent within each packet. The packets flow back and forth in a bidirectional process (see Figure 7.23).

Each TCP node advertises its TCP window size, depending on bytes available in the port area for TCP communication that the process application protocol is using. This process continues to flow in both directions (see Figure 7.24).

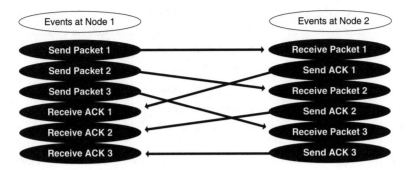

FIGURE 7.23   *The TCP stream.*

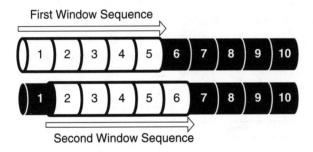

FIGURE 7.24   *The TCP stream windowing concept.*

When one device sends a TCP sequence number and a certain number of data segments, it waits for an acknowledgment from the other endpoint. If the receiving endpoint responds with an acknowledgment (as receiving and processing some of the segments sent by the source node), the source node continues to send segments. If for some reason the destination endpoint does not acknowledge the segments as being received, the source end node throttles back the TCP stream transmission and does not continue to send segments. This is based on a mechanisms called *Positive Acknowledgment and Retransmission* (PAR).

In TCP communication, the protocol requires that each set of segments has some acknowledgment or else a TCP retransmission occurs, and data is again requested. This is a PAR operation and is considered a positive factor in maintaining a connection.

As long as everything is working in a normal fashion, TCP communications flow in a normal manner. There will always be a certain number of sequence numbers and data being sent out and window sizes being advertised on each transmission from endpoint to endpoint.

As the TCP communication starts, it can be viewed from a protocol analysis standpoint. The initial sequence numbers can be viewed by setting a SYN flag inside the header of the TCP. After the three-way handshake occurs, a TCP open state exists. Eventually, if the TCP open communications have completed and all the required data has been communicated through the TCP packets, eventually a TCP connection will be requested for finish or breakdown of normal communications from one endpoint. This is usually the source device that started the communication. If an abnormal communication break occurs, it is a TCP reset. But again, on normal TCP breakdown of communication, a finish request by one endpoint is provided and the destination node replies with a "finish." This is the normal process of TCP stream communication from a TCP open state to a TCP closed stated (see Figure 7.25).

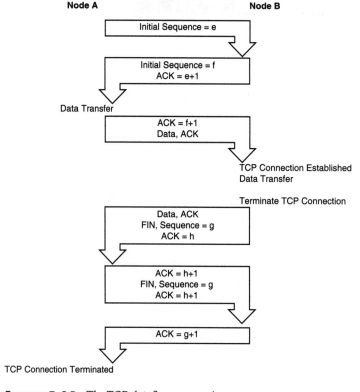

FIGURE 7.25 *The TCP dataflow sequencing process.*

The following list describes the TCP fields that should be reviewed during a network baseline session:

- **TCP Source field and the Destination Port field, 16 bits.** These fields identify the TCP port numbers that are assigned to endpoint hosts. These fields can associate certain application programs at end nodes. Note that a TCP port in a TCP host can be used by multiple endpoint IP hosts.

- **TCP Sequence Number field, 32 bits.** This field indicates the position of the TCP data stream in sequence of dataflow. If the indication is an initial sequence number, the field indicates the start or open state of a TCP communication session.

- **TCP Acknowledgment Number field, 32 bits.** This field displays the sequence number of the sender in the last transmission plus the data received in bytes.

- **TCP Header Length field, 4 bits**. This field indicates the length of the TCP layer header.

- **TCP Code Bits field, 6 bits.** This field indicates how the TCP packet sent should be handled by a TCP router and the TCP destination host node. The following TCP flag code bits apply:

  URG = Urgent

  ACK = Acknowledge active

  PSH = Push TCP data in buffers to maximum process

  RST = The TCP port state of connection should be reset

  SYN = This Flag starts the TCP open state in sequence

  FIN = The TCP data stream is about to close and end

- **TCP Window Size field, 16 bits.** A TCP endpoint host uses this field to notify the other endpoint host of available window buffer size in bytes available as to receive the next TCP transmission.

- **TCP Checksum field, 16 bits.** This TCP field is used for a CRC algorithm as to calculate the value of both the TCP header and data fields to ensure for maximum reliability.

- **TCP Urgent Pointer field, 16 bits.** The urgent pointer field displays the end of any urgent dataflow.

- **TCP Options field and Data fields, variable.** This field area usually holds data. This Options field may point to other upper-layer protocols and may also invoke data padding. The *maximum segment size* (MSS) of a PDU that a TCP packet can handle can also be noted in this field on the initial open state (see Figure 7.26).

```
TCP: - Header —
TCP:
TCP:  Source port = 3158
TCP:  Destination port = 23 (telnet)
TCP:  Sequence number = 4664
TCP:  Acknowledgement number = 1051902686
TCP:  Data offset = 20 bytes
TCP:  Flags = 18
TCP:  ..0.  . = (No urgent pointer)
TCP:  1  . = Acknowledgement
TCP:  . 1  = Push
TCP:  . .0.. = (No reset)
TCP:  . ..0. = (No SYN)
TCP:  .  0 = (No FIN)
TCP:  Window = 1015
TCP:  Checksum = 5A45 (correct)
TCP:  No TCP options
TCP:  [11byte(s) of data]
```

FIGURE 7.26 *A TCP layer trace decode.*

7.2.5 ICMP

The *Internet Control Message Protocol* (ICMP) is an inherent error-based protocol designed into the operation of an IP stack for most IP node configurations. Whether an IP host is an endpoint host, an IP router, or any specific device using an IP-based protocol stack, the device can usually communicate via an internal ICMP.

The ICMP provides a method by which devices using the IP for datagram services can send messages and assist in the control of the IP process when there is an error-based process in an IP environment. It is normal technique for an analyst to filter on the ICMP when analyzing an IP-based network for possible errors. Different ICMP messages can be generated by hosts and other devices in an IP-based network when an IP-based error occurs (see Figure 7.27).

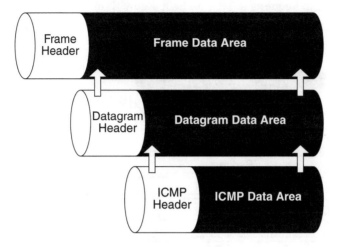

FIGURE 7.27 *The ICMP encapsulation concept.*

For example, one of the ICMP errors considered common is an ICMP redirect, which indicates that a packet is being redirected to another gateway, router, or switch.

Another example is an ICMP destination unreachable error, which indicates that a network, host, protocol, or application port is not available for access (see Figure 7.28).

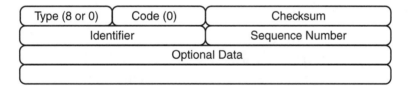

FIGURE 7.28 *The ICMP layer fields.*

These types of occurrences are described in more detail later in this chapter in the section titled "ICMP Analysis."

The following list shows the key message types used in ICMP packet transmission:

- ICMP data message types:

    Type 3. An IP Destination Unreachable

    Type 4. Source Quench (Busy IP Host)

    Type 5. Redirect Required

Type 8. Echo Requests & Type (0) Echo Reply (Pings)

Type 11. IP (TTL) field - Time To Live Exceeded

See Figure 7.29.

Type Field	ICMP Message Type
0	Echo Reply
3	Destination Unreachable
4	Source Quench
5	Redirect
8	Echo Request
11	Time Exceeded for a Datagram
12	Parameter Problem on a Datagram
13	Timestamp Request
14	Timestamp Reply
15	Information Request
16	Information Reply
17	Address Mask Request
18	Address Mask Reply

FIGURE 7.29 *The ICMP message type fields.*

- ICMP control types:

    Type 12. IP Parameter Problem

    Type 13. IP Timestamp Request & Type (14) Reply

    Type 15. IP Data Information Request Type (16) Reply

    Type 17. IP Address Mask Request & Type (18) Reply

- ICMP field internals:

    ICMP Type field

    ICMP Code field

    ICMP Checksum field

    ICMP Datagram Address field

    ICMP Data field

- **ICMP Type field, 8 bits.** This field indicates the ICMP data message type and issue.

- **ICMP Code field, 8 bits.** This ICMP field provides a set of information about the ICMP Type field. This Code field further defines the message type. For example, an ICMP message type of destination unreachable has a code that indicates whether the host, network, or a specific protocol is unreachable.

- Code identifiers:

  0 DU/Network Unreachable

  1 DU/Host Unreachable

  2 DU/Protocol Unreachable

  3 DU/Port Unreachable

  4 IP Fragmentation Required

  5 IP Source Route Failed

  6 IP Destination Network Unknown

  7 IP Destination Host Unknown

  8 IP Source Host Identified

  9 IP Prohibited Communication to Destination Network

  10 IP Prohibited Communication to Destination Host

  11 Type of Service (TOS) Cannot Be Used For Network Area

  12 Type of Service (TOS) Cannot Be Used for Host

  See Figure 7.30

Code Value	Interpretation
0	0 Network Unreachable
1	1 Host Unreachable
2	2 Protocol Unreachable
3	3 Port Unreachable
4	4 Fragmentation Needed and DF set
5	5 Source Route Failed
6	6 Destination Network Unknown
7	7 Destination Host Unknown
8	8 Source Host Isolated
9	9 Communication with Destination Network Administratively Prohibited
10	10 Communication with Destination Host Administratively Prohibited
11	11 Network Unreachable for Type of Service
12	12 Host Unreachable for Type of Service

FIGURE 7.30 *Code identifiers and interpretation.*

- The ICMP message code subvalue type fields:

    ICMP Checksum field, 16 bits. This ICMP field allows for the check sum process for an ICMP packet.

    CMP Datagram Address and ICMP fields, variable. This field contains the specific address of the first 64 bits of original packet involved in ICMP issue. The original IP datagram involved in IP error occurrence is tagged or padded on the end of the ICMP message data. This field also contains ICMP data (see Figure 7.31).

```
ICMP: - ICMP Header —
ICMP:
ICMP:  Type = 3 (Destination unreachable)
ICMP:  Code = 0 (Net unreachable)
ICMP:  Checksum = 180F (correct)
ICMP:  IP header of originating message (description follows)
ICMP:
IP:  - IP Header —
IP:
IP:  Version = 4, header length = 20 bytes
IP:  Type of service = 00
IP:  000.  . = routine
IP:   0 . = normal delay
IP:   .0  = normal throughput
IP:   . .0.. = normal reliability
IP:  Total length = 72 bytes
IP:  Identification = 32973
```

FIGURE 7.31 *An ICMP header decoded by a protocol analyzer.*

7.2.6 Other Key TCP/IP Application-Based Protocols

A range of application protocols in the networking industry rely on the TCP/IP stack for general communications. Specifically, certain applications and applied upper-layer protocols require the use of a transport protocol, such as TCP or UDP, and always require the underlying network layer protocol IP to be present for general transmission. These protocols are considered part of the TCP/IP suite.

The scope of this text does not cover a full discussion of these protocols, because there are other sources available, some of which are mentioned in Appendix B. These other sources can give a more detailed description of these protocol types and their interaction on the internetwork.

The following list describes other TCP/IP that are part of the TCP suite (application as well as other layer protocols):

- **File Transfer Protocol (FTP).** This is an application layer protocol used above the TCP and IP layers for a guaranteed reliable mode of accurate file access and transfer.

- **Trivial File Transfer Protocol (TFTP).** The access and transfer of files between TCP/IP network nodes. The TFTP requires less overhead than standard FTP, but also provides for less overhead.

- **The Telnet Protocol.** This is an application layer protocol used above the TCP and IP layers for transmitting characters in an oriented terminal mode based on keyboard screen data between IP networking nodes.

- **Simple Mail Transfer Protocol (SMTP).** This is an application layer protocol used above the TCP and IP layers for a guaranteed mail transfer process for TCP/IP nodes requiring mail transfer.

- **Remote UNIX (RUNIX) protocol.** A remote UNIX host–based communication protocol for UNIX calls made on the TCP/IP layers.

- **Domain Name Service (DNS).** A database query protocol for obtaining network addresses in an enterprise TCP/IP environment.

- **TCP/IP Common Management (CMOT).** An information-based management protocol used over TCP/IP.

- **X Window Protocols.** This is an application layer protocol used above the TCP and IP layers for complex screen remote draw calls.

- **Network Basic I/O System (NetBIOS).** This protocol is mainly considered part of the IBM and SNA protocol suite. It is used in the TCP/IP suite for connection setup protocol process for naming station addresses, datagram sending processes session setup, maintenance, and session data processing.

- **Routing Information Protocol (RIP).** This is a distance vector routing protocol and is based on 30-second standard updates. The IP-based RIP is used for updating routing information as to enterprise network and device location information required across IP-related routers, gateways, and host systems.

- **Subnetwork Access Protocol (SNAP).** This is standard encapsulation protocol used for protocol node-to-node device stack interpretation. The SNAP protocol is used as a protocol-handling vehicle—that is, as an enveloping protocol.

- **Logical Link Control (LLC).** This is also standard encapsulation protocol used for protocol node-to-node stack interpretation. This protocol is also considered a main part of the IBM and SNA protocol suite and offers polling capabilities. The LLC protocol can also be used for connection setup and maintenance by higher-layer protocols and applications. LLC is seen quite frequently in TCP/IP dataflow (see Figure 7.32).

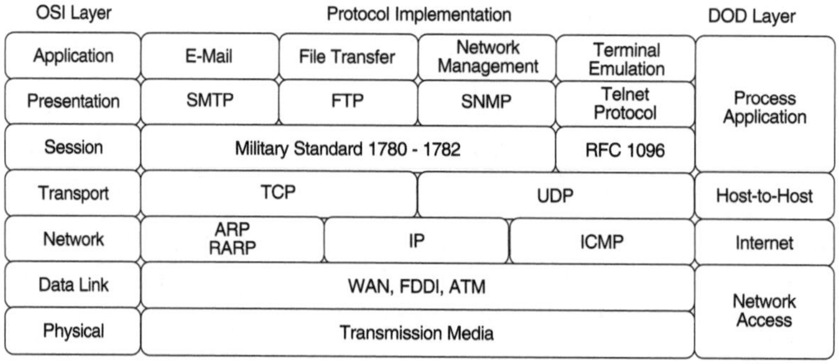

OSI Layer	Protocol Implementation				DOD Layer
Application	E-Mail	File Transfer	Network Management	Terminal Emulation	
Presentation	SMTP	FTP	SNMP	Telnet Protocol	Process Application
Session	Military Standard 1780 - 1782			RFC 1096	
Transport	TCP		UDP		Host-to-Host
Network	ARP RARP	IP		ICMP	Internet
Data Link	WAN, FDDI, ATM				Network Access
Physical	Transmission Media				

FIGURE 7.32 *The DOD model for TCP/IP as compared to the standard OSI model.*

The TCP/IP environment is very complex. To become a master in protocol analysis of this environment involves extensive study and research of the TCP/IP *Request for Comments* (RFCs).

7.3 TCP/IP Protocol Suite Analysis

This section discusses some of the key analysis techniques that an analyst can use when examining the TCP/IP suite. The discussion starts with a general review of analyzing the IP layer or IP.

7.3.1 IP Analysis

When reviewing the IP, keep mind that the key focus of the protocol is to provide an internetwork addressing scheme, along with a measure of length of transfer between two points in an IP-based network. A packet could not traverse an IP-based network gateway or router, unless an IP address was available for an IP address check to transfer a packet across one IP segment to another.

The IP Addressing field clearly identifies the source IP address network and the source host from which the network transmission originates from or is being transmitted to for process. In this case, the source and destination IP addresses are extremely important, especially with the subnetting schemes in place on today's IP-based networks. The key factor is that the IP Addressing fields are the main focal point of the analysis.

An analyst should examine the IP header of any problem type packet by examining the TOS field. If all the flags are inactive, no specialized routing is being used for TOS. If any of the fields are active, perhaps a specific type of service is being assigned to the packet; this may lead the analyst to understand the specific communication design being invoked by the application developer or the IP protocol stack or operation within the specific device.

The next valuable field is the Protocol Type field. Note, however, that most protocol analyzers just display the next protocol being encapsulated in the packet internal view and the Protocol Type field most likely correlates directly to that review.

Another important area is the TTL field. The TTL area of the IP header may enable an analyst to identify issues related to routing loops or delays. The TTL field indicates the amount of time that a packet has spent in an IP-based network or the number of hops traversed. This could show long delays or indicate a routing loop in an IP-based network. The TTL field is usually set upon generation at a default of 64 or 128 second to live or travel across an IP internetwork. Depending on which IP version is invoked, this field can vary in terms of seconds to live on an internetwork. If a TTL packet shows a low TTL of two to three seconds, the packet has traversed a high number of network hops or has spent too much time inside the router.

Remember that the TTL packet is decreased by one for each second that it spends within an internetwork IP path of a routing device, and must also be decreased by one for each device or logical hop that it traverses.

7.3.2 Host or Transport Layer Analysis

When examining the TCP and UDP layers, specific techniques must be used with a protocol analyzer to examine the overall fluency of endpoint-host–to–endpoint host for IP communications. When IP communication commence, both endpoints in a host-to-host transport layer process provide a TCP or UDP port as assigned for general communications. Because of this, an analyst should focus on any problem based in a TCP communication analysis session by investigating what ports are open in the source and destination end-host points for general communication between the two IP nodes. In most cases, a workstation and a server have certain host layer ports open for general application transfers.

7.3.2.1 Host Layer (UDP) Analysis

When examining the UDP, keep in mind that the UDP provides only the function of assigning and allowing access to a port for TCP-based communications. An analyst should closely study the UDP-assigned ports and be aware of what ports are assigned for communication. Also, the Checksum field should be investigated to see whether it is active. If the field is active, data is being verified for integrity. In some cases, this may cause minor latency when the application process has to investigate the data for communications. Most application programs deactivate the field; however, if the Checksum field is active, it was most designed to be active because the process application protocol does not provide for an integrity check on data. This is the reason the field is provided for use, because it will actually check the data via an algorithm between two IP nodes communicating via a UDP port. An analyst should also note the length field in the UDP header.

7.3.2.2 Host Layer TCP/IP Analysis

When analyzing TCP/IP, many different areas must be examined. The first area to focus on when examining general TCP communications is the fluency of the TCP open-to-closed state communication process. An initial TCP communication between two devices can be investigated by filtering on the two devices from a physical or network layer standpoint. Specifically, the analyst can start the session by filtering on the physical MAC address or the IP address for the two communicating devices. If a connection-based problem exists, the following process enables an analyst to examine the overall cycle.

The analyst should investigate the initial sequence of a TCP open communication process. It is important to look for a TCP three-way handshake to occur on a consecutive basis. This should consist of two packets that are initially communicated with initial sequence numbers, and then a third packet without an initial sequence number (which is the end of the three-way handshake). Dataflow should then commence on a consecutive basis in a bidirectional manner. There should be low latency between the two endpoints when communicating back and forth in a transitional phase.

One of the most important areas to examine in this communication is how well the TCP window handles the dataflow from endpoint to endpoint. If the TCP window is initially communicated and advertised at 8K, it should remain open at 8K and should provide communication availability within the 8K-range window. If the 8K window is ever transitioned down to a lower level, such as 1000 bytes or 0 bytes available, this could indicate a possible disconnect or reset is about to occur in TCP communications. It is important for an analyst to keep an eye on the TCP window and the overall float size of the TCP window range.

If the TCP window range is initially advertised at 8K, the TCP window should not float any more than 2000 bytes on each endpoint for adequate handling of a TCP window operation. If there is an excessive float, say from 8K to 1K or 0, this could very well indicate that a larger TCP window size is needed on each endpoint.

The next area that should be investigated in TCP communications is the Flags field for a reset if there is an abnormal breakdown in communications. If this does occur, it is an abnormal operation.

The other area that should be focused on is the TCP finish state. Upon break of a normal TCP open to a closed state communication, a finish bit should be set from one endpoint, and the other endpoint should send another finish bit. This would indicate a normal finish or smooth TCP closed state operation. If a smooth TCP closed state is not achieved and a TCP reset or abrupt TCP close occurs, overall communication flow suffers.

It is also important to note whether sequence and acknowledgment numbers are incrementing in a normal fashion when flowing back and forth during general communications of the TCP open state to closed state. The bidirectional communication process should show the payload of data adding to the sequence and acknowledgment numbers on sequence cycle reverse directions upon transfer. The positive acknowledgment and retransmission mechanism effects should not have to take upon active occurrence unless extensive delays occur. If there are a high number of retransmissions from one point to another, the analyst should examine the delta time to see whether any delays in the internetwork are causing the PAR transmission of the TCP mechanism to take effect.

These are some of the most helpful hints that will assist an analyst to understand the general TCP communications from one endpoint to another. If there is an extensive delay process and the PAR communication appears to take over the overall operation effects of the TCP communications, this may indicate continuous retransmissions and an eventual TCP reset. This type of event indicates an immediate problem that could be related to network delays or inherent slow operations within one of the IP nodes.

In summary, closely examine all the areas noted in a network analysis session, and ensure that focused notes are taken during the TCP/IP analysis session.

7.3.3 ICMP Analysis

The ICMP is an error-based protocol. Because of this fact alone, ICMP dataflow is a main focal point when starting an analysis session on an IP-based network. The inherent operation of the IP-based protocol allows for the ICMP-based errors to be generated upon an actual error occurrence within a device or when actual communication between two devices is affected by an IP-based problem in the overall internetwork. With that said, several ICMP-based errors can be captured by an analyst when correctly and effectively using a protocol analysis approach during network baselining.

Again, if a network is heavily based on the IP, an ICMP error test should be performed when investigating the error levels of the network. This is more of an error level focus on the IP and can be considered an upper-layer protocol analysis technique. At the same time, it is an effective way to examine the IP configuration stability and reliability of IP nodes throughout an internetwork.

The discussion now turns to a brief description of each ICMP-based error protocol generation type.

7.3.3.1 ICMP Ping or Echo Request Reply Sequences

The ICMP Echo Request and Reply sequence is one of the most common ICMP types and is called *ping*. This type allows for the generation capability of an IP node to send out an IP request to another IP node for an IP address to respond back. If the IP device responds back through an ICMP reply, the ICMP request was responded to in a normal manner and the ping is considered active and working. This means that the device was located and in effect "pinged" and operating. If an analyst detects a high numbers of ICMP pings during an analysis session, which is considered a passive network baseline, a network management process is most likely under effect or operation during that given time.

Typically, network management systems use follow inherent approach of using pings to investigate device status or operation on umbrella-based management systems, such as HP OpenView and other hub-based management systems such as the Bay Network Optivity and Cabletron's Spectrum. These are just samples of network management programs that can invoke the ping. Pings are also invoked by actual network management or support personnel to test network delay or propagation sequence. In such a case, this would be a static invoked process for a specific purpose. In most cases, the network analyst is aware of the ping cycle.

7.3.3.2 ICMP Fragmentation Required Message

As noted, the IP can send a datagram up to 65K in size. Because datagrams can be sent which are much larger than the normal physical topology MTU of approximately 1500 bytes for Ethernet, or approximately 4K bytes for Token Ring, most packets will be fragmented based on datagram size. In other words, the sent datagram will be sent in multiple packets. In this case, fragmentation fields are required to traverse different routers, switches, or topology points in a physical blended or uniform topology internetwork architecture.

With this in mind, there is an ICMP error type called "ICMP Fragmentation Required." This type of IP error message is typically generated from an IP-based host, router, or gateway that encounters a packet attempting to be transmitted across a routing or switched channel without fragmentation active when it is required. This is common, for instance, when a Token Ring packet is generated from a Token Ring interface on a router over to an Ethernet interface, and the router interface on the Ethernet side intercepts the packet with a bit set upon the source node that says the fragmentation is not going to be used. In this case, the router turns the packet back to the original source device, saying that the ICMP fragmentation bit is required to traverse, because of the change in topology MTU from Token Ring to Ethernet. An analyst should closely monitor for these types of situations, because they identify topology MTU mismatches and configurations on switches, routers, and hosts in an IP-based internetwork.

7.3.3.3 Incorrect IP Address Mask Error

An incorrect IP address mask error can be an indication that the subnet mask applied to an IP address is incorrect. If an analyst captures an ICMP address mask request packet, this can indicate that an IP address was assigned with the incorrect address as it relates to the interface or device for the IP addressing scheme at the facility. Various configurations can be applied in the subnet masks as they relate to various address schemes active in enterprise internetworks. To verify this symptom as a problem also requires investigation of the IP addressing scheme at the site. In this case, you should note these errors and the devices that generate the address mask request. In this particular case, it could be possible that the default gateway or the settings of the IP addressing scheme in the source device generating the packet prior to the address mask request is causing the problem. It is also possible that the router or switch IP addressing scheme is not compatible with the IP addressing scheme at the site.

7.3.3.4 ICMP Redirect Message

ICMP redirect messages communicate a misconfiguration in an IP routing scheme or the default gateway setting in an IP addressing scheme in an IP-based internetwork. Specifically, an ICMP redirect is a packet generated from a IP gateway or router device when it receives a packet that should be sent in another direction.

The process is as follows: A source device generates a packet to a destination device. If an IP-based gateway or router intercepts the packet and sees that the packet should not be sent through its channel, it sends an ICMP redirect message. As the redirect message is generated outbound, an analyst can capture the message. The message usually indicates the original IP transmission by tagging on the IP header from the original transmission. It shows the original source and destination device at the bottom of the detail area of the packet. This shows how the original transmission was intended to flow. The top of the packet contains an IP header in the normal IP encapsulation mode showing the device retransmitting the packet to the original device. Then, in the middle is an ICMP redirect area that shows the IP router or gateway that should be used for processing the packet through for general transfer.

By investigating this packet, an analyst can see the original IP header transmission from the source to the destination device and can also see the intercepting device returning the packet and identifying within the middle of the ICMP packet, along with the proper router or gateway path to take for route. Upon capture of this type of event, an analyst should investigate the source device for a proper default gateway setting, and should also investigate the site router tables and router configurations within the device returning the packet. There may also be an incorrect setting in that particular router or switch or host, if a host is providing routing via two NICs within a server channel. Such circumstances may indicate that a close review of the routing environment should be performed by the analyst to investigate an IP configuration routing issue. Packets excessively redirected may cause delays on the internetwork, and may prevent ports and hosts from being reached upon transfer for IP communications. Specifically, by intercepting redirects and properly troubleshooting the redirects to cause, it is very likely that connectivity and latency problems will be resolved in an IP-based network.

7.3.3.5 ICMP TTL Expired

The IP header contains a TTL field, which determines the amount of time in seconds that a packet can live in an IP network, and the number of hops that the packet can traverse. The normal default for an IP node upon an IP stack configuration is 64 seconds to live.

If a packet is generated and traverses from a site in New York across a WAN to California, for example, the following scenario could unfold. If a packet leaves New York with 64 seconds to live and traverses the Chicago router, and the Chicago router has a 30-second delay, the packet would have approximately 33 seconds to live. This would account for a 1-second drop for the hop in Chicago plus a 30-second drop for the delay in the Chicago router. If the packet reaches the Salt Lake City router and there is a 40-second delay, the Salt Lake City router would discard the packet because there is no more time to live. In this case, an "ICMP time to live exceeded" packet would have to be sent back to the source device in New York.

An analyst using a WAN analyzer in the Chicago or New York headquarters where the packet originated can capture the TTL expired packet sent from the Salt Lake City router. In this case, the packet would show the original transmission tagged at the bottom of the ICMP analysis packet and it would show the device returning the packet. By investigating the TTL Expired field and understanding the route of the packet, the analyst may be able to identify which router or which area of the internetwork has the highest delay. This is an important investigative process during network analysis. An analyst should thoroughly troubleshoot any TTL expired packets, because they most likely indicate a delay on the internetwork or a misconfiguration of a router or switch device in a large enterprise design.

7.3.3.6 ICMP Destination Unreachable
An "ICMP destination unreachable" packet indicates that an IP node is returning a transmission onto the internetwork because its destination was not reached.

There are several classifications of destination unreachable:

- ICMP destination unreachable network unreachable
- ICMP destination unreachable host unreachable
- ICMP destination unreachable protocol unreachable
- ICMP destination unreachable port unreachable

With all four of these types identified, it can clearly be seen that if a packet is intercepted with this type of event, the packet should be closely reviewed. The packet usually shows the original IP packet source transmission from the source to destination device that was attempted, and the type of protocol, network, or host, that was sought. The vector of the internal ICMP field showing the network, host, protocol, or port unreachable determines which action should be taken.

If a network is unreachable, it most likely that the packet is being returned from a router or switch, and that the network cannot be found or identified because it is not built within the static or dynamic router of the router. Another possibility is the fact that the route is incorrect, or the network is down and not available.

If a host is unreachable, this usually indicates that the host is inactive, nonresponsive, or not functioning on a network. It could also indicate that the host is not a legal address on an IP-based network, or is improperly configured. This can also indicate that the source device is improperly calling on the wrong host.

A port unreachable message could indicate that an application is inactive within a host. This is a very common occurrence in a network analysis session. When an analyst captures ICMP destination unreachable port unreachable conditions, the application type for the port assignment should be investigated. The port should be clearly noted and the device returning the error should be closely noted. Most likely this will be a server with a certain application running with a port that was inactive or too busy at the time to respond. If the problem is intermittent, it could be because of the application load on the port of the host being too heavy, and the port temporarily not being accessible. If this is a consistent error, the application may not be running, or the port may be incorrectly assigned and the application may be misconfigured. It is also possible that the server or NOS operation may be misconfigured.

A protocol unreachable condition usually indicates that a particular protocol is not active at a router, switch, or host device. This requires further investigation of the device reporting the error.

7.3.4 Closing Statement On TCP/IP Analysis

TCP/IP analysis requires a truly investigative technique via protocol analysis during a network baselining exercise. To truly identify the cause of problems requires exact troubleshooting and cause analysis techniques based on protocol analysis results. It is also recommended that the analyst thoroughly study the TCP/IP suite through the RFCs and other documents cited in Appendix B. Extensive knowledge of TCP/IP is helpful when analyzing TCP/IP-based environments.

7.4 IBM SNA And NetBIOS Protocol Suite Analysis

The IBM protocol suite, which was derived directly from the industry migration cycle of the IBM networking architecture, includes two main protocols that are predominant in the IBM networking environment: *Systems Networking Architecture* protocol (SNA), and NetBIOS.

Many other protocols could be considered part of the IBM SNA protocol suite. Some of these protocols are independent of the IBM protocol model and are used in other protocol suites for specific operations. The independent protocols within the suite are mentioned briefly in the following list.

- **Systems Networking Architecture (SNA).** A high-layer data communication protocol for access to the IBM host data resources.

- **Server Message Block (SMB).** The SMB protocol was engaged for use in the IBM OS2 LAN Server networking process for calls from a workstation to a LAN server NOS. The SMB protocol is used as an application layer protocol for the LAN server environment, as required for connection, login, and file access.

- **Remote Program Load (RPL).** The RPL protocol is used as a diskless workstation protocol for IBM Token Ring PROMS.

- **Network Basic I/O System (NetBIOS).** This protocol allows for engaging name-mapping processes and data-sending processes. The NetBIOS is also used to establish and maintain session services. The NetBIOS protocol is also engaged as a connection setup protocol for named station addresses.

- **IBM Network Management protocol (IBMNM).** The IBMNM protocol is also used for functional address communication at Token Ring physical layer.

- **Bridge Protocol Data Unit (BPDU).** The BPDU is engaged for launching updates in *spanning-tree algorithm* (STA)–based communication. The BPDU protocol is also used for identifying an STA topology change in the STA root tree in communication for bridges.

- **Logical Link Control (LLC).** This protocol is popular for encapsulation. LLC is also used as a connection setup and maintenance process to maintain polling in certain computing environments. LLC is engaged for connection setup between workstations and different IBM-based hosts and servers and works well with various higher-layer protocols (see Figure 7.33).

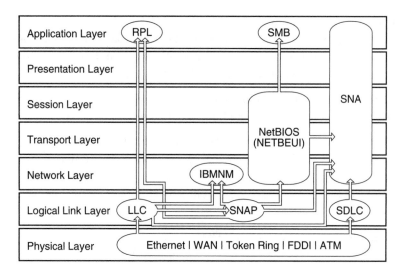

FIGURE 7.33 *The SNA protocol model.*

The protocols in the preceding list are among the most common protocols seen within the SNA and IBM environments. These protocols can be used individually for specific purposes. When running a network baseline session, it may become necessary to engage a network protocol analyzer to individually decode these protocols for a specific purpose.

The two most common IBM-based protocols encountered are SNA and NetBIOS. Based on the predominance of these two protocols as related to the overall protocol suite, the following sections describe these two protocols in the context of network analysis.

7.4.1 SNA Protocol

The SNA protocol was developed within the IBM networking environment. SNA is the protocol responsible for most of the key network communications for endpoints within an IBM enterprise environment. The SNA protocol was originally designed and structured for the IBM host environment. In today's LAN and WAN internetworking infrastructures, a user sometimes requires access to applications that reside on an IBM host environment. The SNA protocol can be used for access when communicating to a host. In most cases, there is a shell or terminal emulator running on the PC workstation on a LAN when this type of communication takes place. On certain topologies, this type of communication is more prevalent than in others, such as the Token Ring environment as opposed to an Ethernet environment. This is because of the natural transition of the IBM host environment, which was present within local area environments that eventually grew from a Token Ring infrastructure.

Keeping that in mind, sometimes an analyst must analyze SNA during a baseline session. The following is a description of each one of the SNA protocol layers. In consideration of the context of this book, the descriptions have been limited to the protocol layers. For more detail regarding SNA operations or SNA protocol layer field configuration issues, refer to the sources cited in Appendix B.

7.4.2 SNA Protocol Suite Interactive Layers Analysis

The SNA protocol suite is based on a seven-layer internetwork communication process model that includes the following layers (see Figure 7.34):

- Physical control/data link control layer

- Path control layer

- Transmission control layer

- Dataflow control layer

- Presentation services/transaction services layer

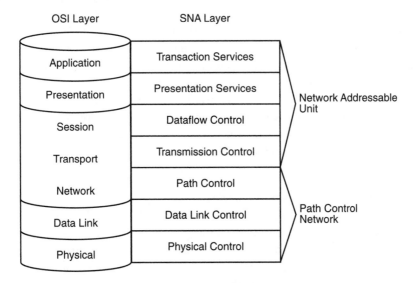

FIGURE 7.34 *Comparing the SNA protocol model to the OSI model.*

7.4.2.1 SNA Physical Layer and Data Link Layer Processes

The SNA physical and data link layers work in an interoperable fashion to ensure that the communication from the local or WAN medium as communicated to an IBM host can be processed as a normal data stream to the physical channel of the IBM host SNA environment. In some ways, these layers are somewhat similar in terms of the standard OSI model for physical and data link control. The physical connection is the main focus of the physical layer, along with the packet assembler and dissembler process. After the packet has been received off the medium and the physical medium-dependent code is interpreted, the packet is then sent up to the data link layer in SNA. In this layer, the transfer process is handled by the data link controller of SNA.

The data link control layer is responsible for the node-to-node, endpoint-to-endpoint SNA device communications for data transfer. This layer ensures a reliable data transfer sequence.

7.4.2.2 SNA Path Control Layer

The SNA path control layer is somewhat similar to the network layer as it relates to the OSI model. The SNA path control layer provides for an SNA packet to be transferred between one path to another. Note, however, that the protocol itself is not designed for a high amount of internetwork routing in terms of today's LAN infrastructures. Another key function of the path control layer is to ensure that each of the two node points involved in an SNA conversation is properly connected through to assist the transport processes. Because of this capability, it is quite common to see the path control layer compared to a transport connection layer in the OSI model. The path control layer is responsible for the compatibility connection sequence function of one node to talk to another node across an SNA internetwork. The route configured between the two SNA nodes, such as a workstation running an emulation program and an SNA host, is a virtual route. The function of actual routing between the two nodes across the SNA internetwork is achieved through the SNA transmission control layer.

7.4.2.3 SNA Transmission Control Layer

The SNA transmission control layer operates in a session mode sequence, such as the session layer protocol in the OSI model. The flow control between two SNA nodes is established and a session is considered active at this layer. If there is a need for any data to be encrypted for security purposes and to be reinterpreted through decryption, that process occurs at this layer. The request and response headers of the SNA packet format are also interpreted at the SNA transmission control layer.

7.4.2.4 SNA Dataflow Control Layer

The SNA dataflow control layer also operates as an area that is responsible for maintaining a session between the workstation emulator and the SNA host. The process of investigating the integrity of the data from endpoint-to-endpoint communications occurs at this layer. The dataflow layer receives each request and provides each response inbound and outbound of each SNA endpoint channel. It is also the responsibility of the dataflow layer to reassemble dataflow sequences for any fragmented messages in the overall communication sequences. The request and response units within the SNA dataflow communication must occasionally send portions of the message. The dataflow layer ensures that the portions of the message are assembled upon reception at each endpoint and broken down for transmission through a dissembler process for generation outbound upon an internetwork transfer. This is one of the key responsibilities of the dataflow layer.

7.4.2.5 SNA Presentation Services and Transaction Services Layers

When the SNA host session is considered physically stable, meaning that the path is established, the transmission control layer has ensured that the nodes are maintaining flow control, and the response sequences are being properly assembled and dissembled. The presentation services and transaction services next come into play. In these layers, the host environment and endpoint environment communicate through certain transactions called back and forth from node to node for each specific application call. When the data is ready to be presented to an application layer process, the presentation services become effective for program-to-program communication. This is where higher-layer application processes and database-interrelation processes take place.

7.4.3 SNA Dataflow Processes

The following is an example of a general scenario of a workstation-to-host communication process. When using a protocol analysis tool such as protocol analyzer during a network baseline session, an analyst can capture the session by either filtering on the workstation running the SNA emulation program, or by filtering on the host channel on the LAN connection, such as a LAN-based SNA TIC connection from an IBM host connection.

An SNA packet would be assembled with key information that can be interpreted on the protocol analyzer. This information may include a key area within the packets called the Data Link Control header for SNA. This header is normally encapsulated inside of a physical frame and captured on the LAN, such as Token Ring frame (see Figure 7.35).

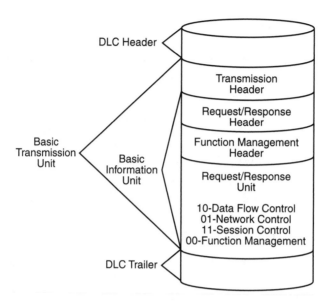

FIGURE 7.35 *How the SNA protocol model field internals are engaged.*

The Token Ring frame includes a Routing Information field, for example, and then pad a protocol called the LLC. The LLC header normally encapsulates the source service access point and destination service access points. Contained within the SNA portion of the Token Ring frame is an SNA transmission header that includes the format, identification, and the required destination and source addresses for the SNA session. Flags are present and identify header information for general communication, which is key to the path control and transmission control layer areas. The request and response header contain bytes of information important for general communication. If any function management data is present within the SNA header, it includes the pointers for a particular function to engage a specific network operation, such as starting an initial connection and performing an authentication process to log on to the host. The SNA dataflow layer is involved in this area, along with the transaction and presentation services. If the data control process is finally going to be set up and locked in for general communications, a request and response unit and a session layer control process is involved. In this case, the SNA transmission control layer and SNA dataflow layer would be key in the communication sequence. If a network control process is required to perform receive/request or response unit cycles as identified, this area carries key information such as testing and network management processes for SNA network management functions.

Relative to the high-level processes for general SNA communications, keep in mind that the SNA architecture design is based on *logical units* (LUs), *physical units*, (PUs), and *system services control points* (SSCPs). The LUs are defined as end-to-end node-to-node communication points across the SNA internetwork. A PU is a device that can have a hardware or software logical configuration, through which communication can be directed for input and output. The SSCP is an area within the SNA internetwork where a host system usually resides, and software and hardware processes are working together to allow for the SNA process to take place. When investigating an SNA packet, it is important to decode the transmission header and the request and response notation, and the management function header, if required. Notations in the frame may indicate certain information related to dataflow control, network control, or session control. The Connection Control field is important to analysis and general decoding sessions. If the connection is going to be maintained on a consistent basis, the LLC is usually consistently engaged as a polling sequence protocol, or in some cases, NetBIOS session services may be involved.

7.4.4 The NetBIOS Protocol

NetBIOS is a communication protocol based on a connection-oriented process, and was originally developed for IBM's PC LAN broadband network. The development cycle was overseen by IBM and Sytec, Inc. Originally NetBIOS was designed to function on read-only memory on the NIC. In today's environments, NetBIOS is loaded within the network card driver area and built in to the firmware and hardware operations of many network interface channels involved in SNA communications.

Other protocols are compatible and work quite frequently with SNA and NetBIOS, such as SMB and other key protocols. Within the NetBIOS communication cycle, four key functions take place.

- Name services
- Session services
- Datagram services
- Miscellaneous functions

The name service allows for the naming processes to take place upon the initiation of the NetBIOS session. The name consists of a number of characterizations, usually within the 16-characterization category. This is where a device attempts to map a logical name to a process for the SNA communication cycle. Three individual calls usually occur during this sequence. They are Add Name, Delete Name, or Add Group Name.

The NetBIOS session service is a process in which a session is usually established through the SNA transmission control and dataflow layer sequences. At times, however, the NetBIOS session is used for straight data transfer, because it allows for a more reliable link than standard NetBIOS datagram services. Data messages are usually variable in length. NetBIOS session services include the following:

- Call

- Listen

- Hang up

- Send

- Receive

- Session status

NetBIOS datagram services allow for a transfer of data, but in a somewhat unreliable manner. This is somewhat similar to the unreliable transfer noted for UDP in the TCP/IP suite. Datagram services allow for fast transfer of a unit of data between two SNA established endpoints for communication. The transmission control layer and dataflow layers are involved, but the actual maintenance is not as critical.

Datagram services are used for the following functions:

- Send datagram

- Send broadcast datagram

- Receive datagram

- Receive broadcast datagram

Other functions in the NetBIOS protocol are also used and fall into a category called miscellaneous functions. These include the following:

- Reset

- Cancel

- Remote program

- Load

- Adaptor link status

- Unlink

The NetBIOS communication sequences vary depending on implementation and the requirements of the application or NOS environment. Some of the key NetBIOS calls that can be interpreted with a protocol analysis tool are noted in the following table. Note that the various protocol analyzers may provide a different display sequence or name for the actual NetBIOS call. Table 7.1 lists some examples.

TABLE 7.1 SOME OF THE MORE GENERIC CALL NAMES

Call Name	Call Function
NAME_QUERY	Call requests a name on the network.
NAME_RECOGNIZED	Call recognizes a name.
NAME_IN_CONFLICT	Call detects a duplicate name.
ADD_NAME_QUERY	Call checks for a duplicate name.
ADD_GROUP_NAME_QUERY	Call checks for a duplicate group name.
ADD_NAME_RESPONSE	Call detects duplicate names after query.
SESSION_INITIALIZE	Call sets up a session.
SESSION_CONFIRM	Call ID's receipt of SESSION_INITIALIZE.
SESSION_ALIVE	Call checks whether session is active.
SESSION_END	Call terminates the session.
DATAGRAM	Call ID's datagram transmitted.
DATAGRAM_BROADCAST	Call ID's broadcast datagram.
DATA_ACK	Call data-only acknowledgment.
DATA_FIRST_MIDDLE	Call data is first or middle in frame.
DATA_ONLY_LAST	Call data is last in frame.
RECEIVE-CONTINUE	Call waiting for outstanding receive.
RECEIVE_OUTSTANDING	Call retransmit last data.
STATUS_QUERY	Call requests status of a remote. name
STATUS-RESPONSE	Call reply to STATUS_QUERY.
TERMINATE_TRACE	Call terminates trace on local/remote.

7.5 SNA Protocol Communications Analysis

Because of the lack of predominance of SNA and NetBIOS protocols in today's networking environments, this text presents only a limited discussion regarding analysis of the SNA protocol suite. When analyzing the SNA protocol suite, it is important to start with a proper filtering approach on the SNA host and on the workstation providing terminal emulation to the SNA host. First, capture the inbound and outbound communications from the SNA host environment.

An analyst will note certain processes within an SNA connection that should be examined. Usually a workstation calls with a link control query setup that can be captured with a protocol analyzer. In certain situations, after the SNA session has been established, a request and response sequence occurs in reverse order, which can be captured and examined to understand the overall function calls of the SNA host. Standard communications occur and involve logical assignment of SNA exchange IDs or physical and logical unit setup processes in general communication. These also can be examined using a protocol analysis approach. Sometimes an SNA host shows itself as extremely busy on a LAN environment. This may be the result of a generated outbound "Receiver Not Ready" frame that can be captured from a LAN configuration. Excessive upper-layer communications related to an application flowing between a workstation emulator and an SNA host may indicate the presence of delays through a high number of segment continue packets. In this event, it is quite possible that the SNA configuration and channel configuration need to be redesigned to allow for more fluent communication to handle the amount of inbound LAN traffic at a certain data rate.

NetBIOS can be used as a reliable connection-based protocol sequence and will still allow for sending data as through the session control or through datagram control sequences. The type of NetBIOS protocol sequence being engaged must be closely examined. An analyst should be able to quickly identify naming services, session services, and datagram services, and decipher the various cycles as related to the SNA communication cycle. During a protocol analysis session, an analyst should watch for the SNA communication to establish a proper connection sequence from an initial standpoint. The connection sequence involves the path control layer and the transmission control layer. After the session has been established and data is available for transfer, the transmission control and dataflow layers will most likely be involved in every transmission. Whenever the application is called upon or a sequence for the application process is engaged, the transaction and presentation services can also be analyzed.

An analyst should keep a close focus on the request and response headers in the SNA communication cycle for these types of sequences, and eventually look for a proper breakdown of normal communication sequences, when the teardown is valid for the SNA session.

7.6 Windows NT Protocol Suite Analysis

The Windows NT protocol suite is comprised of various protocols that were derived from other internetworking protocol suites in the enterprise environment. The Windows NT protocol directly involves the SMB protocol, which was originally developed within the context of the IBM OS2 LAN Server infra-structure, along with the NetBIOS protocol, which is heavily used in the SNA protocol suite. For the network and transport layer protocol communication processes, IP is used for the network layer communications, and TCP is used for general transport connectivity.

The NT protocol suite is designed around the Windows NT peer-to-peer networking services, along with the capability of a Windows NT Workstation, a Windows 98 station, or a Windows 2000 station to communicate to an NT Server. In this type of configuration, the workstation establishes physical com-munications to an NT-based server through a physical topology frame such as an Ethernet or a Token Ring frame. After this type of communication has been established, the IP is used for datagram transfer of units of data across an internetwork channel. The IP address is significant because it provides the capability to route or transfer data across a bridge, a routed or a switched channel in an internetwork. This is the way in which a Windows NT Workstation can communicate to a server on another segment.

After the data communication session has been started, the session is main-tained through engagement of TCP. Standard TCP mechanisms for TCP open state to closed state occur, such as described in the TCP analysis section of this book. A TCP windowing advertisement is used in a consistent process along with TCP sequence and acknowledgment processes.

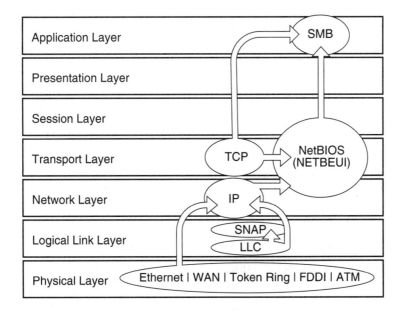

FIGURE 7.36 The Windows NT protocol layer model.

The Windows NT operating system then invokes the SMB protocol. The SMB protocol is extremely important, because it is used for calling on the server in the NT NOS process. The NT NOS process involves a high number of calls through *application programming interface* (API) calls to an SMB processing level, which engages certain areas in the NT operating system as communicating to the SMB protocol functions. This includes sequencing in areas of the SMB protocol sequence calls as related to the NOS, which include communication to areas within the operating system, as follows:

- Redirector

- Transport driver interface (TDI)

- Other protocols within the suite

The following is a brief description of the Windows NT protocol suite processes engaged when taking into account the interaction between the layers. Note that when performing a network baseline session, an analyst may need to capture certain packets between a workstation and a server in an NT protocol analysis session. Not all protocol layers may be active, depending on the function of the particular protocol call, such as a workstation connecting to a server, logging on to a server, or transferring data to an application in an NT Server.

With sequences in which a workstation is just maintaining a connection with an NT Server, for example, the only layers that may be active would be the physical topology layer, the IP layer, and the TCP layer. If actual data is being transferred, the NetBIOS session layer may also be active. In other cases, there may be circumstances during which the NT server is being called on by an NT Workstation for a specific file to be opened and accessed. In this case, the SMB protocol may be active in the packet.

The following is a list of the protocols in the Windows NT protocol suite.

- **IP.** Network layer datagram and addressing services for delivery of data

- **TCP.** Transport-based connection-based protocol operation and reliable end-to-end communication over IP datagrams

- **NetBIOS.** Session layer operations for connection setup protocol processes and for naming station address processes

- **NetBEUI.** Comparable to NetBIOS, but nonroutable

- **Server Message Block (SMB).** Used for Windows NT Workstation–to–NT Server application layer protocol calls in a LAN and WAN environment.

The following is a description of the overall protocol layer interaction scheme designed around the Windows NT protocol suite access from a workstation to a server in an NT protocol operation.

7.6.1 Windows NT Protocol Operations

To truly understand all the protocol analysis events that need to be performed to tune or troubleshoot a Windows NT environment, an analyst must also understand the architecture of the internetwork composite. When examining the NT server-to-client operation, the analyst must take into account how the Windows NT protocol suite matches up against the OSI model.

It should always be noted that the OSI model may apply, but the Windows NT protocol suite is mapped differently across the model. The Windows NT client model includes an area of operation for the general NOS communication directly through the protocol chain to a redirector process. The redirector process then allows for creation of I/O calls through SMB. The SMB protocol then communicates to a subnet protocol stack that includes Layers 3, 4, and 5 (transport, session transport, and network layer protocol stacks). Communication then inherently directs to the network drivers, which involves the NDIS specification and communication with the key network adaptor. The network driver normally provided by Microsoft uses the *Network Driver Interface Specification* (NDIS) interface. This particular interface allows multiple protocol stacks to communicate across the network infrastructure with single or multiple NIC adaptors inside the server or workstation. The NDIS drivers are widely used and are usually internal to the NT distribution software. Note that the NDIS drivers normally operate within the NOS at protocol layer points two and three (see Figure 7.37).

The driver implementation of the NDIS drivers is usually built within the NIC configuration process. The NDIS driver is actually used in a mode where a wrapper *data link library* (DLL) is implemented around the NDIS interface.

Multiple protocols such as NetBEUI, TCP/IP with streams, and IPX/SPX communicate with the NDIS interface. These are normally in the area of the network transport and session layer.

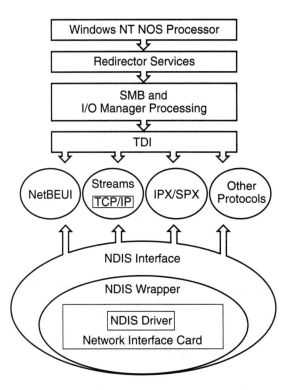

FIGURE 7.37   *The Windows NT processing cycle.*

They then communicate up to a TDI, which communicates to the redirector area of the NOS.

Note that in between the redirector and the TDI, key interaction of I/O occurs and SMB interacts with session, transport and network layer protocol operations.

NDIS allows for the true separation of physical networks from transport protocols. NDIS also allows for different protocol stacks to interactively work on a single NIC adaptor. NDIS also allows for full 32-byte accessing multiprocessing.

Note that the protocol stacks that reside between Layers 3, 4, and 5 are sometimes referred to as the subnet protocol area. The protocol stacks normally used are IP and TCP, or IPX and SPX with NW Link IPX compatible protocol in Windows NT or NetBEUI. These protocols cover the spectrum of the subnet area Layers 3, 4, and 5.

The Windows NT Server does not just support the NDIS interface, but also supports the *Open Data-link Interface* (ODI). The ODI is more inherent to the general Novell and Apple computer environment.

The NDIS specification was developed by Microsoft and is the main internal native driver mechanism used with the Microsoft protocols as related to the OSI model. If the ODI architecture is used, the NDIS drivers would correspond to a portion of data in the data link layer and are written to work with the *link support layer* (LSL). The LSL is a key element of the ODI specification; it allows for the NIC adaptor to be virtually viewed across the logical plane of the network process. In the Windows NT Server environment, the streams interface can be used to encapsulate communication protocols to allow for a uniform transport interface. Streams is an interface that was developed by AT&T in the UNIX environment and allows for a common interface between applications, by providing a package around key network and transport layer protocols, and involves a stream tail and stream head.

All network drivers have an internal capability to operate with a hardware operation of a particular NIC. Key NIC hardware registers are under the control of the driver, such as status registers, memory access, and I/O operation. It is important that the Windows NT Workstation or Server be installed with the correct driver to match the NIC card. It is inherent to the Windows NT Server and NT Workstation operations to engage the capability to bind the NIC card to the NIC driver. Note that Windows NT Workstation and Server software normally includes most of the popular NIC drivers. If the NIC driver is not available, the appropriate vendor must be contacted. Windows NT NIC drivers are written to the NDIS 3.0 specification, which is compliant with the NetBEUI, SPX, IPX, and TCP/IP protocol suites. NDIS drivers are not restricted to 640KB of memory as a typical DOS environment allows. The other major improvement is that the NDIS driver in 3.0 allows for the elimination of the protocol manager, which did engage overhead. Instead of using a protocol manager, Windows NT uses an internal Registry, which is a database within the server, and allows a software module (NDIS Wrapper) to surround the NIC driver. The main internal subnet protocols inherent to the NT Server native mode for Layers 3, 4, and 5 are Layer 3 = IPX and IP; Layer 4 = SPX and TCP; Layer 5 = NetBIOS; Layer Span 3 to 5 = NetBEUI (see Figure 7.38).

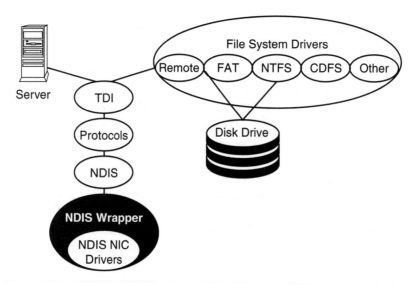

FIGURE 7.38 *The Windows NT NOS server operational model.*

The original implementation of IP was configured to allow for true network layer connectionless service to occur along reliable non-connection-based communication of an IP datagram. The IP datagram process allows for inter-network dataflow to occur and provides for a true unit of measure for data. This is also the same for the standard Network layer IPX protocol in the Novell environment. The key to network layer protocols is that data is packaged for internetwork transfer and internetwork addressing fields. In reference to the transport layer at Layer 4, note that the TCP, UDP, or SPX protocol, allows for some sort of connection to be maintained.

The inherent difference is the capability in the operation of each transport layer protocol. The most popular implementation is to use TCP; it has a full internal capability for data windowing, true connection-based operation, and sequenced and acknowledgment communications, which are considered the most reliable on top of the standard IP datagram service communications. In reference to the session layer or cross-layer 3/4/5 communication processes that are inherent methods to NT, two particular implementations are possible: NetBIOS and NetBEUI. The original implementation of the NetBIOS specification allowed for approximately 17 internal commands for connection-based functions to occur that allowed for the creation, maintenance, and disconnect of certain network client-to-server communications.

The basic NetBIOS commands were originally developed and then extended and so called the NetBEUI. In the late 1980s and early 1990s, NetBIOS and NetBEUI were widely released. The NetBEUI protocol allows for an actual cross-layer transport and session protocol operation to occur; and NetBIOS refers more to the session layer for engaging programming command activity that interacts with the APIs. By separating the transport protocol from the application layer processes of API, it is possible to have the NetBIOS API call support on protocols other than NetBEUI. Specifically, NetBIOS can communicate on top of TCP and IP, which is usually the most popular protocol stack implemented in the Windows NT environment. The NetBEUI protocol is not routable, but does span network Layers 3, 4, and 5. This presents a problem on large internetworks that require packets to be routed across bridges and routers. The NetBEUI protocol is adequate for small LANs that do not require a large amount of interconnections to other networks through bridges or routers. NetBIOS and NetBEUI both allow for establishing naming connections and assignments to provide for protocol calls and session establishment. This process assists with the Windows NT peer-to-peer networking capabilities (see Figure 7.39).

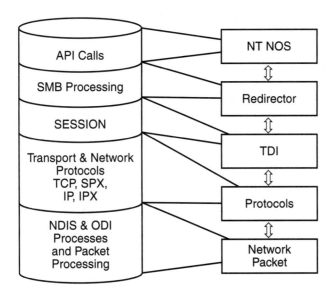

FIGURE 7.39 *Windows NT packet-formation processes.*

In the event that multiple networks are required and interconnection between networks is necessary for communications, NetBIOS should be used on top of the TCP/IP stacks for most implementations. If NetWare interaction is going to be a factor, the NWLink IPX-to-SPX communication can also be used. The Windows NT implementation in NetBEUI/NetBIOS contains extensions over the original NetBEUI designed by Microsoft, IBM, and Intel, and is referred to an the Windows NT NetBIOS frame processes. If the client uses the NetBEUI protocol in its original form, it spans Layers 3, 4, and 5. If NetBIOS operates at the session level, it normally communicates with TCP/IP or the IPX/SPX components of the NWLink design. NetBIOS originally had a limit of connections per active workstation on the network. The new NetBIOS frame implementation removes the limit of connections and permits the NT Server to interact with more stations.

It is important to understand that the TCP/IP suite is also a benefit because it allows Windows NT Servers and client workstations to interact more heavily with the Internet, and allows for applications to be inherently loaded across particular devices with protocols such as FTP, Telnet, NFS, X Window, and other key protocols. Windows NT can also communicate with IBM mainframes via the *Datalink Control* (DLC) protocol, and also allows for LLC interaction. It is also possible that the Windows socket interface, WinSock, will be used in TCP as part of the standard BSD UNIX operation for general communications. Both NetBIOS and WinSock are implemented as DLLs in the Windows environment. One of the key factors that has to be considered is that the Windows NT subnet layer design is intended to allow for communication on the internetwork via the TDI. The TDI interacts above the subnet layer and communicates to the redirector services.

The TDI resides between Layers 4 and 5 and above, and communicates as a uniform interface for network hardware communications to the redirector services. The TDI is critical for transport layer protocol communication to APIs. The redirector is a component operation that resides in the TDI area of the NOS design. The redirector allows the actual communication coming through the protocol to the transport chain and the TDI to be communicated up to the NOS application operations. The redirector component communicates with the TDI by utilizing an I/O request/response director that communicates with an I/O manager. The I/O manager calls upon certain driver entry points within the redirector to create SMB protocol commands that can be communicated through the TDI down through the transport layer, into the network layer, and across the internetwork to the other key clients and communication.

Specifically, between the redirector and TDI, the resulting SMB commands are used interactively to create and process key operating system calls. Most Windows NT file server and print-sharing operations are performed by the SMB protocol operation in this particular area. The main SMB protocol calls are the following:

- High-level, connection-based process services

- Obtaining directory entries

- Reading and writing blocks of data for host file access

- Overall file access

- Manipulating database operations

- Name-registering services across the internetwork

After the redirector, the last area that needs to be considered is the API. The API is the I/O communication area where the NOS is actually operating in an interactive mode with the redirector to create the SMB calls on the network.

The API operation depends on the implementation of the protocol chain within the server and client. In reference to the general NOS calls on the redirector, note that certain internal operations called "named pipes" and "mail-slot application" programming interfaces are engaged to perform the open, read, and write processes for file access and resource access across the internetwork. On the Windows NT Servers, the named pipes APIs are based on OS2 APIs in the original form, and allow for security operations. In the OS2 environment, they are called "first-class" mail slots. In the NT environment, they are called "second-class" mail slots and are used as connectionless message deliver process API calls upon the redirector. Specifically, mail-slot messages are developed and generated between the server and the client to allow for identification of computer services and notification messages. NT clients can call on the name-pipe operation. The name-pipe operation allows for true client identification. This enables the server to service a workstation request based on its *security ID* (SID) to match the request to allow for proper authentication. Generally, the NOS within the NT operating system is used in a full multitasking interaction and communicates to the redirector, which then uses an I/O manager to create the SMB protocol calls through the TDI. The TDI then communicates through the session, transport, and network layer protocol chain of the subnet area, which then uses the NDIS driver (or other driver components in composite) to create a packet sent across the network (see Figure 7.40).

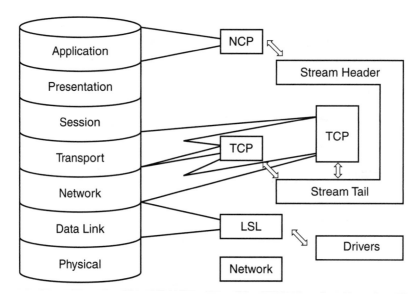

FIGURE 7.40 *Comparing the OSI model to the Windows NT ODI stack engagement.*

The following section discusses the actual protocol layer interaction and fields used on the Windows NT network for analysis.

7.6.2 Windows NT Protocol Suite Configuration

The Windows NT protocol suite includes the standard topology frame that will be used, such as Ethernet or Token Ring. The next process that will engaged is the IP for datagram services, and the transmission control for connection-based processes. If session data is going to be transferred back and forth in pure form, the NetBIOS session layer is engaged. The final focus is that the SMB protocol is used for application access. Earlier in this chapter, during the TCP analysis and SNA/IBM analysis discussions, the other key protocols such as IP, TCP, and NetBIOS were examined in detail. For the purposes of bringing forward a discussion of the SMB protocol, this book now presents the key configuration fields that may be interpreted with a protocol analysis tool when analyzing a Windows NT protocol session and reviewing the SMB protocol. Note that certain analyzers may display the SMB protocols in different sequences that may cause the function names to be displayed differently than as noted here. The following descriptions are the most common terms for the SMB protocol and are used in most network analysis tools.

7.7 SMB Protocol Decoding

The SMB protocol is an application layer protocol that was developed in the IBM PC LAN program operational release that interactively uses NetBIOS API protocol calls for the session layer for final interaction across an internetwork.

The internal functions of the SMB protocol are used to communicate with remote workstation clients to the NT Server, and from client to client for interaction in an internetwork configuration. The Windows NT NOS calls on the redirector, which then communicates to the TDI and intercepts certain calls based on the I/O manager creation of SMB protocol commands. The SMB protocol is also common in the OS2, LanMan, and VINES protocol environments. The protocol may be used for connection-based operations, connection maintenance, and file call operations. Complete file search modes are supported in multiple levels of the file access via different transaction calls (see Figure 7.41).

```
┌DETAIL──────────────────────────────────────────────┐
 SMB:  ───── SMB Transaction Command ─────
 SMB:
 SMB:  Function = 25 (Transaction)
 SMB:  Tree id      (TID) = 0000
 SMB:  Process id   (PID) = 0000
 SMB:  Word count = 17
 SMB:  Transaction name = "\MAILSLOT\LANMAN"
 SMB:  Total size of mail data = 18
 SMB:  Additional information = 0000
 SMB:  .... ....  .... ..0. = Response expected
 SMB:  .... ....  .... ...0 = Do not disconnect TID
 SMB:  Time to wait for completion: 1000 msec
 SMB:  Op code = 1 (Write mail slot)
 SMB:  Priority of transaction = 0
 SMB:  Class = 2 (Unreliable)
 SMB:  Command = 1 (Announcement)
 SMB:  Services = 13
 SMB:  .... ..1. = Server
 SMB:  .... ...1 = Work station
 SMB:  Major version number = 2
                         ─────Frame 557 of 20571─────
 1       2 Set   3Expert 4 Zoom  5         6Disply 7 Prev  8 Next  9Select 10 New
 Help    mark    window  out     Menus     options frame   frame   frame   capture
```

F I G U R E 7 . 4 1 *A protocol analyzer view of the SMB protocol decoded.*

A list of SMB functions and their description follows.

7.7.1 SMB Control Commands

- **SMB Function, 1 byte.** The Function field can be used for any protocol call from a server/client to a complete main operation process on the remote server/client. The Function field is considered the primary operation field of the SMB call.

- **SMB Tree ID, 2 bytes.** The Tree ID is the vector pointer related to disk access on the server/client request command and the associated remote server/client reply command.

- **SMB Process ID, 2 bytes.** This is the internal process ID between the server/client to a remote server/client connection.

- **SMB Multiplex ID, 2 bytes.** This is the internal subvector of the process ID related to the connection between the server/client and the applied remote server/client.

- **SMB Word Count, 1 byte.** This is the specific focus related to the word subvector of the protocol model.

- **SMB Transaction, variable.** This field is used for unique protocol operational event calls between a server/client and remote server/client. The actual transaction event will be unique, depending on whether there is a server/client broadcast occurring, a file search occurring, or a file operation occurring.

SMB protocol commands are divided into four categories:

- **Session control.** SMB control operations allow for the connection and disconnection of key services between the server and the redirector and allow for the interactive communication between these two processes.

- **File commands.** SMB file operations and commands allow for the access of certain key files and directories across the internetwork between client to server and client to client.

- **Print commands.** SMB print processes allow for communication of key print operations across the internetwork infrastructure.

- **Message commands.** SMB messages will allow for transmitting and receiving key I/O information for the NOS-to-client-to-server communications, along with broadcast messages that are critical for internetwork control.

The following is a brief breakdown of the standard SMB protocol commands:

- **SMB Start Setup and More and Tree Request/Response.** This protocol call establishes the initial connection between the redirector process and the shared resources of a server or client. This command is unique because it normally engages the packet-size negotiation for a buffer and also includes the authentication for the account name and the password for the NT domain name, including the native operating system and the native manager version. The Tree connection process allows for the connection sequence to occur for the server/client.

- **SMB Tree Disconnector Break Connection.** This protocol call disconnects the connection between the redirector and the applied shared resources of the NOS and the NT server/client.

- **SMB Logon and Logoff Request Reply Sequences.** This protocol call is normally used for the logon and logoff processes between server/client and server/client nodes.

- **SMB Negotiate Protocol.** This function is used to establish a communication dialect between server/client and server/client multiple nodes. Normally the network program, network version, and the applied DOS versions will be communicated on the negotiation protocol sequence. After the negotiation protocol response has been received, the security mode, Maximum Size of Host Transmit buffer, and virtual circuit assignments occur. The session key is established, along with authentication and the date of negotiation.

- **SMB Transaction Functions.** When the protocol call is a function-equals transaction, the SMB sequence can include unique transactions such as: **MAIL SLOT BROWSE, MAIL SLOT NET/NET LOGON,** and **NAMED/PIPE.** The named-pipe and mail-slot operation commands are used for unique communication for file system operations to communicate with APIs between server/client and server/client. The mail-slot commands are used in a connection second-class mode to locate on the network server/client, and send broadcast and notification messages processes. Transaction commands are unique common sequences; many more transactions can be called in the subvector through the function-equals transaction protocol call.

7.7.2 SMB File Access Commands

- **SMB Get Attributes for Disk File Access and More.** This call allows the file attributes from the remote server/client to be accessed as required.

- **SMB Rename a File and More.** This command requests a server/client to rename a file as required.

- **SMB Delete a File and More.** This command requests a server/client to forward an instruction to delete a file as required.

- **SMB Commit a File and More.** This command allows the server/client to send a write command through SMB for all buffers related to a hard disk operation.

- **SMB Create a Directory and More.** This command allows a server/client to engage a "Make Directory" command.

- **SMB Delete a Directory and More.** This command allows the server/client to engage a "Remove Directory" operation across a particular structure.

- **SMB Open a File and More.** This command allows the server/client to engage an "Open File" operation through assigning a file handle. The "SMB Open and More" file command is the initial open sequence for the function in SMB actual file access. This is where the function would be labeled as an "Open and More" request sequence, and the file and path names would be identified. All key file attributes would be identified within the subvectors of the file path name within the "Open and More" command. Also, the creation date along with the "Read and More" command may be attached. Upon the response of an SMB "Open and More" response sequence, the final attribute assignments will be identified along with the file handle and the current file size. This may also include an SMB "Read and More" response with data bytes read attached to the packet.

- **SMB Create a File and More.** This command allows the server/client to engage an initial creation process on a file.

- **SMB Close a File and More.** This command allows the server/client to close a particular file.

- **SMB Set Attributes in File and More.** This command allows the server/client to set a specific set of attributes.

- **SMB Lock a Byte in Block and More.** This command allows the server/client to lock a set of data blocks in a file.

- **SMB Unlock a Byte in Block and More.** This command allows the server/client to unlock a set of data blocks in a file.

- **SMB Create a Special File and More.** This command allows a server/client to create a special filename and pass it to the redirector process.

- **SMB Create a New File and More.** This command allows the server/client to generate a new file if the assigned file name does not currently exist.

- **SMB Check a Directory and More.** This command allows the server/client to engage an investigation on a directory structure.

- **SMB Read a Byte in Block and More.** This command allows the server/client to request a read on a specific block of data.

- **SMB Write a Byte in Block and More.** This command allows the server/client to write a specific block of data to a file.

- **SMB End of Data Process and More.** This command allows the server/client to terminate a certain node connection as required.

- **SMB Get a Set of Disk Attributes and More.** This command allows the server/client to request hard disk storage statistics on a particular server/client.

- **SMB Search for Directory/File and More.** This command requests the server/client to engage file search operations.

7.7.3 SMB Printing Commands

- **SMB Return Print Cue and More.** This command requests server/client to reengage a print cue operation.

- **SMB Create a Spool File and More.** This command requests the server/client to start a file for printing.

- **SMB Spool Byte Block and More.** This command requests the server/client to write a block of data to a print spool file.

- **SMB Close Spool File and More.** This command requests the server/client to close a specific file that's cued for printing.

7.7.4 SMB Message Commands

- **SMB Get a Machine Name and More.** This command allows a server/client machine name to be requested and mapped to a user.

- **SMB Forward Client Name and More.** This command allows the server/client to intercept a message from a user/client name and add a name to its name table.

- **SMB Send Broadcast Message and More.** This command allows the server/client to send an SMB message to all servers/clients that can intercept on the network.

- **SMB Send Single Block Message and More.** This command allows the server/client to transmit a single block of data with up to 128 characters between two clients.

- **SMB Start Send of Multi-Block Message and More.** This command allows a server/client to send a multiple-block message.

- **SMB End of Send of Multi-Block Message and More.** This command allows a server/client to end a multiple-block transmission message process.

- **SMB Send Text of Multi-Block Message and More.** This command allows for sending text messages of up to 1600 characters.

- **SMB Cancel Forward Process and More.** This command allows a server/client to delete a name from its naming table.

The following is a brief overview of the protocol operational sequencing as normally seen on an NT-based internetwork and the protocol-tracking events between the IP, TCP, NetBIOS protocol, and SMB protocol.

This is just one example of the protocol layering that can occur with these protocol types. The physical layer is normally engaged for general connection processes. Specifically, if Token Ring is used, ring insertion occurs; or if Ethernet is used, the station is active on the network. The connection process between two clients, or a client and server, occurs through the NetBIOS naming services, where a Check Name process occurs, followed by a Find Name for the actual host. After the Find Name has been recognized through the NetBIOS sequencing, the NetBIOS protocol moves to a Session Initialize process, and then a Session Confirm returns from the remote host. After the two clients or client and server have been connected through a NetBIOS session, SMB is engaged for a Negotiate Protocol sequence and a Negotiate Protocol response. The next process that takes place is an SMB Set Up Account and then a Connect Confirm on the setup process. The next process, the SMB transaction sequence, is followed by multiple transactions, that may include file searches, file opens, and writes and applied reads, as required. This is where true application transfer occurs; and applications may be called upon between clients and servers. Eventually a logoff process occurs through an SMB sequence, and a disconnect in the SMB engagement takes place. At that point, the NetBIOS session eventually breaks in normal fashion, completing the protocol event sequence on the internetwork.

7.8 Windows NT Analysis

When analyzing the Windows NT protocol suite, it is important to keep a close focus on the overall topology frame sequence to ensure that the physical layer is solid.

After the physical layer has been determined to be solid and operating, the next area to examine is the IP addressing scheme. As long as the IP addressing scheme is properly operating, any other areas of the IP datagram should next be investigated, such as TTL, for proper fluency and routing across the internetwork channels involved in the Windows NT analysis session.

The TCP layer should be examined for connectivity, positive acknowledgment and retransmission sequencing, as well as window sequencing and true connection maintenance.

If the connection layer appears to be solid, the NetBIOS layer will most likely show true transfer of data and the maximum amount of data transferred between the workstation and server based on the session established between the NT Workstation and the NT Server.

When the server is being called upon for general I/O sequences such as searching for files, finding a file, opening and accessing files within the NT Server, for any process ranging from connection, to logon, to application access, the SMB protocol sequence is active. After the application has been opened, it may decide to invoke transmission of data straight through the NetBIOS session layer or possibly through encapsulation within the SMB protocols.

The results seen in a network analysis session can be affected by the application development team data processes implemented and the implementation of Windows NT against the application in a specific internetworking environment.

In closing, an important note to remember during a Windows NT analysis session is to closely examine the IP, TCP, NetBIOS, and SMB layers for general fluency and overall communications. It is important that the complete protocol stack operation be working in a solid manner. Any improper conditions could indicate that other areas of the internetwork may have problems such as the physical network, or the routing layer network, or even that a switching-based problem exists.

If the application layer has a problem, the protocol communication at the SMB layer will most likely indicate SMB errors or other problems that relate to inherent problems in SMB protocol sequencing. This may indicate NOS-compliancy issues with certain workstation shells such as incompatible service packs or other conditions.

Keep an open mind when analyzing Windows NT, because the protocol suite uses an abstract design that engages many protocol suites that must work together in an interoperable fashion. This is an important fact to remember when performing a network baseline session in an SMB environment.

7.9 DEC Protocol Suite Analysis

The DEC protocol suite is an extremely complex protocol that was derived for terminals to communicate to the DEC mini-host environment. An analyst should keep this in mind when encountering the DEC protocol suite during a protocol analysis baseline session.

In the LAN environment, certain protocols may be active for certain communication sequences that apply. A physical frame is usually encountered and in most cases the physical frame is Ethernet, because DEC is heavily deployed against the Ethernet topology. In an analysis capture, a physical frame is the outside physical header and trailer portion of the packet, such as outlined in the Ethernet frame specifics.

The next area that would be encountered in a network analysis session includes a data link encapsulation protocol such as LLC or SNAP.

For the packet to be routed from one DECnet node to another, the DECnet routing protocol is usually active and clearly shows the source and destination network areas for the DECnet internetwork along with the DEC nodes active for communication.

If a connection is being maintained and stability is required, *Network Services Protocol* (NSP) is usually active. From there, a process application protocol is present in the packet that is active for the LAN workstation's communication sequence as related to the DEC host environment.

In today's environment, it is common to see other protocols present above NSP protocol, such as X Window or SMB, when communicating to a host environment.

Protocols that were extremely predominant in the early days of the DEC mini-computing environment, such as *Local Area Transport* (LAT) protocol, are not as active in today's networking environments. It is more common to see protocols such as SMB at the application layer, because of the low amount of overhead required when calling upon a host environment. The LAT protocol and other protocols used at the DEC application access level, such as *Data Access Protocol* (DAP) are extremely redundant protocols and require more overhead and general communications.

The following is a description of some of the DEC protocol sequencing layer interaction processes that can occur, along with some of the DEC protocol types. Also presented are hints on analyzing the DEC protocol environment.

The DEC protocol suite centers on the DECnet protocols developed in the early 1970s by Digital Equipment Corporation.

First, DEC introduced DECnet Phase I protocol, which was based on PDP systems. Next, DECnet Phase II was introduced, which offered host support for DECnet. VAX process DECnet Phase III was introduced in the 1980s, which added cross-network routing along with network management. The DECnet Phase IV protocol suite was next introduced, which included support for Ethernet LAN and WAN technologies. Next, DEC introduced DECnet Phase V. The LAN and WAN DECnet architecture includes a physical and data process link layer, followed by a key routing layer. Above the routing layer is an end node–to–end node communication layer. The next layer is the session control layer. A network application layer is also present and interoperates with a network management layer. The DECnet phase operations is at the top layer.

7.9.1 DECnet Protocol Layers

The following list describes the major protocols engaged in the DECnet computing protocol suite model:

- **DECnet Routing Protocol (DRP).** This DRP acts as network layer protocol and assists with routing across DEC areas. DRP's intent is to initiate and maintain cross-area router links in a DEC internetwork. DRP is responsible for routing packets from source DEC nodes through DEC area routers that separate DEC areas, and to destination DEC endpoint hosts.

- **DEC Network Services Protocol (NSP).** The NSP ensures that a reliable message process can occur at the transport layer for overall transmission. NSP creates a virtual connection. The main functions of NSP are to establish, process, and destroy DEC links and to provide error and dataflow control. The overall transport process is engaged.

- **DEC Data Access Protocol (DAP).** The DAP allows for remote file access in a DEC environment. The DAP provides a command and reply protocol that allows a DEC workstation to initiate a process to create a files on host. The DAP allows for file access, opening, reading, writes, and closing cycles.

- **DEC Network Information and Control Exchange (NICE).** The NICE protocol is a DEC command/reply protocol that allows network management processes in a LAN and WAN session.

- DEC **Server Message Block (SMB).** This is the application layer protocol described earlier in this a book as developed for the LAN server environment. The SMB protocol can also be used in the DEC environment for remote file access use.

- **DEC Command Terminal (CTERM).** This DEC protocol is engaged for communication with DEC terminals in DEC LAN and WAN environments. It works with the DEC Foundation Services protocol.

- **DEC Foundation Services (FOUND).** The FOUND protocol is engaged when communication require a terminal-handling service on a LAN or WAN session. DEC FOUND can be engaged for initiating and disconnecting logical DEC connections that occur with DEC-based workstations and applications. FOUND works with the CTERM protocol.

- **DEC Session Control Protocol (SCP).** The SCP performs a session operation and is engaged to establish and maintain a virtual connection with DEC NSP sequencing.

- **DEC Maintenance Operations Protocol (MOP).** The DEC MOP is engaged for DEC network maintenance services for device-to-device tracking. MOP can be used for diskless workstation downloading and remote sequence loads.

- **DEC Local Area Transport (LAT) Protocol.** The LAT protocol is designed for terminal I/O process flow between devices in DEC areas that require endpoint-to-endpoint source communication. LAT can function as an interface protocol for a DECnet mini-host to general LAN domain link communication (see Figure 7.42).

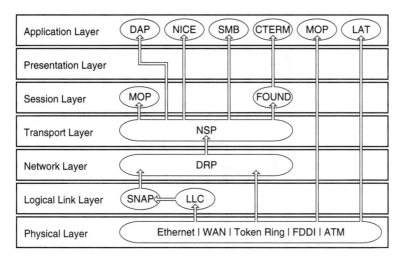

Application Layer	DAP	NICE	SMB	CTERM	MOP	LAT
Presentation Layer						
Session Layer	MOP			FOUND		
Transport Layer			NSP			
Network Layer			DRP			
Logical Link Layer	SNAP — LLC					
Physical Layer	Ethernet I WAN I Token Ring I FDDI I ATM					

FIGURE 7.42   *The DECnet protocol suite.*

The following items are important to analyze in the DECnet protocol suite:

- **Physical stability analysis.** It is critical that the physical layer supporting DECnet protocol communication be healthy. An analyst should always verify the physical frame carrying the DEC protocols.

- **DEC LAT error analysis.** The DEC LAT protocol may exhibit error information that a protocol analyzers can capture. DEC LAT errors are noted when they occur in the LAT decode layer. WAN analysts can locate DEC LAT errors by paging through the data trace. Any DEC node and area addresses must be noted when analyzing the DEC protocol suite.

- **DECnet Routing Protocol analysis.** The DRP protocol includes information such as addressing for nodes and DEC areas and the hop count between areas and costs to DEC networks. It is important to examine the DRP header internals for protocol errors such as excessive hop counts or high costs in route.

- **DEC connection analysis.** An analyst should examine connection integrity in the NSP and SCP layers in a DECnet environment. A connection should be set up, communication take place, and the session breakdown occur normally.

- **DEC polling analysis.** The DECnet nodes will notify each node of the node location and continue updates with Hello Timer packets. A protocol analyzer can capture errors in the Hello Timer values if the Hello Timer values are not correct and updates occur out of sequence, DEC devices may encounter routing errors. It may be possible to reconfigure the timer values if they are incorrect (see Figure 7.43).

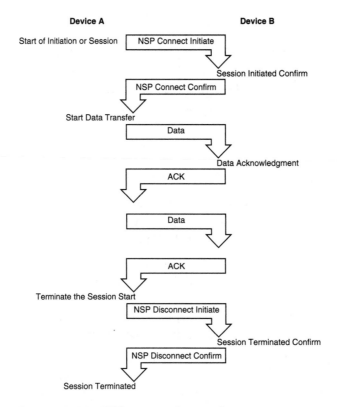

FIGURE 7.43 *DECnet protocol sequencing.*

To fully understand and examine the decodes of any DECnet protocol in the suite requires a close review of the specific protocol. The references listed in his book enable an analyst to further research the DECnet protocols (see Appendix B).

7.10 AppleTalk Analysis

The AppleTalk protocol suite is usually encountered in internetworking environments that use a heavy amount of Apple Macintosh workstations. The AppleTalk protocol is common for network-based industry applications such as art design and other innovative applications that are popular in the Apple computer and Macintosh computing environment. The AppleTalk node-to-node communication processes can be based on peer-to-peer transfers.

The following discussion provides a brief history of the AppleTalk protocol, along with a description of the AppleTalk protocol types.

We have also presented a set of AppleTalk Analysis techniques. We have limited the discussion of AppleTalk protocols to general areas. The AppleTalk protocol suite varies in actual implementations, because of the current market presence of many other protocols such as Windows NT that are more predominant in industry site configurations. In fact, there are really only two main implementations, Phase I and Phase II. In the 1980s, Apple unleashed the original AppleTalk protocol, Phase I. The AppleTalk Phase I protocol was designed for Macintosh peer-to-peer LAN-based communications. In the late 1980s Apple unleashed Phase II. The AppleTalk Phase II operation offers expanded support for internetworking. The AppleTalk zone mapping system is increased to 255 zones. Phase II supports Token Ring overlay implementations.

The AppleTalk internetwork addressing scheme encompasses nodes, network zones, and ports. A workstation corresponds to an AppleTalk node. The AppleTalk network is grouped into a zone. An AppleTalk router device is called a port.

The physical layers of an AppleTalk network usually rely on the topology for support. Most of the time, AppleTalk is resident over topologies such as Token Ring, Ethernet, or the LocalTalk. The AppleTalk-based networking involves the engagement of a set of sequenced protocols that rely on the physical frame of a particular topology for communication, such as Ethernet or Token Ring. The AppleTalk data link layer usually engages an encapsulation protocol such as LLC or an AppleTalk protocol for the data link layer, such as *Link Access Protocol* (LAP). The AppleTalk protocol has subcomponent layers such as TokenTalk, LAP, EtherTalk LAP, and LocalTalk LAP layers.

After the network layer protocol communication sequencing has been established between an AppleTalk workstation and an operating system server, the DDP is usually active for decoding. This is the network layer protocol that allows for investigation of the AppleTalk node network layer addressing scheme and processing of an AppleTalk packet across an AppleTalk router or switch.

At the OSI transport layer, the AppleTalk *Routing Table Maintenance Protocol* (RTMP), AppleTalk Echo Protocol, AppleTalk Transaction Protocol, and Name Binding Protocol are active. For AppleTalk nodes to map addressing and cross-links to devices on the network, other protocols are critical at the network and transport layer such as *Zone Information Protocol* (ZIP) and *Name Binding Protocol* (NBP).

The AppleTalk protocol engages session layer operating by suing AppleTalk Data Stream Protocol, ZIP, the AppleTalk Session Protocol, and the *Printer Access Protocol* (PAP).

The AppleTalk architecture engages presentation services through AppleTalk Filing Protocol and Postscript. After the application process has been engaged, the required application-based protocols in the AppleTalk environment, such as *AppleTalk Filing Protocol* (AFP) or other custom protocols such as SMB, can even be used for sequencing above the AppleTalk network layer. The AppleTalk architecture also allows for application calls through AppleShare File Server and the AppleShare Print Server Protocols.

7.10.1 AppleTalk Protocol Types

- **DDP.** A network layer protocol engaged to activate addressing for transfer across AppleTalk zones and used to transfer data between AppleTalk nodes on an internetwork. The DDP layer includes information on addressing and hop counts traversed.

- **LAP.** The LAP protocol is used as a main logical link for an AppleTalk node to link upper-layer protocols with the physical medium.

- **SNAP.** This encapsulation protocol is engaged to package ULP protocols for protocol stack link configuration.

- **AEP.** The AEP protocol engages the capability to link Echo or Ping process for AppleTalk nodes for identification and timing links.

- **ZIP.** The ZIP protocol is engaged to provide a process to cross-map NBP binding to the AppleTalk network routing links to zones.

- **NBP.** The NBP protocol translates an AppleTalk name to specific zone for data sockets.

- **RTMP.** This protocol assists with AppleTalk routing updates between AppleTalk routers. RTMP can also be used as a route discovery protocol for routers.

- **PAP.** The PAP protocol is engaged to link printer dataflow in a route of stream mode to print devices.

- **ASP.** The ASP protocol is engaged at the session layer and is used for AppleTalk session establishment, connection, maintenance, dataflow, and disconnects.

- **AppleTalk Data Stream Protocol (ADSP).** The ADSP protocol provides for a connection-linked socket to provide for a data stream to process between AppleTalk nodes.

- **AppleTalk Data Stream Protocol (ATP).** The ATP protocol is used to provide a transaction of data between two specific sockets in AppleTalk endpoint nodes.

- **AFP.** The AFP protocol engages a file access and file mode transfer cycle at the application level (see Figure 7.44).

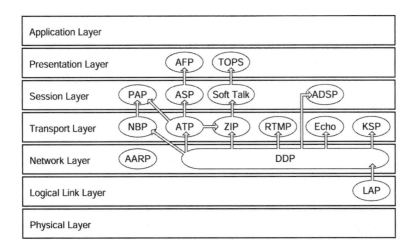

FIGURE 7.44 *The AppleTalk protocol suite model.*

7.10.2 AppleTalk Protocol Suite Analysis

An analyst should engage a focused view when analyzing the AppleTalk protocol suite. The interaction of the protocol suite is complex. It is important to keep a focused view on the ZIP communication. The ZIP is involved in the communication of the internal zones in an AppleTalk internetwork environment. The ZIP is used to translate between the AppleTalk network numbers and zone names. Any ZIP packets should be examined for proper addressing between nodes. An analyst should also review the NBP protocol. The NBP is used as a name relational transfer mapping process across the AppleTalk internetwork to link devices to names and zones. This protocol allows AppleTalk network stations to refer to different types of services through a cycle of mapping AppleTalk character names. Most processes within an AppleTalk internetwork are named and have NBP designations. NBP packets can be captured and decoded to examine the addressing information. When an AppleTalk node user cannot locate a particular service, there can be various misconfigurations present within a device. By analyzing NBP, an analyst can locate misconfigurations. The RTMP is a key protocol to examine for problems with routing lengths and wait times in the AppleTalk layers. An analyst should closely review and RTMP updates for proper routing convergence. By analyzing RTMP, an analyst may locate routers that have configuration concerns. RTMP holds key information on wait time, routing length, routing hops, and router location.

The AFP contains key information on AppleTalk resources for file access to AppleTalk nodes. An analyst can decode AFP to examine node request for certain file pointers and file accessed method required. An analyst can review AFP to examine and evaluate file access fluency (see Figure 7.45).

If there are connectivity issues, an analyst can review the ASP. The ASP protocol can be checked for proper device connection initiation, connection, transmission, and breakdown (see Figure 7.46).

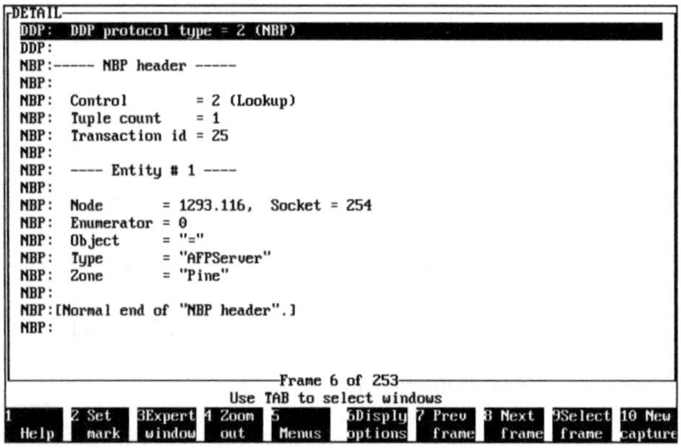

```
┌DETAIL────────────────────────────────────────────────────────┐
│DDP:  DDP protocol type = 2 (NBP)                               │
│DDP:                                                            │
│NBP:----- NBP header -----                                      │
│NBP:                                                            │
│NBP:  Control       = 2 (Lookup)                                │
│NBP:  Tuple count   = 1                                         │
│NBP:  Transaction id = 25                                       │
│NBP:                                                            │
│NBP:  ---- Entity # 1 ----                                      │
│NBP:                                                            │
│NBP:  Node       = 1293.116,  Socket = 254                      │
│NBP:  Enumerator = 0                                            │
│NBP:  Object     = "="                                          │
│NBP:  Type       = "AFPServer"                                  │
│NBP:  Zone       = "Pine"                                       │
│NBP:                                                            │
│NBP:[Normal end of "NBP header".]                               │
│NBP:                                                            │
│                                                                │
│                      ─────Frame 6 of 253─────                  │
│                       Use TAB to select windows                │
│ 1      2 Set  3Expert 4 Zoom  5       6Disply 7 Prev 8 Next 9Select 10 New │
│  Help   mark  window   out     Menus  options   frame  frame  frame capture│
```

FIGURE 7.45 *An example of an AppleTalk protocol trace.*

```
DLC:    Source°=Station APPLE0F0E6A
DLC:
RI:     ————————Routing Indicators————————
RI:
RI:     Routing Control = E3
RI:            111..... = Single-route broadcast, non-broadcast return
RI:            ...0 0011 = RI length is 3
RI:     Routing Control = 58
RI:            0.... .... = Forward direction
RI:            .101... = Largest frame is unspecified maximum value
RI:            .... 1000 = Reserved
RI:
LLC:    ————————LLC Header————————
LLC:
LLC:    DSAP = AA, SSAP = AA, Command, Unnumbered frame: UI
LLC:
SNAP    ————————SNAP Header————————
SNAP
SNAP    Vendor ID = 080007 (Apple)
SNAP    Type = 809B (AppleTalk)
SNAP
DDP:    ————————DDP Header————————
DDP:
DDP:    Hop count° = 0
DDP:    Length° = 60
DDP:    Checksum° = 0000
DDP:    Destination Network Number = 0
DDP:    Destination Node° = 225
DDP:    Destination Socket° = 1 (RTMP)
DDP:    Source Network Number° = 3148
DDP:    Source Node° = 42
DDP:    Source Socket° = 1 (RTMP)
DDP:    DDP protocol type = 1 (RTMP data)
DDP:
RTMP:   ————————RTMP Data————————
RTMP:
RTMP:   Net° = 3728
RTMP:   Node ID length = 8 bits
RTMP:   Node ID = 31
RTMP:   Tuple 1 : Cable range = 3728 to 3728 (Version 2)
RTMP:   Tuple 2 : Net 3732, Distance = 3
RTMP:   Tuple 3 : Net 3731, Distance = 2
RTMP:   Tuple 4 : Net 3730, Distance = 1
RTMP:   Tuple 5 : Net 3722, Distance = 0
RTMP:   Tuple 6 : Net 3723, Distance = 0
RTMP:   Tuple 7 : Cable Range = 3724 to 3724 (Version 2)
RTMP:   Tuple 8 : Cable Range = 3726 to 3726 (Version 2)
RTMP:
RTMP:   (Normal end of  RTMP Data )
RTMP:
```

FIGURE 7.46 *An example of an AppleTalk protocol trace.*

For more details as to information on the AppleTalk protocols contained within the suite, refer to the sources cited in Appendix B.

7.11 Banyan Protocol Suite Analysis

In today's networking environment, the Banyan protocol suite is not predominantly deployed across large LAN and WAN internetworks. This protocol, however, was extremely popular throughout the 1980s and early 1990s, especially in large government infrastructures throughout the world. This was because of the stability available through reliable interconnection of large server environments spread across diverse global infrastructures. The Banyan *Virtual Networking System* (VINES) protocol suite was introduced by Banyan Systems, Inc. The Banyan VINES network architecture includes a set of protocols drawn from the Xerox XNS suite and the TCP/IP. The Banyan suite also includes protocols from the SNA environment.

The server infrastructure within a Banyan environment has the capability for a strong interconnection via the StreetTalk processes for server-to-server communications. When investigating the Banyan protocol suite, it not unusual to encounter other protocols common to other protocol suites. Many of the protocol layers within the Banyan protocol suite are somewhat similar to other industry protocols.

When decoding a Banyan packet, a physical layer protocol topology frame header is present from the local area topology where the Banyan protocol suite is captured in a network baseline session.

After the physical layer protocol has been investigated in a packet, a data link protocol is present for encapsulation, such as the LLC or SNAP. The data link layer engages *VINES fragmentation protocol* (VFRP).

In most cases, the *VINES Internet Protocol* (VIP) is engaged, which is very common to standard IP operations. The VIP, *Vines Routing Update Table Protocol* (VRTP), and ARP operate at the network layer.

When a transport layer connection is required for maintenance, in most cases the *Sequence Packet Protocol* (SPP) is engaged. The *VINES Internet Control Protocol* (VICP) works mainly at the transport layer along with SPP and other TCP/IP-related protocols, and AppleTalk-related routing protocols.

An analyst encounters application protocol layers engaged on top of the VINES protocol suite, such as SMB protocol or other application layer protocols for workstation-to-server calls in a Banyan environment.

Some of the other key Banyan application layer protocols that may be encapsulated for general communications are the Matchmaker Protocol, FTP, and the VINES StreetTalk protocol for server synchronization.

7.11.1 VINES Protocol Types

The following list describes the Banyan VINES suite protocols:

- **VIP.** The VIP is used for network layer operations and data-transfer services.

- **VRTP.** The VRTP is used in the VINES internetwork environment to maintain routing information between routers.

- **VICP.** The VICP is engaged to broadcast errors and network topology changes to VINES nodes active with VIP.

- **VINES Interprocess Communication Protocol (VIPC).** The VIPC is a transport layer protocol used for providing connection services.

- **SPP.** The SPP transport level protocol is engaged to establish a virtual connection, process data transfer, and maintain a connection operation.

- **VFRP.** The VFRP allows for breakdown decoding and reassembly of the network layer packets for transmission to the data link layer, the physical layer, and any higher layers.

- **VINES MAIL Protocol.** The MAIL protocol is engaged for transmission of messages in the VINES email system.

- **SMB.** The SMB protocol is also used in the VINES suite for application file access.

- **VINES MATCHMAKER.** The MATCHMAKER protocol is used by the VINES upper layers for operating node program-to-program communication. MATCHMAKER also supports RPC calls. The MATCHMAKER packet-tagging techniques allow for linking functions: File, FTP, Server, Echo, Router, Background, Talk, and Network Management (see Figure 7.47).

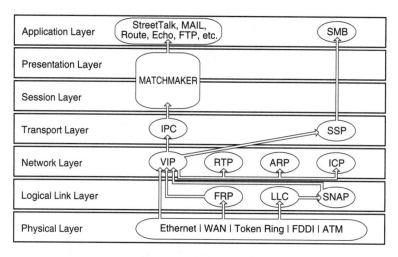

FIGURE 7.47 *The Banyan protocol model.*

Certain VINES protocols have specific functions. The following is a combined synopsis of their interaction.

The VFP allows the main VINES protocols to communicate with different hardware in the internetworking environment, for example. The VFRP protocol interacts with the VIP to determine the required packet size for hardware connections. At the network layer process area, the VIP, the VRTP, the VARP, and the VIPC work together to ensure node-to-node communication. The VIP works with the VRTP to establish connection between source and destination VINES nodes. The VRTP protocol is responsible for updating all the VINES servers and routing nodes with information relating to routing metrics. The VINES Address Resolution Protocol (VARP) works to assign the required addressing schemes. The VIPC is important, because it interrelates most of the key information between nodes as far as general integrity of communication between client nodes. This VIPC protocol tracks any errors in communication between nodes, and can specifically be analyzed for error data. At the transport layer, the SPP is used to set up and maintain a virtual connection between any two specific VINES nodes in an internetwork. The higher-layer application protocols such as the *Remote Procedure Call* (RPC) protocol and SMB are next engaged.

7.11.2 Banyan Protocol Suite Analysis

The first focus in a Banyan VINES analysis session should be a physical layer review. The physical layers must have true integrity. Errors at the physical layer can cause higher-layer communication errors in the VINES process. It is important that a VINES analyst examine the workstation-to-server connections and operation of the server routing update tables and server addressing environments. By determining that VIP packets communication fields are proper, an analyst can verify the key network health points in a VINES internetwork. The VIP layer includes addressing information to ensure that the nodes and servers can be identified. It is important that all addressing be verified in a VINES environment.

The VRTP packets contain information related to server internal addressing, and are used to maintain address information throughout a VINES internetwork. The VINES network communication is based on a cross-site WAN update scheme whereby servers update other servers in the internetwork regarding the services with which they are associated. The StreetTalk naming system is based on a database synchronization between each server. It is important that each server update other servers on changes to the addressing environment.

The VINES RTMP packets contain address information regarding VINES network numbers and subnetwork numbers. As noted, RTMP packets are engaged for routing updates as to key routing information for VINES-based routers. An analyst can capture VRTP packets and decode for information on site routers. The analyst should evaluate the VRTP updating sequence for updates to occur every 90 seconds. When performing a baseline study of a large enterprise WAN internetwork for VINES, the StreetTalk database should be checked on all key host and any interchannel packet communication for server-to-server sync process must be examined.

The VINES IP has metric values on transport hops between VINES nodes, which require examination. The VINES IP header includes most of the information for examining addressing from network and subnet information as noted. An analyst should examine the IP header to determine what address communication is occurring. If two nodes are having a communication problem, the analyst should use the protocol analyzer to filter on the nodes. Next an analyst should perform analysis and decode the IP headers, and record the internal information such as the network number, subnet number, protocol type, and Transport Control fields. The VINES StreetTalk database should update approximately every 12 hours. The StreetTalk database can be analyzed with proper filters applied on the protocol analyzer.

To truly understand the VINES protocol suite may require further research of the VINES protocol (see Figure 7.48). Appendix B lists references to the VINES material.

```
┌DETAIL─────────────────────────────────────────────────────────────┐
│DLC:  Ethertype   = 0BAD (Banyan VINES)                             │
│DLC:                                                                │
│VIP: ----- VINES IP Header -----                                    │
│VIP:                                                                │
│VIP: Checksum = FFFF (Null checksum)                                │
│VIP: Packet length = 34                                             │
│VIP:                                                                │
│VIP: Transport control = 1F                                         │
│VIP:          0... .... = Unused                                    │
│VIP:          .0.. .... = Does not contains RTP redirect message    │
│VIP:          ..0. .... = Do not return metric notification packet  │
│VIP:          ...1 .... = Return exception notification packet      │
│VIP:          .... 1111 = Hop count remaining (15)                  │
│VIP:                                                                │
│VIP: Protocol type = 2 (Sequenced Packet Protocol - VSPP)           │
│VIP:                                                                │
│VIP: Destination network.subnetwork  = 01000013.0001                │
│VIP: Source network.subnetwork       = 001E86AF.80DE                │
│VIP:                                                                │
│VSPP: ----- VINES SPP Header -----                                  │
│                    ─────Frame 16 of 332─────                       │
│                    Use TAB to select windows                       │
├────────────────────────────────────────────────────────────────────┤
│     2 Set  3Expert 4 Zoom 5       6Disply 7 Prev 8 Next 9Select 10 New│
│ Help  mark  window  out   Menus   options  frame  frame  frame capture│
└────────────────────────────────────────────────────────────────────┘
```

FIGURE 7.48 *An example of a Banyan VINES protocol trace.*

7.12 Routing Technology Protocol Analysis

When performing a network baseline, a key process is to examine how the overall internetwork routers in the enterprise environment communicate to each other in a stable and reliable manner. An enterprise facility that incorporates more than one network segment will use a router or a switch to separate the segments.

In most networking environments, there are no longer simple networks, but rather internetworks comprised of many segments, which may require routers to separate the different logical segments. Many of the routers found in today's environment can communicate to each other and update each other regarding device location and routing vectors as related to location of various networks and devices throughout the complete enterprise configuration. Routing protocols are used for two main reasons. One reason is to determine internetwork routes, and the second reason is to provide a transfer of information between different networks. The actual determination of internetwork routes is based on a complex set of measurements within the specific routing protocol. Routers communicate with other routers by using specific algorithms for determining the optimal internetwork routes between multiple networks. Routers maintain a subset of routing tables, to store all the key information to be used in obtaining the correct addressing for different routes between the different routers.

A group of measurements and categories, called "routing metrics," are used to determine some of the routing parameters; these usually vary from router type to type. For example, a Bay router works different from a Cisco router. All routers normally maintain complex routing tables with all the key information on the other routers on the internetwork. The routers share this information periodically by updating each other through some sort of routing information protocol. The routers communicate with each other and continue to keep the updates current between the different routers. Consequently, when a node on one network wants to transfer information to a node on another network, if the complete routing table is current, the source node can obtain the most efficient route. At times, certain routing algorithms may not be efficient, and this can cause the updates from table to table in routers and file servers not to be performed on a proper time sequence. This can temporarily cause a routing loop, which is not an unusual occurrence on large internetworks that do not support some of the complex routing algorithms that may be required (see Figure 7.49).

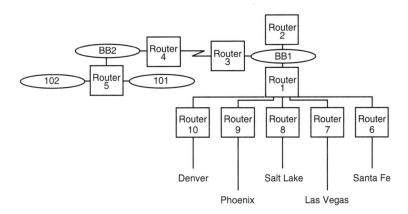

FIGURE 7.49 *Routing layout concepts.*

It is important for all the network routers housed within a specific location to communicate to each other in a proper way. If all network routers are contained within one location, this is considered an "interior" location. If Company A from one location wants to communicate to Company B at another location, it is likely that they will be separated by routers that use an "exterior"-based routing communication cycle for updates.

When interior routers communicate to each other, such as the routers within Company A, they use an interior routing–based protocol. When routers communicate across different interior-based routing systems, they use an exterior-based routing protocol (see Figure 7.50).

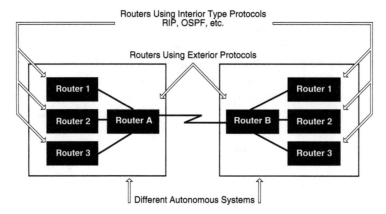

FIGURE 7.50 *How routing protocols synchronize.*

Routing technologies also vary when taking into account the types of protocols that can be used to update various routers for internetwork segment location and device location. These routing update protocol sequence processes are usually broken into two types: distance vector protocols and link-state-based routing protocols.

When enabling a routing protocol configuration within a facility, it is first important to determine the difference between an interior and exterior system.

Routing algorithms within internal-based system routers can be designed to allow for changes in network size and network delays, including bottlenecks and even lows or peaks in network bandwidth utilization factors. Some routers have groups of complex routing algorithm configurations, and other basic algorithms are in some standard basic routers. Most routers should be able to maintain either a dynamic or a static routing information table. Dynamic routing is used when routers are updating each other because of general information changes and operation changes on the particular networks involved. Static changes are usually modified by the network design group and can be configured so that the router operates in a standard way in certain areas. Many routers can support static and dynamic routing.

Any protocol should have a centralized algorithm that enables routers to always maintain tables of the precalculated, most efficient routes within standard internetwork layouts. There should also be distributive algorithms in order for internetwork routes and time changes on the network to be calculated on a dynamic basis.

Most routers should be able to provide a multipath approach to allow traffic to flow in multiple areas throughout a large internetwork. The term "collapsed backbone" refers to the situation in which the external networks throughout an internetwork actually join within the backplane of a large comprehensive router; that router then serves as a complete backbone between the networks.

Many routers today function efficiently with complex internetworks. These routers can identify performance issues in an internetwork traffic flow and provide reliability when delays and high-bandwidth utilization occur. Most routers should be able to calculate whether a packet needs to be communicated in a different route. These routers should be able to make a decision dynamically on whether an alternative route would be more efficient in relation to load or communication cost factors.

At times, routers also may need to adjust their packet size on the network to accommodate communication load factors throughout an internetwork. In today's complex internetworks, router technology needs to take into account bandwidth utilization to allow for this type of transfer.

Interior-based routing-based protocols can have a dynamic or a static route, depending on the type of routing protocol engaged. One of the more common routing protocols for interior-based routing updates is RIP. This protocol was originally developed to operate in the BSDI version of UNIX and was standardized in the late 1980s in different RFCs.

7.12.1 RIP

The RIP has been enhanced and there are now two versions: Version 1 RIP and Version 2 RIP. Version 2 now supports variable-length subnet masking, which allows for interoperability across different routing schemes in a more enhanced fashion for addressing flexibility.

The RIP usually updates on a very frequent basis and advertises the distance to a device based on routing hops and the vector based on thenetwork point-to-point path.

Each router involved in a RIP updating sequence, or RIP communication sequences between two routers, updates on specific intervals. Most RIP update intervals are set for 30 seconds, which is considered standard. Certain RIP intervals are set for 60 seconds, which is custom for specific RIP protocol variances such as Novell RIP.

The only concern with regard to RIP is that the shortest path first or time metric to a certain network is ignored. There are no internal calculations within a RIP-based routing protocol of what the shortest path is to a device. This can be of concern when a RIP calculation is being performed.

If a device is located two hops away through a set of Fast Ethernet channel networks rather than hop away through a shared Ethernet channel, for example, the RIP takes the shortest hop, which would be the shared Ethernet channel. In this case the shared channel would actually be a slower channel for general communications, but the convergence of the route would occur in this manner. When RIP determines a final route through the distance vector process, this is called "convergence."

Other protocols in an interior-based system, such as OSPF and *Extended Interior Gateway Routing Protocol* (EIGRP), which is proprietary to the Cisco environment, use a link-state-based protocol that is more sensitive to overall internetwork delays.

In a link-state-based protocol system, the changes in routing environments are based on the status of the physical speed of the linked internetwork of routers in the networking environment. When the router is originally launched or refreshed, it will usually participate in the routing protocol sequence through a Hello sequence or Update sequence of its state to other routers in the internetwork. Updates are usually sent on hourly intervals and are somewhat custom configured, depending on the enterprise design.

If the state of a router changes, the advertisement is performed via a link-state advertisement chain update. This is important because the router can create and maintain a consistent database in a link-state-based routing designs such as OSPF or EIGRP. Link-state protocols can evaluate the corresponding shortest path first and time metric to a specific router. Each router can use link state changes to pass information to neighboring routers to update the complete internetwork interior-based router scheme.

The link-state database is maintained in a consistent basis, which differs somewhat from the routing information table base in a RIP-based scheme. There are constant calculations against the path of the destination to each network, which does engage some overhead against the current hardware router system performing the hardware configuration for the routing environment.

In most cases, however, this is a standalone router and does not cause any load. The key factor to remember regarding link-state-based protocols is that if an interface on a router goes down, this information is usually propagated across the complete internetwork at once.

If there is a redundant path configuration available, routing convergence takes place and a recalculation of the shortest path first to the new route is established. Because of these calculations, a small load may be imposed on the routers involved, but this not considered a negative situation.

In most link-state-based routing environments, the network has the inherent capability to allow for contiguous networks to be recognized and identified through variable-length subnet masking. It is also possible to summarize all the routing updates within one routing table update. The rule of thumb ranges from 50 to 150 interface routers per area to be designed within a particular area.

Other routing protocols are available today, depending on the exterior or interior requirement.

When performing network baselining, it is important to understand that an analyst must capture routing protocol updates when investigating the sequencing between two routers to investigate the routes that may be static or advertised on the routers. If there is a problem with a router or switch on a network during a network baseline, an analyst may encounter an abnormal transmission in the routing update packets sent from one router to another. In this type of situation, the validity of certain routing tables may be abnormally refreshed, and route validity changes could occur frequently within the interior-based routing system. An analyst should be able to quickly capture routing updates from certain routers, and identify whether sequences are normal.

When examining a RIP-based router such as a Novell server or standard IP-based router running 30-second RIP, for example, the RIP update sequences should occur in this time interval. If for some reason the updates occur every 1 to 2 seconds, this is an abnormal condition in a distance vector system based on standard RIP.

Another example would be if in a link-state-based routing system, an abnormal change was detected and an *link state advertisement* (LSA) was being sent every two to three minutes; this would also be abnormal because link-state changes are normally sent on half-hour or hourly sequences.

With these facts in mind, note also that the RIP updates or any type of routing protocol update, such as OSPF, will be communicated inside the physical topology frame and must be investigated through packet analysis via a protocol analysis session.

Two other terms need to be defined: *intradomain* domain (within the same area or domain) and *interdomain* (in different areas or domains).

As a final note regarding baseline techniques, it is important for an analyst to be able to decode the different routing algorithms present within the internal packets of the routing protocols captured with a protocol analyzer. A protocol analyzer can pick up the routing protocols and enable the analyst to decode the fields for the respective routing protocols. At times, it is an advantage to be able to capture a particular packet between two networks, and display the packet to obtain information on how the packet was transferred from one network to the other. Key information probably will be found in the packet's Routing Protocol fields relating to how long the time transfer took between the two networks. Also encoded in the protocol packet is information on the number of delays between the network and the respective hops between the complete internetwork traffic cycle.

Novell RIP packets encode the time required to traverse a network in terms of units called TICKS, for example. Data in the RIP packets also encode the number of networks passed through on the transfer from Network A to Network F in the Hops fields in the packet. This type of information is critical during actual troubleshooting of internetwork traffic route issues.

Again, the focus here is that routing protocols provide for a determination of internetwork routes, and the actual transfer of information between those particular networks. An analyst can decode routing information packets to obtain key information about internetwork traffic flow. The discussion now turns to a general description of some of the key routing protocols available for inter-communication between interior- and exterior-based routing schemes.

7.12.1 Routing Protocol Types

Following are descriptions of some key routing protocols in the internetworking environment. The routing protocols should not be confused with the protocols used to route data at the network layer, such as IP. Routing protocols are internetwork protocols used in certain internetworking environments to allow for communication and calculation of routes between respective routers connecting networks. These protocols include protocols such as the RIP, OSPF, and other routing protocols that are proprietary used by certain router manufacturers, such as the Cisco's EIGRP from Cisco Systems Inc.

The key routing protocols are as follows:

- Interior Gateway Protocol (IGP)
- Exterior Gateway Protocol (EGP)
- Routing Information Protocol (RIP)

- Open Shortest Path First (OSPF)

- OSI ES-to-IS and IS-to-IS Protocols

- Cisco's Extended Interior Gateway Routing Protocol (EIGRP)

7.12.1.1 IGP and EGP

In the IP networking environment, the term *gateway* can describe routers. Some routers are used to move packets between networks under the same network management control on the Internet, and are termed *core routers* or *interior routers*. The protocol used to route between the interior routers within a specific network management scheme is the IGP.

Exterior Gateway Routing Protocols are used for routing between the interior routers on one independent internetwork to other exterior routers on another independent internetwork. EGP is a dynamic protocol that allows for this transfer. EGP updates based on the number of networks that can be reached, and is also used at a regular interval for updating those routers. The information within EGP packets varies depending on the subset of the protocol.

7.12.1.2 RIP

The RIP was developed in the Berkeley and Xerox development environment. This protocol has been used in a large subset of high-end computing environments. Most of these major computing protocol subsets use a derivative of RIP, but not in exact form. RIP is normally used in interior-based routing systems. RIP is based on a distance vector scheme. The RIP is intended to efficiently route packets. RIP was intended for smaller networks. RIP has a 16-hop count limit. Large networks frequently must exceed the 16-hop count limit. RIP uses a simplistic algorithm for metrics and for updating multiple routes. At times, RIP may have problems and effect incorrect updates in the routing tables for large networks. When router resets occur in a RIP environment on large internetworks, incorrect routing tables may be the result. Update mismatches can occur when tables are not updated for 60 seconds, which is the standard RIP update interval. Newer routing protocols are more robust in complex internetworks, but RIP remains an efficient protocol for most of the more standard-size internetworks.

7.12.1.3 OSPF

OSPF was developed by the Proteon Corp., along with major educational institutions. This protocol was developed as a link-state routing protocol, used mainly in interior-based routing systems, and is extremely dynamic for routing algorithms between large internetworks. The OSPF protocol is regarded as one of the popular protocols for use in large internetworks. The OSPF routing protocol takes advantage of some of the strengths of RIP. It conforms to the basic structure within the RIP environment, but it also addresses some high-end techniques applied to the protocol algorithm. Instead of updating routers throughout an internetwork on the standard every 30 to 60 seconds, for example, the OSPF routing protocol updates on-the-fly when there are problems between any routers. This feature eliminates most occurrences of routing loops. In an OSPF scheme, routers can recover quickly and update the internetwork-linked routers.

Another advantage of OSPF is that it allows for multiple path routing dynamics and can route on-the-fly to the most efficient route. This protocol also works with higher-end applications to decide routes on the dynamics of a particular application process. The OSPF protocol includes a feature called TOS routing, in which an application can dictate to the IP TOS and allow the internetwork routing protocol (OSPF) to dictate a packet and give it priority on its route and identification path. This capability to work with upper-layer applications allows OSPF to dynamically route between destinations in a large internetwork on an application's request. OSPF can also engage load-balancing techniques to carefully calculate ways to balance traffic over multiple routes on an internetwork. This is an essential capability if low delay factors are to be achieved throughout the internetwork.

7.12.1.4 OSI ES-to-IS and IS-to-IS Routing Protocols

The International Standards Organization has developed a group of different routing protocols to communicate across OSI protocol environments. The protocols are based on *end systems* (ES) and *intermediate systems* (IS). End systems are devices that do not route; intermediate systems are routing devices. These devices can exist in areas called routing domains. It is possible for an ES to route to an IS in the same area through the ES–to–IS version protocol. An IS version can route to another IS device in the same area through the IS-to-IS version protocol. IS-to-IS is a derivative of DECnet Phase V routing. If an ES or IS device needs to communicate across areas, the *Interdomain Routing Protocol* (IDRP) is used. There are Level 1 and Level 2 routers. Level 1 routers can talk to Level 2 routers, and normally, Level 2 routers communicate only with other Level 2 routers. This provides an organized approach for internetwork routing.

7.12.1.5 Cisco's EIGRP

EIGRP is a proprietary protocol developed by Cisco Systems. EIRGP is intended for large internetworking environments. The internal configurations for a router using EIGRP can be extensively customized. EIGRP has a large group of settings for custom environments. Its metric settings allow for custom multipath setups with auto-switching on-the-fly to other routes when failures in a route occur. A feature called holddown is used to prevent a router from automatically reestablishing routes on a bad link. Routing loops can be prevented by a feature called split-horizon, which stops redundant updates on bad routes.

7.13 Closing Statement on ULP Analysis

This chapter has presented some of the major protocols along with the key routing protocols that can be examined with a network protocol analyzer. The key to understanding protocol analysis at the upper layers is to maintain a set of network baseline mechanisms, as previously discussed in this book.

To become proficient at analyzing specific protocols, an analyst must keep a library of current reference material on each protocol suite. An analyst should always have a set of reading or reference materials from NOS vendors and application vendors available when examining any key protocol environments such as Novell, NT, or TCP/IP.

It is important to remain current on updates and changes to any configurations of the fields of the protocols, because these parameters change quite frequently upon new releases of operating systems, new applications, and internetwork change requirements.

This is an extremely dynamic industry and an analyst must have sufficient reference material available to analyze the protocol suites that may flow on top of the various topologies of an internetwork.

This book now moves to a description of each one of the major topologies in the physical network area of LAN and WAN environments. Each topology is discussed in terms of its architecture and the proper analysis and baseline techniques related to each topology environment. To truly baseline any large enterprise environment, an analyst must understand the physical topology and the upper-layer protocols being investigated. It is a mandatory for an analyst to thoroughly use an analyzer across the complete spectrum of site protocols in a network baseline study to properly evaluate an internetwork infrastructure from an enterprise standpoint.

Case Study 6: TCP/IP Baseline Analysis

A client in the financial industry contacted the LAN Scope analysis team to monitor an application that was experiencing extensive corruption of its database records for financial information. The client, a financial brokerage institution, provided investment capability for clients in the areas of mutual funds, general stock and bond operations, and other financial instruments.

The application in question was an investment-based application, which kept customer records online for the financial institution. The information included personal data on customers as well as their financial history with the financial institution. Complete tracking information was utilized in this application against all financial transactions involved with the client. This was considered a major business application because it impacted the general business flow of the company.

In the past, this type of information was maintained on the mainframe in a mini-host environment and was considered 100% stable. A recent rollout and push to move the application against the LAN as a mandate was instituted, which prompted some concerns about the stability of the application along with its rollout across the internetwork infrastructure.

There were concerns about using the LAN, but again it was a mandate to deploy the application across the LAN based on the distributed access of remote offices supporting the client infrastructure throughout the world.

At the time LAN Scope was contacted, the application was in an early rollout phase, with only approximately 100 users. More than 1,200 users at multiple locations were targeted for the final rollout stages of this application. The main concern was that users were experiencing intermittent corruption in certain database areas that appeared to show anomalies, and therefore the application was not 100% accurate. Fortunately, this application was in a predeployment testing phase and not considered production at the time, (see Figure CS6.1).

The application was only being used at the headquarters facility and was in a test phase. In other words, the information was also being directly input into the mini- and mainframe host environment via terminal servers, so that the client records could be verified upon corruption to any of the data files.

The output from the host environment was periodically checked against the LAN records in the database using an automated test program provided by the new application vendor. Periodic nonconsecutive information was located in output reports for comparison of the databases that showed the anomalies in data results between the host processor area and the new LAN-based application area.

Based on this concern, it was necessary to immediately troubleshoot why the corruption was taking place. The LAN Scope analysis team was requested to perform this exercise.

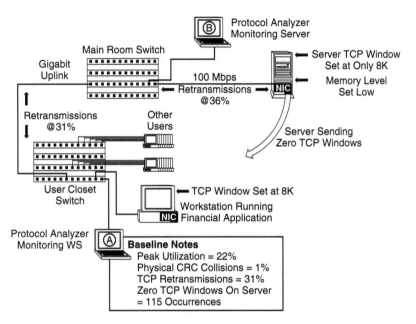

FIGURE CS6.1 *Monitoring an application which was experiencing extensive corruption of it's database records for financial information.*

LAN Scope conducted an entrance briefing with the client and the vendor of the application, during which we reviewed the topology, architecture, and application event cycles involved. We utilized application characterization processes after we performed a rapid baseline on the application characterization areas of the topology where the application movement was taking place. After we had completed the baseline notes, it was clear that the overall utilization levels were not of concern, the protocol percentages appeared to be normal, and the physical error rates related to the physical Ethernet topology were nominal.

The overall architecture was extremely robust and based on Fast Ethernet, with gigabit uplinks throughout the facility. With this noted, we also detected an extremely high level of TCP/IP, noted at 95%. This application was based on a network and transport layer of utilizing IP for general datagram transfer and TCP for transport connectivity stabilization. The application layer was built on a custom design of engaging a custom application engine.

With this noted, the LAN Scope analysis team focused on decoding the actual application events, looking for any stability problems related to connectivity. We noted during our initial application characterization phases that the application showed a high number of connectivity-based errors in the connection layer statistics of our network analyzer.

A high number of TCP window-size exceeded errors were noted. This type of error indicates that a TCP window stream has been affected by a TCP window not being available to handle communications. This type of event is an extreme problem when a connection state is considered active and open in a TCP port transmission.

As explained previously, TCP operates in the following manner. A connection is established between two endpoints across an internetwork. Each end is considered a TCP host endpoint for communications. The TCP connection starts with a three-way transmission process, which is considered a handshake, and a TCP port is considered open and active on the two endpoints. When the port is open, a size of available TCP buffering capability on each end is advertised through what is called a TCP window. This can be translated to exact data in bytes. This is the area in each endpoint, or workstation, or server being reviewed in this manner, that is available for TCP stream transmission between the two points. This area allocates in bytes and its availability and size is also directly tied to memory and resources in the PC (and operating system.)

The default TCP window being advertised for this particular application was noted at 8K between the workstation and the server. This is exactly related to the number of bytes available. The TCP communication which occurs back and forth is always updated by sequence and acknowledgment numbers to update each TCP end transmission. The process is also noted as engaging with a TCP open state to a TCP closed state. When a TCP session is opened, an initial sequence number is identified; and when a TCP closed state ends, a finish request is brought from one node to another and confirmed by the other end. If a TCP reset occurs abnormally, it can indicate a breakdown in TCP communications. If critical data is being sent back and forth, and a TCP reset occurs, it is very possible that the TCP transport connection could experience loss of data and thus create a direct loss of data input to any application utilizing TCP at the upper layers for transport. This could then cause database corruption.

The LAN Scope analysis team noted that during a database transmission and final record lock on a transmission of a particular client's financial records, that TCP connection errors and TCP window-size exceeded errors were both common. The exceeded errors indicated that one endpoint had a TCP window size that was exceeded and was not available any further for receiving or transmitting TCP information to the other endpoint. In this case, we noted that the event took place consistently in the LAN file server in the main computer room that handled the database application for the financial record-keeping process. This particular file server had only an 8K TCP window configured. The file server configuration was noted as having a robust level of memory, a high-speed Ethernet full duplex, along with a high-speed channel access design. The overall CPU processing levels appeared to less than 25%.

The main concern here was that the overall Ethernet channel and general network layer communications appeared to be stable. The application appeared to be operating in a fluent manner. There were no application errors from the vendor noted in the application process.

From our review, it appeared as though the transport layer was of concern, because of the network analysis results being received during the session. Again, one analyzer was positioned at the user area where the investment records were being entered from a user platform on a workstation. The user was then connected to a half-duplex Ethernet channel link through a port on the switch on the user floor. An uplink was then provided via a Gigabit Ethernet channel to the main computer room where the server was connected to a full-duplex Ethernet channel operating in a normal manner. All Ethernet statistics on the switched port showed low utilization, along with our baseline statistics. The only areas that appeared to be affected were the transport layer or connection-based layer statistics on our network analyzer.

Upon decoding all the symptoms, we immediately noticed that the server was dropping from an 8K window to a zero window after approximately two to three minutes of general transmissions. This appeared to take place on high user access when 20 to 30 users connected using the application. Upon lower user counts, it appeared as if the TCP window floated between 8K and 2K. When the 20-user threshold was applied, it appeared as though the server's TCP window's handling capability would be exceeded in the server, and connection breaks were frequent, noted as TCP resets on any ports active on the server. The server also would continue to have a TCP window-size exceeded error on any ports that were considered open at the time. Specifically, ports that were already open would not be able to float between the 8K and 2K range, and would float from 8K to 0 bytes available. Any new ports would not be properly synchronized through a TCP open state and would almost immediately be reset and would not allow transmission to start.

We immediately brought our findings to the MIS team for review. The MIS team, the application vendor, and the LAN Scope analysis team sat down to develop a synopsis, based on this information.

Our immediate findings were that we would require an upgrade of the TCP window size on the server of a minimum of 32K, just to handle the main users in the facility.

For predictive analysis as to the application rollout, future studies were required for application characterization and placement of users throughout the facility.

It was quite possible that this application would require a multiserver environment for different locations, based on the user-count levels. Because of the robust transfer of the application related to packet size and requirements on TCP port handling, it was likely that servers would be required in a distributive fashion based on 64K TCP window size, along with much higher memory levels of 1 and 2 gigabytes of memory, just to handle application dataflow.

To resolve the issue at this site for further testing and verification, we had the MIS team upgrade the server's TCP window via a Registry change in Windows NT to 32K. We also had a memory upgrade applied of 1/2 gigabytes to the LAN server, and the application was retested.

The LAN Scope analysis team immediately found that the TCP window was no longer being exceeded, and the 100+ users deployed were able to connect continuously to the server without causing a situation in which the server could not handle multiple TCP ports open without incident. There were no reset concerns and no further TCP resets took place. All ports were opened with a proper open state and a proper finish state for general TCP communications.

This allowed the initial application testing phase of the migration to continue at the facility and to be fine-tuned. Also the database records were shown and verified
on multiple cycles against the host's mini-computer output and were shown to be consistent and accurate on an ongoing basis at the LAN server. This application was tested for another three to four months before we were requested to perform application modeling and rollout requirements for other locations for the financial institution.

We considered this initial process an excellent testing cycle, using network baselining and application characterization combined to troubleshoot the TCP port connectivity issues. The TCP has an extremely robust communication-handling capability for transferring data. One of the requirements to support TCP handling capabilities is a focused approach to characterizing application rollouts and also adjusting certain TCP parameters that may be required. In the early phases of TCP rollouts in the early 1970s, the TCP parameters for protocol stacks were released in such a way that TCP parameters could be modified easily to allow an accurate configuration.

When TCP became an industry standard, many different parameters could be adjusted for TCP port operation. As more and more operating systems became prevalent, certain TCP configuration parameters were considered hard-configured and were not allowed to be modified. This was because some stability was required on TCP stack uniformity. The only concern here is that many applications today require TCP for transport modifications and require different configuration flavors as related to TCP parameters. Many of the operating system vendors have had to move forward and offer parameter-change capabilities in the protocol stack of their operating system or workstation design. In recent years, the NOS and applications vendors have noted this concern and have redesigned their TCP configurations to be more flexible for application vendors and MIS teams that require TCP handling capability.

This exercise was positive because the implementation of proper network baselining methodology, along with application characterization and troubleshooting processes, identified the TCP-based issues and assisted the site MIS team to produce a successful application rollout.

Case Study 7: NetWare Baseline Analysis

One of LAN Scope's clients was experiencing a problem with a new application, and requested that the LAN Scope analysis team review the application process. Our client indicated to us that the application was running on a file server that had recently been upgraded to a Novell NetWare 4.x release, and that he thought the problem was possibly more related to the operating system release rather than the application.

The LAN Scope analysis team began this cause-isolation analysis exercise with an entrance briefing, during which we reviewed the network topology and the problematic symptom history. We also reviewed the migration history of the server as well as future migration plans for the server.

The application implemented on the server was an accounting-based application. The MIS team stated that the application had been used in other server environments at other locations without incident, and did not think that the application was causing the problems being experienced.

The specific symptom being experienced was users being disconnected frequently from the server, which was utilizing a Novell 4.x release and maintaining an SPXII connectivity between the workstation and the server when utilizing the application.

A high number of printing processes was associated with this particular accounting process and the SPXII protocol was required for connectivity stability by the application vendor.

Other parameters noted were that the file server utilized for this application was based on a robust hardware platform, but it was also noted that the server had not received any upgrades for internal hardware design prior to the 4.x implementation. It was noted, however, that the server did receive a connection upgrade from a 100Mbps half duplex to a full-duplex connection in the main computer room Ethernet-switched environment (see Figure CS7.1).

The LAN Scope analysis team took these facts into consideration upon performing our network analysis exercises. Our first exercise was to use the process of rapid baselining, during which we closely monitored certain points of workstation usage throughout the facility against the server. Next, we engaged a vector point of analyzing the main server in the computer room environment. We made this decision because the number of symptomatic complaints against this particular server were so widespread, along with the fact that the servers running this application at other sites did not have problems.

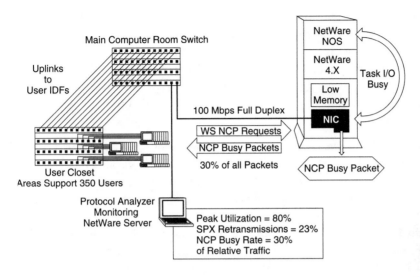

Figure CS7.1 *NetWare Baseline Analysis on a new application.*

We also requested information regarding comparable configurations on the other servers for hardware and software, NOS release, and other parameters that were supporting the application. We wanted to get a complete picture of the server environments that were not experiencing the application problem and wanted to compare them to the unique server that was exhibiting application problems.

We started in the main computer room and closely monitored the server through a port-mirroring process on the Ethernet switch. We closely monitored the server for general utilization levels on the Ethernet channel. We noted that utilization levels on the 100Mbps full-duplex ports were extremely high, ranging between 50% to 60% for an average, and peaking in the 70% to 80% range. This was of concern on such a high-speed channel. We noted that there were more than 350 users connecting to the application throughout the enterprise infrastructure.

The general protocol statistics showed a high number of inbound broadcast frames from other Ethernet areas within the domain. Overall the traffic levels were extremely high against the server. We examined the physical Ethernet level, which did not show any major problems.

We next moved to upper-layer protocol analysis decoding and utilized specialized filtering against the server. It is quite common in the Novell environment—whether in standard Network Core Protocol or in NCPB—for a Novell NetWare server that when experiencing heavy I/O task load at the server application processing level to be able to generate outbound to the network a transmission frame for responses to workstations that indicate when the server is busy.

Specifically, when a NetWare request comes inbound to a NetWare 3.x NCP-based standard server or a 4.x-based NCPB server environment, there is a field set where the server can reply back and say that the operating system is too busy to respond at this time. This is referred to as a NetWare Core Protocol "delay" or NetWare Core Protocol "busy" flag, which also can be indicated in the NetWare Core Protocol burst response fields. In standard NetWare Core Protocol, an inbound request is noted as a 2222, and a normal reply is noted as a 3333. If a 9999 is sent on an outbound standard NetWare Core Protocol reply from the server, this indicates that the server is busy. A NetWare Core Protocol burst response is set at 7777 with a busy flag set, responding to the workstation.

Normally a workstation mechanism shell allows for a back off of outbound transmission when this process reply is received from a server. Depending on the workstation image configurations, which may vary within a facility, however, it is possible that continued transmissions will take place. Other parameters can also be modified in the IPX and SPX levels at the workstation shell or image area and will cause a workstation to continue to retransmit.

If the server is continuously busy and the transport level is based on SPX and the connection is maintained consistently, this impacts the server with inundated requests for the information to be returned. Depending on a modification of IPX and SPX retry timers, workstations can eventually time out. The normal process is that a NetWare workstation connects to a server and then logs on to the server environment. When application file access is required, an open event for certain files may occur, and the information should flow back and forth.

In standard NetWare Core Protocol, each request is provided with a reply interpacket transfer for the overall complete file transfer cycle. In NCPB, one request is sent out and multiple replies can be brought down from the server in a sequence mode, and then another request can be brought forward. This is a less-intensive process, because it allows the workstation to only request for certain sequences of the total transfer, and for the server to provide multiple replies. This type of situation can cause a maximum traffic level to also be impacted against the Ethernet channel.

In this particular case in this site environment, the Ethernet channel was not of concern. Both standard NetWare Core Protocol and NCPB could be fully applied to the Ethernet channel. The main concern here was that the overall internal server platform, once closely reviewed, was a major issue. In our base-line analysis exercises, we continued to monitor the NetWare Core Protocol operations via upper-layer protocol decoding. We found that the NetWare Core Protocol busy frames were responsible for more than 30% of all replies out of the server, even in the NCPB operation design. The client had recently implemented the 4.x release against the server without taking into account various memory and hardware platform upgrades that were performed at other sites on servers that were housing this application.

It was clear from reviewing information from the other servers that differences did exist. This server had approximately 25% less memory than the other servers that received the upgrade and also had a much older general platform design on processor and other bus configurations.

Based on these concerns, along with other NetWare modification parameters that were not consistent, we requested that a server build be applied to this facility that was comparable with the other facilities. The MIS team immediately concurred with our recommendations because we were able to display the output of our trace analysis results, showing a high number of NCP busy packets being generated by the server. With these clear results at hand, the client immediately applied a new hardware configuration against this facility. The new hardware configuration for the server allowed higher memory and CPU modifications as for an immediate implementation that was considered 100% compatible with the application and comparable to the other site locations.

We reanalyzed the issue and found that the NCP busy rate dropped from 30% of all frames to only 2% to 3% of frames upon extremely heavy access. The overall user community stopped complaining about the issue, and the help desk calls were brought down to a minimal level.

Overall, the accounting application was now operating in a much more positive fashion.

In this particular case, the findings were that the Novell 4.x release was applied on a server that was not properly resourced for the upgrade. By performing rapid network baselining and by investigating the NetWare ULPs following a technique to pattern match on the NetWare Core Protocol outbound busy frames based on our previous experience, we quickly resolved this concern.

Case Study 8: Windows NT Analysis

The LAN Scope analysis team was requested to perform a baseline analysis exercises for large pharmaceutical company that was in the process of rolling out multiple NT Servers as an overall migration change from Novell NetWare to NT. Recently the site had only been using 2 NT-based servers and just completed a rollout of approximate 25 additional servers across their enterprise infrastructure. The servers were carefully implemented in a proper NT rollout with primary domain and backup domain controllers properly placed, and the NT trust configuration properly designed. This was based on the entrance briefing notes that we received.

We also noted in the entrance briefing that there were a high number of symptomatic problems in which users were experiencing slow performance and sluggish traffic levels after the NT rollout. Prior to the rollout, most of the users were still accessing the applications in the environment, which were basic office suite applications in a Novell operating system environment. The users stated immediately that they thought the new NT environment was not performing properly.

The NT environment up to the rollout was based on only one to two servers being tested in one area of the enterprise internetwork. The complete site node configuration interacting with the new NT server environment involved an immediate move from approximately 100 users to more than 2,000 users. This rapid change of user access having problems was of immediate concern (see Figure CS8.1).

In our entrance briefing meeting, the LAN Scope analysis team reviewed the internetwork configuration, the topology configuration, architecture, and the application environment overlay. We reviewed the symptomatic history and the recent migrations at the site. We also looked at any planned migrations for the near future.

Because the problems occurred immediately upon rollout and there were no problems logged in the test environment, we intuitively had concerns based on our previous experience in the NT environment with other clients.

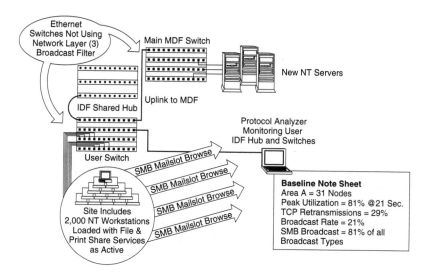

FIGURE CS8.1 *Subject for a Windows NT analysis.*

We deployed our protocol analyzers in two to three user areas that were experiencing performance problems in user IDF closets. We ran through standard baseline characterization, and noted average to peak utilizations to be in check; however, with peak transitions occurring in the 80% level for brief, but bursty periods of 1.2 to 2 seconds. This was noted on different switched Ethernet channel areas and shared Ethernet areas throughout the facility. All the standard Ethernet characterizations for utilization, protocol percentages, and Ethernet error rates all appeared to be within check. It was just that certain protocol percentages in broadcast form that appeared to be bursty as related to the TCP/IP, NetBIOS, and SMB protocol stack normally engaged for Windows NT.

Upon final decode in various site IDF closet session areas, it appeared that most of the bursty transitions pointed to a definite concern with SMB broadcast levels. After completing standard utilization, protocol percentage, and physical error rates, our focus was upper-layer protocol decoding. In the broadcast percentage statistics of our protocol analyzers for all the areas tested, we noted that SMB showed bursty protocol sequences and intermittent transitional burst transfers of 22% broadcast that quickly coincided with utilization peaks of 70% plus in the areas being sampled. We stopped all our network analyzers and synchronized time sequences and parameters for display view. We turned on network utilization within the data-trace review along with relative time, and upper-layer protocol data viewing on SMB.

We noted that all peak saturation levels that we were concerned about, and that would be considered transitional and high in the broadcast level, had SMB protocol as active. In this case, we also noticed immediately that SMB vector type was noted as a SMB Mailslot Browse, which we were familiar with from previous exercises. Upon Windows NT implementations in peer-to-peer NOS environments, it is normal to have file and print share services as active, which will cause periodic SMB Mailslot Browse commands to occur. This type of browse or broadcast is usually necessary for peer-to-peer networking.

In this particular environment, based on the primary and backup domain controller layout and file and print share application configurations, browsing services were not required. Peer-to-peer networking was not engaged and the browse services were extremely high. The rollout increase from 100 users to more than 2,000 users generated a higher SMB browse broadcast frame process on a consecutive basis that was not in direct parallel with the requirements for this particular network.

What was actually occurring in the facility was that extremely high SMB broadcast levels had been induced in different Ethernet physical shared areas and switched areas throughout the facility. Because the facility was not yet engaging broadcast Layer 3 filtering in any area, and the site MIS team also was not aware of the SMB broadcast level, what was occurring was an effect of an outbound local and wide area network storm sequence of SMB broadcasts that were not expected. These traffic levels were negatively impacting other areas of the network such as standard data transfers and usage for other business applications throughout the facility.

This type of SMB broadcast was immediately pinpointed as the cause of the problem that was affecting performance throughout the facility.

We immediately requested that the file and print share services were turned off for the devices and workstations where peer-to-peer networking services were not required, and only left on in the server environments where it was required. The NT support team at the site closely reviewed the situation and immediately understood what parameters were required for change control to modify this configuration and adjust the SMB broadcast levels to a minimum for SMB Mailslot Browse operations.

Upon implementation of the changes, the LAN Scope analysis team was asked to re-analyze the issue. We moved through the site to analyze different Ethernet areas and found that the broadcast levels had dropped from 26% to 3% for SMB.

We immediately noted that we had a success measurement vector that compared with the previous sampling session during the troubleshooting phase. We provided our findings to the site and we requested that the application environment be closely monitored and reviewed by the help desk and also that the user community be interviewed.

We noted that performance appeared to be enhanced throughout the facility upon immediate implementation of the change. It took several days before all the issues were communicated in a clear fashion, because of perception issues that were already present about possible slow performance in the new Windows NT Server environment. After the MIS team had communicated a change-control modification to the user community, the user community felt more comfortable with the new NT environment. General access of the NT environment continued in a positive fashion, and the issues were resolved through the baselining exercises that LAN Scope performed for this client.

This type of occurrence is still common in NT implementations, because this operating system has strong inherent capabilities that can be applied in a variety of ways, depending on specific requirements of the client. Even though this is a simple problem, this type of concern is a problem that could likely occur in critical NOS environments that are using heavy Windows NT infrastructure.

Network baselining was extremely useful in this particular exercise, along with the process of investigating upper-layer protocols related to the Windows NT protocol stack, which utilizes a heavy amount of SMB transaction calls for general access across the workstation and server platforms.

Case Study 9: Routing Baseline Analysis

A large advertising firm based on the West Coast contacted LAN Scope regarding a routing problem. They were using a high number of applications that were based on AppleTalk and Novell server operating system environments. Most of the application data was housed on various Novell file servers within the infrastructure, even though different AppleTalk networks were segmented and connected throughout the facility.

The advertising firm, located in the suburbs of Los Angeles, had a four-office location design against the enterprise internetwork architecture. Each independent office had different advertising departments, such as Development, Design, Sales, and so forth placed in each one of the offices. The offices were considered similar in operation but as distributed to location, depending upon advertising sales requirements.

The different location offices were connected through Novell multiprotocol routers for an initial configuration throughout the facility. Most of the Novell NetWare file servers at the facility had been in place since the mid-1980s, but had been upgraded for hardware, software, and NOS release. Much of the server environment was still based on 3.x in many of the different Novell areas (see Figure CS9.1).

Based on the inherent operation of the business and the migration cycle of the network, there were many different servers implemented in distributed fashion throughout the four facilities. Also, the Novell servers were not controlled by any centralized MIS department. Each location had its own MIS administrator, and they worked with each for general connectivity and transfer of information related to advertising design, sales models, and so forth.

Eventually the total Novell server environment climbed to more than 60 Novell file servers for the complete company and the wide area sites in the Los Angeles suburbs were still connected through a Novell internal routing process in the Novell multiprotocol router design. Because of the number of Novell file servers across the four sites, there were many different user requirements at each location to access various servers to obtain advertising design files, sales information, or client history files.

Specifically, there was a tremendous amount of interaction across the four sites between users in the workstation environment, which totaled about 800 users and 60 file servers at the four sites. This was also taking place without the servers being centralized for a particular design.

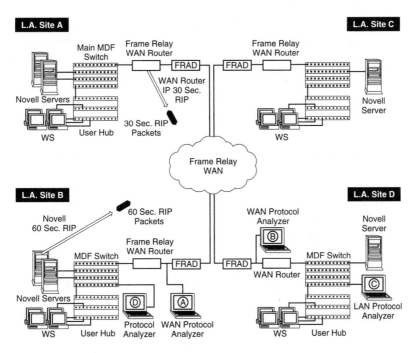

FIGURE CS9.1 *Networking system to receive a routing baseline analysis.*

All the Novell file servers were running SAP on 60-second intervals to update services to other Novell file servers. In this particular layout, they were also running Novell RIP on standard 60-second updates from the original Novell 2.x and 3.x design. The Novell multiprotocol routers were also participating in the Novell RIP updates for general communication.

Stabilization was in place in the facility, and most of the workstations throughout the facility were able to locate different Novell file services or applications running on different file servers, because the Novell SAP and RIP processes were provided clear 60-second updates as to all the distance vector routing protocol tables in the various servers. RIP in a Novell configuration is based on a 60-second update and is based on a distance vector routing protocol sequence. As explained later in this book, the distance vector routing protocols allow for an understanding of the link vector to a particular service or router or device stored in a routing table of a router, and the actual time or metric or distance to that device. In the Novell metrics, the distance vector routing protocol is applied on a 60-second update. What this means is that each one of the file servers and the routers throughout the facility was sending routing updates on 60-second intervals to ensure that each routing table in all the cross-site routers or servers had information related to other servers or routing services through the facilities so that all devices could be located by different workstations or servers as required. Overall, the internetwork in terms of the Novell infrastructure could be considered "hooked" or consistently updated for all services and routing channels available.

Recently the site had a requirement to increase their WAN bandwidth because the T1 circuits were showing extremely high utilization, at the 80% to 90% level. Performance on the WAN was also being perceived as negative by the user community. This problem started to occur over a one-year period during a consistent growth period, when the number of advertising designers increased from 100 to 300.

The MIS team immediately worked on a plan to migrate the facility to a WAN infrastructure based on Frame Relay, which allowed for a Committed Information and Burst Channel rate to be implemented across the facility, and to remove the meshed T1 point-to-point architecture between the four offices in the remote Los Angeles location. The implementation was effected through a router and WAN vendor in a positive fashion. WAN routers were implemented at each site and the Novell multiprotocol routers were removed. The four sites were interconnected through the new WAN routing scheme. The routers were considered to be a robust platform and had an extremely high throughput rate that would allow for a much higher performance level. Also the bandwidth levels were actually doubled by the Frame Relay intersystem switching cloud design between the facilities provided by the WAN vendor.

As soon as the wide area implementation was completed, connectivity problems started to be exhibited that were not present in the preceding design. Specifically, there was an immediate problem with certain workstations finding certain file servers or services that were previously available.

Even though the WAN levels appeared to show a positive bandwidth increase on the platform configuration, the main concern was that designers could not connect to file servers or get critical files, along with the sales team not being able to transmit important information. These problems were immediately present upon implementation of the new WAN platform, which was cut-over in just one business weekend.

The LAN Scope analysis team was immediately contacted to troubleshoot this issue. We arrived on-site with an emergency troubleshooting focus. We conducted a quick entrance briefing with the client, reviewed the previous topology and architecture configurations, as well as the migrations that took place with the WAN. Because this was a client of ours, and we understood the internetwork intimately, we immediately proceeded with troubleshooting exercises. We placed a WAN analyzer between two of the key locations where two of the WAN router channels were implemented. We also placed LAN analyzers against the LAN areas within those particular environments, which were based on Token Ring and Ethernet architecture. Several file servers were closely monitored by the LAN analyzers. The WAN channel was monitored via our two WAN protocol analyzers.

Our immediate focus was to examine utilization levelson the WAN medium, to verify the bandwidth concerns. WAN utilization levels appeared to be in check, with utilization below 30% between all sites, which was extremely low compared to the vendor reports for the previous T1 circuits. We examined protocol percentage levels and noted normal percentages as expected for AppleTalk and Novell NetWare. Our main concern was that the TCP/IP RIP appeared to be prevalent, which was not noticed before in previous analysis sessions.

We moved into our upper-layer protocol process to examine the routing updates between the new routers that had been implemented. We noticed that RIP updates were occurring on a consistent basis between the two routers. We also noticed that certain RIP updates were also seen on the LAN, on a consistent basis.

Upon further investigation of our analysis data, we finally observed that the statistical screen of our network analyzer showed a high number of routes confirmed and route cancelled errors, where routes were being recycled on the new WAN routers. We also saw a high number of NCP "file server not found" errors in the upper-layer NetWare Core Protocol decoding process.

With this type of occurrence, we further analyzed the NetWare Routing Information updates and noticed that they were occurring on 60-second intervals. The routing updates were also examined on the routing channels between the WAN routers. The new WAN routers that were being sampled showed a 30-second update sequence.

From these findings, we closely reviewed the configuration and found a condition to be present at this facility that we had handled before at other sites. The Novell implementation of Routing Information Protocol is based on a standard 60-second update. The new routers that were implemented against the WAN were based on a 30-second update. The new WAN router and the Novell file servers at each one of the four remote sites were intermittently canceling the routes by flushing the routing tables in the routing update configuration against the new standard IP RIP on the new router platforms for the WAN. This caused an intermittent condition in which certain routes would be unavailable and also made specific devices unable to be located in the router tables. This problem would be prevalent when certain workstations would have a default router point to the WAN router to find a remote server that housed an application or key sales information for the facility.

Based on this finding, we recommended to the MIS team that they adjust the new routers throughout the infrastructure to a 60-second RIP forced update. The other option was to modify the servers to IP-based 30-second RIP updates. With this implementation being of concern because of different patch upgrades and NOS upgrades required throughout the facility in the future, the client decided to back off the WAN routing scheme from an IP-based routing scheme to a Novell-compliant RIP scheme of 60-second intervals. They thought this was a simpler modification and contacted the WAN vendor.

The WAN vendor applied the configuration to the WAN router protocol scheme for a 60-second update. This allowed for a more consecutive routing information distance vector update between all of the Novell servers running RIP and the new WAN routers between the four sites.

We immediately reapplied a post baseline review of the facility, and found that all servers were being located and all key services and applications could be accessed from all four location offices. With this finding, we immediately identified that the Novell and IP RIP incompatibility had been the issue, and provided a final report to the client.

Our technical synopsis was that the WAN routing scheme, although implemented on a standard IP-based 30-second RIP update scheme was normal, but it was not 100% compatible with the current configuration of the Novell SAP and RIP scheme.

The final finding was that the modifications had to be applied either to the Novell server environment or the new router environment. The fact was that modifying the Novell server environment was more complex than modifying the router environment, until the future Novell migration cycles were completed, such as NetWare 4.x and NLSP implementations that were planned.

This baselining exercise was successful because we performed a standard baseline to verify the WAN channels and used upper-layer protocol analysis against the Routing Information Protocol updates and general upper-layer Novell protocol communication for server location vectoring. The baseline analysis process allowed for an immediate cause analysis of this particular issue.

CHAPTER 8

Ethernet

In the early 1970s, the industry introduced networking structures that provided distributed access via local area networks (LANs) to different hosts for resource access. This functionality directly diverged from the centralized processing associated with the mainframe and mini-computing environments. One of the first LANs to be developed was the Ethernet topology network. Ethernet development began in the early 1970s as part of a combined effort of the Digital, Intel, and Xerox Corporations (sometimes referred to as *DIX Consortium*). Xerox was involved from the network developmental side of the collaborative effort. The Xerox development team called the original network platform design XWire. *Digital Equipment Corporation* (DEC) spearheaded the transceiver for the NIC circuitry. Intel mostly developed the chips necessary for the *network interface card* (NIC) to create the Ethernet end-to-end NICs. Overall, the DIX Consortium worked together to create the main components for the initial Ethernet LAN.

Initially, opinions differed as to what to name this new topology network. Although Xerox developed the network structure for the cabling system and the endpoint-to-endpoint communications, and called the network XWire, the Consortium finally decided on the name *Ethernet*. The person most responsible for naming this topology, as the story goes, is Mr. Bob Metcalf, a development engineer for Xerox. It seems that Bob had a very specific idea as to how the Ethernet network would be designed from a physical layout perspective—that is, data flowing through the walls at a fast rate. The story is that Bob actually visualized the data flowing as the gas ether, and that streams of ether gas were visualized as a backdrop to the sky in which the Greek sun god Helios was flying in a chariot. Therefore, the name *Ethernet* became the final name for the Ethernet specification. Regardless of whether this is entirely true, the Ethernet network was introduced in the late 1970s.

The Ethernet topology layout specifications and frame types have evolved extensively since the initial development. In 1980, the DIX Version One (V.1) was introduced. The DIX Ethernet V.1 frame type included an internal Ethertype field. In 1982, the DIX Version Two (V.2) was released. The Ethernet Raw frame type version was introduced, which included a length field. In 1985, the Ethernet IEEE-accepted version frame type was introduced with an internal 802.2 LLC encapsulation mode active. In 1993, the Ethernet SNAP frame type was released, and introduced the SNAP organization and vendor fields as internal to the encapsulation design.

8.1 Understanding Ethernet Architecture Design and Layout

This section presents some of the main architecture specifications for the Ethernet physical layout, such as thicknet, thinnet, 10BASE-T, and 100BASE-T. This is a general discussion of specifications for configuration and layout.

8.1.1 Ethernet 10BASE-5: Thicknet

Several different topology layout and design standards comprise the Ethernet physical infrastructure. The original version of the Ethernet topology is based on a bus layout LAN topology. The original version is quite often called *thicknet*, also known as the 10BASE-5 standard. The 10BASE-5 layout is based on a LAN that utilizes 10Mbps engaging baseband transmission with a maximum of 500 meters in total length for the bus. The cable used for 10BASE-5 is extremely large in diameter and is based on a thick coax cabling type that is a quarter-inch in diameter. The main configuration is based on a bus layout, in which the main cable is run from workstation, point to point, throughout a building. The LAN devices such as workstations and servers with an Ethernet 10BASE-5 NIC connect via a drop-link cable to the main cabling bus on the thicknet bus. At each end of the main thicknet cable is a 50ohm termination point N connector. The reason for the 500-meter length is to allow for the proper capacitance to ensure true signal integrity and low attenuation. If a cabling implementation for 10BASE-5 were to exceed 500 meters, it is quite possible that the *carrier sense multiple access collision detection* (CSMA/CD) mechanism of the Ethernet LAN NICs that is used for network access may not work properly, which could cause physical Ethernet problems.

In the 10BASE-5 Ethernet topology, repeaters are specified as allowed if necessary to extend the segment length. The specification calls for no more than four repeaters in a complete 10BASE-5 bus layout, which limits the complete thicknet segment to 2,500 meters (the maximum length for the overall thicknet bus extension). This would be true if using a straight bus extension of standard repeaters or a multiport repeater layout (see Figure 8.1).

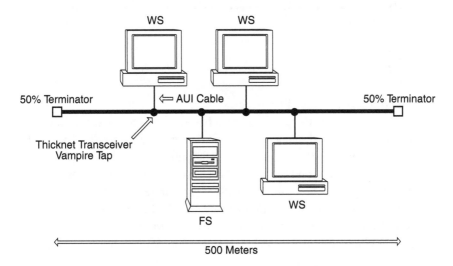

FIGURE 8.1 *A thick Ethernet 10BASE-5 bus segment layout scheme.*

In 10BASE-5 Ethernet, any workstation connecting to the cabling medium must connect through an external transceiver, which provides the *medium attachment unit* (MAU) interface for the physical layer. The external transceiver has an *Attachment Unit Interface* (AUI) 15-pin connector on the 10BASE-5 NIC, which provides for a connection to a drop cable that can be up to 165 feet in length. The drop cable is an extension cable usually run down an internal wall channel and then connected to the main thicknet cable run within the building infrastructure. For the drop cable to connect to the thicknet cable, a special connector called a *vampire clamp* is utilized. The thicknet 500-meter segment length specification allows for up to 100 workstations to interconnect on the segment. The maximum distance allowable between any two transceivers or devices connecting through the drop cables from the AUI connection to the thicknet is 8.2 feet (see Figure 8.2).

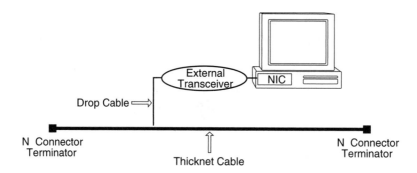

FIGURE 8.2 *A 10BASE-5 device connection scheme.*

8.1.2 Ethernet 10BASE-2: Thinnet

The next Ethernet LAN layout scheme based on bus topology is called *10BASE-2,* also called *thinnet.* The name *thinnet* is descriptive of the smaller cabling medium for the transmission. The thinnet cable utilizes RJ58 coax cable. The transmission is still based on a 10Mbps baseband transmission mode. The specification called *10BASE-2* is deciphered as 10Mbps based on baseband transmission with a maximum length of approximately 200 meters. The 10BASE-2 configuration has a bus layout with the cabling being run throughout a facility from workstation location point to point (see Figure 8.3).

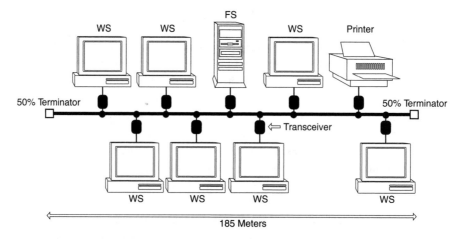

FIGURE 8.3 *A 10BASE-2 thinnet segment layout.*

On a floor with 30 workstations, for example, at one endpoint of the main thin-net cable run would be the first workstation where the end of the cable would connect to that first workstation. That endpoint would be terminated. The cable would then continue to flow through the wall from workstation point to point and connect to each workstation until it reaches the 30th or last workstation. A 50ohm terminator is also applied to the last connection at the end of each main cable. Each workstation is directly connected to the thinnet cable through a (T) BNC-type connector tapped into the thinnet cable. Because the cable is smaller in diameter than thicknet, a BNC-T adaptor connection can be utilized. This adaptor connector is spliced into the middle of the cable. This connection scheme physically resembles a T connector, with the bottom of the T point of the connector connecting directly to the Ethernet 10BASE-2 NIC at the work-station. The top part of the T connects in line with the main cable run.

The thinnet specification allows for a maximum length of 185 meters, or 607 feet. Many NICs have been designed to operate on longer specifications. Modifications in the Ethernet architecture NIC design allow for an end-to-end communication process enhanced by the circuitry on the NIC. Repeaters are also valid in the 10BASE-2 thinnet configuration and are based on a specific distance extension. In the thinnet specification, no more than four repeaters can be used to extend an Ethernet segment to a maximum of 925 meters.

An Ethernet thinnet segment configuration is designed for connection of no more than 30 nodes. This directly relates to the maximum length of 185 meters. With 185 meters the maximum length because of the smaller diameter of the RG58 coax cable, there is an inherent lower capacitance level to truly maintain signal integrity. If the cable is implemented at a length longer than 185 meters, it is quite possible that attenuation of the signal will occur, as well as subse-quent loss of signal properties. This is why the number of stations per Ethernet segment is limited to 30 in a thinnet configuration (see Figure 8.4).

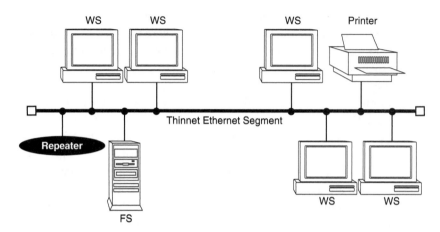

FIGURE 8.4 *10BASE-2 device connection scheme.*

8.1.3 Ethernet 10BASE-T: Twisted Pair

As the networking industry evolved, the next platform release of the Ethernet topology was based on a requirement for a more progressive and workable solution for implementing and supporting the physical topology within the corporate infrastructure. The Ethernet bus layout types 10BASE-5 and 10BASE-2, although a workable LAN solution, are somewhat cumbersome when implementing and expanding an Ethernet internetwork. Troubleshooting the Ethernet bus topologies is also quite awkward and complex, because the bus main cabling is usually physically run throughout a facility in a complex manner. The cable travels through the wall infrastructure to reach areas where different workstations and network devices that require connection to the Ethernet network are positioned. When problems occur, at times the troubleshooting process can actually require pulling the cabling from the wall infrastructure to examine and troubleshoot different connection points, such as thicknet vampire clamps and drop or thinnet T connectors.

With this in mind, the Ethernet design engineers, including Ethernet NIC providers and other product manufacturers, designed an Ethernet topology that would be based on a centralized star-like layout wiring scheme. The Ethernet topology that emerged from this vendor design effort was the *10BASE-T*.

10BASE-T represents an Ethernet network with a 10Mbps data rate. It also uses a baseband transmission method, but on twisted-pair wiring. The 10BASE-T scheme is based on a star layout with a centralized hub located within one area of the LAN environment. The hub is usually placed in a centralized wiring closet or hub room for the main central point of interconnection of individual cables connected to all the devices in the Ethernet network site.

It is important to remember that when Ethernet was originally introduced to the industry, most of the implementations were based on peer-to-peer networking, and there was not a high concentration of multiple server structure designs that required placement of centralized servers. Most of the networking needs actually centered around resource sharing between PCs in more of a peer-to-peer approach. The main thrust of the 10BASE-T implementation in the early stages was to provide a centralized hub, star wiring scheme that would normally be positioned within one computer room. From the centralized hub, cables were run outward and dispersed to each location using twisted-pair wiring. The original 10BASE-T cabling types included standard phone cabling, which was run from the centralized hub in the main computer room directly out to the Ethernet workstations.

As noted, many of the original 10BASE-T layouts utilized Category 3 *unshielded twisted pair* (UTP), which is the same cabling that was normally used for phone communications throughout most corporate enterprise infrastructures. Note that in today's environment, Category 5 cabling is the most common when implementing standard and Fast Ethernet networks (see Figure 8.5).

UTP 10BASE-T Hub

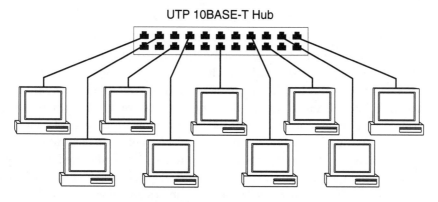

FIGURE 8.5 *A 10BASE-T Ethernet layout scheme.*

One of the main reasons this particular Ethernet topology design became so popular was because most industry clients could buy an Ethernet 10BASE-T star-based hub and utilize the phone cabling systems already housed within their building as a point-to-point wiring scheme to implement the Ethernet network.

If additional connections for workstations to the Ethernet network were required, the solution was as simple as adding a phone jack and running a UTP cable from the workstation point to the 10BASE-T hub point in the building phone closet. Overall, this was a simple and cost-effective solution to building a LAN.

The 10BASE-T architecture maintains certain specifications and standards. The main 10BASE-T Ethernet hub, for example, should be placed within the main computer room wiring closet or in the phone closet within the facility. The centralized wiring hub would actually provide connection for all the network devices and workstations being connected for transfer to the Ethernet network. Many of the first 10BASE-T hubs released were designed on 8-, 16-, and 24-port designs. For an Ethernet hub with an 8-port design, all 8 ports are connected to a device via UTP cabling schemes. If additional devices above the 8 count are required for connection to the network, most 10BASE-T hubs allow for a specific port to provide for an uplink cable to be used to connect another hub for expansion. The hub is positioned in the main closet, and the cables run directly out to the desktop. The length of the cable was originally specified for no more than 100 meters. The actual type of connection on the hub is an RJ45 standard connector or phone jack.

Within the 10BASE-T hub, internal circuitry was designed to allow the Ethernet network to still function as a shared medium in an individual cable run in a star layout design, just as in a bus architecture. The transfer communication from port to port for Ethernet node interaction would be handled by the hub circuitry. The 10BASE-T internal circuitry was based on a backplane with port-to-port replication repeater circuits that would allow for transfer of data from port to port. In the initial release of the 10BASE-T hubs, the ports were fairly passive in terms of circuitry design and were not highly advanced. In today's Ethernet environment, 10BASE-T and 100BASE-T hubs and switches, which are much more advanced than the initial star hub design are in use (see Figure 8.6).

The initial Ethernet 10BASE-T cabling scheme was extremely cost-effective, but it was susceptible to electrical interference, depending on where in the facility the cables were run. Any cables running over areas or equipment that generate electrical magnetic interference could cause problems in the quality of transmission. Overall, however, the standard implementation of 10BASE-T in the mid-1980s was positive, because the traffic levels of most LANs were fairly light. At the time of the initial 10BASE-T Ethernet product release, usually less than 50% of capacity was actually utilized. This was because the node counts were also fairly low and LAN networking was just starting to evolve as an important implementation for the computing industry.

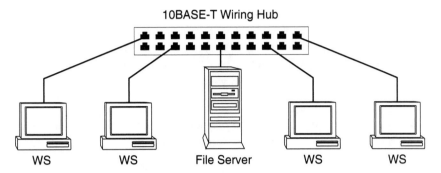

10BASE-T Wiring Hub

WS   WS   File Server   WS   WS

FIGURE 8.6 *A 10BASE-T device connection scheme.*

It should be pointed out that there were definitely electrical differences in place for the 10BASE-T hub and NIC technology in terms of how the network topology operated. There was usually an electrical charge on the wire, which differs somewhat from the bus transmission process. In the 10BASE-T technology, the type of 10BASE-T hub being utilized influenced these electrical differences. Certain Ethernet 10BASE-T vendor hubs allowed for signal regeneration and signal amplification upon input and output of the hub ports as related to transfer to and from the Ethernet hub. This design made it inevitable that the Ethernet signals would be propagated across the 10BASE-T network in a more enhanced way than in the bus types (because of complex regeneration schemes within the 10BASE-T hubs). Note that with 10BASE-T, it's possible to use multiport repeaters to extend the 10BASE-T network.

During the early product releases and implementation of Ethernet 10BASE-T, many different vendors were providing the hubs. There was fierce competition to provide higher amplification of signal, low signal attenuation, high capacitance, and longer extension of cabling runs past the normal Ethernet specification. Many different Ethernet NICs, hubs, transceivers, and connectors were introduced, offering enhanced capability as to higher node counts and longer cabling lengths than specified by the Ethernet implementation.

This enhanced capability would work fine, as long as a company implementing the Ethernet 10BASE-T network would used the same vendor for the hub and Ethernet NICs. However, many companies used different vendors for their Ethernet NICs and Ethernet hubs, thus leading to a hybrid design within their respective companies. To create an even more complex situation, many Ethernet vendors produced products that would allow the different Ethernet topologies—10BASE-T, 10BASE-2, 10BASE-5, and 10BASE-F—to interconnect through unique transceivers, hubs, and multirepeaters. Although these devices provided connectivity, many times they would cause problems such as signal loss and point-to-point connection problems that resulted from variances in the design scheme that made the cross vendors incompatible.

This "situation" mainly resulted from the inherent business race by the Ethernet product vendors to try to provide the most workable solution for Ethernet. Even though an industry standard and set of specifications were in place, many industry vendors overwrote the specifications and stated that their product would work in an enhanced manner. This led clients to buy the product with the highest-level features as quoted on the product statistical sheets. At times, a certain client would find that the new high-rated device would not work well when implemented in a common Ethernet network with another vendor's product. Such occurrences caused many problems that then had to be troubleshot and resolved. The original Ethernet specification really turned out to be a wide-open implementation because of the different manufacturers involved in a product rollout race to capture the market.

8.1.4 Ethernet 10BASE-F: Fiber Optic

Another popular 10Mbps Ethernet topology infrastructure option is *10BASE-F*. The 10BASE-F specification is based on a 10Mbps data rate with baseband transmission over fiber cabling systems. This version of the Ethernet topology is also based on a star-shaped wiring scheme similar to 10BASE-T. The 10BASE-F layout features a centralized hub that is usually placed within a wiring closet or phone closet. The difference is that the use of fiber rather than UTP cabling makes it possible to extend the 10BASE-F cabling scheme. The original release of 10BASE-F was based on the use of 50 or 100 micro fiber-optic cable.

With the original implementations of Ethernet 10BASE-F, multiport repeaters could be used to extend 10BASE-F hubs via connections to expand the network. The 10BASE-F hub drop cables could extend as far as 1.3 miles. Therefore, fiber-optic cabling could be used to increase the overall electrical energy generation source to the endpoint Ethernet workstation. The industry clients quite often used the 10BASE-F topology to implement an extension from one Ethernet 10BASE-T network area to another. It was common to see 10BASE-T hubs connected to a 10BASE-F repeater hub through a transceiver connection. Such a setup allowed a 10BASE-F hub to connect to another 10BASE-F hub for building-to-building crossover connections that would allow for extensions of the main 10BASE-T Ethernet LAN network to other buildings.

Thus, a simple extension of the Ethernet network without partitioning or sepa-rating the network with bridging and routing technologies was possible (see Figure 8.7).

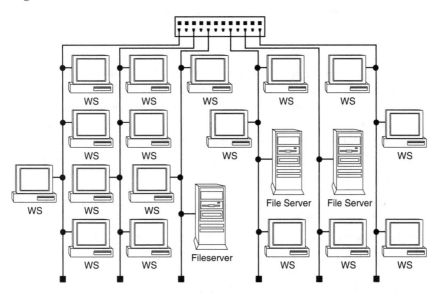

FIGURE 8.7 *A 10BASE-F thinnet repeater layout scheme.*

8.1.5 Closing Statement on 10Mbps Ethernet Topology Architecture

The discussion thus far has covered the standard implementation of 10Mbps baseband transmission Ethernet. Later in this chapter, you will learn about 100Mbps Fast Ethernet and 1000Mbps Gigabit implementations. The discussion now turns to a detailed review of the workstation, server, and Ethernet node access methods. Note that the original access method is still a valid access method utilized in Fast Ethernet layouts in certain configurations.

8.2 Ethernet Access Methods

The Ethernet topology is based on a contention-based access method. This process is termed *contention-based* because the Ethernet NICs within worksta-tions connecting to an Ethernet network contend to use the medium. Because the transmission of the Ethernet physical signal is based on baseband, this means that only a single station's signal fully propagates on the medium in a specific unit of time. Whether the Ethernet topology type is 10BASE-5, 10BASE-2, 10BASE-T, or 10BASE-F, the station utilizes an access method to contend for the right to transmit on the network.This access method is called *carrier sense multiple access collision detection* (CSMA/CD).

The CSMA/CD operation is a LAN medium access system based on an algorithm invoked by the Ethernet architecture and built within an Ethernet NIC. All the nodes that want to transmit on the network or the specific workstations thereof and the connected NICs invoke a process to request a transmit on the network. This involves a designed capability where the Ethernet NIC can listen for the opportunity to transmit on the network. In this listen mode, the Ethernet NIC tries to sense whether a signal is on the Ethernet medium (called a *carrier*).

As noted earlier, the Ethernet network is a baseband transmission medium. Again, this means that only one specific node transmits in any specific time period, usually broken down into fractions of a second. Many different Ethernet nodes or workstations can communicate to each other and use the medium within one second. It is common for 20, 30, 40, 50, or even 60 devices to process an end-to-end conversation within one second. In designs such as the older thicknet 10BASE-5 architecture, the Ethernet NIC could actually sense an occurrence, called a *collision*, taking place on the medium.

Because the Ethernet access architecture is based on contention, if two Ethernet NICs transmit to each other on the medium and another device attempts to transmit to another device at the same time, a collision might occur. An Ethernet *collision* can be defined as an event that occurs when two or more Ethernet workstations attempt to transmit on the Ethernet cabling medium at close intervals in time and Ethernet packet signals from different nodes collide on their actual travel en route across the physical medium.

If the two Ethernet NICs are transmitting to two different destination nodes, it is possible that their frames may arrive on the cabling medium at the same time. If this occurs, a collision occurs—that is, the Ethernet frames collide. When this happens, the Ethernet packet being transmitted can be truncated, causing the Ethernet frame structure to be shortened and the CRC field within the frame to possibly become corrupted. In most cases, the packet intended for the destination node will not arrive, and the transmitting Ethernet source nodes involved in the collision need to retransmit the packet. The process is known as a *reestablishment of transmission*. The transmitting nodes detect the collision and move through a process during which they requeue the frame and attempt to retransmit. The Ethernet nodes that detect the collision back off and attempt to requeue the frame for transmission.

The event cycle of accessing the Ethernet medium through CSMA/CD operates as follows: A specific Ethernet workstation attempts to transmit on the network. This transmission process is invoked when the workstation's upper-layer protocol or an application within the workstation invokes a protocol event sequence, or protocol chain operation, in which a *protocol data unit* (PDU) is processed down to the Ethernet NIC level through the PC. Next, in the PC platform and NIC, an Ethernet frame is formed. The Ethernet frame is used to encapsulate or envelope the PDU with the necessary Ethernet headers to form an Ethernet packet.

Then the Ethernet packet is queued for transmission. In this case, the Ethernet NIC takes over the responsibility of attempting to transmit the packet on the network. When the actual packet transmission occurs, the Ethernet NIC sends an outbound frame onto the network. Prior to this process, a set of events called the Ethernet *transmission access process* occurs. Note also that when an Ethernet NIC receives a frame, this invokes the Ethernet *receiving access process* (see Figure 8.8).

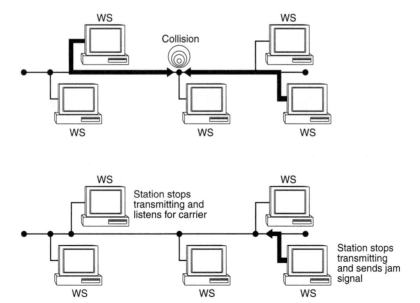

FIGURE 8.8 *An Ethernet collision event.*

The full collision event cycle can affect general communications on the Ethernet network channel. Devices using the medium for communication can be affected in a negative manner when collision rates exceed the 1% to 2% level. When utilization on an Ethernet network increases above the 65% level, collisions levels generally increase; these collisions then negatively affect performance by decreasing effective throughput (see Figure 8.9).

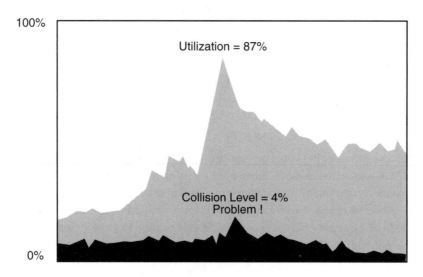

FIGURE 8.9 *High utilization can affect the physical Ethernet collision rates.*

The discussion now turns to a more detailed review of the Ethernet access process engaged by devices such as workstations, servers, and other devices transmitting or receiving packets across the Ethernet medium.

8.2.1 Transmission Process for Ethernet Node Access

When an Ethernet node wants to transmit on an Ethernet medium, whether a workstation or a server, a process to start the transmission occurs in either the workstation shell or the network operating system on the server. Specifically, the server NOS or workstation shell is involved with an application interaction, in which a PDU is queued for transmission. A portion of data is queued for transmission on the network, and the device next attempts to form the packet through the protocol chain in that device.

A workstation application queues a unit of data for transmission, for example, and the shell image of the workstation invokes a protocol chain process. During this process, the data travels through the protocol sequencing of the workstation in the processing chain and is queued for transmission upon the network.

The workstation shell links the data to the workstation NIC. Next, the Ethernet NIC utilizes an Ethernet frame to formulate a structure required for transmission around the data, and the data is entered into the Data field of the Ethernet frame.

An Ethernet packet is then formed and queued for transmission. Next, the NIC on the Ethernet node attempts to transmit the packet on the network to the destination station. In the packet transmission queuing process, the Ethernet packet is ready for transmission, but the Ethernet NIC moves into a stage called *slot time*, during which the NIC waits for approximately 51.2 microseconds.

The word *approximate* is stressed because, as stated earlier, the design of the process in Ethernet NICs from different vendors varies widely; the specification is somewhat loose in this particular area. Once the Ethernet packet has been slotted and is ready for transmission, the Ethernet NIC then listens for a carrier. While listening for the carrier, the Ethernet NIC tries to sense a carrier on the medium. The Ethernet NIC listens for any type of signal present on the medium. In most cases, the NIC circuitry includes an internal or external transceiver that allows for carrier sense to take place. If no carrier is sensed during this stage, the Ethernet NIC transmits the packet onto the network to the destination station. If the Ethernet NIC does sense carrier, it moves into an additional wait time of approximately 9.6 microseconds. After this wait time, the packet is then transmitted onto the network by the NIC.

After the packet has been transmitted onto the network, if everything is working perfectly, a destination station receives the packet and processes it for operation. If for some reason the packet is transmitted onto the network at the exact same time as another device transmits, and the packet is involved in a collision with another device, the two devices involved in the collision sense the collision process. The stations involved in the collision then back off and perform a random algorithm sequence that invokes a unique circuitry pattern operation cycle. The detecting Ethernet NICs sends a quick 32- to 48-bit signal, a time jam, to clear the medium.

The Ethernet NICs then randomly run a number-generation system and attempt to requeue the packet for transmission. The purpose of randomly generating a number is to attempt to ensure that the packets involved in the collision do not transmit at the exact same instance upon retransmission, which would cause another collision. In most cases, because of the random number-generation process to requeue the packet for transmission, the packet is retransmitted at a different instance than the packet involved in the preceding collision. In most cases, the packet eventually arrives for reception at the destination device.

During the backoff algorithm, a counter is incremented and a random number-generation process occurs. If for some reason a collision does occur again, each station again backs off and performs the random number-generation process before its next retransmission occurs. This process repeats up to 16 times at the physical layer before the device does not retransmit again. If this occurs, the upper-layer protocol process in the workstation must sense that the data event did not occur and must reprocess the complete transmission. This is one of the main reasons that application vendors attempt to implement an extremely efficient process application layer protocol or a transport protocol when utilizing the Ethernet medium for transmission to ensure final data transfer (see Figure 8.10).

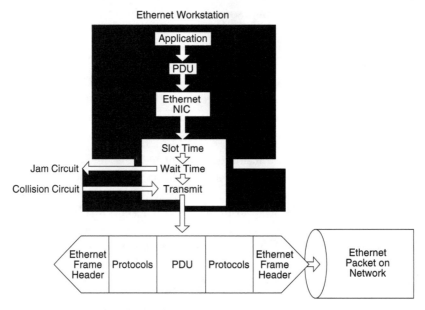

FIGURE 8.10 *The Ethernet data-transmission process.*

8.2.2 Receiving Process for Ethernet Node Access

In the Ethernet environment, a process takes place in which an Ethernet NIC or workstation receives a packet. First, the Ethernet NIC investigates a packet to ensure that it is intended for its station. An Ethernet investigates the packet, examining the address during the first phase of the process. It reviews the address for an exact address match to the Ethernet NIC and it also reviews the packet to see whether the packet is set for broadcast or multicast. If the packet sent to the destination station is addressed for the specific device, it is processed. If the packet is generated for a broadcast or multicast ID, the device in most cases processes the packet. Note that Ethernet NICs in standard configuration normally interrogate every packet that passes the node point or hub/switch port.

When a packet is received by an Ethernet NIC on a hub or switch port, or even the bus type medium, for example, the NIC begins the receiving process. After the first investigation process has occurred, during which the destination station provides a match for the respective node address or broadcast, it then passes the packet to the second phase of investigation. In the second phase, the Ethernet NIC examines the packet for a valid frame size and valid CRC field. If the length of the packet is within the Ethernet frame size specification and the CRC check is valid and stable, the Ethernet NIC then processes and links the packet to the upper-layer protocol sockets in the protocol chain of the particular workstation or server. If for some reason the frame size does not match or the CRC is corrupt, the NIC receiving the packet discards the packet and does not process it to the upper layers.

In the Ethernet mechanism topology function, there is no guaranteed way for the Ethernet NIC to respond and let the transmitting node know that this occurrence did take place. This is an inherent problem in Ethernet transmission, because there is no true connection stability mandatory in the Ethernet frame architecture. In the Ethernet IEEE frame type, which engages the *Logical Link Protocol* (LLC) protocol, and the Ethernet *Subnetwork Access Protocol* (SNAP) frame type, there is the capability to provide connection stability, but is not often used because of overhead costs. Custom algorithm operation features that can also address this issue are available from Ethernet switch and product vendors.

The discussion now turns to a description of the Ethernet addressing system. Further descriptions are presented on the Ethernet frame structures and how the packaging of an upper-layer data unit is employed when an Ethernet frame encapsulates data for an Ethernet packet to be formed (see Figure 8.11).

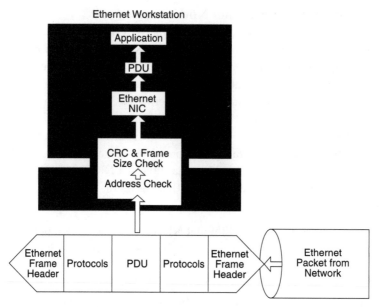

FIGURE 8.11 *The Ethernet data-receiving process.*

8.3 Frame Addressing

The Ethernet frame architecture uses a very simple addressing scheme involving a 6-byte hexadecimal address applied to an Ethernet NIC. The 3 bytes of the leftmost portion of the address are used for the manufacturer code, such as 3Com, Cisco, Bay, and so forth. This is the hexadecimal address that applies to the various well-known manufacturer codes. A protocol analyzer usually decodes the Ethernet manufacturer ID for the analyst in the display view and also presents the Ethernet manufacturer NIC type for view.

The lower 3 bytes are the unique hexadecimal address that applies to the specific Ethernet NIC. The Ethernet addressing scheme is hard-coded by the manufacturer (which differs from Token Ring). Most Ethernet NICs include a physical component that enables one to locally administer or override the address. There are other unique ways to cause Ethernet devices to assume different addresses, but these methods are used more at higher layers, such as the network IP or IPX addressing layer, to provide for unique addressing schemes. At the physical layer, a very simple methodology is normally used (see Figure 8.12).

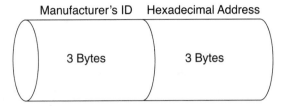

Manufacturer's ID   Hexadecimal Address

3 Bytes   3 Bytes

FIGURE 8.12 *The Ethernet physical addressing scheme.*

8.4 Physical Transmission Signal Code Processes

At the physical layer, the Ethernet transmission process uses Manchester encoding on the cable medium. *Manchester encoding* is a digital encoding system that uses bi-phase encoding, in which the first half byte of a period of the signal and the second half byte of the signal are linked. A clock signal is invoked where a synchronization occurs between the first and second half of the byte signal. Next, a resultant signal code is formed for transmission from the station NIC or hub/switch adaptor port, and the signal is generated on the Ethernet physical medium.

8.5 Higher-Layer Management

The Ethernet topology is a highly robust topology that provides rapid transmission, making it very popular for this specific reason. Other LAN topologies, such as Token Ring, that use deterministic access methods and also process frames at the physical layer cannot always compete with Ethernet's frame-per-second-generation rates because of the overhead involved with the enhanced physical mechanisms. To compete, a Token Ring NIC requires a much more complex design in the circuitry, which in the early release of Token Ring NICs created higher costs.

The design of the original Ethernet NICs inherently lacked an internal Ethernet physical design for network management. The Token Ring architecture, as explained later in this book, has a truly inherent circuitry design that makes it possible to provide fault redundancy and use physical frames at the physical level for transmission. These processes allow Token Ring NICs to manage each other with regard to fault redundancy and error recovery. This is also present in other physical LAN topologies such as *Fiber Data Distributed Interface* (FDDI). The Ethernet NIC mechanism has no inherent design capability in the NIC or the basic Ethernet frame structure for default management processes to operate.

Because of this, the Ethernet NICs have only become intelligent since the late 1980s and early 1990s through the combined implementation of the *Simple Network Management Protocol* (SNMP) operation with Ethernet NICs, hubs, and switches.

SNMP, a protocol coresident within the TCP/IP protocol suite, is utilized as a way to manage different Ethernet devices. A simple process is invoked in which an SNMP *Management Information Base* (MIB) agent is placed on the Ethernet NIC, hub, switch, or other Ethernet devices in the firmware design. The MIB agent can hold important SNMP statistics on the device on which it is applied. The Ethernet NIC then can be managed by an SNMP central station that communicates to Ethernet MIBs.

The process involves an SNMP console being implemented on the Ethernet network that utilizes SNMP to manage other devices on the Ethernet network. The protocol invokes software operations that transmit requests and queries to all Ethernet NICs and devices on the network such as a hub or switch that have a MIB firmware agents designed on circuitry of the device.

The Ethernet device or NIC can then respond to the SNMP queries with certain physical attributes such as frames transmitted, bytes transmitted, collisions, and other specifications such as CRC errors on the Ethernet NIC. This process makes it possible to implement a network management system on an Ethernet hub or switch that can query all Ethernet NICs in a 10BASE-T or 100BASE-T architecture. SNMP queries can also be used for calling on higher-information MIBs such as IP or TCP statistics. The key point is that SNMP along with RMON technology has made the Ethernet environment intelligent and manageable, which has brought success through industry acceptance (see Figure 8.13).

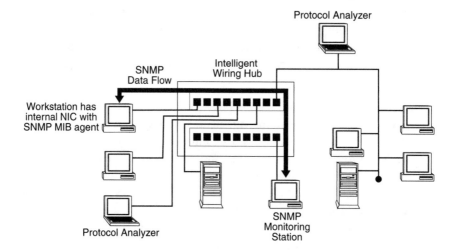

FIGURE 8.13 *How monitoring an Ethernet network can be achieved with both a protocol analyzer and an SNMP management system combined.*

In an Ethernet environment, you should always combine the use of protocol analysis with any site management systems for hubs or switches that engage SNMP or RMON technologies when performing a network baseline. At certain times, you should use network management systems that utilize SNMP and other information-gathering tools, such as RMON specifications, along with standard protocol analysis. The following section describes Ethernet frame types.

8.6 Ethernet Frame Types

The evolution of different Ethernet topologies, such as 10BASE-5, 10BASE-2, 10BASE-T, and Fast Ethernet, also necessitated frame structure. This differs somewhat from other topologies; Token Ring and FDDI, for example, have fairly standard singular-frame structures that have not changed. Note also that the *Institute of Electrical and Electronic Engineers* (IEEE) supports the premise that the Ethernet frame structure should continue to be enhanced so as to be more stable and uniform.

The various Ethernet manufacturers constantly strove to provide uniformity and common design. Their purpose was to benefit the consumer by keeping Ethernet NICs and other Ethernet products within specification. Despite their efforts, many of the enterprise internetworking environments as implemented have evolved to a point where they are still utilizing hybrid Ethernet topologies and different Ethernet frame types. This results from certain variances that exist in final design of Ethernet products by certain vendors in contrast with industry specifications and standards. Because of this fact alone, the question arises as to whether multiple Ethernet frame types create any benefit.

Four Ethernet frame types are considered standard. It is the author's contention, however, that there are only two standard Ethernet frame types: Ethernet II and Ethernet Raw. The other available Ethernet types use technologies that evoke extra Ethernet header frame format fields used for encapsulation or the insertion of other protocols.

The Ethernet frame type called *IEEE Accepted*, for example, uses a 802.2 LLC header inside the Ethernet frame. Although a standard and IEEE-accepted Ethernet frame type, it is my view that this is just an Ethernet frame with the LLC protocol being used for encapsulation and protocol chain handling. There is another frame type called *Ethernet SNAP*. This type is the IEEE-accepted version with a further encapsulation mode for protocol chain processing, invoking the Subnetwork Access Protocol internally for encapsulation inside the Ethernet frame.

Either way, the industry views the Ethernet architecture as having four main frame types. For the purposes of the industry specifications, the following sections describe the four main Ethernet frame types.

8.6.1 Ethernet II Frame Type

The Ethernet II frame type was the earliest frame type. It was released at the same time as the 10BASE-5 thicknet architecture. The Ethernet II frame type is a simple frame comprised of a Preamble for the overall frame to be processed in and out of Ethernet NICs, along with a Destination and Source Address for identification of the Ethernet nodes, a Type field that indicates the type of protocol processing for the Ethernet frame, and a Data field that holds data, along with a simple *frame-check sequence* (FCS).

The Ethernet II frame type Preamble is configured for an 8-byte configuration. The Destination Address and Source Address are each configured for a 6-byte address configuration. The Type field is noted at 2 bytes. The Data field usually varies between 46 and 1500 bytes in size. The frame-check sequence is a standard CRC process designed at 4 bytes in size. The industry specification for the total allowable frame length of an Ethernet II packet is from 64 bytes to 1518 bytes (see Figure 8.14).

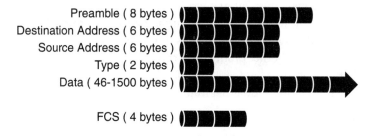

FIGURE 8.14 *The Ethernet II frame type.*

8.6.2 Ethernet 802.3 Raw Frame Type

The next frame type, Ethernet 802.3 Raw, was released with the thinnet and 10BASE-T topology architecture. This is a very common frame type that does not use any type of internal encapsulation such as the LLC header or SNAP header. The Ethernet 802.3 Raw frame type is called "raw" because it does not include these encapsulation methods. Because of this fact alone, certain industry standards groups considered the frame type nonreliable from end-to-end transmission. Again, there is no way in the Ethernet basic access method for transmission and reception of data from node to node for the source device to know that the destination device received the packet. In other topologies such as Token Ring and FDDI, there is a method in which a packet is returned to the original source station. When this occurs, the source station knows that the transmission was completed. This is part of the reason for enhancing the Ethernet frame type in the IEEE-accepted version (described next).

The 802.3 Raw frame type includes a standard Preamble. The Preamble differs from the standard Ethernet II frame type because the Preamble is 7 bytes. There is 1 byte attached and allocated for a *starting frame delimiter* (SFD), which makes for a total 8-byte Preamble. The physical Ethernet addresses are still based on two 6-byte frame sequences—that is, the Destination is 6 bytes and the Source Address is 6 bytes. The Type field was removed in the 802.3 Raw frame type and replaced by a Length field, which identifies the actual length of the frame. This was done so that the protocol chain processing of Ethernet nodes when handling the frame could identify the length of data encapsulated within the Ethernet frame immediately for protocol vectoring and rapid acceleration. The Data field is deployed as variable at 46 to 1500 bytes. The frame-check sequence is 4 bytes in size. The 802.3 Raw frame format can pad the data length at times (see Figure 8.15).

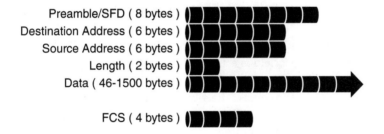

Preamble/SFD (8 bytes)
Destination Address (6 bytes)
Source Address (6 bytes)
Length (2 bytes)
Data (46-1500 bytes)

FCS (4 bytes)

FIGURE 8.15 *An Ethernet 802.3 Raw frame type.*

8.6.3 Ethernet 802.3 Frame Type with 802.2 LLC Internal

This particular frame type is the main IEEE-accepted frame type. The IEEE and the industry Ethernet manufacturers provided an Ethernet frame type that is more reliable for transmission. The resultant solution was that the Ethernet manufacturers in the IEEE approved a frame type that utilizes the 802.2 LLC protocol specification attached to the Data field.

The 802.2 LLC protocol specification is a connection-based protocol implemented inside this Ethernet frame type. Note that the 802.2 LLC protocol is a standard protocol. It is a separate communication protocol that can carry data and provide for reliable transmission across multiple networking media. It also has internal fields such as *Source Service Access Points* (SSAP) configured for a destination and source endpoints utilizing LLC. The two *Service Access Points* (SAPs), called SSAP and DSAP, can communicate with each other in connection-based processes (Type 1), unacknowledged connection-based processes (Type 2), and acknowledgment-when-required processes (Type 3). There are also methods and variances of configuration of LLC's implementation where the actual use of LLC in communication makes it possible to maintain a connection. Because of this alone, the industry vendors considered the insertion of the LLC header as a way to allow different protocols, applications, and NOS vendors to make the Ethernet frame available for a connection-based cycle. By engaging custom processes of LLC's use in Ethernet, it is possible to allow for source and destination Ethernet nodes to be aware of transmissions that were received on transmission outbound and reverse cycles. This particular process is not always invoked, and the LLC mode is used mainly for standard encapsulation in most transmissions.

The 802.3 IEEE-accepted frame format uses a Preamble that is standard and somewhat similar to the 802.3 Raw Preamble. There are 7 bytes allocated for the Preamble with 1 byte for an SFD. The Source and Destination Address fields are based on sizes of 6 bytes each for the physical Ethernet source and destination address. The Length field is 2 bytes in size. Prior to the Data field encapsulation, the SSAP of LLC and the *Destination Service Access Point* (DSAP)of LLC, along with the Control field, are implemented. The SSAP field is a 1-byte field, the DSAP field is a 1-byte field, and the Control field is a 1-byte field. The total LLC header is 3 bytes. The Data field in an 802.3 IEEE-accepted frame is 46 to 1500 bytes. The 4-byte frame-check sequence is also engaged. The Ethernet frame size for this type is still 64 to 1518 bytes. In the IEEE standard frame format, padding is normally not used (see Figure 8.16).

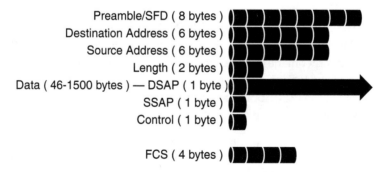

FIGURE 8.16 *Frame Type with 802.2 LLC.*

8.6.4 Ethernet 802.3 SNAP Frame Type

The fourth Ethernet frame type that is popular is the 802.3 *Subnetwork Access Protocol* (SNAP) Ethernet frame type. In this particular frame type, an enhanced encapsulation process is engaged. A further encapsulation process is used, in which the SNAP fields for Organizational code and Ethernet type are deployed within the overall encapsulation process of the Ethernet frame. The LLC encapsulation process is also used.

The SNAP Ethernet frame structure is as follows. There is a Preamble, which again is 7 bytes with a 1-byte SFD. The Destination and Source Address fields are 6 bytes each in length. The Length field is 2 bytes. The next field is the LLC 3-byte encapsulation mode header with an SSAP, a DSAP, and a Control field. The next encapsulation technique is the SNAP Organizational code, which is 3 bytes, along with a SNAP Ethernet type that is 2 bytes. The SNAP header allows for protocol chain processing enhancement, in which an Ethernet NIC can more rapidly and accurately interpret what Ethernet type is active and being used for transmit from another device along with the Organizational code. This allows multiple topologies in internetworking to coexist in a more uniform manner. The next field is the Data field, which is 46 to 1500 bytes, and the frame-check sequence field is still at 4 bytes for the CRC. The SNAP type frame size is limited to 64 to 1518 bytes (see Figure 8.17).

The key factor here is that this is the most enhanced and robust version of the Ethernet frame types. This is currently the most common Ethernet frame type used for node-to-node general transmission.

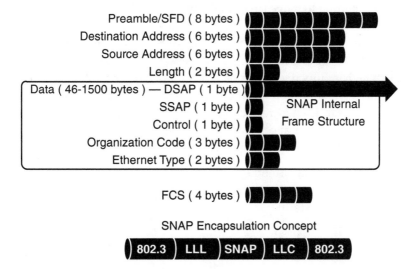

FIGURE 8.17 *The Ethernet SNAP frame structure.*

8.6.5 Closing Statement on Frame Type Analysis

When utilizing a protocol analyzer in a network baselining session, various features are available that enable an analyst to review the frame type immediately. Some analyzers have statistical modes that can immediately identify the type of frame active for transmission for each device even before the analyzer trace capture is stopped. A node device address is usually present in the statistical active screen and shows the type of Ethernet frame being transmitted. Some analyzers may require the trace to be stopped and saved for the internal data of an Ethernet frame header to be displayed and decoded. When viewing the internals of any particular packet, it is important to review the Ethernet frame header to determine the frame type. If an Ethernet II, 802.3 Raw, 802.3 IEEE-accepted with LLC encapsulation, or SNAP frame type is active, it is very easy to see this by viewing the Ethernet frame header.

The following section describes the general architectural changes associated with the Fast Ethernet environment, and compares some of the older Ethernet shared architecture. The discussion then turns to a detailed description of Switched Ethernet. This chapter closes by presenting ways to perform network baselines on the Ethernet topology.

8.7 Fast and Ethernet Switching Architecture

As the implementation of Ethernet-based networks started to accelerate during the early 1990s, the requirement for network topologies to support larger amounts of dataflow became a major issue. Specifically, the applications and network operating systems that were being designed and deployed in the early 1990s were starting to move larger PDUs more quickly. This was because NOSs and applications were designed with larger data-packaging and -handling features, and the networking PC and server hardware platforms were built with the capability to move data at higher bits per second internally, which translated to a higher outbound frame-per-second rate. This evolution directly affected network utilization on all LAN topologies. With regard to the Ethernet 10Mbps architecture, an increased use of the available capacity started to occur; this increased the physical collision rate and negatively affected effective throughput and network performance.

Early in the 1990s, faster Ethernet products that could move data at higher rates were developed and released. Ethernet technology was developed to increase the data rate to 100Mbps. Eventually, through certain specialized vendor features and full-duplex technology, even higher data rates were available (such as 200Mbps and higher). During this same period, Ethernet moved from just a shared area network mode to an individual mode functionality, in which the device could have a direct single channel to a device (called an *Ethernet switch*). Ethernet switching is discussed in much more detail later.

Many events played a part in the advance of Ethernet technology. First, there was the advanced engineering of the PC *central processing unit* (CPU). Some of these advances were related to the increase in speed ratings of various processors, in workstations, and in servers. This would include the move to Pentium, Celeron, AMD series, and other high-performance processors. The higher speed rating of these technologies led to an immediate and inherent capability for end nodes such as Ethernet workstations and servers to transmit more rapidly. These changes invoked a higher FPS rate, which affected an overall faster data rate on the Ethernet medium. In summary, faster processor technology drove the need for higher bandwidth.

Another reason Ethernet technology advanced is directly related to the number of node counts, which began to increase throughout the worldwide network infrastructure. Many companies started to see the benefit of having a LAN, and started to deploy more and more workstations and servers on the LAN. This increase in node count required high-performance Ethernet devices and systems with technological advancements that could handle the higher capacity.

As the new processor technology hit the industry along with increasing node counts, the collision level on standard shared Ethernet became a factor. Collision levels started to increase and became a major problem, which led to a direct need for new Ethernet technology to address the higher collision concern. One solution was to increase capacity; another was to introduce Ethernet switching. There is a definite negative performance curve where effective throughput decreases when utilization and associated collision levels decrease in the shared Ethernet LANs. It is well documented that when Ethernet utilization levels reach the approximate 30% to 40% level, the overall effective throughput of data transfer starts to decrease. Note that when shared Ethernet utilization levels start to exceed 60% to 80%, the physical collision levels of the Ethernet medium, which is an inherent normal operation, start to be disruptive and can increase above the 5% level. Such an occurrence can negatively impact network protocol layer communications, and eventually the upper-layer communications also have fluency problems. In such a case, physical errors further increase.

This phenomenon is called the Ethernet *bounce effect*. What occurs is that the increase in upper-layer utilization results from more applications being in use. This increase, in effect, causes an event to take place. The event can be considered a utilization ball that is bounced on the Ethernet physical layer where collision levels start to increase and then negatively affect the upper layer (thus as a ball bouncing on the physical medium).

Another reason for the Ethernet technology advancements is the need to increase effective throughput. As noted earlier in this book, effective throughput directly relates to the amount of data transmitted in a certain amount of time. Perfect network communications occur when the most amount of data is transmitted in the least amount of time, otherwise called *maximum dataflow energy* (MDFE). The MDFE was starting to decrease in the industry when more applications and higher dataflow was implemented on the Ethernet 10Mbps medium; therefore, the requirement for higher-speed Ethernet and the 100Mbps data rate was recognized, along with the need for faster Ethernet channel processing within the Ethernet NIC.

The next big concern driving Ethernet technology advancement is the requirement for Ethernet networks to be separated. It is a clear fact that each type of shared Ethernet network has the maximum node count applied, whether it be 10BASE-5, 10BASE-2, 10BASE-T, or Shared Fast Ethernet. All shared Ethernet types apply a maximum number of nodes that can be deployed; these maximums affect the final applied traffic levels that can be overlaid on the Ethernet medium (capacity). At a certain point, the Ethernet network must be extended through proper technology or separated and connected to another Ethernet network. This process is called *partitioning* or *segmentation*. These processes allow capacity levels to be split across more Ethernet individual network segments.

8.7.1 Fast Ethernet Technology

Fast Ethernet was one of the first technological advancements that addressed some of the concerns that had been surfacing in the Ethernet community for increased dataflow requirements. This section discusses how the 100Mbps technology compares to the standard 10Mbps technology. Recently Gigabit Ethernet has been introduced at 1000Mbps (discussed later in this chapter).

The following discussion does not take into account switching architecture or half- or full-duplex technology. This following is a simple comparison of standard and Fast Ethernet.

The data rate for standard Ethernet is 10Mbps. As noted earlier, there are different shared Ethernet topology configurations such as 10BASE-5, 10BASE-2, 10BASE-T, and 10BASE-F. The standard data rate for Fast Ethernet is 100Mbps. The Ethernet vendors designed Ethernet NICs that had faster processing capabilities. At the same time, the vendors introduced Ethernet hubs that also had ports or adaptors that operated at a faster capacity. The adaptor for an Ethernet hub in a Fast Ethernet environment uses a much more complex port-circuitry design. The hub port operates almost exactly as an Ethernet NIC and is considered an Ethernet adaptor (as related to the circuitry of an Ethernet port).

In standard and Fast Ethernet, the frame types are still similar in design and are compatible. All four frames types work on both standard and Fast Ethernet. As mentioned, standard Ethernet is rated at 10Mbps; Fast Ethernet is rated at 100Mbps. In today's infrastructure, the standard Ethernet cable support for 10Mbps and 100Mbps is normally implemented on Category 5. Note, however, that 10Mbps Ethernet operates up to 30% to 40% levels without any attenuation or signal loss on standard Type 3 or even Type 4 cable. Most infrastructure environments today are wired with Category 5 cabling to accommodate both data rates. The 100Mbps Ethernet technology devices definitely require Category 5–certified cable for transmission. This is because a 100Mbps data rate is performing at a more rapid frame-per-second generating capability and the physical signal is moving at such a fast rate that true capacitance and low attenuation are definitely required.

Note that in the Fast Ethernet and Shared Ethernet architecture, the overall collision domain definitely differs. The collision domain is designed as the cable distance between two specific nodes in an Ethernet shared medium architecture. Note that the Ethernet collision domain for standard Ethernet at 10Mbps is rated at 3,000 meters, or 9,842 feet. In 100Mbps Ethernet, the collision domain is decreased to 412 meters, or 1,352 feet. This is because there is an immediate requirement for a shorter length of cable to allow for capacitance of the overall signal propagation at the faster rate.

Another factor to consider is that the Ethernet chipset timing parameters on the NIC and the port adaptor circuits in the hubs changed because the data rate changes and the requirement for the faster CSMA/CD processes where occurring. First of all, the timing of Fast Ethernet NIC slot timing for transmission decreased from 52.1 microseconds to 51.2 nanoseconds. There are also many differences in the adaptor design in 100BASE-T as compared to 10Mbps topology.

The adaptor design in the 10Mbps topology utilizes a standard NIC with circuitry that evokes a PDU insertion through the LLC layer and *medium access control* (MAC) layer to an the Ethernet packet formed and sent through the *physical signaling layer* (PLS) on the NIC. The signal is then processed through the *physical medium attachment* (PMA) layer of the NIC, which is connected to the medium. The *medium dependent layer* (MDL) then processes the packet outbound for medium transmission.

In 100BASE-T topology, a more complex scheme is invoked. The 100Mbps Ethernet NIC card operates an LLC process and inserts the PDU in an Ethernet frame. The Fast Ethernet NIC then processes the packet through a reconciliation layer and then processes it out to the *media independent interface* (MII) port to the 100BASE-T type of transceiver. The type of transceiver depends on the type of Ethernet cabling medium and the circuitry involved. If there is a separate 100BASE-T transceiver, an MMI port that can connect a 40-pin connector to different transceivers is active. Normally, the transceivers combine onboard the NIC, and the standard processing NIC circuitry and the transceiver are combined within one card for a 100BASE-T NIC. The 100BASE-T NIC transceiver portion of the NIC design, whether onboard or separated, includes the *physical coding sublayer* (PCS). The PCS links to the *physical medium attachment* (PMA) layer, which then connects to the *physical medium dependent* (PMD) layer, which then processes through an *auto negotiation* (AN) layer for a 10Mbps or 100Mbps data rate sensing operation, and then connects to the MDI for transmission (see Figure 8.18).

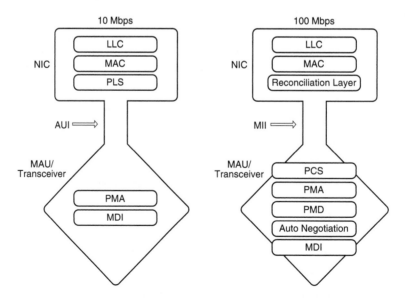

FIGURE 8.18 *The differences between an Ethernet 10Mbps and an 100Mbps adaptor.*

8.7.2 Half- and Full-Duplex Operations

In standard and Fast Ethernet architecture, another introduction to improve the overall data rate is the capability for half- and full-duplex connections. The cabling scheme of the RJ45 scheme allows for either half- or full-duplex connections. A half-duplex connection utilizes an adaptor port assignment connected to the NIC, to where only a transmit-and-receive process is performed on a one-on-one operation. An Ethernet workstation or server transmits up to the port, and then the port transmits any packets back down to the NIC. In a full-duplex design, all four wires in the cabling link between the node and the port are engaged in a bi-directional phase, and a full-duplex communication capability is in place so that the cards can receive and transmit at the same time (see Figure 8.19).

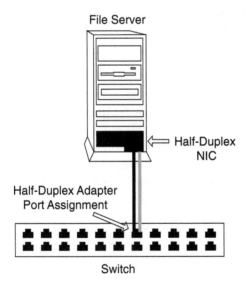

FIGURE 8.19 *An Ethernet half-duplex adaptor scheme.*

In a full-duplex NIC-to-port design, the collision circuitry is eliminated, and the Ethernet NIC and Ethernet port operate in a collision-free environment. The CSMA/CD process is not involved. The hub architecture internal engineering circuitry allows for separation from port to port. This particular process enables Ethernet switching (see Figure 8.20).

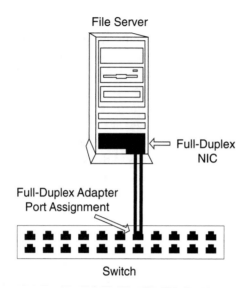

FIGURE 8.20 *An Ethernet full-duplex adaptor scheme.*

8.7.3 Shared Ethernet and Repeater Architecture Technology

Before moving into a description of Ethernet switching, it is important to reinforce the discussion of shared Ethernet. Shared Ethernet is basically the same term that can be applied to 10BASE-5, 10BASE-2, 10BASE-T, and 100BASE-T. Specifically, this is when Ethernet nodes share the medium. In this particular case, they are part of the same collision domain.

In actual design, an Ethernet shared design can be considered a repeater (see Figure 8.21).

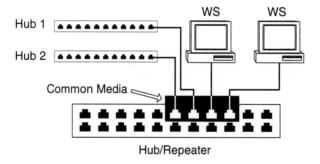

FIGURE 8.21 *An Ethernet shared media adaptor concept.*

In an eight-port shared Ethernet hub, for example, the device repeats the signal from port to port to port. That means that every Ethernet NIC connected to an Ethernet shared hub or repeater hub sees the packets that are transmitted in specific time intervals in almost direct parallel on each port. There are slightly different time slices in which the different NICs will see a packet, but essentially all packets transmitted in and out of the Ethernet NIC are seen in parallel across the shared or repeater Ethernet area or common collision domain. This is considered *Shared Ethernet architecture*. In this particular design, CSMA/CD technology is active, and only half-duplex connections apply (see Figure 8.22).

In a Fast Ethernet 100Mbps environment, as noted, the collision domain is smaller than the Ethernet collision domain in 10Mbps Ethernet (see Figure 8.23).

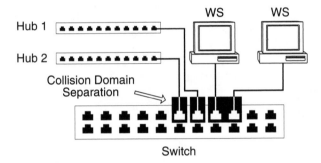

FIGURE 8.22 *Separating an Ethernet collision domain.*

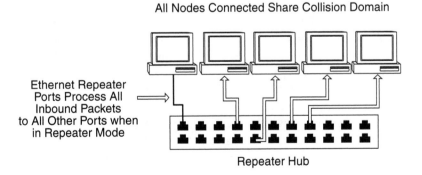

FIGURE 8.23 *A shared media area against an Ethernet collision domain.*

As the Ethernet architecture evolved, the Shared Ethernet media concept became a concern, and full-duplex connections and separated or "switched" connections for important devices became popularly required. This led to Ethernet switching (see Figure 8.24).

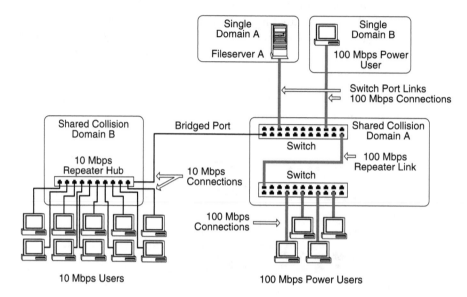

FIGURE 8.24 *An Ethernet internetwork with a 10/100Mbps connectivity scheme split by multiple collision domains.*

8.7.4 Ethernet Switching

In the early 1990s, Ethernet switching became a very popular product offering in the industry for Ethernet implementation. *Ethernet switching* is based on the process in which each port of an Ethernet hub can act as a switched port for connection to an Ethernet device that has its own connection and is isolated from the other ports on the Ethernet hub. In other words, the device is not an Ethernet hub anymore, but rather an Ethernet switch. The switch architecture is based on the fact that there is high-end switching backplane within the Ethernet switch. The backplane separates the circuitry of each port from one another across the Ethernet switch internal architecture. This separation of port design allows the device to function as a switch. Essentially, each port on the switch is provided a brief timeslot for backplane access. The circuitry within the Ethernet switch moves quickly and cycles access availability to each switch port. This allows Ethernet devices connected to the switch ports to have access to the backplane for a particular time slice within the overall multiplexing between ports. This switch process design requires an isolation in the circuitry design so that each port essentially has its own point of presence or connection to the Ethernet backplane present within the Ethernet switch. This backplane is called the *Ethernet switch backplane* or *fabric backplane*.

The first company to market an Ethernet switch was Kalpana, which introduced the first Ethernet switch in the late 1980s/early 1990s. This switch was considered a Generation 1 Ethernet switch. It was a basic physical layer switch that would allow for separation between Ethernet ports as connected to the Ethernet switch. This was a simple physical device that examined the Ethernet packet as it entered the Ethernet switch, reviewed the physical header, and then forwarded the packet immediately to the outbound port as required, based on the physical Ethernet frame header. In this case, the physical header was being processed through the inbound switch circuitry and was also being processed on the outbound port before the trailing edge of the Ethernet frame was even completely processed through the inbound port. This was called *Generation 1 Ethernet switching*. This was a positive design at the time, because it allowed for an immediate speed increase in accessing the Ethernet medium.

For example, a 10BASE-T architecture design exists with two hubs, Hub 1 and Hub 2. Server A and Server B were placed on Hub 1. Due to a protocol event in the NOS, all the users on Hub 1 had reason to access Servers A and B. At approximately the same time, the users on Hub 2 also had to access Servers A and B. Note that the users on Hub 2 were connecting through a bridge/router link that separated Hub 1 and Hub 2 by a bridge/router module. In this case, it is almost inevitable that the users on Hub 1 would have faster access to Server A and Server B. In an Ethernet switched architecture, a main Ethernet switch with eight ports could be deployed. The Servers A and B could be placed on two of the switching ports and the Ethernet Hubs 1 and 2 could be placed via an uplink cable on two of the other switched ports on the eight-port hub. This would allow more rapid access to Servers A and B on the Ethernet switch from users on both Hub 1 and Hub 2.

In Generation 1 Ethernet switching, one of the key drawbacks was that after you started to place the Ethernet physical switches within an infrastructure design, the devices that may have been separated by a bridge or router then started to become part of one complete common collision domain segment. Unless a bridge or a router that was used to separate the Ethernet switches deployed, the switch essentially forwarded the full Ethernet packet without any error-checking, and eventually the Ethernet Generation 1 switching design became an issue. The issue was that some of the Ethernet packets with errors were propagated between floors that were previously separated by bridges or routers. Although the speeds in the data-rate forwarding of an Ethernet switch were faster, because of the operation of a physical device forwarding cycle, the actual propagation of errors also became an issue (see Figure 8.25).

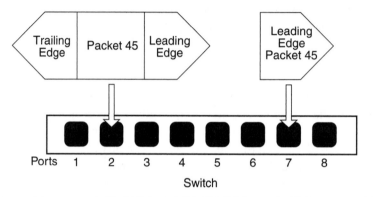

FIGURE 8.25 *Ethernet "cut-through," or Generation 1, switching.*

Because of these drawbacks, Ethernet Generation 2 switching was introduced and became popular. Note that the Ethernet Generation 1 switching was based on a straight "cut-through switching" mode (or what is called *cut-through and forwarding the frame mode*). There is no storing or error-checking process in Generation 1 switching. This is just an on-the-fly process where the packet is forwarded in one port and out another port.

Ethernet Generation 2 switching, introduced in the early 1990s, presented a solution by invoking a process called *store-and-forward*. The store-and-forward process in the Ethernet switch performed an error check on the Ethernet CRC field and checked the length of the frame. If a packet was brought into the Ethernet switch, and if the switch adaptor port examined the frame header and found an improper Ethernet frame size or a corrupt CRC field, that Ethernet packet would be discarded and would not be forwarded to the destination port on the switch. In such a case, this was a positive factor because errors seen on Segment 1 would not be seen on Segment 2 and so forth. This was also a nega-tive because the devices on Segment 1 would continually retransmit the pack-ets to the port and there was not an intelligent way for the sending device to know that the Ethernet switch was not forwarding the packets.

From a protocol analysis standpoint, an industry analyst could just see the retransmissions as being high and possibly identify an Ethernet-switched store-and-forward configuration as being the reason for the turning back of the bad packets. The solution would be to resolve the issue of the packet generation with the corrupted CRC by investigating the source device or NIC in the Segment 1 area causing the problem (see Figure 8.26).

Ethernet Switch Generation 2 Store and Forward Mode

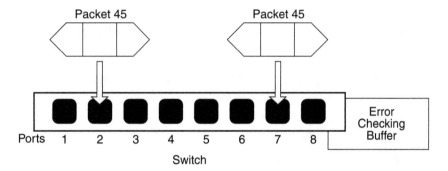

FIGURE 8.26 *Ethernet "store-and-forward," or Generation 2, switching.*

Another one of the drawbacks of Generation 2 switching was that the store-and-forward process required inherent overhead processing in the Ethernet switch. This slowed down the switch, making it operate more slowly and affected the Ethernet switch architecture in such as way that the switch required more memory and higher-speed backplane operations to make the switch operate in a faster design. This required an enhancement to the overall backplane or design of the Ethernet switch, which eventually led to another technology: Generation 3 switching.

In Generation 3 switching, the cut-through and store-and-forward modes became an optional configuration for the client who wanted to implement the switch. In doing so, vendors also released a higher-speed backplane and memory upgrades, along with firmware and software upgrades, to allow the switch circuitry to operate faster in forward frames. A faster operation and the higher fabric backplane between each one of the ports made implementation of store-and-forward possible, which allowed error-checking to be resident, but which also allowed such a fast operation in process cycle that the delays associated with the store-and-forward operation was not a factor.

A major industry concern that surfaced after Generation 3 Ethernet switching was the capability to provide for some sort of network management or isolation of each switched port on an addressing sequence basis (see Figure 8.27).

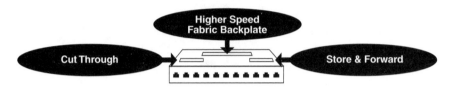

FIGURE 8.27 *Ethernet Generation 3 switching.*

These issues led to *Generation 4 Ethernet switching*. Specifically, some vendors were concerned that the clients needed to address each switched port by an IP-specific address. This would be of concern if a specific server or critical device were directly connected to the Ethernet switch. Because of this, the Ethernet switch designs were changed so that the Ethernet switch itself could investigate the network layer area of a packet and perform IP addressing assignment or IPX addressing assignments, or general network Layer 3 protocol addressing on the switched ports.

Another requirement that surfaced at this time was the capability to implement high-speed network management capabilities to manage each one of the switched ports to identify whether certain conditions existed at the endpoints connected to the switch, such as a packet not being processed. It was also important that the switch provide the capability to quickly view the individual switch ports from a centralized network management point and to review the switch's operational capacity with regard to how certain ports were operating from a packet-forwarding and packet-error standpoint. As a result of these requirements, industry designers implemented network management within the switch. This solution involved just invoking SNMP along with the RMON 1 and 2 specifications within the switch. Thus, by implementing a higher-speed backplane, combined with cut-through and store-and-forward, along with network layer addressing and network management, the switches released during the Generation 4 phase in the mid-1990s addressed the requirements with these positive enhancements (see Figure 8.28).

Note, however, that the overall processing rates did appear to slow down briefly upon introduction of these devices. The vendors immediately addressed this concern by continuing to increase the design of the switch high-speed backplane to a point where the actual backplane operated in a Gigabit data-rate range. This backplane speed enhancement—that is, the increased speed rating of the fabric backplane—created an increased capability of the switch port circuitry to provide the Generation 4 switching features at high speed.

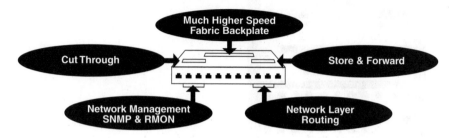

FIGURE 8.28   *Ethernet Generation 4 switching.*

The overall evolution of Ethernet switching was really becoming a positive factor in the industry, and Ethernet switching became heavily implemented throughout the enterprise environment.

The current phase of Ethernet switching implementation found in today's networking environment is the Generation 5 Ethernet switching architecture design. *Generation 5 switches* are based on a design in which the Ethernet switch looks like a centralized cage or hub. Modular blades are used as switch blades for the switch. Specifically, we have evolved to a point where internetworking can be done within one box. Routing, switching, bridging, different topology blades, and so forth can all be implemented within one particular switch. The older generation of stackable switches are still a useable solution in user IDF areas, but it is quite popular to buy a centralized Ethernet switch and place it within a main MDF computer room that has multiple switch blade capabilities. Specifically, one switch blade can be used for 10Mbps Ethernet connected to older Ethernet devices, another switch blade can be used for Fast Ethernet direct connections to main computer room servers, another for Gigabit Ethernet uplinks between user IDF closet switches, and another as a wide area router module.

Other topologies could also be introduced within an Ethernet switch centralized cage architecture, such as Token Ring. In such a case, an internal switch router module could provide separation between the different topologies. Overall, we have evolved to a point where we are internetworking within one box. This new Generation 5 module switched architecture design of a hub chassis is bringing us to a point where the complete internetwork is being consolidated to one or two centralized devices that operate a complete enterprise environment (see Figure 8.29).

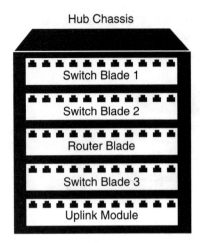

FIGURE 8.29 *An Ethernet switch using Generation 5 switching.*

8.7.5 1000Mbps Gigabit Ethernet Technology

A key factor propelling the Ethernet forward is the continuing reengineering of the overall speed rating of the switch backplane architecture. Today, Ethernet switch backplanes can operate at more than 20 gigabits per second. Many of the Ethernet architecture requirements today also include the capability for Gigabit Ethernet connections with a high-speed 1000Mbps channel for data rate.

Ethernet Gigabit architecture does not work well within a shared architecture environment because of collision domain restrictions. It only is workable in a switched environment, and it is extremely positive for a user area–to–main computer room uplink channel design link. Even with the faster desktop computers and servers in the environment, it is still somewhat complex and abstract when considering the designing of Ethernet NICs for Gigabit 1000Mbps channels direct to the desktop.

Gigabit Ethernet is the state-of-the-art industry Ethernet channel design. Even though Gigabit Ethernet can be designed for half- and full-duplex operations, its final design is based on true full-duplex connections with fiber interconnection schemes. Single-mode and multimode fiber can be utilized for connections, but definite meter lengths must be maintained and followed closely per each specific Gigabit Ethernet product's manufacturer's specifications.

Although copper link solutions obviously are workable, the maximum allowable length is so short that it is not workable for a shared architecture or even for interconnection schemes. As the industry is evolving, further copper solutions for Gigabit are being developed. At this point, no more than 50–100 meters are usually implemented on a copper scheme. In reference to the Gigabit Ethernet uplink, normally lengths of up to 500 meters work in a positive fashion.

The 1000Mbps Ethernet NIC is based on utilizing a *Gigabit Medium Independent Interface* (GMII). The GMII interface is also be utilized with a *Gigabit Medium Dependent Interface* (GMDI). The key here is that the propagation of the signal of a Gigabit Ethernet has a very low variance of frequency, and the bit budget of the minimum length of transmission and propagation of bit transfer is extremely sensitive.

The extension of Gigabit links sometimes can be accomplished through gigabit repeaters, but again this is a solution that must be very carefully implemented. The 8/10B coding techniques are utilized for the overall 1000MB technology. Through shortwave technology, the capability to utilize a proper wave length specification for multimode and single-mode fiber is possible. The fiber channel design is extremely sensitive, and again 1000Mbps Ethernet is normally positively implemented in Gigabit uplinks and straight point-to-point connections.

8.8 Examining Protocol Analysis and Troubleshooting Techniques for Ethernet

When performing a network baseline study in the Ethernet topology environment, a protocol analyzer is a key tool for isolating certain concerns that relate to Ethernet packet analysis, frame structure, and so forth. Also, the use of Ethernet tools such as network management systems that use SNMP, RMON 1 and RMON 2 also assist in gaining metrics relevant to the network baseline process.

As previously discussed in this book, it is important to perform a network baseline session measuring standard workload characterization measurements. Certain important techniques are required in a workload characterization process.

First, it is critical to ensure that utilization is checked in a standard mode for average, peak, and historical views, and that node-by-node utilization is also investigated. It is then important to examine protocol percentages.

When examining protocol percentages, it is important to quickly view the percentage of 802.3 protocols. The 802.3 percentages should be fairly low in standard Ethernet, because standard Ethernet frames should not be present on the network unless they are carrying upper-layer data. Unlike Token Ring or FDDI, in which physical error frames that would carry normal frame communication can be present, Ethernet frames are only present in standard form and are not considered Ethernet packets unless they are carrying upper-layer data. A high percentage of pure 802.3 or Ethernet II frames showing in protocol percentages as present in breakout indicate a possible error condition.

As noted earlier, it is then important to investigate the Ethernet physical layer. The discussion now turns to how to analyze standard Ethernet physical frames for error categories that are important in Ethernet. Some of these descriptions apply to the standard 10Mbps Ethernet environment, but those are also still important from an analysis perspective when performing an investigation. Certain Ethernet frame types are also important to 100Mbps Fast Ethernet; these items are discussed in the following section.

8.8.1 Ethernet Physical Analysis

When performing a network baseline session, certain Ethernet error types need to be quickly captured and analyzed to truly verify the physical health of the Ethernet topology. The type of errors seen and the quantity of errors will vary as to their effect on the Ethernet medium's capability to support upper-layer protocol dataflow. Note also that there are specific techniques for troubleshooting standard Ethernet cabling in the Ethernet bus types 10BASE-2 and 10BASE-5 and star types 10BASE-T and 10BASE-F that require the use of *time domain reflectometers* (TDR) and specialized cabling tools. This book does not address these techniques. For further information about these techniques, see the manuscript sources in Appendix B, "Reference Material."

The following section describes the main error types that can be captured with a protocol analyzer and isolated through decoding Ethernet frame types, and reviews statistics on some Ethernet analyzers and management-based systems.

8.8.2 Local Collisions

A *local collision* is the Ethernet packet that has been captured by a protocol analyzer as a result of a normal Ethernet collision event. Ethernet collision levels should not exceed 2% in most standard Ethernet environments if the physical topology is stable. The protocol analyzer usually displays the Ethernet percentage related to the Ethernet collision level as related to overall traffic—that is, the number of Ethernet collisions as relative to absolute traffic. If percentages reach 3% to 5%, it is possible that the overall upper-layer protocol fluency will be affected. An Ethernet physical local collision is defined as a packet shorter than the normal physical minimum length of 64 bytes and which has a corrupted CRC field. The CRC field is usually corrupted and the addresses may even be truncated because the Ethernet collision process causes the packet to be smacked or truncated upon occurrence. When a protocol analyzer captures the packet, sometimes the address fields cannot be read quickly. In this type of situation, it is important for an analyst to view the frames prior and post capture of the Ethernet collision event. In other words, if the Ethernet collision frame captured is noted at analyzer frame 32, frames 31 and 33 should be investigated, because quite often the same two devices will attempt to retransmit, or transmit prior to the collision event. Also, the Ethernet analyzer or management system statistical mode collision counters need to be closely monitored. Any collision levels of more than 2% should be investigated through a detailed protocol analysis review of the captured data (see Figure 8.30).

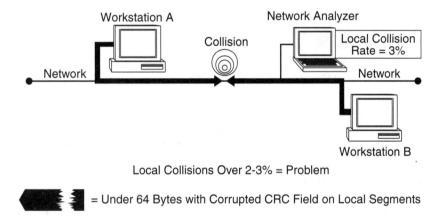

FIGURE 8.30 *A local collision event on the physical Ethernet medium.*

8.8.3 Remote Collision

A *remote collision* is a packet that occurs on a remote segment. Some protocol analyzers have an inherent design whereby they can mark a collision as remote. Although this is a valid error, it is rare for a protocol analyzer to display a remote collision. The analyzer will need a specific Ethernet chipset design that is truly specific to Ethernet physical medium analysis. Most of the analyzers in today's marketplace only analyze from the data link layer up, and do not provide true physical Ethernet medium analysis. Some cable testers are available and provide an enhanced view of the Ethernet medium, and some of the more hardware-based and enhanced protocol analyzers also provide this capability. A remote collision is defined as a collision similar to a local collision event, but one that occurred on a remote segment. It is less than 64 bytes in length and has a corrupted CRC. The only difference is that it occurs on a remote segment. The protocol analyzer can track this by continuously monitoring certain addresses that traverse remote segments, and then tracking a packet that has a partial address from a remote segment that has a corrupted CRC and is shorter than 64 bytes in length (see Figure 8.31).

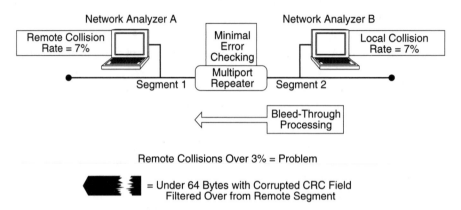

FIGURE 8.31 *A remote collision event on the physical Ethernet medium.*

8.8.4 Late Collisions

Late collisions occur in Ethernet topologies with layout configurations that exceed the normal meter length for this particular specification. Late collisions were common in the thicknet and thinnet environment when clients exceeded the normal length limits on their implementation of the Ethernet physical bus architecture. A *late collision* is defined as a packet larger than 64 bytes that has a corrupted CRC. What normally occurs with late collisions is that two Ethernet NICs on each end of a segment can't sense the carrier because the medium is too long for the circuitry to sense the signal. In such an event, a late collision is captured and considered a long packet with collision properties in the analyzer. In some cases, this is actually captured as an event called *jamming* (see Figure 8.32).

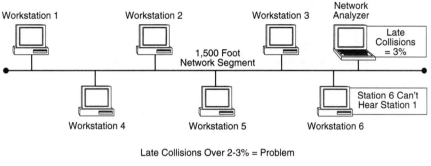

FIGURE 8.32 *A late collision event on the physical Ethernet medium.*

8.8.5 Cyclical Redundancy Check and Alignment Errors

All Ethernet transmission and receiving processes can check the CRC field. The CRC field is a 32-byte field and is normally based on a 32-byte CRC check. If an Ethernet frame is transmitted with a corrupted CRC field or a station receives a corrupted CRC field, certain events occur (as previously described). A bad CRC field in an Ethernet frame affects the data-transmission and -receiving capability between the two Ethernet nodes. If a protocol analyzer captures a packet that has a normal length with a corrupted CRC field, it is very possible that the NIC transmitting the packet, or a device that passed the packet such as a bridge or router, has a problem. In such a case, the analyst must capture the packet and investigate the source device. It may be necessary to replace the NIC or upgrade the driver and then to re-analyze the situation. CRC errors should not exceed the 3% to 4% level in most analysis conditions (see Figure 8.33).

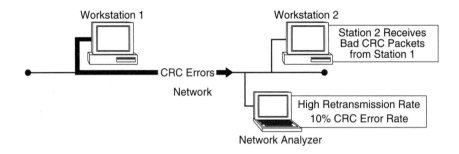

CRC Errors Over 2-3% = Problem

= Packet Contains Corrupted CRC Field

Bad Packet
Field

FIGURE 8.33 *A CRC error event on the physical Ethernet medium.*

8.8.6 Long and Short Packets

An analyst should be aware that long and short packets can be generated on an Ethernet network upon the malfunction of a NIC or the malfunction of an adaptor port on a switch, hub, or router. In this case, a *long packet* is defined as a packet exceeding the 1518-byte specification. A *short packet* is a truncated packet under the 64-byte level. Short packets can obviously be associated with local or remote collision events. Long packets are usually associated with late collisions or jamming conditions. The point here is that there is a standard Ethernet specification for an Ethernet NIC to process a frame and that one of the Ethernet NIC investigation modes noted on the receiving approach is to investigate the frame size. Long or short packets captured can usually be viewed on a protocol analyzer in a display mode by looking at packet size and packet size counters. Also, the trace can be decoded after it has been captured and saved, to review a frame to see the actual size of the Ethernet frame header. Again, packets under 64 bytes are considered shorts or runts; packets exceeding 1518 bytes are considered long packets (see Figure 8.34).

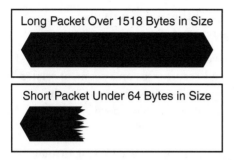

FIGURE 8.34 *An Ethernet long and short error event on the physical Ethernet medium.*

8.8.7 Jabber

Jabber refers to a condition that occurs when an Ethernet NIC is performing a backoff algorithm and attempts to send a quick jam signal to clear the medium. When the jam signal is sent to clear the medium, the device senses a collision. It is supposed to be sent for no more to 32–48 bit times. If the signal is set for a longer time period and continues on an ongoing basis, this is an occurrence streaming signal of Manchester signal encoding that could flood the Ethernet medium and possibly prevent normal communication across the Ethernet channel. This is what's known as a *jabber condition*.

A protocol analyzer would pick this up as a continuous transmission from one or more devices that would be corrupted code and would be an ongoing occurrence. It could also possibly be viewed as a long frame occurrence on a continuous basis from one device in a statistical display mode of a protocol analyzer (see Figure 8.35).

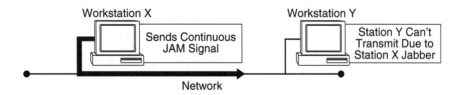

Jabber: Station Sends JAM Signal Over 32 to 48 Bit Times in a Continuous Fashion

FIGURE 8.35 *An Ethernet NIC jabber error event on the physical Ethernet medium.*

8.8.8 Summary Statement on Physical Ethernet Analysis

The following list summarizes these types of error occurrences:

- **Local collisions.** When excessive local collisions occur, an analyst should look for high utilization overload occurrences on a segment related to application or user counts being applied. It is also possible that the design limits of the Ethernet infrastructure have been exceeded or that the cable segment is too long.

- **Remote collisions.** If remote collision rates are active on an analyzer, it is possible that a remote segment may be overloaded related to application loading, or it may be misconfigured as connected to the local segment when the analyzer is picking up a remote collision occurrence. It is also possible that there is a problem with the device that separates the two segments such as the router, switch, repeater, or hub.

- **Long and short packets.** If long or short packets are encountered, it is likely that the NIC, or the adaptor to which the NIC is connected, has a circuitry problem. The NIC, the hub/switch port adaptor, or the NIC drivers may need to be replaced. A bad transceiver can also cause this condition.

- **Late collision.** When a late collision is encountered with a protocol analyzer and a source address is located, an analyst should look at the source NIC to examine the NIC design and its capability to interoperate on the Ethernet medium with other Ethernet NICs. It is preferable to implement the same type of Ethernet NICs throughout an infrastructure. Implementing a high number (over 50%, for example) of Ethernet NICs from different vendors will likely introduce problems, because many vendors vary in their design of Ethernet architecture. Usually when late collisions occur, it is possible that the NIC has a bad wait timer circuit or an oversensitive circuit in its carrier sense operation for CSMA/CD.

- **Jabber.** When jabber conditions occur, they usually appear on an analyzer as a continuous transmission of a long packet, and a NIC has most likely failed or the transceiver is not operating properly. This is usually a physical condition in a NIC or the transceiver. Sometimes the port adaptor of an intelligent hub or switch can also cause this problem.

- **CRC errors.** CRC alignment errors are generally caused by bad NICs or drivers; if captured on a protocol analyzer in a consistent basis from one device, this usually indicates that the device's associated NIC, NIC driver, or hub/switch adaptor port should be replaced. The condition should be addressed through troubleshooting, replacement, or reconfiguration and should then be re-analyzed.

8.8.9 Closing Statement on Analyzing Standard Ethernet

The preceding discussion provided a review of how to closely analyze standard Ethernet. Note that late collisions and remote collisions are events common to older shared Ethernet bus types of the topology. These error types are not usually seen in Fast Ethernet, Switched Ethernet, or full-duplex Ethernet.

It is still important to note that CRC errors, local collisions, short- and long-frame generation, along with conditions related to NIC or port jabber, are still possible problem factors with a Fast Ethernet and Switched Ethernet architecture.

The following section describes Fast Ethernet and switching review analysis.

8.9 Fast Ethernet and Switching Review Analysis

Many of the tools and management systems available for protocol analysis of Ethernet make it possible to perform a switched analysis review. It is important that an analyst understand that certain parameters have to be configured on the analyzer to properly examine a Fast Ethernet channel.

It is important, for example, to understand whether a Fast Ethernet protocol analyzer is configured for half-duplex or full-duplex. This is an important setting as to ensure that the analyzer is properly connected to the monitored medium.

The actual type of Ethernet *Media Dependent Interface* (MDI) being connected to for analysis is another important factor. When connecting a protocol analyzer to a 100Mbps Ethernet network, for example, there are 100Mbps MDI differences between 100BASE-TX, 100BASE-FX, and 100BASE-T4. 100BASE-TX allows for a standard two-pair Category 5 cabling interface connection. 100BASE-T4 allows for four-pair Category 3 and 4 cabling connection. And 100BASE-FX allows for a one-pair multimode connection. It is important to understand that there will be an actual configuration for connection as to MDI type parameter and that this must be applied to the analyzer before capturing data.

8.9.1 Ethernet Product Specifications as Related to Site Cabling Structure

Many Ethernet devices found in enterprise infrastructures today are based on Fast Ethernet and switching architecture. In certain cases, Fast Ethernet technology is combined in a shared architecture design.

When analyzing a Fast Ethernet shared architecture, an analyst must understand the standard specification for collision domain designs implemented for clustered shared Ethernet. In a Fast Ethernet environment, the design collision domain diameter is extremely tight. The analyst must always check the site cabling specifications to ensure compliance with the specific vendor Ethernet hub providing the Fast Ethernet shared connection and the industry specifications.

Specifically, when examining a Fast Ethernet environment, it is important to understand that the collision domain for Fast Ethernet has to be within specification. Therefore, the first focus is to ensure that the diameter of the collision domain is correct and the proper cabling specifications are followed in direct correlation with the specific product manufacturer for the Ethernet switch, bridge, or router.

8.9.2 Utilizing Ethernet Management Systems as Combined with a Protocol Analyzer

Fast Ethernet and switching environments can be quickly monitored from a network baselining perspective by reviewing the actual switched statistics. By using certain network management statistics that invoke programs based on SNMP, RMON 1 and RMON 2, queries, and responses, an analyst can view certain switched statistics remotely; these can provide certain baseline metrics that are part of the overall network baseline study.

When utilizing a network management system, it is possible through an inband Ethernet channel process to query a certain switch, hub, or router in an Ethernet environment. In the case of an Ethernet switch, it is possible to review, on a port-by-port basis, the switch statistics for the packet forwarding rate per port, the in and out packet count per port, and other port statistics for key items such as Ethernet physical attributes and metrics present in the Ethernet SNMP MIB or RMON agent. It is also important to view statistics on Ethernet switch ports from site management systems that may use half-duplex adaptors, such as CSMA/CD collision and CRC statistics.

This is an important way to start the network baseline exercises when reviewing an Ethernet environment. Just invoke the available Ethernet device network management systems. Attempt to ensure that all features of the network management system relevant to the study of the Ethernet switching environment within an enterprise configuration are properly used during a network baseline study (see Figure 8.36).

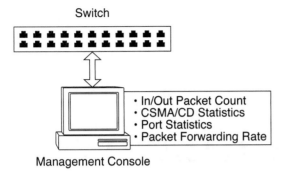

Switch

In/Out Packet Count
CSMA/CD Statistics
Port Statistics
Packet Forwarding Rate

Management Console

FIGURE 8.36   *The use of a switch management system to obtain network baseline results.*

8.9.3 Ethernet Collision Domain Analysis Techniques

The next step that should be performed in a network baseline exercise when examining a Fast Ethernet environment from a physical standpoint (as opposed to a standard Ethernet environment review) is to closely examine each collision domain.

This examination requires sectional collision domain baselining, which is the process of ensuring that each collision domain is carefully analyzed. Each shared collision domain should have local collision levels of no more than 2%.

If an Ethernet switch has segmentation or partitioning designs where certain switch ports are clustered together to form a shared area such as Ports 1–4, that is collision Domain 1. This type of clustered collision domain area can be closely analyzed by using a Ethernet mini hub. An Ethernet *mini hub* is a simple device that can provide a simple uplink to the Ethernet switch and then allow a certain number of devices to be connected to the hub. Next, the Ethernet protocol analyzer can be plugged into the mini hub. The four-port shared area has now just been extended down to the mini hub for analysis. Protocol analyzer positioning is critical in this type of situation (see Figure 8.37).

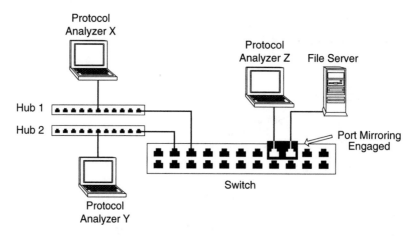

FIGURE 8.37 *A protocol analyzer positioning process in an Ethernet internetwork layout.*

8.9.4 Ethernet Port Mirroring Analysis Techniques

If certain devices require analysis on an Ethernet switch and all the ports are switched, those ports can possibly be viewed through *port mirroring*.

The port mirroring analysis technique is very important; it is a special method that allows an analyzer to be plugged into a switch port, allowing the analyzer to view the traffic of a device connected to another port on the same switch. Specifically, the traffic in and out of a specific port for a certain device can be viewed or replicated on another port through port mirroring or port replicating. This is a feature that must be allowed as a monitoring feature and provided by the switch manufacturer. Port mirroring is not always enabled as active by default, and is not a feature available on all Ethernet switches.

To invoke port mirroring usually involves specialized commands. These commands vary from manufacturer to manufacturer. What is key here is that the traffic in and out of one port can be mirrored or forwarded to another port and closely monitored with a portable Ethernet protocol analyzer. Again, certain parameters or commands may need to be invoked in the vendor-switched management system to allow this to take place.

After the port mirroring has been applied, the analyzer should be properly configured for the type of connection being monitored. If the connection is based on a certain data rate, the analyzer has to be set for the data rate—that is, 10 or 100Mbps. If the device connected to the port being monitored is set for half- or full-duplex Ethernet, the analyzer must also be set for that type of duplex. The Ethernet channel connection must also be properly configured on the analyzer.

Several switches on the market make a roving analysis port a possibility. This is a port on the back of the switch into which an analyzer can be plugged out of band and plugged into the switch. Sometimes certain switch parameters in a soft configuration or through hardware switches are available, making it possible to examine each port quickly from the back of the switch. This is not as common as port mirroring being enabled in most switch management–based systems.

Switched-based management system port mirroring is popular, because it usually is something that can only be invoked by engaging the switch management system. Most manufacturers in the Ethernet industry have made this a requirement, because it obviously requires the implementation of the switched management system.

When a switch is implemented within an Ethernet enterprise environment, it is important that the applied management system also be used so that a proactive approach can be available for network baselining and for network monitoring of the switch (see Figure 8.38).

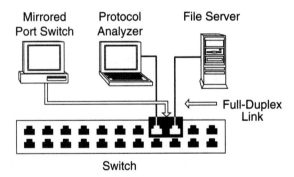

FIGURE 8.38 *A Ethernet port mirroring process for protocol analysis.*

8.9.5 Ethernet Switch Configuration as Related to Network Baselining

Another area to consider is the concerns associated with certain Ethernet switches set up for store-and-forward. As noted previously, if a switch is set up for store-and-forward, and Hub 1 is connected to Port 2, and certain devices on Hub 1 have packets with CRC errors being transmitted into the switch, and the switch is set for store-and-forward, all packets being forwarded into Port 2 that have CRC errors will be discarded.

The only way that an analyst can identify this occurrence is to perform a proper collision domain analysis on Hub 1. If network, transport, or application layer retransmissions are excessively high and appear to be correlated to devices that also have high physical CRC error rates, very possible those devices are invoking the upper-layer retransmission rate.

8.9.6 Ethernet Switch Uplink Analysis as Related to Network Baselining

Another concern is uplink characterization. As noted in Ethernet environments, there is the capability to configure an Ethernet switch in the main computer room and then have an Ethernet switch in a user area. The Ethernet switches would be connected by an uplink connection cable or fiber extension. The cable could be a standard Category 5 uplink cable and should be rated for the proper length to provide capacitance of data rate applied. The same issues apply for fiber uplinks required for Fast or Gigabit Ethernet uplinks. It is important to ensure that the fiber meets the specifications of the switched devices at each end of the uplink for SMF or MMF fiber types along with length.

Also note that the uplink could be an extension of repeater circuits in the two switches and the two Ethernet switches which would extend the collision domain.

The uplink can also be considered a separated switched uplink, which would actually be separated by two bridging circuits in each switch. In this case, the uplink would be considered a switched uplink channel.

The analyst must understand the configuration of the Ethernet architecture layout to apply the Ethernet protocol analyzer properly.

If the Ethernet collision domain is just being extended through a repeater uplink, it is not necessarily a requirement to analyze the uplink. The uplink channel can be monitored on either one of the collision domain ends, because it is one common collision domain between the two switches.

If the uplink is a switched uplink, the uplink has to be closely monitored. To analyze the uplink, port mirroring can be engaged at either one of the endpoints by implementing an analyzer at one of the ports at one of the switches on either end. Then port mirroring should be activated against the port handling the uplink between the two switches. This way, the analyst can monitor the uplink. This procedure can be performed on both ends of the uplink.

If Ethernet uplinks are being used in a site design, it is important that they be monitored during the network baseline study. This monitoring enables an analyst to understand the amount of traffic from one user area up to a main computer room Ethernet switch within a main computing environment.

The user environments from area to area within a corporate infrastructure may vary in terms of utilization levels.

If an analyst monitors the uplink for Hub 1 in User Area 1 and shows an uplink utilization of 20% average and 40% peak, for example, this is one particular notation for the network baseline exercise. If an analyst monitors the uplink for Hub 2 in User Area 2 and notes that the utilization is 70% with a 99% peak, it is very possible that this particular user area requires partitioning or separation of the hub environment to lower the utilization levels on the switched uplink to the main computer room switch port. In this case, the uplink for User Area 2 could be completely flooded and could cause saturation levels on the main computer room switch in the site environment.

It is also important for the analyst to be aware of the different types of uplinks for various cabling systems. Category 5 cabling systems can be used for UTP-based systems, or fiber can be used. Based on the uplink type channel, a certain type of media interface may be required on the analyzer for connection and analysis of the particular channel (see Figure 8.39).

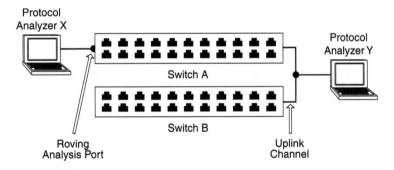

FIGURE 8.39 *Ethernet switch uplink analysis.*

8.9.7 Ethernet Switch Latency and Operation as Related to Network Baselining

The next area of concern in Fast and Switched Ethernet analysis is generally interpacket latency or delays that may be present between the Ethernet hubs and switches within the different areas of the computing environment. Usually there is an Ethernet hub in the main computer room, along with Ethernet hubs present in each one of the user areas. In today's computing environment, many of these hubs can be straight Ethernet switches or Generation 5 combined internetwork hub and switching devices (see Figure 8.40).

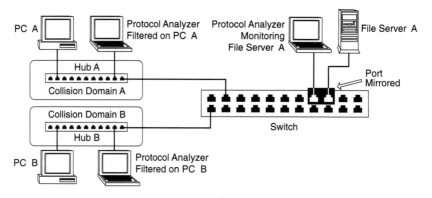

FIGURE 8.40 *Measuring cross-domain latency and effective throughput during a network analysis session being performed on an Ethernet internetwork.*

The key is that there can be many different collision domains present in shared Ethernet; in certain other cases, an Ethernet environment may be purely switched. What is important is the examination of differences in time between point to point in network communications. We must all remember that maximum dataflow energy—that is, transmitting the most amount of data in the least amount of time with the truest integrity of data—is perfect network communication.

With this in mind, an analyst should always examine each Ethernet collision domain separately. Each collision domain must be investigated for standard baseline measurements such as utilization, protocol percentages, and error levels.

The next factor that should be examined is the timing differences between Ethernet collision domains. Data-transfer performance ratings should be investigated, such as effective throughput. With this taken into account, it is important to again note that timing and effective throughput must be monitored and measured between point-to-point Ethernet areas within an enterprise site Ethernet architecture.

8.9.8 Protocol Analyzer Positioning in Ethernet Networks as Related to Network Baselining

When performing a network baseline exercise, an analyst should plan out the Ethernet baseline project by first obtaining an understanding of the Ethernet architecture design, layout, and implementation within the specific site. When the analyst understands the configuration, he can choose the analyzer positioning points.

Consider, for example, a site configured with one main computer room switch in an area called the MDF as the main computer room with an MDF switch (MDFS1). The site has two servers, X1 and X2. Three uplink cables are attached to the main MDFS1 from User Areas A, B, and C. This setup presents at least eight monitoring points. Each one of the three collision domains for the shared Ethernet in User Areas A, B, and C is an analyzer positioning point (so, points 1, 2, and 3 are identified). The next three monitoring points are the uplink channels from User Areas A, B, and C. The analyst would have to position an analyzer in the main computer room and perform port mirroring against ports assigned to uplinks from User Areas A, B, and C, which would introduce analysis positioning points 4, 5, and 6. The analyst could then perform a port mirroring against each one of the main servers in the computer room to see how they are performing in the closest point within the MDF computer room. This would introduce analysis positioning points 7 and 8 for the servers X1 and X2.

Interpacket delta time for X1 and X2 could be measured as responding within the closest Ethernet switching environment in the computer room via analysis points 7 and 8. Then the analyst can determine from the uplink characterization statistics from MDF area as seen from the User Areas A, B, and C, via analysis points 4, 5, and 6. Last, the analyst can examine the user areas closely via analysis points 1, 2, and 3 and perform a collision domain baseline review of users accessing the servers from each area of the Ethernet internetwork.

Another example is an analysis of a pure switched Ethernet environment. In this case, the analyst may have to choose certain Ethernet users to study within the switched areas of User Areas A, B, and C. In other words, if the user areas were not shared and were switched, it may be intrusive to the baseline process to study each one of the ports. The analyzer positioning point chosen would have to apply to respective users who are using traffic at normal high levels and are busy at that particular time of the analysis session. The analyst then can rove certain users who are representative of the Ethernet switching area in User Closet A and maybe closely monitor one or two users in that area.

The analyst then can take the next analyzer and position it in User Closet B, and can choose two or three users who are also busy and monitor their switched uplinks. The analyst can then move through the complete Ethernet environment with this type of approach. All user area IDF uplinks should be closely monitored in the main computer room by monitoring uplink channels from a port mirroring exercise.

All main servers and hosts must also be monitored closely for interpacket delta time, response time, and general analysis via port mirroring in the main computer room.

The next technique to be used sitewide is Ethernet end-to-end EFT performance analysis. This type of analysis is achieved by engaging the effective throughput analysis techniques discussed previously in this book.

It is important, for example, to filter workstation users who are accessing servers in the main computer room. To do so, an analyst may want to position an Analyzer 1 (from a port mirroring exercise perspective in a switched Ethernet environment) on the User Closet A uplink to the MDF. The analyst would position Analyzer 2 on the switch in User Closet A and perform a port mirror analysis against a specific user workstation. The analyst would then place Analyzer 3 in the main computer room on a port mirroring exercise against the main switch in the MDF and position it on the server being accessed in the main computer room and port mirror against the server. This would allow for three analysis positioning points.

Next, the analyst could use an application characterization process and have the user connected to Closet A engage an application. The analyst should synchronize all three analyzers so that the complete Ethernet physical frame translation between all the switched environments can be analyzed. Even without discussing the upper-layer protocol analysis outcome generation results from this study, the analyst may be measuring certain characteristics about the Ethernet latency delays of different Ethernet switch manufacturers. The analyst can examine the common Ethernet product implementations and understand the latency from the user's connection to the Ethernet switch in Closet A. The analyst might also determine the actual delay in latency and throughput between the uplink from User Closet A to the main computer room, as well as the amount of interpacket latency from the actual server that receives the frame from the uplink in the main computer room on the same switch.

Using protocol analysis methodology, an analyst can understand the following:

- The interpacket latency in the user's workstation and the effective throughput of the user's workstation

- The same type of metrics as related to the user closet switch (A)

- The same type of metrics as they apply to the uplink between (A)

- The same metrics as they apply to the MDF switch backplane processing rate on the main computer room switch in the Ethernet channel in the main computer room

- The Server metrics for EFT and interpacket latency

This discussion points out the importance of analyzer positioning. Protocol analyzer positioning is critical in a Switched and Fast Ethernet environment when performing a network baseline study. It is also important when employing general analysis techniques.

8.10 Closing Statement on Ethernet Analysis Techniques

This chapter presented the key Ethernet architecture principles involved to understand the Ethernet architecture and topology infrastructure. We have also discussed some of the key baseline analysis techniques for studying standard Ethernet, Fast Ethernet, and Switched Ethernet environments.

When viewing an Ethernet environment, it is important for an analyst to understand that the physical frame architecture is not built with a high amount of intelligence as related to communicating network management–based processes.

An analyst must always keep in mind that performing a network baseline in an Ethernet environment may involve a combined process of using all the tools available for a network baseline. If a management system is available to view the internetwork hubs in the enterprise, this management system should be invoked, and as many baseline statistics that can be gathered from that management system should be extracted for the network baseline report.

The analyst should also understand that it is critical that any switched or router-based management systems in the Ethernet enterprise management environment be engaged.

It is a fact that a protocol analyzer is the primary tool for performing a network baseline exercise in the most accurate manner, and it is critical to know how to position the analyzer against the architecture of the Ethernet environment.

It is also important to keep in mind that, with Ethernet having different topology types in terms of layout, there may be hybrid Ethernet designs interconnected within a site. The analyst must take this into account and may need to deploy physical Ethernet techniques along with Switched and Fast Ethernet monitoring techniques when required.

The analyst may also encounter different devices within the Ethernet environment. In this case, the analyst must understand the management statistics and the use of those devices.

All manuals that are available for the specific Ethernet devices will be helpful. An analyst must always remember that a half- or full-duplex link may be encountered in a study, and an analyst must be ready to adjust the connection type option and the data rate on the protocol analyzer.

With all these factors taken into account, an analyst should be able to perform a successful network baseline exercise against the Ethernet architecture with the methodology and techniques presented in this chapter.

Case Study 10: Standard and Fast Ethernet Network Baseline Analysis

To perform a network baseline, you must follow many steps, including these main ones:

1. Review the network configuration and any of its problems.

2. Perform a network baseline and data-acquisition planning session.

3. Produce a final project plan for the network baseline process.

The following complex case study discusses a standard and Fast Ethernet network baseline recently performed by the LAN Scope analysis team.

The client was a small college in Florida with a medium-sized Ethernet internetwork of approximately 400 users with multiple shared and switched segments. As noted, the Ethernet internetwork at this site was based on a shared media Ethernet 10BASE-T architecture combined with 100BASE-TX Fast Ethernet shared and switched architecture.

Several software applications critical to the college's business operation were experiencing performance problems. One of the main problem applications tested students prior to their admission. The testing took place in an education center, where students used PCs and an educational testing program. The program tested the students' literature assessment, reading, mathematical skills, and scientific skills. This test was the final requirement before admission.

During the middle of the testing program, the application would either intermittently disconnect or fail for some of the students. In certain cases, a particular student's test data was intact; in other cases, test data was corrupt. Obviously, a serious networking problem existed. The networking problem also affected (in an extremely negative way) the normal business operations and schedule of the college because many of the students had to be retested.

After the college contacted LAN Scope, I personally became involved in the project planning cycle for the network baseline. We requested specific information on the network configuration and the symptomatic history. We also requested the application profiles. The college's MIS team provided diagrams, problem logs, and reviews of application deployment. Our analysis team then developed a project plan.

During our first meeting with the college's MIS team, we learned that the educational center workstations used for the testing were based on a set of Ethernet connection cabling runs to a 10BASE-T shared Ethernet architecture in a floor-distribution network facility closet. The network closet in the testing area internally housed a network rack with four Ethernet shared hubs and one switched/shared 10Mbps Ethernet hub for partitioning and uplink purposes. The four shared hubs could handle 24 ports per hub. Therefore, 24 students could connect and test via each hub.

Each hub was then connected to the closet Ethernet switch within the educational center computer room closet. Specifically, the closet switch provided 10Mbps switch connections to each of the four shared Ethernet hubs. The switch in the educational room closet provided a 10Mbps Ethernet uplink channel cabling run to a main computer room. The main computer room provided a connection from the uplink closet cabling run to the main computer room via a shared Ethernet hub within the main computer room. This shared Ethernet hub was being used as a group shared area, which provided multiple closet connections to link to the main computer room. From the computer room main shared hub, another uplink channel Ethernet link internal to the computer room connected to a switched computer room Ethernet switch. This switch directly connected to the main file servers in the computer room. The site file servers were connected via switched Fast Ethernet full-duplex connections to the main switch in the computer room. This same main server switch also connected to an additional middle rack-mounted shared 10Mbps Ethernet hub in the main computer room.

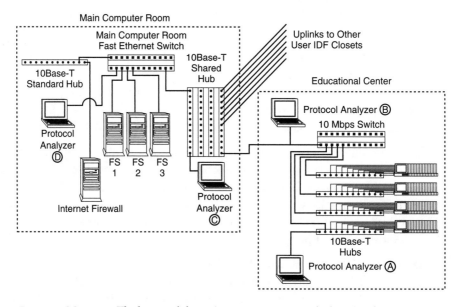

FIGURE CS10.1 *The layout of the main computer room and educational center workstations.*

This layout clearly used both a mix of shared Ethernet at 10Mbps for the student connections along with switched connections in the educational center–floor network closet. The layout also used a switched connection for 10Mbps to the main computer room, and another shared Ethernet area in the main computer room for centralized wire-cabling grouping. The main file servers were connected to a high-speed 100Mbps switch, which was also connected to the internal computer room main shared hub that grouped closet uplinks.

Immediately obvious to us, the overall Ethernet channel appeared to be mismatched in terms of data-rate design. We noticed another mismatch in the Ethernet shared media and switched media configuration. As noted earlier in Chapter 8, "Ethernet," shared Ethernet media uses a technology referred to as *carrier sense multiple access collision detection* (CSMA/CD). The shared areas in the educational center provided student access to the medium, but all students on each particular hub competed for the medium. On the switched channels for the educational closet along with certain uplinks in the computer room, a pure switched channel was provided. The data rates at 10Mbps (or 10 million bits on the wire per second) provided only a limited frame-per-second rate-generation capability as compared to the 100Mbps connections used for the site file servers. We reviewed all these conditions closely before deploying our network analyzers to the college to perform the network baseline. Based on the symptomatic occurrences noted—such as disconnects and slow performance—and the site design layout, we developed the following baseline plan.

We placed a network analyzer in the educational room network closet to perform a focused network baseline on each of the shared Ethernet hubs that were providing connections to the student areas. We placed another network analyzer on the Ethernet-switched uplink channel to the main computer room. We placed a third network analyzer on the shared Ethernet hub in the main computer room, and a fourth network analyzer on the switched Ethernet hub that provided connections to the main file servers along with the uplink from the shared hub in the main computer room.

This fourth network analyzer was configured for different port-mirroring sessions, to review each one of the servers and determine how they communicate back to the shared Ethernet hub in the main computer room.

We started the network baseline session by performing basic network characterization at each of the analyzer positions. We next engaged specific analysis, simulating high usage of the application by requesting the student population in the testing area to use the application (to reproduce the problem event).

Several students and teachers participated. All four analyzers were synchronized for network absolute time to ensure that all trace file data captured would be compatible in time measurements. At the initial launch of the application, a consultant was deployed in the testing area to take notes of any symptomatic occurrences (disconnects or slow performance). At the same time, a structured application analysis was made on one user running just the application. Our analyst monitored specific events, such as the application launch time as well as the access to the educational literature module and the scientific mathematical modules. Certain metrics were reviewed, such as cumulative bytes moved along with relative time for each event cycle. Chapter 5, "Network Analysis and Optimization Techniques," presents more information on application characterization analysis methodology.

We then conducted an additional wide-open session with no capture filters applied to a maximum-user testing situation. The focus of this test was to fully understand the effects of high usage on the application. We also wanted to determine whether high usage overloaded either the shared media hubs in the educational closet or the uplink to the computer room.

We conducted three sets of tests. We closely reviewed the problem log in the computer room for any reports of problems experienced by the simulation team. We also closely reviewed the application-selected test for each application event, including how the events were reviewed related to application characterization, along with the math group simulation workload characterization results such as average bandwidth and peak transitional bandwidth, effective throughput, and response time.

Chapter 5 presents the measurement techniques applied during this analysis exercise.

After we had completed the session-testing capture operations, all four analyzers were stopped, and each trace file was carefully saved. We brought all four network analyzers to a central review area at the college.

Analyzer one, which focused on the shared Ethernet areas and was used to rove all four Ethernet hubs of the educational center, showed extremely high utilization and saturation levels, ranging from 92% to 95% of the available 10Mbps shared Ethernet capacity on each of the four hubs. The peak transitions were marked, noted between 2.5 and 3.5 seconds at saturation of the Ethernet shared area. Long acknowledgment times were noted as received from the workstations and from the servers on both ends. Disconnects related to the connection layer protocols were evident by TCP window connection *TCP Resets* (TCP RST) in the TCP layer. The TCP layer transported the application.

Chapter 5 presents detailed information on these analysis techniques.

Analyzer two, on the switched uplink channel between the floor closet and the main computer room connection, also showed low throughput alarms along with long acknowledgment time errors.

In the main computer room, on the main shared Ethernet hub analyzer position, analyzer three showed extremely high peak utilization saturation on the shared hub in the computer room, with levels noted between 88% and 92%, at time intervals ranging from 1.5 to 4.5 seconds.

The switched Ethernet analyzer four, which monitored the server providing the application access in the computer room via port mirroring, showed a high number of long acknowledgment times from the resulting testing stations accessing the server, along with minor application errors in the application fluency, as related to the application access. Excessive TCP disconnect errors were evident as well as latency in the TCP communication channel.

From a cross-review of all the trace files, we developed a list of analysis result factors:

Result Factor 1: The Ethernet design in the educational resource support center clearly showed that the Ethernet hubs were overconcentrated in terms of connection population as related to the applied application usage when the maximum student count was simulated. This clearly showed that even though the 24 ports may have been considered an adequate design, further separation of node counts as to partitioning was required, or a switched design would be required to allow the application to perform at a normal level. The application used protocol data-unit sizes of approximately 1400 bytes and full Ethernet packet sizes on transfer. This particular size of data moving at an extremely rapid delta time interval from the workstations (between 1ms and 5ms) caused a contention for the medium that was extremely high. We immediately concluded that the Ethernet hubs within the educational center closet needed to be partitioned by a one-half or one-third split per area.

Result Factor 2: The second analyzer on the uplink channel showed excessive errors, which clearly indicated that the switched uplink channel would be better on a 100Mbps capacity design to provide for a maximum capacity channel between the main educational closet and the main computer room where the file servers reside.

Result Factor 3: The third analyzer in the main computer room showed an inefficient design that used a shared Ethernet hub in line with a switched channel to the file servers in the main computer room. We immediately concluded that the shared Ethernet hub should be removed or possibly reconfigured into a clustered switch design in the computer room.

Result Factor 4: The fourth network analyzer showed no major abnormal symptoms, because the servers were connected at 100Mbps full duplex. We concluded (or actually reconfirmed) that the channel from the main computer room switch providing access to the servers should immediately be connected to a switch in the computer room at the same data rate of 100Mbps, which would provide direct uplink and downlink connections to all site user area network closets (such as the educational center computer room network closet). The main goal here was to eliminate the shared Ethernet hub in the main computer room as an intermediate passthrough route in the end-to-end Ethernet channel.

From all the issues identified and the conclusions drawn, the LAN Scope analysis team developed a final network baseline report. Our recommendations included the following:

- The shared Ethernet hub architecture in the educational network closet was extremely concentrated and required a three-way partition on each 24-port hub. Three additional shared hubs were required, and there were available ports on the Ethernet switch in the educational room closet that could be used for the purpose.

- The Ethernet-switched uplink channel could be configured for a 100Mbps data rate. We immediately recommended a 100Mbps uplink channel for the main computer room.

- The main computer room shared Ethernet hub area was not providing any clustering or switching and actually provided an extremely high collision domain. This was a negative situation on all points of presence from certain network user-area closets in the college (as it relates to having a shared Ethernet hub in the main computer room). We recommended removing this hub and implementing a high-speed Ethernet switch that could provide uplink and downlink channels between the user closets within the college, including the educational center and other areas, to the main computer room. This implementation provided immediate switched access to the servers within the file server room area.

These recommendations comprised our main set of recommendations in the final network baseline report. We did, however, isolate other issues—such as application fluency problems related to read/write overlaps and file transfer conditions—that allowed for some fine-tuning of the application.

This case study shows how we used network baseline analysis to isolate problems in a shared and Fast Ethernet environment in an exact, rapid, and accurate manner. The overall data acquisition for this particular network baselining process lasted only several days. The decoding and reporting also lasted several days.

A key factor of this case study was that this problem had been occurring for almost six months and had been causing extensive business problems. Proper network baselining planning and data acquisition, a close review of the data extraction, accurate problem isolation, and a proper reporting process enabled us to quickly resolve the issues.

This case study clearly shows that network baselining along with protocol analysis is an extremely useful way to resolve critical issues. The case study also clearly demonstrates that network baselining can improve network performance and ensure infrastructure stability and reliability by providing a more clear and direct path for a network's migration.

Case Study 11: Ethernet Switching Analysis Problem

Ethernet switching has become more and more popular over the past several years because it provides high-speed access to critical devices and eliminates, in certain circumstances, shared Ethernet mechanisms such as *carrier sense multiple access collision detect* (CSMA/CD, which involves a large amount of collision and contention for the medium). The strong interest in Ethernet switching and its benefits has resulted in rapid deployment of Ethernet switches. Ethernet switches are being deployed within large internetwork infrastructures on an ongoing basis. Because many applications require Ethernet switching channel access for additional requirements (capacity, for example), some MIS teams must deploy switches so quickly that certain configuration parameters may not always be defined prior to implementation. When this occurs, an incompatibility may exist between certain devices connected to the Ethernet switches. An improper implementation of an Ethernet switch, with regard to network positioning, may also occur.

The LAN Scope analysis team recently performed a network baseline for a law firm that occupies several floors of an office building in the Los Angeles area. The firm had lately implemented multiple Ethernet switches throughout its network configuration. Prior to the Ethernet switching implementation, the network followed a multi-year cycle (with the Ethernet network originally based on a thinnet bus Ethernet and 10BASE-T hub architecture). The firm eventually migrated to a blended network architecture that allowed for both 10Mbps and 100Mbps user connections and switched connections across certain floors. The design was based on a multi-floor architecture that used different Ethernet switches to provide connection and separation between the floors, and Ethernet bridges provided the floor interconnection separation.

When we started the network baseline study, we noted symptomatic occurrences of errors (intermittent disconnects) present on certain floors. This type of problem was not present in the preceding Ethernet shared architecture design, which was based on Ethernet bridging separation. There were also a high number of symptomatic occurrences of intermittent disconnects on critical network file servers in the main computer room.

The LAN Scope analysis team immediately assessed the situation and performed an entrance briefing of the site configuration. We reviewed the site topology maps for the LAN and WAN configuration, along with the server configurations for hardware and software builds. We also reviewed the switch and router configurations. We noticed immediately that the switch design incorporated multiple-vendor product platforms. The facility also used multiple-vendor network interface cards and switch configurations. We reviewed the symptomatic history along with the application data movement profiles within the facility. We then proceeded to the network baseline plan.

The multi-floor layout was based on a three-floor scheme. We noted that on the first floor of the law office, the Ethernet internetwork was a basic user 10/100BASE-T hub configuration that provided access to the first-floor closet location. This was the point of presence where all user connections, whether rated as 10Mbps or 100Mbps workstation connections, could connect to the Ethernet hub internetwork. The 10BASE-T and 100BASE-T hub in the first-floor closet also provided an Ethernet-switched module that connected to the main computer room on the third floor.

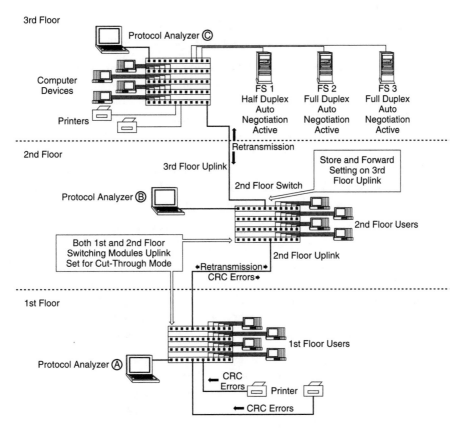

FIGURE CS11.1 *Three-floor layout of the Los Angeles Law Firm.*

A similar configuration for users in the law firm was provided on the second floor. The third floor housed a main computer room Ethernet internetwork hub switch that provided the uplink and downlink channels to the first- and second-floor 10/100Mbps BASE-T hubs. A switch in the third-floor computer room also provided direct connections to main file servers on certain Ethernet switch modules, along with connections to wide area network routers and firewalls for access to the Internet.

I developed a focused project plan to use the LAN Scope analysis team in the following manner. One consultant placed an analyzer on the first floor in the user area and performed a standard network baseline of the user closet network domain on the first floor. Another consultant placed a second analyzer on the second floor to perform a network baseline of the user closet network domain on that floor. I placed a network analyzer in the main computer room on the third floor to review general network baseline statistics.

All three baseline sessions involved a review of network utilization in an average and peak transitional mode. They also included a review of Ethernet node-by-node utilization breakouts and applied protocol percentages along with a more detailed protocol percentage review for protocol types. Some of the site Ethernet connections and devices configured at 10MB half duplex were reviewed for physical Ethernet error types that apply to 10Mbps half-duplex CSMA/CD operation, such as CRC errors and collision rates. Any pure switched connections rated at 100Mbps full duplex were not reviewed for collision, because collision operation is disabled in this mode.

After completing the initial baseline sessions, we examined all three analyzers for the trace file information. It was evident from the trace file data that excessive physical errors were generating from two devices noted as printers on the first floor. These physical errors were abnormal and showed an excessive generation rate of 200 errors per minute on one port and approximately 350 errors on another port. The two physical error analysis events were filtered in the network analyzer and saved as separate results for further review.

On the second floor, we noted a high number of physical errors across all 10Mbps ports for user connections. After further decoding the trace analysis results from the second analyzer on the second floor, we noted that we could not read the addresses of the frames involved in the collision event, but that the collision events appeared to be occurring across all ports on the second floor.

The third-floor analyzer showed a high number of long acknowledgment times along with an excessive retransmission rate of more than 33% on communication from users on the first and second floor to the third-floor main computer room. It was interesting that the analysis results from the third-floor baseline session connecting to the main computer room hub did show excessive protocol-based errors, but that the third-floor users were not experiencing disconnects.

Because of this unique occurrence, we focused our analysis on the first- and second-floor Ethernet baseline sessions (because of the excessive number of physical errors encountered). We noted again that high retransmission levels affected the network and transport layers and therefore the upper-layer fluency showed low throughput on application dataflow.

After closely examining the physical traces from the first floor, we noted that the Ethernet-switched configuration required review. We reviewed the Ethernet hub and switch configurations for the first and second floor in a comparative analysis. After extensive review of the switching parameters, we found that the Ethernet switch on the first floor, which was a different vendor type than on the second floor, was configured for cut-through switching on the uplink switch connection to the switch module on the second floor. The second-floor Ethernet switch showed a store-and-forward configuration on a partial setting on the uplink to the third floor, but did not use store-and-forward on the connection as received from the first floor. Actually, two Ethernet switching port modules were implemented for the first- and third-floor connection on the second-floor switch.

We immediately identified the cut-through switching configuration between the first and second floor as a possible channel for propagation of any Ethernet physical frames to be propagated up the second-floor area if occurring on the first floor. Chapter 8 discusses Ethernet cut-through switching in more detail.

At this point, we further decoded the traces and identified frames in the second-floor trace results; these showed the physical addresses of the printers from the first floor generating onto the second-floor medium. We isolated this information by using exact data-trace analysis and the "paging-through-the-trace" methodology, and thus concluded that the cut-through switching configuration was incorrect for the site configuration. We also concluded that a store-and-forward Ethernet switching configuration would be more correct and optimal for Ethernet switching separation between the first- and second-floor Ethernet switching uplink channel.

We also determined that the two devices causing the errors had physical Ethernet NIC operational modes on the hardware channel, and we replaced the Ethernet NICs in the printers on the first floor.

With this reconfiguration in place, we then retested the first, second, and third floor with all three network analyzers synchronized throughout with absolute time set. We conducted another rapid baseline session that lasted approximately two hours. After completing that session, we stopped the analyzers and reviewed the trace results. We noted, upon review of the Expert and the monitoring screens, the absence of physical errors. We also noted that the retransmission levels from the second- to third-floor switched uplink dropped from 33% to 2%, which is a normal rate for Ethernet traffic.

The users at the site also stated that applications were operating faster and that application launch and access times were more rapid. We surveyed the first and second floors, and received no additional performance complaints from the users. However, we did receive complaints regarding intermittent disconnects for certain file servers located in the main computer room. Because of this condition, we focused the latter part of our study on the main computer room.

We deployed multiple network analyzers in the computer room and set up port mirror sessions on three main file servers. Via the network baseline process, we reviewed each main file server. We reviewed the utilization of the network medium, protocol percentages, and error rates. We noted that CRC errors were generated on high-burst sequences from all three file servers on an intermittent basis. This intermittent CRC physical generation was present in the trace results, but again was only occurring in an intermittent nature and did not relate to any high-utilization occurrence from the servers or high-burst sequence of data. What we did notice was that the overall TCP sequencing for any TCP connections also intermittently broke and showed definite disconnects in TCP resets in communication.

This occurrence prompted us to closely review the Ethernet server hardware configurations as well as the Ethernet switch configurations in the computer room. From this review, we determined that two of the servers were set at 100MB half duplex, and one server was set at 100MB full duplex. This difference alone influenced our decision to closely review the switch port configurations. All the Ethernet switch port configurations for the main computer room were set on Auto-Negotiation. In the Ethernet specification, Auto-Negotiation allows for a multiple poll and link pulse state sequence that involves multiple states where different NICs can auto-negotiate with a port for a certain data rate to sense the port activity between the switch and the Ethernet NIC being applied for a compatible data rate. Although this technology is under specification and is considered a solid Ethernet specification rule, there can be problematic circumstances with this type of configuration. In my experience, I have found that under certain conditions when multiple-vendor NICs and switch products are used in design at a site, it is possible that the Auto-Negotiation sequence may not work on a consistent basis. Note, however that this should be a definite workable configuration if all specifications are followed. However, the reality is that it is sometimes better to configure a hard-coded link speed and duplex-speed setting for both the switch port and the NIC being applied.

Based on this concern and the configuration issue found at the site, we immediately applied a 100Mbps full-duplex configuration for each server and hard-coded the switch configuration in both the server NICs and in the switch ports on the main computer room switch.

We reapplied the setting and again baselined the third-floor switch area. It was noted immediately that the physical error generation and disconnects were now eliminated. We closely reviewed this occurrence as well as the user groups throughout the third floor. After interviewing the users and reviewing our trace analysis results, which now showed a nominal physical error rate (less than 1%), a retransmission rate of less than 5%, and an extremely high throughput level that increased from 100Kbps to approximately 700Kbps on transfer, we concluded that we had resolved most of the issues at the site.

We next moved to a final off-site data-decoding session, in which we reviewed and verified our data and developed our baseline report for the facility.

In this case study, it was obvious that the network analysis sessions were extremely positive, along with the network baseline methodology being applied at the same time. This was an extremely effective way to review the Ethernet environment in a rapid fashion to resolve the issues and at the same time to achieve enough data to produce a baseline study.

Note that in parallel with all these sessions, we were performing statistical charting on a network baseline platform that allowed for charting of utilization, protocol percentages, and frame-per-second fluctuations. These charts were saved and attached to our main baseline report to the client. Our final baseline report presented a focused review of our session by introducing an executive summary of the issues along with a characterization of each area, and a focused list of each issue identified with a clear-cut recommendation. We then attached all our baseline charts and closed our baseline report with a technical migration recommendation to implement a more uniform Ethernet switching design along with a list of other site-wide recommendations that would benefit the site. Some of the recommendations involved workstation platform upgrades, hardware upgrades, and redeployment of certain applications across different servers for a better balance and higher performance of access. We also found conditions in our traffic results that pointed to WAN problems, which required further review of WAN performance in a later session.

The main fact presented here is that by conducting the network baseline and protocol analysis (following the proper methodology), we resolved a set of critical issues that were affecting this particular environment.

CHAPTER **9**

Token Ring and
Switched Environments

The Token Ring architecture was developed in the early 1980s. Throughout the early phases of development, many companies participated in the evaluation of different design and circuitry possibilities for a LAN based on the deterministic operation. The Token Ring topology was created and released by IBM and Texas Instruments, although other companies, such as Madge, were also directly involved in the final evolution of the design.

In 1985, the *Institute of Electrical and Electronic Engineers* (IEEE) released the 802.5 design specification for the Token Ring LAN. The Token Ring topology is designed as a physical star, but is called a logical ring. Various devices connect across an electrical ring that interconnects through a device called a *Multi-Station Access Unit* (MSAU). The network devices connecting to the MSAUs are connected through lobe cables.

As mentioned earlier, the actual layout of the Token Ring LAN design configuration was based on a physical star. At the time of introduction, the Token Ring network was contrary to the initial introduction of the Ethernet topology, which was introduced in a bus layout configuration.

The Token Ring network configuration also has an extremely inherent fault-redundant operation. The fault redundancy is built in to the physical wiring scheme and the NIC-to-NIC LAN operations. The Token Ring network is considered fault-redundant and more of a stable LAN topology. It is a fact that this fault redundancy does introduce a small amount of overhead applied to the overall data traffic load. If a Token Ring LAN is operating in a normal and stable mode, however, the fault-redundancy circuitry and associated operations usually are not active, and the physical traffic overhead is minimal and causes little impact as to utilization load.

On a Token Ring network, data is transmitted in a baseband transmission mode, similar to Ethernet. One of the main differences is that the access method for Token Ring is based on a deterministic method, as compared to the contention-based method CSMA/CD process utilized in the Ethernet LAN environment.

The original Token Ring architecture was introduced to the industry in 1985 at a 4Mbps data rate. In 1989, 16Mbps Token Ring was introduced. In the mid-1990s data rates of 32Mbps and even higher (specifically, 100Mbps) were introduced for industry implementation. However, these higher Token Ring data rates were not well received. This was because by the time they were available for Token Ring, there were already more advanced data rates in operation with other network topologies. These topologies included Fast 100Mbps Ethernet, 100Mbps FDDI, and 155Mbps and 622Mbps ATM. There were also high-cost issues associated with implementing the higher data rates in Token Ring topologies and in upgrading existing Token Ring LANs.

9.1 Token Ring Design and Layout

The Token Ring design physical attributes are based on a star layout. The Token Ring network design is based on a physical communication medium entity. The actual upper-layer protocols and application data are packaged within Token Ring–based specification frames that flow on top on the Token Ring physical network, and thus create a final networking architecture. Certain components are standard as originally introduced in the Token Ring design, and are still present in the more advanced Token Ring architecture products available today. To introduce the main concepts of the Token Ring, I will use the initial design specifications to explain the physical layout.

The Token Ring network architecture is based on an operation that occurs on the Token Ring NIC card. Essentially, the Token Ring NIC is the network. The Token Ring NIC contains a complex set of circuits that operate together and are known as the *Token Ring agent*. The Token Ring agent chipset was designed to interpret and process data for inbound and outbound transmission. The Token Ring NIC agent processes all Token Ring packets and separates the actual *Protocol Data Unit* (PDU) from the Token Ring frame up to the upper-layer protocol unit chain processing of a workstation or a server connected in a Token Ring LAN environment. For purposes of technology terms, note that a

Token Ring station is also referred to as a *ring station*. In summary, the Token Ring NIC agent performs all the handling and interpretation of data communicated inbound to and outbound from the Token Ring NIC.

To describe the Token Ring LAN connection scheme, the Token Ring NIC card is a ring station and is interconnected to a Token Ring hub cabling scheme through a cable run called the *lobe cable*. As mentioned earlier, the Token Ring hub scheme is based on a centralized hub scheme based on an MSAU. The initial design of the MSAU was released in an IBM product called the IBM 8228. The IBM 8228 MSAU hub was built on an 8-port device port design. This was because in 1985, the internetwork community was still progressing at a fairly slow pace. Many LANs required only 8 to 20 devices for interconnection. The initial MSAU had an 8-port design that allowed for 8 devices to be connected.

For example, this specifically meant that a site could have seven workstations and one file server could access one MSAU. Inside the MSAU was an internal circuitry path called the *main ring path* (MRP). This was a path that created an electrical ring inside the actual MSAU. The cabling of each particular port had a direct run out to the specific ring station. The cable, called the lobe cable, was the link between the ring station and the centralized MSAU wiring scheme (see Figure 9.1).

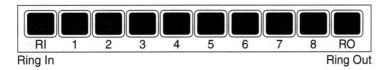

Ring In   Ring Out

FIGURE 9.1   *A Token Ring MSAU.*

If for some reason the Token Ring centralized MSAU wiring scheme required more devices to be connected to the Token Ring network because of expansion needs, there was a *Ring-In* (RI) and *Ring-Out* (RO) port designed for cabling links into additional IBM 8228 MSAUs. The RI and RO port allowed for expansion of the Token Ring MSAU centralized wiring scheme through a very simple process. The Ring-Out port of one MSAU could connect to the Ring-In port of another MSAU, and thus extend the MRP of Token Ring LAN. When this process is used, however, the RO port of the second MSAU should link back to the RI port of the initial first MSAU in the MRP link, and thus create a final main MRP complete loop or electrical ring. The last MSAU RO MRP cable link to the first MSAU RI is required because the Token Ring cabling scheme is built on a four-wire inherent cabling path that creates an MRP that can utilize a backup path. The MRP uses only two wires of the MRP, called the *primary MRP path*; an additional two wires in the MRP are called the *backup secondary data path*. The backup MRP cabling link is not invoked unless a fault redundancy ring is required. The fault redundancy of the cabling process is further described later in this chapter.

As noted earlier, the actual main ring path specification allows for a physical ring and an electrical ring to be in place from an overall design standpoint. The devices connected to the network through the lobe cables communicate with each MSAU port, and all the data seen on one port is also replicated through the MSAU and the complete MRP to other ports on the Token Ring network.

The Token Ring network is definitely a shared medium based on baseband transmission. When the Token Ring network physical wiring scheme was initially designed, one of the first concepts was to introduce a centralized wiring scheme from a positioning point within a building infrastructure. This was to fulfill the requirement to allow for a troubleshooting process that would be simple if an issue occurred on the physical medium. Because of this, all the hubs or MSAUs were required for placement within a patch panel. The patch panel would then be placed within the wiring closet. This layout was normally a common process for actual implementation design as based on the implementation of the Token Ring network. Most of the Token Ring networks that were implemented between 1985 and 1990 were introduced through the IBM product sales network. Because of this, many of the specifications required for layout of the physical Token Ring were implemented through procedures developed by IBM engineering teams and through associated IBM documentation. Some of this documentation is noted in Appendix B, "Reference Material."

With all the MSAUs being physically placed within a patch panel and also being physically positioned within a wiring closet, this created a centralized wiring process within a building that was extremely structured from a cabling system standpoint. All the lobe cables would run out to the physical workstations or ring stations placed throughout a facility.

The lobe cables, when connected to a ring station, came back directly to the patch panel within the wiring closet. The patch panel would then have patch cables that would link down directly into the MSAU ports that would be utilized for device connection. Each one of the mounted MSAU hubs in the rack would then be interconnected to each other through the RI and RO ports in the Token Ring MSAU rack. Again, the last MSAU would link back to the initial MSAU to complete the ring. This is based on the four-wire inherent cabling fault-redundant path (see Figure 9.2).

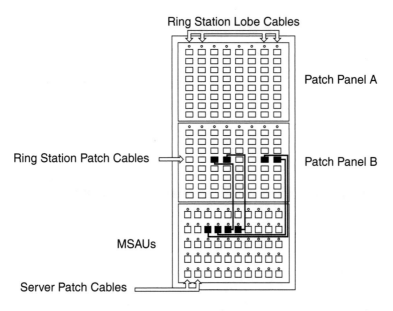

Ring Station Lobe Cables

Patch Panel A

Ring Station Patch Cables

Patch Panel B

MSAUs

Server Patch Cables

FIGURE 9.2   *A standard Token Ring patch panel.*

The fault redundancy in the MRP cabling scheme comes into play when the MRP primary ring path loop is broken for any reason. This would include an MRP cabling break in the linked RO-to-RI cabling between MSAUs. This type of issue could be resolved by just removing the bad cable. The MSAU RI and RO ports of all the initially designed MSAUs included an inherent self-shorting data connector process that was built in to the loop design of the physical port of the MSAUs. The initial IBM 8228 MSAUs were simple in overall circuitry and based on mechanical relay process. Therefore, if a cable were to be damaged or if there was a bad cable between any of the MSAUs, it was possible for a technician to remove the bad cable. The RO and RI ports would automatically self-short and use the backup secondary path of the MSAU MRP cabling scheme (see Figure 9.3).

Throughout the industry, many companies implemented a Token Ring LAN and did not utilize the proper cabling for a true four-wire scheme or did not link the last MSAU in the MRP to the first MSAU for the backup path to be available in implementation. When this occurred, the removal of a bad cable would not allow the backup path circuitry to be invoked by the fault-redundancy cabling and RI and RO MSAU port operation. In this case, this would cause problems in the overall recovery of the physical Token Ring medium.

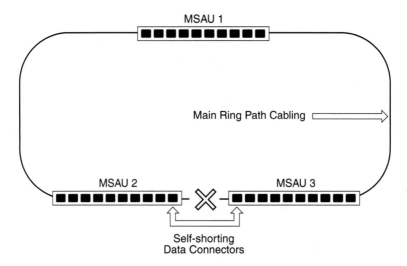

FIGURE 9.3 *The fault redundancy built in to the Token Ring wiring scheme.*

Overall, the Token Ring network is based on a physical star and a logical ring concept that is one of the most fault-redundant and unique LANs in the market (see Figure 9.4).

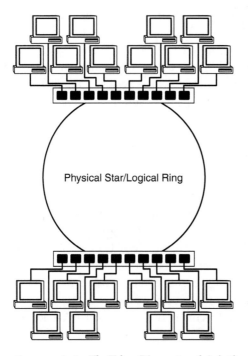

FIGURE 9.4 *The Token Ring network is both a physical star and a logical ring.*

9.2 Understanding Token Ring Network Operation

Now that the Token Ring network cabling layout and structure have been discussed, the following is a discussion of the operation of the Token Ring network. The technical discussion that follows specifically describes how ring stations gain access to the Token Ring LAN deterministic medium along with how ring stations (RS) can communicate with other stations.

Because the Token Ring network was introduced in direct parallel to compete with the Ethernet LAN environment, certain features are built in to Token Ring and are considered enhancements to the Ethernet topology. This, of course, depends on the view of the industry analyst.

Note that the Token Ring LAN-structured centralized wiring scheme and fault redundancy are considered a plus in the local area networking environment. It is important to remember that the mainframe processing environment and mini-computer environment offered stability and a certain amount of guaranteed uptime as related to *Mean Time To Repair* (MTTR) and stabilization in the computing environment.

When the Token Ring LAN was initially introduced, LANs were considered unreliable in terms of stabilization and performance. Many MIS managers were concerned as to what the correct LAN topology should be for deployment. Many of the large banking and conservative institutions that utilized IBM host mainframes and mini-computers for processing business data moved forward with the Token Ring network for a LAN topology because of the inherent fault redundancy of the physical operation.

The following is a discussion of the physical Token Ring medium operations that are extensive as compared to Ethernet. Particular operations inherent to the design allow a Token Ring network to still offer a stable foundation for upper-layer protocol data transfer even when physical errors occur in communication. These features allow for a higher level of reliability and stability for upper-layer protocols to operate on. In other words, the Token Ring foundation was extremely stable as compared to the Ethernet topology upon initial release.

In today's environment, note that the Ethernet environment has advanced to where it can be completely managed and is considered stable. But again, this is because of the implementation of other technologies used in parallel with the Ethernet standards, such as *Simple Network Management Protocol* (SNMP) and RMON specifications, to manage the Ethernet internetwork technology.

The Token Ring topology, upon initial release, was without question considered to be the most fault-redundant and stable technology for a LAN type, and was widely implemented throughout the infrastructure.

The following section discusses the physical Token Ring architecture operations that allow the Token Ring network to function.

9.2.1 Token Passing Theory

In a Token Ring network design, a token circles around a physical electrical ring. The token is a 3-byte frame composed of a Starting Frame Delimiter field, an Access Control field, and an Ending Frame Delimiter field. This token frame circles around the ring on a continuous basis after the Token Ring network is active and operating. To activate a Token Ring network, two devices with inserted Token Ring NICs must be active on a physical Token Ring LAN. The initial device starting communication on the Token Ring will release the token. This process is described in detail later. After the token has actually been released, it circles the ring. Every device on the ring sees the token as it passes its NIC point on transfer. The normal timing cycle for a token to circle the ring is usually 10ms at a minimum.

If a device wants to transmit on the ring, this will be because an upper-layer protocol process invokes a request for communication. The upper-layer protocol process is engaged by the application or network operating system. This could be a workstation or a server that wants to communicate. The protocol chain processing in the upper-layer channels of the device cause a process to occur in which a Token Ring frame is composed with data and processed for request for transmit. At this point, the device wanting to transmit generates a vector command for its Token Ring NIC to copy and grab the token when it passes its node point to communicate on the ring. This allows for the start of access and data transfer on the physical medium. The device NIC then takes the token and appends the token to the actual Token Ring data frame for transmission. At this point, the Token Ring data frame will be sent out onto the Token Ring network MRP in an outbound transmission cycle. The Token Ring frame contains fields to assign a source and a destination station address.

The Token Ring frame will be interrogated by every Token Ring station as it passes through the ring. A certain interrogation process occurs, during which each Token Ring station's NIC interrogates a portion of the Token Ring frame— the starting delimiter, and then the frame control field, and next the associated destination address of the actual Token Ring frame.

If the Token Ring frame has certain valid attributes available in the frame control field (discussed later), and the Token Ring frame also has a destination address match with the Token Ring node investigating, the respective Token Ring node then sees that it is the respective destination station where the Token Ring frame is intended for as related to transmission (see Figure 9.5).

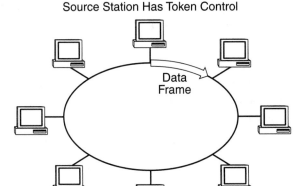

FIGURE 9.5 *Token passing.*

The Token Ring NIC in the destination device then processes the actual Token Ring frame received from the source device for extraction of the upper-layer protocol or physical data communication. Upon completing the processing of the frame, the destination Token Ring station releases the original Token Ring frame back out onto the ring for forwarding cycle retransmission back to the source station. When the source station receives the Token Ring frame, it then automatically reviews certain fields within the Token Ring frame, called the addressing and frame status fields. The access control field identifies whether the destination station received the frame, and whether the destination station recognized the frame, and copied the frame in for processing. After this final review of transmission cycle has been completed by the original source station, it then releases the token back out onto the ring for another station to grab the token to transmit.

In summary, the Token Ring architecture process of Token Ring passing theory is as follows:

A token is passed around the ring. A source station that wants to transmit grabs the token, appends data to the token, and creates a data frame. The data frame is transmitted from the source station to the destination station. The destination station then examines the frame, copies the frame in for processing, and then releases and forwards the frame back to the source station, which then investigates the frame to ensure that it was processed correctly. The frame is then stripped of all data, and a simple token is released back out on the ring so that another station can transmit—thus, the operation of a deterministic medium.

The access of any ring station, which can be any workstation or server on the ring, to communicate on a Token Ring network is determined by its access to the ring as based on and determined by the ring station's capability to gain access to network via the token.

It should now be clear that if there is extremely high utilization in place on a Token Ring network and because of the inherent deterministic operation, eventually the speed of data transfer may be affected.

Specifically, the speed at which each Token Ring device has the capability to receive a token and transmit may be slowed down by high utilization levels and load on a Token Ring network.

In the original design of a Token Ring network architecture, a 255+ node count design was allowed for implementation. In today's networking operating system environment, in conjunction with the high-loading applications being deployed, only much lower node counts can be utilized in a layout as capable of supporting higher data rates.

9.2.2 Dataflow Direction and NAUN Process

The Token Ring network operates on a process in which data is always transmitted in a downstream or clockwise fashion. This is called *downstream Token Ring data transmission*. Because transmission is always in a downstream mode, a device communicating on the ring in an upstream mode would be improper.

But there is a concept called the *nearest active upstream neighbor* (NAUN); this concept is very important for fault-redundancy troubleshooting and associated physical Token Ring management.

At any time when a device that is counterclockwise or upstream from a device is active or inserted into the MRP, it is referred to as the NAUN device.

If a device is one port directly above the Token Ring device downstream, and both devices are operating, for example, the device directly upstream would be considered the NAUN. If for some reason the device one port upstream from the particular device is turned off and is inactive, the next device upstream would be considered the NAUN device (see Figure 9.6).

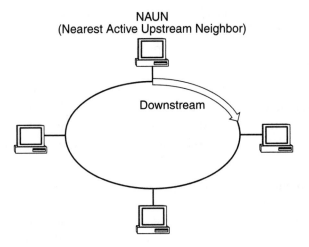

FIGURE 9.6   *Token Ring NAUN.*

The NAUN is an important concept for troubleshooting in fault-redundancy processes of the management cycle. This is due to an inherent operation called *neighbor notification* (explained later), during which each device on the Token Ring network maintains a register of its upstream neighbor address for troubleshooting processes. Therefore, the concept of a NAUN is very important for overall troubleshooting processes.

9.2.3 Token Ring Address Schemes

In the Token Ring network architecture, the addressing schemes are unique as compared to the Ethernet architecture and are more complex and offer more flexibility from an overall design standpoint.

The three types of addressing are as follows:

- Individual

- Group

- Functional

9.2.3.1 Individual Addressing

Individual addressing refers to the individual address of the Token Ring NIC card. This is somewhat similar to the Ethernet addressing design, although local administration of the physical Token Ring address is possible.

The Token Ring individual physical address is based on a 6-byte addressing scheme, in which the leftmost 3 hexadecimal bytes represent the manufacturer code, and the 3 rightmost hexadecimal bytes represent the actual physical hexadecimal address.

In certain cases, in the individual addressing scheme of Token Ring, manufacturers such as IBM or Madge may release a card to a company and just implement the NIC with the physical address assigned by the manufacturer, which is also verified with the IEEE. This is considered the *universally assigned address*.

Some companies required the ability to locally administer the address to create unique addressing schemes for management purposes. This requirement was addressed by the Token Ring specification, so manufacturers would allow customers purchasing a Token Ring NIC to assign a unique address that could compare to phone numbers or cubical numbers throughout company layouts. This was considered extremely flexible from an addressing system standpoint, but could easily pose a problem if not maintained properly. Specifically, if there is a duplicate address on a Token Ring network, a station cannot enter the ring. This can only be a problem with locally administered addresses. Because of this, many companies have chosen to use universal administration.

9.2.3.2 Group Addressing
Group addressing allows for a group to be defined on a Token Ring network.

A set of stations on the ring could be the local post office, for example; another set of stations on the ring could be the local legal office; and another set of stations on the ring could be the local medical office. A network operating system or an application could invoke a process where a broadcast to a specific group of devices was created.

Obviously, these would be technical group address assignments for a specific technical function in the application or the operating system. But the capability was there for group addressing to be assigned. In this case, a Token Ring station, if part of the group, would have a combined or parallel function running in which it would be assigned as part of the group. If this group addressing function were active, the station could then understand the group addressing destination address and process the frame for the cycle.

9.2.3.3 Functional Addressing
Functional addressing involves the functions that were built in to the initial Token Ring card design operation—that is, a function would be operating in a station that would be important. The functional assignment could be compared

to a function such as legal or medical operations. In technical terms, there could be a specific function that the device is running parallel to its individual operation, such as a LAN manager, an active monitor, or an error monitor. These functions are considered standard in the Token Ring physical functional addressing system.

The main methodology of functional addressing was that the initial design vendors wanted to be able to manage the physical ring.

When certain devices were implemented on the ring, for example, they would be able to run combined or parallel management functions in direct operation with their normal individual function. In other words, a device could have a unique physical address that would be considered the individual address. The same device could also have an assigned functional address where the device would perform a function that would be supported by or support the rest of the ring. In this case, some standard functional addresses were common (see Table 9.1).

TABLE 9.1 EXAMPLES OF STANDARD DEVICES WITH THEIR CORRESPONDING FUNCTIONAL ADDRESSES

Standard Device	Functional Address
Active monitor	C00000000001
Ring error monitor	C00000000008
Ring parameter server	C00000000002
Configuration support server	C00000000010
Bridge	C00000000100
LAN manager	C00000002000

All these addresses are common functional addresses. Many other functional addresses are reserved for future use. This is a common term used in IBM technology.

Functional addressing allowed manufacturers and NOS application manufacturers to develop functions on the ring for design where they could utilize unique management systems.

What is being introduced here is the capability for manufacturers of network operating systems and other key products in the industry to use a design technique to manage the ring that could be inherent to their own particular operation or capability.

9.2.4 Token Ring Signaling Methods

The Token Ring physical medium signaling method uses differential Manchester encoding, which differs from the Manchester encoding used in the Ethernet LAN environment. The coding occurs at the physical layer.

Simply put, there is a binary 1 and 0 reverse process cycle that utilizes a blended cycle against a binary code of nonreturn to zero and eventually results in differential Manchester encode—and thus the Token Ring physical signal used on the cabling medium (see Figure 9.7).

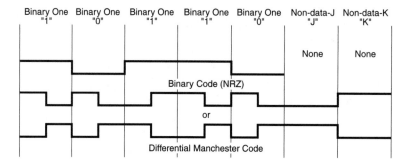

FIGURE 9.7 *The Token Ring physical signal method.*

9.2.5 Token Ring 4Mbps Technology Versus 16Mbps Technology

One of the last areas to discuss before moving into the internal operations of the Token Ring architecture is the comparison between 4Mbps technology and 16Mbps technology. Because there was not a heavy implementation of 32Mbps and higher Token Ring data rates, this discussion concentrates on comparing 4Mbps and 16Mbps technology.

The main difference between 4Mbps and 16Mbps technology is that a 4Mbps Token Ring frame has a maximum frame size of approximately 4500 bytes. In a 16Mbps technology a NIC has the capability to process a frame up to 18000 bytes in size. It is common to see Token Ring frame sizes at the 4Mbps size (4500 bytes), even in a 16Mbps environment. Increasing the packet size allows for the creation of a much larger PDU for transmission (see Figure 9.8). Most of the network operating system vendors along with the application vendors that utilize Token Ring for physical transmission never saw a strong requirement for increasing the PDU size, because most endpoint Token Ring nodes did not have the capability to process the data at such a large size because of data rate-handling restrictions. This is the reason that the PDU remained in the 4500 byte frame size area, even on a 16Mbps data rate network (see Figure 9.9).

The other key difference is that the 16Mbps data rate has a much higher frame-per-second rate-generating capability on board the NIC. The actual frame-per-second rate capability between a 4Mbps and 16Mbps card varied from vendor to vendor. The fact is that a 16Mbps data rate card has a much faster processing rate compared to a 4Mbps data rate card, as related to frame-per-second rate.

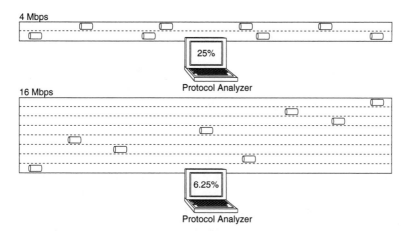

FIGURE 9.8 *A Token Ring network not overutilized and not in need of a capacity upgrade.*

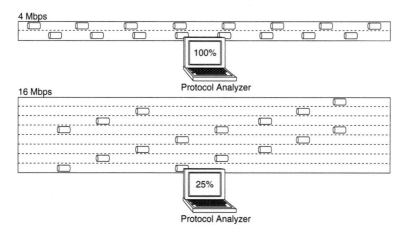

FIGURE 9.9 *A Token Ring network overutilized and in need of a capacity upgrade.*

Another noticeable difference is the actual implementation of the *Early Token Release* (ETR) technology. This was introduced around the same time that the 16Mbps technology was introduced. ETR technology allows for two frames to travel on the ring in one given instance. This is not two data frames, but just two frames.

In an ETR transmission, for example, the sending station grabs a token off the ring and forms a data frame through the append operation and sends a frame to the destination station. The destination station at that point starts to process the frame. During this time cycle, the source station immediately releases the token. This differs from the process engaged in the original 4Mbps design, in which the token was held until the original frame was transmitted back for interrogation and the token was released. The early released token is then sent out to the ring for any station waiting to transmit. The station wanting to transmit can then grab the token and start to build a frame for transmission on the ring. This is similar to a bank drive-in operation with multiple drive-through lanes, where one client is processing a transmission with a bank teller in the window, while another person is preparing his financial transaction in the drive-through system. Moving to the technical aspects, the original destination station receiving the frame processes the transmission and then sends the frame back to the original source station. If the original source station receives the frame within a time period considered valid, it does not move into an abort sequence cycle to stop the transmission of the original frame that was sent outbound upon the early token release cycle. Therefore, the station that received the token early can append data and transmit a frame for a faster process (see Figure 9.10).

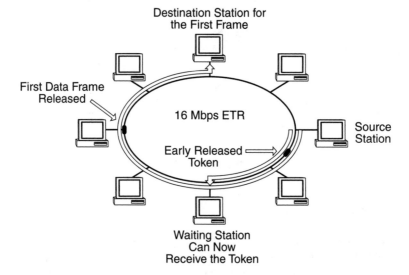

FIGURE 9.10 *The Token Ring ETR concept.*

The ETR process effects an increase in speed of the overall Token Ring operation. Note, however, that if the original source station does not receive the frame back from the destination station for any reason, such as ring latency or the fact that the frame was not received by the destination station, the source station aborts the initial ETR transmission. This event is called an *abort sequence cycle*. Timers called *Token Ring protocol timers* are active and manage this complete cycle for general operations.

Note also that in a network architecture using ETR, all the Token Ring cards should be active or inactive for early token release to operate in a true enhanced process. In many implementations, part of the NICs implemented in certain Token Ring networks may have early token release as active and other cards do not. Such a situation can cause an imbalance in Token Ring timing that can cause problems at the physical layer, such as ring recovery or ring purge operations and unstable neighbor notification rates.

Note that in most cases, so long as the split in ring balance is not excessive, such as if one or two stations are using early token release and the rest are not, this is not a major issue. A Token Ring network with an ETR mixed design implementation becomes a timing problem issue when the split approaches a 50% to 50% level on ETR active and ETR not active.

To explain further, the reason for the mix of early token release technology is vendor release cycles. In 1989 many of the Token Ring NICs were released with early token release as optional. In 1991 through 1992, many cards were released with the early token release option as active and set as the default. In mid-1994 to 1995, many cards were released with early token release as active and set for hard default—that is, the configuration was permanent and could not be changed. In this case, the industry just implemented Token Ring cards as they purchased them, and the phenomenon occurred in which Token Ring networks were deployed with NICs applied with a mixed setting of ETR both on and off.

Through many different troubleshooting processes in the late 1990s, the LAN Scope analysis team has addressed this concern by advising many clients to evaluate the Token Ring network through the process of examining neighbor notification timing and examining ring recovery processes to determine whether there is an early token release mismatch. If neighbor notification timing is varied of center of 7.00 seconds and shows 6.5- to 7.5-second area variances and there are high counts of ring recovery occurrences processes, these may indicate an ETR mismatch. If an early token release mismatch is suspected, verifying the process requires a complete audit of the Token Ring NICs throughout the Token Ring network area.

9.2.6 Token Ring DTR and Switching

Token Ring technology advanced quickly in the late 1990s. Today, Token Ring switching provides a low-cost way to allow a Token Ring network to be enhanced through higher performance.

The Token Ring switching products used today were developed through a migration of *Dedicated Token Ring* (DTR) switching. A DTR switching platform allows capacity to be increased by allowing a certain ring station to have a dedicated port for access. A single ring can then be increased further by engaging full-duplex adapter technology. Token Ring switching modules within an intelligent hub architecture allow for creating internal Token Rings to the specific hub. The switch process design allows an implementer to design more rings, by dividing ring stations across separate and internal rings. This process enables a designer to manage bandwidth allocation. The DTR process allows for a separate ring to be designed for one station. The lobe-cabling link can be engaged as a separate Token Ring loop between a station NIC and a port on the Token Ring switch. In this mode of Token Ring switching, stations normally operate in half duplex. A device can also use a full-duplex NIC if the switch port has a full-duplex adapter circuit. The full-duplex adapter can engage all four wires in the lobe cable and allow the dedicated loop to operate at 32Mbps.

Advancements in Token Ring switching and DTR have introduced the capability for overloaded rings to be divided into much smaller rings. The Token Ring product vendors have now introduced the capability to increase the data rate for Token Ring to more than 100Mbps. Implementing this type of Token Ring technology is very costly and requires certain management schemes.

9.2.7 Main Token Ring Frame-Type Structures

Another important feature of the Token Ring topology is that the Token Ring frame structure is built on three different frame types that can interact with each other on a consistent basis. This differs from Ethernet, which has four different data frame types that can be involved in communication from one point to another.

One of the frame types in the Token Ring topology is the Token Frame, which is a 3-byte frame that circles the ring for ring station access and control.

There is also a Token Ring data frame type that is divided into two sub-categories:

- Token Ring data frame with vector Data category
- Token Ring data frame with vector TR MAC category

The Token Ring data frame carries actual upper-layer data, and the Token Ring Data frame with an internal MAC header carries actual data related to the physical Token Ring medium for control. The third frame type is a Token Ring Abort Sequence frame, which can be used for an abort operation such as the ETR abort cycle.

9.2.8 Devices That Can Manage the Physical Ring

In the initial release of the Token Ring network, certain devices were deployed with functional addressing active for physical management on the ring. This was prior to the implementation of SNMP and RMON technology in the Token Ring environment, and represented a communication method for managing the physical ring. Much of the functionality of these roles was based on the use of a management system introduced by IBM, called the LAN Network Manager System. Note, however, that two of the initial physical functional address assignments are still common throughout the Token Ring network today: the Standby Monitor and the Ring Error Monitor. Many of the other initially assigned functional addresses are not present in today's operation, unless implemented in a proprietary environment such as an IBM host structure.

For the ring to operate in a consistent and stable fashion, certain management roles were applied to the Token Ring technology. Local management roles were roles considered important to the local ring. Ring management server roles were roles of management that would synchronize and operate throughout different rings that were communicating with each other through Token Ring bridges or routers.

On a local ring, there was always the requirement for a *standby monitor* (SM) role. An SM is a device with a functional operation that runs in tandem with a local individual addressing scheme. All devices on each ring are called standby monitors. This is because almost any device actively inserted and running on a Token Ring network is active in the SM role and is always "standing by" to become the *active monitor* (AM).

The next important role is the AM. The AM is the most important role of a physical local ring management process. A device running as an AM can also function as a general ring station. The AM functional address can be assigned and run in direct parallel with the combined assignment of the individual assignment of the local device. Specifically, this means that a server, workstation, router, or even a LAN printer could act in the AM role. The active monitor is the main communication manager on the local ring and is designated the AM role through an operation called the *token-claiming process*. This process allows the AM role to be assigned dynamically and is noted as the first device active on the ring with the highest address. In most cases, this is the server. The token-claiming process is described later in this chapter.

The device assigned the AM role will have seven responsibilities. These include maintaining the ring master clock, initiating neighbor notification, monitoring neighbor notification, maintaining proper ring delay, monitoring token and frame transmission, detecting lost tokens or frames, and purging the ring. This is obviously an extremely important process for overall Token Ring management cycles. The processes related to the discussion of these roles will be clear as we move further in this chapter and discuss the architecture cycles of the ring (see Figure 9.11).

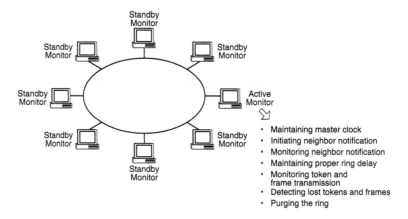

FIGURE 9.11 *The main responsibilities of the Token Ring active monitor.*

The next role that was important in the initial release of the Token Ring physical management processes was called *configuration report server* (CRS). This CRS implementation was introduced to allow for certain configurations to be immediately cross-loaded from and to certain ring stations when management was required on the ring. Some of these configurations were items that would be collected for statistical purposes, such as NAUN changes or new active monitor MAC frame transmissions.

Another management function also in the past was the *ring parameter server* (RPS). An RPS is a special server that would run in combination with a local assigned address where one device would be the RPS. The RPS had the capability during ring initialization cycles, when a workstation would insert on a ring, to download to a new station a logical ring number, a soft error report time value, or a ring parameter version level. It could also monitor the ring station by querying the address, the microcode level of the NIC, and the NAUN's address. This information was combined within the RPS function.

Another function still used today and also assumed by many protocol analyzer management systems is the *ring error monitor* (REM). The ring error monitor has the express purpose of collecting physical Token Ring errors. This is why it is so important to the management system and the functionality of the network protocol analyzers. The REM can collect Token Ring soft and hard errors generated by the Token Ring inherent finite state machine operation of a Token Ring NIC. During certain processes in a Token Ring NIC, soft errors are generated prior to a hard error failure. These processes are described later in this book. The point here is that the REM is a functional address that is assigned. After this address has been assigned, it is combined directly with an individual device. Any device assuming the REM function can capture all errors on the ring, whether they are soft or hard. Again, this is an address that is still important to today's operation of the Token Ring environment.

The *LAN bridge server* (LBS) function was implemented in the early Token Ring operational stages to allow all Token Ring bridges to intercommunicate bridge statistics for the number of frames transmitted through a bridge and lost and discarded frames transmitted as processed.

Another function is the *LAN reporting mechanism* (LRM). This function can almost be compared to a *Management Information Base* (MIB) in today's SNMP environment. This was a function that could be implemented on any device throughout a Token Ring physical network. If a device was running an LRM function, it could collect certain statistics and communicate back and forth with a LAN manager console (thus, the comparison with an SNMP console communicating with a MIB). In this case, an LRM agent was considered for implementation as a functional operation to be designed into all Token Ring NICs and management hubs. This advancement in technology was never really brought to its true potential.

The next main function is the LAN manager function. It is considered the pinnacle of all the management functions of Token Ring architecture and was used for a period of time but in today's environment is not implemented heavily, The IBM LAN network management concept was extremely innovative and allowed for a device to be assigned the LAN manager functional address. This device would be the centralized management system and would communicate with the configuration report servers, ring parameter servers, ring error monitor, LAN bridge servers, and any devices running a LAN reporting mechanism.

Therefore, a complete inherent spider architecture was developed comparable to the SNMP or RMON technologies to allow for physical management in the Token Ring. The interesting fact about this complete phenomenon is that back in 1985, the developers of Token Ring had the ability to physically manage the complete Token Ring environment within the physical layer operations of the overall network topology without involving the upper layers. Many of the network operating system vendors and application vendors did not see the inherent strength of this design. If the Token Ring vendors along with the network operating system and application vendors worked together closely, it is very possible that this management could have reached a higher potential through the implementation of LRMs. Thus, Token Ring networks could have achieved a higher level of respect in terms of network management capability in today's operating system environment. This is a definite fact, and one of the weak spots in Token Ring development as the product started to move forward during the early 1990s. It is therefore my technical opinion that if the network management cycles of the physical Token Ring capabilities of the Token Ring topology were developed in a more aggressive manner, the Token Ring architecture would be much more popular from an implementation and usage standpoint.

Because of the lack of attention to this area as well as other design areas, such as intelligence in the Token Ring hub architecture, other LAN topology products advanced more rapidly in terms of deployment against the Token Ring topology. The other major concern was the speed of Token Ring, which also would have had to be considered by the design teams while also concentrating on physical Token Ring management.

The Token Ring architecture is obviously a very stable and fault-redundant operational technology. To illustrate how strong the fault operation is, the following is a discussion of the actual architecture cycles and processes that occur at the Token Ring physical communication level (see Figure 9.12).

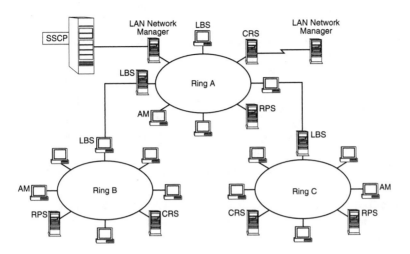

FIGURE 9.12 *The Token Ring management scheme that was designed for the physical layer.*

9.3 Understanding Token Ring Physical Communications

Certain communication processes occur at the Token Ring physical level. These processes occur as part of the Token Ring physical management cycles inherent to the Token Ring topology fault-redundant design.

The following Token Ring processes are described here:

- Ring insertion
- Token claiming
- Priority access
- Neighbor notification
- Ring purge
- Beaconing
- Finite state machines
- Token Ring protocol timers

9.3.1 Ring Insertion

Ring insertion is a five-phase process that occurs to ensure the attachment of a new ring station to the physical ring. Although there are five steps, they are known as Phase 0 through Phase 4 (as part of an IBM naming convention).

In Phase 0, the Token Ring NIC sends a physical signal to the Token Ring MSAU port. This signal activates a mechanical relay in the port. The port then activates as open. At this point, an active lobe link is considered in place between the Token Ring NIC and the Token Ring MSAU port. A simple Lobe Test MAC frame is released from the NIC and transmitted up to the port and looped back down to the NIC connecting. This signals that the NIC port is active and available for communication. The lobe test MAC frame cannot be seen by a protocol analyzer on the main ring path (see Figure 9.13).

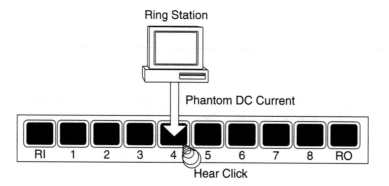

FIGURE 9.13 *Phase 0 of the Token Ring insertion process.*

In the second step, Phase 1, the Token Ring NIC listens or attempts to sense an *Active Monitor Present* (AMP) MAC frame. This is one of the 25 MAC frames described later in this chapter. In this phase, a new Token Ring NIC upon insertion onto the ring listens for an AMP frame. This frame indicates that an AM is present on the ring. If there is no AM device present, the new station's Token Ring NIC vectors into a state in which it eventually generates a new Active Monitor Present frame and becomes the AM. If an AM is already operating on the ring, the new device logs the vector to not send an AMP frame, and it moves to Phase 2.

In the third step, or Phase 2, the Token Ring NIC transmits a frame up the lobe path and onto the MRP of the Token Ring, called a Duplicate Address Test MAC frame. This frame has a source address that equals its own address, and a destination address that also equals its address. Therefore, the frame is transmitted on the ring and circles the downstream fashion of the ring, and should be received by the source station attempting to be inserted on the ring. This would ensure that there is no other station on the ring noted with a duplicate address. If the frame does not come back to the source station, another station must have received the frame and will be the assigned duplicate device on the ring. This particular device copies a frame in error and generates a soft error frame called a Frame Copied Error. A device attempting to insert on the ring will stop the ring insertion process as active and will attempt to reinsert. If this process is not resolved, it can be a cyclical ongoing process, and the device will never insert on the ring. This can be viewed with a protocol analyzer just by monitoring the ring insertion process (see Figure 9.14).

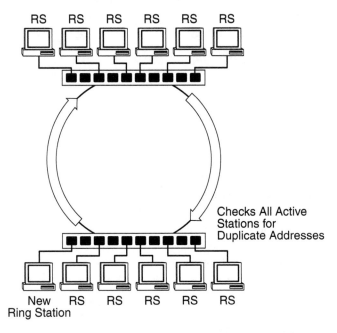

FIGURE 9.14 *Phase 2 of the Token Ring insertion process.*

The fourth process, or Phase 3, of inserting on the ring is referred to as participating in neighbor notification. In this case, the new ring station participates in neighbor notification. This process occurs every seven seconds and is described later in this chapter. When neighbor notification is active on the ring, the new station just sends out a standby Monitor Present MAC frame and lets all the other stations know that it is active on the ring. It also records its nearest active upstream neighbor address in its UNA buffer upon the cycle (see Figure 9.15).

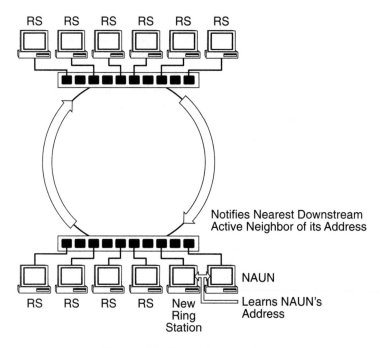

FIGURE 9.15 *Phase 3 of the Token Ring insertion process.*

The last process of ring insertion, or Phase 4, is called *request initialization*. During this process, the new ring station inserts onto the ring and sends a Request Initialization MAC frame outbound. This frame was used heavily in the early phases of Token Ring operation for ring insertion cycles, in which a ring parameter server would download certain initialization parameters to the station. In today's environment, hub management systems can take advantage of this particular Token Ring specification outbound cycle; in most cases, however, they will not invoke any retransmission back to the station. In this case, most of the new Token Ring NICs just continue to operate on the ring as normal. At the end of Phase 4, the station is now considered active and operating on the ring (see Figure 9.16).

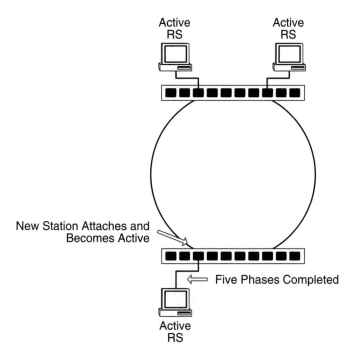

FIGURE 9.16 *Phase 4 of the Token Ring insertion processes, which indicates that a new ring station is now actively inserted into the ring.*

9.3.2 Token Ring Claiming or Active Monitor Contention

A standard physical process occurs called Token Ring claiming, which, for simplicity purposes, could be called active monitor contention. The actual specification, however, is referred to as Token Ring claiming.

This process occurs when a new device on the ring, or an existing device on the ring, contends to become the AM. This is the process of how a device is assigned the dynamic active monitor role.

Token claiming takes place when one of the following three conditions occurs:

- When a new station attaches to the ring and does not detect the active monitor

- If a standby monitor detects the absence of an active monitor on the ring and cannot detect an Active Monitor Present frame for a certain amount of time as related to two timers: the T-Good Token or T-Receive Notification

- If an active monitor cannot detect any frames on the ring for a period of time related to a timer called T-Receive Notification

When any one of these three circumstances occurs, the active monitor contention cycle starts, and the token-claiming process is active.

A station can operate in two main modes as active when in the token-claiming process:

- Claim token transmit mode

- Claim token repeat mode

In a claim token transmit mode, an actual device is contending for the role and is transmitting certain frame cycles to become the active monitor, and is in contention to become the active monitor.

In a claim token repeat mode, a station is aware that the active monitor contention cycle is occurring, but is not contending to become the active monitor.

The token-claiming process determines whether a station is in a transmit or a repeat mode and is based on the following operation. An originating station detects that there is an Active Monitor Present frame problem, based on one of the three conditions previously described. In this case, the originating station generates a Claim Token MAC frame on the MRP, which is one of the standard 25 MAC frames. This frame includes its address in a Data field that has a Claim Token MAC vector.

Every station receiving the frame must investigate a Frame Control field with a MAC vector, and investigate the type of process and data inside the Data field. Therefore, when the frame is transmitted outbound onto the ring, the next downstream station investigates the frame. It compares its address to the address of the Source Station field of the frame transmitting the Claim Token MAC frame. In this case, if its own station address is lower, it drops into a claim token repeat mode. The next station down the ring performs the same cycle. If its station address is lower, it also drops into a repeat mode and appears passive in the process. If the third station downstream compares the source Claim Token MAC address to its address and determines that it is higher, it engages a process in which it is active in a claim token transmit mode and is going to contend for the role. At this point, however, it waits and lets the frame continue to be passed around the ring.

Considering that all the rest of the stations on the ring do not have a higher address, eventually the original frame reaches the frame that transmitted the original Claim Token frame. This original source station then releases the token for one cycle. This station remains active in the claim token transmit mode. This token then circles the ring, and all devices in the claim token repeat mode just pass the token on for processing. The one device that did move into a claim token transmit mode takes the token and activates a claim token transmit process. This Claim Token frame that will be generated by the device contending will eventually reach the source station that originally sent the Claim Token MAC frame. This device then compares its address to the station contending and sees that it is lower, and drops into a claim token repeat mode. Thus, it is lowering its priority and is clearly not going to win the role of active monitor. This process causes the original frame to continue to move back to the second station that contended with a claim token transmit mode, and this station releases the token for one cycle.

If no stations contend for the role after three cycles of this process, eventually this station becomes the active monitor on the ring. Upon doing so, it generates a frame called *New Active Monitor Present*, which is one of the standard 25 MAC frames (see Figure 9.17).

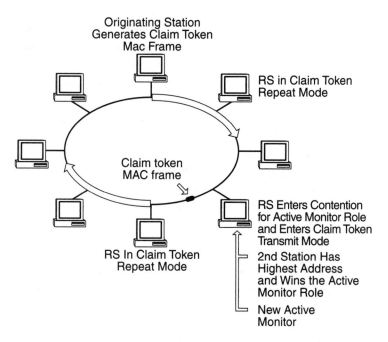

F IGURE **9.17** *The token-claiming concept.*

9.3.3 Priority Access

Within the Token Ring architecture, there is always an Access Control field contained within the token frame and the data frame. In the Access Control field are three priority bits of note; these have the capability to assign a priority to a Token Ring transmission. Note from the outset that this process is normally not invoked by application or upper-layer operating system manufacturers because priority is normally maintained in the upper-layer protocol sequencing. Note also that it was very innovative in the design that priority is capable at the Token Ring physical level.

If this is invoked and captured on a protocol analyzer as active, it is possible that this could be part of a problem if other applications are not using priority access.

The process is as follows: A basic token frame transmitted on the network has an active Access Control field. The Access Control field contains a set of bits called the *priority bits*. The priority bits are three bits from 0 to 7 in priority in binary settings. If a station on the ring had an upper-layer process that wanted to invoke priority, it would grab the token and reserve the priority of the token. For example, priority 5 would be a 101. In this case, the token would be released on the ring. If no other station contended for the token at a level higher than 5, the station would receive the token back and take the reserve priority and append data to it and create a data frame through the append operation, and the Access Control field in the data frame would have a priority 5 as active. In this case, this station could transmit and receive back and forth to a destination station at priority 5 on a consistent basis. It would have to consistently release the token on every cycle. If there were another device on the ring that had a priority 6 or 7 contending capability, it could possibly reserve the token and then take the token control away from the two devices transmitting a priority 5. This is not a normal cycle and is not common in normal communications, due to the inherent problems that could occur based on this cycle. But it is a fact that this process can take place. With that said, normally the priority is set at 000 consistently at the physical level. Another priority feature available in Token Ring architecture is the monitor bit. The monitor bit is also in the Access Control field. This bit is set as an active zero on outbound transmission from any Token Ring source device. When this device passes the active monitor on the ring, which always will occur on one particular ring cycle, the active monitor has the responsibility of setting this bit to a one. When this happens, the frame is then passed on through the ring. If the original source station receives the frame back, the token is released on the ring.

But if for any reason the original source station is turned off or has a problem, and the frame is passed on the ring for a second cycle and the active monitor detects a frame when the Access Control field monitor bit is set to one, it discards the frame and then purges the ring. This allows for each station on the ring to have equal priority and to prevent data frames from continuously circling the ring.

9.3.4 Neighbor Notification

Neighbor notification is one of the more important processes in the Token Ring physical operation that interrelates with fault redundancy in the troubleshooting processes of Token Ring. The process is on a seven-second cycle. Due to a timer called T Neighbor Notification, the assigned active monitor sends out an active monitor present frame. This is a consistent operation engaged from the early release days of the Token Ring and is still consistent on a local Token Ring.

The Active Monitor Present frame invokes a cycle in which the Token Ring MAC vector on the next downstream station notes the occurrence of the neighbor notification. In this case, it will record the upstream neighbor address buffer from the source address of the Active Monitor Present frame. The Active Monitor Present frame then circles the ring, and a token is eventually released. The next station down the ring then takes the token and transmits a *standby monitor present* frame. This is just indicating its particular address to its downstream neighbor, which will record in its Upstream Neighbor Address buffer the Address and the Source Address field of the Standby Monitor Present frame. This continues around the ring until each device records the address of the upstream neighbor on the ring. This causes a neighbor notification event to occur in a seven-second cycle on every ring.

If a protocol analyzer is set for a MAC capture filter and it is connected to a Token Ring physical ring, the neighbor notification cycle is seen immediately on seven-second intervals. It is then possible to determine which is the active monitor and how long it takes for the neighbor notification cycle to occur.

On a healthy Token Ring, a certain amount time is specified for a neighbor notification cycle to occur. This amount of time is called *ring poll time*. Specifically, it should take no more than 2 to 2.5 seconds for a physically healthy operating Token Ring to perform neighbor notification. It should then recur on a seven-second interval.

If a protocol analyzer detects that neighbor notification is not occurring in seven-second intervals—specifically, longer or shorter intervals than seven seconds—it is possible that a major physical problem exists on the ring. Most likely in this occurrence, other frames will be present, such as physical soft errors and a high number of Ring Purge MAC frames. There may also be a physical Beaconing frame condition present. Some of these conditions usually coexist when there is an unstable neighbor notification cycle (see Figure 9.18).

```
━━━ SUMMARY VIEW ━━━━━━━━━━━━━━━━━━━━━━━━━━━━━━━━━━━━━━
 1            Broadcast      MADGE000001   MAC   Active Monitor Present
 2   0.020    Broadcast      00000000002   MAC   Standby Monitor Present
 3   6.906    Broadcast      MADGE000001   MAC   Active Monitor Present
 4   0.011    Broadcast      00000000002   MAC   Standby Monitor Present
 5   6.916    Broadcast      MADGE000001   MAC   Active Monitor Present
 6   0.012    Broadcast      00000000002   MAC   Standby Monitor Present
 7   6.915    Broadcast      MADGE000001   MAC   Active Monitor Present
 8   0.013    Broadcast      00000000002   MAC   Standby Monitor Present
 9   1.028    Broadcast      MADGE000001   MAC   Ring Purge
10   0.000    400000000001   00000000001   MAC   Duplicate Address Test
11   0.000    Broadcast      MADGE000001   MAC   Active Monitor Present
12   0.000    400000000001   00000000001   MAC   Duplicate Address Test
13   0.010    Broadcast      00000000002   MAC   Standby Monitor Present
14   0.000    Config Srv     00000000001   MAC   Report SUA Change
15   0.015    Broadcast      00000000001   MAC   Standby Monitor Present
16   0.000    Param Server   00000000001   MAC   Request Initialization
17   0.000    Config Srv     MADGE000001   MAC   Report SUA Change
18   0.000    Param Server   00000000001   MAC   Request Initialization
19   0.000    Param Server   00000000001   MAC   Request Initialization
20   0.000    Param Server   00000000001   MAC   Request Initialization
━━━ Frame 1 of 225 ━━━━━━━━━━━━━━━━━━━━━━━━━━━━━━━━━━━━━
 1      2       3       4       5       6        7       8       9      10
HELP   MARK                          MENUS   DISPLAY   PREV   NEXT           NEW
                                             OPTIONS   FRAME  FRAME       CAPTURE
```

FIGURE 9.18 *An analyzer data trace that presents the Token Ring neighbor notification process.*

9.3.5 Ring Purge Process

Another important operation in the Token Ring architecture communication cycle is the ring purge process. The ring purge process is an inherent part of the fault-redundancy cycle. The Token Ring architecture was built in such a way that the device assigned as the active monitor has the capability to purge the ring and to cause a reset across the physical NICs connected to the ring. The reset is a very quick process that resets the physical buffers and usually does not disrupt the upper-layer protocol operation of applications or network operating system functions. This is usually a very rapid process that occurs in less than a one-second interval, during which the complete ring can restabilize. Most upper-layer protocols will not time out or disconnect if the ring purge process does not occur too frequently.

If ring purge processes occur at a rate of more than 50 ring purges per hour, this is considered a possible unstable condition. If they start to occur at 100–200 times per hour, this is an even more unstable situation. When ring purge counts approach 1000–2000 per hour, the physical ring is usually unstable and other upper-layer protocols are disconnecting and applications are generally affected. When ring purges do occur at high levels, it is always a physical condition that has caused the problem and a physical problem should be troubleshot in conjunction with this occurrence. In some cases, excessive upper-layer application loading can affect the process, but usually the physical layer is the main concern of this particular type of occurrence.

The ring purge process generally occurs for certain physical conditions. One condition is when the active monitor has its Any Token Timer expired, noted at 10ms. This would mean that no token or frame has been transmitted by the active monitor in 10ms. Therefore, the active monitor should purge the ring and reset the physical state.

Another occurrence is when the ring recovery process continually occurs and has to be set back to a normal repeat mode after a ring purge process. When the active monitor detects a monitor bit set to one, and a frame has cycled the ring more than once, it is normal to see the ring purged. Another occurrence is any of the error conditions that take place due to the active monitor present role, such as a disruption of timing on the ring and proper execution of a Token Ring process, lost tokens or frames, or other error conditions considered excessive.

The discussion now turns to how the soft error process of fault redundancy of Token Ring is designed and operates.

9.3.6 Soft Error Counting and Fault Redundancy Operation

As noted earlier, the Token Ring architecture is extremely fault-redundant. Built within the Token Ring chipset of every Token Ring NIC is the capability to perform a soft error assembly process when an error occurs and to generate the error out onto the ring. After this process occurs, the Token Ring NIC is supposed to recover and continue operating.

This is an intelligent cycle for error recovery and is an enhanced version of the Token Ring topology features as compared to other LAN topologies such as Ethernet. In other words, the Token Ring NIC can detect an error, package the error for transmission to a station that can log the error, and then recover and continue operating. This is an extremely enhanced feature for fault redundancy.

The process occurs as follows: If any Token Ring station detects an error, it immediately invokes a Token Ring timer called T-Soft Error Report. This timer is normally set at two seconds.

For two seconds, the timer counts, and all the errors that can possibly be assembled are logged into a register for insertion into a Token Ring Soft Error Report packet. At the end of the two seconds, a Token Ring Soft Error Report MAC packet is assembled, and a Token Ring data frame is set on the ring with a MAC vector called Soft Error Report. The Soft Error Report MAC frame is generated onto the ring with an outbound address to C00000000008, called the ring error monitor. Any device assigned as the ring error monitor on the ring, such as a protocol analyzer or a management system, can capture the error.

After the source station has logically transmitted the error, it then resets its physical buffers, recovers, and actually starts operating again as a normal ring station. In certain cases, the active monitor may react to this occurrence depending on level, and purge the ring so that all the stations on the physical ring reset. This is a ring recovery cycle as associated with the soft error generation.

Within the packet, there could be 10 different types of soft errors (described later in the troubleshooting section of this chapter). These errors need to be analyzed closely, because it is possible to isolate a problem before a total Token Ring failure occurs by capturing the error, decoding it properly, and taking action prior to the occurrence. If certain types of Token Ring errors continue to occur, eventually a Token Ring hard error may occur, called a *Token Ring beacon*. When this takes place, the complete Token Ring physical NIC operation ceases, and upper-layer protocols cannot flow.

When Token Ring soft errors are minimal (certain types are not considered high-impact errors), the Token Ring recovers and upper-layer protocols are not interrupted and can continue to operate normally. This is obviously considered a positive situation.

When this complete process takes place and the Report Soft Error MAC frame is communicated on the ring, the frame contains important informational items. These items include the device generating the error, along with the error type and the address of the upstream neighbor. This is where the neighbor notification cycle is so important, because the device generating the error has a transmission process outbound stating that it has seen an error and its address is involved along with its upstream neighbor address, and here is the error type. When interpreting this occurrence, it can be seen that this is a process that creates a circle around the possible area of fault in the ring. This is called a fault domain and is described later in this book.

This illustrates the importance of the Upstream Neighbor Address buffer logging during the neighbor notification cycle. If dataflow is normal from station to station in a clockwise fashion, and eventually one station device has an error generation outbound, the problem is most likely within that device or the device upstream (its NAUN) in the area of fault. Specific fault domain troubleshooting techniques are discussed later in this chapter.

9.3.7 Beaconing

The last process to be discussed before moving into the physical Token Ring frame structure, Token Ring protocol timers, and the troubleshooting and associated baselining techniques, is the beaconing process.

The beaconing process was designed into the Token Ring architecture as a way for Token Ring cards to automatically recover from major physical Token Ring problems and remove a physically bad NIC from the ring. Note, however, that the process was never truly enhanced through network design features that were possible in the engineering of Token Ring cards from certain vendors.

If this area were addressed, this is another area where the Token Ring architecture implementation node count would have increased and eventually become more popular. This is another weak point from the Token Ring design camp and is considered a major weakness in the overall troubleshooting process of the Token Ring architecture. It is my position that if the vendors and associated engineering teams had paid more attention to the operation of this particular feature, they could have designed the most fault-redundant network in the history of local area technology.

The specific process is that there is a cycle in which a Token Ring NIC can detect a hard error. To do this, the Token Ring NIC has an internal operation occur during which its finite state machine and internal operations detect an error that is nonoperational or considered hard. This particular error is detected through an excessive count of soft errors or other events that take place on the Token Ring NIC, or its associated NIC, or within a fault domain around a particular NIC generating the hard error. This hard error is called a beacon. What occurs is that the Token Ring NIC, when moving into this state, generates a packet called a Physical MAC packet with a Beacon MAC vector. There are four beacon MAC types, and all four usually generate a Token Ring failure occurrence on the ring that will cause an outage.

The Token Ring Beacon MAC frame is formed, and a frame called a *data frame* is transmitted onto the ring, with a Frame Control MAC vector active and a beacon indication inside the Data MAC field. When any frame on the ring downstream receives the Frame Control field with MAC active, it investigates the field and sees the beacon as active.

At this point, it moves into an immediate beacon repeat state and stops operating any upper-layer protocol transmissions. This obviously interrupts all upper-layer protocols and operations on the ring, and stops the rings from operating. This continues for every ring station on the complete ring, and they all move into a beacon repeat state. After eight transmissions from the original source station in the beacon transmit mode process of the original beacon frame in beacon transmitter process, a continued cycle occurs in which eight transmissions are considered the completion of the cycle. After eight transmissions from the beaconing station of the Beacon MAC frame, an isolation process occurs in the circuitry and the overall operation of the Token Ring mechanism. What takes place is that the station beaconing notifies within its transmission who the NAUN is as associated with its connection to the Token Ring network architecture. The NAUN detects the eight cycles of the beacon transmission and immediately removes itself from the ring and starts a testing process. It runs a lobe test MAC frame and a duplicate address test frame process that are part of the normal ring insertion process, as noted earlier.

These two frames test the lobe path and the capability for the frame to transmit one frame around the ring. Then this station, if completing the test, puts itself active back out on the ring in a beacon repeat mode (see Figure 9.19).

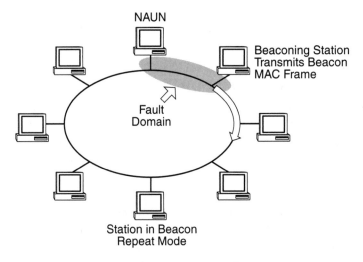

FIGURE 9.19 *The Token Ring beaconing concept.*

Next, the station downstream transmitting the beacon frame performs the exact same process. If it performs the same process and passes the Lobe Test MAC frame and the duplicate address test without failure, both of the stations appear to be stable and the source station to transmit the frame also inserts itself back on the ring as normal. At this point, the active monitor activates a ring purge process and the ring is cleared, restabilized, and starts to transmit a token as normal. In 99% of all cases, the beaconing process recurs almost immediately and continues on an ongoing cycle. This is because the testing cycle in almost all cases is not extensive enough to actually detect the error. If one of the stations had detected an error during the Lobe Test MAC frame or the duplicate address test, it would have removed itself from the ring as part of the normal beaconing operation. In this case, the station that is bad would have been removed and the beaconing condition would have been physically isolated. The ring would continue to operate on its own and a physical device would have been troubleshot and removed by an automatic process of the physical medium.

This is a very positive fault-redundant feature. For the record, in most cases, this is not enough troubleshooting of physical circuitry. More diagnostic tests should have been performed by the two stations in the physical engineering mode of the beaconing process—such as internal diagnostic runs and different cycles that may have been available—to truly remove the station from the ring so that the process would not have to have been troubleshot manually.

In most cases, an engineer or analyst will actually have to associate the two stations that are beaconing and remove them from the ring. This can be done by using a protocol analyzer. In most cases during the period from 1985 through the early 1990s, this was the only way to isolate the beaconing stations on the ring.

The only other way to troubleshoot the issue was by physically locating the devices that were removing themselves from the ring, and just removing the cables from the MSAU.

In the mid 1990s, intelligent hub-based systems were introduced; these have the capability to detect that the two stations generating the process would perform an automatic vector outbound generation of a Remove Ring Station MAC frame and wrap the ports on the actual Token Ring ports that were causing the beaconing conditions. Through this process, the Token Ring management vendors found a way to address the concern by wrapping the ports quickly so that a technician would not have to find the Token Ring stations causing the beaconing condition. Although this addressed the issue, for the record this was a little bit late. The community that was utilizing Token Ring products from 1985 through 1995 had to incur many troubleshooting problems and outages prior to the implementation of automatic port fault wrapping for beaconing conditions. This is again a major weakness in the evolution of Token Ring design.

9.3.8 Token Ring Timers

The Token Ring protocol has 14 timers used in the Token Ring architecture. This discussion does not examine the interoperation of each Token Ring protocol timer. Note that within the design of a Token Ring card there is an operation called a finite state machine. A *finite state machine* is an interesting operation that is active in the Token Ring architecture and allows for the Token Ring card to inherently interrelate the mode of a Token Ring communication process in direct conjunction with a Token Ring failure mode. Many different finite state machines can occur and each Token Ring vendor can invoke a finite state machine differently. This is actually the process of how a Token Ring card will vector from one point to another and act as related to an error or transmission.

With that said, it should be mentioned that there are different protocol timers that allow the cards to operate. These timers vary in data-rate design as related to different timing intervals. For the purposes of this book, the following timers are active. Refer to Appendix B for other sources that explain timer operation. A top protocol analyst in a Token Ring analysis session should understand the operation of the internal cycles of these timers. They are extensive and require considerable reading and study to truly understand their operation and effect on Token Ring network operations.

The following are the key timers:

- T_Attach
- T_Claim Token
- T_Any Token
- T_Physical Trailer
- T_Good Token
- T_Response
- T_Soft Error Report
- T_Transmit Pacing
- T_Beacon Transmit
- T_Escape

- T_Ring Purge

- T_Neighbor Notification

- T_Neighbor Notification Response

- T_Receive Notification

Note that all the timers have one common thread. Each timer activates at a certain point, and each timer has an action. There is always a condition that cancels the timer and a certain duration during which the timer runs.

For general discussion purposes, a few examples of the key timers are presented. The T_Any Token is a timer used to set the amount of time that an active monitor can wait before it detects a starting delimiter sequence from either a token or a frame on the ring. If the active monitor does not see any type of starting delimiter from a token or a frame, it assumes that the ring is not operating. It times out after 10ms and activates an automatic ring purge condition. Another example is the T_Attach timer, which is used to set the amount of time that a timer can stay in the ring insertion process. This timer is activated in Phase 1 when the monitor check process occurs in ring insertion. The timer times out in 18 seconds if the ring insertion process encounters any problems and is not completed. The timer is cancelled earlier if the process completes. When the timer times out, this reactivates the ring insertion process. These are just a few examples of how the Token Ring timers operate.

9.3.9 Token Ring Frame Structure

Three types of frames are used for communication on the Token Ring network:

- The token frame

- The data frame

- The abort sequence frame

9.3.9.1 The Token Frame

Three fields are engaged in the Token Ring frame: the Starting Delimiter field, the Access Control field, and the Ending Delimiter field. The starting delimiter is a sequence of approximately 8 bits, 0–7. These bits allow the code to be sensed on inbound and outbound transmissions on the Token Ring NIC. The ending delimiter is the ending portion of a token frame that is an 8-byte sequence built on a 0–7 bit cycle for transmission inbound and outbound of a NIC (see Figure 9.20).

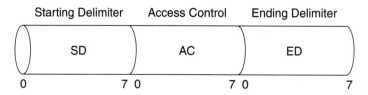

FIGURE 9.20 *A token frame.*

The Access Control field includes 8 bits. Bits 0 to 2, the left three first positions, are called priority bits. The middle or fourth bit is called the token bit. The fifth bit is called the monitor bit, and the last three bits are called the priority reservation bits (see Figure 9.21).

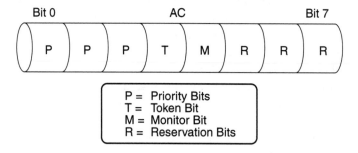

FIGURE 9.21 *The internal field of an Access Control field.*

9.3.9.2 The Data Frame

The Token Ring data frame has multiple fields: Field 1 is the first byte and is called the Starting Delimiter. Field 2 is the Access Control field. Field 3 is called the Frame Control field and defines whether the frame is a data frame with Token Ring physical Medium Access Control data, or upper-layer data called Logical Link Control data. Frame 4 is a 6-byte address for the Destination Address field of the Token Ring NIC. Field 5 is the 6-byte Address field for the source address of the Token Ring frame transmitted. Field 6 is the Routing Information field. This is a variable-length field from 2–18 bytes. Field 7 is a variable-length field that identifies the actual Information field that carries the data, such as the actual upper-layer protocol data or the physical Medium Access Control field. Field 8 is the 32-bit CRC field. Field 9 is a 1-byte sequence indicating the Ending Delimiter field, and field 10 is called the Frame Status field, which includes whether a frame was copied and a frame was understood for frame processing (see Figure 9.22).

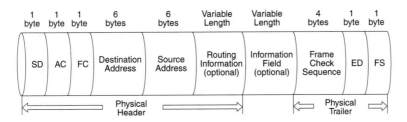

1 byte	1 byte	1 byte	6 bytes	6 bytes	Variable Length	Variable Length	4 bytes	1 byte	1 byte
SD	AC	FC	Destination Address	Source Address	Routing Information (optional)	Information Field (optional)	Frame Check Sequence	ED	FS

Physical Header ⟷

Physical Trailer ⟷

FIGURE 9.22 *A Token Ring data frame.*

9.3.9.3 The Abort Sequence Frame

The abort sequence frame is a simple starting delimiter and ending delimiter tagged together and is considered a 2-byte sequence for general transmission (see Figure 9.23).

Bit 0			SD			Bit 7		Bit 0			ED			Bit 7
J	K	0	J	K	0	0	0	J	K	1	J	K	1	1	E

FIGURE 9.23 *An abort sequence frame.*

9.3.10 Description of 25 MAC Frames

The Token Ring protocol architecture has 25 MAC frames that are used for communication at the physical layer, as follows:

- **Standby Monitor Present.** This frame is used by neighbor notification for a ring station to notify its address and to log its upstream neighbor address during neighbor notification.

- **Active Monitor MAC Present.** This frame is used by the active monitor present to start the neighbor notification cycle.

- **Ring Station Initialization MAC.** This is a frame sent outbound on the ring and in the station insertion process by a new ring station entering the ring.

- **Initialized Ring MAC Station.** This is a frame sent by the ring parameter server if a certain ring station inserting on the ring is going to require certain ring initialization parameters.

- **Lobe Test MAC.** This is the frame used in the ring insertion process to test the lobe path.

- **Duplicate Address Test MAC.** This is the frame sent during the ring insertion process and during the beaconing process to test the ring for duplicate addresses on the ring, and to also, during the beaconing process, test the overall capability for a station to transmit around the ring in one cycle.

- **Beacon MAC.** This is the frame indicated upon transmission of a hard error of fault occurrence.

- **Claim Token MAC.** This is the frame used by a station that detects the loss of an active monitor and wants to contend for the role of an active monitor cycle.

- **Ring Purge MAC.** This frame is transmitted by the active monitor and causes every physical station on the ring to reset its physical layer and causes ring recovery to take place.

- **Report Neighbor Notification MAC Incomplete.** This frame is transmitted on the ring during the neighbor notification process and indicates the situation where the NAUN T_Neighbor Notification timer has expired. In this case, this means that the neighbor notification cycle could not complete and there may be a fault domain isolation process to indicate the error.

- **Transmit Forward MAC.** This is a frame that can be transmitted outbound from a LAN management console or new management-based systems to test the station's availability on the ring.

- **Report Transmit Forward MAC.** This is a station that can be transmitted by a LAN manager console or a new management station from where the NIC must respond to the Transmit Forward MAC frame. The two previous frames work together in a manner comparable to a ping process in the IP environment.

- **Report Active Monitor MAC Error.** This is a frame generated by the active monitor when it detects a problem in process in its own operation. This would indicate a problem in the active monitor cycle.

- **Report Soft Error MAC.** This is the frame generated by any ring station when it encounters an error and packages an error for generation on the ring. This frame includes valuable information and must be decoded by an analyst as to the type of soft error.

- **Change Parameter MAC.** This is a frame generated by the ring station onto the ring, normally when a CRS is active (which is not used in the industry at this time).

- **Remove Ring Station MAC.** This is a frame that can be transmitted by a management station CRS or many of the new management systems that automatically remove a ring station from operation. This causes a Token Ring NIC to automatically deactivate for certain port adapters to wrap on intelligent Token Ring hub architecture.

- **Request Ring Station MAC State.** This is a frame that can be transmitted by LAN management stations and CRS and new management stations to request the state of a MAC frame. If a Token Ring NIC receives this frame, it responds with a following frame.

- **Report Ring Station State.** This frame is transmitted by the ring station in response to the Request Ring Station State. This frame responds with the state of operation, such as functional addresses and other operations active in the ring.

- **Request Ring Station Attachment MAC.** This frame is transmitted on the ring by a new LAN management station or an old LAN manager to request the attachment of a ring station. This would directly relate to the type of functions run by the station.

- **Report Ring Station Attachment MAC.** This is the response from the NIC to a Request Ring Station Attachment frame from the management station.

- **Request Ring Station Address MAC.** This is the twenty-first MAC frame in the subset, in which a management station or a LAN manager can request the address of a station. This is used by new management systems to quickly query an address of a Token Ring NIC.

- **Report Ring Station Address MAC.** A Token Ring NIC must respond with the twenty-second MAC frame type, called Report Ring Station Address, and the address is responded back through this transmission.

- **Report NAUN Change MAC.** This is the twenty-third MAC frame change type. This is when a station involved in a ring insertion area of the Token Ring sees a new NAUN active and reports a NAUN change from its nearest Upstream Neighbor Address buffer.

- **Report New Active Monitor MAC.** This particular frame is transmitted by the active monitor when it becomes the active monitor through the active monitor contention or token-claiming process.

- **Response MAC.** This frame is normally transmitted from one frame to another when there is a syntax error in the respective transmission. This normally occurs upon transmission and ring insertion in abnormal conditions, or in abnormal conditions of physical conditions.

9.4 Troubleshooting Token Ring Physical Faults and Errors

When troubleshooting a Token Ring network generating soft or hard errors, it is important that an analyst capture all Soft Error Report MAC frames, Beacon MAC frames, and Ring Purge frames. These types of frames carry the information that holds the main error type and information that may need to be further decoded. These types of frames point to the fault domain. The Token Ring *fault domain* can be defined as the assigned logical area of hard fault. This area is assigned by the Token Ring NIC-to-NIC communication and architecture. It is inherent in Token Ring architecture for NICs to utilize the beaconing process to isolate a hard failure to a hard fault domain. A Token Ring NIC can also use the report soft error generation to create a soft area of fault.

9.4.1 Analysis and Troubleshooting of Token Ring Fault Areas

A logical area of soft or hard error fault or a fault domain will include three subareas:

- The station transmitting the Beacon or Soft Error Report MAC frame

- The beaconing or soft error reporting station's recorded NAUN address

- The medium used for connection between the error-generating ring station and its NAUN

When examining a Token Ring fault domain area, it is critical to analyze and isolate the actual location of failure cause. To capture, analyze, and isolate a point of failure within a fault domain, an analyst must focus on both Beacon and Soft Error Report MAC frame types via protocol analysis in a network baselining session.

In certain cases, the internal data areas within a Beacon or Soft Error Reporting MAC frame may point an analyst to a specific network device or failure areas on the Token Ring. In other cases, an analyst may have to perform certain manual troubleshooting steps as interleaved with rapid post analysis to isolate an issue identified to a fault domain. When troubleshooting a fault domain, an analyst must remember to examine the Beacon or Soft Error Report MAC frames through a protocol analysis session. To troubleshoot the internals of the frame, the analyst must record the reporting address and the NAUN address to assign a fault domain. Next, the analyst can start the manual troubleshooting by isolating one fault domain to two lobe areas as possible source of failure. The analyst should remove one lobe area cable link from the fault domain assigned by actually detaching one of the lobe cables from the Token Ring hub. Next, the analyst should re-analyze the ring. If the Beacon or Soft Error Reporting MAC frame is gone, the problem is in the removed lobe area. If the frames are still present, the analyst should reconnect the first suspect lobe area and disconnect the second lobe area and re-analyze the ring. The problem frames should not be present any further in the trace.

If a group of devices or a complete Token Ring network is experiencing problems or issues, it is possible that the MRP has an internal failure. If all the MSAUs or hubs are properly configured in the wiring racks and the MRP cross-hub RI and RO out cables are connected properly, the analysis of the MRP is relatively simple.

The proper way to troubleshoot and analyze a suspected MRP problem is to start by isolating the ring to a certain MSAU or hub area. It is important to understand that the main MSAUs, hubs, or the RI and RO cabling can be the cause of failure in an MRP outage. The analyst should start by isolating the first MSAU or hub in the rack by disconnecting its RI and RO cables. Next the analyst should re-analyze the removed and isolated hub area by verifying that the stations connected to it can properly perform basic ring insertion and communicate across the ring. If the MSAU or hubs in the MRP being used in the Token Ring network do have specific diagnostics, they should also be engaged. If the first MSAU or hub area tests positive, the next MSAU or hub area should be reconnected to the hub area just analyzed by re-attaching the RO cable from the first MSAU or hub to the second MSAU's or hub's RI port. Next, the analyst should re-analyze the new ring with two hubs as interconnected. This analysis and troubleshooting process should continue until a problem in the MRP is encountered in post analysis. The problem MRP hub or cabling area will be located, when an area that is reconnected causes a high amount of Soft Report Error MAC frames or a single Beacon MAC frame to be generated. This troubleshooting cycle involves an elimination cause-and-analysis process (see Figure 9.24).

```
┌─ SUMMARY VEIW ──────────────────────────────────────────────────
│ 613 0.019  Broadcast  IBM1E004FA   MAC Claim Token
│ 614 0.020  Broadcast  IBM1E004FA   MAC Claim Token
│ 615 0.019  Broadcast  IBM1E004FA   MAC Claim Token
│ 616 0.019  Broadcast  IBM1E004FA   MAC Claim Token
│ 617 0.019  Broadcast  IBM1E004FA   MAC Claim Token
│ 618 0.020  Broadcast  IBM1E004FA   MAC Claim Token
│ 619 0.009  Broadcast  IBM1E002D0   MAC Beacon
│ 620 0.020  Broadcast  IBM1E004FA   MAC Beacon
│ 621 0.019  Broadcast  IBM1E004FA   MAC Beacon
└──────────────────────────────── Frame 619 of 828 ──────────────
┌─ DETAIL ────────────────────────────────────────────────────────
│   MAC: ---- MAC Data ----
│   MAC:
│   MAC: MAC Command:
│   MAC: Source: Ring station, Destination: Ring Station
│   MAC: Subvector type: Beacon Type - Streaming signal, Claim Token
│   MAC: Subvector type: Physical Drop Number 00000000
│   MAC: Subvector type: Upstream Neighbor Address IBM1E004FA
│   MAC:
│
└──────────────────── Frame 619 of 828 ──────────────────────────
                      Use TAB to select windows
  1      2       3       4      5       6        7      8      9      10
 HELP   MARK                  MENUS  DISPLAY   PREV   NEXT          NEW
                                     OPTIONS   FRAME  FRAME        CAPTURE
```

FIGURE 9.24 *An analyzer data trace showing a MAC beacon event affecting the Token Ring network main ring path.*

9.4.2 Analyzing Token Ring Error Reporting and Decoding

When performing a network baseline, one of the key analysis issues is to troubleshoot the physical medium of the LAN. This is usually the fourth or fifth step in the baselining process, as mentioned earlier in this book under "Workload Characterization Measurements."

When involved in a Token Ring environment, certain Token Ring physical errors can be encountered, such as the 10 types of soft errors in a Soft Error Report MAC packet, or a physical Token Ring beaconing condition encountered when decoding a Beacon MAC frame. Troubleshooting these errors requires the use of a protocol analyzer. The protocol analyzer will have to be connected to the network and requires the capability of capturing a Token Ring error types and displaying the error for decode. There is a certain method for capturing and decoding Token Ring errors with an analyzer in such a condition. To actually decode the error types, an analyst needs to understand each error type and the occurrence of each error, and the vector for action if this error occurs.

The following is a description of key Token Ring soft errors along with key Token Ring beaconing errors. These error analysis descriptions should be used in direct association with the baseline process, which is introduced later in this chapter as related to baselining and performing workload characterization measurements in Token Ring.

9.4.2.1 Soft Reporting Error MAC Frame Analysis

When a ring station encounters a soft error, it increments its internal soft error counter and starts a Token Ring protocol timer (T_Soft_Error_Report). After two seconds, the timer expires and the ring station generates a Report Soft Error MAC frame. High occurrences of certain soft errors can cause ring performance and connectivity problems. Certain soft errors are considered more serious than others. When recording soft errors, an analyst must be aware of the level of seriousness and the possible failure cause for each type of soft error. Certain soft errors can point to an actual network component failure cause. The Report Soft Error MAC frame transmitted actually contains the soft error type, the reporting ring station's NIC address, and its respective NAUN's NIC address. When performing an analysis session for error recording, the proper way to decode a Report Soft Error MAC frame is to note the type of soft error and any associated addresses in the MAC frame, such as the reporting address and the NAUN. The soft error internal field in the MAC frame is a 12-byte field, and 10 of the bytes actually represent soft error types. The soft error types are divided into two main subtypes:

- Isolating error types

- Nonisolating error types

Isolating error types report ring station internal error counters as collected that can be isolated to final cause. *Nonisolating error types* are errors that cannot be easily decoded. The following is brief description of the main error types and the associated analysis methods:

- **Internal error.** This error type identifies that the sending ring station has encountered an internal error. If this error type is recorded frequently, the reporting ring station NIC may be encountering a close-to-failure error. It is recommended to remove and replace the NIC from the device sending station, and the ring should be re-analyzed.

- **Burst error.** This error type identifies that the sending ring station has encountered a signal transition error. This occurs frequently during ring insertion. If this error type is recorded frequently, the reporting ring station NIC may be encountering a bad lobe cable or bad port on the MSAU. It is recommended to remove and replace any questionable components from the device sending station connection, and next the ring should be re-analyzed.

- **Line error.** This error type identifies that the sending ring station has encountered a signal transition error. This occurs frequently during ring insertion. If this error type is recorded frequently, the reporting ring station NIC may have encountered an internal checksum hardware error, and the NIC may be at fault. It is recommended to remove and replace the NIC from the device sending station connection, and next the ring should be re-analyzed (see Figure 9.25).

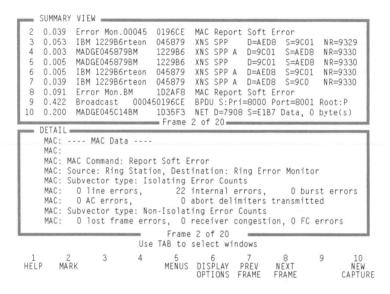

```
SUMMARY VIEW
 2  0.039  Error Mon.00045  0196CE  MAC Report Soft Error
 3  0.053  IBM 1229B6rteon  045879  XNS SPP    D=AED8  S=9C01  NR=9329
 4  0.003  MADGE045879BM    1229B6  XNS SPP A  D=9C01  S=AED8  NR=9330
 5  0.005  MADGE045879BM    1229B6  XNS SPP    D=9C01  S=AED8  NR=9330
 6  0.005  IBM 1229B6rteon  045879  XNS SPP A  D=AED8  S=9C01  NR=9330
 7  0.039  IBM 1229B6rteon  045879  XNS SPP A  D=AED8  S=9C0   NR=9330
 8  0.091  Error Mon.BM     1D2AF8  MAC Report Soft Error
 9  0.422  Broadcast     000450196CE  BPDU S:Pri=8000 Port=8001 Root:P
10  0.200  MADGE045C14BM    1D35F3  NET D=7908 S=E1B7 Data, 0 byte(s)
                            Frame 2 of 20
 DETAIL
    MAC: ---- MAC Data ----
    MAC:
    MAC: MAC Command: Report Soft Error
    MAC: Source: Ring Station, Destination: Ring Error Monitor
    MAC: Subvector type: Isolating Error Counts
    MAC:   0 line errors,     22 internal errors,     0 burst errors
    MAC:   0 AC errors,        0 abort delimiters transmitted
    MAC: Subvector type: Non-Isolating Error Counts
    MAC:   0 lost frame errors, 0 receiver congestion, 0 FC errors
                        Frame 2 of 20
                 Use TAB to select windows
    1       2      3      4      5       6      7      8     9     10
  HELP    MARK                       MENUS DISPLAY  PREV   NEXT        NEW
                                         OPTIONS FRAME  FRAME      CAPTURE
```

FIGURE 9.25 *An example of a MAC soft error captured from LAN protocol analysis sessions during a network baseline study.*

- **Abort delimiter transmitted error.** This error type identifies that the sending ring station has encountered a recoverable internal error that forced it to transmit an Abort Delimiter frame. If this error type is recorded frequently, the reporting ring station NIC may be encountering a close-to-failure error. It is recommended to remove and replace the NIC from the device sending station, and the ring should be re-analyzed.

- **AC error.** This error type identifies that the sending ring station has encountered a condition in which a frame received from the transmission cycle could not set the address recognized or frame copied bits. If this error is occurring, it is possible that the reporting station's NAUN has a failure. The station's NAUN can be removed, and the reporting station

NIC can also be removed to isolate the failure. It is recommended to remove and replace the NICs as required from the devices, and then the ring should be re-analyzed (see Figure 9.26).

```
7/14/97                LANalyzer Network Analyzer                    8:20
Press ALT-T to toggle between summary modes            Trace Decode
                          c:\xln\lanz\802.5
Frame: Number: 16           Length: 52 bytes
      Frame Status: Address not recognized, frame not copied
      Receive Channels: Errors
802.5: AC: Frame Priority=0  Monitor Count=0  Priority Reservation=0
FC: MAC Frame               Attention Code=0
Station: MADGE1060BF              - - - -> RingErrorMon
Major Vector Command:                      Report Error
Total Vector Length:                       34 bytes
Source class:                              Ring Station
Destination class:                         Ring Error Monitor
Subvector Length: 8 bytes
Isolating Error Counts:                    Line Error          0
                                           Internal Error:     0
                                           Burst Error:        0
                                           ARI/FCI Error:      0
                                           Abort Delimiter:    0
Subvector Length: 8 bytes
Non-isolating Error Counts:                Lost Frame:        32
                                           Receive Congestion: 0
                                           Frame Copied Error: 0
                                           Frequency Error:    0
                                           Token Error:        0
Subvector Length: 6 bytes
Physical drop Number:                      00000000
Subvector Length: 8 bytes
Upstream Neighbor's Address:               IBM2CB4E1
```

FIGURE 9.26 *An example of a MAC soft error captured from LAN protocol analysis sessions during a network baseline study.*

- **Lost frame error.** This error type identifies that the sending ring station has encountered an error that indicates that an originating ring station generated a frame onto the ring to a specific address and did not receive the frame back from the destination device. If this error type is recorded frequently, the reporting ring station NIC may not be copying frames properly, or the destination device may be the failure point. It is recommended to remove and replace the NICs involved, and then the ring should be re-analyzed.

- **Receiver congestion error.** This error type identifies that the sending ring station has encountered a situation in which it could not copy a frame addressed to its NIC address. This occurs because of lack of buffer space within the destination NIC and because of low processing resources in a destination station. There can also be low resource design issues on routers and bridges that cause this error. This error is also common when an application is flooding data too frequently to an under-resourced endpoint. If this error type is recorded frequently, the reporting station NIC may require a resource upgrade as to memory, NIC, or NIC driver. The ring design should be closely examined and re-analyzed.

- **Frame copied error.** This error type identifies that the sending ring station has encountered a situation in which it has copied a frame that may have the same address as its own address, like a duplicate address. If this error type is recorded frequently, the reporting ring station NIC may not be copying frames properly, or a duplicate address is attempting ring insertion and is failing. The ring should be analyzed for any device attempting ring insertion with a possible duplicate address assigned. It is recommended to remove duplicate assignments and to replace any suspect NICs involved, and then the ring should be re-analyzed.

- **Frequency error.** This error type identifies that the sending ring station has encountered an attempt to process a frame that does not contain the proper ring clock frequency. It may indicate either a bad active monitor or ring electrical problems. If this error type is recorded frequently, the AM should be replaced and the ring should be re-analyzed. If the issue continues, the ring electrical grounding for the hub racks should checked, along with complete MRP being analyzed.

- **Token error.** This error type identifies that the sending ring station has encountered a token error. This error is generated by the active monitor in the event of other ring issues. Usually, the Active Monitor initiates ring recovery and issues a new token. This error type is common when other ring stations detect and generate burst and line errors onto the ring. Usually, token errors are not an issue. If this problem is continuous in generation, it is recommended to remove and replace the AM NIC from the device sending station connection, and next the ring should be re-analyzed (see Figure 9.27).

9.4.2.2 Technical Notes on Hard Beacon MAC Frame Analysis
Beacon-based MAC errors are the more critical type of errors and are considered hard. When a hard error occurs, the Beacon MAC frame usually indicates the point of fault domain and the devices involved. On occurrence of a beacon hard error, a Token Ring network takes on the form of engaging the beaconing repeat process, as noted earlier. It is important to bypass the fault area for the ring to operate. The bypass may occur dynamically because of the beaconing cycle built in to the architecture.

```
6/15/96            LANalyzer Network Analyzer                    8:21
Press ALT-T to toggle between summary modes         Trace Decode
                          c:\xln\lanz\802.5
Frame: Number: 64            Length:52 bytes
     Frame Status: Address not recognized, frame not copied
     Receive Channels: Errors
802.5: AC: Frame Priority=0  Monitor Count=1  Priority Reservation=3
FC: MAC Frame                Attention Code=0
Station: MADGE14674F              - - - - -> RingErrorMon
Major Vector Command:                     Report Error
Total Vector Length:                      34 bytes
Source class:                             Ring Station
Destination class:                        Ring Error Monitor
Subvector Length: 8 bytes
Isolating Error Counts:                   Line Error         0
                                          Internal Error:    0
                                          Burst Error:       0
                                          ARI/FCI Error:     0
                                          Abort Delimiter:   0
Subvector Length: 8 bytes
Non-isolating Error Counts:               Lost Frame:        0
                                          Receive Congestion: 81
                                          Frame Copied Error: 0
                                          Frequency Error:   0
                                          Token Error:       0
Subvector Length: 6 bytes
Physical drop Number:                     00000000
Subvector Length: 8 bytes
Upstream Neighbor's Address:              IBMOF223
```

FIGURE 9.27 *An example of a MAC soft error captured from LAN protocol analysis sessions during a network baseline study.*

Most intelligent Token Ring hubs isolate the beaconing devices and wrap the ports involved. Most protocol analysis tools along with ring monitoring tools enable an analyst to troubleshoot and quickly identify any hard beacon errors causing a ring to experience failure-based issues. The analyst should just record the beaconing device and the NAUN address and assign a fault domain. The devices can be removed and the ring can be re-analyzed. Troubleshooting of the MRP may also apply when the beacon process occurs on a network.

9.5 Network Baselining in a Token Ring Environment

Because the Token Ring network is extremely fault-redundant in its own inherent operation, various techniques can be used to immediately isolate a Token Ring physical problem. This is an important fact, because of the general methodology of workload characterization network baseline measurement cycles.

The Token Ring inherent fault-redundant operation enables an analyst to move quickly with a protocol analyzer and capture certain types of packet traffic dataflow. The analyst can then examine the dataflow in such a way as to isolate whether the problem is in the physical Token Ring network or in the upper-layer protocol areas.

In all LANs, it is important that the LAN topology deployed be stable and operate with a strong foundation for upper-layer protocol dataflow to operate properly. This is critical for applications being used on the network along with the operating systems controlling the applications.

When starting a network baseline in a Token Ring environment, the following general processes can be used. This discussion also presents some specific processes that directly relate to some of the Token Ring troubleshooting processes already discussed.

The following sections discuss five steps that outline the methodology for baselining a Token Ring environment.

9.5.1 Step 1: Token Ring Workload Characterization Baselining Methodology

An analyst should immediately deploy a network protocol analyzer to perform a utilization characterization measurement process against a shared Token Ring network area. In this case, as long as it is a shared Token Ring and not a switched Token Ring environment, the ring will show an average and peak utilization that can be quickly measured and noted for general network baseline statistics. The procedures discussed earlier in this book under "Workload Characterization Measurements" fully apply.

In the Token Ring environment, a key factor to take into account is that the topology is deterministic. Because it is not contention-based, it can sustain higher peak utilization for a longer duration before upper-layer protocols time out. Because of this fact, an analyst should not just determine that peak utilizations are not a problem. The point here is that peak saturation levels in the area of five to six seconds could possibly be sustained at saturation levels of 95% and above without upper-layer protocols timing out. This is a condition somewhat determined based on the operating systems and applications deployed.

In most cases, an analyst should always attempt to keep peak utilization on a Token Ring network, when considering segmentation and redesign, in the area of 65% to 75%, maximum. For the record, however, higher peak saturation levels can be sustained on a deterministic medium.

One fact is that the actual speed of access to the medium for each device that has to gain access to the token will be slowed down by higher utilization levels. So with that said, it proves beneficial to just design Token Ring so that it can sustain higher application loading levels with smaller segments if they are going to be implemented in a shared design versus a switched design.

9.5.2 Step 2: Token Ring Workload Characterization Baselining Methodology

When performing network statistical node-by-node utilization, it is always important to monitor on a Token Ring environment what the actual utilization levels are on a device-by-device basis. This is because a shared medium is being monitored. This would not apply to a switched link. In this case, the importance here is that on a shared medium, if there is one device on a Token Ring absorbing an extremely high level, it is possible that it could negatively affect the deterministic token-passing cycle and cause a physical problem or an upper-layer problem. The analyst will be able to quickly identify the device further by performing the third typical workload characterization measurement of protocol percentage breakout.

In a switched Token Ring environment, it is also important to understand that by roving a Token Ring switch and measuring each one of the dedicated Token Ring switched links, it is possible to understand whether proper distribution is applied against the switch. In certain cases, it is possible that a small Token Ring network connected to a switch may have a higher level of traffic on it and may still require further segmentation across another additional switched port. Keep in mind that Token Ring switched ports are not just used for connecting one particular device, but are at times used for segmenting rings; and in some cases, the rings may need to be partitioned further. Therefore, it is important to always perform a node-by-node utilization comparison against a Token Ring switched pattern when using a protocol analysis system or a management system.

9.5.3 Step 3: Token Ring Workload Characterization Baselining Methodology

Protocol percentage measurements are very important in Token Ring. If the 802.5 percentage exceeds 4% to 5%, it is very possible that the Token Ring medium is having a recovery problem. This can be seen very early in a Token Ring monitoring session from a management system or a protocol analyzer. An analyst should be able to understand that the 802.5 percentage is going to be primarily comprised of Token Ring MAC-based packets that are communicating. In a normal healthy Token Ring network, a Token Ring MAC trace should just show neighbor notification every seven seconds. Even in the busiest Token Ring environment, this normally would account for only 2% to 3% of maximum traffic.

If the 802.5 protocols are seen in a protocol measurement screen of a management system or protocol analyzer at percentages of 8% to 10% or higher, this is an immediate flag that there are problems in the physical Token Ring level. Further isolation with the next step needs to be performed for error isolation.

9.5.4 Step 4: Token Ring Workload Characterization Baselining Methodology

Error isolation and ring purge review are the next key areas that require analysis. In the physical Token Ring analysis area, the analyst has to closely examine the Token Ring physical operation after performing the first three steps by applying a capture MAC filter with a protocol analyzer in a capture system of the analyzer or a management system. This just enables the analyzer management system to perform the role of remote error monitoring, capturing Report Soft Error packets along with Token Ring Purge packets as active. Another parameter may need to be adjusted on certain analyzers to capture Ring Purge packets. The key factor is to first monitor the ring purge count on the ring. If the ring purge count exceeds 200 to 300 ring purges per hour, an immediate identification and further investigation of the physical MAC traffic at a detailed level is required. This means that the ring is possibly having a problem on physical ring recoveries that are affecting upper-layer protocol fluency.

The next level is to investigate any Token Ring Report Soft Error packets. As noted earlier, many different Report Soft Error packets may be encountered; however, the 10 specific types that occur for various reasons are important for analysis. The ones that occur at low levels during normal ring operations are Token Ring, line, burst, and token errors. Other errors, such as internal errors and abort errors, are serious and may be an indication that a Token Ring NIC is about to fail completely and move into a finite state machine vector as a beacon MAC vector and cause the complete ring to go down. In this case, an analyst should immediately examine this area.

The way to perform a MAC capture filter is to start the analyzer on a MAC capture filter and to run the analyzer for at least 10 to 15 minutes, stop the capture, and save the trace. The analyst should then open up the trace and examine all the packets. If the physical layer is clean of soft errors and beacon errors, there should be a simple neighbor notification sequence occurring every seven seconds, and the ring poll time should occur for no more than 2.5 seconds. This is a normal cycle. If a high number of Report Soft Error packets area seen along with a high number of ring purges, this indicates nonfluency in the Token Ring physical area.

If a high number of ring management frames such as Request Ring Station State or Address are also seen, this indicates management systems that are active and may be disrupting traffic. In today's environment, new intelligent hubs' management systems introduce some management frames from the older Token Ring structure processes that may at times absorb traffic levels that may be unnecessary if a client is also using coexisting SNMP RMON-based systems.

Either way, when focusing on the physical layer, an analyst should trouble-shoot any Report Soft Error packets that are considered serious and take action as described earlier in this chapter.

If a beaconing condition is found, an analyst should immediately locate the beaconing device and its nearest active upstream neighbor and remove these devices. The medium should then be immediately re-analyzed.

All physical soft error analysis steps apply as noted earlier in this chapter for isolation and cause analysis.

If the physical layer is found to be a problem, the issue should be troubleshot and the network should be re-analyzed starting from step 1 of the workload measurement process, to ensure a clean physical Token Ring that shows clear neighbor notification and minor ring insertion events are encountered.

The *Token Ring rotation time* (TRT) timing measurement is also a good indica-tion of how fast Token Ring frames are being processed. The definition of TRT is the amount of time it takes for a single token to circle the ring. The normal TRT levels should be between 5 and 150 microseconds. TRT is an excellent measurement statistic to use if available on an analyzer when performing physical analysis for troubleshooting the general health of a Token Ring network.

9.5.5 Step 5: Token Ring Workload Characterization Baselining Methodology

In this step, the analyst should closely monitor the ring for general Token Ring frame MAC communication processes. This involves basically using the same MAC data trace that was taken in step 4 and further examining the interaction of the Token Ring physical MAC communication. Neighbor notification is all that should normally be seen in a clean Token Ring operation. There will be ring insertion processes when new devices insert on the ring, and possibly a brief set of frames showing a line and burst error sequence along with small occurrences of token errors from the ring active monitor. Other than that, a clean physical Token Ring should just show neighbor notification and ring insertion cycles, and possibly token claim events when new active monitors are assigned. This should not be an ongoing occurrence.

After this step is completed and everything is found to be operating in a solid Token Ring physical state, the next layer to move on to is upper-layer protocol analysis. In this case, if the steps noted earlier were followed properly, this would conclude the methodology for analyzing a physical Token Ring architecture. It should be mentioned that other innovative steps can also be deployed, such as analyzing Token Ring rotation time. Token Ring rotation time should be no more than 125 microseconds and is typically seen in most networks today between 5 and 150 microseconds, maximum.

9.6 Closing Statement on Baselining Token Ring Environments

The key methodology in analyzing and baselining Token Ring environments is really based on an analyst's understanding the inherent operation of the Token Ring architecture. That is why so much time has been spent in this chapter explaining the Token Ring architecture. If an analyst understands how a Token Ring network works, a protocol analyzer will be a valuable way to quickly monitor the physical medium system, because Token Ring network operations clearly generate the required information for analysis when failures occur. In other words, the Token Ring Soft Error packets, the Token Ring general MAC communication, and other Token Ring packets such as the Token Ring Purge packet actually indicate how the Token Ring is operating.

If an analyst understands the inherent internal operations of Token Ring architecture, he can quickly determine whether the Token Ring physical layer is a problem.

The analyst can determine whether the topology needs to be addressed in a physical isolation cause area problem or whether a ring partitioning or resegmentation design is required.

An analyst can feel comfortable after analyzing the physical Token Ring layer through step 5. It is important to next move through the baselining process with the standard upper-layer protocol procedures, as noted earlier in this book. These procedures include analysis and baseline steps such as analyzing the size of the packets, effective throughput, response-time analysis, and analyzing the phases of network communication. The next step also includes performing trace analysis at a deep data-decoded level that allows for data extraction of upper-layer problems.

Note that if a Token Ring network is operating in a physically stable manner, any problems being exhibited on the ring can clearly be associated as problems related to upper-layer occurrences on the ring, such as design, layout of application, or NOS operation.

Case Study 12: Token Ring Analysis Problem

The Token Ring architecture is based on an extremely fault-redundant topology design. Fault redundancy is built in to the wiring scheme, inside the NIC design, along with the Token Ring frame communication processes that are also present to allow for Token Ring physical NIC card–to–NIC card end-to-end communication. The complete architecture is considered an intelligent topology as compared to other topologies such as standard Ethernet, in which no inherent physical frame management protocols are engaged, such as *Simple Network Management Protocol* (SNMP) or RMON technologies.

One of the most interesting Token Ring cases encountered by the LAN Scope analysis team involved a Token Ring internetwork that was troubleshot by our team several years ago. Through the general troubleshooting process as well as consistent site visits for consecutive network baselining, the Token Ring internetwork, which had a significant number of performance problems, is now considered stable, reliable, is and performing at a high level.

The client was a large medical practitioners' office in Washington, D.C. The facility location included different medical offices as well as administrative support offices for the practice. The Token Ring internetwork was based on a three-floor design. Each ring had a specific Token Ring network assigned to each area. The first-floor ring, for instance, was based on the main area where the medical practitioners operated. The second-floor ring was dedicated to general administration, including finance, accounting, and other varying functions. The third-floor ring was dedicated to the executive offices and other general support areas for the medical practitioner's operation.

The original Token Ring configuration for the facility was implemented in 1989. At that time, Token Ring was still considered fairly new in terms of enterprise internetwork design. In fact, this was one of the first 16Mbps architectures to be implemented in the Washington, D.C. area. Not only were the rings based on a 16Mbps architecture design, but they also included a partial implementation of *Early Token Release* (ETR). Multiple speed ratings of Token Ring are currently implemented against the industry architecture. At the time of this particular implementation in 1989, there were only two speeds available in Token Ring: 4Mbps and 16Mbps. The ETR design is an additional feature where the Token Ring NICs allow for the token to be released earlier after a data transmission, thus speeding up the overall performance of the physical topology for the Token Ring network.

The original configuration in this facility was based on an approximate 90-user design, with 30 users per ring. In 1996, the site began to experience extensive performance problems. When our analysis team was contacted regarding this issue, we immediately deployed our team to baseline the network and troubleshoot any performance problems to cause.

When we arrived at the site, we conducted an entrance briefing with the MIS team members at the site to review the internetwork design. The first thing we noticed was that the user counts had increased to a level where each ring now handled approximately 80 to 120 users. The rings were separated by a somewhat unique bridging/routing process called *internal file server routing*. Specifically, some of the file servers were used as bridges between the specific rings. The file servers were also being used for general access for logon services, file and print services, and certain application access processes. Upon reviewing the configuration, we also noticed that the site had a mixed set of Token Ring hub types, including the main IBM 8228 design as well as a third-vendor product based on active port operation and other design specifications. It was also noted that the site was using varied types of cabling schemes throughout the facility. This was a result of changes over an extended period of time, during which various types of cabling were installed on an "as-needed" basis to allow additional nodes to be connected to the main ring.

One of the primary complaints that was discussed during the entrance briefing was that users were experiencing sluggish performance and frequent disconnects when using the network. The problem was noted as intermittent, but consistent throughout most application usage at the site.

Based on information gathered during the site briefing, the LAN Scope analysis team immediately developed a project plan to use a rapid baseline process to review each one of the three rings. The initial project plan also called for a thorough review of the performance of the users' workstation applications and the workstations themselves, based on a brief application-characterization exercise from the user area.

On the second-floor ring, we noted that an area was implemented where some of the site file servers were placed on the second-floor ring for general access, and that two additional file servers were engaged to separate floors one and two, and three via internal server-based routing.

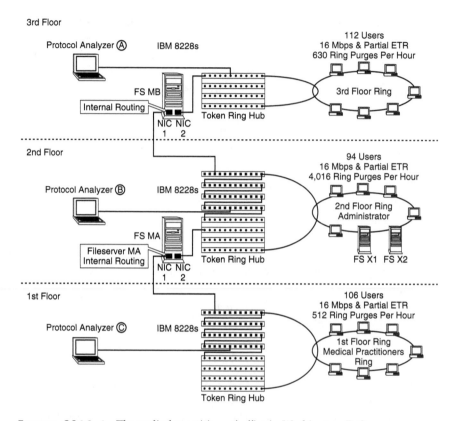

FIGURE CS12.1 *The medical practitioners' office in Washington, D.C.*

The initial baseline process was engaged against all three rings. Three specific network protocol analyzers were used in parallel on all three rings. Each ring was first investigated for overall utilization notations for average, peak, and historical bandwidth. Node-by-node bandwidth was next investigated, and then the protocols were measured for percentage distributions on each ring. The physical errors were next monitored based on the Token Ring *Soft Error Report* (SRE) MAC category, along with a review for possible physical beaconing conditions related to the Token Ring architecture. The Token Ring physical *Medium Access Control* (MAC) layer frame communication was next investigated using a capture MAC filter on each ring. This chapter presented a detailed discussion of the Token Ring architecture processes.

Based on these initial tests, the following information was found while baselining the environment. Floors one and three showed extremely high ring insertion rates of expected user counts of 100+ users. Many of the user node-by-node utilization measurements showed fluctuating usage of the shared Token Ring bandwidth. The average utilization on the first floor was noted at 38%; however, the peak percentage was noted at the 89% level for a duration of 4.2 seconds. It was noted that the second floor showed an extremely high utilization level also at 96% for a 9.1 second interval. The third-floor ring showed an average utilization of 17%, but with a peak percentage of 94% for a 6.4 second interval. These notations were extremely critical, taking into account the peak saturation levels and the long time durations noted. These high saturation levels were an immediate warning flag that connection-based protocols could possibly time out and negatively affect application fluency upon application access from any user on the first or third floor.

An interesting finding from the workload characterization baseline process was that all three rings showed a fluctuating MAC percentage protocol level of 3% to 9.8% on the protocol layer percentage review. Further investigation yielded that the physical SRE MAC error rate was also abnormal, showing MAC SRE packets generating excessively on the second-floor ring at 8%, and at levels on the first and third ring ranging from 2% to 3%.

Through investigation of the MAC layer on all three floors, the following was noted. Floor one showed an extremely high number of line, burst, and receiver congestion error rates throughout the ring. Ring three showed the same type of condition. The receiver congestion rates on both floors one and three were extremely high as associated with the file server NIC cards that were connecting floors one and three. Specifically, most of the congestion appeared to be on traffic passing in and out of the ring for these two user rings.

When examining the second-floor ring, the Medium Access Control soft error packet analysis along with the general MAC layer review showed an extremely high line and burst error rate, also coinciding with high receiver congestion rates on the internal routing server channels acting as bridges between floors two to one and two to three. It was also noted that there was an extremely high internal error rate generating from three specific stations on the ring.

Based on the workload characterization baseline measurements and the error analysis and MAC percentage findings, the LAN Scope analysis immediately focused our attention on examining the physical layer.

Through a more discrete analysis, we found on the second-floor ring that even the general process of neighbor notification, which should occur in a seven-second interval, was occurring at a three to four second interval at an abnormal rate. The ring purge rate was noted at over 4,000 ring purges per hour. Such an excessive rate usually indicates a ring that will not operate or handle stabilization for normal connectivity or upper-layer application flow. The ring purge rates on rings one and three were also high, at approximately 500 to 600 ring purges per hour.

Through further analysis, we observed that with the neighbor notification rates, even when falling within the normal seven-second interval range, the timing intermittently appeared to fluctuate between 6.9 and 7.1 seconds. This immediately was identified as a possible mismatch related to ETR. It is typically best to have all cards either configured with ETR on, or configured with ETR off. When there is a high percentage of cards split between the two settings, timing mismatches can occur on the physical layer.

Based on these findings, we immediately focused on a way to segment the rings by a percentage level that would allow for a lower utilization level capacity at the peak level, and thus allow for a more stable situation for further analysis.

The internal errors that were associated with the three devices on the second floor ring were identified as NICs that needed to be replaced, with the ring then being re-analyzed.

After reviewing our Level 1 findings from our troubleshooting process after approximately two days into the network baselining cycle, the LAN Scope analysis team presented the following short-term recommendations:

- We recommended that the customer have all rings split by a 50% ratio. The second-floor ring, which had approximately five servers connected to the ring, was targeted for an additional ring, noted as a server backbone ring. This would introduce a new site-wide Token Ring layout configuration with a total of seven rings.

- We recommended an immediate migration change for the three NICs generating an internal error. This migration was critical, because it was possible that these cards were causing intermittent beaconing conditions or other failures in the Token Ring area of the second floor. This was a major concern, because one of the NICs was present on a main application server.

Based on our immediate recommendations, the customer moved forward with the following design configuration. A Token Ring internetwork switch was redesigned and brought into the facility; this allowed for separation of the three rings via a Token Ring switched uplink design. All the three main rings were split by a 50% ratio. Each floor in the facility was split into a two-ring configuration. An uplink via Category 5 channeling design was brought to the second floor. A rack-mounted Token Ring switch was configured, and each one of the rings was connected via a proper configuration to the Token Ring switched ports.

On the second floor, the two rings were also brought directly into the switch. A server ring was created off another port for two of the file servers that were used minimally. Some of the site intelligent hubs that were based on standard IBM technology were used for staging the configurations. By reviewing the site layout and documentation, we noted that some of the older non-IBM-type hubs in the facility that were not compliant with the IBM architecture were found to be injecting DC Phantom current abnormally on the main ring path. They were removed from the design.

The critical main file servers at the facility, which were previously routing, were redesigned to a one-card configuration operation and were brought directly into the switch. As a result, these rings had no contention for the token and effectively had a *Dedicated Token Ring* (DTR) loop off the switch.

The planned design appeared to be positive. The network did initially operate in a stable fashion in a cutover testing session that was engaged prior to the next business week.

The LAN Scope analysis team arrived early on the Monday of the second week of the study, and reviewed the configuration prior to cutover for business that particular day. The ring appeared to show stabilization on all rings at the general physical characterization levels and showed very low error rates across the ring. There were no soft error report packets. All file servers were checked for general operation and configuration. All the file servers, with the exception of file server Main2A, were operational.

We began troubleshooting the file server Main2A with a protocol analyzer connected to the proper switched port. We installed another MSAU and examined the traffic between the server as connected to the Token Ring switched port. It appeared as though the server in question was experiencing problems upon the ring insertion process. We contacted the vendor and were informed that the Token Ring card had to be set for a specific speed and that the port on the Token Ring switch should not be set for Auto Speed Detect. Based on this configuration change and the hard-coding of 16Mbps, the server immediately began to function properly on the ring. We were therefore able to certify the ring for operation.

The users began to access the new Token Ring infrastructure at approximately 10 a.m. on the second business week. All application levels appeared to be operating at a higher performance level. The users stated that the environment appeared to be more rapid in terms of logon response and general application access. Overall, the environment appeared to be extremely stable.

We redeployed our protocol analyzers across all three rings. It was noted immediately that the ring purge rate levels had significantly decreased. The first-floor and third-floor rings showed ring purge levels no higher than 10 ring purges per hour. The second floor ring showed a rate of 50 ring purges per hour, which is minor.

After seeing stabilization, we then proceeded with our normal baseline process. The utilization levels on Ring 1A showed an average utilization of 6% with a peak of 38%. Ring 1B showed an average utilization of 18% with a peak utilization of 52%. On the second-floor rings, 2A and 2B, comparable uses were noted, with Ring 2A averaging 14% utilization and peaking at 39%, and Ring 2B averaging 17% utilization and peaking at 42%. The small server backbone ring for the two minor file servers showed an average utilization of 9% with a peak of 22%. Rings 3A and 3B also showed normal utilization levels, with 3A showing an average utilization of 11% and a peak level of 31%, and Ring 3B showing an average utilization of 19% and a peak level of 61%.

All the other main file servers were monitored for interpacket response time by monitoring their response to requests from the other rings being monitored. There appeared to be no problems present in this area, so these rings were not closely baselined at that point. With all utilization levels appearing to be in check, we noted that protocol percentages at the MAC level were well below 1% on all the site's seven rings.

Our next step was to examine the Token Ring physical error rate on all rings across the facility. All the rings appeared to be stable, with the exception of an intermittent line and burst error rate that ranged between 2% to 3% on all seven rings.

After a further review of the facility cabling, we immediately identified that most of the cabling in the facility was based on IBM cabling Type 1, but there had been some introduction of UTP wiring schemes with media filters that appeared to be noncompliant. Upon further review, we concluded that some of the cabling needed verification.

We continued our testing and noted that the Token Ring frame communication appeared to be extremely stable. We also ran standard application testing from certain rings from specific user areas. On floor one, we tested users accessing the general medical database application for the practitioner operation. The application appeared to launch within a 10-second period, which was noted by the user to be extremely rapid; before LAN Scope's implementations, the same type of launch took almost two minutes. This was just a general note by the user; however, our post-protocol analysis review did show a definite 12-second interval for the launch sequence. Upon accessing the application operating the database, all the general cumulative bytes, relative time sequences, and utilization effects appeared to be normal. We also noted this same positive condition on all other applications that were tested, such as word processing and accounting-based applications on other floors. Overall, we noted a successful outcome for this phase of the baseline process.

By the following business evening, the practitioner MIS team had a cabling audit performed at the facility and found that approximately 13 cables were out of specification. These cables were immediately replaced.

On our final day at the site, we closely reviewed all the rings again for physical testing and found that the line and burst error rate was nonexistent, and at a very low level and only present upon ring insertions.

Overall, this facility was stabilized and brought to a much higher performance level. It is still based on a Token Ring topology design. New protocols have been introduced into the facility based on new operating system deployment and new application deployment. As the site continues to grow, it may become necessary to implement a center backbone network based on a higher-speed platform for capacity channel design. Any future migration changes will be based on application deployment and not on an urgent requirement to stabilize the facility. In other words, now that the facility is operating in a reliable fashion, the only migrations that may be required will be a result of application growth.

We are continuing to work with the facility as new applications are introduced, to measure the impact of each application and the network's capability to accept the application. If an eventual migration is required for higher capacity, other directions may have to be considered, such as Fast Ethernet or other design architecture modifications such as an ATM backbone. Either way, the client had a requirement to stabilize the facility still using the Token Ring fault-redundant features. These requirements were met through the network baselining exercises. We considered this a successful project, in which the network baseline process was used to troubleshoot, stabilize, and increase the performance in the facility.

CHAPTER 10

Fiber Data Distributed Interface

The *Fiber Data Distributed Interface* (FDDI) network is a fault-redundant, point-to-point, high-speed LAN topology design. The FDDI network is based on a 100Mbps data-rate standard, although higher data rates can be achieved and are discussed later in this chapter. The design of a FDDI network is physically based on an infrastructure design that utilizes two physical rings. One ring is utilized as a primary ring; the second ring is utilized as a backup ring connection electrical link.

The nodes or stations that interconnect to a FDDI network can connect to either the primary or the backup ring at the same time, or just to the primary ring. The FDDI specification allows for approximately 500 stations to be interconnected to the FDDI network. The cabling distance of a FDDI network in a standard configuration should be no more than 200 kilometers. The maximum distance between two respective FDDI nodes on a FDDI ring can be no more than two kilometers. The FDDI internetworking protocol model design is based on a layering scheme that mainly relates to the *Open System Interconnection* (OSI) model at the physical and data link layer. Four layers operate as compared to the two layers of the OSI model.

The four layers are as follows:

- FDDI Physical Independent layer (PHY)

- FDDI Physical Media Dependent layer (PMD)

- FDDI Medium Access Control layer (MAC)

- FDDI Station Management layer (SMT)

NETWORK PERFORMANCE BASELINING

524

Three companies developed FDDI's overall architecture: Sperry, Burroughs, and Advanced Micro Devices. These three companies formed a consortium to introduce the technology that was developed between 1983 and 1998 when the standard was approved. The *American National Standards Institute* (ANSI) formally certified FDDI after review by its X3T9.5 Committee.

10.1 FDDI Network Architecture and Topology Specifications

The FDDI topology is a LAN design based on a dual-ring fault-redundant approach. FDDI has a star layout design with a point-to-point network configuration, in which each device connected to the network is attached to the main FDDI ring in a counter-attached dual-ring topology design. The dual ring that interconnects to each one of the specific devices on the FDDI is called the *trunk ring*. The primary and the secondary ring (the dual-ring technology) work together in a counter-rotating mode. The counter-rotating rings enable a support analyst to easily reconfigure a FDDI ring when a problem occurs.

FDDI actually works through an electrical ring design, but is laid out as a logical star. This is somewhat similar to the Token Ring LAN configuration. The following section further describes the architecture details.

10.1.1 FDDI Architecture-Specific Technical Notes

The FDDI ring cables that interconnect FDDI devices actually move through an infrastructure, such as a building, in a star topology design. The main FDDI network is still an electrical ring. A FDDI network is mainly used as a backbone technology. Because of its use as such, FDDI rings are usually designed and implemented within one main computer room. FDDI has all the technology necessary to be fully configured as a local area network (LAN). Therefore, a FDDI network in a large corporate infrastructure can serve as a backbone technology and can also provide direct LAN connections to the desktop. Most companies have thus far limited their implementation of FDDI to its backbone role because of the physical wiring restrictions and costs. Even so, they can still interconnect other LAN topologies with a FDDI ring via modules in internetworking technology–based hubs. Most of the backbone technology for FDDI networks is used to interconnect to main file servers or key hosts within main computer rooms. Quite often, the main FDDI backbone ring interconnects to other LAN technologies so that users can access a FDDI host via other LAN technology end routes, such as Ethernet.

An end user might connect to an Ethernet LAN or a Token Ring LAN (in most cases), for example, and then route, switch, or bridge over to a FDDI backbone within a main computer room. This is a common implementation of the FDDI network because of the high-cost structures and implementation issues involved with using the FDDI topology for direct end-user connectivity.

One of the key characteristics of the FDDI architecture is that certain nodes that interconnect to the FDDI network can change the ring length of the FDDI network in terms of its complete operational configuration.

As stated previously, one of the main rings on a FDDI network is considered a primary ring and usually handles all data transfer. The secondary ring is mainly used for fault redundancy and normally handles only data-intensive transfers during high-speed transfer cycles.

All the nodes interconnected to the FDDI network are active nodes. A device is a node if it has at least one connection to either the primary or the secondary ring on the FDDI network. For a device to be an active node, it should have a FDDI MAC agent on the FDDI NIC. Further discussion of the FDDI MAC agent appears later in this chapter. If the MAC agent is processing and active, a device is considered an active node on a FDDI network.

Two types of nodes are considered active for configuration and connection to a FDDI ring structure: *single attachment stations* (SAS), and *dual attachment stations* (DAS). A SAS connects to one ring, and a DAS connects to both the primary and the secondary ring.

The FDDI architecture allows other devices to interconnect with FDDI network in extension and fault-redundancy configurations. An optical bypass device for a FDDI network is one common implementation of such. This type of device maintains an emergency connection in the event of a node fault. Certain devices can inherently have an optical bypass design connected within their node in case certain processes fail. In such a case, the FDDI ring can continue to operate through the node connection, even if the device fails.

When multiple devices have to connect to the FDDI internetwork, a FDDI concentrator is used. The FDDI concentrator can connect to the dual-ring configuration or to a single-ring configuration. A *single attached concentrator* (SAC) connects to the single ring; a *dual attached concentrator* (DAC) connects to the dual-ring architecture.

Four main interconnection schemes apply to FDDI port configurations on a FDDI device or design. Port A is considered a ring port for interconnection to the backup ring. If a SAC or a DAS connects directly to the backup ring, it connects through Port A. If a device, such as a SAS or a DAS, is going to connect to a primary ring, it uses Port B. If a device, such as a concentrator, is going to connect to the ring on the primary ring, it uses Port B. In most cases, DASs and DACs connect to both rings, which is the most common configuration; and in such cases, Ports A and B are both used. The dual-redundancy technology offers the advantage of the counter-rotating fault-redundancy inherent in the architecture.

Most DAC and SAC concentrators have a Port M. This is the connection port on a concentrator for an end-node device to actually connect to the FDDI topology (as noted before, through a concentrator link). If a device is going to a concentrator, the device will have a Port S, which connects to Port M on the concentrator.

Specifically, the normal link process for an endpoint device to interconnect to a FDDI ring is for the device's Port S connector to link and interconnect to Port M on a SAC or DAC concentrator. Then the concentrator will have interconnection ports, such as Ports A and B, which provide the final connection directly to the main FDDI ring (see Figure 10.1).

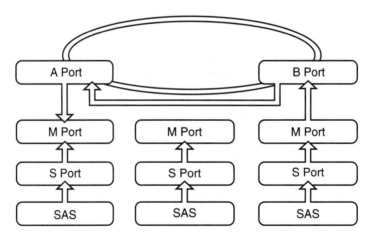

FIGURE 10.1 *Applying the primary ring FDDI concentrator connections to the layout scheme.*

All active SAS and DAS devices have a MAC agent operating. The FDDI MAC agent enables interconnection processes, address verification, fault-redundancy verification, and interconnection and cross-communication operations with *Station Management layer* (SMT) agents inherent in a FDDI device. (More details on this subject appear later in this chapter.) Note that connecting a specific single device to just one of the FDDI ring paths is normally not recommended. An SAS should connect through a concentrator link, for example. This type of interconnection scheme can be used, but might cause faults and failures on the FDDI ring.

You should actually use DAS or DAC devices to connect to both rings. When this setup is used, multiple end ports interconnect to the main ring, ensuring a clean A and B connection to both the primary and the backup secondary ring (see Figure 10.2).

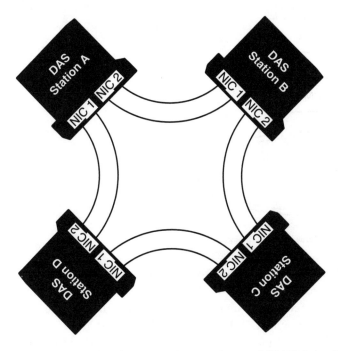

FIGURE 10.2 *Applying a DAS connection to a full FDDI ring layout.*

Another advantage of DAS-based stations is that they usually have both a MAC agent active as well as a SMT layer operation active, which allows for a full set of physical management operations to be active (as is inherent in the FDDI design). This is not to say that some SAS-based designs will not also have an active SMT layer that can also be an active component of the SAS device architecture (see Figure 10.3).

The DAC type concentrators usually fully comply with all the FDDI specifications and allow for the cleanest connection to the FDDI ring. Also, dual attachment stations inherently enable you to configure and lay out a fault-redundant architecture within a specific site. DACs normally support a fully physical media-dependent operation that allows for a full A and B port interconnection and uses both *media interface connections* (MIC) and the standard FDDI (ST) and (SC) connectors for physical media fiber links.

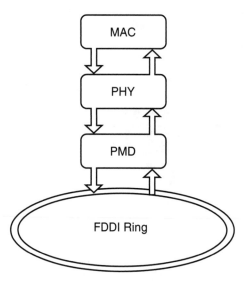

FIGURE 10.3 *An internal SAS device.*

SACs are usually less intelligent than DACs, but will allow for the interconnection of a device to the ring. A SAC is generally implemented on configurations when budget resources are limited. As stated earlier, the preferred approach when designing a FDDI LAN is to use DACs that allow for a fully redundant A and B port connection to the main FDDI ring. The DACs then can provide multiple access end ports for SASs and DASs to interconnect to the concentrator, and can then link directly into the main FDDI ring.

10.1.2 Final Summary Technical Notes on FDDI Architecture Specifications

The following items are some of the key FDDI architecture technical specifications:

- **FDDI data rate.** 100Mbps.

- **Signal encoding process.** NRZI with 4B/5B block coding.

- **FDDI media type interconnection scheme**. Fiber MMF and SMF. Shielded twisted-pair/data grade unshielded twisted-pair.

- **Clocking scheme.** Distributed and cross-linked transmit and receive clocks operating in direct parallel.

- **Maximum frame size.** 4500 bytes or 9000 symbols.

- **Frame format.** MAC frame format: Preamble, Starting Delimiter, Frame Control, Destination Address, Source Address, Information field, Frame Check Sequence, Ending Delimiter, Frame Status field.

- **Priority levels for operation as assigned with access.** Eight levels of asynchronous deterministic operation, which is considered standard, along with synchronous if required.

- **Priority handling.** Station priority can be considered active.

- **Access protocol.** *Timed Token Rotation Time* (TTRT) protocol and token passing methodology.

- **Network transmission.** The token is captured by extracting it from the ring and stripping it from the network into the station. The station transmits data frames as required, and then releases the token. A token release is normally provided immediately after data transmission is completed or after timer THT expires.

- **Maximum length of standard configurations.** 200 kilometers. In certain cases, a unique configuration may apply in accordance with vendor's specification.

- **Maximum node count.** 500 nodes.

- **Maximum distance between stations.** 200 kilometers.

- **Physical topology.** Logical star hierarchical ring.

10.2 FDDI Ring State Technical Process

When the FDDI ring is operating, the ring can be configured in different states (from a layout and design perspective). The FDDI operational state changes based on occurrence. The following is a brief description of the primary ring layout and design possibilities, along with certain descriptions of FDDI operational states.

The main FDDI network operational states are as follows:

- FDDI single ring with trees

- FDDI dual rings with trees

- FDDI dual rings without trees

- FDDI dual homing ring configuration

- FDDI wrapped ring

10.2.1 FDDI Single Ring with Trees

This implementation is configured in a design where a FDDI network is using a single ring. Multiple devices can be interconnected via M ports on a concentrator. This is not the most popular design, because fault redundancy is not inherent to the operation within a single ring architecture.

10.2.2 FDDI Dual Ring with Trees

In this type of configuration, both the primary and the secondary rings are used. A DAC design is normally directly connected to the main primary and secondary ring via the A and B port connection method. Any specific devices that are going to interconnect to the main FDDI ring will usually only be DAS-type devices. Specifically, any devices that are going to directly connect to the ring and not use a concentrator import normally use a DAC configuration rather than an SAS-type connection to ensure a fault-redundant implementation. Any SAS devices that are going to connect are linked to the main FDDI dual ring through a DAC connection. With this type of configuration, it is important to ensure that a pure dual ring is maintained; devices can have both SAS and DAS connections via a DAC concentrator, however, to form the tree off the dual ring (see Figure 10.4).

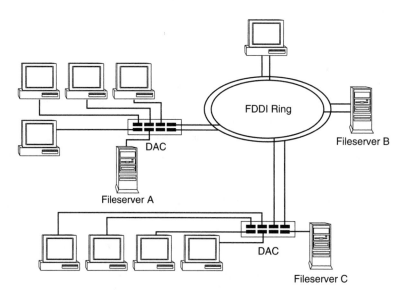

FIGURE 10.4 *A FDDO network layout using a pure dual ring design.*

10.2.3 FDDI Dual Ring Without Trees

In this configuration, a main FDDI ring is designed and engaged primarily as a pure backbone architecture. This type of configuration is based on a dual ring without any trees linked to the configuration. In this configuration, only DACs and DAS devices that are considered critical are interconnected to the both the FDDI primary and secondary ring configuration.

This setup would be based on a configuration where a FDDI layout is in a main computer room. In this case, the main servers or hosts would have primary Port B and secondary Port A connections directly to the ring. Generally, no trees are configured as a concentrator link between the main server or host even though a DAC connection is valid. This would allow for a pure DAS to dual ring full loop interconnection operation.

10.2.4 FDDI Dual Homing Ring Configuration as Related to Station Interconnection

The FDDI design can also allow a critical server, such as a host or a main file server, to have direct resource interconnections via two different connection links to the FDDI ring.

One specific design could allow for two DAC concentrators to be connected to both the primary and the secondary rings of the main FDDI full loop ring, for example. A main file server could also have two FDDI NICs, which would then interconnect to the two different DACs via M ports. This layout would then allow two different points of presence through two different concentrators for the main server to link into the FDDI ring. In this type of situation, one link from the server would be maintained in a constant operational state; the other one would be maintained in a withheld or quiet link state. In this case, the main active link state that is operating would be the primary link. In case of any failure of operation in that particular device or FDDI NIC, the dual homing link would take over and become the active link, and would move from a quiet or withheld state to an active link state. This is a popular configuration for fault redundancy (see Figure 10.5).

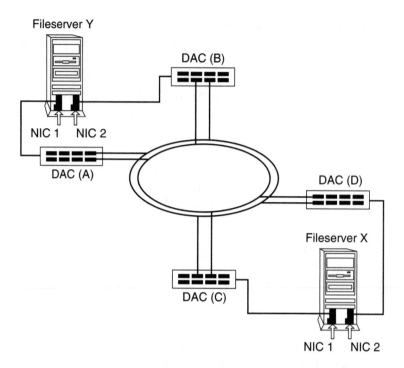

FIGURE 10.5 *FDDI ring layout that engages dual homing.*

10.2.5 FDDI Wrapped Ring Configuration Port

In the case of a failure of a FDDI node or device connected to the main ring, it is possible for devices, such as DACs or DASs, to allow for immediate recon-figuration and for the main FDDI ring to be wrapped. When a FDDI ring wraps, a loop occurs where the main and primary ring connect at a failure point to effect a wrapped condition.

In such a case, the FDDI node technology in the DAC or DAS invokes an oper-ation where an electrical trigger signal is sent to the FDDI network connection. Certain dual-ring technology components allow an actual bypass process to take place where the concentrator or station will allow light to stream through the bypass optical break and actually move the ring into a wrapped state process. In certain types of device configurations, this might require manual reconfiguration; in other cases, true inherent automatic reconfiguration can take place. This depends on the specific type of FDDI device and technology as implemented for wrapped state configurations (see Figures 10.6 and 10.7).

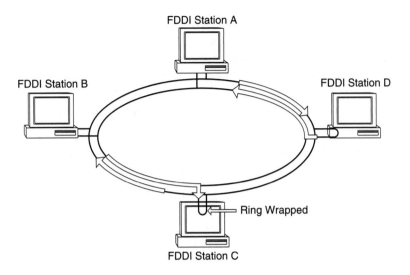

FIGURE 10.6 *Wrapped state configuration.*

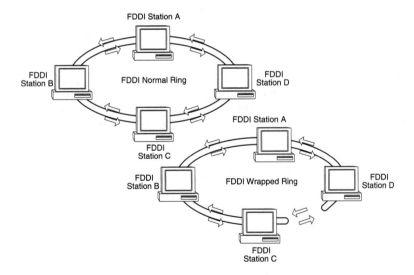

FIGURE 10.7 *Wrapped state configuration.*

10.3 FDDI Physical Operation Technical Descriptions

The following is a description of the main FDDI layer operational modes and processes that can take effect when a device is connected and active on a FDDI network. The following descriptions apply to both directly connected station configuration NICs, such as a SAS or DAS, and to concentrator connections, such as SACs and DACs, as they interconnect to a main FDDI single- or full-loop ring.

All FDDI NIC connections can have certain layer operations that are active. The following descriptions relate to these layer interconnection schemes.

The following four operational layers operate within the FDDI physical connection area:

- FDDI Physical Media Dependent layer (PMD)

- FDDI Physical layer (PHY)

- FDDI Medium Access Control layer (MAC)

- FDDI Station Management layer (SMT)

This example represents the processing chain that engages when a FDDI NIC receives a FDDI packet from the medium for handling: The main interconnection of the FDDI NIC operation scheme from the physical medium up through the protocol chain includes a process where signals are either transmitted or received through a PMD layer. The optical signals are then converted into electrical signals that are passed on to the PHY layer for operation. The FDDI PHY layer then processes the physical signals, which are based on FDDI symbols, and translates these into the final FDDI frame or packet format. The FDDI MAC layer processes the FDDI packet and frame field to extract the actual data transferred, which is either passed to the SMT if the data is based on physical operations or to the upper-layer protocol sockets if pure data is being transmitted. Figure 10.8 shows how the internal FDDI NIC internal operational areas relate to the OSI standard model.

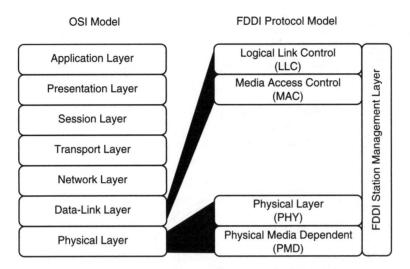

OSI Model   FDDI Protocol Model

FIGURE 10.8 *How the internal FDDI NIC internal operational areas relate to the OSI standard model.*

10.3.1 Physical Media Dependent Layer

The PMD layer is the closest connection point of the FDDI NIC from a station or concentrator as it interconnects to the FDDI main ring fiber loop connection. This is the actual physical media-dependent area of the physical network operation. Key operations are required for the FDDI NIC to convert optical signals brought from the medium or being sent onto the medium to and from the physical electrical format as related to media transmission. An optical signal is used for final transmission on the FDDI medium for overall transfer of data.

Specific technology allows a FDDI NIC to connect to the actual media. The PMD layer includes internal operations that allow for optical signal processing.

These areas include the optical transmitter, which processes the FDDI-applied waveform in a spectral-width format, and also has internal capabilities to operate with a center wavelength operational power meter through a *light emitting diode* (LED) operation to process through a final laser diode for transmission. Figure 10.9 shows the FDDI PMD operational areas.

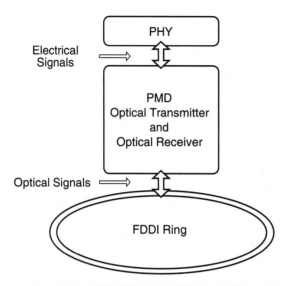

FIGURE 10.9 *FDDI PMD operational areas.*

The optical receiver circuit provides the same type of circuitry operations as the receiver circuit. Optical bypass switches can also be involved in the interconnection of this type of configuration. The main media type of connections normally utilized in a PMD layer can include both fiber and cabling specifications. A standard *media interface connection* (MIC) can be used, or the standard FDDI (ST) and (SC) fiber connectors can be used (see Figures 10.10, 10.11, and 10.12).

FIGURE 10.10 *A standard FDDI MIC connector.*

FIGURE 10.11 *A FDDI (SC) connector.*

FIGURE 10.12 *A FDDI (ST) connector.*

10.3.2 FDDI Physical Layer

The FDDI PHY layer is the area that provides the internal operations of the circuitry to allow for the optical signals from the FDDI medium to be processed through the FDDI NIC channel up to the protocol-processing layer. In the PHY layer, the primary FDDI operations occur on the FDDI NIC and relate to the interconnection between the PMD layer and the uplinked FDDI MAC layer. Specifically, the FDDI PHY layer is the area where technology operations occur that link the PMD fiber link operations to the FDDI MAC layer frame processing area operations. Figure 10.13 shows the internal operations of the FDDI NIC physical operational area circuits.

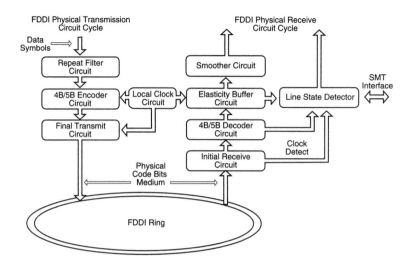

FIGURE 10.13 *The internal operations of the FDDI NIC physical operational area circuits.*

The PHY layer allows for the encoding and decoding of the actual physical symbols on the FDDI medium to be processed on reception from the fiber medium and upon transmission from the MAC layer. Having said that, both transmit and receive circuits are active in the PHY layer. On the FDDI PHY layer receive circuit, optical signals are received from the FDDI medium via the FDDI PMD layer on the receive function and then processed through a PHY receive circuit, which then simultaneously processes signals through a 4/5 B signal decoder circuit and through a line state detector. The line state detector interfaces in a parallel operation with the FDDI SMT layer interface. The PHY 4/5 B decoder circuit then processes the signals through an elasticity buffer and into a smoother circuit. The data is then passed up to the FDDI MAC layer.

On the FDDI PHY transmit circuit, FDDI frames assembled within the FDDI MAC layer are set for transmit and are passed to the FDDI PHY layer. The FDDI PHY layer performs an operation to break the frame down into electrical signals and then composes actual FDDI symbols for transmission on the medium. The signals are sent from the FDDI MAC layer to a FDDI PHY layer repeat filter. Next, the signals are processed by a 4/5 B line encoder, which associates the signal with a clocking signal, and then the final signal is passed to the PMD layer for transmission onto the FDDI medium.

In this case of signal transmission and reception, a FDDI NIC will utilize a certain coding on the medium. The encoding for the signal is *nonreturn to zero inverted* (NRZI) on ones. In this coding scheme, a logical one (1) is represented by a transition from the signal's current operation state to its next state in an interval mode. In the next case, a logical zero (0) is represented when there is no transition for the overall signal for process on the medium. These signals are interleaved through a local clocking signal, and the final signal is processed.

10.3.3 FDDI Medium Access Control Layer

The FDDI MAC Layer is one of the more important areas on the FDDI NIC. This importance results because the FDDI NIC MAC layer is responsible for assembling a packet for transmission and from reception to the upper-layer protocol area chain within a particular FDDI device.

The FDDI MAC layer interacts heavily with the PHY layer and also operates in direct correlation with the FDDI SMT layer. The physical FDDI MAC layer provides four main high-level functions when transferring FDDI frame information to signals on a reverse receive and transmit cycle in and out of the FDDI NIC to the upper-layer protocols, as required.

The following four functions are invoked:

- Error checking processes

- Address recognition review

- Data interpretation of the FDDI frame and packet internal data

- Access of the FDDI NIC to the medium

Figure 10.14 shows the internals of the FDDI MAC agent.

The FDDI signals, when being interpreted on a receive process, come from the FDDI PMD and PHY layers and then are passed through the FDDI MAC layer before moving to the upper-layer protocols. When the signals are received on an inbound MAC receiving cycle, error-checking processes activate and compilation starts, where a FDDI frame and packet are assembled for processing. The FDDI MAC layer engages address recognition to verify the source and destination FDDI node addresses. Next, the FDDI layer starts the interpretation of the type of data being presented for processing. The valid data types can include SMT layer data associated with control of the FDDI physical ring or upper-layer protocol data. The FDDI layer starts the interpretation of the class of traffic as the FDDI frame is processed. Any data that needs to be extracted for the SMT layer or for the upper-layer protocols is then separated by the FDDI MAC functional operations.

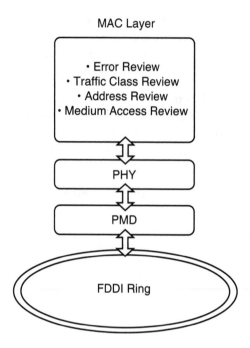

FIGURE 10.14 *The internals of the FDDI MAC agent.*

On an outbound transmit cycle, the FDDI MAC layer receives data from the upper-layer protocol chain processing layer or the FDDI SMT layer. In this case, the FDDI MAC layer then must perform an immediate data-type inter-pretation to assign a class of traffic and to assign the proper addresses and formulate the FDDI frame formatting that will surround the upper-layer protocol data unit or the SMT layer internal frame data. Certain error-checking fields are assigned as active, and the FDDI packet is formed for transmission and processing down through the FDDI PHY layer for signaling transfer to FDDI symbols, and then for final processing through the FDDI PMD layer for the optical signal to be formed for transmission. In the transmission operation, the FDDI MAC layer engages the operational steps for the FDDI node to gain access to the FDDI medium. In this operation, the FDDI MAC layer invokes certain timers required for access. The FDDI access method is presented in detail later in this chapter.

10.3.4 FDDI Station Management Layer

The FDDI SMT layer is an important operational layer that runs in direct parallel with the FDDI MAC and PHY layer operational areas. The SMT layer utilizes certain operations to effect a fault-redundant cross-management of the device nodes as part of the complete FDDI network. Later in this chapter, a full detailed section is presented on the FDDI SMT layer and the effects on FDDI NIC operations.

10.4 FDDI MAC Network Access Methods

The FDDI MAC layer actually assigns access methods. When this process occurs, the operation may affect certain FDDI frame operations. The FDDI internetwork architecture is based on the deterministic access that is somewhat comparable to the Token Ring access methodology. For a FDDI device or node to connect to the FDDI ring, the FDDI TTRT must be active and operating.

10.4.1 Types of FDDI Access

The FDDI technology allows for the following three types of access to the overall available bandwidth:

- Synchronous bandwidth

- Asynchronous shared bandwidth

- Batch bandwidth

The first class of bandwidth, noted as synchronous bandwidth, is not normally invoked in a common FDDI configuration. If invoked, this would be a case where a device could have complete operation and control over the FDDI ring in a continuous synchronous format. The second class of service, noted as asynchronous shared bandwidth, is a process where the deterministic access method does not engage any priority and all devices with FDDI NIC connections have equal access based on the TTRT.

The third class of service is only applied in the case of a condition where there is leftover bandwidth. In this condition, a specific device will have already transmitted its normal data sequence and then can utilize any leftover bandwidth for engaging batch transfers. This is another mode that is not commonly engaged for general data transfer in most FDDI configurations.

10.4.2 FDDI MAC Timed Token Passing Access and Data Transmission Operations

To access the FDDI network, a FDDI NIC card for a device must gain control of the FDDI token. For a FDDI device to transmit data, the device's NIC must capture the token by using extraction stripping process. After the FDDI NIC has captured the token, it performs a combination process where a set unit of data is formed into a frame and processed from the FDDI MAC layer and is then processed through the PHY layer and sent to the PMD layer; a FDDI packet is next transmitted out onto the main FDDI ring. When a FDDI device transmits a data frame out onto the ring, it has control of the asynchronous bandwidth for a short period of time. It cannot hold the bandwidth in an asynchronous mode for a continuous cycle; otherwise it would be considered as operating in a synchronous operation. In the asynchronous process, the FDDI MAC timers associated with TTRT protocol sequencing determine the amount of time that the device can transmit on the FDDI ring before it must release the token back onto the main FDDI loop for other FDDI nodes to utilize the ring for data transfer.

After the source station has completed the process of transmitting data out onto the ring, in most cases it then must release the token out onto the ring so that other devices can transmit data. Certain protocol timers are associated with this type of transmission cycle. A timer called the *Token Rotation Timer* (TRT) of a device normally monitors the amount of time that a device can actually transmit on the ring as related to when it must finally release the token for other nodes to gain access to the medium.

During most cycles, a device connecting to the FDDI ring just grabs the token and performs a source data transmission on the ring, and then releases the token when it has finished transmitting. In certain other cases, a FDDI-connected device can activate a timer called the *Token Holding Timer* (THT), which allows a device after completing an initial transmission cycle to again transmit for an additional period of time. In this case, after the THT has expired, the source device must finally release the token to ensure an asynchronous operation on the main FDDI ring.

The following example describes a typical FDDI MAC timer interaction. A FDDI station, when interconnected to the ring, invokes a FDDI NIC operation when an upper-layer protocol transmission is required for packet transmission. This also can be invoked by the FDDI SMT layer for physical node ring management processes. The FDDI NIC loads an immediate *T_Request* (T_REQ) timer value that activates the TTRT process, which then engages the TRT time cycle that the device attempts to use for transmission. The FDDI NIC after loading the T_REQ time value in a register, and completing a process called *token bidding*, next loads the time value determined by TTRT into the *T_Operational* (T_OPR) timer register. The T_OPR register actually becomes the individual FDDI station NIC's TRT value. In this case, the NIC now has been assigned a TRT timer value that it will utilize for its transmission time cycle. After the TRT has been activated, the station attempts data transmission. Note that each station performs transmission out onto the ring through the process of utilizing the loaded TRT timer value to engage an assigned data transmission cycle. If the station's data transmission cycles are completed, the station can then utilize any extra time that may be available as based on the original TRT time cycle. Additional time would be assigned to a THT timer, which would be activated and allow for an additional transmission cycle. At this point, other timers would interrelate to the final transmission time cycle, such as the T_MAX and T_MIN timers, which may invoke a station to immediately release a token, if required.

Assume, for example, that one station (B1) FDDI NIC is set at a TRT of 10ms and three other stations are bidding with the station to determine the final TTRT of the ring. If the first station is labeled as B1, after the token has been received by station B1 and a data frame has been composed, the B1 station would start the transmission. It would transmit onto the ring and send one FDDI frame for a complete cycle. After its THT timer has expired, it would then release the token out onto the ring so that another station could transmit.

If only eight months of time were utilized for transmit, that would mean that its token holding timer would hold an additional two months for transmission. Depending on protocol operation, the station could release the token immediately or transmit for another two months. If for some reason it attempts to transmit and eventually the token holding timer expires, other timers can be activated, such as T_MIN and T_MAX, and the final *Timer Valid Transmission* (TVX) will activate an immediate release of the token out onto the ring so that stations B1 and B2 can to transmit.

Various contention processes occur on the FDDI token passing scheme when required. These contention processes are involved with the final TTRT as determined by all the devices as they are configured on the FDDI ring for communication. All the FDDI device NICs interconnected to the ring must participate in a process called *token bidding*, which determines the final TTRT utilized across the ring.

The various manufacturers of FDDI NICs might have specific preset values designed into the FDDI NIC card hardware and software structure that allow for a different T_REQ and T_OPR values to be set. These values can affect the final timer for bidding, which is called *T_BID*, and the final TRT of a device's particular NIC. The values for T_REQ timer and the loaded T_OPR timer can vary from manufacturer to manufacturer. Specifically, certain FDDI NICs can attempt to transmit faster than others and will have certain targets in design for how long they will hold the token when transmitting on the ring before they release the token as compared to other FDDI NICs. Due to this possible variance in FDDI NIC technology, it is important that a common time be assigned for the main FDDI ring TTRT value. To ensure that the process is equal for asynchronous bandwidth control, the token bidding process is engaged.

The following is a description of a typical token bidding scheme and data-passing process as it would occur on a FDDI medium in a real network configuration. All stations on a FDDI ring normally must go through a bidding process and a claim process to connect and become an active station on the FDDI network. When a station is powered up and is the first station on a ring, its T_REQ loads the T_OPR operational value register, which determines its TRT. The T_REQ value is also loaded in the T_BID register for each station when a device is connecting to the ring that must go through a bidding process.

Consider this example: Station X1 activates and connects to a FDDI network and becomes the first station connected on the network. Immediately after this process, stations X2 and X3 can become active as related to connection for the FDDI medium. Assume that station X1 transmits an initial FDDI MAC Claim frame on the ring based on a T_REQ and T_BID value set that determines the a final TRT of 30ms. If station X2 receives the Claim frame from station X1, it activates an immediate bidding contention. Station X2 compares its address to the incoming station from X1.

If the destination address of the frame does not match the station of X2, it next compares the source address to the incoming frame. If the address of the inbound source frame from station X2 has a high or low address, this may then activate other timers. The actual timing values are compared also in the frame structure, and the T_REQ values are compared. Station X2 checks the frame control field and examine the Frame Control field for the address state to identify whether the X1 station is using a long or short address identification for a 16- or 48-bit address setting.

Station X2 next compares its Destination Address field to the incoming frame from station X1. If the destination address of the frame does not match the station X2, it next compares the source address of the incoming frame to its own address, and then it sets the higher flag if the address of the Claim frame is higher than the address of the station; otherwise, it sets the lower flag. A higher flag setting indicates to the MAC state machine that the Claim frame with the higher address was received, and the lower flag indicates a lower address. The first four bytes of the received frame contain the T_BID value of station X1, which is examined next. It compares stations X1 T_BID value at 30ms with its own T_BID of 70ms.

Its own value is higher and it sets the higher flag indicating the higher value. Station X2 validates that the frame from station X1 is legal in size. This frame-check sequence operation is verified. In this case, because a higher claim comparison has been made, the receiver process in station X2 indicates that its transmitter is set to repeat the frame and it does so by setting a unique flag called *higher claim*. Station X2 then sets its T_NEG = T_BID received and repeats the station X1 Claim frame on the main FDDI ring. In this case, station X2 is not bidding or is in contention. Station X1's Claim frame next reaches station X3, which is in a quite flat state. Station X3's NIC state machine operation applies the same operation as X2 did in the preceding process. Specifically, station X3 compares the T-BID received from station X1 at 30ms with its own T_BID at 20ms and finds it has received a lower-claim complement number. Then it sets the lower-claim flag, indicating to the transmit state machine to strip the station X1 Claim frame from the ring and transmit its own Claim frame.

At this point, station X1 is losing to station X3 and station X3 is starting to win the bid process in determining the ring final TTRT time. Station X1, which was transmitting its own Claim frame, receives the Claim frame from station X3. After the station X3's Claim frame is received and checked for validity, station X1 defers the bid process and drops out as a bidder and repeats X3's Claim frame. Station X1 sets its T_NEG timer to equal 20ms, as noted from station X3's T_BID as received, and sets its higher-Claim frame, and its NIC state machine stops transmitting its own Claim frame and repeats the Claim frame from station X3. At station X2, a similar situation occurs and it changes its T_NEG timer, which was noted at 30ms from a previous contention with station X1 to a resolved T_NEG timer of 20ms, acknowledging that X3 is the lowest value and is determining the final FDDI ring TTRT.

When Station X3 receives back its own Claim frame, it knows that it has won the claim process. At that point, station X3 sets a receive state machine of "My Claim Flag Indicator" for the transmitters to stop transmitting any Claim frame and notes that it has won the claim process. The station X3 transmitter then sets its T_OPR timer to T_NEG and resets its TRT to T_OPR. Station X3 clears its late counter of any value and then issues a nonrestricted token. At this time, station X3 has won the claim process and it may not immediately begin transmitting data before issuing the token. The first token rotation is usually engaged just to synchronize the various timers and flags in the different FDDI stations and to notify all active FDDI stations that the claim process has been successfully terminated (see Figure 10.15).

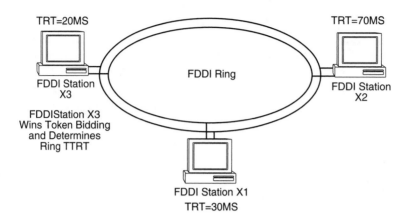

FIGURE 10.15 *The FDDI token passing and bidding process.*

Note that at times it is possible that the FDDI cross-ring claim resolution may occur where certain stations may bid with the same T_BID. If equal T_REQ bids are present from two or more stations, the longer address configuration usually takes precedence over the final transmission. A 48-bit address FDDI Claim frame with a T_REQ bid of 60ms usually wins the bid against a 16-bit address in FDDI with a 60ms T_BID and T_REQ bid set.

All FDDI stations when transmitting and receiving data perform an extensive data- and error-analysis process. All FDDI NIC MAC agents verify destination and source addresses, and examine a FDDI frame transfer process for proper structures as to CRC alignment and FDDI frame integrity (see Figure 10.16).

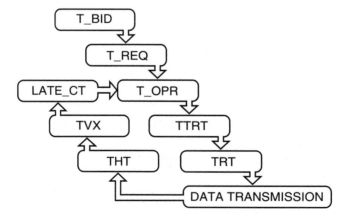

FIGURE 10.16 *Main FDDI timers and variables with their associated operation links.*

10.5 FDDI MAC Frame Format

The following is a brief description of the FDDI MAC frame format specifications. The FDDI token format engages a starting delimiter with a Frame Class field with an additional ending delimiter. A FDDI frame is composed of a a maximum of 4500 bytes, which includes 8 bytes of preamble. The Preamble field is engaged for clock recovery purposes and for the synchronization of the incoming and outgoing symbols as processed through the FDDI PHY receiver and transmission circuits. The Source and Destination Address fields in a FDDI frame normally take up 2 to 6 bytes each, depending on whether the station is engaging a 16-bit addressing scheme or a 48-bit addressing scheme, which in turn affects the final Information field size (which varies between 4478 to 4486 bytes). Figure 10.17 shows the data frame format.

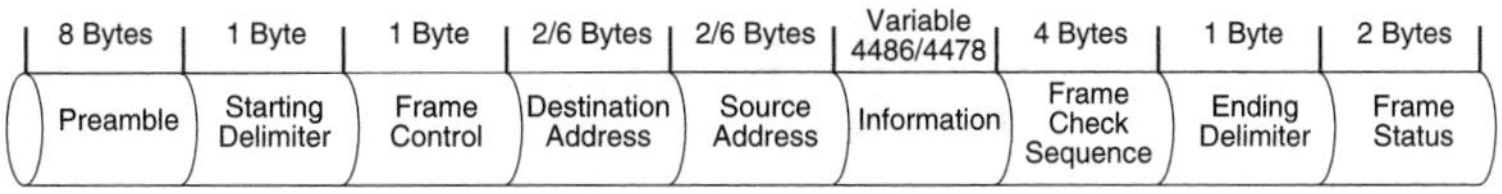

8 Bytes	1 Byte	1 Byte	2/6 Bytes	2/6 Bytes	Variable 4486/4478	4 Bytes	1 Byte	2 Bytes
Preamble	Starting Delimiter	Frame Control	Destination Address	Source Address	Information	Frame Check Sequence	Ending Delimiter	Frame Status

FIGURE 10.17 *The FDDI data frame format.*

The configuration fields in a FDDI frame are set as follows:

- **Preamble (PA).** 8 bytes in length.

- **Starting Delimiter (D).** 1 byte in length.

- **Frame Control (FC).** 1 byte in length.

- **Destination Address (DA).** 2 to 6 bytes, depending on 16- or 48-bit addressing.

- **Source Address (SA).** 2 to 6 bytes, depending on 16- or 48-bit addressing.

- **Information (PDU).** Variable 4478 bytes to 4486 bytes in length.

- **Frame Check Sequence (FCS).** 4 bytes in length.

- **Ending Delimiter (ED).** 1 byte in length.

- **Frame Status (FS).** 2 bytes or more. This field includes a frame error indicator, address recognized indicator, and a frame copied indicator.

10.6 FDDI Station Management Layer

As discussed earlier, a FDDI NIC layer allows for control of the FDDI MAC processes. That layer is somewhat similar to the Token Ring MAC layer. The FDDI *Station Management* (SMT) layer is a higher-layer type of operation that intercommunicates with the FDDI MAC and PHY layers. The SMT layer also has extensive capabilities for cross-device management of the FDDI network as a whole. The FDDI SMT interconnects with a PHY layer by engaging certain physical connection management processes. These processes involve operations, such as link junction–level management, that further invoke operations such as "station initial state open," "single active to form connection," "network response to exchange," "synchronize link," and "station link active." In other words, the FDDI SMT layer can invoke functions that operate on interaction with the PHY layer but affect the PMD layer. These SMT-to-PHY processes are invoked by the physical connection management operations that reside in the SMT layer operational cycles (see Figure 10.18).

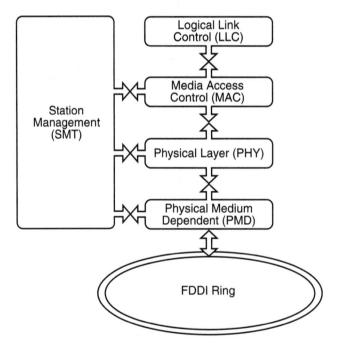

FIGURE 10.18 *The FDDI SMT layer as cross-mapped to the other FDDI NIC functions.*

The physical connection management process can also monitor the state of the FDDI ring by invoking link confidence tests and link error monitoring tests. These special operations allow for monitoring of the FDDI NIC insertion cycle, the FDDI station configuration mode, and also are used for the monitoring of the FDDI NIC as it is interconnected to the network. Actual line states can be monitored by a device's SMT layer, which can invoke certain signals through the PHY layer to generate operations on the PMD layer. The line states that can be monitored by the SMT layer are operational states such as active line state or unknown line state and other states related to the FDDI medium connection process (see Figure 10.19).

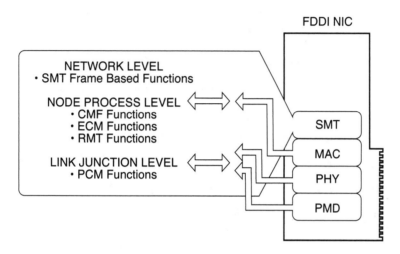

FIGURE 10.19   *The internal areas of the FDDI NIC SMT agent operation.*

The SMT layer can also perform management on the FDDI ring with the ring node management sublayer operations. In this case, the SMT layer interacts with the MAC layer on the FDDI NIC. The SMT layer is communicating mainly to the MAC layer. This is a functional area of the SMT processes that ensures that a FDDI NIC station is inserted into the FDDI ring and is properly configured. Certain operations are performed to ensure that device key statistics are communicated through SMT channel circuit operation functions such as configuration management, path functions operations, entity coordination management processes, and ring management processes. In this particular area, important functions are monitored such as the state of the FDDI NIC as related to FDDI MAC operations for stability. Directed beacons and subbeacon isolation operations are monitored, along with trace operations and duplicate address isolations. These operations are described in detail in the section titled "Methods for Analyzing and Troubleshooting FDDI Networks," later in this chapter.

At the network level, the SMT layer can monitor the node-to-node communications on the FDDI ring as a whole. Certain types of communication related to operations are performed; these are somewhat similar to the Token Ring MAC layer operations on a Token Ring network.

10.6.1 Station Management Layer Processes

On a FDDI network, the SMT layer can invoke key processes, including the following:

- Station Management Neighbor Information Frame (NIF)

- Station Information Frame (SIF)

- Station Management Layer Echo Frame (ECF)

- Station Management Layer Resource Allocation Frame (RAF)

- Station Management Request Denied Frame (RDF)

- Station Management Layer Report Frame (SRF)

- Station Management Parameter Management Frame (PMF)

- Station Management Extended Services Frame (ESF)

The following sections describe how the SMT layer can engage functions that affect the complete FDDI ring operation (see Figure 10.20).

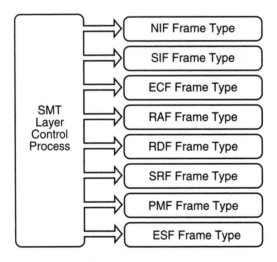

FIGURE 10.20 *FDDI NIC operational processes that can be generated by SMT frame types.*

10.6.1.1 SMT Neighbor Notification Protocol Operations

In this case, the SMT layer engages operations through the FDDI MAC layer to form certain frames that invoke cycles for Neighbor Notification. The Neighbor Notification protocol is engaged when a new station enters the FDDI NIC ring.

The new station should participate in Neighbor Notification by sending an SMT *Neighbor Information frame* (NIF) to request that it can become part of the operational FDDI ring. A FDDI NIF frame request can include information about the upstream and downstream neighbors (UNA and DNA).

Certain cycles occur in a FDDI NIF operation: Normally, a station such as H1 transmits a request that includes a NIF identification onto the ring. Station H2 receives the NIF request and transmits a NIF response onto the ring identifying its own address. Station H3 also receives the NIF request and responds with its address. This process continues around the ring. This cycle allows for the new device inserting on the ring to be aware of the other devices. The process also allows the complete FDDI ring addressing scheme to be recycled so that all active stations are aware of the upstream and downstream neighbor addresses associated as to interconnection on the FDDI loop. This process is engaged by the FDDI SMT layer, which forces the FDDI MAC layer to transmit the necessary NIF frames, as required.

10.6.1.2 SMT Status Reporting Protocol Operations
The FDDI SMT layer can also perform a process known as generating *Status Reporting frames* (SRF) by engaging the Status Reporting Protocol. When unexpected or dynamic changes on the ring are encountered, the changes can be communicated back and forth to different nodes via the SRF protocol sequence. These are very important frames from a protocol analysis perspective.

10.6.1.3 SMT Parameter Management Protocol Operations
The FDDI SMT layer can engage a process called *Parameter Management Protocol*. In this operation, an SMT *Parameter Management frame* (PMF) can be sent out for ring management purposes. In such a case, the FDDI SMT engages a PMF cycle through the FDDI MAC layer. The FDDI MAC layer transmits an SMT PMF with "get request" subvector on the main ring to a specific device. In this type of operation, another station can respond with a PMF with a "get response" subvector to the source querying station. This inherent SMT operation engages a management cycle based on a query-and-response cycle utilizing the Parameter Management Protocol process.

10.6.1.4 SMT Echo Process
SMT Echo frames are engaged to perform an operation similar to an ICMP ping. The FDDI SMT layer can invoke a FDDI devices's NIC MAC layer agent to transmit an Echo request frame to a certain device. The device receiving the SMT Echo request frame normally then responds with an SMT Echo reply frame.

10.6.1.5 SMT Resource Allocation Process

SMT frames can be generated for advertising SMT resources as available between nodes. In such a case. the FDDI SMT layer can generate *SMT Resource Allocation Frames* (RAF). The SMT RAF can be engaged to cause a FDDI NIC to process communications as to the resources available on the network to determine the capability for asynchronous or synchronous transfer.

10.6.1.6 SMT Extended Services Process

SMT frames can be generated for engaging an advertisement of extended services available in communication between FDDI nodes. In such a case. the FDDI SMT layer can generate *SMT Extended Services frames* (ESF).

10.6.1.7 SMT Request Denied Process

In certain cases, when a FDDI device cannot respond to a certain type of SMT frame, it can transmit an SMT *Request Denied frame* (RDF) and ignore the requested SMT operation. When a RDF frame is captured with a FDDI protocol analyzer, it may indicate an operational incompatibility with an SMT operation between multiple FDDI active devices or NICs.

10.6.1.8 SMT Status Information Process

Within the SMT layer operations, there is also the capability for the status of a FDDI NIC as related to its operational mode and general configuration on the FDDI network to communicate certain key information through SMT *Status Information frames* (SIF). The FDDI SMT layer on one NIC can communicate to the SMT layer on another NIC to determine certain communication cycles on the ring through SIF frame formats. This is a communication layer capability unique in the FDDI operations and allows for unique inherent management capability through the FDDI SMT layer.

10.6.2 FDDI Station Management Layer Frame Format

The FDDI Frame Information field can encapsulate an internal field that carries the Station Management layer Information frame data and the applied header. The FDDI SMT layer assembles a unique protocol data unit for the SMT process and inserts it within the data field of an SMT layer frame format (see Figure 10.21).

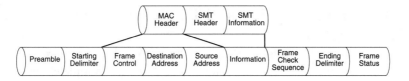

FIGURE 10.21 *The main FDDI frame format can carry the required SMT information to effect an SMT process on the FDDI network.*

The following SMT fields are engaged:

- **SMT Frame Header.** Total normal standard length, 20 bytes (7 fields engaged).

- **Field 1.** SMT frame class, 1 byte. This field identifies the SMT frame-based operation (NIF, SIF, ECF, RAF, RDF, SRF, PMF, or ESF).

- **Field 2.** SMT frame type, 1 byte. This field identifies whether the SMT frame is an announcement, a request, or a response.

- **Field 3.** SMT version ID, 2 bytes. This field indicates current SMT version. This varies from time to time accordingly to industry releases.

- **Field 4.** SMT transaction ID, 4 bytes. This field displays an SMT request/response sequence.

- **Field 5.** SMT station ID, 8 bytes. This field identifies a FDDI station ID.

- **Field 6.** SMT PAD, 2 bytes. This field marks the alignment of the SMT frame.

- **Field 7.** SMT data length, 2 bytes. This field identifies the SMT data field length.

The FDDI SMT layer is extremely important from a protocol analysis standpoint. If an analyst is monitoring a FDDI backbone ring or a LAN ring that is utilizing SMT operations, the SMT layer may inherently communicate some of the key configuration and operational issues that may be taking place on the FDDI medium. It is important during a network baseline study for an analyst to filter the SMT layer by utilizing a protocol analysis approach described later in this chapter. It is also important to finally note that there is a heavy interaction between the FDDI SMT layer and FDDI MAC layer.

10.7 Methods for Analyzing and Troubleshooting FDDI Networks

When analyzing and troubleshooting a FDDI network, it is important to first ensure that the analyzer that is going to be utilized is completely FDDI compliant. Because both a primary and backup ring connection is possible in configuration, based on the FDDI ring specifications, it is important to ensure that an analyzer can connect to both rings. Specifically, because variances in the FDDI connection types can exist—as related to the options of MIC, ST, and SC connections—it is important to ensure that the physical medium-dependent connectors are available along with the analyzer tool connection cables.

When analyzing a FDDI LAN, it is important to ensure that the network is monitored for high efficiency throughput, low delay, and latency. This is necessary because, in most cases, a FDDI network is providing backbone technology capability. It is important that the network delay be minimal when devices communicate across the FDDI medium. The queuing delays must be minimal and the final transmission time must be executed in a mode that allows each device an equal asynchronous time cycle. The final endpoint-to-endpoint transfers must be achieved at a high effective throughput level.

As mentioned previously, various timing factors are important in each FDDI NIC, such as a queuing delay, because they affect final transmission capability. It is important to ensure that FDDI NICs receive frames properly in a rapid fashion, process all frames through upper-layer protocol cycles, and then the NIC must transmit all responses back rapidly. Usually standard transmission times apply, based on the TTRT, finally determined through token bidding and associated with the T_BID and T_OPR timers and variable registers of each specific FDDI NIC interconnected to the ring. As noted earlier, heavy interactions may occur, associated with different FDDI NICs as they activate a connection to a main FDDI ring. If a FDDI NIC has an extremely low or high T_BID and T_OPR value finally loaded into the TRT, this may affect the overall operation of the complete FDDI ring. It is important that an analyst understand that each device on a FDDI ring must be closely monitored during events such as token bidding, claiming, and neighbor notification via protocol analysis. A standard transmission time normally takes place when a FDDI NIC is transmitting on a ring. A FDDI NIC can normally transmit within 80 nanoseconds-per-byte range. This translates to approximately a 32 to 38 milliseconds time period to transmit a 4500-byte- or 9000- symbol-based frame. Although this is not considered a standard, it is considered a common goal when a vendor designs a FDDI NIC. This range for transmission ensures low latency and low propagation delay on the internetwork.

The minimum ring latency should always be no more than 100 microseconds. In most cases, a FDDI ring complete with all devices active should provide a much lower ring latency level than 100 milliseconds; and in most cases, the ring latency should be no more than approximately 3.4 to 10 milliseconds. This is the normal ceiling level for ring latency.

The following section presents the key steps required to properly perform a network baseline on a FDDI network.

When analyzing a FDDI network, it is important to understand that the network is based on a high data rate, at 100Mbps minimum, and has the capability to perform at a high throughput level. The main focus of a FDDI baseline is to perform the network statistical measurements that will enable the analyst to identify any performance-inhibiting factors present within a FDDI network layout or design. The FDDI network topology should provide the highest throughput and performance foundation so that upper-layer protocols have a strong foundation for throughput and performance for general data transfer. With this in mind, certain measurements apply to a FDDI network baseline.

The following is a brief review of the workload characterization measurements that an analyst should use in a FDDI analysis study.

10.7.1 FDDI Bandwidth Utilization

When performing bandwidth utilization measurements in a FDDI network, keep in mind that it is a deterministic medium. Because it is deterministic and operates somewhat similar to the Token Ring environment, it is important to understand that utilization levels must be monitored in a specific manner. Utilization levels can be achieved at a higher level and the network will still sustain operations because of inherent fault-redundant operations and sequencing processing that occur at the FDDI MAC layer and the SMT layer. These layers assist in allowing the FDDI network to continue to operate in a stable fashion even when high utilization loads impact the medium. The key factor is that if there are high number of nodes on a FDDI network and utilization is showing high peak utilization saturation, it may be beneficial to consider whether there would be any options as to segmentation. There may be possible advantages in breaking up a FDDI network into more separate networks by implementing a FDDI router, switch, or bridge between the networks. The segmentation process may allow each device node on the FDDI rings to receive a more even distribution of the token from the deterministic process. This would only be required on extremely high saturation levels above 80% to 90%. Keep this in mind that all standard utilization measurements apply in a FDDI baseline study, such as average utilization, peak utilization, and historical measurements.

10.7.2 FDDI Node-to-Node by Utilization

It is important to closely monitor node-to-node by utilization when examining a FDDI network. This is necessary because on a FDDI network there may be concerns as to the overall token passing scheme if certain devices have any problem circumstances in the FDDI NIC that might cause a high token rotation time or a negative effect on the TTRP of the complete ring. By closely examining node-to-node by utilization, an analyst might quickly determine whether any node is absorbing a high amount of bandwidth. It is possible that the physical FDDI NIC operation and design of the NIC is causing this occurrence. When analyzing the physical FDDI medium, an analyst might further isolate the problem to a specific node that exhibits an extremely high bandwidth level, leading the analyst to the exact cause of a problem (in this case, related to FDDI cross-ring performance on the deterministic medium).

10.7.3 FDDI Protocol Percentage Measurements

When performing protocol percentage measurements in the FDDI network, it is important to extract any high levels of FDDI protocol percentages in the MAC or SMT layers. If percentages above the 4% to 5% level are seen in the MAC protocol, or above 6% to 7% in the SMT protocol, the composition of these protocol types should be further investigated. Specifically, a detailed analysis of the MAC processes and the SMT management processes should be performed. If extremely high levels of the MAC or SMT layers are noted, this may indicate a FDDI ring that is moving through states considered nonoperational or recovery states that require further physical layer analysis.

10.7.4 FDDI Physical Layer Detailed Analysis

The next area to focus on during analysis of a FDDI ring is related to a basic monitoring process of the physical layer. Monitoring the physical layer on a FDDI ring requires a close understanding of the FDDI MAC operational timer processes and the FDDI SMT layer processes.

To closely examine the FDDI physical layer, an analyst should engage a FDDI protocol analyzer and activate a filter in a capture mode for both the FDDI MAC layer and the SMT layer. Some protocol analyzers may require the activation of the FDDI Void and Claim capture filter along with the general FDDI MAC and SMT filters, because these are sometimes considered separate on certain analysis platforms.

An analyst should examine any MAC communication from the FDDI NICs to other FDDI NICs, along with any SMT layer communication between NICs. This examination enables an analyst to understand how the FDDI NICs are connecting to the FDDI medium and also how devices are participating within the FDDI main ring standard TTRT. Any FDDI NICs that have high effected TRT or high T_OPR timers may be able to be identified as devices they are causing performance problems on the ring. Any FDDI NICs or FDDI concentrators having hardware problems may be able to be identified by excessive levels of the FDDI claim processes.

High void frame rates may indicate delays in translational frame transfer from one topology to another, such as FDDI to Ethernet. Any high-traffic occurrences in the SMT layer usually shows the subframe type for SMT sublayer types, such as SRF frames that can be further decoded to analyze the problem encountered. Based on the analysis performed in these areas, an analyst may be able to identify a physical FDDI problem and address the issue either by replacing or reconfiguring a device, and then by re-analyzing the LAN.

Other key technical notes are important when examining the FDDI physical layer operations and processes.

An analyst must closely monitor the standard FDDI token rotation processes. When analyzing the physical layer of a FDDI network, an analyst should closely monitor the actual ring latency. As noted, in most cases the FDDI ring latency should be less than 3.5 microseconds for general operations. The ring latency should be no more than 100 microseconds. This allows for a proper asynchronous spread of transmission. Also, each device should not have to transmit and hold the token for any more than 80 milliseconds for normal transmissions. Any level higher than this would be extremely high. The low timing value for a device that is going to be transmitting on a FDDI ring should not typically be lower than 8 milliseconds. The spread between 8 and 80 milliseconds is key, because variances do exist between the various FDDI NIC cards available. When monitoring a FDDI ring with a protocol analyzer that can engage a latency timer that will monitor token rotation time across the ring, it is important to note that the token rotation time should be no higher than 100 microseconds between FDDI NICs. When a FDDI NIC is attempting transmission, the time for transmission including the transmission and the token holding timer operation and final release of the token should be no more than 8 to 80 milliseconds. Typically, these timing levels are at the lower end of the spectrum.

After the transmission areas have been monitored via network analysis, an analyst should take a step back and take a bird's-eye view of the timing situation. Again, the key is low latency and high performance and high throughput on a FDDI technology. If problems are seen in the TRT or the amount of transmission timing, it is possible that such occurrences affect the overall performance levels of the complete ring. If higher timing levels and values are identified, the analyst may need to review further a FDDI NIC or the NIC software drivers.

After these areas have been reviewed, the analyst must next use a protocol analyzer on the FDDI medium and invoke a general FDDI MAC capture or display filter, depending on the mode of analysis. If the data has already been captured in one large trace file, the analyst can invoke a display filter to view the MAC layer. Certain FDDI MAC operations are key when reviewing the FDDI ring.

The following types of processes should be closely reviewed with a FDDI protocol analyzer when analyzing a FDDI ring for physical layer analysis of the MAC and SMT layer process cycles.

After a MAC layer is operating in a FDDI beacon state, a directed beacon may be active. When a directed beacon continues to occur, it can be considered a stuck beacon operation. After a stuck beacon operation occurs, the NIC itself may remove a fault within the node from the FDDI ring. This could cause the FDDI device to move into a FDDI trace function, which performs a testing of the device NIC.

In a trace function, the device encountering a stuck beacon operation performs a loopback path test. If the device passes that test, the device reenters the ring. The trace operation usually isolates the problem to a fault domain.

On duplicate address concerns, the SMT functions activate to assist in detecting situations related to duplicate addresses. Such situations can prevent a ring from becoming fully operational during MAC claim and beacon processes. When situations arise in which duplicate stations are present on a FDDI network, it is possible that more than one station might win the claim process and issue a token. This is more likely to occur if stations are utilizing 16-bit addresses, which are locally administered. With 48-bit addresses, this normally does not occur. If a duplicate address occurrence takes place, a jam beacon may be present in the analysis data of the FDDI ring.

After the FDDI MAC layer analysis has been completed, the final focus before moving to the upper-layer protocols is to analyze any SMT layer operations taking place on the ring. These types of operations include key areas that require further analysis in the SMT layer.

An analyst should always perform analysis of the *Neighbor Notification Protocol* (NNP). This may show conditions where certain devices may not be participating in the neighbor information process. If a certain device is not transmitting NIF frames, that may indicate a problem with the FDDI NIC.

The SMT SRF-type frames may carry unique data about a node's operations and are a key factor in FDDI physical layer analysis. The SMT layer SRF Link Confidence Test errors may indicate that a FDDI NIC cannot insert upon the ring. Through analyzing SRF frame via network analysis, the device that cannot insert can be identified. The SMT layer SRF Link Error Reporting Errors frames may indicate a problem with the flow of traffic through a port in a FDDI station NIC or concentrator. The SMT layer SRF MAC Errors frames may indicate a FDDI NIC cannot process a frame through copy functions or a frame is invalid and in error, or a duplicate address found. These conditions can identify possible misconfigured FDDI station NICs or concentrators. The SMT layer SRF Trace frames may indicate that a certain FDDI NIC or concentrator is operating in a fault mode.

The SMT layer assists in reporting on high FDDI MAC claim rates. High FDDI MAC claim rates indicate a constant change in the overall token bidding scheme and the ring order. The SMT layer can also assist in reporting on the frequent occurrence of stuck beacon and directed MAC frames. If a directed or stuck beacon frame is captured, the source device should be isolated and the analyst should replace the FDDI NIC or concentrator and the ring should be reanalyzed. The SMT layer may also assist in the reporting of trace occurrences. If the trace function is active on a FDDI ring, there may be conditions where a device is isolating a fault domain. An analyst should note the source and destination addresses to mark the fault domain.

The processes previously noted are the most important areas to analyze during a standard FDDI network baseline process. The analyst should also apply a ring performance analysis approach as required. Chapter 4, "Quantitative Measurements in Network Baselining," and Chapter 5, "Network Analysis and Optimization Techniques," discussed this process when the concepts for measuring effective throughput and timing were introduced. Based on a full stability review of the FDDI physical layer showing a positive output, an analyst can then move to the upper-layer protocol analysis step, which is described next.

Based on initial workload characterization steps being performed in a positive manner, an analyst can then move to analyzing the upper-layer protocols. This is where an analyst closely focuses on the FDDI medium from a full analysis perspective and examines the upper-layer protocol areas. In this case, the analyst should examine the protocol data unit carried by the FDDI frame by utilizing the methodologies presented earlier in this book to perform a full workload characterization review of the FDDI packets. This completes the approach necessary to analyze a FDDI medium in a positive network baseline process (see Figure 10.22).

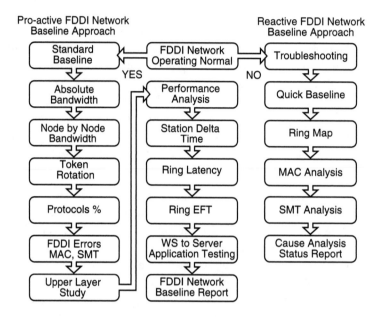

FIGURE 10.22 *The processes for performing both proactive and reactive analysis in a FDDI network baseline study.*

10.8 Closing Statement

The FDDI LAN topology is extremely fault redundant. When applying a proper network baseline approach, an analyst can perform the required methodology and extract the relevant workload characterizations such as utilization, protocol percentages, and associated physical analysis techniques to ensure that the ring is stable. If problems still exist after the ring has been verified stable, these problems most likely reside in the upper-layer protocol area.

If problems are located on the FDDI physical ring, they most likely will show in the physical layer MAC analysis or in the physical layer SMT layer analysis reviews at the network baseline stage. Further analysis of any other FDDI specifications may be required, as related to the variances possible because of manufacturer-specific designs and layout configurations.

The most important point to be made in this chapter is that most FDDI issues can be resolved by analyzing the MAC and the SMT layers, and the upper layers can be focused on from a main network baseline perspective.

Case Study 13: FDDI Timing Analysis

The *Fiber Distributed Data Interface* (FDDI) architecture allows for a network topology architecture that is extremely fault redundant, but that can also operate at an extremely high data rate. The FDDI data-rate design is much higher than standard topology ring architecture, such as the Token Ring specification. FDDI allows for a 100Mbps data rate on a single ring configuration and in custom dual configurations can allow for up to 200Mbps data-rate transmissions. Further specifications on the FDDI architecture and general topology specifications are presented later in this book. The discussion now focuses on a specific case study based on FDDI analysis.

The LAN Scope analysis team was contacted by a client who was experiencing excessive performance problems on a small FDDI backbone ring. Although the ring was small as to node-connection count, it was still a critical main ring for database access at the company's headquarters.

Upon arriving at the site, the LAN Scope analysis team immediately held an entrance briefing to review the FDDI ring configuration and specification. The ring was based on a 24-device connected configuration. The FDDI ring was operating in a normal fashion until several months prior to our engagement. The ring recently started to exhibit performance problems after two new database servers had been introduced into the facility.

The main facility internetwork was based on a split Token Ring and Ethernet shared architecture for user access through different floors of the facility for general operations. The FDDI ring in question contained the main file servers that were used for access to a custom database application for product tracking related to the site business operations. The applications that were experiencing slow performance were originally designed to operate on a digital VAX environment. The host environment for the application at this site was configured with *Digital Equipment Company* (DEC) mini-computers that were used for operations on this particular ring.

The NICs were all originally based on connection to a DEC host platform. Two new custom hosts of a specific server type were brought into the facility. The new host hardware platforms were designed to support a new type of the database being used at the facility. The vendor of the new database also brought the hardware configuration for the host as part of the package platform for the company.

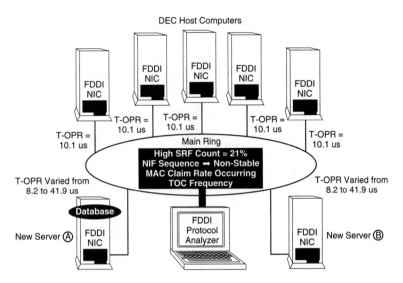

FIGURE CS13.1 *The Network for a manufacturing company based in Detroit, Michigan.*

This customer was a manufacturing company based in Detroit, Michigan, which developed a specific type of motor part having to do with infrastructure for engines used throughout automotive manufacturing plants in the United States.

Upon arriving at the site and meeting with the internal MIS team, the LAN Scope analysis team reviewed the general configuration. The internal MIS team immediately informed us that the two new database servers were the cause of the problem. Our initial focus was not to examine these servers as to the specific cause, but to generally review the FDDI ring from an initial baseline perspective, and then to closely examine the servers' operation (see Figure CS13.1).

We first connected a network protocol analyzer configured for FDDI topology analysis to the main FDDI ring. We noted the important workload characterizations such as utilization and protocol percentages as an initial focus. We observed that the average ring utilization was only 2% with a peak of 12% for 2.1 seconds as related to utilized capacity. The protocol percentages were normal, with DECnet showing at 70% and NetBIOS at 10%, and a TCP/IP showing at 20%. We immediately identified that there was a fluctuating percentage of *Station Management Protocol* (SMT) for FDDI at the physical layer, noted between 2% and 12%. Upon our review of the protocol statistics, this appeared abnormal.

Based on this concern, we then examined the physical layer of the FDDI from a general operation perspective. We set filters to examine physical FDDI beacon frames, *Medium Access Control* (MAC) beacon frames, claim frames, void frames, and general SMT types for conditions such as examining SMT *neighbor information frames* (NIF), SMT *status reporting frames* (SRF), and other conditions in the station management protocol category.

Our analysis immediately showed that the MAC layer appeared to be stable. There were no excessive beaconing conditions, claim conditions, or excessive void rates at the FDDI MAC level.

The higher percentage definitely appeared to be in the SMT frame-based layer. It appeared that the SRF count was high along with a nonstable NIF configuration sequence occurring upon operations. We also noticed that the claim rate appeared to be occurring on a more frequent basis than normal at the MAC level.

We then started to decode some of the general FDDI physical layer frames that were present. When we examined the FDDI frames for general operation information, we noted that upon NIF operation request and claim rate occurrences, all the DEC machines showed a requested *Timed Token Rotation Time* (TTRT) of 10.1ms, which appeared to be well within normal specifications. However, it was immediately evident that the valid transmission time and final determined bid time was as high as 41.9ms. This was excessive for general operations for FDDI claim sequencing.

We immediately decided that we should further examine the general claim process on the ring. The claim process in FDDI is a process where the stations across a FDDI ring can bid to determine the TTRT. This determines the amount of time that each station is allocated to transmit on a FDDI ring in an asynchronous process for equal communication, and also the time available for an additional transmission for a node based on the *Token Holding Timer* (THT), if additional time is required.

We noted that most of the stations on the ring in the original DEC configuration were using a token operational loaded timer of approximately 10ms for a *Timing Bid* (T_BID) operation. This T_ BID configuration is typically loaded upon the original configuration of a bid cycle.

After the two new devices had been introduced into the facility and their database server operations had become involved in the bidding process, they appeared to bid at a sequence rate that showed an intermittent change in bidding operation from 8.2 seconds. This rate rose intermittently and flagged solid at 41.9 seconds. This appeared to be an event that recurred and the nodes appeared to fluctuate with regard to their timing request on the token bidding processes. Every time this happened, it appeared that there was also an additional claim operation on the ring. This was odd. It showed that eventually what was occurring was that the new host station FDDI NICs were causing intermittent fluctuation in the complete bidding process and transmitting claim frames at an intermittent, different level and causing an abnormal operation. Other stations on the ring, such as DEC stations, would stabilize at a 10.1ms TTRT at a lower level and then eventually would increase into a higher level of 41.9ms.

Our investigation showed that because of the inconsistent claim operation of the new host environment NICs based on the database servers, their *T Operational Timers* (T_OPR) might be problematic. During the first rotation, we noted that they initialized at an 8ms level, but on the second rotation they changed their T_OPR and T_BID timers to approximately 41.9ms. We observed that eventually the actual physical level of FDDI was resetting at an asynchronous level across the ring at 41.9ms and continuing to operate for a period of time during which upper-layer protocols would operate on a ring that was utilizing a final negotiated TRT of 41.9ms.

We then verified our analysis of this condition and saved it in our trace analysis results. We then contacted the vendor of the new database application. They contacted their hardware vendor, and through further investigation it was determined that the particular FDDI NICs had a problem that caused this exact type of condition. Eventually, we even found conditions where a FDDI MAC Beacon Trace event was engaged and affected by the fluctuating TTRT situation. This condition, as analyzed, was abnormal and acknowledged as so by the FDDI NIC vendor. The new FDDI NICs were shipped to the facility and the LAN Scope analysis team oversaw the implementation of the new cards.

We re-analyzed the FDDI ring and found that the requested T_BID and TTRT and associated TRT of the new FDDI cards was 8ms and always consistent. This allowed the negotiated TTRT on the ring to eventually become 8ms and the valid transmission time to be much lower across the FDDI ring.

General operational performance immediately increased across the facility and appeared to show stable operation.

This type of analysis would not have been possible without discrete protocol analysis review and except through the method of reviewing the FDDI workload characterizations.

Many of the MIS support team members were concerned that periodic peak utilizations were occurring and were not being captured in the management systems. They also thought that there were perhaps too many devices on the ring.

In this case, it was a simple condition of two new FDDI NICs that were operating abnormally during the token bidding process of the claim cycle of FDDI.

In this particular case, our network baselining methodology proved to be 100% successful in verifying the site's operation and stabilizing the facility to a higher performance level.

CHAPTER 11

Baselining and Analyzing ATM

In the late 1990s, the networking industry started to release robust appli-cations, introducing applications that caused high utilization loads on networks and required a higher available capacity level on LANs and WANs. In addition, more end users within companies were starting to use the inter-network infrastructures. In direct parallel, the overall data components of the network also increased at the same time. As the application growth increased in direct concert with the number of users, the industry required higher speed network topologies. In response, network vendors began developing them, introducing technologies that provided high data throughput and high-speed transfer between different point-to-point schemes within global internetwork infrastructures.

Some of the key high bandwidth and broadband technologies even currently available today still only allow for specific, set data rates and specific components that are somewhat restrictive. A definite need existed for more of a broadband network topology that would enable innovative connectivity, high data throughput, and high data transfer, but that could also communicate to other LAN network topologies such as Ethernet, Token Ring, and so forth. The networking industry responded to this need by developing a new networking topology called *Asynchronous Transfer Mode* (ATM).

Both LANs and WANs can use ATM. Specifically, ATM can be used as just a LAN-based topology or as a backbone and uplink technology. ATM networks can serve as the medium infrastructure for high-speed data transfer of both

LANs and WANs. The ATM network is one of the more robust network topologies used in networking infrastructures.

This chapter describes the key architectural concepts and the methodology for baselining and analyzing an ATM network.

11.1 Introduction to ATM

The ATM technology is based on a connection-sequenced process that allows for extremely robust communication. ATM is associated with general broadband technologies. The ATM network can provide the combined transfer for key datasets such as data, video, circuit emulation, multimedia, and voice. ATM networks can transfer all types of new and innovative communication media technologies in combined or different stream cycles (see Figure 11.1).

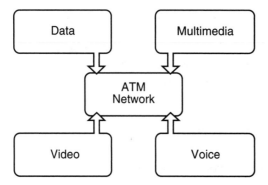

FIGURE 11.1 *How an ATM network can handle multimedia traffic flow.*

The foundation of the ATM network architecture is based on the transfer of an ATM cell. An *ATM cell* is a small component comparable to a packet, but is a fixed unit and is set at a 53-byte unit design. The typical ATM data transfer rates normally range from OC3 155Mbps to OC12 622Mbps. The overall consolidation of different information components for transfer—such as data, voice, circuit emulation, and multimedia—makes ATM a highly robust transfer mode.

The ATM network is extremely flexible in terms of design; the network designer can use both a *permanent virtual circuit* (PVC) and a *switched virtual circuit* (SVC) design.

The ATM network is compatible with other high-speed topologies such as the *Synchronous Optical Network* (SONET). Originally, ATM was based on a platform designed around *the Broadband Integrated Services Digital Network* (BISDN).

The *ATM Forum* (ATMF) categorizes ATM as a functional release. Key benefits of ATM include its high speed, high throughput, and low latency capability for overall network transfer. Also, it allows for a protocol-independent interconnection scheme between multiple network technologies. ATM is truly a high-speed broadband networking technology.

11.2 ATM Connection Schemes and ATM Cell Design

The ATM connection scheme is based on a process that uses an endpoint-to-endpoint communication design. Fundamentally, the endpoint-to-endpoint communication scheme is based on what is known as an *ATM Transmission Path* (ATM TP). The ATM TP is the primary, highest level ATM channel link from one device to another device that is communicating within an ATM network. Within the TP, devices intercommunicating through the ATM network can use assigned subpaths.

The second level down in the ATM communication path design after the TP channel is the *ATM Virtual Path* (ATM VP). The VP is comparable to a link known as the *Virtual Channel Connection* (VCC). The ATM VP is the path between two specific devices; these devices are assigned a link through the ATM internetworking hardware. The ATM VP has an internal sublayer capability to link and carry both a *Virtual Channel Identifier* (VCI) and a *Virtual Path Identifier* (VPI) to establish a wide range of different links through the ATM main network TP channel. Figure 11.2 shows the ATM transmission path. Figure 11.3 shows how the ATM TP uses a VPI and a VCI to establish a connection.

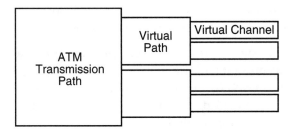

FIGURE 11.2   *The ATM transmission path.*

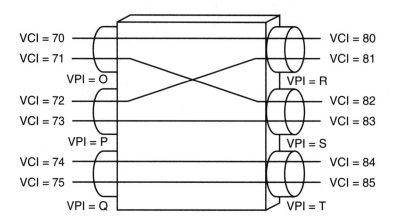

FIGURE 11.3 *ATM TP using a VP and a VCI to establish a connection.*

The following section briefly describes the main connection schemes used as the interfaces between ATM devices.

11.2.1 ATM UNI and NNI Connection Schemes

On an ATM network, assigned connections are usually either a *User-to-Network Interface* (UNI) connection or a *Network-to-Network Interface* (NNI) connection.

The ATM UNI connection is used when an endpoint such as a device is connected to an ATM switch and then to an ATM network. Normally, UNI connections are used for PCs, servers, workstations, and other key devices in an ATM network. You can set up the UNI connection through both a PVC hard-coded connection or on an SVC dynamic process connection.

If two specific ATM network point of presence devices, such as ATM switches, are going to require connection, or if the ATM network topology is going to be used for WAN connections, an NNI connection is usually preferred. The ATM NNI connections are normally provided via an internal connection within a LAN, or on a WAN through carrier-based designs.

The key point to remember is that when ATM networking devices connect to other devices, they typically connect through the NNI path. When endpoint devices (such as servers and workstations) connect to the ATM networking devices (such as switches), they connect through the UNI connection scheme (see Figure 11.4).

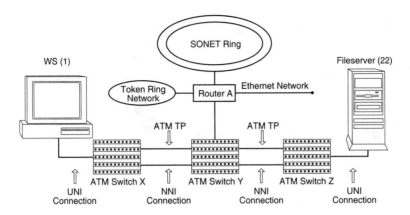

FIGURE 11.4 *UNI and NNI connections.*

The following example shows the main high-level scheme of the overall ATM connection: For a workstation on an ATM switch to connect to a server on another ATM switch, an end-to-end ATM TP channel must be formed. For the TP to actually be achieved, an ATM VP will have to be assigned. The VPI and VCI that form a final VCC determine the ATM VP. The VCC is considered the route identifier for the VP. The final ATM TP assignment between any two devices on the network, which holds the VP and VCC connection, is only possible through addressing identification. The ATM cell VPI and VCI fields, which are carried in the 5-byte header of the 53-byte cell, determine the addressing assignment.

The ATM cell is based on a 53-byte design and has a 5-byte overhead. Within the 53-byte cell with the 5-byte overhead separated, a 48-byte data payload is assigned separately. During point-to-point networking, certain key fields in the ATM cell are used.

As mentioned earlier, the ATM cell header contains a 5-byte field area. The ATM cell header key fields include the Generic Control field, the Virtual Path Identifier field, the Virtual Channel Identifier field, the Cell Loss Priority field, along with the Header Check Control field. As noted, the ATM cell is 53 bytes in size, 48 bytes of which are for the actual data payload assembled by the ATM processing mechanisms (as discussed in more detail later this chapter). Figure 11.5 shows an ATM cell.

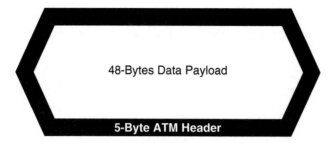

FIGURE 11.5 *An ATM cell.*

Other ATM header components that enable the VCC to identify a route and to assign a virtual path include the following:

- The first field is a 4-bit generic control field used for flow control sequencing.

- The VPI is an 8-bit field used to assist in assigning the final VP. This VPI is generally used to establish network-to-network connections, frequently for the final path assignment and then for the UNI final connection. The 8-bit assignment applies to a UNI connection. An NNI connection results if a network-to-network connection is being used for the VPI. In this case, the VPI can be 12 bits in length.

- The VCI assigns the final channel to the virtual path (normally assigned as a 16-bit field).

- The Cell Loss Priority field is a 1-bit field used to identify whether the actual cell can be discarded upon certain traffic overload conditions.

- The Header Control field is an 8-bit field normally used to detect or correct any errors in the transfer of cells between point-to-point connections. Figure 11.6 shows an ATM cell's internal fields.

After any device has received the ATM cell, the ATM device must process the cell, whether it is an endpoint device or an ATM switch. Endpoint ATM devices are usually PCs or workstations that include an ATM NIC. In this case, an ATM NIC would provide for the processing of the cell in both the transmission and receiving cycle. If the device is an ATM switch, the ATM circuitry is much more enhanced than in end-device ATM NICs. An ATM switch involves a design for multiple ATM network connections for UNI devices that are going to connect to the main ATM network via the ATM switch. Within the ATM switch, internal ATM adapter circuits are assigned to each ATM port and are normally present in ATM modules. The ATM modules then interconnect to an ATM switch backplane. Each ATM switch within the network eventually connects to other ATM switches and devices via an ATM uplink channel through NNI and UNI channel connections.

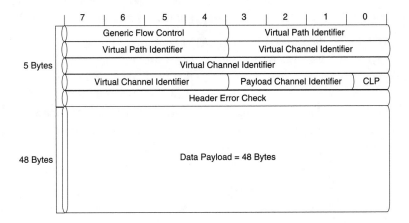

FIGURE 11.6 *The internal fields on an ATM cell.*

Within any ATM transmission or receiving process, certain circuitry must be available in both the ATM UNI devices and the ATM NNI devices and switches. The circuitry usually includes subcircuits to handle the processing of the ATM cell on both a transmission and receiving cycle. The ATM devices that process the ATM cell in the transmission and receiving cycle investigate the ATM cell.

11.3 ATM Operational Function Layers

The following standard layers must operate in an ATM NIC or an ATM switch port:

- The ATM Physical (ATM PHY) layer

- The ATM layer

- The ATM Adaptation layer (AAL)

The ATM PHY is the lowest layer closest to the ATM medium. This layer is responsible for transmitting and receiving the cells, and provides for the final data transfer processes of the ATM signal on the medium. It also includes two sublayers: the *Physical Medium* (PM) layer and the *Transmission Convergence* (TC) layer.

The ATM middle layer processes the cell after the ATM data stream passes through the physical layer on both the transmission and receiving cycle. The ATM layer separates the cell or combines the cell with the actual header information for transfer, or strips off the header transfer information upon receiving the ATM cell. This layer separates the physical layer from the actual processing AAL for handling the ATM *Protocol Data Unit* (PDU) in a 48-byte data payload.

The AAL handles the transfer from the ATM layer up to the upper-layer protocols, or assembles the upper-layer protocol data and puts together the payload required to transfer data streams down to the ATM layer for header assembly. The AAL is responsible for the investigation of the PDU and also invokes a process called *Segmentation and Reassembly* (SAR) for data transfer handling and composition for communication between two ATM endpoint nodes. Figure 11.7 displays the ATM protocol layer model.

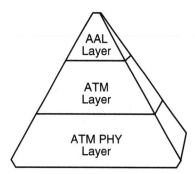

FIGURE 11.7 *ATM protocol layer.*

11.3.1. ATM PHY Layer Technical Operations

The ATM PHY layer contains both a TC layer and PM layer. The PM layer operates close to the actual fiber medium. Contained within the PM layer are certain circuits that enable reception and transmission of the physical signal: the physical medium circuits and the bit timing circuits for transfer of the ATM signal on the fiber medium.

The TC layer, a layer above the PM layer but a sublayer of the PHY layer processing sequence, involves other circuits such as the cell to frame transmission control circuit, cell boundary process circuitry, cell rate processing and smoothing circuits, and cell header processing to and from the ATM layer. Figure 11.8 displays the ATM PHY layer operations.

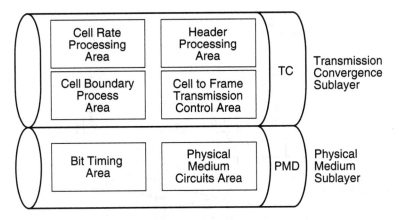

FIGURE 11.8 *ATM PHY layer.*

11.3.2 ATM Layer Technical Operations

The ATM layer is responsible for the interpretation of the ATM header and the processing of the ATM PDU and pass through routing of data with the AAL and composure of the ATM cell. The ATM layer involves circuitry such as multiplexors to handle the amount of transfer as related to extreme cell transfer. The layer also includes VPI and VCI processing circuits. The ATM layer engages generic flow control handling circuits for overall flow sequencing between two ATM endpoints and includes cell header processing to extract an ATM payload from a PDU or to import a PDU into a cell.

Note again that the ATM layer has to perform VPI and VCI tagging for address resolution and mapping. The ATM layer is responsible for ATM cell translation and for final cell transfer tagging. Figures 11.9. and 11.10 displays the ATM layer main operational modes and the VPI and VCI address processing.

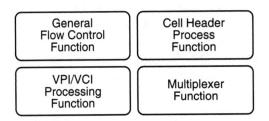

FIGURE 11.9 *ATM layer modes.*

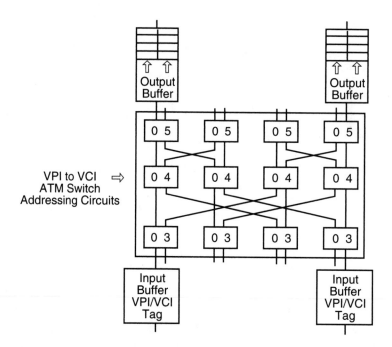

FIGURE 11.10   *VPI and VCI address processing.*

11.3.3 AAL Technical Operations

When moving into the ATM layer, the AAL is extremely critical to the overall final cell transfer process. The AAL includes the following two subareas:

- The Convergence Sublayer (CS)

- The Segmentation and Reassembly (SAR) layer

When an ATM cell has been brought through the ATM PHY layer and the ATM layer on a receiving cycle, it is brought up to the AAL. The AAL must break down the ATM PDU and provide transfer of the data stream up to the upper-layer application layers. In this particular case, the AAL SAR sublayer performs the data translation between the PDU and the final cell based on the processing from the ATM layer. Then, the ATM CS sublayer takes over the final processing.

The CS sublayer invokes circuits that include assignment and extraction operations for handling the ATM AAL type, the data properties, the timing, and the common process assigned to the ATM data transfer. These types of circuitry and operational cycles engage to transfer the ATM payload data up to the application layer. Figure 11.11 shows the ATM AAL main functions.

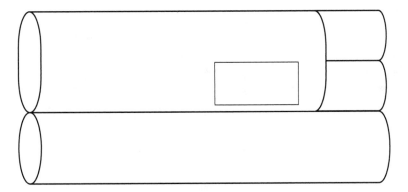

FIGURE 11.11 *ATM AAL main functions.*

On the outbound cycle for transmission, the *network operating system* (NOS) and the application components operating within the device provide the ATM AAL with a data stream from the NOS and application processing cycle. The ATM AAL takes the data stream and breaks it down into 48-byte payloads for transmission by processing the data through the CS sublayer circuits and assigning a data process, timing, an ATM process code, and an AAL type for overall transmission. The ATM cell is then processed through the AAL SAR sublayer so that the PDU data stream is translated into actual ATM cell units of 48-byte data payloads for transfer through the ATM layer and the ATM PHY layer and then onto the medium.

The following AAL types can be assigned:

- AAL 1
- AAL 2
- AAL 3 and 4
- AAL 5

Figure 11.12 presents the main AAL types.

The following AAL service classes can be assigned:

- Class A
- Class B
- Class C and D
- Class C and D and X

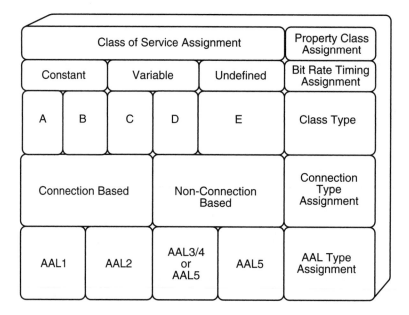

FIGURE 11.12 *AAL types.*

The following AAL classes can be assigned:

- **Class A.** This is a constant bit rate assignment and is normally used for voice. Connection processes are engaged and timing is required.

- **Class B.** This is normally a variable bit transmission rate process engaged for video transmissions. Connection-based processes are maintained and timing is required.

- **Class C.** Variable bit rates are assigned for high variable transfers such as bursty data transfers in video and other high-transfer media. Connection-based processes are engaged; and in Class C, timing is not required.

- **Class D.** Variable bit rate transfer is provided for unique sequences that involve transfer, such as bursty applications where connections are required and timing is not required. This is similar to Class C.

- **Class X.** This class is normally traffic-independent and timing is not required, as it is for open class design in unique operations.

Figure 11.13 shows the main AAL classes.

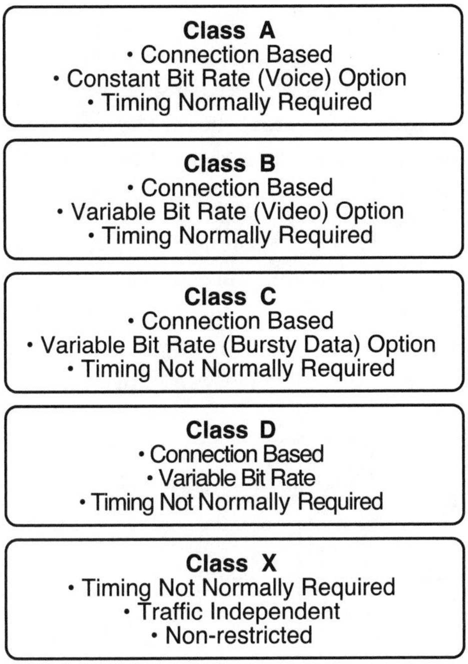

Class A
• Connection Based
• Constant Bit Rate (Voice) Option
• Timing Normally Required

Class B
• Connection Based
• Variable Bit Rate (Video) Option
• Timing Normally Required

Class C
• Connection Based
• Variable Bit Rate (Bursty Data) Option
• Timing Not Normally Required

Class D
• Connection Based
• Variable Bit Rate
• Timing Not Normally Required

Class X
• Timing Not Normally Required
• Traffic Independent
• Non-restricted

FIGURE 11.13 *Main AAL classes.*

These various AAL classes are used to assign a type and processing mode to data being transferred. Based on the AAL type assignment, the AAL CS sublayer area ensures that the proper timing, data properties, and common process are assigned to mark the final AAL type to a cell. The timing and data properties are affected, based on the AAL type. During an active ATM end-to-end communication session, both endpoint nodes have to understand the service mapping of the AAL type configuration.

When a workstation makes the data transfer to a server through an ATM network, if the request is being performed by a PC and the AAL type is already assigned, the PC attempts to transfer the data from the PC application layer through the ATM NIC by engaging the AAL, the ATM layer, and the ATM PHY layer to transfer the ATM cell onto the network. After the cell has been sent out onto the ATM TP for the ATM network, an ATM switch must investigate the cell and transfer it through the ATM TP on an assigned VCC via a final VP. All the required information to complete the final data transfer from an ATM node is encapsulated in the ATM cell header.

When an ATM cell is received by a device, the AAL service class is investigated by the device AAL to ensure the proper processing of the cell data to an application. The AAL type ensures the synchronization between the applications on each end of two ATM devices communicating across the ATM physical network so that each endpoint node can understand the processing of the ATM dataflow.

It is important to understand that the dataflow is assigned from an application process to an ATM data stream, which is then processed into a 48-byte data payload. The ATM devices that process the payload must move data through the AAL to the ATM layer and out to the ATM PHY layer on the network. Figure 11.14 shows the ATM cross-layer flow process.

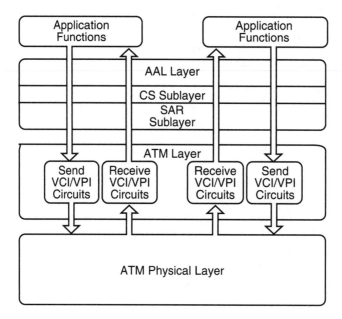

FIGURE 11.14 *ATM cross-layer flow process.*

When two ATM devices are communicating, such as a server and a workstation, each endpoint always communicates with the highest layer such as an application or NOS software module. The application endpoint, such as the server application running or the user shell running, then must communicate through the device-specific AAL, ATM layer, and ATM PHY layers at their endpoints. On transmission after the ATM cells have been generated, the ATM cells are received on the ATM network via UNI connections. Next the ATM cells must transfer through an ATM switch via an NNI connection.

The ATM switch backplane fabric circuits process the ATM cells to interpret the final VCC or VP connection link for assignment as to the link through the network switching channels for NNI connections between multiple ATM switches. This process allows for the ATM final TP to be engaged so that it provides an endpoint-to-endpoint final communication process for two ATM devices.

Figure 11.15 shows the ATM dataflow cycle of a transmission process.

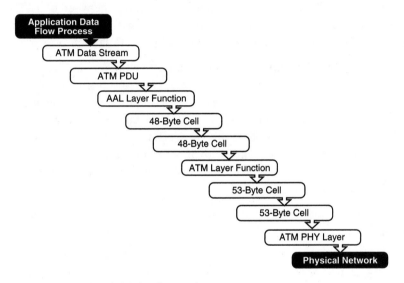

FIGURE 11.15 *ATM dataflow cycle.*

Figure 11.16 shows an ATM endpoint-to-endpoint dataflow sequence.

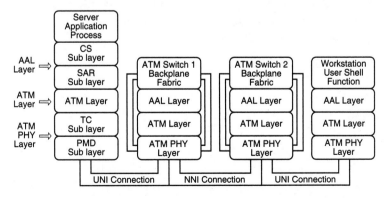

FIGURE 11.16 *ATM endpoint-to-endpoint dataflow sequence.*

11.4 ATM Connection Assignment Sequencing

As noted earlier in this chapter, an ATM connection can be assigned through both a PVC and an SVC.

In a PVC connection for two ATM devices, the assignment is preestablished and preassigned in a configuration. A PVC circuit is established for connection between a set of ATM devices or ATM switches within an internetwork configuration. The ATM VPI and VCI addressing components are used to establish a predetermined VP and final VCC assignment for a link between two ATM devices. This would be considered a hard-designed or hard-coded endpoint-to-endpoint PVC assignment for an ATM-based network layout.

In some cases, it is necessary for dynamic connection on demand sequencing to be available via SVC assignment for ATM devices to connect to the ATM network. The SVC assignment process is engaged in unique ATM network–designed networks that require a dynamic assignment of an ATM address to a device in an on-demand cycle. In this case, a device engages a switched virtual address resolution sequence with an ATM switch. The process of assigning an ATM address involves several steps for an ATM device to connect to an ATM network.

The following example steps you through an ATM device SVC connection process:

1. The initial step for a SVC setup is noted as the Phase (1) Call Sequencing Process. In this phase, a device attempts to start an SVC setup with an ATM switch through a UNI connection by sending a Setup message. Certain sequences of communication occur between the ATM UNI–connected device and the ATM switch. The Phase (1) sequences include Call Initial Reference message, Calling Node Address message, Traffic Mechanism Linking message, Call Sequencing message, Call Processing message, and VPI and VCI assignment.

   Figure 11.17 displays Phase (1) of the SVC connection process.

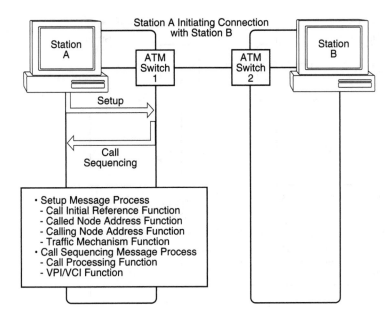

FIGURE 11.17 *Phase (1) of the SVC connection process.*

2. In Phase (2) of the process, the endpoint ATM workstation device has an initial setup active for connection to an ATM switch. Eventually this switch connects to another switch, which sets up a connection for the final VP to the other endpoint being attempted for connection, such as a server.

    Other Setup messages must occur to allow the Phase (2) SVC process to engage, such as the Setup message, which includes another Call Reference message, a Call Party Address message, a Call Party Address Assignment message, a Traffic Characteristic Link message, Quality of Service Assignment message, and a final VIP and VCI assignment. The final endpoint, such as a server, sets up its connection with the other endpoint ATM switch and performs a Call Proceeding Call Reference, and then sends a Call User Deciding to Accept Call Assignment message.

    Figure 11.18 displays Phase (2) of the SVC connection process.

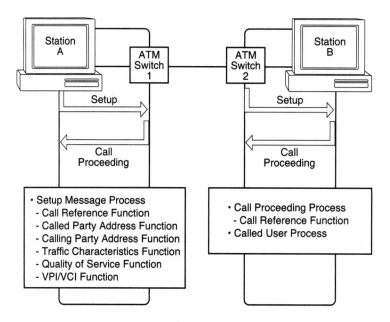

FIGURE 11.18 *Phase (2) of the SVC connection process.*

3. Phase (3) of the ATM SVC process is where the final endpoint device (such as the server) provides the actual acknowledgment that the connection is valid. In this case, the endpoint provides a Connect Message Assignment that links to the Call Reference Call Party Address message and indicates call acceptance through a Connect Acknowledgment Call message.

   Figure 11.19 displays Phase (3) of the SVC connection process

4. In Phase (4), the last step of the process, the original endpoint workstation, such as the UNI device, acknowledges that it has seen the assigned acknowledgment from the remote device (the server). In this case, the workstation just provides another Acknowledgment message to the endpoint server that it has acknowledged the workstation's request that it is connected, for the final SVC setup process.

   Figure 11.20 displays Phase (4) of the SVC connection process.

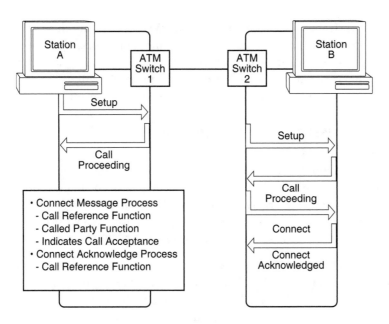

FIGURE 11.19   *Phase (3) of the SVC connection process.*

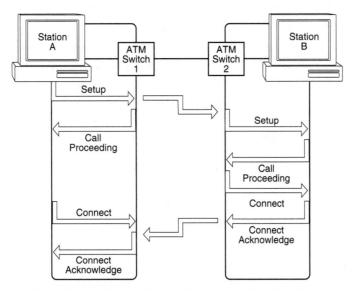

Station B Informs Station A That It Is Now Ready for Data Flow Transfer

FIGURE 11.20   *Phase (4) of the SVC connection process.*

In closing, in ATM networks a predetermined PVC connection can be assigned, which in some cases is considered more stable and more workable from a support standpoint in many large networks. On the other hand, for many dynamic situations that may require many different users to attach to the ATM network, SVC assignments could apply for a valid connection assignment.

11.5 ATM Addressing Assignment and Convergence Operations

It is important to understand that in an ATM network, certain devices are required to connect to an ATM server on a dynamic basis to obtain addresses of other devices on the internetwork. This is called *address convergence* or *address resolution for network topologies*. The approach used in an ATM network is to perform a process called ATM *LAN Emulation* (LANE).

In ATM networks, the LANE process is very important when ATM networks are connected to other LAN topologies such as Ethernet, Token Ring, and through routers or switches in a large ATM infrastructure. For instance, many Ethernet and Token Ring LANs are already in place and operating in the corporate environment. The users on these networks may just need a high-speed transfer mechanism for data transfer from one point of a building to another (or in other words, a high-speed backbone).

As a solution, many industry clients are using ATM technology for a transfer point between key points within a building, such as two separate floors. ATM network technology is being used in this case as a backbone link. In this type of design, there may be the requirement to provide interconnection on certain floors of Ethernet or Token Ring LANs to an ATM switch. In this case, the switch allows for Ethernet and Token Ring modules to have an assignment connection to the ATM switch. Within the back of the ATM switch is an ATM backplane that processes transfer of the Ethernet or Token Ring frames, via frame translation and PDU extraction, to an ATM cell transfer for an ATM uplink to another switch. The ATM switch uplink is considered a backbone component of the ATM building network.

In this type of layout, the devices on the Ethernet or Token Ring LANs have to locate the remote server on another Ethernet or Token Ring LAN in a building that is using an ATM backbone for a data transfer link between two ATM switches. To do so, the device attempting to communicate through the ATM backbone must perform an address linking or convergence process through the ATM LANE cycle.

The ATM LANE process occurs as follows:

1. A workstation connects to a physical local router or ATM switch and performs a physical outbound packet transmission process such as an *Address Resolution Protocol* (ARP) query to locate the remote device. In most cases, the local router runs an ATM *LANE Client* (LEC) circuit to provide the initial ATM address mapping.

2. The local router then takes the Ethernet frame and assigns an immediate LEC link to obtain the ATM address identifier required to start the ATM connection. In certain cases, the LEC may need to locate a *LANE Emulation Server* (LES).

3. The LES circuit holds the main ATM network address table. In certain cases, the LEC and LES circuits are combined within one device, such as a main ATM switch.

Figure 11.21 shows the ATM LANE process.

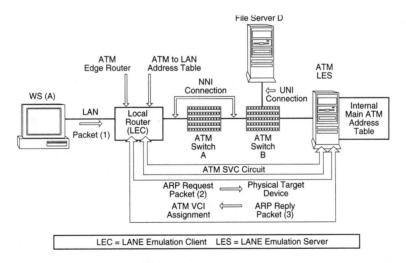

FIGURE 11.21 *ATM LANE process.*

In summary, a workstation connects to a local ATM router or switch that has an LEC circuit. The device generates an ATM query for an ATM assignment of a VCI connection to a remote LANE server on another ATM switch, or a specific separated LANE server process that is running on a host.

The key is that the ATM LEC communicates to the ATM LES to obtain the final ATM identifier address mapping that provides a physical address assignment to the remote PC that wants to connect to the remote server on the other side of an ATM NNI connection. This process is noted as ATM LANE.

Another ATM addressing assignment process is to engage a cross-site ATM Edge router or Edge switch design. In this case, each router or switch connected to the ATM network has an LEC circuit within each module. Also, one specific main module within the ATM switch can provide an LEC circuit. Figure 11.22 shows the ATM LES-to-LEC communication cycle.

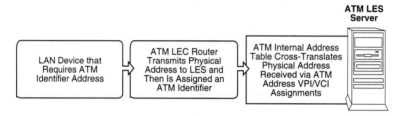

FIGURE 11.22 *ATM LES-to-LEC communication.*

The key is that all devices on Ethernet or Token Ring LANs connected to switch modules for their specific topology are connected into an internetworking hub or switch device. The main internetworking device handles the ATM switch connection and can provide an immediate LEC assignment for ATM addressing identifier resolution. An ATM LANE server circuit may be implemented on a central ATM switch within the main ATM backbone network. In this case, usually an ATM switch runs LEC circuits on all switch modules. This design allows for providing a cross-site ATM address mapping scheme for LAN address queries to resolve with ATM address identifier mapping in the main ATM switches handling the LES circuit. The ATM LES circuit then responds back with the ATM addressing to the LAN devices.

Note that when this process occurs, the ATM switch handling has to maneuver a high amount of VPI and VCI tagging to provide the final address mapping. The VCIs and VPIs are going to be bundled to assign a final VP and VCC for the overall sending of data through the ATM final transmission path. Figure 11.23 shows how an ATM switch cross-maps the VPI and VCI ATM cell fields for addressing and data transfer routing.

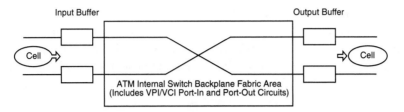

FIGURE 11.23 *How an ATM switch cross-maps the VPI and VCI ATM cell fields for addressing and data transfer routing.*

The ATM switches maintain an in-depth address table for ATM assignments as related to the routing entry. The connection table includes an assignment of each port that will have an assignment of a VPI and a VCI for the possible type of data being used as related to the AAL type. When an ATM switch receives a cell on an incoming port, it processes the VPI and VCI from the cell header and provides an immediate mapping assignment via a VCC through the ATM switch, which provides for transfer out the other ports within the ATM switch fabric. The ATM cells are transferred through the ATM switch rapidly on a high-speed transfer process.

11.6 Analyzing ATM-Based Networks

When reviewing an ATM network, it is important to understand that the workload characterization measurements are extremely critical. It is also critical that the analyst be prepared with the proper ATM analyzer. Certain types of connectors may be required for the ATM analyzer to connect to the ATM fiber medium at the site. It is important that the analyst understand the type of ATM connection required to apply the ATM protocol analyzer for data capture. For example, an ATM connection could be a UNI connection or an NNI connection. The analyzer most likely must be set up for either a UNI or an NNI connection mode. Another concern is to ensure that the analyzer being utilized is properly set up for the correct PVC or SVC connection mode. Certain software and firmware codes exist for the type of ATM UNI or NNI connection that may be applicable, based on the type of vendor assignment and design within the ATM devices connected.

All this information must be noted prior to setting up the ATM analyzer for capture. This enables the connection of the ATM analyzer in a quick and rapid manner and can help speed the network baseline process.

An analyst should request the ATM address information and ATM connection mapping sheets from the support personnel at the site. This type of documentation is usually available from ATM vendors for the ATM connection schemes used from device to device between UNI and NNI connections, along with the type of ATM UNI or NNI code assigned. This documentation enables an analyst to set up the analyzer and understand decodes more rapidly. Note that certain cables, specific cable connectors, or ATM connection pods may be required for connecting the ATM analyzer to an ATM network circuit.

After the analyzer has been connected to the ATM analyzer and can capture ATM cells, specific methodologies must be used for a normal workload characterization baseline exercise on an ATM network. The techniques described in the following sections apply when analyzing an ATM-based LAN.

An analyst should start by performing the following standard measurements:

- Average and peak bandwidth utilization

- Node-by-node utilization for all ATM circuits

- Protocol percentages and types

- ATM PHY layer analysis

- ATM layer review

- AAL review

- Review of upper layer protocol data units.

Figure 11.24 shows the ATM network baseline process phases.

11.6.1 Analyzing ATM Link Utilization

An analyst must understand that when measuring ATM utilization, both PVC and SVC circuits have to be measured. SVC circuits typically show a higher amount of utilization because of the call setup process that occurs during certain transmission cycles.

The key point is that the ATM network has to be monitored for standard utilization from an average, peak, and historical standpoint, depending on the type of analyzer used.

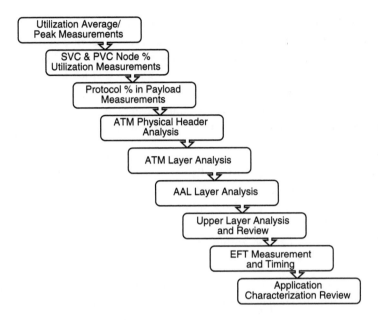

FIGURE 11.24 *ATM network baseline process phases.*

Most analyzers allow for at least an average and peak bandwidth measurement to be captured. In ATM network analysis, an analyzer tracking the ATM Cell-Per-Second (CPS) rate normally measures utilization. The utilization is linked to the available capacity, such as an OC3 (155Mbps) or OC12 (622Mbps). An ATM analyzer calculates and displays the average and peak utilization based on the number of cells present on the medium in state of time as related to the absorbed capacity.

Peak utilization transitions can occur very quickly on an ATM network because of the high transfer capability. In certain cases, ATM switches may have a backup overflow when trying to transmit data out onto a slower LAN connection such as Ethernet or Token Ring off the ATM medium. On outbound transfer from an Ethernet-or Token Ring–based LAN onto an ATM backbone, the transfer of data occurs much more rapidly. An analyst more likely sees bursty and high peak utilization on the ATM NNI rather than on the ATM UNI links.

The key to ATM utilization analysis is to capture all transitional peaks that occur and to properly measure a peak utilization for the period of time. Again, higher utilization levels normally are seen on ATM switch–to–ATM switch links, such as NNI channels, because there is more of a wide open capacity channel. This occurs because NNI links are wide open and no slower medium LAN network bottlenecks block bursty data transfers. ATM switches have to slow down the data rate when moving data back onto a Ethernet or Token Ring LAN.

11.6.2 Analyzing ATM Endpoint-to-Endpoint Utilization

When measuring ATM networks from an endpoint to another endpoint, it is important that an analyst understand that he must extract the relative utilization breakout for each PVC and SVC assignment as compared to the complete ATM TP utilization within an ATM network composite.

If a complete site network baseline is being performed, the analyst should take this into account and perform a very structured analysis against the ATM network as a whole. This measurement methodology enables the analyst to understand each main UNI and NNI connection. At a minimum, within a main site, each NNI connection should be closely sampled between the ATM switches. These are considered node points within the ATM backbone network.

If an analyst is measuring a specific ATM network backbone, the ATM analyzer should allow for extracting the node-by-node utilization for all the devices transmitting on the ATM network.

Each main VCC connection should be broken out for its relative utilization of the main ATM TP absolute utilization. In this type of case, when reviewing the data from a transmission path internal process on an NNI connection, the focus is to examine what virtual channel connections or virtual path assignment utilization factors are being utilized as relative to the complete absolute usage of that particular NNI channel.

11.6.3 Analyzing ATM Protocol Percentages

When looking at protocol percentages, the process could be as simple as reviewing the types of upper-layer protocols being transferred across the ATM link, depending on the ATM analyzer used.

Most ATM analyzers allow for a breakout of the upper-layer PDUs and a percentage marking as required. In this case, normal workload characterization processes apply.

If the ATM analyzer can also break out the AAL percentages from the ATM layer, it would be beneficial to note the AAL types and percentages. In most cases, the protocol percentage measurement process is fairly simple in ATM analysis.

11.6.4 Measuring ATM Physical Layer Error Levels

Most ATM analyzers allow for a brief review of the physical ATM data stream from the physical media-dependent layer on an inbound or outbound transmission cycle from the ATM medium.

If the ATM analyzer is properly connected to the medium on a UNI or NNI connection, the analyzer should extract key information for the analyst to review. The physical ATM error information includes header checksum errors, cell loss, and other key occurrences.

One critical error to check for is cell loss. If any cells are missing on reception from the overall data stream, this can affect the integrity of the endpoint-to-endpoint communications. Sometimes an ATM switch provides rapid transmission between two ATM switch points such as the NNI channel. On eventual retransmission back onto an Ethernet or Token Ring slower LAN medium, the cells may not be processed as rapidly because of the slower medium connection capability. In this case, the ATM switch port-to-cell buffer load may eventually increase within the ATM switch. If this occurs, ATM cells can be discarded or cells can be processed in an overflow mode from the buffer and not be processed onto the target LAN. This is called a cell leak or a cell loss condition.

When performing an ATM baseline session, some analyzers can detect cell loss by counting the ATM cell stream as processing the overall cell headers on a consecutive basis. If cell loss above a 1% level is detected, it is very possible that the upper-layer protocols may not retransmit and the data integrity of an application data stream can be affected. An analyst should monitor cell loss very closely.

When performing ATM physical analysis techniques, it is important that any errors in the header Error Check field of the ATM cell be identified. Most analyzers quickly identify ATM header control errors upon processing. It is possible that ATM cells on normal dataflow through an ATM internetwork transmission path could eventually get corrupted because of high-speed transfer cycles. This can happen in normal ATM networks where devices are not even failing. For instance, ATM cells can get corrupted during extremely high data loads upon the network as a whole. Note that ATM cells can get corrupted when failures occur in certain ATM devices and components.

When an ATM protocol analyzer starts to detect a high amount of cell corruption on a consistent ATM channel, it is very possible that a particular ATM channel may have a problem. It is also possible that there can be a major issue on either endpoint as related to the ATM switches if connecting two NNI points. This can also be an issue on a UNI connection when a device is connected through an ATM NIC up to an ATM switch port. In this case, the user endpoint for the ATM connection being used for capture via the network analyzer should be investigated for physical hardware operation, configuration operation, and possible review and replacement and reanalysis of the link.

In summary, it is important for an analyst to understand that if a high number of cell header errors are encountered, extreme cell corruption may exist and may be affecting the upper-layer protocol process.

Because of the high data rates, it is important that the physical layer of the ATM network be extremely stable. An ATM network must provide a proper foundation transfer for all upper-layer protocols. This is critical in an upper-layer analysis session.

Certain ATM network analyzers also allow for a brief review of the ATM PHY layer and close monitoring of the ATM medium. This is not always the case with all industry tools; but again, some analyzers do enable this type of close review of the ATM medium. Figure 11.25 displays the key areas to review during ATM PHY layer analysis.

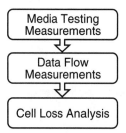

FIGURE 11.25 *Key areas to be reviewed during ATM PHY layer analysis.*

If an ATM medium has a problem affecting ATM signal transmission, the physical layer might be encountering physical media-dependent errors that would be reported to the analyzer. An analyst should keep a close watch on this concern.

11.6.5 Analyzing the ATM Layer

When an analyst is utilizing a network analyzer during an ATM session, it is possible to use the analyzer to track the VPI and VCI assignment for addresses. It is also possible to verify the header checksum area and cross-verify cell loss and error control. It is important to match cells to data streams upon processing up through the ATM layer to the AAL. Types of cell mapping errors or eventual transfer errors from the ATM layer to the AAL can be captured in ATM layer analysis. Some analyzers indicate these types of problems. These error types may indicate a problem with an ATM NIC or an ATM switched port. It is important for an analyst to closely review an ATM analyzer for statistics that may show problems when data is processing through the ATM layer. Figure 11.26 displays the key areas to review during the ATM layer analysis.

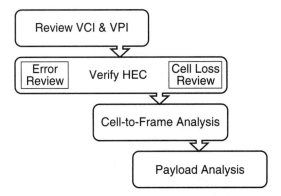

FIGURE 11.26 *Key areas to review during the ATM layer analysis.*

11.6.6 Analyzing the ATM AAL

An analyst must realize that the ATM AAL transfer is extremely critical, because the application data is integrated with the ATM cell on transmission and receiving modes. In this type of process, the ATM AAL takes the PDUs and extracts them from the cells on inbound receiving cycles and transfers them to data streams. On an outbound transmission, the data stream is broken down or segmented by the SAR layer into ATM cells for transfers. When monitoring UNI and NNI connections, certain analyzers can indicate problems that may relate to the ATM AAL SAR layer process. Most ATM analyzers can investigate the CRC field, the payload sequencing, PDU matching, and general SAR processes of transfer from the data payload to the ATM stream for the application. An analyst should closely monitor these processes. Figure 11.27 shows the key areas to review during the AAL analysis.

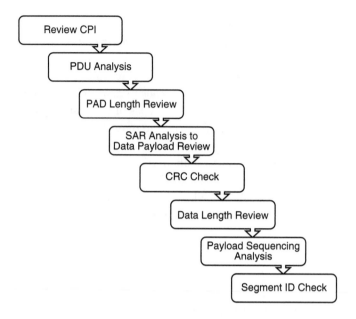

FIGURE 11.27 *Key areas to review during the AAL analysis.*

The analyst may have to closely review the ATM AAL SAR process. Processes with an AAL SAR cycle of the ATM AAL can be because of software and upper-layer application configuration issues and improper NOS configurations. These types of problems can cause further issues as related to the ATM TP design. A high number of retransmissions in the data cycle in general at the network and connection upper-layers may possibly be invoked by a high number of ATM PHY layer cell retransmissions. ATM cell retransmission can occur because of problems with the ATM SAR circuitry or SAR software configuration within a specific ATM point.

The analyst must carefully review the SAR data stream–to–cell sequencing on a consistent basis. The main way that this can be monitored is to closely review whether a high number of physical layer retransmissions occur and whether the assigned ATM connections appear stable. If connections are not stable, it is possible that the AAL SAR process may have problems.

The investigation of the AAL segment type, the sequence number, and multiplexing identification numbers is critical. Certain analyzers identify immediate problems in this area and may report them to the analyzer statistical screen or within the analyzer data.

If improper AAL types are found to be assigned, this also may affect the processing the SAR cycle. If data is missing from a payload, an analyzer may also encounter missing data or missing data payload errors; the analyst must quickly review this area. The PDU size should never be less than 8 bytes and should never exceed 65KB for an overall stream. After the stream has been broken down, it is transferred in 48-byte payloads.

11.6.7 ATM Protocol Analyzer Positioning Within an ATM Network

When analyzing an ATM network, an analyst must understand the importance of the positioning of the ATM analyzer. On ATM LAN segments, the analyzer should be positioned on devices that are going to connect via a UNI connection to an ATM switch, along with positioning analyzers on the ATM NNI to NNI connections. An analyst should use multiple positioning points so that ATM endpoint-to-endpoint transmission cycles can be monitored. An analyst should keep a close eye on ATM switch port flooding because this could possibly cause a lock on an ATM TP PVC or SVC circuit. These types of circuit locks normally don't occur on ATM NNI connections but may occur on ATM UNI connections. Figure 11.28 shows how to position an ATM analyzer during a network baseline session.

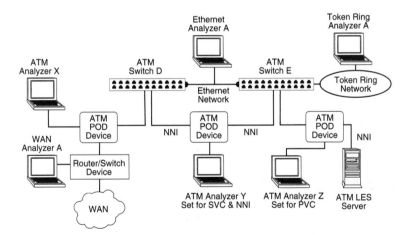

FIGURE 11.28 *Positioning an ATM analyzer during a network baseline session.*

After the analyzers have been properly positioned on the network, the analyst should look for key factors such as ATM cell delays. This would include conditions where an ATM switch is overloaded, and there is not enough switch memory applied for proper port buffering between ATM channels and LAN channels. This can affect the final SAR process on endpoints. If an ATM switch is improperly configured or improperly deployed in terms of an overload of connections, this could cause propagation delays on an ATM NNI-to-UNI channel. Additional delays could be present because of a slow switched backplane fabric in an ATM switch or router device as related to the number of connections or load against the switch, and an eventual physical mismatch and overflow of data could affect the source and destination device as related to final application dataflow integrity. Cell loss and overload are critical and could affect the integrity of the final data stream for transfer.

Figures 11.29 and 11.30 represent the concept of cell loss analysis.

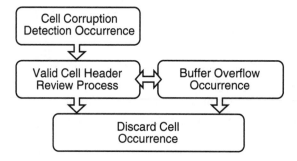

FIGURE 11.29 *Cell loss analysis.*

FIGURE 11.30 *Cell loss analysis.*

An analyst should keep in mind that the ATM network was designed for high transfer data rate and high throughput process. Therefore, it is very important that the connection schemes be properly designed. If Ethernet and Token Ring networks are properly connected to an ATM switch, the next factor that must be considered is the amount of Ethernet and Token Ring connections that are going to be transferred through an ATM switch on an eventual TP channel from an ATM switch to another ATM switch.

One key method an analyst can utilize as a measurement technique is to perform a close analysis between all key ATM switches in the overall ATM network that are providing endpoint-to-endpoint LAN connections on the ATM uplink or backbone. Effective throughput must be monitored along with utilization levels. If low utilization levels and capacity levels appear to be in check and throughput appears to be high, this would be a positive factor. When measuring the NNI connection, throughput should be easily achieved at well over 2000Kbps to 3000Kbps.

When measuring a UNI connection, throughput is somewhat susceptible to the LAN or endpoint device connections. In certain cases, each port connected to an ATM switch, such as an Ethernet LAN or a Token Ring LAN, must be monitored for utilization levels.

If a 16Mbps Token Ring LAN is connected to a port on an ATM switch, and the utilization levels of the Token Ring LAN port on the ATM switch for the UNI connection are showing extremely high levels of 80 to 90%, this would be negative. These types of saturation levels could indicate that the overall ATM switch port is also experiencing buffer overload when the ATM switch is attempting retransfer of data back onto that respective slower speed Token Ring LAN. This situation could cause a buffer overflow and eventually the ATM switch fabric would not be able to handle the data for the port assignment. An eventual flood of the switch port could cause cell loss and loss of integrity of the upper-layer PDUs. This type of an issue can sometimes be addressed by installing additional memory in the ATM switch and upgrading the switch configuration to handle a higher number of configurations. Another consideration could be to deploy additional ports and then segment the Token Ring LAN to be connected across multiple ATM ports for proper balancing. This would further reduce the level on the ATM TP for the specific ports assigned to the Token Ring LAN devices and therefore cell loss may not be a major factor. It is also important that the ATM NNI connections be balanced as well. Figure 11.31 displays an ATM LAN utilization and an EFT occurrence.

Overall, the complete ATM TP must be carefully considered from a design standpoint. When performing a proper network baseline study, an analyst can find ways to balance an ATM network on a more accurate basis to provide a higher performance level on the TP channel on the ATM backbone or ATM uplink design.

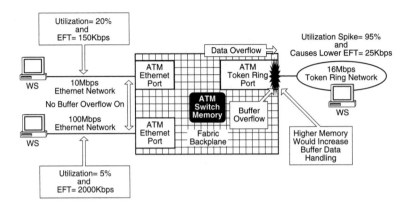

FIGURE 11.31 *ATM LAN utilization and EFT occurrence.*

As the industry moves forward to deploy more ATM endpoint connections such as server connections with direct ATM cards, which will provide a UNI connection directly to an ATM switch, more critical review of application balancing and endpoint-to-endpoint design will have to be considered. In current ATM backbone and uplink designs, these issues are not considered major factors, but balancing is critical.

ATM network baselining procedures are critical and must be performed in an exact manner, and the steps noted earlier in this chapter should be closely followed. It is important to take proper technical notes and to have all the ATM documentation available for a proper ATM network baseline study to be completed.

Case Study 14: ATM Performance Analysis

Asynchronous Transfer Model (ATM) is a connection-oriented topology service that can be utilized for local area, wide area, or broadband internetworking. Many different upper-layer protocols can work with ATM for general communication from node to node. The ATM internetwork architecture is based on a three-layer design comprised of the ATM physical layer, the ATM processing layer, and the ATM adaptation layer. In the ATM transfer process, a fixed-cell mechanism is utilized for packaging data instead of the frame structures used by other topologies, such as Ethernet and Token Ring.

For the purposes of this case study, the bottom line is that the ATM topology allows for a higher performance level based on the rapid processing of transmitting a fixed data unit of transfer on a per-transmission basis. The actual ATM data rate achieved can be analyzed by closely monitoring cell transfer versus frame transfer.

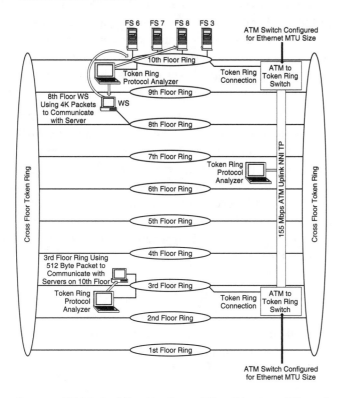

FIGURE CS14.1   *Migration from a Token Ring to an Ethernet architecture.*

This case study involves a LAN Scope client who was involved in a long-term migration from a current Token Ring architecture to a future Ethernet architecture in the user and server areas to increase performance on their internetwork channels between the users areas and key file servers at the enterprise facility. The migration also involved a structured plan to implement an ATM backbone channel between all user and file server areas.

The LAN Scope analysis team was contacted to study and test an ATM channel that was recently staged as a parallel channel to a cross-floor Token Ring network backbone that had been in production for several years. When we arrived at the site, we met with the MIS team members for an entrance briefing. We were briefed that the site had a 10-floor layout with multiple Token Ring networks for user access that were interconnected via cross-floor parallel Token Ring backbones configured through building riser channels. The network had been in place for three years and had been operating in a proper manner up to the point of our visit. We were also told that there recently had been an increase in the number of applications deployed against the LAN, which previously had been on mini- and mainframe host environments. Specifically, at this time the LAN was starting to be used for the processing of critical business dataflow for the company. The company in question was a finance company that provided transfer services between different banks in the Los Angeles area.

Upon reviewing the internetwork design and the symptomatic notes from our entrance briefing, we noted that a high number of performance problems were recently being experienced on the new ATM staged channel between the third and tenth floors. On the tenth floor, the client staged a main computer room that housed most of the main file servers for the facility. The other floors contained user network closets with Token Rings based on 16Mbps architecture. Some of the floors had one or two Token Rings, depending on user-count connection requirements for the specific floor.

A cross-floor Token Ring traversed the complete tower of the headquarters facility so that each floor user-based Token Ring network would have an interconnection to the tenth floor server room. The server room contained two Token Ring backbone rings that were in place to house the servers that provided resources for the users throughout the facility.

We learned in the site entrance briefing that a vendor had approached the company MIS team with a proposal to introduce an ATM backbone architecture between the floors. The main MIS team members thought that this type of implementation was perfectly in line with the projected migration cycle for a company that wanted to maintain a Token Ring topology within the user area, while increasing performance for general backbone and server point-to-point architecture. We noted in the entrance meeting that the client also intended to connect some of the file servers directly to a Token Ring ATM switch or via direct ATM on the tenth floor. The backbone architecture between all the floors was intended to be eventually based on ATM.

Based on the intended architecture direction, the client and associated vendor staged one ATM link between a third-floor user ring and one of the tenth-floor server rings as a parallel cross-floor backbone link for testing. The vendor equipment was staged with an ATM–to–Token Ring switch on the third floor and another ATM switch on the tenth floor that connected to one specific server ring, as a link down to the third-floor switch. An ATM *Network-to-Network Interface* (NNI), using a 155Mbps channel data rate, was utilized for the connection between the two ATM switches. One specific ring on the third floor was chosen for testing because the ring users engaged heavy access to a specific file server on the tenth floor.

Immediately upon implementation of the channel, the users on the third floor started to complain about performance. The users complained that when they logged on to the network, they had normal performance access; however, it appeared that whenever they accessed applications or general transfer, performance was definitely slower than when they were connected to the preceding Token Ring channel. This obviously confused most of the MIS team members, because they expected to see an immediate increase in performance. This also confused the ATM switch vendor. The vendor did provide technical support on the issue, but thought that their initial configuration from the third-floor Token Ring via ATM switch on the third floor was proper, and that the conversion from the tenth-floor ATM switch back to the Token Ring backbone on the tenth floor was also properly configured as related to para-meters for the switch and the ATM NNI *transmission path* (TP) cross-floor link.

The LAN Scope analysis team was asked to review the issue. We immediately deployed a protocol analyzer on the third-floor and tenth-floor Token Rings. We had an ATM analyzer available for testing, but we did not see a need to immediately deploy the analyzer in the initial stages of testing. Based on our knowledge of ATM, what we were first looking for was a general benchmark of performance of the application data transfer from one workstation Token Ring node on the third floor to the file server node on the tenth-floor backbone ring. However, the customer did request that we analyze the AT NNI channel on the link.

Based on this request, we did insert an ATM protocol analyzer in line with the staged ATM uplink for general testing purposes. This enabled us to have a three-position analyzer testing point design on our network baseline and troubleshooting process. Analyzer 1 was positioned on the third floor user ring; analyzer 2 was positioned on the ATM NNI uplink channel between the third and tenth floor; and analyzer 3 was placed on the tenth-floor server ring. The tenth-floor server ring access testing was planned based on an exact server, so we carefully set up a filter for the file servers MAC address on the third position analyzer. We wanted to run a specific set of testing patterns that included a standard workload characterization process to establish a rapid baseline, and we also wanted to focus on cross-floor performance issues. We engaged the third-floor analyzer, analyzer 1, and set up a filter against a specific user who was complaining about performance. We left the ATM analyzer on wide-open capture filtering on the uplink channel.

We asked the user on the third floor to launch a set of applications that had recently been experiencing performance problems. We noticed immediately that the user was experiencing certain performance problems, and we did see certain alarms activate on both the third-floor analyzer and the tenth-floor analyzer. We stopped our test briefly, deactivated the node filters, and decided to perform our normal rapid base-lining procedure to ensure that we had the proper measurements for characterization on the overall channel.

On the third-floor ring, we found an average utilization of 25% with a peak of 52%. We found the protocol percentages to be normal, and the Token Ring error rate stable. The Token Ring frame communication showed a normal ring purge rate and stabilization.

We closely monitored the tenth-floor ring and found similar conditions. On the tenth-floor ring, we found an average utilization of 41% with a peak of 72%. There were no abnormal saturation peaks, or protocols out of range. There were also no abnormal Token Ring physical errors or frame communications. The uplink analysis results on the ATM NNI showed clear utilization, well below 5% of the overall 155Mbps OC3 channel. We also noted that the protocol percentages appeared to be in line with the percentages of upper-layer protocols seen in the general Token Ring environment at the facility. There was a percentage-based mix of TCP, NT, and NetWare protocols as related to the different server environments across the facility. The ATM link also showed a 53-byte cell-forwarding process that was operating perfectly, and forwarding at approximately 20,500 cells per second. All general characterization checks appeared normal.

We then moved back to a more enhanced process of checking the application transfer via the third- and tenth-floor analyzers. We asked the user to launch the application a second time and more closely monitored the general symptoms on our analyzer. We consistently noted a high number of low effective throughput alarms and long acknowledgment times from the server. We noted that the application being accessed was on a expected Novell file server. We also noted that protocol layer decodes for the *Sequence Packet Exchange* (SPX) layer were showing a high number of acknowledgment and sequence latency-based errors (in that the acknowledgment numbers were not updating on a frequent basis), and they were also showing an extensive delay from the tenth-floor response back to the third-floor area.

During this session, we were closely investigating the artificial intelligence–based statistical screens on the analyzers that were utilized on the third- and tenth-floor Token Rings.

We stopped and saved the traces on all three analyzers. We next closely examined the data trace of the analyzer positioned on the third floor for general transfer. We turned on the summary and internal windows of the packet analysis areas within the trace. We noticed that the user, when launching all the application files, appeared to be using extremely small packet sizes. The packet sizes were noted at well under 600 bytes, specifically less than 576 bytes. This immediately caught our eye, based on our previous experience with this client's specific dataflow. Specifically, previous studies with this client showed that all Token Ring users throughout the facility normally used a much larger packet size, ranging from 2000 to 4000 bytes, for general communications to the Novell file servers at the site. The Novell file servers were utilizing a burst mode protocol process along with *Large Internetwork Packet Exchange* (LIPX). Even when Sequence Packet Exchange was used, SPX II was engaged for larger packet-size processing.

Based on our observations, it was immediately evident to us that the *maximum transmission unit* (MTU) for Token Ring was limited on the third-floor ring. We examined the tenth-floor Token Ring trace data results and also identified that the server was communicating to the workstations on the third floor at an extremely small packet size when using the ATM channel.

We reexamined the initial launch sequence of our trace analysis results from the third floor. We noticed that when the workstation on the third floor requested a packet size of approximately 4K via Novell packet-size negotiation of Get Maximum or Big Packet Size, a packet-size reply was returned to the third-floor workstation limiting transfer to approximately 576 bytes. This appeared to be more in line with the standard Novell *Internetwork Packet Exchange* (IPX), or SPX1 parameters. Further review of this condition, showed that the maximum packet size was limited, even upon negotiation of outbound workstation requests for a large packet size. This was confusing because all the normal configurations of the third- and tenth-floor Novell nodes allowed for this type of packet-size negotiation to occur.

Further investigation of the tenth-floor traces appeared to show anomalies on the packet-size general transfer between the ATM to Token Ring switch to the server on the tenth floor. This prompted our team to request configurations of the ATM–to–Token Ring switches from the vendor. Upon review of these configurations with the vendor, we could clearly see that there was an automatic configuration for a maximum MTU that was smaller than a maximum Token Ring size of approximately 4K. Further investigation showed that the vendor had recently upgraded the ATM switch configuration from ATM to Ethernet *LAN Emulation* (LANE) to ATM Token Ring LANE. LANE is a process that allows an ATM switch to map a topology node to a particular ATM identifier address in a particular cycle. At certain times in the LANE process, the actual size of a packet can also be affected as negotiated based on topology MTU specifications.

When a LAN station sends a frame to an ATM switch, the switch utilizes a *LAN Emulation Client* (LEC) and a *LAN Emulation Server* (LES) to map the type of communication that will occur based on the ATM edge switch or design.

In this particular case, the recent upgrade from ATM Ethernet LANE to Token Ring LANE should have allowed for maximum packet-size increase to 4K. Apparently the patch did allow for compatibility with the Token Ring topology, but kept the maximum MTU below the 4K range and limited the general packet size to an Ethernet MTU of approximately 1500 bytes.

Through further investigation of this situation and in comparison with Novell parameters for the IPX and SPX protocol stack in the NICs of the nodes involved, we clearly found an incompatibility in the ATM switch parameters with the Novell NIC drivers and protocol stack operations.

We contacted a Novell technical support channel and found out that there had been a series of calls on this particular problem for this type of vendor switch. In this
circumstance, it was found that the SPX protocol stack, when limited to the Ethernet MTU channel, would default to below a 576-byte connection or forwarding rate on an SPX type-1 connection-based process. Specifically, SPX 1 was considered as engaged and any attempted LIPX negotiation was defaulted to standard IPX.

This definitely accounted for a smaller packet-size configuration anomaly that was somewhat due to contributing factors of both the vendor protocol stack having an incompatibility with the ATM switch, along with the ATM switch capability to forward a proper Token Ring packet in normal negotiation sizes.

The ATM switch vendor was contacted upon our final findings and was able to provide a firmware patch that allowed for a maximum MTU negotiation of 4K across the ATM NNI channels. This patch, as related to software and firmware, was implemented on the site ATM switches using a flash code.

The LAN Scope analysis team then reanalyzed the condition, utilizing the same type of application testing. Upon investigation of the third- and tenth-floor testing nodes, we immediately noted that 4K packet sizes were being negotiated and a standard Novell burst mode protocol was now being engaged for communication to each one of the Token Ring packets over the channels that entered the ATM switches. The cell-forwarding rate increased to more than 35,000 cells per second and appeared to show a much higher performance channel. When we contacted the users on this recent migration implementation related to our exercise, they also noted a higher performance level.

In this case, our network baseline technique and combined ATM testing proved extremely successful.

CHAPTER **12**

WAN Topologies

When performing a network baseline study on a *wide area network* (WAN), an analyst must be properly prepared with the necessary WAN documentation prior to beginning the study.

The WAN documentation that should be compiled prior to performing a WAN network baseline study should include WAN layout diagrams, WAN router configuration specifics, WAN networking configuration sheets for equipment such as DSU and CSU connectivity devices, and WAN carrier circuit information. Specific notations for addressing schemes between LAN sites interconnected through the WAN should also be included in the documentation.

WAN networks are composed of connectivity schemes that interconnect multiple LAN-based sites. Because of this, it is important for an analyst to have a handle on the configuration, layout, and the network baseline results of any LANs interconnected through a WAN being analyzed.

With the rapid deployment of new internetwork technology, LAN and WAN network infrastructures are changing quickly in the global environment. There is an ongoing cycle of deployment of multiple network nodes and devices along with the parallel rapid deployment of many different applications and network operating systems across separate LANs. This process increases the data workload and applied network baseline review cycles that must be performed on LANs and WANs by network designers, implementers, and network support teams. The application deployment alone occurs on such a consistent basis that frequent LAN and WAN network baselining must be performed on an ongoing basis.

It is beneficial to perform WAN baselining samples both before and after application deployment. This helps an analyst to understand how certain WAN mediums and other associated LANs that are interconnected by the WAN networks are affected by application deployment (see Figure 12.1).

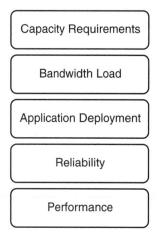

Capacity Requirements

Bandwidth Load

Application Deployment

Reliability

Performance

FIGURE 12.1 *Factors to consider when performing a WAN network baseline study.*

This chapter presents the necessary architecture descriptions for some of the key WAN network topologies that are popular and utilized throughout the global infrastructure in today's networking environment.

We first discuss dedicated circuit technology, including fractional T1 and T1 circuit architecture, along with methods for troubleshooting and analyzing T1 WAN circuits. Next, we discuss ISDN architecture technology, along with analysis methods that can be used to properly troubleshoot and analyze an ISDN WAN link. This chapter closes with a description of the Frame Relay architecture, along with a discussion of techniques on how to analyze and troubleshoot Frame Relay networks.

Keep in mind that many factors are involved in designing, implementing, troubleshooting, and analyzing a WAN medium. Most WAN network designs have specific bandwidth requirements that must be in place to support the required application deployment and network communication dataflow between key LAN sites. The cost of an overall WAN and its design and support processes are also major factors when deciding on a final WAN design.

Wide area networks must be stable, reliable, and provide high performance. At the highest layer of visibility, WANs must always be available. This is because many of our WAN topologies today support access to different LAN sites that connect distributed servers. In this case, servers are placed across different LAN sites and hold specific resources that must be accessed by users from different LAN locations. Simple centralized server positioning and processing is no longer widely used, and many diverse client/server applications are deployed across WAN mediums. Because of this, there are many different options for WAN types and topologies.

12.1 Dedicated Circuit and T1 Architecture Technical Overview

Dedicated circuit technology has been popular for quite some time. From the mid-1980s through the early 1990s, it was quite popular to use digital lease-line architecture for interconnection between LAN-based sites. Two LAN sites could engage a leased WAN link that would allow for digital transmission across the line. *Dataphone Digital Services* (DDS) were available in full- or half-duplex communications and were utilized for lower data rates from 2.4Kbps up to 56Kbps. With DDS transmission, the digital signals are carried inside the WAN communication leased channels and then are transferred from LAN to LAN across metropolitan areas.

The digital leased-line scheme evolved to a more enhanced WAN digital transmission design option with the introduction of the T-carrier system. The T-carrier system was introduced by the Bell Laboratories development team. Many different vendors participated in the enhancement of the T1 specification. The T1 technology evolved over a period of time and was an important solution in solving capacity and connectivity problems between different local area sites (see Figure 12.2).

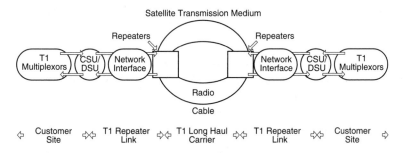

FIGURE 12.2 *A basic T1 circuit layout design scheme.*

The initial T1 circuit is based on a 1.544Mbps digital circuit link between two sites. The T1 circuit cabling layout is normally based on a four-wire path copper system that allows for point-to-point interconnection schemes between two sites. The T1 circuit signal transmission design is not limited to just copper-based media and can be engaged across fiber optics, microwave, and other cabling systems.

The T1 point-to-point connection scheme is simplistic in design, and allows for interconnection between two sites through a scheme connecting a *data terminal equipment* (DTE) and *data communication equipment* (DCE) process.

The initial transmission signal design for a *digital signal* (DS) channel included a circuit allocation assignment of DS0 circuits and circuit upgrades from that point. The *DS0* channel is the foundation of the digital T1 services network. A DS0 channel is rated at 64Kbps and can be multiplied 24 times with framing applied to create the T1 DS1 signal, noted as 1.544MB.

The T1 circuit DS1 design can be interleaved on a 28-circuit multiplex scheme, which allows for a T3 circuit allocation of 44.73Mbps, and which utilizes multiple channels for intercommunication. Other higher DS multichannel designs such as T4 and other circuitry are used throughout the industry. The T1 circuit design is the most widely used digital channel option for interconnection between point-to-point locations.

If more WAN bandwidth is required, multiple T1s can be interconnected by adding more direct-circuit, point-to-point links from site to site. It is also possible to create high-bandwidth links between sites by multiplexing multiple T1 channels from LAN site to LAN site through a *High-Speed Serial Interface* (HSSI) module in routers at each endpoint (see Figure 12.3).

A LAN interconnected to a WAN is usually linked through a passthrough device such as WAN router. The router usually has a LAN module that connects the LAN segment to the WAN router, such as an Ethernet network module. The router usually also has a WAN module that links to a WAN transmission circuit interface via a T1 port. The T1 port then usually connects to a WAN transmission device such as a channel bank multiplexer or a simple *digital service unit/channel service unit* (DSU/CSU), which then connects to the carrier WAN line. Within the WAN router, a process occurs in which *protocol data unit* (PDU) streams are extracted from the Ethernet frames entering the LAN module interface. The data streams are then converted into a signal with applied framing for WAN transmission via the WAN router and WAN module. The WAN module applies the final LAN PDU–to–WAN signal conversion via frame-to-signal translation to produce a framed data stream such as the T1 frame.

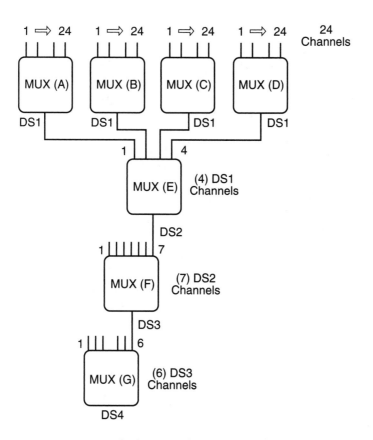

FIGURE 12.3 *Multiplexing can be used to create a multiple-circuit interleaved, but incremental, T1 tiered WAN design scheme.*

The T1 WAN channel signal circuitry design engages a data-to-signal framing technology that operates at three different levels: positive voltage, negative voltage, and ground reference point. The T1 digital signal alternates in bipolar mode based on transition of continuous ones and zeros, which reverse in polarity. The one value on the signal is known as a V pulse and a consecutive one is considered a negative V pulse. Zeros are normally generated as straight zero values. The signals reference a master clock signal to create the final T1 synchronous signal on the overall channel. The digital coding scheme engages a *Bipolar 8 to Zero Substitution Signal* (B8ZS), which is utilized as a code in the pulse stream. The B8ZS is used to ensure the proper transmission for zero bytes within the point-to-point transmission. After data has been formatted in a T1-specific frame for transmission across the digital T1 circuit, multiplexing is next used in a tier design, which includes interleaving multiple DS channels at one site that would then be multiplexed into a final T1 DS combined signal. The following format process forms the actual T1 final frame data stream: The data is formatted in 8-bit patterns for transmission at an 8KHz data-sampling rate of 8 bits per sample, which creates a 64Kbps data rate (and that directly relates to a 64Kbps per DS0 channel data rate). The 64Kbps DS0 channel is multiplexed by 24 channels in a full T1 frame to create a 1.536Mbps T1 frame. The 1.536Mbps T1 frame is then supplemented by an additional bit that is added and is normally labeled as the 193rd bit to complete the T1 framing process.

This formatting process allows for one framing bit to be assembled in addition to the 24 DS0 channels and creates the T1 DS1 signal. With this process, the 24 DS0 channels, which are rated at 64Kbps, equal 1.536Mbps and with one framing bit at 8Kbps, equal the final T1 data rate of 1.544Mbps.

Note that the European assignment of digital leased-line transmissions is normally designed around a 56Kbps circuit transmission due to different framing methods. The European methods for transmission engage 7 data bits with 1 parity bit assigned, which changes the data rate achieved from 64Kbps as used in the United States to 56Kbps, which is normally used in Europe (see Figure 12.4).

Channel #1	Channel #2	. . . .	Channel #24	F
Bits 8	8		8	1

Per T1 Channel	8 Bits x8 KHz Sampling Time Period
	64 Kbps per Channel x24 Total DS0 Channels
	1,536 Kbps of Data per Frame +8 Kbps T1 Framing
American DS-1 Transmission Rate:	1,544 Mbps

Per T1 Frame	24 Channels x8 Bits per Channel
	192 Bits +1 Framing Bit
Framing Bit or 193rd Bit	193 Bits per Frame

FIGURE 12.4 *A standard T1 frame used in the 24-channel, 64Kbps DS1 frame format.*

Note that T1 circuits and digital leased communication are susceptible to noise and interference that can occur depending on how the lines are configured from a point-to-point location. Cross-talk related to magnetic fields can be a major interference. This results because the lines are not properly positioned from the point-to-point layout. Another major concern is envelope delay distortion. In this case, attenuation can occur and frequency changes can be affected on an ongoing basis. Phase jitter is also a concern, in which zero crossing interference can take effect as related to the signal voltages, which can be negatively affected. To address most of these concerns, most T1 circuits are provided with a conditioning process through T1 channel (C) and digital (D) conditioning. The C and D conditioning is usually provided within a *digital service unit* (DSU) and *channel service unit* (CSU). The DSU/CSU devices provide the main interconnection scheme from a WAN router to the T1-carrier circuit medium.

When deploying a T1 circuit, you must consider overall LAN and WAN management concerns. The design team must understand many issues, including the topology layout for interconnection between the LAN and WAN points, how the circuits are going to be connected, and the LAN-to-WAN bandwidth requirements. The T1 switching gear must be configured. The T1 circuit-handling devices such as the DSU and CSU must be properly configured and implemented within each site of the LANs being interconnected on the WAN. The proper WAN routing protocols must be engaged and configured between multiple routers to ensure cross-site WAN router convergence of addresses among multiple locations. The cost of the WAN hardware and software is also a major factor, as related to the overall layout of the T1 dedicated circuit. T1 fractional circuits can be designed as available as a portion of the T1 circuit allocation. Fractional T1 circuits are available in 64K DS0 increments up through a 1.544Mbps design. Popular fractional T1 circuits are commonly designed in the area of 128Kbps, 256Kbps, 512Kbps, or 768Kbps. Various T1 fractional designs and configurations can be assigned, according to the bandwidth requirements, between LAN sites.

12.2 Troubleshooting and Analyzing T1 Circuits

When performing a WAN network baseline study on a specific WAN circuit type, all standard workload characterizations must be considered (as discussed later in this chapter in the section titled "Closing Notes on WAN Network Baselining"). This discussion now focuses on the specific methods for testing and analyzing WAN T1 channels.

When performing a network analysis session against a WAN medium that includes a circuit such as a digital leased line or T1 and fractional T1 circuits, specific network analysis techniques must be used. One of the first techniques that should be engaged for testing the physical health of a dedicated line T1 circuit is to engage a T1 analyzer with a line-quality tester that utilizes a *bit error-rate testing* (BERT) option. When transmission takes place on a T1 circuit, signal-to-bit errors may occur, and the value of a bit can be affected or changed on the T1 medium. Certain external factors can create problematic occurrences, such as noise on the WAN circuit or line, which can cause either end-site router to interpret a T1 signal incorrectly. The T1 signal and the applied framing can be affected. An analyzer BERT is a testing method that can be used to verify the integrity of the WAN link platform, WAN connectivity devices such as DSUs/CSUs, and WAN routers. It is critical that the complete WAN channel has true integrity from a connectivity and transmission level. This is because each LAN endpoint will be affected by the capability of the transmitters and the receivers throughout the complete WAN (see Figure 12.5).

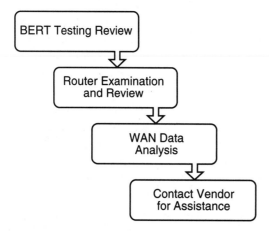

FIGURE 12.5 *The initial process that should be followed for testing and analyzing a T1 or dedicated leased line.*

Most WAN protocol analyzers include data-analysis features as well as internal BERT optional features. Most WAN protocol analyzers connect to the exterior side of a bridge or router via a specific cabling interface. After the WAN analyzer has been connected to the WAN channel link, it can be in either an active or passive position for capturing data traveling across the WAN channel. In a passive mode, the analyzer just captures data for analysis. The WAN analyzer can also emulate a transmitter or a receiver device within the connection path between multiple LAN points connected across a T1 dedicated WAN link.

Local transmitter devices are referred to as DTE or the user equipment on the interior LAN on the transmitter side. The end-user equipment is connected to the local side of the LAN, which then engages the WAN router and circuit to be a transmitting DTE. The WAN side of the router has a DTE and a DCE component. Each WAN network channel has at least one local and remote end. The local LAN endpoint of the WAN network channel is considered the DTE side. The remote end of the WAN network from the local side viewpoint is considered the DCE side.

A WAN protocol analyzer is placed on the exterior side of a LAN and is usually connected between a WAN router port and the WAN circuit via specialized cabling connections.

Many different cabling interfaces can be used. The type of cabling connection for the WAN protocol analyzer usually depends on the WAN equipment chosen for design, such as the router. The most common interfaces are the V.35 interface, the *Electronic Industry Association* (EIA) 232C interface, and the standard EIA-422, EIA-449 interface (see Appendix B, "Reference Material").

When using a WAN protocol analyzer to examine *upper-layer protocol* (ULP) data packets, note that a type of T1 framing encapsulation shows in the analyzer data trace as a DTE or DCE for the source and destination device in the T1 frame header decode. Most WAN analyzers also allow full decoding for T1 frame formats for standard T1 through D4 and extended superframe. Note that at least two WAN protocol analyzers should be used on each end of the T1 WAN channel.

After the WAN protocol analyzer has been engaged and a WAN data trace has been captured and saved, the data should be viewed. The process of actually viewing the WAN ULP-based data is further described throughout the book. As for the T1 frame header, the data packet format displayed in the analyzer usually shows a DTE or DCE as the source and destination.

Next, the analyzer usually displays the data link control layer, the network layer, and other ULP layers held within the encapsulated packet.

When conducting a WAN baseline process (as discussed in the section titled "Closing Notes on WAN Network Baselining"), an analyst must first examine the key workload characterization statistics. These statistics include T1 channel utilization for average and peak levels on the channel. Next, the device node-by-node utilization from each LAN site as applied to a T1 WAN channel should be reviewed and noted by examining the network layer of packets for end-node device identification fields along with statistical screens from the T1 WAN packets captured.

The T1 WAN channel protocol percentages must also be examined as to how different protocol types are applied to each T1 WAN channel. This is critical to understanding the split of usage of different operating systems and applications used across multiple LAN sites throughout the WAN.

It is next critical from an analysis and troubleshooting standpoint to examine the physical integrity of the complete T1 WAN channel. When examining a WAN T1 channel, many areas must be investigated. All general DTE or DCE device operation and hardware diagnostics should be performed. All vendor-specific tools and WAN protocol analyzer BERT features must be engaged. Those testing BERT should be used to test line integrity for transmitting and receiving data with lower error rates. All endpoint LAN bridges, routers, and switches must be examined for general diagnostics. They must be examined for their capability to pass the T1 WAN signal to and from the LAN network to produce and interpret all ULP data streams with true integrity. The WAN router and DSU/CSU equipment must provide proper data-rate buffering speeds, which are critical as to timing and throughput.

The WAN protocol analyzer involved in the network baseline study can be used to carefully examine T1 WAN data frame headers for CRC field health to ensure that there is no corruption. An analyst should carefully examine the integrity of the WAN protocol encapsulation engaged and the handling of protocol layers and ULP data with regard to the final formation of a T1 frame for WAN transmission (see Figure 12.6).

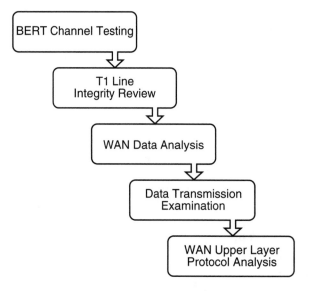

FIGURE 12.6 *The final process in WAN T1 analysis methodology that should be followed during a WAN network baseline study.*

Most WAN analyzers can identify any problem issues with T1 signal framing and WAN T1 packet framing, along with issues related to addressing for DTE to DCE.

After these areas have been examined from an analysis and testing standpoint, an analyst should decide whether BERT is required on the T1 WAN channel. If the initial testing on the physical layer via T1 protocol analysis shows CRC errors, framing errors, or signal statistical errors, BERT should be done. When performing a BERT on the T1 channel, note that a brief outage may be required while testing is performed because BERT is an active generation testing mode operation. BERT is designed to thoroughly test the integrity of the WAN. An analyzer displays the results of a bit error-rate test after sending a transmission with a number of bits across the WAN T1 and then measuring the number of errors or erroneous bits sent and comparing that number to the industry average. A BERT is designed to take into account that approximately 100,000 bits of data are sent or received for every error bit sent or received. Thresholds can be analyzed as to the T1 channel health for acceptability in testing. Any errors in BERT mode of more than 3% can indicate a problem. If more than a 3% error rate is present, further verification testing should be performed by the circuit vendor. Most analyzers that include BERT can test a variety of standard interfaces. An analyzer BERT can usually test different data rates. The analyzer BERT mode engages generation test patterns sent across the link.

To test the true integrity of the link, an analyst should conduct BERT during business off-hours. WAN analyzers with BERT display the error counts and display the results in various statistical modes. Certain data and clock polarities usually need to be selected to properly emulate the WAN T1 configuration for channel transmission design and DTE/DCE mode. Most WAN analyzers have a specific setup for T1 channel-clocking configuration options to fit the actual T1 circuit configuration. The T1 WAN data rate can usually be configured for the proper T1 configuration. WAN analyzers can be set to handle testing for half or full duplex. Dataflow control parameters can also be set to examine transmit and receive processes across the WAN T1 medium. Specific and unique test patterns can be designed and set for continuous or different intervals, depending on configuration. WAN analyzers with BERT can be configured to process different block sizes. The WAN analyzer can be set to trigger and report error alarms. Most WAN analyzers can monitor different lead status information by checking the LED monitoring mode of a WAN analyzer in a BERT mode.

BERT allows for data patterns to be looped back across from a DTE over to another DCE. Specific data patterns can be sent from the BERT mode to enable an analyst to examine the reliability of the WAN between the DTE and DCE. Most WAN analyzer BERT modes can test for wideband jitter, maximum wideband jitter, maximum bandwidth jitter, and threshold variances. Different T1 line codes and frame formats can also be examined. When performing a BERT, error injection is important. T1 channel ports can be injected with errors that can force errors to the surface, possibly showing that DTE and DCE are not operating properly. It is also possible to examine how certain bridges and routers are operating.

This section briefly reviewed the T1 WAN architecture concepts along with the main testing and analysis procedures that can be followed when performing a WAN network baseline on a T1 or fractional T1 circuit. Appendix B contains further material on T1 architecture standards and specifications.

12.3 ISDN Network Architecture Overview

The *Integrated Services Digital Network* (ISDN) is an option for WAN connectivity that is extremely popular today. ISDN is fairly inexpensive and facilitates interconnection schemes between key point-to-point locations such as a home office and a company headquarters. ISDN links are also frequently used as backup links between main LAN sites on a WAN.

The ISDN and associated new technology directly correlated with ISDN, such as *Digital Subscriber Line* (DSL) networks, provide adequate bandwidth to facilitate data transfer within a very rapid time frame, and in an on-demand cycle. The DSL technology offers higher bandwidth levels through unique, dedicated circuitry that allows for bandwidth scaling. *ISDN DSL* (IDSL) is based on a 144Kbps data rate. *Asymmetric DSL* (ADSL) offers a 640Kbps data rate in one direction and 90Kbps in an opposite direction. Other versions of ADSL offer higher bandwidth levels from 2.0 to 7.1Mbps and higher.

ISDN was developed in the early 1960s and fine-tuned throughout the 1970s and 1980s. It became a very highly used WAN service in the early 1990s, and at this point is used quite frequently throughout the industry for many purposes.

The ISDN is based on a WAN process that uses an all-digital transmission medium for high-speed communications between point-to-point locations in a B-channel design that uses a 144Kbps operation, all the way up to a primary-rate ISDN link that can communicate at 1.544Mbps.

As noted, many advanced circuitry and design options are offered in tandem with ISDN, such as DSL. This chapter covers only the ISDN architecture. For further information on ISDN technology or other technologies used in direct parallel, such as DSL, refer to Appendix B.

ISDN is an extremely cost-effective process for dedicated links, because the connection does not have to be maintained on an ongoing basis, such as with a T1 circuit. T1 and fractional T1 circuits are point-to-point that must always be maintained and paid for by the user directly to the vendor. ISDN circuits can be used on demand, and can still provide high-quality transmission at a digital level. Simultaneous transmissions can be used on combinations of ISDN B and D channel designs. The following section briefly describes the primary and basic rate design architecture specifications for ISDN.

12.3.1 ISDN Basic Rate (B) Channel Design

The *basic rate ISDN design* (BRI ISDN) allows for two B channels to be used for communication at 64Kbps. The two B channels are complemented by one D channel circuit rated at 16Kbps. The 64Kbps rate is considered a standard. Data is transferred over the B channels for communication between the point-to-point locations as required. The D channel is used for data control, data framing, and maintenance of the B-channel links. The interconnection company, such as the phone company or carrier, provides the connection and divides the B-channel circuits for the two B channels in the D-channel communication to complete the ISDN link (see Figure 12.7).

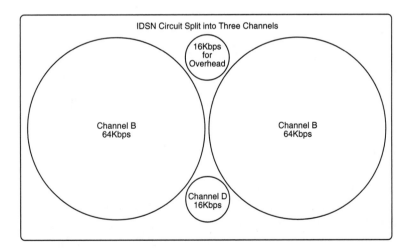

FIGURE 12.7 *The ISDN basic rate design concept.*

The connection point within a facility location is designed in such a way that the endpoint connection device uses an ISDN adapter that has an output port for a PC to connect to the ISDN circuit link terminal adaptor device. Within the ISDN terminal adaptor is a power supply and an ISDN NT1 device circuit. The ISDN NT1 circuit allows for connection from the standard location point of the phone company or carrier connection into the ISDN device. Optional ports usually allow for unique connection based on the type of ISDN configuration. Multiple NT connections can be used for a two-point connection scheme. Normally, an ISDN connector is based on an eight-pin RJ45 adaptor. A PC within a specific location would connect via an ST interface to the NT1 device or the ISDN terminal adaptor, and then a U interface is used for interconnection through the wall. The technology of the ST interface and the U interface and NT1 adaptor can all be combined within a closed ISDN terminal adaptor (see Figures 12.8 and 12.9).

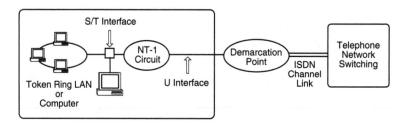

FIGURE 12.8 *The connection scheme from a LAN site to an outbound ISDN circuit.*

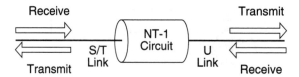

FIGURE 12.9 *The connection scheme from a LAN site to an outbound ISDN circuit along with the ST interface.*

12.3.2 ISDN Primary Rate Design

The primary rate ISDN circuitry and architecture are used for high-speed connections. This is normally used for decentralized locations, such as LAN to LAN for a cost-effective WAN, because it is quite expensive for home or single-location point access. With the new DSL technology, primary ISDN communications are starting to become challenged. The primary ISDN data rate allows for 23 B channels to be interleaved for data transfer with 1 D channel for communication control. The 23 B channels are designed on a 64Kbps allocation for data transfer. This allows the D channel to act as a primary control line for the overall ISDN pipe. Certain cases may require that a primary channel engage an additional link, an H channel, if multiple primary links are going to be multiplexed together between two key sites. In this case, the overall data rates can be increased to a much higher level, such as H12 at 1.920Mbps (see Figure 12.10).

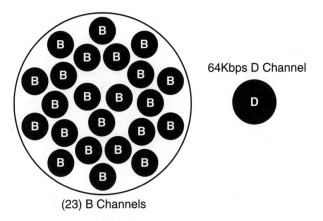

64Kbps D Channel

(23) B Channels

FIGURE 12.10   *The ISDN primary rate design concept.*

Various flavors of the ISDN H design options are available. The primary-rate interface design of ISDN allows for multiple B channels to carry user data, user voice, image and sound, and different multimedia communications over the 23 B channels. ISDN technology also offers broadband ISDN, which is based on the use of digital services in excess of 1.544Mbps speeds.

As noted, 64Kbps is allocated for the D channel in the ISDN primary link and is used for call signaling, setup, and user-packet data transmission in a unique manner for the on-demand callup of the ISDN link. Different signaling methods are used to synchronize the ISDN channels, as required. These signaling methods include *Signaling System 7* (SS7) along with *Digital Subscriber Signaling System 1* (DSS1). In these signaling systems, the carrier uses the systems for control to ensure that the ISDN channels are stable between point to point. These signals are also used for call setup connections and call maintenance. Quite often the control channels are used to ensure that the data transfer is started, the data transfer occurs, the state of communication is valid, the transit delays are low, packet size verification is performed, and transfer requirements are met.

The ISDN network technology is fully scalable in 64Kbps increments and enables users to build clusters of B channels.

A standard ISDN communication process follows this sequence: A user utilizes an ISDN link to establish a setup connection through the D channel to a *central office* (CO). The CO interexchange carrier ISDN D switch acknowledges receipt of the message on the D channel and establishes a B-channel open connection. After the device has established communications through the B channel, the D channel intercepts this process and allows the B channel to send communications into the switch process. The vendor ISDN switch then establishes a setup message with the other end device as requested by connecting to the D channel. The D channel then opens the associated end-device B channel by sending back acknowledgment sequences. After both devices at each end have been connected, the ISDN switch connects the two end-node points to facilitate final data transfer. For ISDN communication to occur, three layers are engaged. ISDN operates at the three communication layers discussed in the following sections.

12.3.3 ISDN Frame Structure for Physical Operations (Layer 1)

The ISDN frame structure is based on a multi-bit sequence process. Each frame carries approximately 48 bits. ISDN uses a configuration with 16 bits for each of the two B channels and 4 bits for the one D channel, for a total of 36 bits. The remaining 12 bits are used for framing and overhead. ISDN frame transmissions of the 48-bit sequence take approximately 250 microseconds to process.

The following is breakdown of the basic ISDN 48-bit frame sequence:

- 8 bits for B-channel 1

- 1 bit for the D channel

- 8 bits for B-channel 2

- 1 bit for the D channel

- 8 bits for B-channel 1

- 1 bit for the D channel

- 8 bits for B-channel 2

- 1 bit for the D channel

ISDN lines must have a *service profile identifier* (SPID). Within an ISDN inter-network, nodes use a SPID to maintain a connection point to the ISDN node. The SPID identifies each node ISDN point and is compared to an address. The SPID addressing process is used with circuit-switched processes rather than packet-switched modes. Another identification mode is the *terminal endpoint identifier* (TEI). The TEI and the SPID identify the individual devices on the ISDN line. TEI addressing is used for multiple devices present on a particular ISDN line (see Figure 12.11).

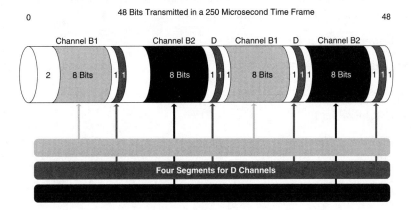

FIGURE 12.11   *The ISDN frame design.*

12.3.4 ISDN Data Link Operations (Layer 2)

Within the ISDN data link layer, different Layer 2 processes are engaged. *Link Access Procedure D* (LAPD) is the protocol used by the D channel to establish call link processes into the ISDN network. The LAPD procedure defines the communication protocol for connection sequences based on the Q.921 standard. The data link layer specifies the overall internal frame structure for the data packet and procedural elements for establishing call connection, data transfer, and call breakdown processes. ISDN Layer 2 can also engage *Link Access Procedure Balance* (LAPB) for packet-switching processes across the network, such as X.25. *Link Access Procedure F* (LAPF) is used for frame-mode bearer services, such as those used under the Frame Relay process.

12.3.5 ISDN Network Layer Operations (Layer 3)

At the network layer, ISDN engages the following:

- Call establishment

- Data transfer

- Call breakdown sequences

In this layer, ISDN performs an end-to-end connection and can use call connection and forwarding. The ISDN network layer can work with LAPB or LAPF processes (noted at Layer 2). Note also that ISDN can rely on upper-layer structures in packet-switching networks. The Q.931 standard allows for supplementary services to take place when using bearer services, such as Frame Relay. Supplementary services can include the following:

- Data-to-number ID

- Dial processes

- Subscriber data ID

- Call line data ID

- Connected line ID

- Call transfer

- Data addressing

- Data transfer

- Data forwarding unconditional

- Call forwarding

- Busy processes

- Line interconnection processes

These are supplementary services that would reside above the Layer 2 area. These services allow ISDN to be completely independent of bearer services. Circuit switching is processed at this layer. ISDN circuit switching allows for signals to flow through a typical analog digital-based system, and to be switched based on requirement. With ISDN, circuits do not need to be constantly established and can be switched when required. PPP is a unique protocol option because subprotocol linking can be used. *Point-to-Point Protocol* (PPP) allows for a fast setup connection and uses the subprotocols that obtain information needed to set up a general TCP/IP connection. PPP is fully compatible with protocols such TCP/IP, NetBIOS, IPX, and SPX. The PPP protocol allows for a large number of concurrent communications.

ISDN communications can integrate with PPP. The PPP protocol allows an end-node ISDN device such as a PC to access the resources of a remote server without being directly connected to be supported across an ISDN channel session. Another ISDN-integrated protocol is standard *Serial Line Internet Protocol*

(SLIP). The SLIP protocol is commonly engaged between IP end-node points and the World Wide Web. The SLIP protocol allows packets to be sent through general communications.

SLIP offers the capability to transfer data via IP datagrams. Variations of the SLIP protocol include the *Compression Serial Line Protocol*, which is engaged for compressed serial communications. The *Multi-Link Point-to-Point Protocol* (MLPPP) allows for communications over serial link like standard PPP, but is not restricted to only one physical link. The MLPPP allows for the data link layer approach that engages the standard PPP in the network layer protocols. The MLPPP allows for more than one PPP standard link from point to point. The MLPPP engages the switched digital services in the ISDN internetwork scheme. MLPPP is compatible with switched communications. Extended versions of MLPPP that allow for more enhanced control and scalable control of each ISDN B channel are available.

12.4 Troubleshooting and Analyzing ISDN Circuits

When analyzing an ISDN circuit, it is important for an analyst to understand that ISDN can be used for standard voice communications, video communications, and other multimedia communications. However, data transfer is the primary use for ISDN links.

An analyst should be prepared and understand what the actual ISDN configuration is set up for with regard to the WAN link configuration that is going to be analyzed. In certain cases, there are ISDN links between a home location and a main carrier location or a company headquarters. ISDN links are also used for specific interconnection across WAN schemes, such as a primary link between two or more LANs within a corporate global infrastructure. In this case, a more sophisticated WAN analysis setup may be required. Either way, the analyst should keep in mind that a proper ISDN analyzer may be required. The analyzer must be able to capture both basic and primary data rates, as required. The following discussion describes the technical approach that an analyst can take when analyzing ISDN WAN circuits for both simple point-to-point connection schemes and for sophisticated LAN interconnection schemes.

The first important step in an ISDN analysis is to perform a standard equipment setup. The following is a brief review of the standard analysis and testing approach taken to review an ISDN circuit.

Most ISDN analyzers will have to set up in a test mode to operate either in a passive or an active mode. In a passive mode, the ISDN analyzer can monitor the ISDN B and D channel links. In an active mode, the ISDN analyzer usually is emulating the line and is actually sending a signal across the link. The analyzer can be set for a basic- or primary-rate configuration. The ISDN phone set configuration must be operable. The main ISDN standard phone set types are AT&T customized, CCITT, Northern Telecom, and NT-1.

The ISDN analyzer may need to be set up to capture an ISDN SPID. ISDN testing handsets can be used for voice communication and clear channel testing. If active bit error-rate testing is going to be used, a circuit may need to be scheduled. The analyzer may need to be set up for either standard Q.921 or Q.931 testing. When the ISDN analyzer is active, it usually keys on whether a standard tone is in place and whether synchronization is active.

An analyst should next check the analyzer to key off the call status and the call type across the D channel configuration. The ISDN analyzer displays whether data is flowing across the B channel.

The ISDN analyzer facilitates standard workload characterization testing. When decoding frames captured with an ISDN analyzer, a full protocol decode level can usually be displayed onscreen.

An analyst should quickly check to see whether ISDN LAPD or LAPF is being engaged for data transmission. An LAPD data header normally shows the process taking place on the ISDN circuit, such as call establishment, data transfer, or call breakdown functions. ISDN BERT analyzers can display additional information, especially in modes when LAPF mode bearer services are engaged for operations such as Frame Relay over ISDN. An analyst can check to see whether signaling methods are engaged, such as the DSS1 or SS7. The analyzer should display any unique protocols such as SLIP, PPP, or MLPPP if they are active on the ISDN layer. After the setup and configuration process has been completed, the first structured step in ISDN network analysis is to perform all standard WAN network baseline measurements. These measurements include the main WAN baseline step measurements, as noted later in this chapter (such as utilization for average and peak transitions). Next, the ISDN channel should be checked for node-by-node ISDN device SPID and TEI usage of the channel. The protocol percentages should be closely noted during the network baseline sampling session. The final area that the analyst should closely check is the ISDN physical layer. All ISDN equipment should be tested for general operations, such as the standard ISDN terminal equipment adaptor 1 or 2 version, along with the NT1 or NT2 adaptor devices. The SPIDs must also be checked for the correct assignments. If the SPID is not correct or the ISDN equipment for the TE1, TE2, NT1, or NT2 is not operational, the data transmission across the ISDN channel may not operate. Any ISDN line-testing test instrument should be engaged and utilized for line testing. There are ISDN testing tools that allow for testing the general leads across an ISDN TE-to-NT-type device path. Most of the WAN protocol analyzers include ISDN testing features for testing lines; these are similar to BERT. An analyst must examine the ISDN channel for LAPD or LAPF processes. It is important to understand whether standard ISDN D channel signaling is engaged or whether a frame bearer service is being engaged. Some of the main issues and problems that can occur on ISDN links include incorrect SPID settings, loss of power for NT and TE devices, block errors, wrong requests by LAPF services, and incorrect ISDN line configurations.

After completing the steps just noted, an analyst can then perform ULP analysis against the ISDN channel. The key is to ensure through ISDN network baselining that the ISDN medium and devices provide the proper foundation for fluent ULP dataflow (see Figure 12.12).

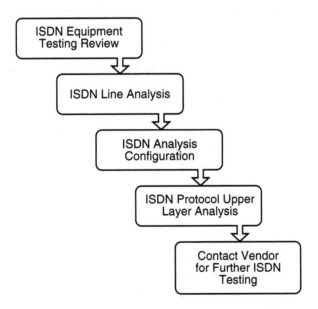

FIGURE 12.12 *How an ISDN analysis session should be approached from a network baseline standpoint.*

12.5 Frame Relay Architecture Overview

Frame Relay was developed based on the original ISDN specification. Frame Relay was also developed as an enhancement to the X.25 packet-switching WAN network. Frame Relay is based on the process of using variable-length frame data components and forwarding the frames from a data stream originating at one LAN endpoint to another LAN endpoint across a WAN internetwork cloud. The actual two-user endpoints communicate with each other through a Frame Relay WAN cloud, but the frames may not transfer over the same dedicated circuit at any particular time. This is based on the fact that the vendors that support the Frame Relay network create a high number of interconnection capability routes between two or more points. These Frame Relay routes are achieved dynamically and can be used by multiple clients whenever the circuit is available on a switching basis.

The packet-switched networks of the initial X.25 packet-switching scheme were reviewed for their overall positive design, and were used along with the ISDN specification as a composite building block for designing and creating the final Frame Relay internetwork system switching-cloud specifications.

The Frame Relay standards were actually developed by the *International Telecommunication Union and Telecommunication Sector* (ITU-T). The different standards for Frame Relay include ITU-T standards as well as ANSI standards.

A specific Frame Relay internetwork scheme can be based on one of two types of connection schemes. A *permanent virtual circuit* (PVC) is based on a hard-coded predetermined configuration between two LAN points. The Frame Relay network can also use a *switched virtual circuit* (SVC) connection scheme, which engages an automatic dynamic connection process that can occur on an ongoing basis.

The Frame Relay network is designed to utilize a Frame Relay access device for connecting LANs to a Frame Relay WAN; this is called a *Frame Relay Assembler Dissembler* (FRAD). The data streams on LANs at end sites are converted in forward and reverse to frame units of data, and the frames are relayed or forwarded to other sites across a Frame Relay WAN in a dynamic fashion. A FRAD device is positioned at the end LAN point at each site location. Specifically, a device such as a workstation or server connects to the local LAN, such as an Ethernet segment. The Ethernet LAN connects to a LAN module in a WAN router. The same WAN router then usually provides an internal backplane connection to a WAN Frame Relay module. The Frame Relay WAN router module converts the LAN PDU to frames for forwarding across the WAN cloud. The WAN router Frame Relay module then interconnects to the local FRAD connection via a WAN port. The FRAD device then connects to the actual WAN circuit via an internal Frame Relay–based DSU/CSU circuit (see Figure 12.13).

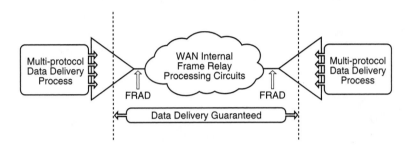

FIGURE 12.13 *A standard Frame Relay WAN connection.*

The connection from the local LAN to the WAN via the FRAD is called the *User-Network Interface* (UNI) connection and is the connection from the DTE to the WAN. As noted, the FRAD then connects to the WAN Frame Relay packet-switching network core cloud. The WAN Frame Relay switching cloud uses many different connections within the frame-switching cloud. The connections in the frame core intersystem switching cloud from FRAD-to-FRAD connections are called *Network-to-Network Interface* (NNI) connections (see Figure 12.14).

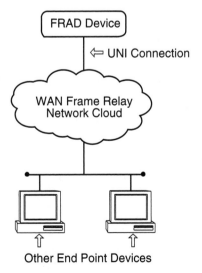

FIGURE 12.14 *An applied UNI scheme.*

The Frame Relay standards allow for data transfer in bidirectional mode along with the assembly and reassembly of data in the proper order. The specification also engages analysis of transmission and applied formatting and operational error conditioning. In Frame Relay transmission, the endpoints do not fully acknowledge every frame. Frame Relay is not meant to operate as a pure connectionless WAN protocol. The Frame Relay network provides a basic connection for transport services that allow for high transfers of data (see Figures 12.15 and 12.16).

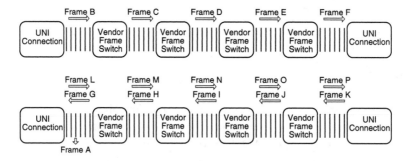

FIGURE 12.15 *How data is forwarded through a Frame Relay switching cloud.*

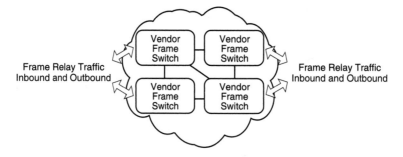

FIGURE 12.16 *How data is forwarded through a Frame Relay switching cloud.*

12.5.1 Frame Relay Frame Fields and Format

The following is a full review of the Frame Relay frame format. A Frame Relay frame includes five main fields:

- Initial Flag field

- DLCI Address field

- Information field

- Frame Check Sequence field

- Ending Frame Sequence field

The Initial Flag sequence is 1 byte in length and consists of 01111110 or 70H.

The Address field includes the *Data Link Connection/Control Identifier* (DLCI) in a high-order and low-order address fields configuration. The high order is 8 bits in length and the low order is 4 bits in length. The Address field also includes a subaddress field that can be used for extension of DLCI addressing. The Address field also has a subfield called a *Forward Explicit Congestion Notification* (FECN) field, which is 1 bit in length, and a *Backward Explicit Congestion Notification* (BECN) field, which is also 1 bit in length. The Address field also includes a subfield that includes a Command Response field for general command processes. The Address field contains a 10-bit address scheme using a bitmap with 8 bits assigned for the first most-significant sequence of the DLCI identifier and 4 bits assigned for the least-significant. The Flag fields are designed to engage with a zero and end with a zero. This process facilitates synchronization and error-free communication and verification that the frame is being processed.

Certain key DLCI addresses are identified for specific assignments. DLCI 0 is usually an LMI channel used for a local management interface. DLCI 1 to 15 is reserved for future processes. DLCI 16 to 991 is usually used for virtual circuits (both permanent and switched circuits). DLCI 992 to 1007 is used for Frame Relay bearer services. This range can also be used for processes related to consolidated link layer management. DLCI 1008 to 1022 is used for future-use assignment. DLCI 1023 is also used for Frame Relay channel layer management, such as LMI.

The Command Response Identification bit is not used by the Frame Relay protocol, but is optional and available for ULP engagement. The *Extended Address* (EA) field is a 2-bit field that allows for an extended support address scheme for higher-order DLCI addresses.

The FECN bit is usually set by the frame WAN intersystem switching network when congestion occurs. The FECN bit is usually set upon a frame being forwarded from endpoint one to endpoint two and normally indicates congestion in the actual direction of data flow.

The BECN bit can also be sent by the frame WAN intersystem switching network when congestion occurs. The BECN bits are usually set when the Frame Relay vendor internal system switching WAN circuits encounter congestion upon forwarding. High counts of BECNs usually indicate congestion in the opposite direction of the original frame-carrying communication. The BECN bits are usually sent by the Frame Relay central system switching network to notify the end LAN point that congestion may be experienced by data traffic in the opposite direction of the frames that are about to be transmitted onto the WAN Frame Relay network.

The *Discard Eligibility* (DE) bit is used when a frame can be discarded based on preference. Note that specific Frame Relay network points may not be required to discard all frames based on the DE setting being active.

The Frame Relay Data Information field is normally set at 1600 bytes maximum but can be set from 1 byte to 1600 bytes. Note that a size of up to 4096 is valid but not recommended. In most cases, much smaller sizes are used to facilitate faster packet-switching processes.

The Frame Check Sequence field is generally used for frame check sequence *cyclic redundancy checks* (CRC), in which each endpoint performs a check by using a polynomial error-checking scheme (see Figure 12.17).

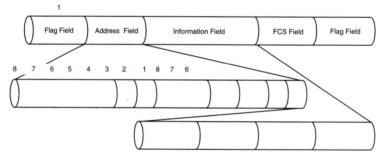

FIGURE 12.17 *The T1 frame format.*

12.5.2 Local Management Interface and Consolidated Link Layer Management

The Frame Relay standards include a unique management process called the *Local Management Interface* (LMI) protocol. The LMI protocol is engaged within the Frame Relay header. LMI is used for the initial assignment of end LAN point as to initial status and configuration when related to the frame *virtual circuit* (VC). LMI is applied via the UNI connection to the frame network. The LMI protocol allows for notification and availability of the VC. LMI engages polling sequences. The LMI processes include the cycle of engaging LMI Status Inquiry messages, which are used to request an LMI status and receive an LMI status response from the end LAN points on the WAN network. LMI is also engaged to confirm the integrity of overall Frame Relay connections. LMI Status messages hold information that notifies end LAN points of the operational status on certain requested information. LMI Link Verification Sequence messages can include status and query data operation. The LMI protocol can be used to verify the frame end-to-end link validity. An LMI status report can be processed when an LMI agent is used to perform an LMI request of status for frame PVC and SVC connections that are active. The LMI frame format uses a standard header, unnumbered frame indicator, protocol discriminator, call reference, message type, and informational element.

Another key process that can be engaged for end-to-end management in Frame Relay is *Consolidated Link Layer Management* (CLLM). The Frame Relay protocol normally relies on the FECN and BECN bits for congestion identification within the internetwork. The CLLM message is carried within a DLCI 1023. When a Frame Relay internetwork is congested, a CLLM message can broadcast a list of DLCIs that are causing congestion in an implicit fashion on the network. The frame format for a CLLM header is included within the Frame Relay header and includes a specific Address field, XID Control field, a Format Identifier, and a Group field. The CLLM frame format also includes a standard parameter to be set for congestion.

12.5.3 Frame Relay Process and Circuit Operations

For Frame Relay communication to engage, a PVC or SCV connection is set up. After the configuration path has been implemented dataflow can engage. PVCs are normally hard-coded and implemented by the Frame Relay vendor for a client. The *Frame Relay Forum* (FRF) has allowed for procedures to be developed with the SVCs for general connection control, including a Setup message, Call Proceeding message, Connect message, Disconnect message, and general release process. The Frame Relay standards were partially built on the ISDN circuit design. On a Frame Relay network, end LAN points normally establish a circuit via a switched setup based on the ISDN B or H channels' foundation of Frame Relay by using the D channel for general control. The Frame Relay network engages the D channel to be utilized for setting up messages for SVC connections and uses the B or H channel for general communication.

With the SVC connection dynamic process, the DLCI addressing scheme is assigned based on signaling messages across the D channel through the FRAD to the central Frame Relay intersystem switching cloud. After the SVC call has been established, and SVC signal requests have been started, data transfer continues via a process based on procedures in the Frame Relay SVC standards.

Frame Relay data review and transfer processes are basic in overall operation. With the Frame Relay protocol chain processing, a receiving cycle is engaged to examine whether a frame is valid. A process then engages to verify the frame check sequence, and then data processing continues. Next, the DLCI Frame Relay addresses are examined. In the address verification process, a logical examination of the DLCI address is engaged, and then the protocol chain of the endpoint device passes the PDU from the Frame Relay header data field portion to the upper-layer application and network operating system area for processing.

The LMI protocol is engaged to monitor intermittent status messages for the virtual circuit. The Explicit Congestion Notification systems are used to pass information from an end LAN point to another end LAN point about the state of the Frame Relay internetwork. These systems notify the state of any potential congestion at internetwork end LAN points within the Frame Relay WAN cloud. Real-time congestion can occur at different points within the Frame Relay intersystem switching WAN cloud and can affect the one specific end LAN point connection, or can negatively affect the entire Frame Relay internetwork. When congestion does occur, the intersystem switching points within the Frame Relay cloud can indicate to end users that the congestion does exist through outbound BECN bit generation (see Figure 12.18).

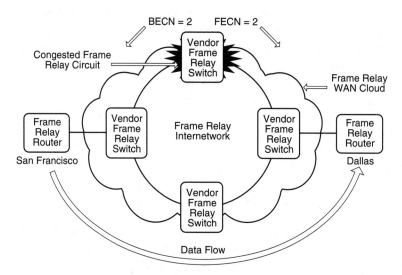

FIGURE 12.18 *Frame Relay Congestion Notification process.*

The Frame Relay FECN bit is normally set in frames passing in the direction of WAN congestion. When FECN bits are received by an endpoint LAN, it usually indicates that the frame has passed through a specific congested area. When the BECN bit is set, it indicates that a congested condition has occurred within the Frame intersystem switching cloud at some point.

The purpose of the congestion notification design is to allow downstream LAN points to be informed of a condition as it is occurring. This should lower traffic delays and should stop the destination LAN points from consistently retransmitting data in the reverse direction, which only increases congestion.

One disadvantage is that the source originator end LAN point has to be aware of the data congestion possibilities. FECN bits do not always provide a true notification function. The principle behind BECN is that if a frame device receives a BECN flag, it should then know that it may be sending data into a WAN network that is encountering internal congestion.

This particular process should allow the sending source device to temporarily suspend communication. The disadvantage of this process is that this is usually received only by the source user if data is flowing in the other direction. If data is being sent by a source device in a half-duplex mode, it is possible that continued congestion may occur, and eventually acknowledgments will not be received. This will be due to continued congestion and the FECN bits being sent on only one end. This type of process cycle could eventually cause WAN Frame Relay timing delays and disconnect events.

The Frame Relay specification engages a unique messaging scheme. The Frame Relay messaging process uses *Consolidated Link Layer Management* (CLLM). The CLLM process is a method for network nodes within the WAN frame cloud to identify congestion. The CLLM scheme allows the DLCI address to be used on a Frame Relay network to identify the "logical channel" between the user and the network. The logical channel has a key significance to that device and the point of address to the Frame Relay cloud. Each end LAN point connected to a FRAD can have a specific DLCI that identifies a unique connection to the Frame Relay WAN. Different DLCIs can be used by different LAN endpoints throughout the Frame Relay internetwork.

12.5.4 Frame Committed and Burst Information Rates

The Frame Relay WAN network offers excellent bandwidth scaling options to increase bandwidth on demand. The Frame Relay *committed information rate* (CIR) allows for a LAN endpoint to have an assigned guaranteed level of bandwidth. The Frame Relay CIR can be defined as the rate of available data that an endpoint LAN node is assigned for passing data on a Frame Relay internetwork. The CIR rate assigned is the bandwidth that should be handled by the Frame Relay WAN network without the occurrences of an issue or problem. If the end LAN point requires bandwidth to be increased on a dynamic demand cycle, the bandwidth allocated through the assigned CIR can be exceeded through the assignment and configuration of *burst information rate* (BIR).

The CIR process allows Frame Relay end LAN points and intersystem switching frame internetwork points or switches to interpret the difference between the actual requirement for bandwidth and availability for data transfer to be achieved for end LAN point–to–end LAN point communications. In most cases, the Frame Relay vendor and the client will agree on a CIR and BIR for configuration between two or more Frame Relay endpoints. After the CIR and BIR subscription has been assigned, data can then be forwarded at the subscribed rate. If there are situations where data has to be sent in an exceeded mode of the CIR, the BIR level should be activated by the Frame Relay WAN. If a Frame Relay end LAN point bandwidth load continues to increase, the actual offered load is increasing.

If offered load increases, the data transmission for required traffic should have the capability to transmit through the Frame Relay WAN with required throughput. This extra bandwidth is usually available; but when congestion levels become excessive on a frame WAN cloud, the inherent congestion control of the Frame Relay network can prevent connection-based problems. This is accomplished by eliminating the congestion and slowing down the connection. A negative factor is that the final data throughput can eventually decrease and retransmission can increase during these sequences. In this case, the Frame Relay initial CIR and BIR design may need to be redesigned. Network baselining is an important process for determining the correct CIR and BIR assignments for connection between multiple LAN points to properly design a Frame Relay–based WAN circuit layout.

Frame Relay is a popular WAN architecture that can accommodate the cross-LAN-site dataflow requirements of current and most future networking-based applications.

12.6 Analyzing and Troubleshooting Frame Relay WANS

When performing a network baseline analysis session or engaging a troubleshooting session on a Frame Relay WAN network, it is critical that the proper type of Frame Relay network analyzer be used. Most Frame Relay analyzers will allow for an immediate configuration and interconnection to the WAN FRAD circuit. A Frame Relay protocol analyzer needs to be placed on the FRAD connection for exterior positioning as related to a bridge or a router placed in a Frame Relay configuration. Inserting the analyzer in the FRAD circuit usually requires a Y cable design that may interrupt the circuit briefly. An analyst should properly plan the insertion of this cable.

Note that there are various unique ways to approach an analysis on a Frame Relay WAN circuit. The main workload characterization methods—as discussed in Chapter 4, "Quantitative Measurements in Network Baselining"— apply when baselining a Frame Relay network. The key statistics should all be examined, such as FRAD circuit utilization for average and peak levels. Next, all DLCIs active on each FRAD circuit should be measured for node-by-node utilization from each LAN site. The FRAD circuit protocol percentages should be examined as to how different protocol types are applied to each DLCI address of a Frame Relay FRAD circuit. Next, it is important to verify the physical integrity of the complete Frame Relay circuit. The Frame Relay header must be investigated from a stability standpoint. It is important then for an analyst to closely examine the Frame Relay LMI communication to ensure that the Frame Relay network is properly setting up communication patterns and that the LMI polling processes are stable (see Figure 12.19).

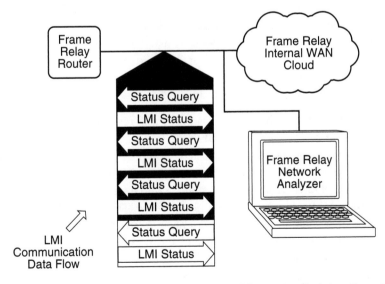

FIGURE 12.19 *How an analyzer can be used for LMI analysis in a Frame Relay WAN network baseline session.*

All Frame Relay communication should be thoroughly investigated for forward and backward congestion notification. The Frame Relay header should be thoroughly checked via protocol analysis for any other problems.

The Frame Relay network, even though it offers extremely dynamic capabilities for setup and dynamic transfer of data through many different switched routes, can present problems if it's under-designed in terms of CIR or BIR WAN channel design. It is important for an analyst to closely examine the bandwidth levels and any associated congestion notification present in the Frame Relay headers. The frame header contains certain information on the integrity of the Frame Relay transfer process. By using a WAN Frame Relay protocol analyzer, important information can be extracted as related to the health and operation integrity of the WAN medium and Frame Relay devices configured in a FRAD end LAN point–to–end LAN point link.

When starting the review of the physical Frame Relay area, again as noted it is important to verify the LMI process. When initial transmission engages, an end LAN point FRAD device will usually generate a message using the LMI process across DLCI 0 for communication. The DTE end point normally generates an LMI status and query message in varying intervals. The standard interval engaged is normally 10 seconds. This cycle allows for establishing the initial link-integrity verification processes and polling. After initial polling, an LMI status inquiry is sent by the DTE to finalize a PVC connection or to establish an SVC circuit. An LMI response is usually received next. The LMI response message includes a list of the DLCIs across the Frame Relay internetwork for the specific site. The status of all DLCIs related to the site FRAD circuit is also included in the LMI response.

It is important to analyze the LMI status query and response messages, because the information contained within the frames presents the DLCI configurations and operational status that are active on the Frame Relay WAN. The LMI protocol header includes LMI Message Type, LMI Information Element, LMI Report Type, LMI Information Element, LMI DLCI Current Sequence Number, and LMI Last Received Sequence Number. The LMI response also presents the FRAD circuit's DLCI identifier as related to the virtual circuit status regarding buffer threshold settings, which can indicate capacity levels and problems. The bandwidth of the DLCI channel is usually indicated in the bottom portion of the LMI header. Next, an analyst should examine the Frame Relay header for congestion notification. Any WAN slowdowns can be verified by examining any congestion notification in the Frame Relay header. It is important to check for any explicit congestion notification in frames that have a header with flags active and to engage FECN or BECN congestion notification (see Figure 12.20).

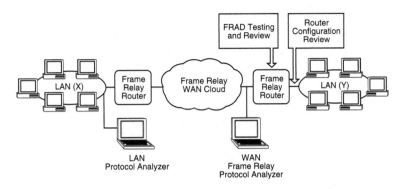

FIGURE 12.20 *The key Frame Relay WAN analysis concepts.*

A Frame Relay protocol analyzer can be used to examine any CLLM messages that indicate WAN congestion via communication across DLCI 1023. Any congestion identified in analysis may also correspond with high end-to-end WAN delta times. If delta response times are high and FECN and BECN flags are active, it is important to note that the issue can be due to upper-layer utilization loading or physical issues. If just FECN flags are active, the issues are usually related to upper-layer loading factors. The BECN flags indicate that possible problems may be present in the Frame Relay intersystem switching cloud (see Figure 12.21).

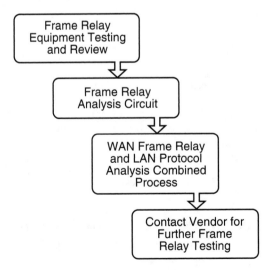

FIGURE 12.21 *The key Frame Relay WAN analysis concepts.*

In summary, when approaching a Frame Relay WAN baseline study, it is first important to perform all standard measurements for workload characterization processes. Next it is relevant to examine the configuration and integrity of the FRAD link. The LMI status frames should be reviewed. An analyst should closely examine the Frame Relay header for the forward and backward congestion settings in the frame header FECN and BECN fields. Last, it is important to verify and correlate response delta time latency and throughput and then to move directly to analyzing upper-layer protocols and data carried within the Frame Relay headers (see Figure 12.22).

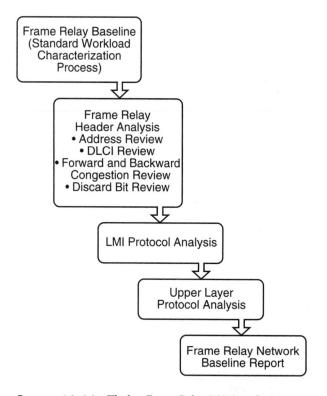

FIGURE 12.22 *The key Frame Relay WAN analysis concepts.*

12.7 Synchronous Optical Network Architecture Overview

This section briefly overviews the *Synchronous Optical Network* (SONET) architecture. This section does not describe troubleshooting methods for SONET. Because of the popularity of SONET networks throughout the industry, however, it is important to present some of the key architecture concepts. Note that

SONET architecture is extremely compatible with high-speed local interconnection schemes between sites that are close within metropolitan areas. Due to high costs, it is somewhat prohibitive to use SONET networks across large geographical spans. Many of the cost levels are starting to come down, and SONET will be a popular interconnection scheme on an ongoing basis for interconnecting high-speed networks that require true broadband connection schemes. This is true for interconnection of both ATM networks and Gigabit Ethernet networks.

The SONET was initially developed by Bell Communication Research, or Bellcore. SONET is recognized both by the ANSI and ITU-T standards groups. The basic SONET signal transmission is based on *Synchronous Transport Signal Level 1* (STS-1). The SONET signal operation processes at 51.84Mbps in its basic configuration. Higher transmission rates can be engaged by multiplexing multiple STS-1 signals. The transmission medium for SONET signals is usually based on *single mode fiber* (SMF) and *multi-mode fiber* (MMF). One of the most common SONET signal levels is the STS-3C interface. The STS-3C operates at 155.250Mbps. The SONET interface signaling scheme utilized is based on the 8B/10B data-encoding scheme.

As mentioned, the basic SONET signal is based on the STS-1 operation at 51.84Mbps. The next SONET level that is utilized is an STS-3, rated at approximately 155Mbps. The levels then increment to STS-9, rated at 466Mbps; STS-12, rated at 622Mbps; STS-18, rated at 933Mbps; STS-24, rated at 1244Mbps; and STS-48, rated at approximately 2488Mbps. The SONET STS-1 frame is based on the 51.84Mbps basic unit transmission process. The SONET frame is constructed with a multiple row-column configuration, including 9 rows and 90 columns. This allows for 810 bytes of communication. The actual frame is transmitted within a minimum period of 125 microseconds that allows for a bandwidth capacity of 51.840Mbps. In the 90 columns of possible data, there are 3 columns that carry the overhead of the frame, known as the *transport overhead* (TOH). The overhead includes processes for management, error checking, and SONET framing operations.

The data payload within the STS-1 frame configuration is inside the 810-byte composite frame structure and includes 87 columns that encompass approximately 783 bytes of data. The 87 columns and 9 rows that are used also include a *path overhead* (POH) pointer for data, which consumes about 9 bytes of overhead, which allows for a final level of 774 bytes of data, for a bandwidth capacity that then relates to an approximately direct 49.54Mbps.

As noted, multiple STS-1 frames can be combined to create the common STS-3 level, which is rated at 155.52Mbps. There is also a special variation of the configuration called STS-3C. The C assignment identifies true concentration with increased payload efficiency.

This bandwidth-building process can also be scaled for increase by multiplexing more STS-1 channels in configuration. The key with SONET networking is to create a WAN design scheme that allows for a true high-bandwidth interconnection between other high-speed topologies in LAN areas to create a seamless *metropolitan area networking* (MAN) design.

12.8 Closing Notes on WAN Network Baselining

When engaging a WAN network baseline process, the first critical step calls for an analyst to establish a proper project plan for data acquisition. The next chapter of this book outlines key methods for network baseline project planning. This process includes establishing goals to understand the WAN design and the available capacity. An analyst then must focus on the actual utilization factors against the capacity. After the utilization factors have been determined and the key workload characterization measurements have been performed, an analyst must next focus on WAN response time and the effective throughput levels being achieved. An analyst should take into account that the WAN is a key medium for interconnection between multiple LANs. A WAN must be properly designed and implemented to handle the dataflow for the business applications that will transverse the WAN channel. Peak utilization becomes a key factor on WAN media because capacity saturation of a WAN medium at more than the 80% to 90% level at times of more than 5 to 7 seconds can cause an outage on the WAN medium. Long duration peaks can cause an eventual overflow on the LAN network endpoints. A true baseline view over a period of time will eventually show transitional peaks and transitional drops in the WAN channel usage traffic model. It is recommended to engage the historical utilization measurement process.

It is critical to understand that many devices may be configured to use the WAN network, but other devices not originally configured or scheduled for in the original WAN design may also be communicating on the WAN. By engaging a node-by-node analysis, an analyst can break out the actual percentage usage according to each LAN endpoint. An analyst may be able to identify devices that are sending broadcast storms affecting the WAN medium. Protocol percentage measurements are important because it is possible that certain protocols may be captured, and these may identify new applications being utilized on the WAN that are unique or not scheduled for in overall planning. As noted throughout this chapter, it is important when performing WAN analysis to closely measure the physical error rate on the WAN medium (see Figure 12.23).

```
┌DETAIL─────────────────────────────────────────────────────────────────────┐
│ DLC:  ----- DLC Header -----                                                │
│ DLC:                                                                        │
│ DLC:  Frame 1 arrived at  14:28:36.3967; frame size is 94 (005E hex) bytes. │
│ DLC:  Destination = DCE                                                     │
│ DLC:  Source = DTE                                                          │
│ DLC:                                                                        │
│ HDLC: ----- High Level Data Link Control (HDLC) -----                       │
│ HDLC:                                                                       │
│ HDLC: Address = 01 (Command)                                                │
│ HDLC: Control field = A6                                                    │
│ HDLC:     101. .... = N(R) = 5                                              │
│ HDLC:     ...0 .... = Poll/Final bit                                        │
│ HDLC:     .... 011. = N(S) = 3                                              │
│ HDLC:     .... ...0 = I (Information transfer)                              │
│ HDLC:                                                                       │
│ X.25: ----- X.25 Packet Level -----                                         │
│ X.25:                                                                       │
│ X.25: General format id = 10                                                │
│ X.25:     0... .... = Qualifier bit                                         │
│ X.25:     .0.. .... = Delivery confirmation bit                             │
│                        ────────── Frame 1 of 4442 ──────────               │
│                          Use TAB to select windows        File: BRGVTX25.SYC│
│ 1       2 Set   3Expert 4 Zoom  5       6Disply 7 Prev  8 Next  9Select 10 New│
│   Help    mark    window   out    Menus  options   frame    frame  frame  capture│
└─────────────────────────────────────────────────────────────────────────────┘
```

FIGURE 12.23 *Data-trace results from a WAN network analysis session.*

When moving into upper-layer analysis, it is important to follow the steps laid out in Chapters 4 and 5 of this book for upper-layer protocol decoding. All WAN sessions should be examined for transferred block and packet sizes. Network timing is critical on WAN networks. All end-to-end file transfers should be examined via file throughput measurements. An analyst must examine the data-transfer integrity across WANs. It is helpful to perform application characterization when performing a WAN baseline (see Figure 12.24).

```
┌DETAIL──────────────────────────────────────────────────────────────────────┐
│ DLC:   ----- DLC Header -----                                                │
│ DLC:                                                                         │
│ DLC:   Frame 19 arrived at  07:28:13.8285; frame size is 66 (0042 hex) bytes.│
│ DLC:   This frame is dated 2 day(s) after capture started.                   │
│ DLC:   Destination = DTE                                                      │
│ DLC:   Source = DCE                                                           │
│ DLC:                                                                          │
│ ROUTER: ----- CrossComm Router/Bridge -----                                  │
│ ROUTER:                                                                       │
│ ROUTER: Header = 00033C000002                                                 │
│ ROUTER:                                                                       │
│ TRING: ----- Short Token Ring Header -----                                   │
│ TRING:                                                                        │
│ TRING: Destination = Station 16009834A1E1                                    │
│ TRING: Source      = Station 16009834BAB1                                    │
│ TRING: Padding bytes = 002A                                                  │
│ TRING:                                                                        │
│ IPX:   ----- IPX Header -----                                                │
│ IPX:                                                                          │
│ IPX:   Checksum = 0xFFFF                                                      │
│                       ────────── Frame 19 of 180241 ──────────              │
│                          Use TAB to select windows       File: ARMIPXWA.SYC  │
│ 1       2 Set   3Expert 4 Zoom  5       6Disply 7 Prev  8 Next  9Select 10 New│
│   Help    mark    window   out    Menus  options   frame    frame  frame  capture│
└─────────────────────────────────────────────────────────────────────────────┘
```

FIGURE 12.24 *Data-trace results from a WAN network analysis session.*

In closing, an analyst must closely examine all WAN addresses in the physical WAN headers, such as a Frame Relay header, and associate these with the network layer addresses and the specific operations of the upper-layer protocols. Time frames of receiving frames from one LAN point to another must be closely monitored, along with key communication sequences, such as connection, logon sequences, polling events, broadcast traffic, and other associated updates such as routing protocol transfers and general broadcast communication (see Figure 12.25).

```
┌DETAIL────────────────────────────────────────────────────────────────┐
│ DLC:  This frame is dated 1 day(s) after capture started.             │
│ DLC:  Destination = DCE                                               │
│ DLC:  Source = DTE                                                    │
│ DLC:                                                                  │
│ FRELAY: ----- Frame Relay -----                                       │
│ FRELAY:                                                               │
│ FRELAY: Address word = 1851                                           │
│ FRELAY:  0001 10..  0101 .... = DLCI 101                              │
│ FRELAY:  .... ..0.  .... .... = Response                              │
│ FRELAY:  .... ....  .... 0... = No forward congestion                 │
│ FRELAY:  .... ....  .... .0.. = No backward congestion                │
│ FRELAY:  .... ....  .... ..0. = Not eligible for discard              │
│ FRELAY:  .... ....  .... ...1 = Not extended address                  │
│ FRELAY:                                                               │
│ FRELAY: ----- Multiprotocol over Frame Relay -----                    │
│ FRELAY:                                                               │
│ FRELAY: Control, pad(s) = 0300                                        │
│ FRELAY: NLPID = 0x80 (SNAP)                                           │
│ FRELAY:                                                               │
│ SNAP: ----- SNAP Header -----                                         │
└──────────────────────────Frame 49980 of 89648────────────────────────┘
                     Use TAB to select windows          File: 10HROPEN.SYC
1         2 Set   3Expert 4 Zoom  5         6Disply 7 Prev  8 Next  9Select 10 New
   Help     mark    window   out    Menus   options   frame    frame  frame   capture
```

FIGURE 12.25 Data-trace results from a WAN network analysis session.

Case Study 15: WAN T1 Circuit Analysis

The LAN Scope analysis team was recently requested to visit a client site in Atlanta, Georgia, that was experiencing problems with a T1 WAN circuit. This was a headquarters facility for a major transportation company in the city. The company had multiple bus transport locations with remote LANs that were used for information processing for such areas as bus station schedule operations, general business operations, daily financial data-application transfer, and other information related to accessing the headquarters transportation operation.

Each remote bus site had a T1 WAN circuit dedicated channel between the remote and headquarters location points, which was utilized for general communication. The T1 circuits that were linked between the headquarters facilities and the remote bus stations were based on a T1 carrier system rated at 1.544Mbps. This involved a multiple point-to-point connection design based on standard T1 architecture utilizing a router and *digital service unit* and *channel service unit* (DSU/CSU) at each end of the TI channel. The DSU/CSU provides the final WAN signal-conversion connection from a router generating digital signals connected to a T1 channel. The general communications for protocol traffic levels were based on a TCP/IP protocol model, also utilizing a proprietary UNIX-based application on a host at the headquarters facility.

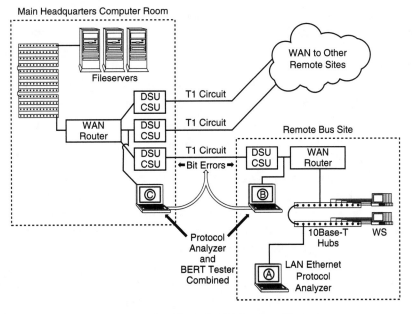

Network with T1 WAN circuit problems.

The primary complaint was that users at a specific remote bus location were experiencing intermittent disconnects on a daily basis along with general corruption of some of the database files transferred. At times, connectivity was not even possible in the early morning hours, and the network appeared to be completely unstable. The problem progressively intensified until it reached the point where an outside consulting team was required.

The LAN Scope analysis team was engaged. After conducting our standard entrance briefing meeting and obtaining the required facts and configurations about the site, the LAN Scope analysis team immediately deployed two WAN network analyzers. We deployed the first WAN analyzer at the headquarters on a specific T1 channel connection; we also deployed another WAN analyzer at the specific remote site. This allowed for an analyzer to be positioned at each end of a WAN T1 channel for testing. In a WAN testing process, we normally would proceed with a *bit error-rate testing* (BERT) process on the physical layer as a first step, but we wanted to first examine the upper layers to ensure that utilization levels were not of concern. The router and WAN support vendor did tell our team that all the client WAN channels appeared to be underutilized at this time.

Upon initial testing, we did notice that the two WAN network analyzers showed a utilization level of less than 10% on the WAN link channel between the two points we were testing. We also deployed an additional LAN analyzer at the bus station to very carefully examine the local area Ethernet LAN segment. This testing session also appeared to show low utilization for the users at the remote facility. We noticed that there were only 12 nodes placed at the facility for access to the remote headquarters, and that the utilization on the 10BASE-T network was extremely stable. The protocol percentages also appeared to be in check, along with a low physical Ethernet error rate.

We next continued testing on the two-position WAN analysis process. We immediately noted that both WAN analyzers exhibited a high number of physical error alarms when monitoring the data transmission across the specific T1 channel. The utilization levels showed an average utilization of 2% with a peak of 8%. The protocol percentages appeared to be normal, and general node-to-node protocol percentages were not of concern because it was just a remote site with 12 users connecting to the headquarters via a direct dedicated circuit via a T1 channel. Our next focus was the physical error-rate issue. Prior to engaging actual error-rate testing against the physical T1 channel, we investigated our testing analyzer tool data and noted that a high number of framing errors were also present in our upper-layer protocol analysis session. The protocol analyzer we were using for the baseline analysis testing had an inherent physical error-rate counter, but did not include an internal BERT process for the physical T1 channel.

In a WAN T1 dedicated circuit, a bit error rate can occur when a value of any of the bits that are forwarded across the T1 circuit by the multiplexing of T1 channels is affected in a negative manner. Among the possible causes of this type of occurrence are noise on the T1 channel line, an improper transmission in the T1 channel bank, or reception of a T1 transmission by either end at the DSU/CSU or inside a bridge or router that provides a connection to the local area medium at the remote site.

Most protocol analyzers allow for an internal BERT process that engages a bit error-rate testing cycle against the link from a true investigative standpoint. A local and remote transmitter device normally processes this type of frame transmission through *data terminal equipment* (DTE) and *data communication equipment* (DCE). A DTE and DCE channel box can also be considered the WAN DSU/CSU, and is usually considered the final exterior connection to the T1 circuit for a WAN vendor.

Another set of our WAN analyzers with BERT active were placed on each of the remote ends of this WAN network channel. We were monitoring a V.35 WAN interface specification channel connection.

We next engaged the analyzers with the BERT mode active in its platform. This enabled us to closely examine the complete WAN end-to-end channel interface from a true testing standpoint. To test the channel, however, we had to inject traffic from the BERT mode that would possibly cause further problems throughout the business day. Because the site was almost nonoperational at the time of our analysis, we planned our testing for the lunchtime period. We set the parameters on our BERT mode in the analyzer to allow for transmission of a test pattern across the link during lunchtime. This data pattern was to be looped between the two sites on a consecutive basis, and we closely analyzed the overall signal health across the link.

Our focus was to examine the predefined bit communication handled across the T1 link, along with the data pattern generation as related to the type of clocking that was being utilized. We also focused on examining the block-size parameters, the timing models, and the general jitter on the link. Immediately upon testing, we encountered a large amount of jitter, as well as a high number of consecutive errors related to the mark parameters for the ones and zeros on the signaling path. The transmission was based on B8ZS, which is a bipolar operation for data transmission across the link. We noted that the pulses appeared to be out of order for normal code processing, and signal code violations were definitely present. When we injected further transmission to increase load, the error rate increased to an even higher level.

We contacted the MIS team, who then contacted the vendor that provided the DSU/CSU and router equipment and requested that they provide technical personnel assistance at the site. The technical team from this vendor provided additional testing tools that checked their equipment at the DSU/CSU and router configuration areas. It was immediately found that the DSU/CSU at the remote site showed error counts upon diagnostics. The vendor deployed another DSU/CSU and requested that LAN Scope retest the channel.

We followed our standard baseline methodology and quickly saw that the upper layers were operating in a normal fashion in terms of utilization and protocol percentages. We also noted that the physical error-rate forwarding errors were no longer present on our upper-layer analyzer. We ran our baseline process for approximately one business day and certified the site as operational and deemed the problem resolved. Based on our final findings, we contacted the site and recommended that all equipment for other bus stations be investigated on a more consistent basis. We noted that this particular WAN vendor was not providing any consistent reports on the overall physical health of the WAN T1 channels. This was unusual, because most WAN network vendors that maintain a client WAN channel do provide such regular reports. In this case, however, there were different vendors over a period of time for the client WAN channels and the remote site equipment, thus creating a problem for parallel and comprehensive support for this client. These issues were addressed, and eventually a testing process was developed in which the DSUs, CSUs, and routers at each remote T1 location were also tested by the WAN network vendor. Specifically, support was brought under one umbrella. In the future, therefore, any physical T1, router, or CSU/DSU problems will be located on a more immediate basis when they occur instead of having to perform a full baseline process.

The bottom line here is that the network baselining process and the methodology deployed against the T1 link was extremely useful in extracting the problem rapidly. We clearly saw that the DTE and DCE were not operating properly upon BERT. Line integrity in the overall transmission did not show a true integrity level for communications. There was no capability for node point one to communicate with node point two on a fluent basis, and it was clear that the upper-layer protocols were not of concern, nor did utilization levels affect the link. It was clearly evident, however, that the signal-frame and the packet-frame formation were negatively affected, which would explain the intermittent problems on the WAN medium. This is a clear example of how the networking baselining process can be successful on a WAN T1 dedicated channel.

Case Study 16: WAN Frame Relay Analysis

The LAN Scope analysis team was recently contacted by a client who had recently implemented a Frame Relay WAN channel between two key locations in the United States. The Frame Relay migration was implemented because of recent performance problems being experienced by users of the WAN link. The headquarters location for the business was in Philadelphia, Pennsylvania, and the remote location was in Seattle, Washington. This new Frame Relay WAN implementation replaced a WAN T1 circuit.

The client was told by their vendor that they would immediately see a performance enhancement based on the capability of Frame Relay to provide a burst channel when the normal *committed information rate* (CIR) was exceeded. The client was briefed that the *burst information rate* (BIR) would allow for an extra burst channel in bandwidth that the previous T1 channel could not provide.

The only concern in this case was that the vendor based the circuit design on a calculated design based on the preceding fractional T1 channel that was in place. The preceding channel was based on a 768K fractional T1 circuit that was not even utilizing a full T1 channel as related to configuration. The vendor automatically assumed that the customer would need no more than a 768K CIR with a burst to T1 maximum on the new Frame Relay channel. This assumption for the Frame Relay channel was not based on any pre-baselining processes or actual measurements, but rather on the preceding hardware configuration at the site.

The client's concern was that they were still experiencing performance problems on the new Frame Relay internetwork cloud WAN link and thought that the problems got even worse since the previous T1 circuit–dedicated channel was removed.

The LAN Scope analysis team deployed a set of two WAN Frame Relay analyzers in the client's Philadelphia and Seattle locations. We also deployed two LAN protocol analyzers on the LAN Ethernet segments at each location, which were communicating with each other for main transfer.

Upon reviewing our initial analysis, the two endpoint WAN analyzers immediately showed an extremely high utilization level averaging between 40% and 48%, and a 92% to 95% saturation on both the DTE and the DCE channels of the WAN Frame Relay circuit.

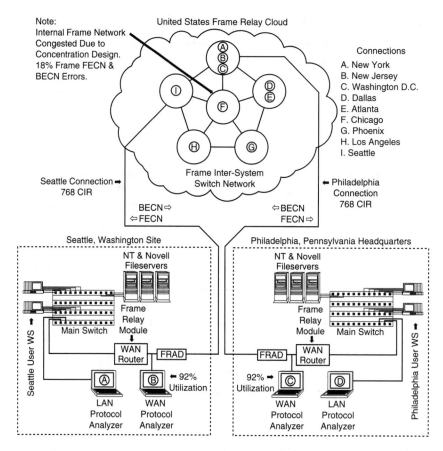

FIGURE CS16.1 *A Frame Relay WAN network channel between Washington and Pennsylvania.*

After identifying the utilization-based saturation levels as to capacity present on the Frame Relay cloud, the LAN Scope analysis further measured and identified the protocol types and found the protocol percentage breakout to be normal. We noted that the Frame Relay physical error-generation level testing showed a large amount of *forward error congestion* (FECN) and *backward error congestion* (BECN) in the Frame Relay headers. These are fields in the Frame Relay header that, when decoded, can indicate possible congestion as to impact saturation of the WAN medium or other channels at the physical layer on a Frame Relay internetwork in transfer.

We immediately noted high error rates of FECN and BECN during our testing session.

Upon further analysis of the internal data, we noted that the upper-layer protocols appeared to be normal and did not show any unusual occurrences in the network, transport, or upper-layer protocol layer processes. Based on information from all our analyzer positioning points in the channel, we thought that the main performance issues were related to capacity, saturation, and perhaps physical error concerns in the physical Frame Relay cloud, such as the vendor frame intersystem switching cloud.

Our main concern was that both the FECN and BECN bits appeared to be set in parallel on analysis of inbound and outbound packets for the Frame Relay cloud communication channel. We again reviewed the analysis session on the Philadelphia WAN exterior analyzer, along with the WAN analyzer positioned on the exterior side of the Seattle link. Both analyzers showed, when compared, that the frames inbound and outbound to Philadelphia were showing FECN and BECN bits set in the headers of the Frame Relay forwarding process at both sites.

Based on this fact, we did not think that the issues were associated with capacity only, but were also possibly related to the vendor intersystem switching cloud. Our thinking was influenced by the number of errors and the excessive level, noted as well over 18%, of all frames communicated.

Another concern was that the saturation levels were extremely high, which indicated that business application-loading levels may have been extremely high, but also that the frame intersystem switching channel was designed incorrectly.

We reviewed the client's configuration and discussed the issues with both the client and the vendor. We realized that the sites were conducting a high amount of communication related to Novell servers and NT Servers across the remote links. The protocol percentage measurements displayed a definite 50% to 50% split at the upper layers.

Based on the most recent implementation and on the fact that no predeployment baseline assessment was provided prior to the implementation, we thought that we had to more closely examine the LAN-to-LAN cross-site network architecture requirements and the communication across the WAN as related to the business application dataflow requirements.

Our team engaged a set of application-characterization and modeling procedures to determine the possible maximum data loading that could affect the WAN channel. In doing so, we calculated, based on utilization levels via application event marking on the LAN and requirements of node counts to engage the application across the WAN between the two sites, that a higher utilization level than a full T1 could be achieved consistently upon high transmission of application-based transfer. (Chapter 4 presents extensive details of application testing methods.) This was based on the fact that both the Philadelphia and the Seattle node counts were based on a LAN limitation of a maximum of 500 users at each site to communicate with different servers at each remote end. The overall high-level architecture was based on a distributed server architecture design that required a large amount of interconnection of different applications that were distributed across both sites.

Based on the fact that approximately 1,000 users in total can interconnect on multiple channels alone, along with the WAN capacity and error levels that were being achieved and additional measurements taken on the two LAN network sites, we determined that an additional Frame Relay circuit would be warranted.

We recommended that an additional Frame Relay circuit be implemented to separate the protocol types of TCP/IP and IPX/SPX at a filtering level using two separate *Frame Relay Assembler/ Dissembler* (FRAD) points. This would allow for immediate identification by splitting the protocol percentages by the NOS types of Novell and NT and provide additional bandwidth with maximum burst bandwidth. This design would also eliminate any concerns related to the physical layer errors being experienced.

The vendor agreed to provide us with an extra FRAD channel configured at the same bandwidth level for the connection between the two sites. This essentially doubled our bandwidth capability and also allowed the protocol types to be separated upon transmission from an organized administrative standpoint.

When the implementation was provided by the vendor, two additional routers were deployed at each site, along with two additional FRAD channel units to allow for the additional WAN channels. The protocol types were split, and the LAN and WAN routers were redefined as to configuration, along with other general parameters that were required.

We immediately noted that a higher performance level was being achieved. The users even stated that the overall WAN between Philadelphia and Seattle was performing excellently.

We redeployed four network protocol analyzers against the WAN and LAN channels for post-analysis network baseline testing. By providing one WAN analyzer at each end of each one of the two Frame Relay channels, we noted that the protocol analyzers in Philadelphia and Seattle both definitely showed a more balanced utilization level—specifically, average utilizations of less than 20% with peak utilizations of less than 50% on both WAN channels. We also noted that the split of protocols showed an extremely accurate level of IPX and SPX as only being present on FRAD channel point one, and IP and TCP present on FRAD channel point two.

In addition, the physical layer of FECN and BECN bits was almost nonexistent as related to bits being active, and the overall Frame Relay header was showing no forward or backward congestion. This eliminated the intersystem switching cloud concerns as to the WAN vendor's operation.

The overall findings from this exercise were that the new Frame Relay WAN circuit was deployed with an improper bandwidth level calculated without proper proactive network baselining engaged. We also found that the Frame Relay intersystem switching cloud was overloaded, based on capacity access required, because of application loading on the channel.

Because the overall capacity was being exceeded, the forward congestion bits were being set on outbound transfer from both the Philadelphia and Seattle sites, which were affecting a large number of backward-congestion bits in reverse directions. This was causing an anomaly that was confusing on analysis, but clearly showed that the overall process of network baselining was successful in extracting the concern.

The process that the LAN Scope analysis team carefully followed enabled us to examine the configuration and integrity of the Frame Relay link, and also to examine field and frame communication. The saturated upper-layer utilization levels immediately pointed out that the problems present in the physical layer Frame Relay forwarding of the FECN and BECN fields were possibly linked to the cause of the problem. This pointed us in the right direction, and therefore we did not focus on the upper-layer application levels or upper-layer protocol area, but rather correctly focused our time and energies on the physical layer and the capacity design of the overall Frame Relay WAN channel.

It was clear that the congestion notification analysis was present. In this case, however, because the utilization levels were so high and because of the architecture at the site, we could immediately refocus our technical methodology in the correct direction.

Our WAN baselining was successful in this area, as well as our troubleshooting efforts.

CHAPTER 13

Network Baseline Planning, Data Acquisition, and Final Reporting

This chapter presents some of the key techniques and methods that an analyst should use when performing a network baseline study. By following these high-level steps, you can ensure the successful completion of a network baseline in both a reactive and a proactive environment.

A network baseline project includes three main stages:

- **Stage 1.** Data-acquisition and baseline-study planning

- **Stage 2.** Data acquisition and active network baselining

- **Stage 3.** Composing and building the network baseline report

For a network baseline program to succeed, an analyst must proceed carefully through these three stages.

Stage 1 is the data-acquisition planning phase—the initial front end of the project. If any one area requires 100% accuracy and thoroughness in terms of detail, it is the step of composing the initial network baseline plan. If key items are properly reviewed and processed, a thorough and technically competent baseline data-acquisition plan can be developed and the final network baseline results for reporting obtained. This chapter identifies the specific steps required when planning a network baseline.

After the initial baseline data-acquisition plan has been composed, the next stage is the actual baseline data acquisition, Stage 2. This active network baseline process is guided by the baseline data-acquisition planning cycle. This is why it is so critical that the first stage of planning the study be 100% accurate and complete.

When an analyst is performing active data acquisition, he must perform many separate steps to ensure that the proper data is captured from the specific network analysis monitoring points. Note that many of these steps must be followed exactly.

After an analyst has completed the data-acquisition process, he starts the final process, Stage 3. In this stage the analyst moves to final network baseline reporting. During the reporting process, an analyst must thoroughly review all the materials (documentation and data) gathered during the baselining process. The analyst must carefully correlate all the information to create a final network baseline report.

This discussion now turns to a detailed analysis of each stage's required steps. Each step is critical to achieving the goal of creating a comprehensive, on-target, and technically competent network baseline report. Figure 13.1 shows the main overall steps required when network baselining.

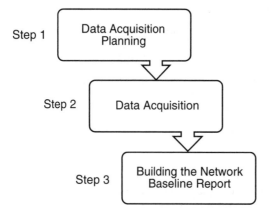

FIGURE 13.1 *Overall network baselining steps.*

13.1 The Project Plan Is Everything

As stated earlier, the *project plan* (also called the *front-end network baseline planning session*) is very critical. When developing a project plan, an analyst must take on the role of network detective, gaining a full understanding of the complete internetwork architecture relevant to the network baseline study. Every network is composed of disparate network topologies and protocols that comprise the complete network architecture.

Consider, for instance, a network using the Ethernet topology and Windows NT for an operating system. Compare that network to a network using Ethernet for the topology but using Novell NetWare for an operating system. These two networks have two different network architectures. Therefore, an analyst must be prepared with a network analyzer that can study the Ethernet topology from a physical layer standpoint and also be able to study the network layer, transport layer, and other key layers (such a the application layer) from a protocol-decoding perspective.

That said, and it merits repeating, an analyst *must* understand the internetwork architecture. To do so, an analyst must engage in a project entrance briefing with all key technical personnel who support the network baseline process. In some cases, an analyst may have to review other areas of the network life cycle (problem history, past migrations, future directions, and so on).

Early on during the planning stage, the analyst must review another key area: *application deployment*. Specifically, such a review is vital because the applications deployed throughout the network may be applied to both the servers and the user workstations that engage the applications.

During the data-acquisition planning stage, an analyst should start with an entrance meeting or briefing. In an entrance briefing, all the key members of the network support team should be present to review the internetwork configuration, symptomatic history, and migration issues, along with application and user profiles. In this type of meeting, a network baseline analyst should take the lead and ask a series of questions regarding the key information required to create a network baseline plan.

The first area of review is the network configuration. An analyst should closely study the internetwork topology by reviewing network diagrams available at the facility (including both LAN and WAN topology diagrams). An analyst should review the types of hubs, switches, routers, and other key devices that provide the actual interconnection and passthrough routes of the topology from a LAN and a WAN perspective.

Certain configuration and operational profiles of main devices, such as switches and routers, may be required throughout the baseline study. An analyst should inventory the total node count along with the actual file server count within the facility.

Next an analyst must understand the type of network operating systems and the placement of key server resources throughout the facility. It is important to understand whether the site is using a distributed or centralized design or both.

After the previously discussed information has been gathered, an analyst should next confirm such details as the cabling layout and other specific items, such as workstation hardware configurations and other details related to the network's physical architecture.

Next the analyst must focus on the workstation. The analyst must understand workstation configuration including such information as software shells, operating shells, application profiles, and other details that relate to the configuration and usage of the workstations. It is also important to understand how the workstations and servers intercommunicate across the network infrastructure.

As the entrance briefing continues, the analyst must next review the network's problem history. An analyst must thoroughly understand the symptomatic history. It is helpful to review network server problem logs, device problem logs, and any Help Desk logged calls that took place in the facility. Key members of the network support staff may hold valuable information. By interviewing specific members of the network staff, a network baseline analyst may be able to understand the symptoms and problems that thread throughout the history of the internetwork's evolution.

During the entrance briefing, the analyst should ask about any recent migrations (*recent* meaning during the past calendar year at the facility, for instance). These would include topology migrations as well as such things as application deployment. The analyst should also take a close look at the planned migration direction for the next calendar year (and possibly even beyond that), to understand how the internetwork may evolve in the near future. Such information enables the analyst, when baselining the network, to possibly obtain data that may assist with fine-tuning the final network migration direction.

An analyst should closely review all main application types deployed at the facility. A network baseline analyst should attempt to understand the general user types as well as the types of applications each user uses on a specific PC. Different user profiles may emerge. One user might use just a word processing application and a general email program, for example. Another user might engage a word processing program along with a high-end application, such as a *computer-aided design* (CAD) drawing application. These two users fit two different user profiles.

After having completed the question-and-answer session with the appropriate network parties, an analyst will gain an initial grasp on the overall internetwork configuration as it currently stands, its problem history, and the anticipated direction for the network. The analyst should also have a handle on the applications currently deployed at the facility as well as some idea regarding the projected future deployment of applications.

From the information discussed throughout this section, the analyst can begin to develop a network project plan. The network project plan must include a full planning stage, during which an analyst chooses specific network analysis monitoring points and uses network analysis tools that will enable the analyst to achieve the network baseline goals.

The final project plan may vary, depending on whether the network baseline study is a proactive study or a reactive study. A *proactive study* refers to a network baseline study being performed on a network that is not having any major problems. A *reactive study* refers to a network baseline study being performed on a network that is experiencing problems at the time of the study.

The following section discusses how to develop your project plan.

13.2 Developing a Network Baseline Project Plan

After the entrance briefing has concluded the analyst should completely understand the internetwork configuration, symptomatic history, and migration direction. The analyst should also have application profiles (deployment and actual user profiles). The final data-acquisition project plan is the next focus of the study.

Before just deploying network protocol analyzers and monitoring equipment, an analyst should understand the types of sampling points necessary to effect relevant data capture with the protocol analyzers positioned throughout the network. An analyst must also understand the sampling time periods necessary to achieve the data capture results for the baseline study.

An analyst must develop a network baseline plan that fits the requirements of the particular internetwork being sampled. An analyst might be called on, for example, to examine areas of the network that are experiencing problems.

In this type of situation, an analyst may decide to immediately deploy network analysis tools in that specific area. (This is an example of being reactive.) Figure 13.2 shows a protocol analyzer positioning process in a network baseline study.

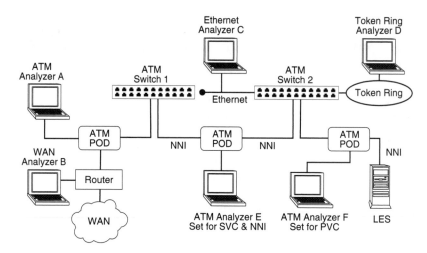

FIGURE 13.2 *Protocol analyzer positioning process.*

In a proactive situation, an analyst may decide to move through the network in a more proactive way and develop a plan that applies to the specific network to ensure that key areas are sampled. An analyst may also decide to develop a sampling session that captures certain application traffic, as required.

Consider this reactive analysis baseline scenario: An analyst is studying a two-segment Ethernet network with approximately 200 users. One main segment is connected through a router and holds a main file server that is having connectivity issues and provides services to the complete site user domain. As noted, the specific file server within the facility appears to have connectivity issues during certain high traffic loads (noted through user complaints). Another server on the same segment is not having any problems. The analyst could develop a network positioning plan to perform a simple network baseline study on both segments, (1) and (2). This would enable the analyst to develop a background baseline view of each main segment, (1) and (2).

The analyst could then study the server for key workload characterization measurements and then focus on details, such as server delta response time and actual file transfer throughput. The analyst could then also study the server that is not having any problems and perform a comparison of the two servers. By reviewing the measurements as well as the proper server documentation, an analyst may then be able to isolate a problem within the server. The issues may relate to the server's network operating system configuration or its hardware build. Software application balancing may also be causing the site connectivity issues.

This preceding network baseline example shows how a baseline project plan could lead to a rapid baseline with a brief sampling session on segments (1) and (2). The problem could be further resolved through cause isolation analysis and close sampling of the problem server.

Consider this proactive analysis baseline scenario: A Token Ring network has a 16Mbps Token Ring backbone. The Token Ring backbone is connected to three user Token Rings running at 16Mbps and uplinked through a Token Ring–switched layout design. If the site experiences no problems, the analyst should plan a full network baseline sampling session on all four main rings, including the backbone. Each ring should then be sampled using standard workload characterization measurements, such as utilization, node-by-node utilization protocol percentages, physical Token Ring error measurements, along with Token Ring MAC review.

The analyst could then proceed to an upper-layer protocol review and study throughput and latency measurements among all the rings. Specific workstations could be sampled for their response time when communicating with certain servers on the backbone ring. Certain servers could also be sampled for their interpacket delta response time on the main backbone ring and how they respond back to the user ring. Application characterization tasks could be run, in which an analyst captures an application on each one of the main subrings for certain user profiles and then closely reviews how applications perform on the subrings when communicating to the servers on the backbone ring. This process generally applies to a proactive study. This type of project planning approach could be applied to a small network with 100 nodes or a large complex internetwork with 5,000 nodes.

The key point is that network analysis positioning is critical, along with network baseline sampling time.

In a proactive study, the network baseline sampling time might spread over a period of a normal business timeframe, such as eight hours for each Token Ring. This type of case presents an example of a proactive view.

In a reactive situation, an analyst may have to adjust the sampling time to a shorter time period to resolve the network issues. In the first example earlier in this chapter, for example, an analyst may have to review the Ethernet segments briefly on a rapid baseline approach for no more than one hour on each segment. The analyst could then troubleshoot the servers on a brief one-hour sample per server. Quite possibly, the issues could be resolved within one business day. Figure 13.3 shows the key steps of the project plan.

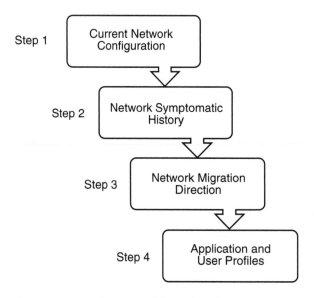

Step 1   Current Network Configuration

Step 2   Network Symptomatic History

Step 3   Network Migration Direction

Step 4   Application and User Profiles

FIGURE 13.3   *Key steps of the project plan.*

These were just two brief examples of project-plan processes that an analyst can use during the network baseline planning stage.

The discussion now turns to a description of the actual data-acquisition process, Stage 2.

13.3 Network Data Acquisition Process

When performing a network data-acquisition process an analyst must keep in mind that the statistical sampling process of the overall network study is critical. It is important to develop a rapid understanding of what is wrong with the network and to develop a set of recommendations and create a focused written report. That said, it is also important to understand that it may be necessary to extract certain quantitative statistical measurements to create the necessary graphs or statistical printouts or associated technical data trace printouts to support the findings in a network baseline report.

Many talented network designers, implementers, and analysts can very quickly assess a network issue and develop a report on a network problem. Any report most likely includes a discussion of the network symptomatic problem, a technical synopsis, and an applied recommendation. Through network baselining, an analyst can utilize specific sampling measurements to develop quantitative technical result documents that can support the findings discussed in a baseline report.

An analyst managing a complete network on a day-to-day basis must understand, from a project management perspective, that statistical analysis is crucial to support the final baseline report. In a proactive network or a reactive network baselining process, an analyst must understand which statistics need to be sampled.

In a proactive study, for instance, measurements should be taken on every network area. These measurements include standard measurements (discussed in Chapter 4, "Quantitative Measurements in Network Baselining," and Chapter 5, "Network Analysis and Optimization Techniques"). Some of these measurements include statistics, such as utilization for average and peak transitions, along with node-by-node utilization and protocol percentages. Error statistics are critical on a per-device basis along with physical traffic associated with certain topologies. Upper-layer protocol statistics as related to timing metrics are critical. This includes measurements to mark metrics, such as the delta time differences and latency between different network segment areas, along with throughput between different segment areas. The main file server and host internetwork response times are also important measurements.

An analyst must take these measurements carefully and develop statistics for quantitative measurement support that he can attach to the final network baseline report. An analyst must always understand that these statistics are going to support the final findings. When performing a network baseline study, an analyst must use an intuitive process to decide which statistics are critical and should be developed for reporting after sampling a certain area. Assume, for example, that an analyst is performing a network sampling session on an Ethernet segment and a high number of physical errors shows up in the initial trace results. The analyst should print the physical trace error results for quantitative statistical support and should attach the results to the final network baseline document.

Other valuable attachments to the final report include network baseline graphs that show, for instance, a high average and a high peak-utilization level.

When performing upper-layer protocol analysis on an Ethernet segment, for example, a high number of low effective throughput conditions are detected. The analyst determines that certain types of file transfers cause the event. The analyst can then develop a printed version of file data output that relates to this concern. The output can include printouts of the low effective throughput statistics along with detailed technical printouts of the files opened and closed during the low throughput occurrence. The analyst can also correlate these low throughput events with the high peak saturation utilization that appears on a graph printed prior to the review of this area.

When completing this stage, the analyst usually has many sets of attachments. The graphs, for example, might support the findings that the particular Ethernet segment is oversaturated and is showing low throughput and high utilization. The attachments represent how application loading is causing low throughput and negative performance on other applications and also affecting the physical Ethernet layer. In this particular case, the analyst develops a technical write-up on the capacity-loading situation that provides a synopsis of the occurrence and also recommends to either partition the Ethernet segment or to introduce switched Ethernet architecture. In this case, the analyst can supplement the network baseline report with all the statistical printouts, such as utilization graphs, physical statistic graphs, effective throughput statistics, and file detail open and close technical printouts for the file movement that caused the utilization peak.

The preceding example shows how critical the data-acquisition statistical mode is to a final network baselining process.

In summary, an analyst must understand that the network baseline data-acquisition stage involves the following key analysis steps:

- Engaging key analysis positioning and capturing points against the topology in the applied architecture.

- Establishing and moving toward a goal during each particular network analysis session in the complete network baseline study.

- Ensuring that the proper analysis and management tools are deployed, properly configured, and set up to gain the required statistics.

- Recording the proper workload statistics and developing technical output reports for graphs, charts, and technical printouts, as required.

- Performing a detailed review of all data gathered in the analysis session, and recording all final baseline information as well as other data including quantitative measurement supports, and ensuring that the data is saved to a proper file for future review.

Figure 13.4 displays the key steps in data acquisition.

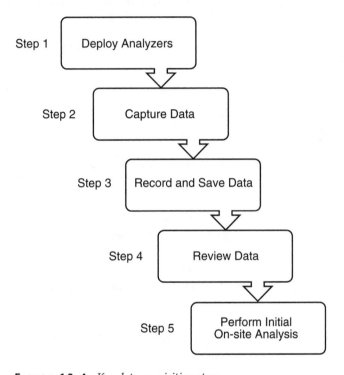

FIGURE 13.4 *Key data acquisition steps.*

The following section shows how an analyst can produce a final report that accurately represents the output of a network baseline study.

13.4 Final Report Building for a Network Baseline Study

When composing the final network baseline report, an analyst must keep in mind that many issues need careful review.

Of primary concern, and to be identified at the outset, is the network baseline report's intended audience. If the network baseline report is to be submitted to a group of technical individuals who just need the main technical information, the report can be developed in a short and to-the-point status memo approach.

If the network baseline is required for an annual baseline study that is going to be considered a blueprint for the direction of the internetwork for the future, a comprehensive network baseline study may be required.

Having grasped an understanding of the audience, the analyst can then guide the overall network baseline composition and writing process to ensure that the audience receives the relevant information from the network baseline study results.

Certain steps must be followed when preparing to develop a final network baseline report, including the following:

1. Problem issue identification and extraction

2. Technical synopsis development

3. Recommendation threading

4. Quantitative baseline data-measurement attachment development

The following subsections briefly discuss these steps.

13.4.1 Problem Issue Identification and Extraction

When an analyst starts to perform the final off-site network baseline reporting-building process, he should first determine whether any issues are considered problems at the site. An analyst can start this process by closely reviewing all the trace files taken from the network baseline stage. The network baseline traces need to be closely reviewed from an internal perspective. The data must be closely reviewed by cross-reading certain trace information from different sessions. It is important to identify problem issues that relate to workload characterization measurements or physical issues, or associated upper-layer protocol issues that may be identified in the study. As any problems are identified, an experienced analyst starts to very carefully extract the issues involved (even keeping a "running issue list"). Each issue should be identified as a problem in a specific trace session.

Any trace that has a problem should be documented along with the area of the trace that shows the problem. An analyst can extract the issues by producing a technical printout of the finding. (As mentioned earlier and as shown here, the analyst must make and keep for future reference technical printouts during the data-acquisition stage.) After the analyst has identified the problem issue, he should list it in a network baseline outline draft of the final report.

The discussion now turns to how an analyst can develop a technical synopsis from the issues identified and extracted from a network baseline session.

13.4.2 Technical Synopsis Development

After the issue has been identified, the analyst must develop a technical synopsis of the problem. As the analyst moves through all the network baseline data for all sessions sampled, eventually a complete list of problem issues emerge; these require a synopsis and applied recommendation.

As noted, an analyst should start the network baseline reporting process by developing a network problem "running issue list." The issue list will most likely consist of network problematic circumstances that occur at the physical, network, transport, or application layer. Any identified issues will most likely be developed on a per-session extraction basis. In other words, the analyst pulls the issues from each separate session as part of a complete network baseline study. In this case, for example, if three segments were studied there may be three separate sets of issues.

The analyst should next perform a cross-review of all separate issue lists and try to determine which issues cross-thread throughout the network baseline study and affect the complete internetwork being studied. Through this methodology, the analyst then can develop a synopsis on each major issue. Some of the issues may require only one synopsis discussion because they may affect multiple segments or multiple network areas. The key factor in this process of the network baselining stage is to next apply a synopsis to each identified technical issue. A *baseline technical synopsis* is defined as a technical review of a network problem's cause and effect. This is where an analyst discusses the actual cause as it relates to the symptomatic effect or network issue (problem) identified during the network baseline stage.

If a physical network problem exists, for example, an analyst can discuss the cause of the network problem as it relates to a failure of a certain type of NIC or an improper NIC driver. This is just one example of applying a technical synopsis to the actual problem event.

After each technical issue is reviewed, a synopsis should be applied. Then, any redundant technical issues and technical synopsis information should be combined for a simplified and streamlined problem issue list that has a technical synopsis applied to each main issue. From this point, the analyst must then move to the process of developing a recommendation for each technical issue.

13.4.3 Recommendation Threading

In this process, an analyst must understand the internals of internetwork design, implementation, and support. This is where the network baseline process moves to the next level in terms of technical skill and knowledge. To provide a recommendation, the technical analyst writing the report must have a solid understanding of these key areas, along with a good understanding of the network analysis baseline results. Recommendations should be clear and technically concise and above all effective. An analyst must determine whether the recommendation is required for a short-term solution or a long-term solution approach so that immediate issues can be quickly resolved. This would mainly include those issues causing network problems. There may also be issues that are not causing major network outages that could be resolved through interim recommendations that involve migration steps, such as the addition/reconfiguration of major equipment, such as bridges, routers, switches, or the reconfiguration of a complete topology or architecture.

After all the issues have been reviewed and the synopsis information has been thoroughly detailed, the analyst should next apply a recommendation for each issue and associated synopsis. If any recommendations are redundant or related to cross-site events, these recommendations can be combined/related to other issues in the report, if required.

One final note: An analyst must ensure that all recommendations are clear and concise. The analyst should ensure that any recommendations requiring design specification or implementation be clearly identified in the network baseline report. This is important so that the network support team understands that such recommendations require immediate action. It is important that actual design specification and implementation planning be well thought out before recommendations are offered.

13.4.4 Quantitative Baseline Data Measurement Support Attachments

After the final report has been composed (that is, all the major issues have been identified and an associated technical synopsis has been applied), and final recommendations have been made, it may be necessary to back up the findings.

An analyst may need to attach proof to substantiate the technical network baseline issues and subsequent recommendations. Technical proof material is important because many support personnel may question the report because of the nature of certain recommendations (especially as to how they affect the internetwork). This is why statistical data acquisition is very important (during network baseline stage). If the project plan is correct and accurate, and the data-acquisition process is completed in a proper manner, the necessary quantitative statistical graphs and data printouts should be available to support any issues discussed in the main network baseline report. An analyst should carefully lay out a table of contents and appendix section of the report to ensure that the attachments support all the issues discussed in the report.

During the network baseline data-acquisition stage, many network attachments may appear to be redundant in nature and not required (graphs, technical trace printouts, and certain statistical screen printouts, for example). Other information may appear to be absolutely relevant to a specific issue discussed. This is where an analyst must apply his expertise and extract from the reporting site files all the printouts and graphs that support the network baseline discussions in the main body of the report. These attachments should be carefully referenced in the network baseline report and cross-referenced to their actual location as attachments.

The analyst may have to go back into the main body of the report and cross-reference the attachments to ensure a complete cross-reference between each technical issue and applied synopsis and recommendation, as well as an associated quantitative measurement statistical printout that supports the finding. This is a critical area of network baseline reporting.

In closing, a key point to mention here is that network baselining is not about producing a large number of graphs and technical printouts that show the overall statistics of the network. Instead, it is crucial for the network baseline report to be on-target from an issue, synopsis, and recommendation standpoint. In other words, the final network baseline report should provide a statistical review of the network sampling session from a workload baseline characterization standpoint for all critical layers, such as the physical, network, and application layer. This is important for each network baseline session sample in the overall network baseline study. When the report reflects all the key network issues and an applied technical synopsis and recommendations are brought forward, it is then time to confirm that the study also includes the proper quantitative measurement statistical printouts to support the findings.

A network baseline report should never be compiled based on just statistical graphs and technical printouts without the proper technical support information (that is, a discussion of the technical printouts within the report itself).

Many network baseline reports consisting of just a series of graphs and technical charts have been delivered in the industry. In such a case, a person reading the network baseline report may find no real value in the measurements if the actual issues are not properly discussed (from an issue, associated synopsis, and applied recommendation perspective).

Note also that if the report is written in a clear and concise fashion and the recommendations are accurate, it is still necessary to support the report with the proper quantitative statistical graphs and printouts in the attachment section.

Figure 13.5 shows the main steps in creating a network baseline report.

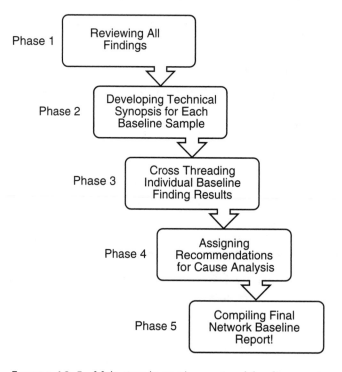

FIGURE 13.5 *Main steps in creating a network baseline report.*

13.5 Closing Statement

This book has presented the key principles and goals of a network baseline study. The early chapters of this book presented the major principles of network baselining. The book then moved to a discussion of the importance of ensuring that a network is stable, reliable, and performing at a high level. Some of the key network analysis tools that can be used in a network baseline study were also discussed. The book then presented extremely detailed information on workload characterization baseline measurements, network baseline process measurements, upper-layer protocol-decoding processes, and problem extraction techniques. Analysis techniques were discussed for network communication analysis along with application characterization. Detailed trace analysis techniques were also discussed. Next, the book moved to a discussion of how a network should be documented. That discussion included some of the key methods used to ensure that a network baseline is properly documented. Also included in this book are chapters with important information on network protocol architecture along with methods and techniques on how to analyze those protocols. Most major LAN and WAN topologies were presented from an architecture perspective with a focus on the technique to analyze and baseline the specific topology.

This closing chapter has discussed the methodology involved when performing a network baseline study along with the steps required to create and deliver a network baseline report.

With all the process methodology offered here, most technical individuals in the industry who are interested in this type of work should be able to eventually plan, perform, and complete their first network baseline against a specific architecture.

The subject matter presented in this book should prove extremely effective as long as all steps and methodologies presented throughout this book are followed properly.

At this point, I want to offer the reader "Best Wishes" in developing the skill set required to be a true network baseline analyst.

The "Art of Network Baselining" is considered a pinnacle area in the networking industry in terms of the technical scope of work involved. This is because an analyst must intimately understand internetwork architecture, design, implementation and support, and this critical process called network baselining!

APPENDIX A

Network Analysis Tool Vendor Contact Information

Antara LLC
747 Camden Avenue
Campbell, CA 95008

Fluke Corporation
6920 Seaway Boulevard
Everett, WA 98203

Ganymede Software
1100 Perimeter Park Drive
Suite 104
Morrisville, NC 27560

Hewlett-Packard
3000 Hanover Street
Palo Alto, CA 94304

Network Associates Inc.
3965 Freedom Circle
Santa Clara, CA 95054

Novell
2180 Fortune Drive
San Jose, CA 95131

Optimal Networks Corp.
2454 Charleston Road
Mountain View, CA 94043

Shomiti Systems Inc.
1800 Bering Drive
San Jose, CA 95112

Wandel and Goltermann
1030 Swabia Court
Research Triangle Park, NC 27709

APPENDIX B

Reference Material

From the following list of sources, you can obtain further information concerning network baselining.

ANSI Core Aspects of Frame Relay ANSI t1.618.

ANSI Encapsulation of ITU-T x.25 over Frame Relay.

ANSI ISDN Signaling Specifications for Frame Relay Bearer Service ANSI t1.617. 1991.

Apple Computer Inc. AppleTalk Phase 2 Protocol Specification, 1989.

ATM Forum UNI Specifications, Prentice Hall: Upper Saddle River, NJ. 1993.

Banyan Systems Inc. VINES Architectural Definition, 1998.

Bellcore 253 Core Sonet Generic Criteria. December, 1995.

Digital Equipment Corp, DECnet Phase IV Routing Layer Functional Specification, 1993.

Horgnig, Charles. *A Standard for the Transmission of IP Datagrams over Ethernet Networks*. RFC 894, April 1984.

IBM Personal Computer Vol 2, Number 8-1 SMB protocols. 1995.

IBM Token Ring Network Architecture, Document SC30-3374-02.

IBM Token Ring Network Problem Determination Guide, Document SX27-3710-3.

IEEE 802.3 (ANSI) Supplement to CSMA/CD, Supplements Consideration for 10Mbps Baseband Networks, Twisted Pair MAU, 10Base-T Institute of Electrical and Electronics Engineers, Inc.

IEEE Standard (ANSI) 1992 Carrier Sense with Collision Detection (CSMA) Access Method and Physical Layer Specification, Institute of Electrical Engineers, 1992.

IEEE, Token Ring Access Method and Physical Layer Specifications, IEEE STD 802.5-1989.

ITU-T ISDN q933, 1191.

ITU-T ISDN, B-ISDN , and ATM AAL Layer Specifications. July, 1992.

ITU-T Sonet References G783,G702, G758,G.781,G787.

Jain, R. *Performance Analysis of FDDI Token Ring Networks*. ACM. SIGCOMM. September, 1990.

Korb, J.T. *A Standard for the Transmission of IP Datagrams over Public Data Networks*. RFC 877, September 1983.

Microsoft Web site.

Mogul, J., and Postel, J. *Internet Standard Subnetting Procedure*. RFC 950, August 1985.

Novell Inc. NetWare Technical Overview, 1989.

Novell NetWare Application Notes, 1995.

Novell NetWare Theory of Operations, 1987.

Postel, J. and Reynolds, J. *A Standard for the Transmission of IP Datagrams over IEEE 802 Networks*. RFC 1042, February 1988.

Postel, J. *Internet Control Message Protocol*. RFC 792, September 1981.

Postel, J. *User Datagram Protocol*. RFC 768, August, 1980.

Postel, Jon, ed., Information Sciences Institute. *Internet Protocol DARPA Internet Program Protocol Specifications*. RFC 791, September 1981.

Postel, Jon, ed., Information Sciences Institute. *Transmission Protocol DARPA Internet Program Protocol Specifications*. RFC 791, September 1981.

Ranade J. and Sackett G. 1989, *Introduction to SNA Networking*, New York, McGraw-Hill.

Sevcik, K.C. and Johnson, M.J. *Cycle Time Properties of the FDDI Token Ring Protocol*. IEEE, Vol SE-13. March, 1987.

Telcordia Technologies (formerly Bellcore). *Key ISDN Documents*. www.telcordia.com/resources/isdn, 2000.

Telenex Corp., *An Introduction to Useful Frame Relay Testing*, August, 1991.

Index

Symbols

A

K-L

The *Technology Series* is a comprehensive and authoritative set of guides to the most important computing standards of today. Each title in this series is aimed at bringing computing professionals closer to the scientists and engineers behind the technological implementations that will change tomorrow's innovations in computing.

Currently available titles in the *Technology Series* include:

Supporting Service Level Agreements on IP Networks, **by Dinesh Verma (ISBN: 1-57870-146-5)**

This essential guide provides ISP managers and engineers practical insight into the procedures required to fulfill their SLAs, and it describes methods and techniques that businesses can use to ensure that the requirements of their service level agreements are met.

Differentiated Services for the Internet, **by Kalevi Kilkki (ISBN: 1-57870-132-5)**

One of the few technologies that will enable networks to handle traffic to meet the demands of particular applications, Differentiated Services is currently being standardized by the IETF. This book offers network architects, engineers, and managers of Internet and other packet networks critical insight into this new technology.

Gigabit Ethernet Networking, **by David G. Cunningham, Ph.D. and William G. Lane, Ph.D. (ISBN: 1-57870-062-0)**

Written by key contributors to the Gigabit Ethernet standard, this book offers critical information to enable network engineers and architects to make cost-effective decisions about how to design and implement their particular network to meet current traffic loads, and to ensure scalability with future growth.

DSL: Simulation Techniques and Standards Development for Digital Subscriber Line Systems, **by Dr. Walter Y. Chen (ISBN: 1-57870-017-5)**

With low-level coverage of xDSL technologies, this book is ideal for computing professionals who are looking for new high-speed communications technology, who must understand the dynamics of xDSL communications to create compliant applications, or who simply want to better understand this new wave of technology.

ADSL/VDSL Principles, **by Dr. Dennis J. Rauschmayer (ISBN: 1-57870-015-9)**

ADSL/VDSL Principles provides the communications and networking engineer with practical explanations, technical detail, and in-depth insight needed to fully implement ADSL and VDSL. Topics that are essential to the successful implementation of these technologies are covered.

Quality of Service in IP Networks, **by Grenville Armitage (ISBN: 1-57870-189-9)**

Quality of Service in IP Networks provides network engineers and architects with the information they need to evaluate existing IP networks and determine how to improve upon traditional best-effort service.

LDAP: Programming Directory-Enabled Applications with Lightweight Directory Access Protocol, **by Timothy A. Howes, Ph.D. and Mark C. Smith (ISBN: 1-57870-000-0)**

If you design or program software for network computing or are interested in directory services, *LDAP: Programming Directory-Enabled Applications with Lightweight Directory Access Protocol* is an essential resource to help you understand the LDAP API, learn how to write LDAP programs, understand how to LDAP-enable an existing application, and learn how to use a set of command-line LDAP tools to search and update directory information.

Directory Enabled Networking, **by John Strassner (ISBN: 1-57870-140-6)**

Directory Enabled Networking is a comprehensive resource on the design and use of DEN. This book provides practical examples side-by-side with a detailed introduction to the theory of building a new class of network-enabled applications that will solve networking problems. It is a critical tool for network architects, administrators, and application developers.

Understanding Public-Key Infrastructure, **by Carlisle Adams and Steve Lloyd (ISBN: 1-57870-166-X)**

This book is a tutorial on, and a guide to the deployment of, Public-Key Infrastructures. It covers a broad range of material related to PKIs, including certification, operational considerations and standardization efforts, as well as deployment issues and considerations. Emphasis is placed on explaining the interrelated fields within the topic area, to assist those who will be responsible for making deployment decisions and architecting a PKI within an organization.

Intrusion Detection, **by Rebecca Gurley Bace (ISBN: 1-57870-185-6)**

Intrusion detection is a critical new area of technology within network security. This comprehensive guide to the field of intrusion detection covers the foundations of intrusion detection and system audit. *Intrusion Detection* provides a wealth of information, ranging from design considerations to how to evaluate and choose the optimal commercial intrusion detection products for a particular networking environment.